# BANKRUPTCY AND
# INSOLVENCY ACCOUNTING

# Bankruptcy and Insolvency Accounting

## FORMS AND EXHIBITS

**GRANT W. NEWTON, CPA, CMA**
**Professor of Accounting**
**Pepperdine University**

WILEY

**JOHN WILEY & SONS**
New York • Chichester • Brisbane • Toronto • Singapore

*Library of Congress Cataloging in Publication Data:*

Newton, Grant W.
    Bankruptcy and insolvency accounting. Forms and
    Exhibits / Grant W. Newton.
       p.   cm.
    Updated annually.
    Includes bibliographical references.
    ISBN 0-471-50863-2
    1. Bankruptcy—United States—Forms.
    2. Bankruptcy—United States—Accounting—
    Forms.  I. Title.
    KF1527.N49   1989
    346.73′078′0269—dc20
    [347.306780269]
    ISBN 0-471-50863-2

Printed in the United States of America

10 9 8 7 6 5 4 3 2

**To Valda, Aaron,
Paul and Danae**

# Preface

This work is designed to provide a broad range of practical guidance for accountants, lawyers, bankruptcy trustees, and creditors of business enterprises in financial difficulty. It is presented in two volumes. This volume, *Bankruptcy and Insolvency Accounting: Forms and Exhibits* contains examples of various forms and exhibits used by accountants and other professionals in bankruptcy cases and out-of-court workouts. The companion volume, *Bankruptcy and Insolvency Accounting: Practice and Procedure,* describes the economic, legal, accounting, and tax aspects of bankruptcy proceedings. Both volumes will be updated annually.

Most of the forms and exhibits in this volume are new. They are included as examples to assist practitioners in serving their clients.

Chapter 2 of this volume contains an example of the use of the bankruptcy prediction model developed by Altman. An example of a bankruptcy petition is presented in Chapter 3. Chapter 4 contains an out-of-court agreement that differs from the one given in the *Practice and Procedure* volume.

Chapter 5 presents two plans—one developed by the debtor and the other by the unsecured creditors' committee. Excerpts from disclosure statements for the two plans are also included. Both statements contain good examples of cash projections that should be studied in conjunction with Chapter 7 of *Bankruptcy and Insolvency Accounting: Practice and Procedure.* Chapter 5 also contains excerpts from a disclosure statement for a plan that was approved by the creditors and stockholders before the petition was filed, and instructions from a chapter 12 standing trustee.

Chapter 6 consists of examples of affidavits, applications, and orders relating to the retention of accountants for the debtor and for the unsecured creditors' committee in both large and small engagements. Other examples included are a petition for fee allowance and an order establishing the procedure for interim payment of fees and expenses.

Examples of cash projections and of the type of information filed with the petition are found in Chapter 7. The chapter also contains several examples of orders that are obtainable shortly after a petition filing to facilitate payment of wages and other expenses, as well as examples of procedures to assist the debtor in preventing payment of unauthorized prepetition expenses. Chapter 8 also describes services that can be rendered by the debtor's accountant and contains examples of forms and instructions for completing operating reports from several different offices of the U.S. trustee.

Chapter 9 contains a report issued to the creditors' committee, while Chapter 10 contains examples of valuations of companies in chapter 11. Audit procedures and reports are shown in Chapter 11. Financial statements for liquidation and going concern purposes are contained in Chapter 12, and Chapter 13 consists of examples of several types of reports that have been issued in chapter 11 cases. Finally, two tax forms used by companies in chapter 11 are located in Chapter 14, and the appendix contains the official bankruptcy forms.

Neither volume of *Bankruptcy and Insolvency Accounting* could have been completed without the assistance of many friends who are professionally involved in reorganization and bankruptcy practice. I am especially grateful to the following individuals for providing information for this volume:

John S. Dubel, CPA, Arthur Andersen, New York
Peter Gibbons, CPA, Price Waterhouse, Philadelphia
William H. Grabscheid, Ernst & Young, Chicago
Barry M. Monheit, CPA, Arthur Andersen, New York
Tim T. Morris, CPA, Deloitte Haskins & Sells, Chattanooga
Martin Nachimson, CPA, Ernst & Young, Los Angeles
David Nolte, CPA, Arthur Andersen, Los Angeles
Michael A. Policano, CPA, Zolfo Cooper, New York
Nancy A. Ross, CPA, Ernst & Young, Chicago
Ronald S. Orr, Esq., Gibson Dunn & Crutcher, Los Angeles
Kurt Schwartz, CPA, Ernst & Young, Los Angeles
Ronald J. Sutter, CPA, Steres, Alpart & Carne, San Diego
David T. Sykes, Esq., Duane, Morris & Heckscher, Philadelphia

Finally, I thank Valda L. Newton for her editorial assistance, and for her patience and understanding during the preparation of this work.

GRANT W. NEWTON

*Westlake Village, California*
*June, 1989*

# Contents

## PART ONE

# Bankruptcy and Insolvency Environment

# The Accountant's Role in Perspective

## EXHIBIT 1-1  PARTIES OFTEN SERVED BY ACCOUNTANTS[1]

A.  Out-of-Court Workouts
1.  Accountant for debtor
2.  Accountant for major unsecured creditor
3.  Accountant for bank or other financial institution
4.  Accountant for major secured lender
5.  Accountant for principal shareholder

B.  Chapter 7
1.  Serve as trustee
2.  Accountant for trustee
3.  Accountant for unsecured creditors' committee, if appointed
4.  Accountant for major bank or other secured creditors
5.  Accountant for Stockholder

C.  Chapter 11
1.  Accountant for debtor-in-possession or trustee
2.  Trustee
3.  Examiner (may involve expanded role)
4.  Accountant for examiner, if court will make such an appointment (Bankruptcy does not provide for such an appointment)
5.  Accountant for unsecured creditors' committee

---

[1] The use of the word "accountant" also includes the rendering of management advisory services or consulting services.

  **6.** Accountant for secured creditors' committee or individual secured creditor

  **7.** Accountant for stockholders' committee or individual stockholder

  **8.** Accountant as "expert witness" for any of the above parties

**D.** Chapters 12 and 13

  **1.** Accountant for debtor or trustee

  **2.** Accountant for standing trustee

  **3.** Accountant for major unsecured or secured creditor

  **4.** Accountant for shareholder or partner (chapter 12 only)

# CHAPTER TWO

# Economic Causes of Business Failures

## EXHIBIT 2-1    ILLUSTRATION OF ALTMAN'S "Z" VALUES

The financial statements of Revco for fiscal year 1986 and 1987 are presented below in Exhibits A–D. Altman's model[1] for predicting bankruptcy failure is as follows:

where $x_1$ = working capital/total assets

$x_2$ = retained earnings/total assets

$x_3$ = earnings before interest and taxes/total assets

$x_4$ = market value of equity/total liabilities

$x_5$ = sales/total assets

The following ratios are used to calculate the "Z" value for 1986 and 1987 (all values are in thousands, except ratios):

| | 1986 | | 1987 | |
|---|---|---|---|---|
| $x_1$ | $=\dfrac{\$639{,}586-253{,}581}{\$986{,}954}=$ | .391 | $\dfrac{\$866{,}515-\$440{,}530}{\$1{,}887{,}787}=$ | .226 |
| $x_2$ | $=\dfrac{\$411{,}729}{\$986{,}954}=$ | .417 | $\dfrac{\$(22{,}419)}{\$1{,}887{,}787}=$ | $-.012$ |
| $x_3$ | $=\dfrac{\$125{,}343}{\$986{,}954}=$ | .127 | $\dfrac{\$109{,}883}{\$1{,}887{,}787}=$ | .058 |

[1] See § 2.62 of the Practices and Procedures volume for a description of Altman's model.

$$x_4 = \frac{\$1,203,370^2}{\$594,424} = 2.024 \qquad \frac{\$(22,384)^3}{\$1,910,171} = -.012$$

$$x_5 = \frac{\$2,743,178}{\$986,954} = 2.779 \qquad \frac{\$2,679,580}{1,887,787} = 1.419$$

$$1986 \;\; Z = 1.2(.391) + 1.4(.417) + 3.3(.127) + .6(2.024) + .99(2.779) = 5.44$$

$$1987 \;\; Z = 1.2(.226) + 1.4(-.012) + 3.3(.058) + .6(-.012) + .99(1.419) = 1.84$$

In using these "Z" values the reader should recall that Altman developed this ratio from manufacturing companies. Thus, it is not entirely appropriate to use it for a retail firm. The asset turnover ratio will most likely be higher for Revco than for manufacturing concern. Considering this factor, it is still interesting to note how much the "Z" value decreased as a result of the LBO.

---

[2] Shares outstanding of 32,414,012 times $37.125 per share at May 31, 1986.
[3] The market value of equity is not known since the stock of Revco is no longer traded on the public exchanges following the LBO. However the book value may be representative of the market value because the assets were restated as of December 30, 1986—the effective date of the LBO. It should be noted, however, that since Revco filed a bankruptcy petition within two years after this date, the deficit in equity may be much larger than reported.

**Exhibit A**  Consolidated Statements of Earnings
*Revco D.S., Inc. and Subsidiaries*
*Periods from December 30, 1986 to May 30, 1987 and June 1, 1986 to December 29, 1986 and*
*Fiscal Years ended May 31, 1986 and June 1, 1985*

| (Dollars in Thousands, Except Per Share Amounts) | December 30, 1986 to May 30, 1987 | Predecessor Corporation (note 1) | | |
| --- | --- | --- | --- | --- |
| | | June 1, 1986 to December 29, 1986 | 52 Weeks Ended May 31, 1986 | 52 Weeks Ended June 1, 1985 |
| Net sales | $991,184 | $1,688,396 | $2,743,178 | $2,395,640 |
| Cost of sales, including occupancy costs (note 5) | 733,344 | 1,249,085 | 2,018,149 | 1,790,731 |
| Warehouse, selling administrative and general expenses | 190,540 | 347,537 | 563,248 | 493,659 |
| Depreciation and amortization | 26,023 | 23,168 | 36,438 | 30,125 |
| Operating profit | 41,277 | 68,606 | 125,343 | 81,125 |
| Interest expense | 64,682 | 19,427 | 28,989 | 14,796 |
| Interest income | (2,030) | (1,481) | (2,465) | (1,777) |
| Unusual items (note 13) | — | (5,018) | (2,815) | — |
| Earnings (loss) before income taxes | (21,375) | 55,678 | 101,634 | 68,106 |

7

**Exhibit A**  Consolidated Statements of Earnings (*continued*)

| (Dollars in Thousands, Except Per Share Amounts) | December 30, 1986 to May 30, 1987 | Predecessor Corporation (note 1) | | |
| --- | --- | --- | --- | --- |
| | | June 1, 1986 to December 29, 1986 | 52 Weeks Ended May 31, 1986 | 52 Weeks Ended June 1, 1985 |
| Income taxes | | | | |
| Federal (note 9): | | | | |
| Current | 76 | 18,545 | 21,501 | 17,441 |
| Deferred | 10 | 6,392 | 14,399 | 5,659 |
| | 86 | 24,937 | 35,900 | 23,100 |
| State and local | 444 | (1,000) | 8,800 | 6,100 |
| | 530 | 23,937 | 44,700 | 29,200 |
| Net earnings (loss) | $(21,905) | $ 31,741 | $ 56,934 | $ 38,906 |
| Net earnings per common share | | $ .97 | $ 1.72 | $ 1.06 |

See accompanying notes to consolidated financial statements.

**Exhibit B**  Consolidated Balance Sheets
*Revco D.S., Inc. and Subsidiaries*
*May 30, 1987 and May 31, 1986*

| (Dollars in Thousands) | 1987 | Predecessor Corporation (note 1) 1986 |
|---|---|---|
| ASSETS | | |
| Current assets: | | |
| Cash, including temporary cash investments | $ 49,632 | $ 45,074 |
| Accounts receivable—trade and other, less allowance for doubtful accounts of $2,826 and $3,074, respectively | 75,689 | 67,554 |
| Notes receivable | 37,164 | 980 |
| Inventories (note 5) | 453,749 | 501,956 |
| Prepaid expenses | 19,462 | 24,022 |
| Net assets of operations to be divested (note 1) | 230,819 | — |
| Total current assets | 866,515 | 639,586 |
| Property, equipment and leasehold improvements, at cost (notes 1, 6 and 10): | | |
| Land, land improvements and buildings | 48,862 | 62,929 |
| Equipment and fixtures | 120,373 | 223,328 |
| Leasehold improvements | 36,315 | 105,388 |
| Construction in progress | 46 | 36,386 |
| | 205,596 | 428,031 |
| Less accumulated depreciation and amortization | 8,388 | 126,684 |
| Property, equipment and leasehold improvements, net | 197,208 | 301,347 |
| Leasehold interests, less accumulated amortization of $4,387 | 160,867 | — |

9

**Exhibit B**  Consolidated Balance Sheets (*continued*)

| (Dollars in Thousands) | 1987 | Predecessor Corporation (note 1) 1986 |
|---|---|---|
| Excess of cost over fair value of net assets acquired, less accumulated amortization of $6,042 and $800, respectively (note 1) | 562,236 | 13,500 |
| Other assets | 100,961 | 32,521 |
| | $1,887,787 | $986,954 |
| **LIABILITIES AND STOCKHOLDERS' EQUITY** | | |
| Current liabilities: | | |
| Current portion of long-term debt | $ 144,141 | $ 4,490 |
| Accounts payable, trade | 141,576 | 155,179 |
| Accounts payable, other | 20,148 | 21,904 |
| Accrued salaries and wages | 24,680 | 22,705 |
| Accrued interest | 48,344 | 7,407 |
| Other accrued liabilities | 28,050 | 35,454 |
| Current portion of restructuring reserve | 29,238 | — |
| Federal, state and local income taxes | 4,353 | 6,442 |
| Total current liabilities | 440,530 | 253,581 |
| Long-term debt, less current portion (note 6) | 1,154,858 | 304,885 |
| Restructuring reserve, less current portion (note 1) | 38,596 | — |
| Deferred income taxes (note 9) | — | 35,958 |
| Holding redeemable preferred stock, $328,406 redemption amount (note 4) | 263,576 | — |
| Holding common stock and common stock puts (note 3) | 2,545 | — |
| Holding common stock subject to put options (note 3) | 10,066 | — |

10

Common stockholders' equity:

| | | |
|---|---:|---:|
| Common stock, par value one cent per share. | | |
| Authorized 7,653,061; issued 5,325,000 (note 3) | 35 | — |
| Predecessor Corporation common stock; par value one dollar per share. | | |
| Authorized 100,000,000; issued 36,742,762 shares (note 8) | — | 36,743 |
| Additional paid-in capital | — | 41,764 |
| Retained earnings (deficit) | (22,419) | 411,729 |
| | (22,384) | 490,236 |
| Treasury stock, at cost (note 3) | — | (97,706) |
| Total common stockholders' equity | (22,384) | 392,530 |
| Commitments and contingencies (notes 10 and 11) | | |
| | $1,887,787 | $986,954 |

See accompanying notes to consolidated financial statements.

**Exhibit C**  Consolidated Statements of Stockholders' Equity
*Revco D.S., Inc. and Subsidiaries*
*Periods from December 30, 1986 to May 30, 1987 and June 1, 1986 to December 29, 1986*
*and Fiscal Years ended May 31, 1986 and June 1, 1985*

| (Dollars in Thousands, Except Per Share Amounts) | Common Stock | Treasury Stock | | Additional Paid-in Capital | Retained Earnings (Deficit) |
| --- | --- | --- | --- | --- | --- |
| | | Shares | Dollars | | |
| Predecessor Corporation (note 1): | | | | | |
| Balance at June 2, 1984 | $36,593 | — | $    — | $38,638 | $371,895 |
| Proceeds from stock option plans | 48 | — | — | 279 | — |
| Compensation on restricted stock plans | — | — | — | 144 | — |
| Federal income tax benefits derived from stock option plans | — | — | — | 133 | — |
| Reclassification | — | (3,145) | (80) | — | — |
| Net earnings | — | — | — | — | 38,906 |
| Cash dividends declared, $.80 per share | — | — | — | — | (29,282) |
| Balance at June 1, 1985 | 35,641 | (3,145) | (80) | 39,194 | 381,519 |
| Proceeds from stock option plans | 102 | — | — | 1,295 | — |
| Purchase of treasury stock | — | (4,376,280) | (98,778) | — | — |
| Treasury stock sold to profit sharing and savings plan | — | 50,675 | 1,152 | 360 | — |
| Compensation on restricted stock plans | — | — | — | 144 | — |
| Federal income tax benefits derived from stock option plans | — | — | — | 771 | — |
| Net earnings | — | — | — | — | 56,934 |
| Cash dividends declared, $.80 per share | — | — | — | — | (26,724) |
| Balance at May 31, 1986 | 36,743 | (4,328,750) | (97,706) | 41,764 | 411,729 |
| Proceeds from stock option plans | 3 | — | — | 81 | — |
| Treasury stock sold to profit sharing and savings plan | — | 48,204 | 1,087 | 660 | — |

| | | | | | |
|---|---|---|---|---|---|
| Federal income tax benefits derived from stock option plans | — | — | — | 2,036 | — |
| Net earnings | — | — | — | — | 31,741 |
| Cash dividends declared, $.60 per share | — | — | — | — | (19,461) |
| Balance at December 29, 1986, before acquisition | $36,746 | (4,280,546) | $(96,619) | $44,541 | $424,009 |
| Post-Merger (note 1): | | | | | |
| Balance at December 30, 1986, after acquisition | $ 35 | — | $ — | $23,511 | $ — |
| Accretions of original issuance discount on redeemable preferred stock | — | — | — | (2,151) | — |
| Amortization of deferred costs on redeemable preferred stock | — | — | — | (417) | — |
| Net loss | — | — | — | — | (21,905) |
| Exchangeable preferred stock dividends | — | — | — | (14,093) | — |
| Convertible preferred stock cash dividends | — | — | — | (5,149) | — |
| Junior preferred stock accumulated dividends | — | — | — | (1,701) | (514) |
| Balance at May 30, 1987 | $ 35 | — | $ — | $ — | $(22,419) |

See accompanying notes to consolidated financial statements.

13

**Exhibit D**  Consolidated Statements of Changes in Financial Position
*Revco D.S., Inc. and Subsidiaries*
*Periods from December 30, 1986 to May 30, 1987 and June 1, 1986 to December 29, 1986*
*and Fiscal Years ended May 31, 1986 and June 1, 1985*

| (Dollars in Thousands) | December 30, 1986 to May 30, 1987 | Predecessor Corporation (note 1) | | |
| --- | --- | --- | --- | --- |
| | | June 1, 1986 to December 29, 1986 | 52 Weeks Ended May 31, 1986 | 52 Weeks Ended June 1, 1985 |
| Net cash flows from operating activities: | | | | |
| Net earnings (loss) | $ (21,905) | $ 31,741 | $ 56,934 | $ 38,906 |
| Interest expense, net | 62,652 | 17,946 | 26,524 | 13,019 |
| Net earnings before interest expense, net | 40,747 | 49,687 | 83,458 | 51,925 |
| Noncash items included in net earnings (loss): | | | | |
| Depreciation and amortization | 26,023 | 23,168 | 36,438 | 30,125 |
| Loss (gain) on disposals of property and equipment | 425 | (101) | 299 | 273 |
| Gains on sales of divisions, net of tax | — | (3,488) | (6,166) | — |
| Deferred income taxes | — | 4,469 | 8,546 | 5,375 |
| Treasury stock sold to profit sharing and savings plan | — | 1,747 | 1,512 | — |
| Working capital provided by operating activities | 67,195 | 75,482 | 124,087 | 87,698 |
| Decrease (increase) in receivables | (8,423) | (22,126) | 5,977 | (21,880) |
| Decrease (increase) in inventories | 103,311 | (79,423) | 6,693 | (19,712) |
| Decrease (increase) in prepaids | 4,844 | (3,245) | 2,355 | (7,654) |
| Increase (decrease) in accounts payable | (52,697) | 57,995 | 7,229 | 7,256 |

| | | | | |
|---|---|---|---|---|
| Increase (decrease) in accrued liabilities | 746 | 342 | 10,923 | (1,241) |
| Other | 3,811 | (2,235) | 926 | (5,923) |
| Net cash flows provided by operating activities | 118,787 | 26,790 | 158,190 | 38,544 |
| Net cash flows from investing activities: | | | | |
| Purchase of Revco D.S., Inc. common stock | (1,253,155) | — | — | — |
| Costs related to the purchase of Revco D.S., Inc. | (5,814) | (6,235) | — | — |
| Purchase of Carls Drug Co., Inc. | — | — | (35,000) | — |
| Additions to property and equipment | (5,420) | (22,276) | (82,415) | (90,173) |
| Additions to computer software | (379) | (1,363) | (1,513) | (2,128) |
| Proceeds from sales of property and equipment | 4,414 | 14,154 | 1,795 | 6,345 |
| Proceeds from sales of divisions, net of tax | 19,700 | 35,358 | 7,978 | — |
| Decrease in restructuring reserve, net of noncash changes | (19,455) | — | — | — |
| Increase in net assets of operations to be divested | (9,678) | — | — | — |
| Decrease (increase) in notes receivable | (13,785) | (23,023) | (30) | 1,487 |
| Interest income received | 1,370 | 1,495 | 2,158 | 1,918 |
| Net cash flows used by investing activities | (1,282,202) | (1,890) | (107,027) | (82,551) |
| Net cash flows from financing activities: | | | | |
| Proceeds from preferred stock issued | 245,117 | — | — | — |
| Proceeds from common stock puts, common stock subject to put options and common stock issued | 36,157 | — | — | — |

**Exhibit D**  Consolidated Statements of Changes in Financial Position (*continued*)

| (Dollars in Thousands) | Predecessor Corporation (note 1) | | | |
| --- | --- | --- | --- | --- |
| | December 30, 1986 to May 30, 1987 | June 1, 1986 to December 29, 1986 | 52 Weeks Ended May 31, 1986 | 52 Weeks Ended June 1, 1985 |
| Proceeds from long-term debt issued | 1,158,750 | — | 261,399 | 11,729 |
| Deferred financing costs | (78,660) | — | (4,197) | (595) |
| Reductions in long-term debt | (150,082) | (2,006) | (5,056) | (4,539) |
| Increase (decrease) in short-term borrowings | — | — | (120,939) | 70,031 |
| Purchases of common stock for treasury | — | — | (98,778) | — |
| Proceeds from stock plans | — | 84 | 1,397 | 327 |
| Compensation on restricted stock option plans | — | 24 | 195 | 367 |
| Federal income tax benefits derived from stock option plans | — | 2,036 | 771 | 133 |
| Interest payments | (24,291) | (18,434) | (22,309) | (14,603) |
| Cash dividend payments | (2,599) | (19,461) | (26,724) | (29,282) |
| Net cash flows provided (used) by financing activities | 1,184,392 | (37,757) | (14,241) | 33,568 |
| Net increase (decrease) in cash and equivalents | $ 20,977 | $(12,857) | $ 36,922 | $(10,439) |

See accompanying notes to consolidated financial statements.

## PART TWO

# Legal Aspects of Bankruptcy and Insolvency Proceedings

# Nature of Bankruptcy and Insolvency Proceedings

**EXHIBIT 3-1   SAMPLE PETITION**

UNITED STATES BANKRUPTCY COURT
FOR THE SOUTHERN DISTRICT OF NEW YORK
REORGANIZATION NO.

EMPLOYER I.D. _____

_____.
Corporation of the State
of New York,                          Original Petition: Under Chapter 11
DEBTOR.

    1. The Post Office Address of _____ is _____.
    2. Petitioner has had its principal place of business within this District for the preceding 180 days.
    3. Petitioner is qualified to file this Petition and entitled to the benefits of Title 11, United States Code, as a voluntary debtor.
    4. Petitioner intends to file a Plan pursuant to Chapter 11 of Title 11.
    5. Attached hereto and made a part hereof as Exhibit "A" is a statement of fees paid and retaining agreements.
    6. Attached hereto and made a part hereof as Exhibit "B" is a pro forma balance sheet as of March 31, 1981.
    7. Attached hereto and made a part hereof as Exhibit "C" is a list of liens encumbering the assets of the Debtor and a statement of bank accounts.
    8. Attached hereto and made a part hereof as Exhibit "D" is a list of creditors by classification.

9. Attached hereto and made a part hereof as Exhibit "E" is a list of 20 largest creditors (excluding insiders or corporations controlled by insiders), together with their names, addresses, telephone numbers and the persons in charge thereof.

10. Attached hereto and made a part hereof as Exhibit "F" is a list of stockholders, together with their names and addresses.

WHEREFORE, Petitioner prays for relief in accordance with Chapter 11 of Title 11, United States Code.

_____

A Corporation of the State of New York

By: _____

President

Dated: April ___, 19_____.

_____

Attorney for Debtor

By: _____

225 Fifth Ave

New York, New York

## R E S O L U T I O N:

I HEREBY CERTIFY that at a meeting of the Board of Directors of

the following Resolution was unanimously adopted:

"RESOLVED, that the appropriate corporate officers are hereby authorized to retain counsel for the preparation, execution and filing of a proceeding for a reorganization under Chapter 11 of the Bankruptcy Code, and that the appropriate corporate officers are hereby authorized to execute all necessary papers, pleadings and documents in connection with said Chapter 11 proceedings."

IN CERTIFICATION WHEREOF, I have hereunto set my hand and seal of the Corporation this ___day of April, _____.

_____(L.S.)

Assistant Secretary

**Exhibit 3-1 Sample Petition**

**21**

# V E R I F I C A T I O N

STATE OF NEW YORK ⎫
COUNTY OF NEW YORK ⎬ ss.
　　　　　　　　　　 ⎭

I, —————, President of ————————— named as Debtor in the above Petition, certify under penalty of perjury that the foregoing is true and correct.

By: ——————————

————————— President

Sworn and Subscribed to before
me on this —— day of April ———.

————————————————
A Notary Public of New York

# EXHIBIT "A"

STATE OF NEW YORK
COUNTY OF NEW YORK:

SHELDON SCHACHTER, being duly sworn according to law upon his oath, deposes and says:

1. That he is associated with the firm of ————————— which firm maintains offices at —————————.

2. The firm of ————————— has been retained by the Debtor herein for the purpose of representation with respect to the filing of an Original Petition Under Chapter 11 relating to Bankruptcy.

3. A full and complete statement of the retention of said firm referred to above is that they were retained prior to the Petition in Chapter 11 for review, discussion and analysis of the problems of the Debtor and for services rendered to be retained with respect to a Petition in Chapter 11 proceedings and all matters relative thereto, and for such further compensation as the Court may allow in accordance with the provisions of the Bankruptcy Code, your Petitioners have received the sum of $100,000 plus $8,500 for costs. Said funds were received from the Debtor.

————————————————

Sworn and subscribed to
before me this ——day of ————.

————————————————
A Notary Public of New York
My Commission Expires on March —————.

## EXHIBIT "B"

ESTIMATED PRO FORMA BALANCE SHEET AS OF _____ AS TO NONTANGIBLE ASSETS ONLY.

### Assets

| | |
|---|---:|
| CASH IN BANKS | $    300,000.00 |
| ACCOUNTS RECEIVABLE | 2,000,000.00 |
| Airplane (cost) | 2,700,000.00 |
| Helicopter (cost) | 700,000.00 |
| | $5,700,000.00 |

### Liabilities

| | |
|---|---:|
| TO TRADE & BANKS UNSECURED | $10,000,000.00 |

(ALL ABOVE ESTIMATED)

## EXHIBIT "C"

### Liens and Encumbrances

Security Interest on Airplane and Helicopter in favor of National Community Bank for debt of approximately $3,800,000.00.

### Bank Accounts

| Name of Bank | On Deposit | Account No. |
|---|---|---|
| National Community Bank | -0- | #00031–752–1 |
| Citizens First National Bank | -0- | #   061–09325 |
| Midlantic National Bank | $600,000 | #142–019–956 |

Exhibit 3-1 Sample Petition 23

## EXHIBIT "D"

## List of Creditors by Classification

|  | *Amount Due* |
|---|---|
| *SECURED* | |
| National Community Bank | $3,800,000.00 |
| 24 Park Avenue | |
| New York, New York | |
| | |
| *PRIORITIES* | |
| Internal Revenue Service | Unknown |
| Holtzville, New York | |
| | |
| State of New Jersey | Unknown |
| c/o Attorney General of the State of New Jersey | |
| Trenton, New Jersey | |
| | |
| Borough of Elmwood Park | Unknown |
| Elmwood Park, New Jersey 07407 | |
| | |
| N.J. State Motor Fuels and Sales Tax | Unknown |
| Division of Taxation | |
| W. State and Willow Street | |
| Trenton, New Jersey | |
| | |
| New York State Motor Fuels & Sales Tax | Unknown |
| Division of Taxation | |
| Albany, New York | |

*UNSECURED*
The complete listing of creditors has not been included.

## EXHIBIT "E"

### List of 20 Largest Creditors

[Names omitted]

## EXHIBIT "F"

### Stockholders of Martin Motor Oil, Inc.

| | |
|---|---:|
| _____.<br>Thompson Drive<br>New York, New York | 50% |
| _____.<br>Thompson Drive<br>New York, N.Y. | 50% |

# Out-of-Court Settlements

**EXHIBIT 4-1  AGREEMENT WITH CREDITORS AND DEBTOR AND DEBTOR'S SOLICITATION LETTER (DISCLOSURE STATEMENT)**

February 28, 19X8

To the Creditors of C_____, Inc.
N_____, Massachusetts and
S_____ Massachusetts

Undoubtedly, you are aware that the debtor is engaged in the retail sale of wearing apparel for men, women, and children. Since December 3, 19X7 we have had a number of meetings with creditors' representatives and their counsel. The purpose of said meetings was to determine whether it would be best to liquidate the assets, or whether we should consider a plan of reorganization that is feasible and in the best interest of creditors, and would allow debtor to remain in business. In order to reach a decision, we had the assets, consisting of inventory, furniture, fixtures and equipment, appraised and the books and records of the company thoroughly examined by the creditors' committee in accordance with its accountants' report, a copy of which is enclosed [omitted].

It is clear that, on forced liquidation and after payment of administration costs and expenses, taxes, and other priority claims, there would be available to general unsecured creditors a dividend of less than 10%. Normally, payment would be made in or within 12 to 18 months after the first meeting of creditors. The national average for costs and expenses in the administration of a bankruptcy estate is approximately 25% of the total realized assets. Therefore, since the appraised assets, including cash on hand, total $56,562.71 and the estimated cost of administration is 25% of that amount, or approximately $14,140.63, there would be left about $42,422.08. If we then deducted all priority claims for taxes, wages, and other amounts owed, the total of said sums would be $25,140.00. There would then be available to general unsecured creditors

$17,282.06 which represents less than 10% of the total due to general unsecured creditors, and would not be distributed until the case is closed, usually 12–18 months after the filing.

After a number of meetings, a plan was proposed which contemplated the formation of a new corporation which would acquire all of the assets of the old corporation.

The officers and directors of the new corporation would be the same as the old corporation, as follows:

| | |
|---|---|
| President and Treasurer: | D_____ T_____. |
| Vice President: | M_____ T_____. |
| Clerk: | R_____ T_____. |
| Directors: | D_____ T_____. |
| | M_____ T_____. |
| | R_____ T_____. |

The stockholders would also be the same in the new corporation as in the old and each would own 25% of the 100 shares of stock outstanding, as follows:

D_____ T_____ 25 shares.

M_____ T_____ 25 shares.

R_____ T_____ 25 shares.

V_____ T_____ 25 shares.

The new corporation's name is to be W_____, Inc. Said corporation will agree to purchase the assets of C_____, Inc. and to pay the following:

(1) All taxes and priorities, in cash, in full.

(2) To pay to general unsecured creditors a sum equal to 20% of the allowed claims in four installments:

a   5% down.
b   5% in 6 months.
c   5% in 12 months.
d   5% in 18 months.

(3) Agree to pay all fees and expenses of the settlement, which are estimated to be in the neighborhood of $14,000 or $15,000, as follows:

a   $5,000 down.
b   Balance in monthly installments of $1,500 until paid.

**Exhibit 4-1    Agreement with Creditors and Debtor**                                    **27**

All of the officers will continue to be employed by the new corporation and to perform the same duties and to receive the same compensation as they had received from the debtor corporation.

The weekly compensation and duties of the officers of W_____, Inc. will be as follows:

| | | | |
|---|---|---|---|
| D_____ | T_____, | Buyer and General Manager | $500.00 |
| M_____ | T_____, | Manager of the N_____ location | $250.00 |
| R_____ | T_____, | Manager of the S_____ location | $150.00 |

The new corporation has entered into an agreement with the debtor corporation and an executed copy is available for examination at this office.

The new corporation, W_____, Inc., is to give, as security for its promise to make payments as heretofore mentioned, the following:

**A**   Trust Indenture and Security Agreement to B_____ R_____ of B_____, Massachusetts, counsel for Creditors' Committee, and I_____ W_____, counsel for the Debtor, as co-trustees, covering all the assets of the debtor, including inventory, accounts receivable, furniture, fixtures and equipment [omitted].

**B**   A pledge of all the issued and outstanding stock of the newly formed corporation.

**C**   D_____ T_____ is to personally guaranty in writing the payment of the amount promised to be paid to the creditors heretofore mentioned. As security for his guaranty, he is to give a mortgage on a house which has been appraised as having a current market value of $45,000 and upon which there is a first mortgage balance of $19,000.

The agreement mentioned will include the usual safeguards with regard to amount of salaries paid to officers and principals of the debtor; a right to declare the entire balance due in the event the company defaults in any payment when due or it sustains a loss beyond the aggregate sum of $15,000; and prohibiting payment of dividends or issuance of additional shares of stock.

The foregoing is a brief summary of the Plan and should not be relied upon for voting purposes. Creditors are urged to read the Plan in full. Creditors are further urged to consult with counsel, or with each other, in order to fully understand the Plan. An intelligent judgment concerning the Plan cannot be made without understanding it.

No representations concerning the Debtor (particularly as to the value of its property) are authorized by the Debtor other than as set forth in this statement. Any representations or inducements made to secure acceptance of the Plan that are other than as contained in this statement should not be relied upon by any creditor. The information contained herein has not been subject to a certified audit. The records kept by the Debtor are not warranted or represented to be without any inaccuracy, although every effort has been made to be accurate.

In order to hasten the distribution referred to above in an out of court arrangement, we have prepared and herewith enclose an acceptance form that could be used in the event a reorganization under Chapter 11 of the Federal Bankruptcy Code is found necessary in order to conclude the settlement.

If you accept our recommendation for an early consummation of the proposed settlement, please execute and return the enclosed acceptance form to this office, together with a statement of your account, showing amount due as of December 3, 19X7.

If you have any questions, please write to this office.

Very truly yours,

I_____ W_____

## Creditors' Agreement

This agreement of February 28, 19X8 by and among C_____, Inc., a corporation duly organized by law and having its principal offices in N_____ in the Commonwealth of Massachusetts, hereinafter called "Debtor," and W_____, Inc., a corporation duly organized by law and having its principal offices in S_____ in said Commonwealth, hereinafter called the "new corporation," and B_____ R_____ and I_____ W_____, both having places of business in B_____ in said Commonwealth, hereinafter called "Trustees," and those unsecured creditors of Debtor who sign this agreement or consent hereto by separate instrument, hereinafter called "Creditors," is made with reference to the following facts:

1   Debtor is indebted to a number of Creditors and desires to effect a settlement of its obligations with said Creditors and an extension of time for the payment of the agreed settlement amount by the new corporation. The new corporation will purchase all the assets of the Debtor, and will give, as security for Creditors, a Trust Indenture and Security Agreement to B _____ R _____, counsel for the Creditors Committee and I _____ W _____, counsel for the Debtor, as co-trustees, covering all the assets of the Debtor, including inventory, accounts receivable, furniture, fixtures, and equipment, and including the usual safeguards with regard to amount of salaries paid to officers and principals of the Debtor; a right to declare the entire balance due in the event the company defaults in any payment when due or it sustains a loss beyond the aggregate sum of $15,000; and prohibiting payment of dividends or issuance of additional shares of stock. Creditors agree with each other and are willing to forego their present rights to enforce present payment of the agreed settlement amount of the terms and conditions set forth hereinbelow.

2   Subject to all the terms, provisions and conditions herein, each and all the Creditors shall and do hereby settle and extend the amount and time of payment of their respective claims as they existed on the effective date of this agreement as defined in paragraph 8 herein, in accordance with the

Exhibit 4-1 **Agreement with Creditors and Debtor** 29

schedule of payments contained in Schedule A which is attached hereto and made a part hereof.

3   From the period beginning on the effective date of this agreement, until the termination date (the date of the last payment to Creditors pursuant to Schedule A), or until such later date or dates as may be agreed on by each individual Creditor, each Creditor agrees that it will not commence or prosecute any action or proceeding against the Debtor or the new corporation, levy any execution, attachment, or any process against the property of the Debtor or the new corporation by reason of the debt owing to such Creditor as of the effective date of this agreement, or file or join in any petition or any proceeding under the Bankruptcy Code or its amendments, 11 U.S.C. §§ 101 et seq. (1978), or any other proceeding having for its object the appointment of a receiver, assignee, trustee or other custodian for the Debtor or the new corporation or the assets of either. However, it is specifically understood, if the amount of the debt of any Creditor is disputed by the Debtor, or the new corporation, that such Creditor may commence and prosecute suit on the disputed claim, but any judgment by such Creditor in connection with such disputed claim shall not be enforced and payment thereof, in the same percentage as is paid to other Creditors hereunder, shall be settled and extended in the same manner as all other debts.

4   The new corporation shall make the payments required by the schedule of payments in accordance with Schedule A to the Trustees; who shall distribute the sum so received to each Creditor in accordance with the time for payments set forth.

5   Each Creditor hereby waives his right to assert in any proceeding at law, in equity or in bankruptcy, that any payment made pursuant to this agreement constitutes an improper, voidable or preferential payment.

6   Nothing contained in this agreement shall be construed or deemed to release or discharge any rights or remedies that any Creditor may now or hereafter have against any endorser, guarantor, or surety who may now or hereafter be liable to any such Creditor upon any debt settled or deferred by the provisions of this agreement, and each such right and remedy is hereby reserved to any such Creditor.

7   In the event that the Debtor or the new corporation becomes a debtor in a proceeding under Chapter 11 of the Federal Bankruptcy Code and proposes a Plan of Reorganization with terms of payment for the debt settled and extended herein in an equivalent (or more favorable amount) to creditors other than those contained in this agreement, then the Creditors who have accepted this agreement shall be deemed to have accepted said Plan of Reorganization in writing without the need for further or separate acceptance. The Ballot For Accepting or Rejecting the Creditors' Agreement and Plan of Reorganization Under Chapter 11, hereinafter "Ballot," which is attached hereto and marked Schedule B, shall also constitute such Acceptance or Rejection of a Plan under Chapter 11 of the Bankruptcy Code.

In this way it is intended to protect each Creditor who executes the Ballot attached as Schedule B, to insure that each Creditor shall receive as much as any other Creditor in the event of a Plan of Reorganization pursuant to Chapter 11 of the Bankruptcy Code.

**8** This agreement shall become binding on all Creditors, Debtor, new corporation, and Trustees in the event ninety-eight (98%) percent in number and dollar amount of unsecured Creditors of the Debtor as of the effective date, who are entitled to join in this agreement, have assented to this agreement by executing and returning to the Trustees the Ballot attached as Schedule B; provided, however, that Debtor may waive the ninety-eight (98%) percent condition by giving written notice to the Creditors that it is waived, in which event this agreement shall become binding upon the Creditors, the Debtor, the new corporation and the Trustees; that date shall be deemed "the effective date" of this agreement.

**9** This agreement shall bind and benefit the parties hereto and each of their respective heirs, administrators, successors and assigns.

**10** Acceptances and/or notices which may be required to be given hereunder shall be given either by certified mail or first class mail, postage prepaid, as follows:

|                         |            |
|-------------------------|------------|
| To the Debtor           | [Counsel]  |
| To the new corporation: | [Counsel]  |
| To the Trustees:        | [Counsel]  |

**11** This agreement may be executed in multiple counterparts.

C_____, Inc., DEBTOR
By: _____
President

W_____, Inc.
By:_____
President

_____
B_____ R_____
Trustee and not individually

_____
L_____ W_____
Trustee and not individually

**Exhibit 4-1   Agreement with Creditors and Debtor**                                    **31**

## SCHEDULE A

### Schedule of Payments to Creditors

All general unsecured creditors shall be paid twenty (20%) percent of their claims as follows:

**1**   Five (5%) percent in cash of the agreed amount of the debt once the agreement becomes binding according to the terms set forth in paragraph 8 of this agreement.

**2**   Five (5%) percent in cash six months from the date of the first payment.

**3**   Five (5%) percent in cash 12 months from the date of the first payment.

**4**   Five (5%) percent in cash 18 months from the date of the first payment.

## SCHEDULE B

**C_____, Incorporated**
**M_____, Massachusetts**
**Ballot for Accepting or Rejecting**
**Creditors' Agreement and Plan of Reorganization**
**Under Chapter 11**

The undersigned, the holder of a general unsecured claim against C_____, Inc., in the unpaid principal amount indicated below, does hereby
[Check one box]        ☐ Accept        ☐ Reject
the Creditors' Agreement dated February 4, 19X8, between C_____, Inc., Debtor, and certain of the holders of general unsecured claims against said Debtor. The undersigned acknowledges the receipt of a copy of said Creditors' Agreement.

The undersigned further consents to the use of this ballot, if a petition is filed for a Reorganization under Chapter 11 of the new Bankruptcy Code, 11 U.S.C. §§ 101 et seq. (1978), for the acceptance or rejection of any Plan of Reorganization which incorporates the terms of the aforesaid Creditors' Agreement of February 4, 19X8, or embodies said terms in principle, or which plan is held not to impair nor materially and adversely affect the interests of the holders of general unsecured claims under said Agreement.

$_____
Amount of claim

Print or type name:     _____
Signed:                 _____
If appropriate     (By:_____
                   (As:_____

Street or Box           _____
City, State, Zip Code   _____

Please sign on the line above (if a corporation, it must be acknowledged by the Secretary of the corporation; if a partnership, this must be signed by a partner; if an individual, then signed by the individual; or, if an individual who is a d/b/a in particular company name, then the individual's signature with the d/b/a must be set forth).

Please return this ballot with a statement of your account (copies of invoices, etc.) so that it will be received on or before March 30, 19X8; allow adequate time for delivery if returned by mail.

Return To:

[Counsel]

# Rehabilitation Proceedings Under the Bankruptcy Code

**EXHIBIT 5-1   SAMPLE DEBTOR'S PLAN**

RONALD S. ORR
DAVID H. KENNEDY
HENRY C. KEVANE
JANINE M. DLUTOWSKI
GIBSON, DUNN & CRUTCHER
333 South Grand Avenue
Los Angeles, California 90071

(213) 229–7000

Attorneys for Debtor

**UNITED STATES BANKRUPTCY COURT
NORTHERN DISTRICT OF CALIFORNIA**

| | |
|---|---|
| **In re:**<br>WORLDS OF WONDER, INC.,<br>a California corporation,<br>Debtor,<br>Tax I.D. No. 94-2960825 | Case No. 4-87-05973-J<br>CHAPTER 11 |

**DEBTOR'S FIRST AMENDED PLAN OF REORGANIZATION**

## Table of Contents

**Exhibit 5-1   Sample Debtor's Plan**                                          **35**

EXHIBITS: [Not included in this volume]

Exhibit A   Asset Purchase Agreement (including the Letter Agreement amendments thereto dated March 24, 1989 and April 7, 1989, respectively) and the following exhibits thereto:

Exhibit G—Certificate of Incorporation of Buyer
Exhibit L—Management Agreement
Exhibit M—Management Consulting Agreement

Exhibit B   Summary of Principal Terms of Liquidating Trust Agreement

Exhibit C   List of Acquired Contracts

*(Editor's Note: A plan outline and voting instructions as contained in the disclosure statement are presented before the plan.)*

## Plan Outline

### 1. Classification of Claims and Interests; Distributions

The following is a summary of the classification of Claims and interests of holders of Debtor's Common Stock ("Interests") and the distributions that will be made to the holders of such Claims and Interests under the Plan:

| Class | Description | Estimate of Total Allowed Claims ($000) | Distribution |
|---|---|---|---|
| 1 | All Priority Claims under Section 507(a) of the Code (other than liabilities assumed by the New WOW, certain amounts secured by Trust Fund Accounts and the Nightingale Fee payable on and after the Closing Date by the Lenders) | $2,480 | Cash in full amount of the Priority Claim or as agreed by Claim holder. |
| 2 | Secured Claims of ABN | $16,100 | The Note, the ABN Note, the Selected Net Assets Adjustment Note (other than the Class 3 residual interest therein) and the ABN Inventory Proceeds (other than the Class 3 residual interest therein), plus the amount, if any, of the Class 2 Distribution Adjustment. |
| 3 | Secured Claims of FNBC, Barclays/American Business Credit, Inc., Centerre Bank, Chicago-Tokyo Bank and First National Bank of Louisville | $67,400 | Pro rata shares of: 60,000 shares of New WOW's Series A Preferred Stock; 150,000 shares of New WOW's Series B Preferred Stock; the Class 3 Interest in the |

Selected Net Assets Adjustment Note, if any; the Class 3 Interest in the ABN Inventory Proceeds, if any; the cash and cash equivalents of the Debtor and its subsidiaries existing on the Closing Date, other than (a) amounts paid to the holders of Class 1 Claims, (b) the Cash Reserve Fund, and (c) the Class 6 Cash Fund; any cash remaining in the Cash Reserve Fund after the Debtor's business has been wound up; the Debtor's accounts receivable existing on the Closing Date; all recoveries by the Debtor of amounts related to voidable transfers, preferences and other transfers, pending lawsuits and any other claims or causes of action of the Debtor existing on the Closing Date; certain other miscellaneous assets of the Debtor not purchased by New WOW; and all of the equity interest in Old WOW; less the amount, if any, of the Class 2 Distribution Adjustment.

| | | | |
|---|---|---|---|
| 4 | All Secured Claims not included in Class 2 or Class 3 | Undetermined | Cash equal to the amount of the Allowed Secured Claim or the property securing such Claim, at the Debtor's option. |
| 5 | All general unsecured Claims of $10,000 or less and all general unsecured Claims voluntarily reduced to $10,000 | $2,500 | Cash from the Class 6 Cash Fund equal to $.10 for every $1.00 of Allowed Claim. |
| 6 | All general unsecured Claims not included in Class 5, including Claims arising as a result of rejection of executory contracts, Claims of the Subordinated Debenture holders, and unsecured and deficiency Claims of the holders of Class 2 and Class 3 Claims | $245,000 | Pro rata shares of Class 6 Cash Fund reduced by the amount of distributions to holders of Class 5 Claims and expenses chargeable against Class 6; and pro rata shares of 45,000 shares of Series C Preferred Stock of New WOW. However, because of partial enforcement of contractual subordination of Claims of Subordinated Debenture holders to Class 3 Claims, holders of Subordinated Debentures will receive only 50% |

**Exhibit 5-1  Sample Debtor's Plan**                                    **37**

| | | | |
|---|---|---|---|
| | | | of the distributions of Series C Preferred Stock otherwise distributable to Subordinated Debenture holders and no portion of the Class 6 Cash Fund. The pro rata amount of each distribution on account of a Class 6 Allowed Claim cannot be determined with any precision. See Section VI(C)(6) below. |
| 7 | All Interests of the holders of the Debtor's Common Stock, all Claims for damages or rescission based on the purchase or sale of the Debtor's securities and all Claims of any person (including Debtor's officers and directors) for indemnification, contribution or reimbursement with respect to Claims related to the purchase or sale of the Debtor's securities | N/A | No distribution. All of the Debtor's existing common stock will be cancelled. |

## 2. Major Terms of the Plan

The Plan provides that the Debtor will sell substantially all of its assets to WOW Acquisition Corp. ("New WOW"), a Delaware corporation recently formed by Eli S. Jacobs ("Jacobs"), pursuant to the terms of an Asset Purchase Agreement dated February 16, 1989. In consideration for the sale of those assets, New WOW will issue Series A and B Preferred Stock to the holders of Class 3 Allowed Claims and Series C Preferred Stock to the holders of Class 6 Allowed Claims under the Plan and will issue to ABN, as the holder of Class 2 Allowed Claims, certain promissory notes in the initial nominal principal amounts of $10,000,000, $2,000,000 and an amount based on certain adjustments to be determined after the Closing Date. New WOW intends to continue the Debtor's business of designing, developing, marketing and selling toys and related products for the retail market and may in the future acquire companies in the toy or other industries.

Following the purchase of the Debtor's assets by New WOW, on the Effective Date, the business of the reorganized Debtor ("Old WOW") will consist of liquidating the Debtor's remaining assets for the benefit of holders of Class 2 Allowed Claims and Class 3 Allowed Claims and winding up the Debtor's affairs in accordance with applicable law. Old WOW, which will be owned by the holders of Class 3 Allowed Claims, will be managed by persons designated by the holders of Class 3 Allowed Claims.

The terms and conditions of the sale of assets to New WOW are described in detail in Section IV below. Distributions will be made in accordance with the classification of Claims and Interests under the Plan, which is described more fully in Section VI below.

TO DETERMINE THE CLASSIFICATION OF YOUR CLAIM(S) OR INTEREST(S) UNDER THE PLAN AND FOR A DETAILED DESCRIPTION OF THE AMOUNT AND TIMING OF DISTRIBUTIONS TO EACH CLASS, SEE SECTIONS VI(B) AND (C) BELOW.

### 3. Tax Consequences of the Plan

Implementation of the Plan may have significant federal income tax consequences for Old WOW, New WOW and the Creditors receiving distributions under the Plan. These federal income tax consequences are discussed in Section VIII below.

### 4. Alternatives to the Plan

Other alternatives to the Plan, including liquidation, may exist. The Debtor does not believe, however, that any reasonably likely alternative provides greater recoveries to Creditors than the Plan. Section IX(C) contains a discussion of these possible alternatives and the reasons for the Debtor's belief that the Plan is preferable to these alternatives.

### 5. Feasibility of the Plan and Management of New WOW

The Debtor expects that New WOW will be managed by the persons and under the terms described in Section V(B) below. The feasibility of the Plan is discussed in detail in Section IX(D) below.

### 6. Conclusion

THE DEBTOR BELIEVES THAT THE PLAN PROVIDES THE GREATEST AND EARLIEST POSSIBLE RECOVERIES TO THE DEBTOR'S CREDITORS. THE DEBTOR HAS CONCLUDED THAT ACCEPTANCE OF THE PLAN IS IN THE BEST INTERESTS OF EACH AND EVERY CLASS OF CREDITORS AND RECOMMENDS THAT EACH CLASS WHOSE VOTES ARE BEING SOLICITED HEREBY VOTE TO ACCEPT THE PLAN.


## VOTING INSTRUCTIONS

### A. Creditors and Record Holders of Existing Debt Securities

IT IS IMPORTANT THAT YOU EXERCISE YOUR RIGHT TO VOTE TO ACCEPT OR REJECT THE PLAN. If you are or may be entitled to vote on the Plan, you have been sent a ballot and instructions for voting with this Dis-

Exhibit 5-1    Sample Debtor's Plan                                              39

closure Statement. You should read the ballot carefully and follow the instructions contained therein. Please use only the ballot sent to you with this Disclosure Statement.

The record date for determining which holders of the Debtor's nine percent (9%) Convertible Subordinated Debentures, due 2012, are entitled to vote on the Plan is April 10, 1989. THE INDENTURE TRUSTEE FOR THE DEBENTURES MAY NOT AND WILL NOT VOTE ON BEHALF OF HOLDERS OF THE DEBENTURES. DEBENTURE HOLDERS MUST SUBMIT THEIR OWN BALLOTS AS DESCRIBED IN THE ENCLOSED INSTRUCTIONS. DO NOT RETURN YOUR SECURITIES WITH YOUR BALLOTS.

To simplify the voting procedure, ballots have been sent to all known holders of Claims, including Disputed Claims to which objections have been or may be filed. The Bankruptcy Code provides that only the holders of Allowed Claims (or Claims which are deemed Allowed) are entitled to vote on the Plan. A Claim to which an objection has been filed is not an Allowed Claim unless and until the Bankruptcy Court rules on the objection. The Bankruptcy Court may temporarily allow a Disputed Claim to which an objection has been filed for purposes of voting on the Plan. Therefore, although the holders of Disputed Claims to which an objection has been filed will receive ballots, these votes will not be counted unless the Bankruptcy Court temporarily allows such Claims for purposes of voting on the Plan.

If a Creditor has an Allowed Claim in more than one Class, it will receive a ballot for each class. IF YOU ARE A MEMBER OF MORE THAN ONE CLASS OF CREDITORS, YOU MUST FILL OUT AND RETURN ALL BALLOTS SENT TO YOU FOR YOUR VOTE TO COUNT IN EACH CLASS.

## UNITED STATES BANKRUPTCY COURT
## NORTHERN DISTRICT OF CALIFORNIA

**In re:**
WORLDS OF WONDER, INC.,
a California corporation,
        Debtor.
Tax I.D. No. 94-2960825

Case No. 4-87-05973-J
CHAPTER 11

## DEBTOR'S FIRST AMENDED PLAN OF REORGANIZATION

Worlds of Wonder, Inc., Debtor and Debtor-in-Possession, proposes the following First Amended Plan of Reorganization pursuant to Chapter 11 of the Bankruptcy Code:

## ARTICLE I

### Definitions

For the purposes of this Plan the following terms shall have the respective meanings specified below. Unless otherwise defined herein, a term used herein that is used in the Bankruptcy Code shall have the meaning assigned to it in the Bankruptcy Code.

1.1 "ABN" means Algemene Bank Nederland, N.V.

1.2 "ABN Allowed Claim" means, collectively, the ABN Allowed Secured Claim and the ABN Allowed Unsecured Claim.

1.3 "ABN Allowed Secured Claim" means the Allowed Secured Claim held by ABN in the Reorganization Case, which shall be deemed allowed in an amount equal to the Total ABN Secured Claim on the Effective Date, reduced by all Permanent Cash Paydowns received by ABN thereon prior to the Effective Date.

1.4 "ABN Inventory Proceeds" means the Net Proceeds of (i) any sales by the Debtor of inventory outside the ordinary course of business (including without limitation any sales of Lazer Tag or ActionMax inventory to the Beekman Group) and of Inactive Inventory (whether or not outside the ordinary course of business) which occur prior to the Closing Date (including without limitation any sales of Mickey Mouse-French inventory), and (ii) any sales by the Debtor of inventory described in Section 1(b)(xi) of the Asset Purchase Agreement whether such sales occur prior to or on and after the Closing Date.

1.5 "ABN Note" shall have the meaning assigned to such term in the Asset Purchase Agreement.

1.6 "ABN Payment" shall have the meaning assigned to such term in the Agreement of Settlement dated September 2, 1988 among ABN, the Committee and the Debtor.

1.7 "ABN Proceeds" means the cash proceeds (other than payments or proceeds of the Note and the ABN Note) received by ABN in respect of its Allowed Class 2 Claims under this Plan on or after the Effective Date and which, prior to the date of determination, are Permanent Cash Paydowns and which ABN is not required to return or refund, including without limitation payments of principal or interest made to ABN in respect of the Selected Net Assets Adjustment Note, payments made to ABN of ABN Inventory Proceeds (but only to the extent such proceeds were paid on or after the Effective Date) and any payments made by the Lenders to ABN under Section 3.8(b), (c) or (e)(1) of this Plan.

1.8 "ABN Special Proceeds Lien" shall have the meaning assigned to such term in Section 3.2.

1.9 "ABN Allowed Unsecured Claim" shall mean the Allowed Class 6 Claim of ABN, which shall be deemed allowed in an amount equal to the amount of ABN payment made by ABN to the Debtor as of the Effective Date, increased

Exhibit 5-1    Sample Debtor's Plan                                                                    41

by the amount of any payments made in respect of any ABN Payment after the Effective Date.

1.10 "Acquired Contracts" means those executory contracts of the Debtor that are included within the definition of "Acquired Contracts" under the Asset Purchase Agreement and are listed in Exhibit C to this Plan.

1.11 "Administrative Claim" means a Claim or portion of a Claim which is a cost or expense of the administration of the Debtor's estate allowed under Section 503(b) of the Bankruptcy Code that is entitled to priority under Section 507(a)(1) of the Bankruptcy Code, including but not limited to any actual and necessary cost and expense of preserving the Debtor's estate and operating the Debtor's business and all fees and expenses of Professionals entitled to compensation pursuant to the Bankruptcy Code.

1.12 "Agreement Re Preference Actions" means the Agreement Re Preference Actions dated February 18, 1989 among the Supporting Lenders, the Buyer and the Debtor.

1.13 "Allowed Claim" means a Claim which (i) has been scheduled by the Debtor pursuant to Bankruptcy Rule 1007 and is not scheduled as disputed, contingent or unliquidated and as to which no proof of claim has been filed; or (ii) is a Claim as to which a timely proof of claim has been filed and as to which Claim no objection has been made within the time permitted by the Bankruptcy Court or which has been allowed by a Final Order.

1.14 "Allowed Secured Claim" means an Allowed Claim to the extent of the value of any pre-petition or post-petition lien on or security interest in property of the Debtor which secures payment of such Claim.

1.15 "Allowed Unsecured Claim" means any Allowed Claim which is not an Administrative Claim, a Tax Claim, Priority Claim or an Allowed Secured Claim.

1.16 "Asset Purchase Agreement" means the Asset Purchase Agreement dated as of February 16, 1989 by and between the Debtor and the Buyer, as amended by the Letter Agreement dated March 24, 1989 and the Letter Agreement dated April 7, 1989, copies of which are attached as Exhibit A hereto and incorporated herein and made part hereof, as it may be properly amended from time to time.

1.17 "Assumed Liabilities" shall have the meaning assigned to such term in the Asset Purchase Agreement.

1.18 "Bankruptcy Code" means the United States Bankruptcy Code, 11 U.S.C. Sections 101 *et seq.*, as amended from time to time to the extent applicable to the Reorganization Case.

1.19 "Bankruptcy Court" means the United States Bankruptcy Court for the Northern District of California or such other Court as may hereafter exercise original jurisdiction over the Reorganization Case.

1.20 "Buyer" means WOW Acquisition Corp., a Delaware corporation.

1.21 "Cash Reserve Fund" means the Trust Fund Accounts existing on the Effective Date; plus two-sevenths of the ABN Payment, to the extent of any payments made by ABN to the Debtor or the Reorganized Debtor in respect thereof prior to or on and after the Effective Date.

1.22 "Claim" means a claim against the Debtor within the meaning of Section 101(4) of the Bankruptcy Code that arose prior to the Confirmation Date.

1.23 "Class" means a category or group of holders of Claims as designated pursuant to this Plan.

1.24 "Class 2 Distribution Adjustment Provision" means the adjustment to the distributions to be made to ABN and the Lenders that is provided for in Section 3.8 of this Plan.

1.25 "Class 3 Interest" means the residual interest of the Lenders in the Selected Net Assets Adjustment Note and the ABN Inventory Proceeds, respectively, provided for in Section 3.8 of this Plan, which is junior and subordinate to ABN's interest therein and arises only when the Remaining ABN Secured Claim is reduced to zero as provided in Section 3.8(d) of this Plan.

1.26 "Class 6 Cash Fund" means an amount of cash equal to five-sevenths of the ABN Payment, to the extent of any payments made by ABN prior to or on and after the Effective Date.

1.27 "Closing" shall have the meaning assigned to such term in the Asset Purchase Agreement.

1.28 "Closing Date" shall have the meaning assigned to such term in the Asset Purchase Agreement.

1.29 "Collection Agreement" shall have the meaning assigned to such term in the Asset Purchase Agreement.

1.30 "Committee" means the Official Committee of Unsecured Creditors in the Debtor's Reorganization Case, as it shall be constituted from time to time.

1.31 "Confirmation" means entry of an order of the Bankruptcy Court confirming this Plan pursuant to Section 1129 of the Bankruptcy Code.

1.32 "Confirmation Date" means the date upon which the Confirmation Order is entered on the docket by the Clerk of the Bankruptcy Court.

1.33 "Confirmation Order" means the order of the Bankruptcy Court confirming this Plan pursuant to Section 1129 of the Bankruptcy Code.

1.34 "Debenture Indenture" means the Indenture dated as of June 4, 1987, between the Debtor and Bankers Trust Company, as Trustee, under which the Subordinated Debentures were issued.

1.35 "Debt Instrument" shall have the meaning assigned to such term in Section 13.5 of this Plan.

1.36 "Debtor" means Worlds of Wonder, Inc., a California corporation.

1.37 "Disputed Claim" shall mean any Claim which has been scheduled by the Debtor pursuant to Bankruptcy Rule 1007 or as to which a proof of claim has been filed to the extent such Claim is not an Allowed Claim.

1.38 "Effective Date" means the Closing Date.

1.39 "Estate" shall mean the estate created in the Reorganization Case pursuant to Section 541 of the Bankruptcy Code.

1.40 "Excess Class 1 Claim" shall have the meaning assigned to such term in Section 5.2 of this Plan.

**Exhibit 5-1   Sample Debtor's Plan**                                                     **43**

1.41 "Excluded Assets" shall have the meaning assigned to such term in the Asset Purchase Agreement.

1.42 "FNBC" means The First National Bank of Chicago as agent for the Lenders under that certain Amended and Restated Loan and Security Agreement dated September 30, 1987 between the Lenders and the Debtor, and not individually.

1.43 "Final Order" means an order or judgment of the Bankruptcy Court which has not been reversed, stayed, modified or amended and as to which (i) the time to appeal or to seek review, rehearing or certiorari has expired (without regard to whether the time to seek relief of a judgment under Rule 60(b) of the Federal Rules of Civil Procedure has expired); and (ii) no appeal or petition for review, rehearing or certiorari is pending or as to which any right to appeal or to seek certiorari, review, or rehearing has been waived.

1.44 "Inactive Inventory" shall have the meaning assigned to such term in the Asset Purchase Agreement.

1.45 "Intercreditor Agreement" shall mean an agreement between FNBC and ABN, in form and substance satisfactory to FNBC and ABN, acknowledging the continuing effectiveness of the Intercreditor Agreement dated September 1987 between the Lenders and ABN to the extent not inconsistent with this Plan and providing for certain notice and reporting obligations of ABN and FNBC with respect to the payments to be made under Section 3.8 of this Plan.

1.46 "Lenders" shall have the meaning assigned to such term in Section 2.3 of this Plan.

1.47 "Lender Proceeds" means the aggregate amount of cash received by the Lenders in respect of their Allowed Class 3 Claims under this Plan on or after the Effective Date and which, prior to the date of determination, the Lenders are not required to return or refund, including without limitation any Net Proceeds of Excluded Assets and any payments in respect of the Series A Preferred Stock or Series B Preferred Stock received by the Lenders and any payments made by ABN to the Lenders under Section 3.8(e)(2) of this Plan.

1.48 "Lender Proceeds Account" shall have the meaning assigned to such term in Section 3.3 (c) of this Plan.

1.49 "Lender's Pro Rata Share" means each Lender's share set forth in the Loan and Security Agreement.

1.50 "Lenders' Unsecured Deficiency Claim" means the difference between the total amount of the Allowed Claims held by the Lenders and the value, as of the Effective Date, of the Lender Proceeds distributable to the Lenders under this Plan. The Lenders' Unsecured Deficiency Claim shall be deemed allowed in an amount equal to $48,200,000 as of the Effective Date; provided that, on motion of the Lenders, the Reorganized Debtor or the Committee filed with the Bankruptcy Court at any time after 13 months, but not more than 15 months, from the Effective Date, the Bankruptcy Court shall, on due notice to the Reorganized Debtor, the Committee and the Lenders, hold a hearing for the purpose of determining whether the Lenders' Unsecured Deficiency Claim should be adjusted upward or downward, as the case may be, to the extent that (i) the net present value as of the Effective Date of (A) the Lender Proceeds actually received by the Lenders on and after the Effective Date until the date of such hearing, plus (B) the fair value of all other property distributed or to be distributed to the Lenders on account of their Allowed Class 3 Claims which has not as of the date of such hearing been converted to cash proceeds and distributed to the Lenders (including without limitation any avoidance actions or other causes of action referred to in Section 3.3 (vii) which are then pending or otherwise unliquidated) is greater than or less than (ii) the difference between the total amount of the Allowed Claims held by the Lenders and $48,200,000.

1.51 "Liquidating Trust" shall mean the liquidating trust that will be created pursuant to the Liquidating Trust Agreement and this Plan, as described generally in Exhibit B hereto, and which will hold the Class 6 Cash Fund (subject to certain deductions and the payment of Excess Class 1 Claims pursuant to Section 5.2 hereof) and the Series C Preferred Stock for the benefit of holders of Class 5 Claims and Class 6 Claims until all objections to the allowance of Class 5 Claims and Class 6 Claims have been determined by the Court by Final Order or otherwise finally resolved.

1.52 "Liquidating Trust Agreement" means the Liquidating Trust Agreement to be entered into by the Debtor and a bank or trust company or other person qualified to act as trustee and selected by the Debtor under which the Liquidating Trust is created.

1.53 "Loan and Security Agreement" means the Amended and Restated Loan and Security Agreement dated September 30, 1987 by and among the Debtor and FNBC as agent for itself and the Lenders.

1.54 "Management Agreement" shall have the meaning assigned to such term in the Asset Purchase Agreement.

1.55 "Management Consulting Agreement" shall have the meaning assigned to such term in the Asset Purchase Agreement.

1.56 "Net Proceeds" means the gross proceeds received from the sale, lease, disposition, liquidation and collection of assets, less amounts actually incurred for (i) necessary and reasonable costs in connection with such sale, lease, disposition, liquidation or collection, including but not limited to, attorneys' fees related thereto if such fees shall have been approved by the holder or holders of any lien on such assets, and (ii) all reasonable and necessary liabilities, charges, offsets and encumbrances required to be discharged with respect to such assets and in connection with the sale, lease, disposition, liquidation and collection thereof, if the foregoing shall have been approved by the holder or holders of any lien on such assets.

1.57 "Nightingale" means Nightingale & Associates, Inc.

1.58 "Nightingale Engagement Letter" means the engagement letter between the Debtor and Nightingale dated April 27, 1988.

1.59 "Nightingale Fee" means the fee payable by the Debtor to Nightingale equal to 3% of the amount of certain net proceeds distributed to creditors of the Debtor after April 1, 1988, that is provided for in the Nightingale Engagement Letter.

**Exhibit 5-1   Sample Debtor's Plan**                                    **45**

1.60 "Note" shall have the meaning assigned to such term in the Asset Purchase Agreement.

1.61 "Old Common Stock" means shares of common stock, no par value per share, of the Debtor which are issued and outstanding immediately prior to the Effective Date.

1.62 "Payment Date" means (i) five business days after the stated maturity of the Selected Net Assets Adjustment Note and (ii) each business day thereafter on which the aggregate amount of Lender Proceeds received by the Lenders, whether by FNBC on behalf of the Lenders or by the Lenders directly, since the prior Payment Date equals the lesser of the then Remaining ABN Secured Claim and $100,000.

1.63 "Permanent Cash Paydowns" shall mean good funds received by ABN or the Lenders in reduction of any obligation owned by the Debtor to ABN or the Lenders that are not required to be returned or refunded to any person or entity.

1.64 "Plan" means this First Amended Plan of Reorganization and any exhibits thereto and any documents delivered in connection therewith, as the same may from time to time be amended by any duly authorized amendment or modification and to the extent permitted therein.

1.65 "Priority Claims" means those Allowed Claims which are entitled to the priority provided for under Section 507(a)(3), (4), (5) or (6) of the Bankruptcy Code.

1.66 "Professionals" means those Persons retained pursuant to an order of the Bankruptcy Court in accordance with Sections 327 and 1103 of the Bankruptcy Code.

1.67 "Pro Rata," as to intraclass calculations, means the ratio of an Allowed Claim in a particular Class to the aggregate amount of all Allowed Claims of that Class.

1.68 "Purchased Assets" shall have the meaning assigned to such term in the Asset Purchase Agreement.

1.69 "Remaining ABN Secured Claim" means (on any date of determination):

(i) The ABN Allowed Secured Claim, *minus*

(ii) An amount equal to the sum of:

(x) the original principal amount of the Note as adjusted by reductions thereto pursuant to Sections 3(b) and (c) of the Asset Purchase Agreement, *plus*

(y) the original principal amount of the ABN Note, *plus*

(z) all Permanent Cash Paydowns received by ABN after the Effective Date with respect to the Total ABN Secured Claim other than cash paydowns on the Note and the ABN Note, *plus*

(iii) Interest on the difference of the amounts determined under clause (i) and clause (ii) from time to time outstanding at the rate of 11% per annum (calculated on a 365-day or, when applicable, 366-day year), compounded annually.

1.70 "Reorganization Case" means the Debtor's case under Chapter 11 of the Bankruptcy Code administered under case number 4-87-05973-J in the Bankruptcy Court.

1.71 "Reorganized WOW" means Worlds of Wonder, Inc., a California corporation, as reorganized on and after the Effective Date.

1.72 "Required ABN Payment" shall have the meaning assigned to such term in Section 3.8 (f) of this Plan.

1.73 "Retention Bonus and Severance Liability" means any liability of the Debtor following the Effective Date under the Retention Bonus Plan approved by Order of the Bankruptcy Court on November 10, 1988, or the Severance Policy of the Debtor approved by the Bankruptcy Court on April 15, 1988, as modified by the Order of the Bankruptcy Court dated November 10, 1988.

1.74 "Section 3(h) Adjustment" means the changes to the terms of the Series A Preferred Stock, the Series B Preferred Stock, the Series C Preferred Stock and the Selected Net Assets Adjustment Note that are set forth in Schedule 3(h) to the Asset Purchase Agreement and which shall be effected if, prior to the Effective Date, the Buyer determines pursuant to Section 3(h) of the Asset Purchase Agreement not to rely on the bankruptcy exception under Section 382(1)(5) of the Internal Revenue Code of 1986, as amended.

1.75 "Secured Creditors" shall mean the holders of Allowed Secured Claims.

1.76 "Selected Net Assets Adjustment Note" shall have the meaning assigned to such term in the Asset Purchase Agreement.

1.77 "Series A Preferred Stock" shall have the meaning assigned to such term in the Asset Purchase Agreement.

1.78 "Series B Preferred Stock" shall have the meaning assigned to such term in the Asset Purchase Agreement.

1.79 "Series C Preferred Stock" shall have the meaning assigned to such term in the Asset Purchase Agreement.

1.80 "Special Proceeds Obligation" shall mean the obligation of the Debtor outstanding on the Effective Date (i) to ABN with respect to and to the extent of the proceeds from the bulk sale of the Lazer Tag and ActionMax inventory subject to a first lien in favor of ABN, used by the Debtor and not paid to ABN on or before the Effective Date as a Permanent Cash Paydown or (ii) to the Lenders with respect to and to the extent of the proceeds from federal income tax refunds subject to a first lien in favor of the Lenders, used by the Debtor and not paid to the Lenders on or before the Effective Date as a Permanent Cash Paydown, in each case as provided in the (Amended) Order (1) Approving Debtor's Business Plan, (2) Authorizing Use of Accounts Receivable Collections and Other Proceeds, and (3) Granting Security Interests and Other Adequate Protection, entered by the Bankruptcy Court on July 5, 1988.

1.81 "Subordinated Debentures" shall mean the 9% Convertible Subordinated Debentures Due 2012 issued by the Debtor.

1.82 "Supporting Lenders" shall have the meaning assigned to such term in the Asset Purchase Agreement.

**Exhibit 5-1  Sample Debtor's Plan**                                           **47**

1.83 "Tax Claim" means the Allowed Claims of governmental units described in Section 507(a)(7) of the Bankruptcy Code.

1.84 "Total ABN Secured Claim" shall mean the amount of the Class 2 Claim for principal and interest in the Reorganization Case, and which is projected to be $32,608,713.08 as of May 15, 1989 (without regard to cash paydowns received as of that date and assuming no further cash paydowns between the date of the Asset Purchase Agreement and the Effective Date which would reduce accrued interest), plus interest on the unpaid principal amount thereof after May 15, 1989 at 11% per annum (calculated on a 365-day or, when applicable, 366-day year), compounded annually.

1.85 "Trust Fund Accounts" shall mean the trust fund accounts established pursuant to the terms of the (Amended) Order (1) Approving Debtor's Business Plan, (2) Authorizing Use of Accounts Receivable Collections and Other Proceeds, and (3) Granting Security Interests and Other Adequate Protection, entered by the Bankruptcy Court on July 5, 1988.

1.86 "Unsecured Creditors" shall mean the holders of Allowed Unsecured Claims.

## ARTICLE II

### Classification of Claims

2.1 *Class 1 Claims.* Class 1 shall consist of all Administrative Claims, all Priority Claims and all Tax Claims.

2.2 *Class 2 Claims.* Class 2 shall consist of the ABN Allowed Secured Claim.

2.3 *Class 3 Claims.* Class 3 shall consist of the Allowed Secured Claims of The First National Bank of Chicago (individually and not as agent), Barclays American/Business Credit, Inc., Centerre Bank, The Chicago-Tokyo Bank, and The First National Bank of Louisville (collectively the "Lenders").

2.4 *Class 4 Claims.* Class 4 shall consist of Allowed Secured Claims other than Class 2 Claims or Class 3 Claims.

2.5 *Class 5 Claims.* Class 5 shall consist of all Allowed Unsecured Claims of $10,000 or less, and all Allowed Unsecured Claims voluntarily reduced to $10,000 prior to Confirmation by the filing with the Debtor of a written election by the holder of the Claim; provided that Class 5 shall in no event include any Allowed Claims of the holders of Subordinated Debentures.

2.6 *Class 6 Claims.* Class 6 shall consist of all Allowed Unsecured Claims, including without limitation (i) Allowed Claims arising from the rejection of executory contracts under Section 365 or 1123 of the Bankruptcy Code; (ii) Allowed Claims of the holders of Subordinated Debentures in respect of the obligations of the Debtor under the Subordinated Debentures (and excluding any claims held by such holders of the kind referred to in Section 2.7(ii)); (iii) the ABN Allowed Unsecured Claim; and (iv) the Lenders' Unsecured Deficiency Claim.

2.7 *Class 7 Claims and Interests.* Class 7 shall consist of (i) the interests of all of the holders of Old Common Stock; and (ii) all Claims for damages or rescission based on the purchase or sale of securities of the Debtor, including without limitation Claims by members of the plaintiff class in the consolidated class actions pending in the U.S. District Court for the Northern District of California styled *In re Worlds of Wonder, Inc. Securities Litigation,* and all Claims of any person, including without limitation any officers and directors of the Debtor, for indemnification, reimbursement or contribution with respect thereto.

## ARTICLE III

### Treatment of Claims and Interests

3.1 *Class 1.* Class 1 Claims are not impaired. Each holder of an Allowed Class 1 Claim will be paid the full amount of its Allowed Claim, without interest, (a) in cash at the later of (i) the Effective Date, or (ii) the date on which such Allowed Claim becomes due and payable pursuant to the terms thereof or the agreement upon which such Allowed Claim is based or (b) upon such other terms as may be agreed upon by the holder of such Allowed Claim and the Debtor. Subject to Sections 5.2 and 13.1 hereof Allowed Class 1 Claims shall be paid (i) first, from the Cash Reserve Fund and (ii) then, upon exhaustion of the Cash Reserve Fund, the Class 6 Cash Fund.

3.2 *Class 2.* Class 2 Claims are impaired. ABN, as the holder of Allowed Class 2 Claims, will receive the Note, the ABN Note, the Selected Net Assets Adjustment Note (subject to the Class 3 Interest therein) and the ABN Inventory Proceeds (subject to the Class 3 Interest therein), plus the amount, if any, of any payments made by the Lenders pursuant to the Class 2 Distribution Adjustment Provision. ABN shall retain a first lien on and security interest in all ABN Inventory Proceeds and all inventory of the Debtor described in Section 1(b)(xi) of the Asset Purchase Agreement or any other inventory held by it following the Effective Date and all proceeds thereof. The Debtor shall assign to ABN on the Effective Date, Debtor's rights under any letters of credit relating to any ABN Inventory Proceeds or any inventory of the Debtor held by it after the Effective Date. ABN shall also retain a first lien on and security interest in all Excluded Assets held by the Reorganized Debtor on or after the Effective Date other than ABN Inventory Proceeds and inventory of the Debtor described in Section 1(b)(xi) of the Asset Purchase Agreement or any other inventory held by it following Effective Date and all proceeds thereof, which lien and security interest shall secure the Special Proceeds Obligation of the Debtor to ABN and which lien and security interest shall be *pari passu* with the lien and security interest granted to the Lenders which secures the Special Proceeds Obligation

**Exhibit 5-1 Sample Debtor's Plan** **49**

of the Debtor to the Lenders provided for in Section 3.3 (the "ABN Special Proceeds Lien").

3.3 *Class 3.*

(a) Class 3 Claims are impaired. The Lenders, as holders of Allowed Class 3 Claims, will receive, on a Pro Rata basis and subject to the Class 2 Distribution Adjustment Provision, (i) all of the shares of Series A Preferred Stock, having a stated value of $1,999,800, to be issued and outstanding on the Effective Date; (ii) all of the shares of Series B Preferred Stock, having a stated value of $11,499,000 (or if the Asset Purchase Agreement closes on the basis of the Section 3(h) Adjustment, $9,999,000), to be issued and outstanding on the Effective Date; (iii) the Class 3 Interest in (A) the Selected Net Assets Adjustment Note, if any, and (B) the ABN Inventory Proceeds, if any; (iv) all of the Debtor's and the Debtor's subsidiaries' cash and cash equivalents held by such entities on the Effective Date other than (A) the Cash Reserve Fund, (B) any amounts to be paid to the holders of Allowed Class 1 Claims, and (C) the Class 6 Cash Fund; (v) any cash remaining in the Cash Reserve Fund after the Debtor has wound up its affairs as provided in Section 5.2; (vi) subject to the terms of the Collection Agreement, the Net Proceeds of all accounts receivable of the Debtor arising prior to the Effective Date; (vii) the Net Proceeds from all recoveries by the Debtor following the Effective Date (A) under Sections 542, 543, 544, 547, 548, 549 and 550 of the Bankruptcy Code and (B) with respect to the Debtor's lawsuits pending on the Effective Date and any other claims or causes of action arising from events occurring prior to the Effective Date; (viii) the Net Proceeds from all other Excluded Assets other than (A) those described in Section 1(b)(v) of the Asset Purchase Agreement and (B) the ABN Inventory Proceeds (subject to the Class 3 Interest therein); and (ix) all of the equity interest in the Reorganized Debtor. The Class 3 Claims are deemed to be Allowed Secured Claims. The Lenders shall retain a first lien on and security interest in all Excluded Assets retained by the Debtor following the Effective Date other than ABN Inventory Proceeds and inventory of the Debtor described in Section 1(b)(xi) of the Asset Purchase Agreement or any other inventory held by it following Effective Date and all proceeds thereof, which lien and security interest shall secure the Special Proceeds Obligation of the Debtor to the Lenders and shall be *pari passu* with the ABN Special Proceeds Lien. In addition, the Lenders shall retain a junior lien on and security interest in all Excluded Assets retained by the Debtor following the Effective Date, which lien and security interest shall secure the obligations of the Debtor in respect of the Allowed Class 3 Claims and shall be subordinate to the lien on and security interest in the inventory of the Debtor and the proceeds thereof held by ABN that is provided for in Section 3.2 of this plan.

(b) Distributions to the Lenders on account of their Allowed Class 3 Claims will be made as follows: (1) the shares of Series B Preferred Stock shall be issued directly to each Lender based upon such Lender's Pro Rata Share; and (2) all other payments or distributions to be made to or for the benefit of the Lenders on account of their Allowed Class 3 Claims (including without limitation any and all Lender Proceeds derived therefrom) shall be paid, distributed, or delivered to FNBC and held by FNBC for the benefit of the Lenders, subject to the Class 2 Distribution Adjustment Provision and Section 3.3(c) of this Plan.

(c) All payments or distributions made to FNBC on account of the Allowed Class 3 Claims (including without limitation all Lender Proceeds derived therefrom) shall be deposited by FNBC for the benefit of the Lenders and ABN into a segregated interest bearing account at The First National Bank of Chicago (the "Lender Proceeds Account"). FNBC shall make distributions to the Lenders or ABN (as the case may be) from the Lender Proceeds Account from time to time and at such times (A) as to ABN, when a mandatory or permissive payment is to be made to ABN under the Class 2 Distribution Adjustment Provision or (B) as to the Lenders, when FNBC determines that the monies remaining on deposit in the Lender Proceeds Account after reserving for (i) payments to ABN under the Class 2 Distribution Adjustment Provision, (ii) the anticipated liabilities of the Lenders to FNBC under the indemnity and expense sharing provisions under the Collection Agreement and/or the Loan and Security Agreement, and (iii) payments to Nightingale under the agreement between the Supporting Lenders and Nightingale referred to in Article IV(ii) of this Plan are adequate to permit a disbursement to the Lenders based upon their respective Pro Rata interests in the monies on deposit in the Lender Proceeds Account.

3.4 *Class 4.* Class 4 Claims are impaired. Holders of Allowed Class 4 Claims will receive in respect of their Claims, at the sole option of the Debtor, either (i) a cash payment, on the Effective Date, equal to the amount of the holder's Allowed Secured Claim or (ii) the property securing such Claim.

3.5 *Class 5.* Class 5 Claims are impaired. Holders of Allowed Class 5 Claims shall receive payment equal to $.10 for each $1.00 of Allowed Claim held by such holder. Holders of Allowed Class 5 Claims will receive distributions in respect of their Claims from the Class 6 Cash Fund as soon as practicable after such Claims are determined by the Bankruptcy Court or otherwise to be allowable.

3.6 *Class 6.* Class 6 Claims are impaired. Subject to the effect of Article IX of this Plan on the Allowed Claims of holders of Subordinated Debentures, holders of Allowed Class 6 Claims will receive a Pro Rata portion of (1) the Class 6 Cash Fund, reduced by (i) the net amount of cash required to be distributed to the holders of Excess Class 1 Claims pursuant to Section 5.2 hereof, (ii) the amount of cash required to be distributed to the holders of Allowed Class 5 Claims, (iii) the expenses chargeable against the Class 6 Cash Fund as provided in Section 6.1 hereof, and (iv) any fees and expenses of the Trustee of the Liquidating Trust, to the extent provided for in the Liquidating Trust Agreement, and (2) all of the shares of Series C Preferred Stock, having an aggregate stated value of $1,499,850, to be issued and outstanding on the Effective Date; provided that no Series C Preferred Stock shall be issued and outstanding and distributable to the holders of Allowed Class 6 Claims if the Asset Purchase Agreement closes on the basis of the Section 3(h) Adjustment. On the Effective

**Exhibit 5-1   Sample Debtor's Plan**                                    **51**

Date, the shares of Series C Preferred Stock to be distributed to Class 6 (if any) will be transferred by the Debtor to the Liquidating Trust and on the 120th day after the Effective Date the Class 6 Cash Fund (subject to the reductions referred to above) will be transferred by the Reorganized Debtor to the Liquidating Trust. Such consideration will be held in the Liquidating Trust for the benefit of the holders of Allowed Class 6 Claims and, with respect to the Class 6 Cash Fund only, the holders of Excess Class 1 Claims which are then remaining unpaid and holders of Allowed Class 5 Claims. Except with respect to payments from the Class 6 Cash Fund on account of Allowed Class 1 Claims or Allowed Class 5 Claims, property held in the Liquidating Trust will not be distributed therefrom until all objections to the allowance of Class 5 Claims and Class 6 Claims have been determined by Final Order or otherwise finally resolved. The amount of the Class 6 Cash Fund distributable to holders of Allowed Class 6 Claims will be distributed to such holders together with the shares of Series C Preferred Stock (if any such shares are to be issued and outstanding and distributed to Class 6 pursuant hereto) to which such holders are determined to be entitled as soon as reasonably practicable but in no event later than 90 days after the Reorganized Debtor shall have furnished to (x) the Trustee of Liquidating Trust, the Committee and the Buyer (A) written notice that all objections to the allowance of Class 5 Claims and Class 6 Claims have been finally resolved and (B) a schedule of the names and addresses of the holders of Allowed Class 6 Claims and the number of shares of Series C Preferred Stock to which each such holder has been determined to be entitled and (y) the holders of Allowed Class 1 Claims (including contingent Claims) that have not then been paid in full written notice of the distribution of the Class 6 Cash Fund.

3.7 *Class 7.* Class 7 interests and Claims are impaired. Holders of Class 7 interests and Claims will receive no consideration under this Plan. All Old Common Stock of the Debtor will be cancelled and extinguished upon the Effective Date.

3.8 *Class 2 Distribution Adjustment Provision.*

(a) *Obligation of Lenders Generally.* The Lenders will be obligated, on the basis of each Lender's Pro Rata Share, to pay to ABN in accordance with the following provisions of this Section 3.8, to the extent of any Lender Proceeds received or held by FNBC or the Lenders, the amount of the Remaining ABN Secured Claim outstanding on each Payment Date. The amount of the Allowed Class 3 Claims shall be deemed reduced, and the amount of the Allowed Class 6 Claims of the Lenders shall be deemed increased, by the amount of any payments made by the Lenders to ABN under Section 3.8(b), (c) and (e)(1) of this Plan. The obligations of the Lenders to ABN under this Section 3.8 shall be several and not joint, and each Lender shall be directly obligated to pay to ABN only such Lender's Pro Rata Share of any Required ABN Payment; provided, however, if at any time it is determined by a court of competent jurisdiction that the provisions of this Section 3.8 are not enforceable against one or more of the Lenders, then the Lenders' obligations to ABN under this Section 3.8 shall become joint and several. Any payments made to ABN by or on behalf of the Lenders under this Section 3.8 shall be applied first against interest on the Remaining ABN Secured Claim and then against unpaid principal.

(b) *Mandatory Payments.* On each Payment Date until the Remaining ABN Secured Claim is reduced to zero by Permanent Cash Paydowns, FNBC will pay ABN, based on each Lender's Pro Rata Share of the ABN Remaining Secured Claim, in cash, an amount equal to the lesser of (i) the Remaining ABN Secured Claim outstanding on such date, and (ii) an amount equal to the difference of (x) the aggregate Lender Proceeds received by or on behalf of the Lenders to such Payment Date, less (y) the aggregate amount of Permanent Cash Paydowns previously made to ABN by or on behalf of the Lenders under Sections 3.8(b), (c), and (e)(1) of this Plan.

(c) *Permissive Payments.* FNBC may, at its option, make cash payments to ABN in reduction of the Remaining ABN Secured Claim, based on each Lender's Pro Rata Share of the ABN Remaining Secured Claim, at any time prior to the payment of the full amount thereof upon 2 days' prior notice to ABN and the Lenders, provided such payments are in the minimum aggregate amount of $100,000.

(d) *Class 3 Interest in Selected Net Assets Adjustment Note and ABN Inventory Proceeds.* ABN shall be entitled to receive in respect of its Allowed Class 2 Claims the entire amount of and interest in the Selected Net Assets Adjustment Note and the ABN Inventory Proceeds, provided that, upon payment in full of the Remaining ABN Secured Claim, the Lenders shall have a residual interest in the Selected Net Assets Adjustment Note and the ABN Inventory Proceeds. Promptly after the Remaining ABN Secured Claim is reduced to zero by Permanent Cash Paydowns, ABN shall assign and endorse to FNBC, without recourse or warranty of any kind, and deliver to FNBC the Selected Net Assets Adjustment Note, which will be held by FNBC for the benefit of the Lenders as their interests may appear. After the Remaining ABN Secured Claim is reduced to zero by Permanent Cash Paydowns, ABN shall deliver to FNBC, for the benefit of the Lenders as their interests may appear, all ABN Inventory Proceeds thereafter received by ABN. FNBC shall hold such ABN Inventory Proceeds and the Selected Net Assets Adjustment Note for the benefit of the Lenders subject to the provisions of Section 3.3(c) of this Plan.

(e) *Disgorgement.*

(1) *By ABN.* From the date hereof until 2 years after the Remaining ABN Secured Claim shall have been reduced to zero by Permanent Cash Paydowns, the Lenders, in consideration of the distributions made to them in respect of their Class 3 Claims, shall indemnify and hold ABN harmless against any obligation to return or refund any ABN Proceeds to the Buyer, the Reorganized Debtor or any other person or entity to the extent that, after giving effect to such refund or return, the aggregate amount of ABN Proceeds received by ABN and not so refunded or returned is less than the aggregate amount of payments made by or on behalf of the Lenders under Sections 3.8(b), (c) and (e)(1) hereof. If any demand, action, suit, proceed-

Exhibit 5-1   Sample Debtor's Plan                                           53

ing or court order requiring ABN to return or refund any ABN Proceeds is asserted or threatened and is likely to create liability of the Lenders under this Section 3.8(e), the Lenders, at their expense, shall have the right to defend any such demand, action, suit, proceeding or court order with counsel selected by the Supporting Lenders. ABN shall reasonably cooperate with the reasonable requests of the Lenders in any such defense. The liability of each Lender for any payment due ABN under this Section 3.8(e) shall be limited to such Lender's Pro Rata Share of such payment.

(2) *By Lenders.* From the date hereof until 2 years after the Remaining ABN Secured Claim shall have been reduced to zero by Permanent Cash Paydowns, ABN shall indemnify and hold the Lenders harmless against any obligation to return or refund any Lender Proceeds to the Reorganized Debtor, Buyer or any other person or entity to the extent that, after giving effect to such refund or return, the aggregate amount of Lender Proceeds required to be so refunded or returned by the Lenders after the Effective Date is greater than the difference (i) the aggregate amount of Lender Proceeds received by or for the benefit of the Lenders prior to the date of determination, and not so returned or refunded, less (ii) the aggregate amount of payments made to ABN under Sections 3.8(b), (c) and (e)(1) hereof. For purposes of calculating the amount of Lender Proceeds received by or for the benefit of the Lenders prior to the date of determination under clause (i) of the preceding sentence, if, prior to the date of determination, the Selected Net Assets Adjustment Note and/or ABN Inventory Proceeds have been assigned and/or delivered by ABN to the Lenders or to FNBC for the benefit of the Lenders under Section 3.8(d) of this Plan, the fair market value of such properties or interests shall be included within the amount of Lender Proceeds received by or on behalf of the Lenders. If any demand, action, suit, proceeding or court order requiring the Lenders to return or refund any Lender Proceeds is asserted or threatened and is likely to create liability of ABN under this Section 3.8(e), ABN, at its expense, shall have the right to defend any such demand, action, suit, proceeding or court order requiring the Lenders to return or refund any Lender Proceeds, with counsel of its choosing. The Lenders shall reasonably cooperate with the reasonable requests of ABN in any such defense. The liability of ABN under this Section 3.8(e) shall be limited to the Lender Proceeds paid over to ABN under this Section 3.8.

(f) *Mechanism for Effecting Payments of ABN Remaining Secured Claim.* FNBC shall make payments on behalf of the Lenders under Sections 3.8(b), (c), or (e)(1) of this Plan by making payments to ABN from monies on deposit in the Lender Proceeds Account. If, at any time when the Lenders are required to make a payment to ABN under Section 3.8(b) or (e)(1) of this Plan (a "Required ABN Payment"), the monies on deposit in the Lender Proceeds Account are not sufficient for the Lenders to meet their obligations to ABN under those sections, (1) to the extent that Lender Proceeds have been distributed to the Lenders on account of their Class 3 Claims, each Lender shall repay to FNBC for payment to ABN from the Lender Proceeds distributed to such Lender the amount of such Lender's Pro Rata Share of the Required ABN Payment, or (2) the first Lender Proceeds received by FNBC at any time when a Required ABN Payment has not been paid in full that are attributable to a Lender that has failed to make payment to FNBC in the amount required to be paid by such Lender under clause (1) hereof shall be promptly paid over to ABN to satisfy such Lender's Pro Rata Share of the Required ABN Payment remaining unpaid. Should a Lender, for any reason, fail or refuse to promptly repay Lender Proceeds to FNBC under this Section 3.8(f) upon the written demand of FNBC for such repayment, FNBC shall be entitled to (A) enforce the repayment obligation in the Bankruptcy Court and/or (B) use such Lender's Pro Rata Share of any Lender Proceeds thereafter received by FNBC to make payments to ABN that will be charged against the obligation of such Lender to pay such Lender's Pro Rata Share of the Required ABN Payment remaining unpaid. Upon written notice by FNBC to any Lender that such Lender must repay to FNBC, for payment to ABN as part of a Required ABN Payment remaining unpaid. Upon written notice by FNBC to any Lender that such Lender must repay to FNBC, for payment to ABN as part of a Required ABN Payment, Lender Proceeds received by or distributed to such Lender in an amount equal to such Lender's Pro Rata Share of any Required ABN Payment in order to make up any deficiency in the Lender Proceeds Account, such Lender shall promptly pay such amount to FNBC for payment to ABN or set such amount aside for the benefit of ABN, regardless of whether such Lender Proceeds were originally distributed to such Lender from FNBC or some other source. Should any Lender fail or refuse to pay or cause to be paid to ABN all or any portion of its Pro Rata Share of any Required ABN Payment, ABN shall be entitled to seek relief in the Bankruptcy Court of any United States District Court in which venue and jurisdiction are proper to (x) enforce such obligation against such non-paying Lender or (y) compel FNBC to perform its duty to enforce such obligation against such non-paying Lender.

## ARTICLE IV

### Conditions Precedent to Consummation of the Plan

It shall be a condition precedent to consummation of this Plan that on or before the Effective Date:

(i) The Liquidating Trust Agreement, in form and substance satisfactory to ABN, the Supporting Lenders and the Committee, shall have been executed and delivered by the Debtor and the Trustee of the Liquidating Trust;

(ii) The Supporting Lenders and Nightingale shall have entered into an agreement providing for the payment of the Nightingale Fee in respect of (A) the Series A Preferred Stock, Series B Preferred Stock, the Net Proceeds of accounts receivable of the Debtor existing on the Effective Date and any other amounts realized by the Lenders in respect of their Class 3 Claims following

Exhibit 5-1   Sample Debtor's Plan                                    55

the Effective Date (which payment shall not be made in the form of any shares of Series A Preferred Stock, Series B Preferred Stock or Series C Preferred Stock) and (B) proceeds of up to $7,000,000 realized by ABN in respect of its Allowed Class 2 Claims after the Effective Date to the extent the Cash Reserve Fund is insufficient to satisfy the amount of the Nightingale Fee applicable to such proceeds realized by ABN at the time such Fee becomes due and payable;

(iii) The Management Agreement, the Management Consulting Agreement, the Collection Agreement and the Intercreditor Agreement shall have been executed and delivered by the respective parties thereto;

(iv) All conditions to the respective obligations of the Debtor and the Buyer under the Asset Purchase Agreement shall have been satisfied or waived; and

(v) An order confirming this Plan shall have been entered, expressly providing in substance the following:

(a) Approving the Asset Purchase Agreement and the instruments and documents to be executed and delivered by the Debtor pursuant thereto, authorizing the execution and delivery thereof by the Debtor and authorizing and directing the performance by the Debtor of its obligations thereunder, including without limitation the transfer of the Purchased Assets to the Buyer pursuant thereto;

(b) Approving the Agreement Re Preference Actions, the Liquidating Trust Agreement and the Collection Agreement, authorizing the execution and delivery thereof by the Debtor and authorizing and directing the performance by the Debtor of its obligations thereunder;

(c) Decreeing and adjudging that the transfer of the debtor's right, title and interest in and to the Purchased Assets by the Debtor pursuant to the Asset Purchase Agreement (i) is a legal, valid and effective transfer of the Debtor's right, title and interest in and to the Purchased Assets and (ii) vests in the Buyer, pursuant to Sections 363 and 1123 of the Bankruptcy Code, Debtor's right, title and interest in and to the Purchased Assets free and clear of all Claims (other than Assumed Liabilities), liens and interests whatsoever, including without limitation any liabilities of the Debtor that may be asserted against the Buyer on the basis of any theory of successor or transferee liability;

(d) Decreeing and adjudging that the partial waiver pursuant to this Plan of subordination rights in favor of the Lenders under the Debenture Indenture that will arise by virtue of acceptance of this Plan under Section 1126(c) of the Bankruptcy Code by Class 3 shall bind all holders of Allowed Class 3 Claims, including any such holder which has rejected or objected to this Plan;

(e) Decreeing and adjudging that the provisions of Section 3.8 of this Plan shall be binding on all Lenders, including any Lender which rejects or objects to this Plan in its capacity as a holder of Allowed Class 3 Claims, and directing any such Lender to perform its obligations under Section 3.8 of this Plan; and

(f) Decreeing and adjudging that by virtue of the acceptance of the Plan by Class 3 under Section 1126(c) of the Bankruptcy Code, FNBC and/or the

Supporting Lenders may enter into the Collection Agreement and all holders of Allowed Class 3 Claims shall be bound by the provisions of such agreement, including any holder which has rejected or objected to the Plan or which refuses to sign the Collection Agreement.

## ARTICLE V

### Means of Execution of the Plan

5.1 This Plan shall be implemented on the Effective Date by the Closing of the Asset Purchase Agreement. On the Effective Date, the following actions shall occur:

(i) The transactions to be consummated on the Closing Date pursuant to the Asset Purchase Agreement shall be consummated;

(ii) Any amounts required to be paid under Sections 365(b)(1)(A) and (B) of the Bankruptcy Code to parties to Acquired Contracts, other than the Debtor, which are being assumed and assigned to the Buyer effective on the Effective Date pursuant to Article VIII of this Plan shall have been paid by the Debtor to such parties;

(iii) All payments or distributions of property to be made on the Effective Date under Article III of this Plan by the Debtor, including without limitation the issuance to the Lenders of shares of Common Stock of the Reorganized Debtor, shall have been made or provided for; and

(iv) The Liquidating Trust shall be established and the Series C Preferred Stock shall be transferred to and vested in the Liquidating Trust pursuant to the Liquidating Trust Agreement.

5.2 The Reorganized Debtor will conduct no business following the Effective Date other than winding up its affairs in accordance with applicable law, which shall include (i) making any payments owing to the holders of Allowed Class 1 Claims to whom payment is not owing until after the Effective Date, (ii) filing all required tax returns, (iii) to the extent consistent with the Agreement Re Preference Actions, commencing and prosecuting avoidance actions under Sections 544, 547, 548, 549 and 550 of the Bankruptcy Code and all other claims and causes of action retained by the Debtor under the Asset Purchase Agreement, including turnover actions under Bankruptcy Code Sections 542 and 543, and continuing the prosecution of all pending litigation, and (iv) collection of ABN Inventory Proceeds and disposing of the inventory of the Reorganized Debtor described in Section 1(b)(xi) of the Asset Purchase Agreement and disposing, liquidating or collecting any other Excluded Assets to be retained by the Reorganized Debtor following the Effective Date. The Reorganized Debtor will pay over to ABN or the Lenders, according to their interests, the ABN Inventory Proceeds and any other Net Proceeds of any Excluded Assets received by the Reorganized Debtor following the Effective Date, subject to the provisions of Section 4(d) or the (Amended) Order (1) Approving Debtor's

Exhibit 5-1  Sample Debtor's Plan                                                         57

Business Plan, (2) Authorizing Use of Accounts Receivable Collections and Other Proceeds, and (3) Granting Security Interests and Other Adequate Protection. The Cash Reserve Fund will serve as the source of payment for all amounts owing to the holders of Allowed Class 1 Claims on or after the Effective Date (including any amount then or thereafter owing in respect of the Nightingale Fee other than amounts to be paid by the Lenders as provided in the agreement referred to in Article IV(ii) of this Plan) and all costs and expenses of winding down the affairs of the Debtor (including fees and expenses of Professionals) and, if all Allowed Class 1 Claims shall have been satisfied in full, prosecuting litigation, including avoidance actions; provided that, to the extent that the Cash Reserve Fund has been fully exhausted at the time that any Allowed Class 1 Claim shall become due and payable on or after the Effective Date (an "Excess Class 1 Claim"), the Class 6 Cash Fund will be the source of payment of such Excess Class 1 Claim. If the Class 6 Cash Fund shall make any payment in respect of any Excess Class 1 Claim, the Reorganized Debtor will deduct from any payments thereafter received from ABN in respect of the ABN Payment that would otherwise be deposited in the Cash Reserve Fund and will deposit into the Class 6 Cash Fund the amount of such payment in respect of an Excess Class 1 Claim. If the Cash Reserve Fund is exhausted prior to the final resolution of all litigation, including avoidance actions, prosecuted by the Reorganized Debtor after the Effective Date, the Lenders, as holders of Allowed Class 3 Claims, shall assume full responsibility for all costs or expenses associated with any litigation then pending. If the Lenders fail to advance the Reorganized Debtor's costs and expenses associated with such litigation, the Reorganized Debtor will assign all of its rights and interest in such litigation to the holders of Allowed Class 3 Claims and the Reorganized Debtor shall have no further obligation with respect thereto. All cash remaining in the Cash Reserve Fund at the time that all Allowed Class 1 Claims (including contingent Claims) have been satisfied in full and the Reorganized Debtor has wound up its affairs in accordance with applicable law shall be paid to the Lenders in respect of their Allowed Class 3 Claims, subject to the Lenders' obligations under Section 3.8.

5.3 The Articles of Incorporation of the Debtor shall be amended, effective on the Effective Date, to change the name of the Debtor in accordance with Section 7(j) of the Asset Purchase Agreement and to prohibit the issuance by the Debtor of nonvoting securities to the extent required by the provisions of Section 1123(a)(6) of the Bankruptcy Code.

# ARTICLE VI

## Objections to Claims; Creditors' Committee

6.1 The Reorganized Debtor shall have the exclusive responsibility for objecting to the allowance of Class 1 Claims, Class 5 Claims and Class 6 Claims, the entire cost of which, including any fees and expenses of the Reorganized

Debtor's counsel and other Professionals, shall be borne by the Class 6 Cash Fund. Following the Effective Date, the Reorganized Debtor shall have the right to file objections to and otherwise contest the allowability of any and all Claims other than a Claim deemed allowed in accordance with the terms hereof. The Reorganized Debtor will cooperate with the Committee in the filing of objections to Class 5 Claims and Class 6 Claims.

6.2 To the extent necessary, appropriate and required under this Plan, the Committee will continue in existence. The Committee shall have the right to investigate and to require the Reorganized Debtor to file any objections to Class 5 Claims and Class 6 Claims which the Committee determines should be filed. The Reorganized Debtor and the Buyer will provide representatives of the Committee access to the books and records relating to the Debtor or its business possessed by each of them to the extent reasonably required by such representatives in connection with reviewing the allowability of Class 5 Claims and Class 6 Claims. The Committee shall have the right to designate, select and retain the attorneys and all experts necessary to investigate the objections to Claims, which may be filed in the name of the Reorganized Debtor or the Committee jointly. All decisions as to the prosecution and settlement of such objections to Claims shall be made by the Reorganized Debtor, upon consultation with the Committee, consistent with applicable law. The fees and expenses of the attorneys and the experts retained by the Committee shall be paid out of the Class 6 Cash Fund in such amounts as may be fixed by the Bankruptcy Court, after notice to the members of the Committee and to the Reorganized Debtor and hearing, from time to time upon proper application therefore.

6.3 A majority of the voting members of the Committee from time to time in office shall constitute a quorum. Meetings of the Committee may be called by its Chairman or any two of its members on such notice and in such manner as he or they may deem advisable. The Committee shall function by decisions made by the majority of the voting members of the Committee in attendance at any meeting at which a quorum is present and acting throughout.

6.4 The individual members of the Committee shall serve without compensation; however, subject to the availability of funds in the Class 6 Cash Fund, counsel for the Committee shall be entitled to apply to the Bankruptcy Court and notice to members of the Committee and the Reorganized Debtor and hearing for reasonable and necessary compensation for services rendered and reimbursement for reasonable and necessary out-of-pocket disbursements incurred with respect to the implementation and consummation of this Plan subsequent to the Effective Date.

6.5 In the event of the death or resignation of any member of the Committee, the Creditor whom he or she represented may designate a successor in his or her place. In the event that such Creditor shall fail to designate a successor within thirty (30) days after such vacancy shall have occurred, the majority of the remaining members of the Committee shall have the right to designate a successor from among the holders of Allowed Class 6 Claims. In the event that the Committee is notified in writing that any member of the Committee is no

Exhibit 5-1   Sample Debtor's Plan                                        59

longer associated with the Creditor by whom he was nominated, such member of the Committee shall be deemed to have resigned from the Committee, and the vacancy shall be filled in the manner specified above. Unless and until such vacancy is filled, the Committee shall function with such reduced membership.

6.6 Promptly following a final determination of all Disputed Class 5 Claims and Disputed Class 6 Claims by Final Order or otherwise, the Reorganized Debtor shall determine the Pro Rata share of each holder of an Allowed Class 6 Claim of the Series C Preferred Stock to be distributed to the holders of Allowed Class 6 Claims (if any shall be distributable pursuant to Section 3.6 hereof) and the Class 6 Cash Fund. The Reorganized Debtor shall thereupon provide written notice to the Committee, the Trustee of the Liquidating Trust, the Buyer and all holders of Allowed Class 1 Claims that have not then been paid in full that the Allowed Class 6 Claims have been finally determined and that a distribution of all of the property held in the Liquidating Trust will be made within 90 days thereafter. The Reorganized Debtor also at such time shall provide the Committee, the Trustee of the Liquidating Trust and the Buyer with a schedule of the name and address of each holder of an Allowed Class 6 Claim, the Pro Rata share of each such holder and the number of shares of Series C Preferred Stock to which such holder shall have been determined to be entitled (if any such shares shall be distributable pursuant to Section 3.6 hereof), which schedule shall also be filed by the Reorganized Debtor with the Bankruptcy Court.

6.7 Upon substantial completion of its functions as designated herein, the Committee shall be dissolved pursuant to Final Order.

## ARTICLE VII

### Cram Down Provision

If the holders of Class 5 Claims or Class 6 Claims do not accept this Plan in accordance with Section 1126 of the Bankruptcy Code, the Debtor will request confirmation of this Plan pursuant to Section 1129(b) of the Bankruptcy Code on the basis that this Plan is fair and equitable as to such holders of Class 5 Claims or Class 6 Claims, as the case may be. The Debtor hereby requests confirmation of this Plan pursuant to Section 1129(b) of the Bankruptcy Code on the basis that this Plan is fair and equitable as to the holders of Class 7 interests and Claims.

## ARTICLE VIII

### Executory Contracts

Any Acquired Contracts which have not been expressly assumed by order of the Bankruptcy Court prior to the Confirmation Date shall be assumed pursuant to Sections 365 and 1123 of the Bankruptcy Code effective on the Effective Date; provided that the Debtor reserves the right at any time prior to the Confirmation Date to delete from the list of executory contracts included in Exhibit C hereto and to reject any such Acquired Contracts which are so deleted. The Debtor will give the other party to any such executory contract which is deleted from Exhibit C appropriate notice thereof. The Confirmation Order will include a finding that, upon assignment to Buyer on the Effective Date of any Acquired Contracts assumed by the Debtor and assigned to the Buyer pursuant to Sections 365 and 1123 of the Bankruptcy Code, there shall be no default by the Debtor under such Acquired Contracts that are uncured on the Effective Date and are enforceable against the Buyer following the Effective Date other than existing defaults that are not required to be cured in order to assume such Acquired Contracts pursuant to Sections 365 and 1123 of the Bankruptcy Code. Any and all other executory contracts and unexpired leases of the Debtor not expressly assumed prior to the Confirmation Date shall be deemed rejected upon entry of the Confirmation Order. Any Claims arising from rejection of any executory contract or unexpired lease shall be forever barred unless a proof of claim relating thereto is filed with the Bankruptcy Court within thirty (30) days after the Confirmation Date.

## ARTICLE IX

### Subordination

The rights of the holders of Subordinated Debentures are subordinated under the Debenture Indenture to the rights of ABN and the Lenders as holders of Senior Indebtedness under the terms of the Debenture Indenture. Notwithstanding anything else herein to the contrary, distributions under this Plan in respect of the Allowed Class 6 Claims held by the holders of Subordinated Debentures shall be made as follows: (i) the Lenders shall, in accordance with the subordination provisions of the Debenture Indenture, receive the Pro Rata portion of the Class 6 Cash Fund and 50% of the shares of Series C Preferred Stock to which the holders of Subordinated Debentures would otherwise be entitled in respect of their Allowed Class 6 Claims; and (ii) the holders of Subordinated Debentures shall receive, as a result of a partial waiver under this Plan by ABN (as the holder of Allowed Class 2 Claims) and the Lenders (as holders of Allowed Class 3 Claims) (such waivers to be effected by virtue of acceptance of this Plan by Class 2 and Class 3, respectively, under Bankruptcy Code Section 1126(c)) of the subordination rights in favor of such holders under the Debenture Indenture, 50% of the shares of Series C Preferred Stock to which the holders of Subordinated Debentures would otherwise be entitled in respect of their Allowed Class 6 Claims.

Exhibit 5-1    Sample Debtor's Plan                                    61

## ARTICLE X

### Retention and Enforcement of Claims

Subject to the Agreement Re Preference Actions and the Collection Agreement, pursuant to Section 1123(b)(3) of the Bankruptcy Code, Reorganized Debtor shall retain and may enforce any and all litigation pending on the Effective Date and all claims or causes of action of the Debtor or the Estate, including without limitation any avoidance action under Sections 544, 547, 548, 549 and 550 of the Bankruptcy Code and turn over actions under Section 542 or 543 of the Bankruptcy Code.

## ARTICLE XI

### Revesting of Property of the Debtor; No Discharge

Except as otherwise provided in this Plan or the Confirmation Order, all property of the Estate, wherever situated, upon the Confirmation Date shall vest in the Debtor and on the Effective Date, (i) in the case of Excluded Assets, shall be retained by the Reorganized Debtor or distributed to certain Creditors as provided in this Plan and (ii) in the case of Purchased Assets, shall be transferred to the Buyer pursuant to the Asset Purchase Agreement. After Confirmation, all property of the Estate, whether retained by the Debtor, distributed to Creditors on the Effective Date or, in the case of Purchased Assets, transferred to the Buyer on the Effective Date, is and shall be free and clear of all Claims, liens and interests, except the Claims, liens and interests of Creditors arising under or provided for in this Plan (including without limitation (x) the liens and security interests of ABN provided for in Section 3.2 of this Plan and (y) the liens and security interests of the Lenders provided for in Section 3.3 of this Plan) or as otherwise provided in the Asset Purchase Agreement. In accordance with Section 1141(d)(3) of the Bankruptcy Code, Confirmation of this Plan shall not operate as a discharge of the Debtor under Section 1141(d)(1) of the Bankruptcy Code.

## ARTICLE XII

### Retention of Jurisdiction

From and after the Confirmation Date, the Bankruptcy Court shall retain jurisdiction for the following purposes:

(a) To hear and determine any and all objections to the allowance of a Claim or any controversy as to the classification of Claims;

(b) To hear and determine any and all adversary proceedings, applications or litigated matters pending on the Effective Date;

(c) To hear and determine any and all applications by Professionals for compensation and reimbursement of expenses;

(d) To hear and determine Claims arising from rejection of executory contracts and unexpired leases;

(e) To enable Reorganized Debtor to commence and prosecute any and all proceedings which may be brought after the Effective Date relating to claims or causes of action which arose prior to the Effective Date or to recover any transfers, assets, properties or damages to which the Debtor or Reorganized Debtor may be entitled under applicable provisions of the Bankruptcy Code, including without limitation under Sections 542, 543, 544, 547, 548, 549 and 550 thereof, except as provided in the Agreement Re Preference Actions;

(f) To liquidate any disputed, contingent or unliquidated Claims;

(g) To enforce the provisions of this Plan;

(h) To enter and implement such orders as may be appropriate in the event Confirmation is for any reason stayed, reversed, revoked, modified or vacated; and

(i) To enter such orders as may be necessary or appropriate in furtherance of confirmation and implementation of this Plan.

## ARTICLE XIII

### Miscellaneous Provisions

13.1 *Arrangements Re Nightingale Fee.* Nightingale shall receive, as the holder of an Allowed Class 1 Claim in respect of the Nightingale Fee, (i) on the Effective Date, a cash payment from the Cash Reserve Fund (or, to the extent funds in the Cash Reserve Fund are insufficient therefor, from the Lenders pursuant to the agreement referred to in clause (iv) of this Section 13.1 or the Class 6 Cash Fund, as applicable), equal to 3% of all cash distributions made by the Debtor after April 1, 1988 but before the Effective Date to ABN in respect of its Allowed Class 2 Claims (excluding certain amounts described in Paragraph 4 of the Nightingale Engagement Letter), (ii) on the Effective Date, a cash payment from the Cash Reserve Fund (or, to the extent funds in the Cash Reserve Fund are insufficient therefor, from the Lenders pursuant to the agreement referred to in clause (iv) of this Section 13.1 or the Class 6 Cash Fund, as applicable), equal to $30,000, representing the amount of the Nightingale Fee deemed to be owing on the Effective Date in respect of the shares of Series C Preferred Stock to be issued and outstanding on the Effective Date, (iii) following the Effective Date, when and as payments are received by ABN (A) in the form of ABN Inventory Proceeds, (B) as principal payments in respect of the Note, the ABN Note or the Select Net Assets Adjustment Note or (C) otherwise in respect of its Allowed Class 2 Claim, a cash payment from the Cash Reserve

**Exhibit 5-1    Sample Debtor's Plan**                                    **63**

Fund (or, to the extent funds in the Cash Reserve Fund are insufficient therefor, from the Lenders pursuant to the agreement referred to in clause (iv) of this Section 13.1 or the Class 6 Cash Fund, as applicable), equal to 3% of each such payment and (iv) at such time as may be provided in the agreement between the Supporting Lenders and Nightingale referred to in Article IV(ii), the fee payable thereunder in respect of (x) the Series A Preferred Stock, the Series B Preferred Stock, Net Proceeds of accounts receivable of the Debtor existing on the Effective Date and any other amounts realized by the Lenders in respect of their Allowed Class 3 Claims following the Effective Date (excluding certain amounts described in Paragraph 4 of the Nightingale Engagement Letter) and (y) proceeds of up to $7,000,000 realized by ABN in respect of its Allowed Class 2 Claims after the Effective Date to the extent that the Cash Reserve Fund is insufficient to satisfy the amount of the Nightingale Fee applicable to such proceeds realized by ABN at the time such Fee becomes due and payable.

13.2 *Release by the Debtor.* On the Effective Date, for good and valuable consideration, including the services rendered by Nightingale and its directors, officers, employees and agents to the Debtor pursuant to the Nightingale Engagement Letter and to facilitate the Debtor's expeditious and effective reorganization, the Debtor shall be deemed to have waived and released any and all claims, obligations, rights, causes of action and liabilities, whether known or unknown, foreseen or unforeseen, then existing or thereafter arising, which are based in whole or in part upon any act, omission or other event or occurrence taking place on or prior to the Effective Date and which may be asserted by or on behalf of the Debtor against Nightingale and its officers, directors, employees or agents.

13.3 *Waiver by ABN of Certain Rights.* ABN, as the holder of Allowed Class 2 Claims, by accepting this Plan, will waive any rights it may have to receive shares of Series C Preferred Stock (i) to which the holders of Subordinated Debentures would otherwise be entitled in respect of their Allowed Class 6 Claims but which, pursuant to the subordination provisions of the Debenture Indenture, would be distributable to ABN, and (ii) to which it is otherwise entitled as the holder of the ABN Allowed Unsecured Claim. The Debtor agrees and acknowledges that the waiver by ABN with respect to its rights to receive Series C Preferred Stock provided for in this Section 13.3 is solely for the purposes of this Plan and does not bind ABN with respect to any other plan of reorganization and that ABN reserves the right to assert such rights and all other rights which it may be entitled to assert in connection with any other plan of reorganization which may be proposed in the Reorganization Case or in connection with any successor case thereto.

13.4 *Agreement by Lenders to Different Treatment.* The Lenders, by accepting this Plan in their capacity as holders of Allowed Class 3 Claims, will agree that, to the extent that their Allowed Claims are entitled to priority in accordance with Section 364(c)(1) or Section 507(b) of the Bankruptcy Code, such Allowed Claims may be treated under this Plan in a manner different from that which the Lenders otherwise could require if the Lenders were to assert the priority of such Allowed Claims to the full extent permitted by the Bankruptcy Code. The Debtor agrees and acknowledges that an agreement by the Lenders to different treatment with respect to such Allowed Claims that will arise upon acceptance of this Plan does not bind the Lenders with respect to any other plan of reorganization and that the Lenders reserve the right to assert such priority in connection with any other plan of reorganization which may be proposed in the Reorganization Case or in connection with any successor case thereto.

13.5 *Surrender of Debt Instruments; Cancellation of Indenture.* Notwithstanding any other provisions of this Plan, no holder of a Subordinated Debenture, promissory note, payment guarantee or other transferable instrument ("Debt Instrument") shall receive any distribution with respect to such Debt Instrument until such Debt Instrument has been surrendered to, or satisfactory evidence of loss has been provided to the Trustee of the Liquidating Trust in the manner set forth in the Liquidating Trust Agreement. As of the Effective Date, the Indenture governing the Subordinated Debentures shall, except as otherwise provided in this Section 13.5, be cancelled and deemed null and void and of no further force and effect. Notwithstanding the foregoing, such cancellation shall not impair the rights and duties under such Indenture as between the Indenture Trustee thereunder and the holders of the Subordinated Debentures. As of the Effective Date, the Subordinated Debentures and the rights of the holders thereof shall be cancelled and shall be null and void, and the holders thereof shall have no rights, and such instrument shall evidence no rights, except the right to receive the distributions provided herein, subject to the provisions of this Section 13.5.

13.6 *Liquidating Trust Agreement, Collection Agreement and Agreement Re Preference Actions.* The Liquidating Trust Agreement, the Collection Agreement, and the Agreement Re Preference Actions will be filed with the Bankruptcy Court prior to the Confirmation Date, will be expressly approved pursuant to the Confirmation Order and will be incorporated into and made a part of this Plan.

13.7 *Interim Distribution of Class 6 Fund.* Nothing herein shall preclude the Reorganized Debtor from filing a motion with the Bankruptcy Court following the Effective Date from time to time, but before all Disputed Class 5 Claims and all Disputed Class 6 Claims have been determined by Final Order or otherwise finally resolved, requesting the Bankruptcy Court, upon notice to the holders of Allowed Class 1 Claims then remaining unpaid, the Committee and the Lenders, to approve an interim distribution from the Class 6 Cash Fund to holders of Allowed Class 6 Claims, subject to an appropriate reserve for the then remaining Disputed Class 5 Claims and Disputed Class 6 Claims and any redetermination of the Lenders' Unsecured Deficiency Claim contemplated by this Plan.

13.8 *Headings.* Headings are utilized in this Plan for the convenience of reference only, and shall not constitute a part of this Plan for any other purpose.

13.9 *Defects, Omissions and Amendments.* The Debtor may, with the ap-

**Exhibit 5-1 Sample Debtor's Plan** 65

proval of the Bankruptcy Court and without notice to all holders of Claims and holders of Old Common Stock but on notice to and consent of the Committee, ABN, the Supporting Lenders and the Buyer, insofar as it does not materially and adversely affect the interest of holders of Claims and holders of Old Common Stock, correct any defect, omission or inconsistency in this Plan in such manner and to such extent as may be necessary to expedite the execution of this Plan. This Plan may be altered or amended before or after Confirmation, as provided in Section 1127 of the Bankruptcy Code, if, in the opinion of the Bankruptcy Court, the modification does not materially and adversely affect the interests of holders of Claims and holders of Old Common Stock. This Plan may be altered or amended before Confirmation in a manner which, in the opinion of the Bankruptcy Court, materially and adversely affects Creditors and holders of Old Common Stock, after a further hearing and acceptance of this Plan as so altered or modified as provided in Section 1126 of the Bankruptcy Code.

13.10 *Governing Law.* Except to the extent that the Bankruptcy Code is applicable, the rights and obligations arising under this Plan shall be governed by and construed and enforced in accordance with the internal laws of the State of California.

13.11 *Notices.* All notices, requests, or demands for payments provided for in this Plan shall be in writing and shall be deemed to have been given when personally delivered by hand, or deposited in any general or branch post office of the United States postal service, or received by telex or telecopier. Notices, requests and demands for payments shall be addressed and sent, postage prepaid or delivered, in the case of notices, requests, or demands for payments, to: Worlds of Wonder, Inc., 4209 Technology Drive, Fremont, California 94538, Attn: President, with copies to: (i) Gibson, Dunn & Crutcher, 333 South Grand Avenue, Los Angeles, California 90071, Attn: Ronald S. Orr, Esq., and David H. Kennedy, Esq., (ii) O'Melveny & Myers, 400 South Hope Street, Los Angeles, California 90071, Attn: Joseph Ryan, Esq., (iii) Murphy, Weir & Butler, 101 California Street, 39th Floor, San Francisco, California 94111, Attn: William Weintraub, Esq., (iv) Chapman and Cutler, 111 West Monroe Street, Chicago, Illinois 60603, Attn: James E. Spiotto, Esq., and (v) Gendel, Raskoff, Shapiro & Quittner, 1810 Century Park East, 6th Floor, Los Angeles, California 90067, Attn: Bernard Shapiro, Esq., and at any other address designated by the Debtor or the Reorganized Debtor by notice to each holder of an Allowed Claim, and, in the case of notices to holders of Allowed Claims, at the last known address according to the Debtor's or the Reorganized Debtor's books and records, or at any other address designated by a holder of an Allowed Claim, by notice to the Debtor or the Reorganized Debtor, provided that any notice of change of address shall be effective only upon receipt.

13.12 *Severability.* Should any provision in this Plan be determined to be unenforceable, such determination shall in no way limit or affect the enforceability and operative effect of any or all other provisions of this Plan.

13.13 *Revocation.* The Debtor reserves the right to revoke and withdraw this Plan prior to Confirmation. If the Debtor revokes or withdraws this Plan pursuant to this Section 13.13, or if Confirmation does not occur, then this Plan shall be deemed null and void and, in such event, nothing contained herein shall be deemed to constitute a waiver or release of any Claims by or against the Debtor or any person in any further proceedings involving the Debtor.

DATED: April 10, 1989
Fremont, California

WORLDS OF WONDER, INC.
Debtor and Debtor-in-Possession
By: /s/   STEPHEN J. HOPKINS
Its: President and Chief
Executive Officer

**Exhibit 5-2 Sample Unsecured Creditors' Committee's Plan** **67**

**EXHIBIT 5-2 SAMPLE UNSECURED CREDITORS' COMMITTEE'S PLAN**

---

RICHARD W. HAVEL
PERRY L. LANDSBERG
SIDLEY & AUSTIN
2049 Century Park East
Suite 3500
Los Angeles, California 90067
(213) 553–8100

**Attorneys for** Official Committee of Creditors Holding Unsecured Claims

UNITED STATES BANKRUPTCY COURT
CENTRAL DISTRICT OF CALIFORNIA

| | |
|---|---|
| **In re**<br>CARE ENTERPRISES, INC.,<br>Debtors. | Case No. LA 88 06398 AG<br>Chapter 11<br><br>OFFICIAL CREDITORS'<br>COMMITTEE'S FIRST AMENDED<br>PLAN OF REORGANIZATION<br>DATED APRIL 14, 1989<br><br>Date: To be set<br>Time: To be set<br>Place: Courtroom C, 8th Floor<br>312 North Spring Street<br>Los Angeles, CA 90012 |

The Official Committee of Creditors Holding Unsecured Claims (the "Committee") proposes the following Plan of Reorganization pursuant to chapter 11 of the Bankruptcy Code:

## ARTICLE I

### Definitions

For the purposes of this Plan, the following terms shall have the respective meanings hereinafter set forth. A term used in the Plan and not defined herein or otherwise in the Plan but that is defined in the Code has the meaning set forth in the Code.

1.01 "Affiliate" means all direct and indirect subsidiaries, partnerships and joint ventures of the Debtor, including those described in the Disclosure Statement accompanying the Plan and all entities that would be deemed an affiliate of the Debtor as that term is defined in § 101(2) of the Code.

1.02 "Allowed Claim" means a claim (a) with respect to which a proof of claim has been filed with the Court within the applicable period of time fixed by the Court, (b) scheduled in the list of creditors prepared and filed with the Court by the Debtor and not listed as disputed, contingent or unliquidated as to amount, or (c) with respect to the Old Debentures and Old Notes, those holders who appear of record on a record date to be fixed, in any event as to which no objection to the allowance thereof has been interposed within the applicable period of limitations fixed in the Plan or the Confirmation Order, or as to which any such objection has been determined by an order or judgment. Multiple proofs of claim filed by a creditor shall be aggregated and shall constitute a single Allowed Claim.

1.03 "Allowed Interest" means as Interest held by shareholders of record on a record date to be fixed as to which no objection to the allowance thereof has been interposed within the applicable period of limitations fixed in the Plan or the Confirmation Order, or as to which any such objection has been determined by an order or judgment.

1.04 "Allowed Secured Claim" means an Allowed Claim secured by a lien, security interest or other charge against property in which the Estate has an interest, or which is subject to set-off under § 553 of the Code, to the extent of the value (determined in accordance with § 506(a) of the Code) of the interest of the holder of such Allowed Secured Claim in the Estate's interest in such property or to the extent of the amount subject to set-off, as the case may be.

1.05 "Bank's Miscellaneous Fees" means the agent fees, letter of credit fees and related expenses which are properly included in and part of the Allowed Secured Claim of the Class 7 creditors, up to a maximum of $500,000.

1.06 "Code" means the Bankruptcy Code, 11 U.S.C. § 101 et seq., and any amendments thereof.

1.07 "Common Stock" means the Class A and Class B common stock of the Debtor.

1.08 "Confirmation Date" means the date on which the Court enters the Confirmation Order.

1.09 "Confirmation Order" means the Order entered confirming the Plan pursuant to § 1129 of the Code.

1.10 "Court" means the United States Bankruptcy Court for the Central District of California.

1.11 "Debtor" means Care Enterprises, Inc., the debtor in this chapter 11 case.

1.12 "Designated Facilities" means the following facilities owned or leased by the Debtor and/or its Affiliates: Salt Lake City, Bountiful, Mt. Ogden, Clearfield, Oren, Valley View, Lakecrest, Palomares, Anza, Alondra, Pomona Vista,

**Exhibit 5-2   Sample Unsecured Creditors' Committee's Plan**                    **69**

Northbrook, Madrone, Colonial (Montebello), Hilltop (Montebello), Escondido, Wyngate, St. Theresa's, Health Care Network Laboratory, Central Home Health (HCN), Watsonville East, Watsonville West, Elmcrest, North Valley and Golden State.

1.13 "Disbursing Agent" means Debtor, Reorganized Care and any entity designated in the Confirmation Order or in the Plan to act in such capacity.

1.14 "Disputed Claims" means alleged claims against the Debtor as to which an objection, including a proceeding to equitably subordinate an Allowed Claim under § 510(c) of the Code, has been filed before 120 days after the Effective Date (or such later date as may be fixed by the Court) by a party in interest and which objection has not been withdrawn or resolved by the entry of a final order.

1.15 "Disputed Interests" means alleged Interests in the Debtor as to which an objection, including a proceeding to equitably subordinate an Interest under § 510(c) of the Code, has been filed before 120 days after the Effective date (or such later date as may be fixed by the Court) by a party in interest and which objection has not been withdrawn or resolved by the entry of a final order.

1.16 "Distributions" means the property required by the Plan to be distributed to the holders of Allowed Claims.

1.17 "Effective Date" means the earlier of (i) 120 days after the Confirmation Date, or (ii) the date on which sufficient funds have been accumulated through sales, financing and operating activities to make the payments called for by the Plan.

1.18 "Estate" means the estate created in this case under § 541 of the Code.

1.19 "Excess Cash" means the net cash provided by all activities of the Debtor and its Affiliates on a consolidated basis, from and after the Effective Date, computed in accordance with generally accepted accounting principles, less the difference, if any, between $5.0 million and the cash available on the Effective Date in excess of the payments called for by the Plan.

1.20 "Indenture Trustees" means the trustees for the Old Notes and Old Debentures.

1.22 "Interest" means the Preferred Stock and Common Stock of the Debtor.

1.23 "Initial Cash Payment" means the sum of $10.0 million, less any payments made by the Debtor, any Affiliates or Reorganized Care to the Class 7 creditors arising from the sales or any other disposition of property occurring between April 1, 1989 and the Effective Date.

1.24 "Loan Agreement" means the loan agreement to be entered into by Reorganized Care governing the terms and conditions of the New Notes and other obligations of Reorganized Care to the Class 7 creditors, which Loan Agreement shall contain covenants, representations, warranties and default provisions which are standard in transactions of a similar nature. The Loan Agreement shall be in the form filed with the Court not less than fifteen (15) days prior to the commencement of the hearing to consider confirmation of the Plan, subject to the filing of such modifications thereto as may be necessary or appropriate prior to the Confirmation Date.

1.25 "Net Available Cash" means all cash available on the Effective Date, less (i) the cash required to make the payments called for by the Plan and (ii) the sum of $5.0 million.

1.26 "Net Reorganization Value" shall mean the net worth of the Reorganized Debtor on a current value basis as of the Confirmation Date as found by the Bankruptcy Court, or if no such finding is made, $40 million.

1.27 "New Collateral" means all property of the Debtor and its Affiliates, other than Original Collateral, Replacement Collateral, Unencumbered Property, or any property which, as a matter of law or as a result of contractual commitments, cannot be made subject to a lien in favor of the Class 7 creditors.

1.28 "New Common Stock" means shares of Reorganized Care's common stock which shall be issued under the Plan and any shares issued in payment of dividends on such shares.

1.29 "New Common Stock Reorganization Value" shall mean the dividend produced by dividing the Net Reorganization Value by $8.0 million. For example, if Net Reorganization Value equals $48 million, then the New Common Stock Reorganization Value will equal $6.00 per share.

1.30 "New Notes" means the promissory notes of Reorganized Care to be issued to the Class 7 creditors under the Plan. The New Notes will be issued in a principal amount equal to the Class 7 Allowed Secured Claims as of the Effective Date, including unpaid interest and attorneys' fees, less the Bank's Miscellaneous Fees and the Initial Cash Payment distributed to the Class 7 creditors on the Effective Date. Interest will accrue from and after the Effective Date at a fluctuating rate equal to the prime commercial lending rate of Citibank, N.A. plus 2% (or 3% while in default), computed on a 360 day year. Interest will be paid on the New Notes monthly in arrears, commencing from and after the Effective Date. Beginning with the last day of the third full calendar quarter following the Confirmation Date, there shall be payable under the New Notes quarterly installments of principal, each reduced by the amount of interest paid during the same quarter, in accordance with the following schedule:

| | |
|---|---|
| 1st quarterly installment | $1.5 million |
| 2nd quarterly installment | $2.5 million |
| 3rd quarterly installment | $2.5 million |
| 4th-11th quarterly installments | $3.5 million |
| 12th quarterly installment (Maturity Date) | Payment of all unpaid principal and accrued interest |

In addition to the foregoing payments, the New Notes may be further reduced by the payment of Net Available Cash and Excess Cash. Net Available Cash, if any, shall be paid on the Effective Date and be applied ratably to the quarterly installments of principal due under the New Notes. Excess Cash shall initially be calculated on the last day of the third full calendar quarter following the Confirmation Date and paid 120 days after the end of such quarter. Thereafter, Excess Cash shall be calculated on a cumulative basis on the last day of each

Exhibit 5-2   Sample Unsecured Creditors' Committee's Plan                71

calendar quarter, and funds shall be deposited or withdrawn from a restricted cash collateral account such that the amount in such restricted account is equal to the amount of Excess Cash. One hundred twenty (120) days after the end of each fiscal year, the Excess Cash held in the restricted cash collateral account shall be disbursed to the holders of the New Notes and applied to the payments due under the New Notes in inverse order of maturity.

1.31 "Old Debentures" means those certain 9% convertible senior subordinated debentures due 2005 issued by the Debtor pursuant to that certain Indenture dated as of June 1, 1985, between the Debtor and Security Pacific National Bank as Trustee.

1.32 "Old Notes" means those certain 16% senior subordinated notes due 1994 issued by the Debtor pursuant to that certain Indenture dated as of September 1, 1984, between the Debtor and Bank of America N.T.&S.A. as Trustee.

1.33 "Original Collateral" means all property which, as of the Confirmation Date, secures the indebtedness of the Debtor and its Affiliates to the Class 7 creditors.

1.34 "Public Debt" means the Old Debentures and Old Notes.

1.35 "Petition Date" means March 25, 1988, the date on which the Debtor filed its chapter 11 petition with the United States Bankruptcy Court for the Central District of California.

1.36 "Plan" means the Plan of Reorganization, as amended in accordance with the terms hereof or modified in accordance with the Code.

1.37 "Preferred Stock" means the authorized preferred stock of the Debtor, including without limitation all Series A Junior Participating Preferred Stock.

1.38 "Pro Rata" means proportionately so that the ratio of the amount of the Distribution made on account of a particular claim or Interest to the Distributions made on account of all Allowed Claims or Allowed Interests of the class in which the particular claim or Interest is included is the same as the ratio of the amount of such particular claim or interest to the total amount of Allowed Claims or Allowed Interests of the class of which such particular claim or Interest is included, subject to the provisions set forth in § 6.06 of the Plan regarding distribution of fractions.

1.39 "Reorganized Care" means Care Enterprises, Inc., as revested with property that was formerly property of the Estate, as provided by § 1141(b) of the Code.

1.40 "Replacement Collateral" means property of the Debtor or its Affiliates, other than Original Collateral, designated by Reorganized Care prior to the Effective Date as substitute collateral for the Class 7 creditors. The Replacement Collateral shall be equal in value to the net proceeds derived from the sale or other disposition of Original Collateral between the Confirmation Date and the Effective Date, less such proceeds as are paid to or for the benefit of the Class 7 creditors.

1.41 "Shareholder Warrants" means the warrants to be issued under the Plan to purchase shares of New Common Stock equal in number to twenty-five percent (25%) of the number of shares of New Common Stock Distributed to the holders of Allowed Claims under the Plan, subject to customary antidilution adjustment provisions, and expiring five (5) years after the date of issuance. The Shareholder Warrants shall have an initial exercise price of $10.00 per share for the first twelve (12) months, which will escalate thereafter by $1.00 per year on each anniversary of the date of issuance. In the event of a merger, sale of all or substantially all of Reorganized Care's assets or other similar transaction respecting Reorganized Care, which shall be defined to exclude transactions with an entity which is an Affiliate of Reorganized Care, the warrants shall be callable after appropriate notice for $.25 per warrant, but will not otherwise be subject to call.

1.42 "Unclaimed Property" means any cash, New Common Stock or Shareholder Warrants which are unclaimed on the 180th day following the Effective Date. Unclaimed property shall include (a) checks (and the funds represented thereby), New Common Stock and Shareholder Warrants which have been returned as undeliverable without a proper forwarding address, (b) funds for checks which have not been paid, (c) checks (and the funds represented thereby), New Common Stock and Shareholder Warrants which were not mailed or delivered because of the absence of a proper address with which to mail or deliver such property, (d) New Common Stock attributable to Public Debt not surrendered prior to the fifth anniversary of the Effective Date, (e) interest and dividends paid, in cash or in kind, on the New Common Stock constituting unclaimed property, and (f) interest on cash constituting unclaimed property.

1.43 "Unencumbered Property" means the skilled nursing facilities owned or leased by the Debtor or its Affiliates in the states of Utah and West Virginia, together with all equipment, inventory, receivables and other personal property used in or arising from the operation of such facilities, and all proceeds, products, rents and profits derived therefrom; provided, however, that if Unencumbered Property is sold or refinanced prior to the Effective Date, then other property of the Debtor or its Affiliates may be substituted as Unencumbered Property to the extent the proceeds of such sale or refinancing are paid to or for the benefit of the Class 7 creditors.


## ARTICLE II

### Administrative Expenses and Unclassified Claims

The holders of Allowed Claims entitled to priority under § 507(a)(1) of the Code, entities entitled to payments under §§ 546(c) or 553 of the Code, and entities entitled to payment of administrative expenses pursuant to §§ 503 and 507(a) of the Code shall receive on account of such Allowed Claims or administrative expenses cash in the amount of such Allowed Claims or administrative expenses (i) on the Effective Date or as soon thereafter as is practicable, or (ii)

Exhibit 5-2   Sample Unsecured Creditors' Committee's Plan                    73

at the option of the Debtor, in accordance with the ordinary business terms of payment of such claims, except to the extent that any such holders or entities agree to different treatment. Notwithstanding the foregoing, professionals employed at the expense of the estate and entitles who may be entitled to an allowance of fees and expenses from the Estate pursuant to § 503(b)(2) through (6) of the Code, shall receive cash in the amount awarded to such professionals or entities as soon as practicable after an order is entered by the Court approving such award pursuant to §§ 330 or 503(b)(2) through (6) of the Code.

The holders of Allowed Claims, if any, entitled to priority under § 507(a)(7) of the Code will be paid in equal quarterly installments over a period of six (6) years after the date of the assessment of such claims, which amount shall bear interest at the rate applicable under non-bankruptcy law to such claims. Reorganized Care may elect, in its sole discretion, to prepay any such claim.


## ARTICLE III

## Designation of Classes of Claims and Interests

Claims and interests are classified as follows:

3.01 *Class 1* (priority): Allowed Claims entitled to priority pursuant to § 507(a)(3), (4), (5) and (6) of the Code.

3.02 *Class 2* (secured): The Allowed Secured Claim of Santa Barbara Savings, which is secured by a lien on Colonial Convalescent Hospital and Hilltop Convalescent Hospital.

3.03 *Class 3* (secured): The Allowed Secured Claim of Home Federal Savings & Loan, which is secured by a lien on Hilltop Convalescent Hospital and Georgian Court Convalescent Hospital.

3.04 *Class 4* (secured): The Allowed Secured Claim of Union Bank, which is secured by a lien on Washington Manor and Cedar Haven Convalescent Hospital.

3.05 *Class 5* (secured): The Allowed Secured Claim of FTC Servicing Corp., as agent, which is secured by a lien on an apartment building located in Phoenix, Arizona.

3.06 *Class 6* (secured): The Allowed Secured Claim of California Federal Savings and Loan, which is secured by a lien on a deposit account located in Los Angeles, California.

3.07 *Class 7* (secured): The Allowed Secured Claim of Citibank, N.A., as agent for Wells Fargo Bank, N.A. and Citibank, N.A.

3.08 *Class 8* (small claims): All Allowed Claims which are $500 or less or which are more than $500 and reduced to $500 by the holders thereof. In order to qualify for inclusion in Class 8, an election by any holder of an Allowed Claim in excess of $500 to reduce such holder's claim to $500 must be made no later than the date by which ballots accepting or rejecting the Plan must be returned as fixed by the Court. Any holder who does not make such election by returning a ballot appropriately marked within such time will be deemed not to have made the election.

3.09 *Class 9* (guarantees): All Allowed Claims arising out of guarantees executed by the Debtor before the Petition Date, pursuant to which the Debtor guaranteed the obligation of any Affiliates.

3.10 *Class 10* (affiliates): All Allowed Claims, the holders of which are Affiliates.

3.11 *Class 11* (trade claims): All Allowed Claims for goods purchased by the Debtor or services rendered to the Debtor, other than legal, accounting or investment banking services, prior to the Petition Date.

3.12 *Class 12* (workers compensation/personal injury): All Allowed Claims for personal injury which are covered by insurance and Allowed Claims for workers compensation.

3.13 *Class 13* (damages): All Allowed Claims other than personal injury claims covered by insurance, which (i) were the subject of litigation pending against the Debtor in a court of competent jurisdiction or before an administrative tribunal as of the Petition Date, or (ii) were scheduled as disputed in the list of creditors filed by the Debtor with the Court.

3.14 *Class 14* (Public Debt and other unsecured claims): All Unsecured Allowed Claims other than claims in Classes 8, 9, 10, 11, 12 and 13. Class 14 includes, without limitation, the Allowed Claims of the holders of Public Debt, the deficiency claims of secured creditors, and those arising from the rejection of executory contracts and leases.

3.15 *Class 15* (equity security interests): Allowed Interests of the Debtor.


## ARTICLE IV

### Classes Not Impaired Under the Plan

The following Classes are not impaired under the Plan

4.01 *Classes 1 and 8.* Except as provided below, Allowed Claims in Classes 1 and 8 will be paid in full in cash on the Effective Date, or as soon thereafter as is practicable, unless otherwise ordered by the Court. Accrued unpaid vacations and sick leave pay, to the extent entitled to priority, will be reinstated and used by current employees pursuant to company policy.

4.02 *Classes 2, 3, 4, 5, 6, 9, 10 and 12.* The Allowed Claims in Classes 2, 3, 4, 5, 6, 9, 10 and 12 shall retain unaltered the legal, equitable and contractual rights to which such claims entitle the holder thereof. If the Debtor is in default to the holder of any Allowed Claim in Classes 2, 3, 4, 5 and 6, the Debtor shall, on the Effective Date, or as soon as is practicable thereafter (i) cure all existing defaults, other than defaults relating to the insolvency or financial condition of the Debtor, defaults arising from the commencement of the Debtor's case or defaults based upon the appointment of or taking possession by a trustee or

Exhibit 5-2   Sample Unsecured Creditors' Committee's Plan            75

custodian; (ii) reinstate the original maturity of the Allowed Secured Claim as though no such default had occurred and pay the Allowed Secured Claim according to that original maturity; (iii) compensate the holder of the Allowed Secured Claim under which there was a default for any damages incurred based upon that claimant's reasonable reliance on the contractual provision under which there was a default or applicable loss; and (iv) comply with all other terms of the obligations without alteration.

## ARTICLE V

## Treatment of Classes that are Impaired Under the Plan

5.01 *Class 7*. The Allowed Secured Claims in Class 7, except for that portion attributable to the issuance of letters of credit, shall receive on account of such claims, and in full satisfaction thereof, the Bank's Miscellaneous Fees, the Initial Cash Payment, the Net Available Cash, if any, and the New Notes. The holders shall retain their Original Collateral and shall also receive a lien on the Replacement Collateral and New Collateral to secure repayment of the New Notes. With respect to the Allowed Secured Claims attributable to letters of credit, Reorganized Care shall pay, annually in advance, a letter of credit fee to the Class 7 creditors equal to 2% per annum of the face amount of letters of credit issued by the Class 7 creditors commencing from the Effective Date to and including the expiration date thereof. The letters of credit shall be cancelled, to the extent no prior draw has been made under said letters of credit, three (3) months after the maturity date of the New Notes. In the event of a drawing under any such letter of credit, the same shall be repaid to the Class 7 creditors within three (3) days after the date thereof. All letter of credit drawings shall bear interest at the prime commercial lending rate of Citibank, N.A., plus 2%, from the date thereof until paid in full. The repayment obligation shall be secured in the same manner as the New Notes.

In order to facilitate the accumulation of cash by Reorganized Care, the Class 7 creditors shall, upon request, release or subordinate their liens and security interests in any Original Collateral sold, refinanced or otherwise disposed of between the Confirmation Date and the Effective Date; provided, however, that the proceeds of any such transaction shall remain subject to liens and security interests of the Class 7 creditors until the Effective Date. To the extent any of the payments made to the Class 7 creditors on the Effective Date are derived from the sale, refinancing or other disposition of Unencumbered Property, then the Class 7 creditors shall, upon request, release their liens and security interests in Original Collateral designated by Reorganized Care having a value equivalent to the total of such payments. In connection with any refinancing prior to the Effective Date of any Original Collateral, Replacement Collateral or New Collateral, the liens and security interests of the Class 7 Creditors may be subordinated to the liens of the new lender.

After the Effective Date, the Class 7 creditors shall receive 100% of the proceeds from the sale, refinancing or other disposition of Original Collateral and Replacement Collateral and fifty percent (50%) of the proceeds from the sale, refinancing or other disposition of New Collateral. All such proceeds paid to the Class 7 creditors shall be applied pro rata against the future quarterly installments due under the New Notes.

5.02 *Class 11*. The holders of Class 11 Allowed Claims shall receive on account of such Allowed Claims, and in full satisfaction thereof, a cash payment on the Effective Date, or as soon thereafter as practicable, equal to 50% of each Allowed Claim. The holder of any Class 11 Allowed Claim may elect, in lieu of a cash distribution, to receive one share of New Common Stock for each $10.00 of such holder's Allowed Claim.

5.03 *Classes 13 and 14*. The holders of Class 13 and 14 Allowed Claims shall receive on account of such Allowed Claims, and in full satisfaction thereof, one share of New Common Stock for each $10.00 of the Allowed Claim. In making the Distribution to the holders of Class 13 and 14 Claims, subordination agreements will be enforced to the same extent that such agreements are enforceable under applicable non-bankruptcy law.

5.04 *Class 15*. All Common Stock and Preferred Stock of the Debtor will be cancelled, annulled and extinguished. The holders of Allowed Interests which are not subject to equitable subordination under § 510(c) of the Code shall receive, subject to $5.05, a Pro Rata Distribution of Shareholder Warrants for the purchase of New Common Stock.

5.05 *Cramdown*. In the event that any impaired Class shall fail to accept the Plan in accordance with § 1129(a) of the Code, the Committee reserves the right to request that the Court confirm the Plan in accordance with § 1129(b) of the Code. With respect to the treatment of Allowed Interests provided for in § 5.04, if (i) less than two-thirds (⅔) in amount of the Allowed Interests (Class 15) actually voting accept the Plan, excluding any negative votes cast by insiders, or (ii) any impaired class of Allowed Claims shall fail to accept the Plan and the Plan cannot be confirmed under § 1129(b) of the Code on account of the provisions for the Distribution of Shareholder Warrants, then the provisions for the Distribution of Shareholder Warrants shall be null and void, and in accordance with the absolute priority rule, the holders of Allowed Interests shall receive nothing under the Plan.

## ARTICLE VI

### Means for Execution of the Plan

6.01 On the Confirmation Date, Reorganized Care shall be revested with all the property that was formerly the property of the Estate (including any claims belonging to the Debtor or the Estate) and Reorganized Care will, subject to § 6.02, continue its business in the ordinary course as it existed prior to the

**Exhibit 5-2   Sample Unsecured Creditors' Committee's Plan**                    77

Petition Date. Except as specifically provided herein, the property of Reorganized Care will be free and clear of all claims, interests, liens and encumbrances. From and after the Confirmation Date, Reorganized Care shall cause its Affiliates to take such actions as may be necessary or appropriate to carry out the terms of the Plan.

6.02 Within 18 months following the Effective Date, unless extended or waived by the board of directors of Reorganized Care and the holders of the New Notes, Reorganized Care will sell or cause its Affiliates to sell the Designated Facilities; provided, however, that Reorganized Care shall have the right to substitute one or more facilities having a reasonably equivalent value for any of the Designated Facilities.

### 6.03  Distributions.

a. The Disbursing Agent will make the Distributions under the Plan, except that the Distributions to holders of Public Debt and Distributions to the holders of Allowed Interests shall be deposited with the Indenture Trustees or stock transfer agent, respectively, who, subject to the rights or claims of each Indenture Trustee under its Indenture and rights of the stock transfer agent, if any, shall deliver such property to holders of the respective securities in accordance with the provisions of the Plan. The New Common Stock to be issued under the Plan shall be deemed duly authorized, fully paid, and non-assessable.

b. To make the Distributions due under the Plan the Debtor shall deliver to the Disbursing Agent, Indenture Trustees and/or stock transfer agent (i) cash sufficient to make all payments called for by the Plan, (ii) the New Common Stock and (iii) the Shareholder Warrants; less amounts placed in the Disputed C/I Reserve. The Disbursing Agent, Indenture Trustees and/or stock transfer agent shall make such Distributions to the holders of Allowed Claims and Allowed Interests entitled thereto under the Plan.

### 6.04  Reserve for Disputed Claims and Interests.

a. On the Effective Date, the Distributions reserved for the holders of Disputed Claims and Disputed Interests shall not be delivered to the Disbursing Agent, Indenture Trustees and/or stock transfer agent, but shall be held by Reorganized Care in a segregated account (the "Disputed C/I Reserve") for the benefit of the holders of the Disputed Claims and Interests entitled thereto under the Plan. Except to the extent that the Court shall determine that a good and sufficient reserve for Disputed Claims is less than the full amount thereof, there will be deposited into the Disputed C/I Reserve an amount of cash and New Common Stock which would have been distributed on account of all Disputed Claims if all Disputed Claims were allowed in the full amount claimed by the holders thereof. With respect to the Distribution of Shareholder Warrants, the Pro Rata calculations required by § 5.04 of the Plan shall be made as if all Disputed Interests were Allowed Interests in the full amount claimed by the holders thereof. In addition to the Shareholder Warrants reserved for the holders of Disputed Interests, there shall be deposited into the Disputed C/I Reserve a number of Shareholder Warrants equal to that which would be distributed to the holders of Allowed Interests if the Disputed Claims in Class 13 and Class 14 were allowed in full and New Common Stock issued to the holders of such claims under the Plan.

b. All New Common Stock held in the Disputed Claims Reserve will be deemed to be issued and outstanding, and with respect to any matter requiring a vote of shareholders, will be deemed to vote on such matter in the same proportions as the votes actually cast by those shares of New Common Stock which have previously been distributed.

c. All dividends which are paid in cash or in kind on account of New Common Stock contained in the Disputed Claims Reserve shall be added to the Disputed Claims Reserve. All cash held in the Disputed Claims Reserve shall be invested in such investments as are authorized by the Court.

d. At such time as a Disputed Claim or Disputed Interest becomes an Allowed Claim or Allowed Interest, the distribution which would have been disbursed had the Disputed Claim or Interest been an Allowed Claim or Allowed Interest on the Effective Date shall be released from the Disputed C/I Reserve and delivered to the Disbursing Agent, Indenture Trustees and/or stock transfer agent for delivery to the holder of such Allowed Claim or Allowed Interest within thirty (30) days. New Common Stock which is issued after the Effective Date upon determination of a Disputed Claim shall be accompanied by the dividend, if any, which would theretofore have been paid on the New Common Stock had it been issued on the Effective Date.

e. At such time as all Disputed Claims in Class 1, 8, and 11 have been finally determined, the balance of the cash not theretofore distributed shall be returned to Reorganized Care. At such time as all Disputed Claims in Class 13 and 14 have been finally determined, any New Common Stock in the Disputed Claims Reserve not required for distribution to the holders of Allowed Claims shall be returned to Reorganized Care together with the Shareholder Warrants representing twenty-five percent (25%) of the number of shares of such New Common Stock. At such time as all Disputed Claims and Disputed Interests have been finally determined, the remaining Shareholder warrants required for Distribution under the Plan shall be distributed Pro Rata to the holders of Allowed Interests.

### 6.05 Unclaimed Distributions.

a. Unclaimed Property shall be delivered to Reorganized Care by the Disbursing Agent and the Indenture Trustees no earlier than 180 days following the Effective Date or at such later date as it is determined that a particular asset constitutes Unclaimed Property. Reorganized Care shall deposit such Unclaimed Property in an Unclaimed Property reserve to be held in trust for the benefit of the holders of Allowed Claims and Allowed Interests entitled thereto under the terms of the Plan. For a period of five (5) years following the Effective Date, Unclaimed Property, including any principal, interest and dividends, in cash or in kind, as may have been paid on account of any such Unclaimed Property, shall be held in the Unclaimed Property reserve solely for the benefit of the

**Exhibit 5-2   Sample Unsecured Creditors' Committee's Plan**        **79**

holders of Allowed Claims which have failed to claim such property. Until the expiration of five (5) years following the Effective Date, Unclaimed Property due the holder of an Allowed Claim or Allowed Interest shall be released from the Unclaimed Property reserve and delivered to such holder upon presentation of proper proof by such holder of its entitlement thereto.

b. At the end of the five (5) years following the Effective Date, the holders of Allowed Claims theretofore entitled to Unclaimed Property shall cease to be entitled thereto, and the Unclaimed Property shall then become the property of Reorganized Care.

6.06 *Distributions of Fractions.* Fractional shares of New Common Stock or Shareholder Warrants shall not be issued or distributed. Instead, each time a Distribution is to be made to the holders of Allowed Claims or Allowed Interests, any fractional interest in New Common Stock or Shareholder Warrants will be distributed according to the following method. All fractions of New Common Stock and Shareholder Warrants which would otherwise have been distributed will be aggregated in separate pools (the "Fractional Pools") on the date of such Distribution. Holders of Allowed Claims and Allowed Interests who would otherwise be entitled to receive fractions will be ranked according to the size of the fractions to which such holders would otherwise be entitled. If two or more holders are entitled to the same fraction (as rounded to the second decimal place), the ranking of such holders will be determined by lot. Based on such ranking, a whole share of New Common Stock or Shareholder Warrants will be distributed to those holders entitled to the largest fractions of each until all of the whole units of New Common Stock and Shareholder Warrants in the Fractional Pools have been distributed.

6.07 *Surrender of Securities.* All Public Debt will be cancelled on the Effective Date of the Plan and shall entitle the holders thereof to the Distribution provided by the Plan. As a condition to receiving the Distribution of New Common Stock provided for by the Plan, any holder of an Old Debenture or Old Note shall surrender such Old Debenture or Old Note to the Indenture Trustees during the period ending at the close of business 180 days after the Effective Date. Thereafter, but prior to the five (5) years following the Effective Date, such holder shall surrender Old Debentures and Old Notes to the Disbursing Agent as a condition to receiving Distributions provided for by the Plan. All Old Debentures and Old Notes surrendered to the Indenture Trustees or the Disbursing Agent shall be conspicuously marked "cancelled" and delivered to Reorganized Care. After 180 days following the Effective Date, the Indenture Trustees shall turn over to the Disbursing Agent their records with respect to the Old Debentures and Old Notes and shall have no further duties or responsibilities with respect thereto.

6.08 *Payment of Indenture Trustee Fees.* Notwithstanding any other provision of the Plan, the Indenture Trustees shall hold and not distribute shares of New Common Stock with an aggregate New Common Stock Reorganization Value equal to 150 percent of their total accrued but unpaid fees and expenses, including their attorneys' fees and expenses (the "Held Shares"). The Held Shares shall secure payment of each Indenture Trustee's respective fees and expenses, including its attorneys' fees and expenses. Each Indenture Trustee may at any time exercise in respect of the Held Stock, in addition to other rights and remedies provided for herein or otherwise available to it, all the rights and remedies under the laws of the State of California at that time and may, in its sole discretion without notice, sell the Held Stock or any part thereof in one or more parcels at public or private sale, at any exchange, broker's board or at any of its offices or elsewhere, for cash, on credit or for future delivery and at such prices or prices and upon such other terms as the Indenture Trustee may deem commercially reasonable, irrespective of the impact of any such sales on the market price of the New Common Stock. To the extent notice of sale shall be required by law, at least ten days' notice to Reorganized Care and the Committee together with publication in any newspaper of general circulation in Los Angeles, California on any two nonconsecutive business days at least ten (10) days before such sale, shall constitute reasonable notice.

Within sixty (60) days of the Confirmation Date, each Indenture Trustee may file, but is under no obligation to do so, a motion for reimbursement of its fees and expenses from the Debtor and Reorganized Care pursuant to 11 U.S.C. § 503(b) If no such motion is made, or upon receipt of payment pursuant to a court order granting such a motion, or upon the entry of a Final Order denying such a motion, Reorganized Care shall redeem within ten (10) days of receipt of an Indenture Trustee's written request to do so, sufficient Held Shares from the demanding Indenture Trustee at the New Common Stock Reorganization Value to fully compensate the demanding Indenture Trustee for all of its fees and expenses then remaining unpaid, including the Indenture Trustee's attorneys' fees and expenses and any fees and expenses arising out of its motion for reimbursement under 11 U.S.C. § 503(b); provided that the Indenture Trustee certifies that no public market exists in which the Indenture Trustee can promptly liquidate sufficient Held Shares at no less than eighty-five percent (85%) of the New Common Stock Reorganization Value to fully compensate the Indenture Trustee for all its fees and expenses then remaining unpaid, including the Indenture Trustee's attorneys' fees and expenses and any fees and expenses arising out of its motion for reimbursement under 11 U.S.C. § 503(b). After receiving full payment of its accrued fees and expenses, including attorneys' fees and expenses, each Indenture Trustee shall distribute Pro Rata the remaining Held Shares in its possession to its respective holders of record as of the record date fixed pursuant to Articles 1.02 and 6.03(a) of the Plan.

## ARTICLE VII

### Discharge

Except as otherwise provided in the Plan and the Confirmation Order, entry of the Confirmation Order acts as a discharge effective as of the Confirmation Date of any and all debts, obligations, liabilities and claims, whether contingent

**Exhibit 5-2 Sample Unsecured Creditors' Committee's Plan** **81**

or otherwise, of the Debtor that arose at any time before entry of the Confirmation Order including, but not limited to, all principal and any interest accrued thereon, pursuant to § 1141(d)(1) of the Code. The discharge of the Debtor shall be effective as to each claim, regardless of whether a proof of claim was filed, whether the claim was an Allowed Claim, or whether the holder thereof voted to accept the Plan.

## ARTICLE VIII

### Retention and Enforcement of Claims

Pursuant to § 1123(b)(3) of the Code, Reorganized Care will maintain and enforce any claims of the Debtor or the Estate.

## ARTICLE IX

### Treatment of Executory Contracts and Unexpired Leases

The Debtor hereby assumes all executory contracts and unexpired leases, whether or not set forth on the Statement of Executory Contracts filed with the Court, which are set forth on Exhibit "1" attached hereto. All executory contracts and unexpired leases not listed on Exhibit "1" are deemed rejected and any proofs of claim thereon must be filed within thirty (30) days after the Confirmation Date.

## ARTICLE X

### Provisions for Inclusion in the Charter of the Reorganized Debtor

Upon the Confirmation Date the persons then holding office on the Board of Directors for the Debtor or any of its Affiliates shall automatically be removed from the Board of Directors. The Board of Directors of Reorganized Care shall immediately as of the Confirmation Date be reconstituted to consist of five (5) members to be selected by the Committee. The new members selected for the Board of Directors and any members of management who must be identified under § 1129(a)(5) of the Code shall be designated in a pleading to be filed with the Court at least fifteen (15) days before the Confirmation Date.

On the Confirmation Date, the newly selected Board of Directors for Reorganized Care shall meet and appoint new management for Reorganized Care, new members for the Board of Directors of the Debtor's Affiliates, and the new management for the Debtor's Affiliates. In selecting new management, the Board shall attempt to retain all such persons in present management as may be appropriate for the continued operations of the Debtor and its Affiliates, and may supplement and/or replace such management as is deemed necessary; provided, however, that notwithstanding the foregoing, as of the Confirmation Date neither Lee Bangerter nor Dee Bangerter may have any place on any Board of Directors, nor any role in new management. As soon as practicable after the Effective Date, the new Board of Directors shall convene a meeting of the holders of the New Common Stock to, among other things, elect a Board of Directors for Reorganized Care.

The Debtor's Certificate of Incorporation shall be amended to prohibit the issuance of non-voting equity securities. Additionally, the Certificate of Incorporation and Bylaws shall be further amended to (i) provide for the cancellation of Interests and the issuance of the New Common Stock and Shareholders Warrants and (ii) eliminate some or all of the anti-takeover measures adopted by the Debtor.

## ARTICLE XI

### Creditors' Committee

11.01 The Committee will continue in its current form after the Confirmation Date and until the Effective Date. The Committee shall have all of the rights, powers and duties set forth in § 103 of the Bankruptcy Code, plus such additional and further rights, powers and duties as may be reasonably necessary in connection with the Plan.

11.02 After the Effective Date, to the extent necessary, appropriate and required under the Plan, the Committee shall continue in existence.

11.03 The Committee shall have the right to participate in (i) appeals from the Confirmation Order; (ii) hearings on proposed modifications or amendments to the Plan; (iii) applications for the allowance of compensation to professional persons; (iv) actions to enforce or interpret the Plan; (v) proceedings regarding Disputed Claim; (vi) proceedings involving other claims by or against the Debtor, or other disputes or issues, to the extent that the Bankruptcy Court retains jurisdiction over such proceedings, including jurisdiction to approve the settlement and compromise of claims that arose prior to the Effective Date.

11.04 The Committee shall not, directly or indirectly, attempt to take part in or exert any influence whatsoever over the business or operations of Reorganized Care or the activities of its Board of Directors.

11.05 The members of the Committee shall serve without compensation, but they shall be reimbursed monthly by Reorganized Care for the reasonable and necessary out-of-pocket expenses incident to the performance of their duties. The Committee may continue to retain its attorneys and accountants previously authorized by the Court, as may be reasonably required by it to perform its duties. Such attorneys and accountants shall be compensated and reimbursed for their reasonable and necessary out-of-pocket expenses on a monthly basis

**Exhibit 5-2 Sample Unsecured Creditors' Committee's Plan** 83

by Reorganized Care. In the event Reorganized Care objects to the amounts requested by such members, attorneys and accountants, it shall be paid the undisputed amount and file an objection to the balance with the Court, which shall determine the amount to be paid.

11.06 Upon substantial completion of its functions as designated herein, the Committee shall be dissolved.

## ARTICLE XIII

### Conditions to Confirmation

Unless waived by vote of the Committee, confirmation of the Plan is expressly conditioned upon: (i) the Committee obtaining, prior to the Confirmation Date, the agreement of the holders of Class 7 Allowed Secured Claims to restructure the indebtedness of certain Affiliates to the Class 7 creditors on terms consistent with the treatment provided in § 5.01 of the Plan; and (ii) Class 11 Allowed Claims totalling in amount to no more than $1,500,000.

## ARTICLE XIV

### Retention of Jurisdiction

Until this case is closed, the Court shall retain jurisdiction to ensure that the purpose of intent of the Plan are carried out. Without limiting the generality of the foregoing, the Court will retain jurisdiction, until the Plan has been fully consummated for the following purposes:

a. Classification and allowance of the claim of any creditor (including claims for administrative expenses) including re-examination of Allowed Claims for purposes of determining acceptances at the time of confirmation, and determination of such objections as may be filed and the allowance of creditors' claims. Failure to object or to examine any claim for the purpose of determining acceptances shall not be deemed to waive the right to object to or re-examine the claim in whole or in part.

b. Rejection of executory contracts that are not rejected prior to confirmation and allowance of claims for damages as to the rejection of any executory contracts.

c. Determination of all questions and disputes regarding title to the assets of the Estate, and determination of all causes of action, controversies, disputes, or conflicts, whether or not subject to pending action as of the date of confirmation, between the Debtor and any other party including, but not limited to, any right of the Debtor to recover assets or to avoid transfers thereof pursuant to the provisions of the Code. Such disputes may be pursued by the Debtor for the benefit of Reorganized Care.

d. Correction of any defect, curing of any omission or reconciliation of any inconsistency in the Plan, Confirmation Order, or any or all documents executed or to be executed in connection therewith, as may be necessary to carry out the purposes and intent of the Plan, on notice or ex parte, as the Court shall determine to be appropriate.

e. Modification of the Plan after confirmation pursuant to the Rules of Bankruptcy Procedure and the Code.

f. Enforcement and interpretation of the terms and conditions of the Plan.

g. Shortening or extending, for cause, the time fixed for doing any act or thing under the Plan, on notice or ex parte as the Court shall determine to be appropriate.

h. Entry of any Order, including injunctions, necessary to enforce the title, rights and powers of the Debtor and to impose such limitations, restrictions, terms and conditions on such title, rights and powers as this Court may deem appropriate.

i. Entry of an Order concluding and terminating this case.

DATED: April 14, 1989

OFFICIAL COMMITTEE OF
CREDITORS HOLDING
UNSECURED CLAIMS BY ITS
CO-CHAIRPERSONS

PYA MONARCH, INC.

By: _____
      Laraine Beck, Credit Manager

R. D. SMITH & COMPANY

By: _____
      John Adams, Vice President

SIDLEY & AUSTIN

By: _____
     Richard W. Havel
     Perry L. Landsberg
Attorneys for Official Committee of
Creditors Holding Unsecured Claims

Exhibit 5-2    Sample Unsecured Creditors' Committee's Plan                85

## EXHIBIT "1"

A. Softward Licensing Agreement with Collier-Jackson, Inc.

B. Master Lease Agreement with Comdisco, Inc. for telephone equipment.

C. Software Licensing and Development Agreement with Automated Programming Technologies, Inc.

D. Equipment lease with Maryland National Leasing Corporation.

E. Purchase Agreement with Development Corp. of America and Ralph E. Hazelbaker.

F. Automobile lease agreement (three) with Galles Rental.

G. Duplicator lease agreement with Eastman Kodak Company.

H. Telephone equipment lease agreement and amendments with AT&T Information Systems.

I. Software Licensing Agreements (two) with Infocentre.

J. Software Agreement and Customer Support Services Agreement with Hewlett-Packard.

K. Agreement for equipment sale with Amcare Microsoftware Systems.

L. Agreement for AMS License Programs with Amcare Microsoftware Systems.

**EXHIBIT 5-3   SAMPLE DISCLOSURE STATEMENT BY DEBTOR (SELECTED ITEMS)**

This exhibit consists of selected provisions for a disclosure statement prepared by the debtor. In order to illustrate all of the items that were included in the disclosure statement the table of contents of the disclosure statement precedes the following excerpts:

Applicability of Federal and Other Securities Laws
Certain Federal Income Tax Consequences of the Plan
Confirmation and Consummation
Recommendations and Conclusions
Income Statement for Year Ending December 31, 1988. (Exhibit D)
Projected Capitalization of New WOW as of June 1, 1989 (Exhibit E)
Estimated Distributions to Holders of Class 2 and Class 3 Claims (Exhibit F)
Comparison of Plan vs Liquidation Proceeds (Exhibit G)
Financial Projections of New WOW (Exhibit H)

## DISCLOSURE STATEMENT

### Table of Contents

Exhibit 5-3    Sample Disclosure Statement by Debtor                                    87

**Exhibit 5-3    Sample Disclosure Statement by Debtor**                                89

**Exhibit 5-3    Sample Disclosure Statement by Debtor**                    **91**

               **iii.** Notes and Assumptions to the Projected State-
                   ment of Income Through March 31, 1994

   **E.** Certain Risk Factors In Owning Capital Stock of New WOW

      **1.** Inherent Uncertainty in the Statement of Projected
         Financial Performance

      **2.** Volatility and Product Acceptance in the Toy Industry

      **3.** Seasonality

      **4.** Competition

      **5.** Material Costs

      **6.** Limitations of Patent, Trademark and Copyright
         Protection

      **7.** Risk of Losing Licensed Rights

      **8.** Government Regulation and Industry Standards

      **9.** Product Liability and Other Insurance

    **10.** Accounts Receivable

    **11.** Subcontracting of Manufacturing and Assembly Work
         to Foreign Producers

    **12.** Ability to Attract Management

    **13.** Dependence on Key Employees

    **14.** Required Financing

    **15.** New WOW to be Highly Leveraged

    **16.** Interest Rates

    **17.** Use of Revenues for Acquisitions and Other Ventures

    **18.** Availability of Tax Net Operating Loss Carryovers

   **F.** Acceptance

   **G.** Confirmation

   **H.** Confirmation Hearing

   **I.** Consummation

 **X.**   Recommendation and Conclusion

### Exhibits

Financial Projections of New WOW                                              H
Order Re Disclosure Statement Dated April 10, 1989                            I

## VII
## APPLICABILITY OF FEDERAL AND OTHER SECURITIES LAWS

### A. Issuance of New WOW Preferred Stock and Class 3 WOW Stock Under the Plan

Section 1145 of the Bankruptcy Code exempts the issuance of securities under a plan of reorganization from registration under the Securities Act of 1933, as amended ("Securities Act"), and state securities laws if three principal requirements are satisfied: (i) the securities must be issued by the debtor or its successor "under the plan" of reorganization; (ii) the recipients of the securities must hold a claim against the debtor, an interest in the debtor or a claim for an administrative expense against the debtor; and (iii) the securities must be issued entirely in exchange for the recipient's claim against or interest in the debtor, or "principally" in such exchange and "partly" for cash or property. The Debtor believes that, under Section 1145 of the Bankruptcy Code, the issuance of the Series A Preferred Stock, Series B Preferred Stock, and Series C Preferred Stock of New WOW (collectively "New WOW Preferred Stock") and the Common Stock of Old WOW ("Class 3 WOW Stock") under the Plan satisfies these requirements and is, therefore, exempt from the registration requirements of federal and state securities laws.

### B. Post-Consummation Transfers of Plan Securities

All resales and subsequent transactions in the New WOW Preferred Stock and Class 3 WOW Stock to be issued pursuant to the Plan are exempt from the securities laws, except for certain transactions by "underwriters." (Holders of New WOW Preferred Stock should be aware, however, that significant limitations on transfer of such shares (discussed in Section IV(C)(8)) are set forth in Article Fifth of the Certificate of Incorporation.) Section 1145(b) of the Bankruptcy Code defines four types of "underwriters":

(i) persons who purchase a claim against, an interest in, or a claim for administrative expense against the debtor with a view to distributing any security received in exchange for such a claim or interest ("accumulators");

(ii) persons who offer to sell securities offered under a plan for the holders of such securities ("distributors");

(iii) persons who offer to buy such securities for the holders of such securities, if the offer is (a) with a view to distributing them, or (b) made under a distribution agreement ("syndicators"); and

(iv) a person who is an "issuer" with respect to the securities, as the term "issuer" is defined in Section 2(11) of the Securities Act.

Exhibit 5-3    Sample Disclosure Statement by Debtor                               93

Under Section 2(11) of the Securities Act, an "issuer" includes any person directly or indirectly controlling or controlled by Old WOW or New WOW, as the case may be, or any person under direct or indirect common control with Old WOW or New WOW, as the case may be.

Whether a person is an "issuer," and therefore an "underwriter," for purposes of Section 1145(b) of the Code, depends on a number of factors. These include: (i) the person's equity interest in a reorganized debtor or its successor under a plan; (ii) the distribution and concentration of other equity interests in a reorganized debtor or its successor under a plan; (iii) whether the person, either alone or acting in concert with others, has a contractual or other relationship giving that person power over management policies and decisions of a reorganized debtor or its successor under a plan; and (iv) whether the person actually has such power notwithstanding the absence of formal indicia of control.

An officer or director of a reorganized debtor or its successor under a plan may be deemed a controlling person, particularly if his position is coupled with ownership of a significant percentage of voting stock. In addition, the legislative history of Section 1145 of the Bankruptcy Code suggests that a creditor with at least 10% of the securities of a debtor could be deemed a controlling person.

Resales and subsequent transactions in the New WOW Preferred Stock or Class 3 WOW Stock by the holders of Class 3 Claims may not be exempt from federal and state securities laws, since the holders thereof may be deemed controlling persons of New WOW and the Lenders will be a controlling person in the case of Old WOW.

To the extent that persons deemed "underwriters" receive securities pursuant to the Plan, resales by such persons would not be exempted by Section 1145 of the Code from registration under the Securities Act. Persons deemed to be underwriters may be able to sell securities without registration subject to the provisions of Rule 144 under the Securities Act, which would permit the public sale of securities received pursuant to the Plan by statutory underwriters, subject to volume limitations and certain other conditions.

GIVEN THE COMPLEX, SUBJECTIVE NATURE OF WHETHER A PARTICULAR HOLDER MAY BE AN UNDERWRITER, THE DEBTOR MAKES NO REPRESENTATIONS CONCERNING THE RIGHT OF ANY PERSON TO TRADE IN NEW WOW PREFERRED STOCK OR CLASS 3 WOW STOCK TO BE DISTRIBUTED PURSUANT TO THE PLAN. THE DEBTOR RECOMMENDS THAT EACH POTENTIAL RECIPIENT OF THE NEW WOW PREFERRED STOCK AND CLASS 3 WOW STOCK CONSULT HIS OWN COUNSEL CONCERNING WHETHER OR NOT RESALES OR OTHER TRANSACTIONS IN PLAN SECURITIES ARE LAWFUL UNDER APPLICABLE SECURITIES LAWS.

## 1. Control Persons

As of the date of this Disclosure Statement, the Debtor has no reason to believe that any recipients of New WOW Preferred Stock and Class 3 WOW Stock might be deemed to be control persons, except the Lenders, as holders of Class 3 Claims.

## 2. Syndicators, Accumulators and Distributors

No arrangements for resale of securities issued pursuant to the Plan are known to the Debtor which would make any person a syndicator, accumulator or distributor.

## 3. Ordinary Trading Transactions

All resales by an entity other than an issuer (including resales by an entity that otherwise could be characterized as a syndicator, accumulator or distributor) of securities issued pursuant to the plans of reorganization generally would be regarded as exempt from registration under the Securities Act so long as the sales are made in "ordinary trading transactions." In the view of Debtor's counsel, a transaction generally will be considered to be an "ordinary trading transaction" if it is made on an exchange or in the over-the-counter market at a time when the debtor is a reporting company under the Securities Exchange Act of 1934, as amended (the "Exchange Act") and does not involve any of the following factors:

> (a) (i) concerted action by recipients of securities issued under a plan in connection with the sale of such securities, or (ii) concerted action by distributors on behalf of one or more such recipients in connection with such sales or (iii) both;
> (b) informational documents concerning the offering of the securities prepared or used to assist in the resale of such securities other than a disclosure statement and any supplements thereto and documents filed with the Securities and Exchange Commission ("SEC") by any debtor pursuant to the Exchange Act; or
> (c) special compensation to brokers and dealers in connection with the sale of such securities designed as a special incentive to the resale of such securities (other than the compensation that would be paid pursuant to arms-length negotiations between a seller and a broker or dealer, each acting unilaterally), not greater than the compensation that would be paid for a routine similar-sized sale of similar securities of a similar issuer.

The views of the SEC on the matter have not, however, been sought by the Debtor and, therefore, no assurance regarding the current position of the SEC can be given.

It is possible that resale transactions which include one or more of the above factors could constitute "ordinary trading transactions," but that determination would have to be carefully made on a case-by-case basis, and the Debtor's counsel and New WOW's counsel have not sought any advice from the staff of the SEC with respect to such transactions.

EACH RECIPIENT OF SHARES OF PREFERRED STOCK OF NEW WOW AND CLASS 3 WOW STOCK SHOULD SATISFY HIMSELF THROUGH CONSULTATION WITH HIS OWN LEGAL ADVISORS AS TO WHETHER THE ISSUANCE OR TRANSFER OF SUCH STOCK IS LAWFUL UNDER THE SECURITIES LAWS AND WHETHER OR NOT THE VIEWS OF THE SEC SHOULD BE SOUGHT.

Exhibit 5-3    Sample Disclosure Statement by Debtor                                    **95**

## C. Current Information

Within 120 days after the last day of its first year on which it has a class of equity security held of record by more than 500 holders, New WOW will be required to comply with the reporting requirements of the Exchange Act. The Debtor is informed that New WOW believes it will be required to comply with such reporting requirements at the time that its Series C Preferred Stock will be held by more than 500 holders of record. This is expected to occur at the time the Series C Preferred Stock is distributed to the ultimate beneficial holders following final determination and allowance of all Class 6 Claims. New WOW has informed the Debtor that it intends to comply with such requirements if, and at such time as, the Series C Preferred Stock is held by more than 500 holders of record. Under these requirements, New WOW will file with the SEC, among other things, Annual Reports on Form 10-K, Quarterly Reports on Form 10-Q and other information.

## D. Certain Transactions by Stockholders

Under Section 1145(a)(4) of the Bankruptcy Code, stockbrokers are required to deliver a copy of this Disclosure Statement (and supplements hereto, if any, if ordered by the Bankruptcy Court) at or before the time of delivery of securities issued under the Plan to their customers for the first 40 days after the Effective Date. This requirement specifically applies to trading and other after-market transactions in such securities. The Debtor does not believe that any such transactions by stockbrokers will be effected for the first 40 days after the Effective Date.

# VIII
# CERTAIN FEDERAL INCOME TAX CONSEQUENCES
# OF THE PLAN

THE FOLLOWING DISCUSSION IS A SUMMARY OF CERTAIN OF THE MORE SIGNIFICANT FEDERAL INCOME TAX CONSEQUENCES OF THE PLAN TO THE DEBTOR, NEW WOW AND HOLDERS OF CLAIMS AND INTERESTS. THE TAX CONSEQUENCES TO HOLDERS MAY VARY BASED ON THE INDIVIDUAL CIRCUMSTANCES OF EACH HOLDER. MOREOVER, THE TAX CONSEQUENCES OF CERTAIN ASPECTS OF THE PLAN ARE UNCERTAIN DUE TO THE LACK OF APPLICABLE LEGAL PRECEDENT AND THE POSSIBILITY OF CHANGES IN LAW. NO RULING WILL BE OBTAINED FROM THE INTERNAL REVENUE SERVICE WITH RESPECT TO ANY OF THE TAX ASPECTS OF THE PLAN AND IT IS NOT CLEAR THAT A RULING COULD BE OBTAINED ON CERTAIN ASPECTS. IN ADDITION, NO OPINION OF COUNSEL HAS BEEN OR WILL BE OBTAINED BY THE DEBTOR OR NEW WOW

WITH RESPECT TO THE TAX ASPECTS OF THE PLAN. ACCORDINGLY, EACH HOLDER OF A CLAIM OR INTEREST IS STRONGLY URGED TO CONSULT WITH HIS OWN TAX ADVISOR REGARDING THE FEDERAL, STATE AND LOCAL TAX CONSEQUENCES OF THE PLAN.

## A. G Reorganization

As discussed in Section IX(D)(5) below, the projections of New WOW's future performance assume that New WOW's federal taxable income can be offset with the Debtor's net operating loss ("NOL") carryovers. Such carryovers will be available in the amounts assumed in the projections only if the transaction contemplated by the Plan qualifies as a tax-free reorganization described in Section 368(a)(1)(G) of the Tax Code (a "G reorganization") and the bankruptcy exception set forth in Section 382(1)(5) of the Tax Code (the "Bankruptcy Exception") (described below) applies. Among the more material consequences of treating the transaction as a G reorganization are that New WOW will succeed to the NOL carryovers of the Debtor, and the Debtor will recognize no gain or loss upon receipt of New WOW Preferred Stock, cash and other property and the assumption by New WOW of the Assumed Liabilities in exchange for the Purchased Assets. Furthermore, if the transaction qualifies as a G reorganization, the Subordinated Debenture holders and any other Creditors whose Claims constitute "securities" (for federal income tax purposes) of the Debtor will recognize no gain or loss on the receipt of New WOW Preferred Stock in exchange for their Claims, as more fully discussed below.

The Debtor believes that the transaction contemplated by the Plan should qualify as a G reorganization. It is important to note, however, that numerous legal issues concerning G reorganizations in general and the Plan in particular have not been addressed, either statutorily, judicially, or administratively, in a manner that can make the determination of a G reorganization status free from doubt. Furthermore, whether the requirements for a G reorganization will be satisfied depends in part on certain factual determinations. Although the Debtor believes the facts support G reorganization status, the Debtor's evaluation of such facts remains subject to challenge.

The uncertainty surrounding G reorganizations could also influence New WOW's decision regarding whether it will rely on the Bankruptcy Exception (described below) and consequently could result in the reduction in the consideration distributable to certain Creditors as described in Section IV(C)(7) hereof. In the event New WOW elects not to rely on the Bankruptcy Exception and the consideration is so adjusted, the transaction in all likelihood will not qualify as a G reorganization.

If the transaction does not qualify as a G reorganization for any reason, New WOW will not be entitled to deduct the Debtor's NOL carryovers from its otherwise federal taxable income. In addition, the transaction would be treated as a taxable purchase and sale of assets, and the Debtor would recognize gain or loss equal to the difference between the fair market value of the consideration (including Assumed Liabilities) received from the sale of the Purchased Assets

Exhibit 5-3   Sample Disclosure Statement by Debtor                                    97

and the Debtor's adjusted tax basis in the Purchased Assets. In the event any gain is recognized, such gain should be offset by the Debtor's current NOLs and thus should not result in an actual tax liability. Furthermore, holders of securities would be treated in a manner similar to holders of claims that do not constitute securities.

## B. Other Tax Consequences

Unless indicated otherwise, the following discussion assumes that the transaction contemplated by the Plan qualifies as a G reorganization.

### 1. Tax Attributes of the Debtor and New WOW

For federal income tax purposes, the Debtor has substantial NOL carryovers which, after the reductions and subject to the risks discussed below, should be available to offset future income of New WOW. NOL carryovers reported on the Debtor's federal income tax return for the year ended March 31, 1988 were approximately $150 million. Based on the information available at the date hereof, the Debtor estimates that after the reductions in its NOL carryovers described in Section VIII(B)(2)(b), "Bankruptcy Exception" and Section VIII(B)(3), "Reduction in the Debtor's Tax Attributes Resulting From Discharge of Indebtedness," the NOL carryovers available to New WOW after consummation of the transaction contemplated by the Plan will be at least $60 million. These carryovers will begin to expire, if not previously utilized, in 2003.

The ultimate extent of the reductions referred to in Sections VIII(B)(2)(b) and VIII(B)(3) will depend on, among other things, the value of the New WOW Preferred Stock and other property distributed to holders of Claims pursuant to the Plan, the total amount of Claims, the amount of interest accrued during a certain period, and the application of the Stock-For-Debt Exception and Bankruptcy Exception (both described below). Although the Debtor believes its estimate of the NOL carryover figure is reasonably accurate, the amount is subject to adjustment upon receipt of additional facts or upon audit by the Internal Revenue Service (the "IRS").

### 2. Utilization of the Debtor's NOL Carryovers by New WOW

#### a. Section 382 in General

Section 382 of the Tax Code provides rules governing the utilization of a corporation's NOL carryovers following significant statutorily prescribed changes in ownership of a corporation's equity (an "ownership change"). The Plan generally provides, among other things, for the transfer of the Debtor's operating assets to New WOW, and for the distribution of New WOW's capital stock to parties other than the Debtor's historic shareholders in a transaction that the Debtor believes should qualify as a G reorganization. Therefore, the Tax Code provides that an ownership change will occur with respect to the Debtor, and the continued availability of the Debtor's NOL carryovers will be subject to the limitations and reductions provided under Section 382 of the Tax Code.

Unless the Bankruptcy Exception (described more fully below) applies to the transaction contemplated by the Plan, Section 382 provides that following an ownership change with respect to the Debtor, the amount of post-ownership change annual taxable income of New WOW that can be offset by the Debtor's pre-ownership change NOL carryovers generally cannot exceed an amount equal to the value of the Debtor immediately before the ownership change (subject to various adjustments) multiplied by a prescribed long-term tax-exempt rate, currently 7.29% (the "Annual Limitation"). The Debtor believes that an ownership change will occur in connection with the Plan and, unless the Bankruptcy Exception (discussed below) applies, the use of the Debtor's NOL carryovers by New WOW will be subject to the Annual Limitation.

### b. Bankruptcy Exception

Section 382(1)(5) of the Tax Code, setting forth the Bankruptcy Exception, provides that the Annual Limitation will not apply to limit New WOW's deduction of the Debtor's NOL carryovers if the stock of New WOW owned by those persons who were shareholders of the Debtor immediately before the ownership change, together with certain stock of New WOW owned by Creditors of the Debtor, comprise 50% or more of the value and voting power of all of the stock of New WOW immediately after the ownership change. Stock received by Creditors of the Debtor will be included in the 50% calculation if the stock was received in satisfaction of a Claim that (i) was held by the Creditor since June 21, 1985, or (ii) arose in the ordinary course of business and is held by the person who at all times held the beneficial interest in such Claim.

The Debtor believes that the Bankruptcy Exception will apply to the ownership change that will occur in connection with the transaction contemplated by the Plan. It is important to note, however, that, as is the case with determining whether the transaction will qualify as a G reorganization, there are significant unresolved legal and factual issues, as well as disputable factual determinations surrounding the Bankruptcy Exception and its application to the transaction. Therefore, application of the Bankruptcy Exception is not free from doubt. Furthermore, if the Bankruptcy Exception applies, any ownership change with respect to New WOW occurring within two (2) years of the ownership change with respect to the Debtor will have the result of reducing to zero the Annual Limitation that would otherwise be applicable. Such an ownership change could, although would not necessarily, result from the exercise by New WOW or the holders of New WOW Preferred Stock of the redemption right or obligation with respect to such stock.

Although the Annual Limitation will not restrict the deductibility of the Debtor's NOL carryovers if the Bankruptcy Exception applies, the Debtor's NOL carryovers will nevertheless be reduced by (i) any interest paid or accrued by the Debtor during the three taxable years preceding the taxable year in which the ownership change occurs (as well as interest paid or accrued during the portion of the taxable year of the ownership change preceding the ownership change) with respect to any Claim which is converted into stock, (ii) 50% of the amount that would have reduced the Debtor's tax attributes but for the ap-

Exhibit 5-3   Sample Disclosure Statement by Debtor                    99

plication of the Stock-for-Debt Exception contained in Section 108(e)(10) of the Tax Code (discussed below), and (iii) discharged indebtedness not qualifying for the Stock-for-Debt Exception. See Section VIII(B)(3), "Reduction in the Debtor's Tax Attributes Resulting From Discharge of Indebtedness." The expected effect of these reductions is reflected in the estimate of the Debtor's NOL carryovers set forth in Section VIII(B)(1), "Tax Attributes of the Debtor and New WOW."

### c. Annual Limitation

If the transaction contemplated by the Plan does not qualify for the Bankruptcy Exception, the Debtor estimates that, based on the current long-term tax-exempt rate, the Annual Limitation for the years following the Closing Date will be in the range of $1 million to $2 million.

### d. Section 269

In addition to the limitations on the use of NOL carryovers set forth in Section 382, Section 269 of the Tax Code authorizes the IRS to disallow any deduction of the Debtor's NOL carryovers if New WOW is determined to have acquired the Debtor's assets principally for tax avoidance purposes. Whether New WOW is acquiring the Debtor's assets principally for tax avoidance purposes is primarily a question of fact. However, due to the substantial financial undertaking by the holders of New WOW Common and Preferred Stock and the anticipated continued operation of the Debtor's historic business, the Debtor believes that the IRS is not likely to challenge the deductibility of the Debtor's NOL carryovers under Section 269 and, if such a challenge were made, that the IRS would not succeed. Nonetheless, there can be no assurance that the IRS will not challenge the utilization of the Debtor's NOL carryovers by New WOW on the basis of Section 269.

## 3. Reduction in the Debtor's Tax Attributes Resulting from Discharge of Indebtedness

Under the Tax Code, the Debtor generally must include in gross income the amount of any discharged indebtedness realized during the taxable year, except to the extent payment of such indebtedness would have given rise to a deduction. However, Section 108 of the Tax Code provides that, if the discharge of indebtedness occurs pursuant to the Plan upon Bankruptcy Court approval, the amount of discharged indebtedness will not be included in income. Instead, unless the Stock-for-Debt Exception (described below) applies, the amount of discharged indebtedness will be applied to reduce certain tax attributes of the Debtor, in the following order: NOL carryovers, credit carryovers, capital loss carryovers, and the bases of the Debtor's depreciable property. Alternatively, the Debtor may elect to reduce the basis of depreciable property prior to the reduction of other tax attributes.

Under the Plan, holders of Class 1 Claims will be paid the full amount of their Claims. The treatment of such Claims should not, therefore, constitute discharge of indebtedness of the Debtor, except to the extent that previously deducted interest is not required to be paid. In contrast, the satisfaction of the Class 2, 3, 4, 5 and 6 Claims will result in discharge of indebtedness, and the Debtor's tax attributes will be reduced by the difference between the consideration received by such Creditors and the amount of the discharged indebtedness except to the extent that (i) the Stock-for-Debt Exception, described below, is applicable, or (ii) the Claims discharged would have given rise to a deduction had they been paid in full.

The Stock-for-Debt Exception of Section 108(e)(10) of the Tax Code generally will apply to prevent a reduction in the Debtor's tax attributes arising from a discharge of a given Claim where such Claim is discharged in exchange for New WOW Preferred Stock or a combination of New WOW Preferred Stock and cash and/or other property unless (i) the amount of New WOW Preferred Stock transferred to an unsecured Creditor in exchange for his Claim fails to meet the proportionality test described below, or (ii) the stock transferred to any Creditor in exchange for his Claim is considered nominal or token. In applying the Stock-for-Debt Exception, the legislative history to the Bankruptcy Tax Act of 1980 provides that where a Claim is surrendered for both New WOW Preferred Stock and cash and/or other property, the amount of the Claim treated as satisfied for the cash and/or other property equals the amount of cash and fair market value of such other property, thereby eliminating any reduction in tax attributes that would arise if the indebtedness was deemed to be cancelled for property and stock on a pro rata basis.

The proportionality test will generally be satisfied with respect to New WOW Preferred Stock issued to a particular unsecured Creditor if the ratio of the value of the New WOW Preferred Stock received by such Creditor to the amount of the Claim cancelled or exchanged in consideration therefor (the "Stock-for-Debt Ratio") is not less than 50% of a smaller ratio computed for all unsecured Creditors participating in the transaction. Although the computations are subject to adjustment upon receipt of additional facts, the Debtor believes that the lowest Stock-for-Debt Ratio for any unsecured Creditor will equal or exceed 50% of the Stock-for-Debt Ratio computed for all unsecured Creditors generally, and as a result the proportionality test should be satisfied with respect to all unsecured Creditors receiving New WOW Preferred Stock.

The Debtor believes that the Series A and B Preferred Stock to be distributed to the holders of Class 3 Claims in exchange for their Claims should not be considered nominal or token. Due to the absence of authority, however, it is less clear whether the Series C Preferred Stock to be distributed to the holders of Class 6 Claims may be considered nominal or token, although the Debtor believes that such stock also should not be considered nominal or token.

The Debtor's estimate of the reduction in its NOL carryovers arising from the discharge of indebtedness is reflected in the figure set forth in Section VIII(B)(1), "Tax Attributes of the Debtor and New WOW." The amount of the reduction could exceed the Debtor's estimate, and depends on, among other things, the ultimate determination of the fair market value of property distributed in cancellation of Claims and whether the Stock-for-Debt Exception applies.

**Exhibit 5-3   Sample Disclosure Statement by Debtor**                    **101**

## 4. Tax Consequences to Creditors

### a. Tax Consequences to Creditors Generally

A Creditor will recognize ordinary income to the extent any cash or fair market value of property received pursuant to the Plan is allocable to interest income, and such income has not already been included in such Creditor's taxable income. The determination as to what portion of amounts received will be allocated to interest is unclear, and may be affected by, among other things, the rules in the Tax Code relating to accrued market discount. Creditors should consult their own tax advisors as to the amount of any consideration received under the Plan that will be allocated to interest.

In the event amounts allocable to interest are less than amounts previously included in such Creditor's taxable income, the difference will result in a loss. Any amount not attributable to interest will be attributed to the Claim surrendered or cancelled pursuant to the Plan, and will be treated as discussed below. The following discussion refers to amounts received that are not allocable to interest income.

If a Creditor receives New WOW Preferred Stock in exchange for a Claim with respect to which such Creditor previously claimed a bad debt deduction, a subsequent sale of the stock may give rise to ordinary income under Section 108(e)(7) of the Tax Code.

### b. Creditors (Other than Class 7 Claimants) Not Receiving New WOW Preferred Stock

A Creditor who receives cash and/or non-cash property other than New WOW Preferred Stock in satisfaction of his Claim generally will recognize gain or loss on the exchange equal to the difference between the Creditor's basis in the Claim and the amount of any cash and fair market value of any non-cash property received that is not allocable to interest. The tax basis of any non-cash property received will equal the fair market value of such property. The character of any recognized gain or loss will depend on the status of the Creditor, the nature of the Claim in his hands and the holding period of such Claim.

### c. Creditors Receiving New WOW Preferred Stock

The tax consequences to a Creditor who receives New WOW Preferred Stock, or New WOW Preferred Stock and cash and/or non-cash property, in satisfaction of his Claim will depend in part on whether such Creditor's Claim constitutes a "security" for federal income tax purposes. To the best of the Debtor's knowledge, the only Creditors that will be deemed to own securities for federal income tax purposes will be the Subordinated Debenture holders. However, certain other Creditors may be treated as holders of securities. All Creditors who will receive New WOW Preferred Stock should consult their own tax advisors as to the status of their Claims as a security for federal income tax purposes.

Holders of securities generally will recognize any gain (*i.e.*, the excess of the cash and fair market value of non-cash property received—including the New WOW Preferred Stock but not including amounts allocated to interest income—over the holder's tax basis in the security) to the extent of the cash and fair market value of such property other than the New WOW Preferred Stock. No loss will be recognized by holders of securities. The basis of non-cash property (other than New WOW Preferred Stock) received by a holder of a security will equal the fair market value of such property and the basis of New WOW Preferred Stock received by such holder will equal his basis in the security surrendered, decreased by the fair market value of cash and non-cash property (other than the New WOW Preferred Stock) received and increased by the amount of interest income and other gain recognized. In the event the transaction contemplated by the Plan does not constitute a G reorganization, holders of securities will be taxed in a manner similar to holders of non-securities, as described below.

Holders of non-securities will recognize gain or loss equal to the difference between the amount of the holder's basis in his Claim and the sum of the cash and fair market value of the non-cash property received for such Claim (including the fair market value of New WOW Preferred Stock), excluding amounts allocable to interest. The character of any gain or loss will depend on the status of the Creditor, the nature of the Claim in his hands and the holding period of such Claim. Such holder's basis in the non-cash property will equal the fair market value of such property.

### 5. *Tax Consequences to Holders of Class 7 Interests*

A holder of a Class 7 Interest generally will recognize loss equal to the amount of his basis, if any, in his Interest. The character of any such loss will depend on the status of the holder, the nature of the Interest in his hands and the holding period of such Interest.

### 6. *Importance of Obtaining Professional Assistance*

AS INDICATED ABOVE, THE FOREGOING IS INTENDED TO BE A SUMMARY ONLY AND NOT A SUBSTITUTE FOR CAREFUL TAX PLANNING WITH A TAX PROFESSIONAL. THE FEDERAL, STATE AND LOCAL TAX CONSEQUENCES OF THE PLAN ARE COMPLEX AND, IN SOME CASES, UNCERTAIN. ACCORDINGLY, EACH HOLDER OF A CLAIM OR INTEREST IS STRONGLY URGED TO CONSULT WITH HIS OWN TAX ADVISOR REGARDING THE FEDERAL, STATE AND LOCAL TAX CONSEQUENCES OF THE PLAN.

## IX
## CONFIRMATION AND CONSUMMATION

The Bankruptcy Code requires the Bankruptcy Court to determine that the Plan proposed by the Debtor complies with the requirements of the Bankruptcy Code, including:

**Exhibit 5-3   Sample Disclosure Statement by Debtor**     **103**

(a) The Plan complies with the applicable provisions of Chapter 11 of the Bankruptcy Code;

(b) The Debtor, as proponent of the Plan, has complied with the applicable provisions of Chapter 11 of the Bankruptcy Code;

(c) The Plan has been proposed in good faith and not by any means forbidden by law;

(d) All payments to be made for services or for costs and expenses in connection with the Reorganization Case have been disclosed to the Bankruptcy Court and are found to be reasonable;

(e) Adequate disclosure has been made with respect to the identity and affiliation of any individual proposed to serve, after confirmation of the Plan, as an officer, director or voting trustee of the Debtor or New WOW;

(f) The provisions of Section 1129(a)(6) regarding the need to obtain approvals from any regulatory commission with jurisdiction over the rates of the Debtor are inapplicable to the Debtor;

(g) The Plan satisfies the "best interests" of Creditors test;

(h) The Plan has been duly accepted by each Class, or at least one Class that is impaired under the Plan has accepted the Plan and the Plan does not unfairly discriminate and is fair and equitable to Creditors and Interest holders;

(i) The Administrative Claims and Priority Claims will be paid in full in cash or on such other terms as may be agreed upon; and

(j) The Plan is feasible so that its confirmation is not likely to be followed by liquidation or the need for further reorganization.

THE DEBTOR BELIEVES THAT ALL THE REQUIRED CONDITIONS WILL HAVE BEEN MET AT THE TIME OF CONFIRMATION AND WILL SEEK RULINGS TO THAT EFFECT FROM THE COURT AT THE HEARING ON CONFIRMATION OF THE PLAN.

In addition, the Plan must be accepted by the requisite number of votes of Debtor's creditors ("Creditors"). Even if the Creditors vote to accept the Plan, the Court has an independent duty to evaluate the matters described above, particularly to determine that the Plan is feasible and that it meets the "best interests" test, as discussed below.

## A.   Classification of Claims and Interests

The Bankruptcy Code requires that a plan of reorganization place each creditor's claim and each stockholder's interest in a class with other claims or interests that are "substantially similar." The Plan establishes seven classes of Claims and Interests. Under the Plan, Claims which are secured or entitled to priority are placed in separate classes from unsecured Claims (except that, for purposes of the Plan, the Lenders have consented to different treatment for the portion of their Claims entitled to priority under Sections 364(c)(1) and 507(b) of the Bankruptcy Code). For a detailed description of the classes of Claims, see Section VI(B).

The Debtor believes that the Plan's classification of Claims and Interests fully complies with the requirements of the Bankruptcy Code and applicable case law.

## B. "Best Interests" of Creditors

Notwithstanding acceptance of the Plan by Creditors or the absence of any objections to confirmation, the Bankruptcy Court must independently determine that the Plan is in the "best interests" of all of the classes of Creditors and equity security holders impaired under the Plan. The "best interests" test requires the Bankruptcy Court to find that the Plan provides to each member of an impaired class of Claims property having a value at least equal to the value of the distribution each such Creditor would receive if the Debtor were instead liquidated in a Chapter 7 proceeding on the Effective Date of the Plan.

To apply the "best interests" test, the Bankruptcy Court must first calculate the aggregate dollar amount that would be generated from liquidation of the Debtor's assets in a hypothetical liquidation on the Effective Date of the Plan under Chapter 7 including the amount of cash held by the Debtor and its subsidiaries and the value of any projected recoveries on actions against third parties (the "Liquidation Value").

To determine amounts that would be available for distribution in a Chapter 7 liquidation, the Liquidation Value must be reduced by (a) the claims of Secured Creditors to the extent of the value of their collateral and (b) the costs of liquidation, including administrative costs and expenses of both the Chapter 7 and Chapter 11 estates. The Debtor's costs of liquidation would include the compensation of a Chapter 7 trustee and counsel and other professionals retained by the trustee; all unpaid expenses incurred by the Debtor during the Chapter 11 proceedings (such as compensation for attorneys, financial advisors and accountants) that are allowed in the Chapter 7 proceeding; litigation costs; asset disposition expenses; and claims arising from the Debtor's operation during the Chapter 11 and Chapter 7 proceedings. In addition, the liquidation itself would trigger certain priority claims, such as claims for severance pay, and would accelerate other priority payments that would otherwise be payable in the ordinary course of business. These priority claims would be paid in full out of liquidation proceeds before the balance would be made available to pay Allowed Unsecured Claims or to make any distribution in relation to holders of Interests.

After estimating the Liquidation Value and costs of liquidation, the Bankruptcy Court must ascertain the potential Chapter 7 recoveries by Secured Creditors, Priority Claimants, Unsecured Creditors and Interest holders and then compare those recoveries with the distributions offered to each Class of Claims or Interests under the Plan to determine if the Plan is in the best interests of the Creditors and Interest holders in each Class.

For the Bankruptcy Court's consideration and to assist creditors' evaluation of the Plan, the Debtor has prepared a detailed liquidation analysis which is

**Exhibit 5-3  Sample Disclosure Statement by Debtor**                    **105**

discussed in Section IX(C) below. Based upon this analysis, the Debtor believes that there would be no distributions available in a Chapter 7 proceeding for Class 7 Claims and that the Class 6 Cash Fund (representing five-sevenths ($\frac{5}{7}$) of the ABN Payment), which would be the only potential source of any recovery by the holders of Class 5 Allowed Claims and Class 6 Allowed Claims, would be reduced by the liquidation costs incurred in the Chapter 7 proceeding, thereby significantly reducing the amount of any funds available for distribution to the holders of Class 5 Allowed Claims and Class 6 Allowed Claims in a Chapter 7 proceeding. Class 1 Allowed Claims might be paid in full if the Debtor seeks to or is compelled to satisfy them from the five-sevenths ($\frac{5}{7}$) of the ABN Payment that would otherwise go to the holders of Class 6 Claims under the Plan, while holders of Class 3 Allowed Claims would receive substantially less recovery. The holder of Class 2 Claims would also receive less absent the Class 2 Distribution Adjustment described in the Plan.

A COMPARISON OF DISTRIBUTIONS TO CREDITORS UNDER THE PLAN WITH THE PROCEEDS FROM A LIQUIDATION OF DEBTOR'S ASSETS IS SHOWN IN EXHIBIT G. WHILE IT IS IMPOSSIBLE TO DETERMINE PRECISELY WHAT WOULD BE RECEIVED IN A LIQUIDATION, THE DEBTOR HAS ESTIMATED THE POTENTIAL DISTRIBUTIONS TO CREDITORS AFTER DISCOUNTING ASSET VALUES IN CONSIDERATION OF THE FACTORS DISCUSSED IN SECTION IX(C)(1) BELOW. BASED ON THIS ANALYSIS, THE DEBTOR BELIEVES THAT EVERY IMPAIRED CLASS WILL RECEIVE DISTRIBUTIONS UNDER THE PLAN WHICH ARE AT LEAST EQUAL IN VALUE TO THE DISTRIBUTIONS THAT THEY WOULD RECEIVE IN A CHAPTER 7 LIQUIDATION, AND THEREFORE THE PLAN IS IN THEIR BEST INTERESTS.

### C.  Alternatives to the Plan

If the Court does not confirm the Plan, alternatives available to the Debtor would be either a liquidating Chapter 11 plan providing for the liquidation of the Debtor's assets on a piecemeal basis, conversion of the Debtor's Chapter 11 case to a case under Chapter 7 of the Bankruptcy Code, or attempting to solicit another buyer for the assets or business of Debtor as a going concern. In addition, the Secured Creditors could take steps to foreclose on their collateral.

Another possibility is that other parties in interest might have an opportunity to file another plan of reorganization. Although a plan could be confirmed even though not accepted by every impaired class if it meets the requirements of Section 1129(b) of the Bankruptcy Code (see Section VI(G)(4) above), the Debtor believes that any such plan could likely result in costly and time-consuming litigation. Moreover, the Debtor does not have sufficient funds to continue to operate during the proceedings that would lead up to another confirmation hearing, nor it is likely that any source of borrowing would be available to Debtor to provide additional operating funds. Further, the Debtor believes that under any alternative plan, holders of Class 5, Class 6 and Class 7 Claims would receive no distributions except, possibly, Class 5 and Class 6 would receive a portion of the ABN Payment.

## 1. *Liquidation Alternative*

Under a Chapter 11 liquidation on a piecemeal basis, the Debtor would cease its operations and sell its assets to a liquidator. If the Debtor were liquidated under Chapter 7, a trustee would be appointed to supervise the liquidation. Depending on the nature of available markets at the time of disposition, Debtor's inventories and related intangible assets could potentially be sold as ongoing product lines to another toy manufacturer or they could be closed-out at reduced prices to existing retail customers.

The remainder of the Debtor's assets would be sold piecemeal, or in the case of cash and accounts receivable, turned over to the Lenders on a basis comparable to that provided in the Plan. The recovery from tangible assets such as prepaid expenses, leasehold improvements and furniture and fixtures in a liquidation would be significantly less than their value on the Debtor's books. Exhibit G shows the Debtor's estimate of the amounts recoverable in a liquidation, and the Debtor's tangible assets other than inventory have been heavily discounted to reflect their questionable liquidation value.

Taking into account the difficulty in locating possible purchasers and the time required to negotiate terms, obtain Bankruptcy Court approvals, and implement the liquidation, the Debtor estimates that under the most favorable circumstances, a Chapter 7 liquidation would take a minimum of six months to one year to conclude, once a decision to liquidate had been made.

Assuming that under the best conditions the liquidation could be completed within six months, the Debtor believes that the total proceeds to be realized from a Chapter 7 liquidation, including proceeds from the sale of inventories, collection of receivables and sale of other assets would be approximately $28,400,000. The amounts realized could vary significantly, however, depending both on the time required to complete asset sales and the market value at the time of sale, among other significant considerations.

The administrative and priority expenses (as described above) which have either been incurred or would arise as a result of liquidation, including the expenses associated with the sale of assets and the conclusion of the Chapter 7 case, would further reduce the total liquidation proceeds approximately $5 million, to $23,400,000. Depending on the length of time required to conclude the liquidation and the Claims asserted against the Debtor, this amount could vary significantly from the Debtor's estimate.

After payment in full of priority, tax, and administrative Claims, the funds realized from liquidation would be insufficient to satisfy Allowed Secured Claims. As summarized in Exhibit G, the Debtor estimates that in the event the liquidation could be accomplished in six months, Creditors would realize up to approximately $13,300,000 less from liquidation of the Debtor than they would

**Exhibit 5-3  Sample Disclosure Statement by Debtor**                     **107**

realize under the Plan. Again, there is no assurance that the liquidation values could be realized.

## 2. Offer of Competing Bidder

In connection with soliciting potential purchasers as described in Section III(C)(8) above, the Debtor received and ultimately rejected an offer from a company believed by Debtor to be solely owned by Mr. Isaac Perlmutter. The major terms of Mr. Perlmutter's offer were: (i) payment of $23,500,000 in cash on closing the transaction in exchange for substantially all of the assets of the Debtor, except school accessories, and some of the proprietary rights licensed by the Debtor; (ii) a down payment of $10,000,000 either to be held in escrow or to be secured by a letter of credit and to be credited against the purchase price, which amount would have been paid to the Debtor if Mr. Perlmutter breached the agreement and failed to consummate the sale; (iii) a requirement that the Debtor pay Mr. Perlmutter $1,250,000 if the sale was not consummated for reasons other than a breach by Mr. Perlmutter; (iv) the Debtor's agreement not to sell any products after entry of a preliminary order approving certain provisions of an agreement with Mr. Perlmutter, which order would have been sought within three days of execution of an agreement documenting the terms of sale; (v) the Debtor's agreement to seek expedited Bankruptcy Court approval for the sale as an emergency sale under Bankruptcy Code Section 363(b), rather than as part of a plan of reorganization; and (vi) payment to the Debtor of a 5% royalty on sales of products introduced by Mr. Perlmutter's company in 1989 for five years, with a guarantee that a minimum of $2,500,000 would be paid during this period.

Mr. Perlmutter's offer would have required the Debtor to operate at levels sufficient to ship all its assets to Mr. Perlmutter during the 90-day period following closing of the transaction, and to pay all royalties, taxes and other costs incurred in connection with the sale. It is the understanding of Debtor's management that Mr. Perlmutter did not intend to continue operating the Debtor's business from its Fremont, California headquarters, and that he would have offered jobs to only a few of the Debtor's employees. The Debtor's management rejected Mr. Perlmutter's offer for a variety of reasons. Foremost, the price he offered, after reduction for the Debtor's expenses in selling its assets pursuant to the transaction, including severance and other expenses associated with shutting down operations, would have resulted in a substantially lower recovery to the Creditors than the offer of New WOW, which was ultimately accepted by the Debtor. Also, Mr. Perlmutter would have required the Debtor to stop selling its products—in effect for the Debtor to cease operating—at the time of entry of a preliminary order approving certain provisions of the agreement. At the same time, Mr. Perlmutter wanted the Debtor to seek emergency approval of the Bankruptcy Court for the sale. Had such approval not been obtained, cessation of the Debtor's business operations at the time of entry of the preliminary court order would have severely limited the Debtor's ability to attract another investor or buyer. Even if the Bankruptcy Court approved the sale to Mr. Perlmutter, the Debtor believes that its or the Lenders' ability to collect its accounts receivable would have been damaged by the Debtor's cessation of operations. In addition, Mr. Perlmutter was unwilling to be contractually bound to purchase the Debtor's assets as part of a plan of reorganization if an emergency sale was not approved by the Bankruptcy Court. Moreover, it was unclear whether Mr. Perlmutter had any intention of operating the business and assets acquired from the Debtor as an ongoing business. For all of these reasons, the Debtor's management rejected his offer.

Although Mr. Perlmutter has indicated in pleadings filed in the Bankruptcy Court that he is willing to offer $3,000,000 more for the Debtor's assets than his understanding of New WOW's offer upon which the Plan is based, the Debtor has not received such an increased offer from Mr. Perlmutter. In addition, the Debtor has been informed by the Supporting Lenders, who, together with the other Lender, are the only Creditors who would benefit from such an increased offer, that they continue to support the Plan (as described in the next Section).

### 3. Secured Creditors' Position Regarding Alternatives to the Plan

The Supporting Lenders and ABN have agreed to support and seek confirmation of the Plan. Nevertheless, in the event a different plan of reorganization is proposed or the Debtor is liquidated under Chapter 7, the Supporting Lenders and ABN have reserved the right to assert, without regard to the Purchase Agreement, the terms of the Plan, or any agreement or understanding with New WOW, both (1) their pre-petition and post-petition security interests in essentially all of the Debtor's property and (2) the full amount of their Priority Claims against the Debtor under Sections 364(c)(1) and 507(b) of the Bankruptcy Code. Consequently, to the extent the Secured Creditors would assert the full amount of their Priority Claims in connection with a different plan or in a liquidation of the Debtor, in addition to claiming all of the proceeds of their collateral, they would be entitled to receive any and all additional consideration or value received by the Estate up to, and possibly exceeding, $40 million, before any distributions to Unsecured Creditors other than the Class 6 Cash Fund, which in any case would be subject to the deficiency Claims of the Secured Creditors and to the Claims of Unsecured Creditors on a pro rata basis.

### D. Feasibility

The Bankruptcy Code requires that Confirmation of the Plan not be likely to be followed by the liquidation of the reorganized company or the need for further financial reorganization. For purposes of determining whether the Plan meets this feasibility standard, the Debtor has analyzed the ability of New WOW to meet its obligations under the Plan while retaining a sufficient amount of cash to carry on its operations. As part of this analysis, New WOW has prepared financial projections of its performance for each fiscal year of the five-year period ending March 31, 1994. Based on an analysis of these projections,

Exhibit 5-3    Sample Disclosure Statement by Debtor                        **109**

as well as an analysis of the proposed management structure and strategies for the acquired business as described below, the Debtor and New WOW believe that the Plan is feasible.

## 1. Management of New WOW

New WOW will be managed by experienced toy industry executives. Members of the Board of Directors who will be active in management include Joshua Denham, a 22-year toy industry veteran, Franklyn S. Barry, Jr., a 16-year toy industry veteran, and David Edelman, who has extensive experience in consumer goods distribution. Additionally, Arthur Dorf, who is expected to join the management of New WOW as Vice President of Operations, has spent nearly 10 years in operations and engineering in the U.S. and the Orient with Mattel, Inc., a leading toy company.

The Debtor believes that New WOW management specifically has expertise in those functions where breakdowns led to the Debtor's bankruptcy petition in 1987. Failure to manage the product development process closely, failure to control product quality, and failure to manufacture and deliver products in a timely manner were among the causes of the Debtor's financial problems, and are areas where New WOW management has extensive experience. New WOW is planning to offer positions to the managers of functions where the Debtor excelled, providing continuity in certain areas. For example, Vice President of Marketing and Product Development Paul Rago, Director of Engineering James Sachs and members of the field sales force, among others, will be asked to remain with New WOW.

## 2. Product Strategy of New WOW

New WOW plans to build its product strategy around existing lines such as "Teddy Ruxpin" and "Boppers" which have multi-year potential, while at the same time diversifying into new technologies and new product categories. It is expected that each year's new products will include items which apply technology to traditional toy subjects, as well as products which use more traditional plastic, fabric and metal processes. New WOW believes that this simultaneous identification with technology and careful diversification will lower the financial risk associated with new products as well as help ensure that adequate profit margins can be realized across the entire line. At the same time, this strategy will provide important continuity with the past.

## 3. Customers and Markets

New WOW intends to aggressively broaden its U.S. distribution beyond the toy supermarkets which provided a substantial portion of the Debtor's fiscal 1989 sales volume. Particular emphasis will be on discount stores, large chains and traditional department stores. New WOW believes that within two years it will be possible to expand its U.S. distribution to be comparable to that of other similarly sized U.S. toy companies.

New WOW also intends to expand into international markets, beginning with

Canada and the United Kingdom in fiscal year 1990. With foreign markets comprising over 60% of world toy sales, this is believed to be an area of potentially rapid growth.

New WOW plans to use direct advertising to children, supplemented by parent-directed media for software products. The aggressive use of media has been for the Debtor, and will continue to be for New WOW, an important part of marketing success with the consumer and the trade.

### 4. Near-Term Strategy of New WOW

For the transition years, fiscal years 1990 and 1991, New WOW intends to proceed deliberately to regain credibility with customers, suppliers and employees. The bankruptcy process has damaged the Debtor's reputation, and it is important that New WOW deliver products and execute its advertising and promotion plan as promised to its customers, and provide stable and predictable schedules for its suppliers.

### 5. Financial Projections

In conjunction with developing the Plan, financial projections have been prepared which may be helpful to holders of Claims in reaching a determination whether to accept or reject the Plan. The projections, in the form of financial statements for each of the five fiscal years in the period ending March 31, 1994 (the "Projection Period"), are based on assumptions concerning future events and circumstances. The assumptions discussed below are key factors upon which the financial results of New WOW will depend during the Projection Period.

NO REPRESENTATIONS CAN BE MADE WITH RESPECT TO THE ACCURACY OF THE PROJECTIONS OR THE ABILITY TO ACHIEVE THE PROJECTED RESULTS. MANY OF THE ASSUMPTIONS UPON WHICH THESE PROJECTIONS ARE BASED ARE SUBJECT TO MAJOR UNCERTAINTIES. SOME ASSUMPTIONS WILL INEVITABLY TURN OUT TO BE INCORRECT. IN ADDITION, UNANTICIPATED EVENTS AND CIRCUMSTANCES MAY OCCUR AND, ACCORDINGLY, THE ACTUAL RESULTS ACHIEVED THROUGH THE PROJECTION PERIOD WILL VARY FROM THE PROJECTED RESULTS AND THE VARIATIONS MAY BE MATERIAL.

   a. *Basis of Presentation.*

The pro forma and projected financial statements of New WOW, attached as Exhibit H to this Disclosure Statement, including the following:

· Projected Pro Forma Balance Sheet with Pro Forma Reorganization adjustments as of June 1, 1989 (Exhibit H-1).
· Projected Pro Forma Balance Sheets for each of the five fiscal years in the period ending March 31, 1944 (Exhibit H-2).

**Exhibit 5-3    Sample Disclosure Statement by Debtor**                    **111**

- Projected Statement of Income for each of the five fiscal years in the period ending March 31, 1994 (Exhibit H-3).
- Projected Statement of Changes in Shareholders' Equity for each of the five fiscal years in the period ending March 31, 1994 (Exhibit H-4).
- Projected Statement of Cash Flows for each of the five fiscal years in the period ending March 31, 1994 (Exhibit H-5).

The pro forma and projected financial statements are unaudited. However, they have been prepared on the basis of generally accepted accounting principles.

b. *Summary of Significant Accounting Policies and Assumptions.*

Significant accounting policies and assumptions are discussed in the following paragraphs.

(i) *Notes and Assumptions to the Projected Pro Forma Balance Sheet with Pro Forma Reorganization Adjustments as of June 1, 1989 (Pro Forma Balance Sheet).*

The Pro Forma Balance Sheet represents the financial statement effects of the Plan relating to New WOW. It has been prepared as of June 1, 1989, as if the Plan had been confirmed by the Bankruptcy Court, and the transaction described in the Purchase Agreement had been consummated on May 31, 1989.

The Projected Pre-Transaction Balances are based on Debtor's current projections of balances at May 31, 1989. There is no certainty that such balances will be accurate and the balances are subject to change should the transaction close on a different date.

Pro Forma Reorganization Adjustments reflect the elimination of pre-closing debt, effective June 1, 1989; capitalization requirements as described in the Plan; consideration paid, liabilities assumed and fair value of assets acquired as of June 1, 1989; and estimated purchase price adjustments in accordance with Accounting Principles Board Opinion No. 16 ("APB16"). In accordance with APB16, the values of Series A, B, and C stock classes are recorded at fair market value. The Pro Forma Balance Sheet also assumes that all of the authorized shares of New WOW Common Stock will be issued and outstanding as of the Closing Date. It is possible, however, that, as described in Section V(A)(1) above, only 225,000 shares will be so outstanding. Issuance of less than the full amount of authorized shares of New WOW Common Stock will not have a material adverse impact on the projected capitalization set forth in Exhibit E or the projections set forth in Exhibit H. In addition, short term debt reflects $2,500,000 in initial funding of working capital which is anticipated to be provided by an asset-based revolving credit facility.

(ii) *Notes and Assumptions to the Projected Pro Forma Balance Sheets for each of the five fiscal years ending March 31, 1994 (Projected Pro Forma Balance Sheets).*

Due to the seasonal nature of the toy industry, the working capital needs of the business vary significantly from month to month, and balance sheets presented at a point in time may not be indicative of balance sheets at other points in the year. As the projections indicate, March 31 is among the lowest points in the fiscal year in terms of working capital needs.

Accounts receivable are assumed to be collected in an average of 90 days during the Projection Period, a typical level for companies selling to New WOW's customer group.

Inventories are stated at the lower of cost or market using the first-in first-out method. In fiscal year 1990, inventory includes approximately $6,700,000 of close-out inventory acquired from Debtor, which has the effect of depressing inventory turnover in year one. Following fiscal 1990, inventory turns are assumed to range from three to four turns.

Property and equipment is depreciated over a five-year period using the straight line method. Property and equipment increased during the Projection Period as net additions exceeded depreciation expense. Capital additions during the Projection Period are considered normal replacements of productive assets, except for the addition of a new computer system at a cost of $750,000 during the ten months ended March 31, 1990. There are no other major capital expenditures assumed.

Fiscal year-end balances do not reflect the existence of short term borrowings. Seasonal working capital requirements based on detailed quarterly and monthly projections demonstrate the need for short-term borrowings at certain times of year (particularly in the August through October period).

The projections assume working capital availability in the form of an asset based revolving credit facility of $35 million to meet cash and letter of credit requirements for operation of the business.

Peak projected cash usage during the Projection Period occurs in November 1989 at which time approximately $31 million is outstanding on the revolving credit facility to meet cash requirements. New WOW believes that, at all times during the Projection Period, capitalization, including the revolving credit facility, provides adequate resources for operations.

Long term debt is comprised of the ABN Note and the Selected Net Assets Adjustment Note.

Dividends are payable annually on May 15 at a rate of 8% of the face amount of the various classes of Preferred Stock. The Series A Preferred Stock is redeemable at the option of the holder after March 31, 1991 (or such other date as may be one year and ten months from the Closing Date), and the projection assumes that such redemption at face value occurs at that time. The projection demonstrates that adequate cash is likely to be available to redeem Series B and Series C Preferred Stock at face value at the option of the holders at a time beyond the Projection Period.

(iii) *Notes and Assumptions to the Projected Statement of Income for the four year and ten month period ending March 31, 1994 (Projected Statement of Income).*

**Exhibit 5-3    Sample Disclosure Statement by Debtor**                    **113**

· *Revenues*

Revenue estimates for the ten months ending March 31, 1990 have been projected based upon estimates of customer demand as of February 28, 1989. They include sales of discontinued products in the amount of $9.4 million. Revenue growth in subsequent periods is based upon 10 percent annual growth in domestic product sales and 20 percent annual growth in international sales and foreign licensing revenues, reduced somewhat in the second fiscal year to adjust for the non-recurring sales of discontinued products.

· *Costs and expenses*

Excluding the costs attributable to closeout sales and international sales and licensing revenues, costs of goods sold as a percentage of revenues are 55.7 in fiscal year 1990, 54.5 in fiscal year 1991, and 53.5 thereafter. The fiscal year 1990 cost of goods sold is based upon current product cost estimates of the Debtor. Subsequent year improvements are attributable to planned cost reductions on certain key products.

The variable selling expense component of selling, general and administrative expense will remain constant as a percentage of sales through the Projection Period. Fixed general and administrative expenses will grow at an annual rate of 5 percent, except for the annual management consulting fee described in Section V(B)(3)(a) above, which is consistently calculated throughout the period. Beginning in September 1989, facilities expense has been reduced by an annualized amount of $500,000 to reflect reduced warehouse space following disposal of closeout inventory. Beginning with fiscal 1991, administrative expense has been reduced by an annualized amount of $400,000 to reflect economies realized by transferring computer operations from an outside service bureau to in-house personnel.

· *Non-operating income (expense)*

Net interest expense includes interest on all long term and short term debt, including the Selected Net Assets Adjustment Note, the ABN Note, and revolving credit debt required to operate the business according to the projections. Interest rates are assumed to be 13.5% on short term borrowings, New WOW's estimates of the prime rate on the Selected Net Assets Adjustment Note and 11% on the ABN Note. Cash balances in excess of $200,000 will be invested with an expected yield on stock investments of 9%.

· *Income taxes and net operating loss carryovers*

The projections assume that, for federal income tax purposes, the Debtor's net operating loss carryovers (after their reduction resulting from discharge of indebtedness discussed in Section VIII) will be available to offset New WOW's projected taxable income during the Projection Period. Such carryovers will be available only if the transaction contemplated by the Plan qualifies as a tax-free reorganization described in Section 368(a)(1)(G) of the Tax Code and if the Bankruptcy Exception set forth in Section 382(1)(5) of the Tax Code (described in Section VIII(B)(2)(b)) applies.

In accordance with generally accepted accounting principles, the projections include provisions for income taxes based upon applying the appropriate statutory income tax rates to income before income taxes for financial reporting purposes. Such taxes are partially offset by the utilization of federal NOL carry-overs. The net 10% tax utilized in the projections consists of state income and franchise taxes, as New WOW is not expected to have net operating loss carry-overs available to offset state and franchise income taxes, and federal Alternative Minimum Tax. See Section VIII. If such NOL carryovers are not available to New WOW (see Section VIII (A)), New WOW would incur a tax on its federal taxable income at a maximum current rate of 34%.

### E. Certain Risk Factors In Owning Capital Stock of New WOW

Discussed below and in other sections of this Disclosure Statement are certain risk factors which, in the opinion of New WOW, should be of importance to persons receiving securities in New WOW under the Plan in evaluating the impact of the Plan, including the ownership of securities issued pursuant to the Plan, the likelihood of receiving dividends on such securities and the future financial performance of New WOW. These risk factors should not, however, be regarded as constituting the only risks involved in connection with the Plan, the ownership of securities issued pursuant to the Plan, the likelihood of receiving dividends on such securities or the future financial performance of New WOW.

#### 1. Inherent Uncertainty in the Statement of Projected Financial Performance

The projections contained in Exhibit H, including the Projected Pro Forma Balance Sheets and Projected Statements of Income, Changes in Shareholders' Equity and Cash Flows of New WOW, project financial performance for New WOW for fiscal years 1990 through 1994. Material risks are inherent in such projections of future financial performance. For example, such projections represent a prediction of future events based upon certain assumptions that are an integral part of the projections and may not prove to be correct. These future events may or may not occur and, therefore, the projections may not be relied upon as a guarantee or other assurance that the actual results will occur. Because of the numerous risks and inherent uncertainties which will affect the operations of New WOW, the actual results of New WOW's operations will undoubtedly be different from those projected and such differences could be material and adverse.

#### 2. Volatility and Product Acceptance in the Toy Industry

Because of the rapid product turnover which characterizes the toy industry, steady year-to-year performance is not likely for a single company. It is difficult to forecast which toy products will meet with consumer acceptance and not lose their popularity or be displaced by competing products developed by others. As a result, there is inherent uncertainty in New WOW's ability to accurately forecast its financial performance or growth in any year until that year's product line

Exhibit 5-3    Sample Disclosure Statement by Debtor                      **115**

is determined and early trade reaction is known. New WOW may not always be able to respond to changes in consumer demand and tastes because of the significant amount of lead time and financial resources needed to bring new products to market. The inability to respond quickly to market changes could have an adverse impact on New WOW's financial performance.

### 3. Seasonality

The toy industry is seasonal due to heavy consumer demand for toys during the December holiday season. New WOW expects that a large percentage of its customer purchase commitments will be received in the first half of the year, after the major toy industry fairs, for shipment in the third and fourth calendar quarters. As a result, much of New WOW's manufacturing, packaging and distribution must be completed during short time periods, and operating results and working capital requirements will vary significantly from quarter to quarter. There is no assurance that New WOW can maintain sufficient flexibility with respect to working capital needs, manufacturing capacity and supplies of raw materials, tools and components to minimize the effects of unanticipated shortfalls in seasonal demand. In addition, orders placed by customers in the toy industry are typically terminable until such time as they are shipped.

### 4. Competition

New WOW will operate in a highly competitive environment. Many of the companies with which New WOW will compete will be larger and more diversified than New WOW and will have available to them substantially greater financial and other resources. Conversely, the relatively low barriers to entry in the toy industry allow new competitors easy access to the marketplace. These competitors may force price reductions or decrease New WOW's market share, which may adversely affect New WOW's financial performance.

### 5. Material Costs

A number of events—currency exchange, plastic prices, foreign labor rates, etc.—could cause product costs to rise and New WOW's gross margins to drop. Adverse developments in one or more cost elements could have a material adverse impact on New WOW's financial performance.

### 6. Limitations of Patent, Trademark and Copyright Protection

Rights to products acquired under license agreements or developed by New WOW may not have patent, trademark and/or copyright protection. To the extent such protection is not available, New WOW runs the risk that a competitor would be able to market products of a somewhat similar nature that may be more appealing to consumers. Where such protection is available to New WOW, it may not have adequate resources with which to wage protracted litigation to protect its rights under patents, trademarks or copyrights owned by it or used under license agreements. In either case, New WOW's financial performance could be materially adversely affected.

## 7. Risk of Losing Licensed Rights

New WOW will acquire the rights to manufacture and sell toy products, including "Teddy Ruxpin," pursuant to license agreements with third parties. There are existing disputes with Alchemy, as described above, the outcome of which could reduce the value of New WOW's license agreement with Alchemy. In the event New WOW defaults on its obligations under any such agreements (including the failure to make payment of royalties), such license agreements could be terminated and New WOW could lose the right to sell that product.

## 8. Government Regulation and Industry Standards

The toy and game industry is highly regulated by governmental safety laws and regulations. The Federal Hazardous Substances Act together with other federal legislation and various federal regulations establish testing procedures and, among other things, standards for the size, shape and materials to be used in toys and games. Several states also require prior testing of some toy and game products. In addition, the American Society for Testing and Materials ("ASTM"), a voluntary industry organization, has established nationally recognized safety requirements for toys and games that are generally adhered to by the toy industry. An independent federal agency, the Consumer Products Safety Commission ("CPSC") monitors federally mandated safety laws and regulations as well as ASTM's voluntary standards. New WOW's failure to comply with these or other applicable federal, state or trade standards, laws or regulations, could result in New WOW's having to recall a product, and could subject New WOW to other governmental enforcement proceedings.

## 9. Product Liability and Other Insurance

Liability claims may be asserted against New WOW by persons allegedly injured by products manufactured or sold by New WOW. If such claims arise, New WOW will be required to satisfy such claims or to defend against actions where liability is disputed. New WOW expects to purchase product liability insurance against such risks, but cannot be assured that such insurance will be available to it or, if available, that the cost thereof will not be so high as to have a material adverse affect upon New WOW's earnings. Recoveries by claimants in such matters are frequently large and, should such a judgment be rendered against New WOW in an amount in excess of its insurance coverage limits, or if New WOW is in the future unable to obtain product liability insurance, New WOW's financial condition and results of operations could be materially adversely affected.

## 10. Accounts Receivable

Competitive conditions could force New WOW to extend more generous terms of sale, including increases in the time in which accounts receivable are required to be paid. Such an increase would increase interest costs and working capital requirements and could adversely affect New WOW's financial performance.

Exhibit 5-3   Sample Disclosure Statement by Debtor                    **117**

## 11. Subcontracting of Manufacturing and Assembly Work to Foreign Producers

New WOW expects that most of New WOW's products initially will be manufactured in Hong Kong, China and Taiwan by unaffiliated subcontractors, and that only minor subcontracting will be with domestic manufacturers. New WOW's reliance on foreign manufacturers creates a risk to its operations resulting from, among other things, fluctuation in foreign currencies against the U.S. dollar, manufacturing and shipping delays, increased shipping costs, acts of foreign governments, labor disputes, civil unrest and strife, increased cost to New WOW of supervising manufacturing and shipping, the absence of easy access to redress through foreign legal systems, and the cost of pursuing legal action in foreign countries, all factors over which New WOW has no control. In addition, such reliance may subject New WOW to an increased risk of adverse action by the United States Government in the form of import quotas, import duties and tariffs and currency devaluation.

## 12. Ability to Attract Management

Debtor believes that the success of New WOW is dependent, in large measure, upon its ability to attract and retain experienced management personnel, including certain members of the Debtor's current management. Because of the uncertainties with respect to the Confirmation of the Plan, New WOW has, to date, been unable to make all the commitments necessary to attract or retain all such management personnel, and there can be no assurance that New WOW will be able to do so.

## 13. Dependence on Key Employees

Debtor believes that the success of New WOW will be dependent in large part on the services of the people listed in Section V(B). The inability of New WOW to reach agreement with them concerning their employment, or the subsequent loss of their services as a result of death, disability or otherwise, could have a material adverse effect upon the business of the Company.

## 14. Required Financing

New WOW expects to obtain bank financing arrangements in connection with the acquisition of Debtor's assets and future operations. No such financing arrangements have been concluded as of the date hereof, and there can be no assurance that such financing will be available or, if available, that it can be obtained without terms that may have a material adverse effect on New WOW's projected financial performance.

## 15. New WOW to be Highly Leveraged

At the Closing, pursuant to bank financing agreements that New WOW expects to enter into, New WOW anticipates that its lending banks will be granted a security interest covering substantially all of the assets of New WOW as security for New WOW's repayment of the loans made thereunder. As a result of typical restrictive covenants which may be contained in New WOW's bank financing agreements, severe restrictions may be imposed on New WOW's ability to sell, borrow against or otherwise convert its assets to cash while any portion of the loans remains outstanding. The bank financing agreements may also specify certain events of default which, if they occurred, would permit the banks to foreclose on the collateral for the loans.

### 16. Interest Rates

New WOW's projections assume various interest rates as disclosed in the projections and the accompanying assumptions. To the extent that average interest rates are substantially higher, particularly in the first two fiscal years, New WOW's financial performance could be adversely affected.

### 17. Use of Revenues for Acquisitions and Other Ventures

New WOW may, in the future, use a portion of its working capital or incur additional debt for the acquisition of other businesses or for entering into other joint venture arrangements with other companies. Persons receiving securities issued pursuant to the Plan may not have an opportunity to review any such acquisition or joint venture arrangement before the occurrence of such an event and there can be no assurance that any such acquisition or joint venture will prove successful. Such a use of working capital or incurrence of debt or such acquisitions or joint ventures may therefore have a material adverse effect on the projected financial performance of New WOW.

### 18. Availability of Tax Net Operating Loss Carryovers

The projections of New WOW's future performance are based in significant part upon the continued availability and utilization of the Debtor's substantial NOL carryovers. There is, however, no authority governing many tax aspects of transactions such as the one contemplated by the Plan. No ruling will be obtained from the IRS and neither the Debtor nor New WOW will obtain an opinion of counsel on this topic. Consequently, although the Debtor believes the description of the tax consequences of the Plan contained in Section VIII above is accurate, there can be no assurance that the tax consequences therein described will obtain if the transaction is challenged by the IRS.

If the transaction does not qualify as a tax-free reorganization, or if the Bankruptcy Exception (described in Section VIII(B)(2)(b)) does not apply, New WOW will be unable (or will be severely limited in its ability) to deduct the Debtor's NOL carryovers from its otherwise federal taxable income. The same result would in all likelihood occur if New WOW decides not to rely on the Bankruptcy Exception and the consideration distributable under the Plan is reduced as described in Section IV(C)(7) hereof. This may, among other things, affect New WOW's ability to pay dividends on the New WOW Preferred Stock.

Even if the transaction qualifies as a tax-free reorganization and the Bankruptcy Exception does apply, certain provisions of the Tax Code may affect the amount of NOL carryovers which will be available to New WOW if certain

**Exhibit 5-3 Sample Disclosure Statement by Debtor** **119**

events occur, including circumstances beyond the control of New WOW, such as changes in the ownership of the capital stock of New WOW.

### F. Acceptance

As a condition to confirmation, the Bankruptcy Code requires that each Class of holders of Claims or Interests accept the Plan, with the exceptions described in Section VI(G)(4). The Bankruptcy Code defines acceptance by a class of holders of claims as acceptance by holders of two-thirds in dollar amount and a majority in number of claims of that class, but for this purpose counts only those who actually vote to accept or to reject the plan. The Bankruptcy Code defines acceptance of a plan by a class of holders of interests (e.g., equity securities) as acceptance by two-thirds of the number of shares, but for this purpose counts only shares actually voted. Holders of claims or interests who fail to vote are not counted as either accepting or rejecting the plan. Each holder of a security issued under an indenture is entitled to vote with respect to such security. An indenture trustee cannot vote on the Plan on behalf of such holders.

Classes of claims and interests that are not "impaired" under a plan are deemed to have accepted the plan. A class is "impaired" if the legal, equitable, or contractual rights attaching to the claims or interests of that class are modified, other than by curing defaults and reinstating maturities or by payment in full in cash. THE FOLLOWING CLASSES ARE IMPAIRED UNDER THE PLAN: CLASS 2, CLASS 3, CLASS 4, CLASS 5, CLASS 6 AND CLASS 7.

### G. Confirmation

The Bankruptcy Code permits confirmation of a plan even if the plan is not accepted by all impaired classes, as long as at least one impaired class of claims has accepted it. These "cram-down" provisions for confirmation of a plan, despite the non-acceptance of one or more impaired classes of claims or interests, are set forth in Section 1129(b) of the Bankruptcy Code and are discussed in Section VI(G)(4) above.

The Debtor believes that the Plan meets the tests described in VI(G)(4) as to Class 1, Class 2, Class 3 and Class 4, and therefore that the Plan can be confirmed even if it is rejected by Class 5, Class 6 and Class 7.

### H. Confirmation Hearing

The Bankruptcy Court will hold a hearing on confirmation of the Plan commencing on May 3, 1989, at 2:00 o'clock p.m. in Courtroom 215, 201 Thirteenth Street, Oakland, California. The hearing may be adjourned from time to time without notice except as given in open court.

Any objection to confirmation of the Plan must be in writing and state the grounds therefor, and must be filed with the Bankruptcy Court and served upon the attorneys listed in § 6 of the Order Re Disclosure Statement, attached as Exhibit I hereto, on or before April 28, 1989.

## I. Consummation

The distributions provided for in the Plan will be made as soon as practicable after the Effective Date of the Plan. Section VI(C) contains a description of the anticipated amounts and timing of distributions to the various classes of Creditors.

## X
## RECOMMENDATION AND CONCLUSION

The Debtor believes that acceptance of the Plan is in the best interests of each and every Class of Creditors and Interest holders and recommends that each Class vote to accept the Plan.

Dated: April 10, 1989.
     Fremont, California

                Worlds of Wonder, Inc.

                Signed: /S/   STEPHEN J. HOPKINS————
                By: Stephen J. Hopkins
                Its: President and Chief Executive Officer

**Exhibit 5-3    Sample Disclosure Statement by Debtor**                    **121**

**Exhibit D**    Worlds of Wonder, Inc. Income Statement
For the Year Ending December 31, 1988 (Unaudited)

| | |
|---|---:|
| REVENUE: | |
| Gross Sales | $  58,220,370 |
| Returns | (23,032,549) |
| Allowances | (3,924,378) |
| | |
| Net Sales | 31,263,443 |
| COST OF SALES | |
| Product | 24,841,056 |
| Tooling | 2,811,658 |
| Warranty | 3,573,706 |
| Overhead | 8,441,186 |
| Other (including inventory writedowns) | 36,399,056 |
| | |
| Total Cost of Sales | 76,066,662 |
| | |
| Gross Profit | (44,803,219) |
| SALES VARIABLES: | |
| Promotions | 41,258 |
| Advertising | 11,648,616 |
| Co-op Advertising | 1,268,295 |
| Point of Purchase Advert. | 2,928,342 |
| Missing Kids Donation | 26,386 |
| Commission | (511,581) |
| License and Royalties | 712,619 |
| Bad Debt | 8,048,034 |
| Freight Outbound | 1,418,032 |
| | |
| Total Sales Variables | 25,580,001 |
| | |
| Contribution Margin | (70,383,220) |
| | |
| General and Administration | 23,788,457 |
| Allocations | (3,691,724) |
| | |
| Operating Loss | (90,479,953) |
| Interest Income (Expense) | (9,900,589) |
| Other Income/(Expense) | (22,833,557) |
| WOW Int'l Licensing Fee | 0 |
| | |
| Loss Before Taxes | (123,214,099) |
| Bankruptcy Costs | 3,505,588 |
| Income Taxes | (2,471,474) |
| | |
| Net Loss | ($124,248,213) |

**Exhibit E**   Projected Capitalization of New WOW as of June 1, 1989
(Dollars in Thousands)

| | |
|---|---:|
| Current Liabilities: | |
| Short Term Debt | $ 9,500 |
| Accounts Payable | 500 |
| Other | 1,945 |
| Total Current Liabilities | 11,945 |
| | |
| Long Term Debt | 4,000 |
| | |
| Shareholders' Equity: | |
| Series A Preferred Stock | 1,931 |
| Series B Preferred Stock | 10,628 |
| Series C Preferred Stock | 1,386 |
| Common Stock | 25 |
| Total Shareholders' Equity | 13,970 |
| | |
| Total Liabilities and Shareholders' Equity | $29,915 |

**Exhibit 5-3  Sample Disclosure Statement by Debtor**                                123

**Exhibit F**   Worlds of Wonder, Inc.
Estimated Distributions to Holders of Class 2 and Class 3 Claims
(Millions)

|  | ABN | Lenders | Total |
|---|---|---|---|
| Balance on the Filing Date (Without Interest) | $28.7 | $78.5 | $107.2 |
| Less: Amounts Paid Through 02/24/89 |  |  |  |
|   Special Proceeds | 12.2 | 11.1 | 23.3 |
|   Inventory Closeouts | 4.2 | — | 4.2 |
| Total Paydowns | 16.4 | 11.1 | 27.5 |
| Ending Balance at 02/24/89 | 12.3 | 67.4 | 79.7 |
| Add: Accrued Interest | 3.8 | — | 3.8 |
| Net Balance With Interest | 16.1 | 67.4 | 83.5 |
| Less: Projected Proceeds |  |  |  |
|   Inventory Closeouts | 12.8 | — | 12.8 |
|   ABN Note | 2.0 | — | 2.0 |
|   Selected Net Assets Adjustment Note | 1.3 | 0.7 | 2.0 (1) |
|   Present Value of Preferred A and B Stock | — | 12.6 | 12.6 (2) |
|   Other Distributions | — | 5.9 | 5.9 |
| Total Projected Proceeds | 16.1 | 19.2 | 35.3 |
| Class 6 Claims for Deficiency(3) | $–0– (4) | $48.2 | $ 48.2 |

(1) Based on estimated principal amount of $2,000,000.
(2) Calculated as the stated value of Series A and B Preferred Stock and increased by all dividends to which holders of the Series A and B Preferred Stock are entitled discounted to present value at a 10% rate (this reflects "best case" assumption that all dividends will be paid).
(3) Subject to adjustment if assumptions used to calculate "Projected Proceeds" change.
(4) Before payments of up to $7 million required under the ABN Settlement. ABN shall have a deficiency claim in the amount of any payment required to be made by it under the ABN Settlement.

**Exhibit G**    Worlds of Wonder, Inc.
Comparison of Plan vs. Liquidation Proceeds Estimated
Distributions to Creditors
Based on February 24, 1989 Projections (Dollars in Millions)

| | Plan (1) | | Liquidation Alternative | |
|---|---|---|---|---|
| **CASH AND RECEIVABLES** | | | | |
| Cash Including Cash Held by FNBC at 2/24/89 (2) | $ 3.6 | | $ 3.6 | |
| Projected Receivables Collections (After Deductions for Broker TV) | 16.3 | | 14.3 (3) | |
| Estimated Recovery from Pending and Potential Litigation | 3.5 | | 3.5 | |
| Projected Cash Disbursements to Plan Effective Date (4) | (13.1) | | (13.1) | |
| Royalties on Product Sales | –0– (5) | | (2.0) | |
| Chapter 11 and /or 7 Administrative/ Priority Costs (6) | (1.6) | 8.7 | (5.0) | $1.3 |
| | | | | |
| **INACTIVE INVENTORY PROCEEDS** | | 10.0 | 9.0 | 9.0 |
| | | | | |
| **ASSETS PROCEEDS (7)** | | | | |
| Active Inventories | | | 14.5 | |
| Prepaid Expenses | | | 1.0 | |
| Other Assets | | | 1.0 | |
| Estimated "Assumed Liabilities" | | | (3.4) | |
| | | | | |
| Total Assets Proceeds | | | $13.1 | 13.1 |
| | | | | |
| Net Present Value to Secured and Unsecured Creditors of the ABN Note, the Selected Net Assets Adjustment Note and Preferred A, B and C Stock to Be Issued by New WOW (8) | | $18.0 | – | – |
| | | | | |
| ⁻ TOTAL ESTIMATED DISTRIBUTIONS TO CREDITORS (9) | | $36.7 | | $23.4 |

**Exhibit 5-3   Sample Disclosure Statement by Debtor**            **125**

## SUMMARY OF ASSUMPTIONS

1. Assumes the consideration for the Purchased Assets described in Section IV(C)(1)–(6), and not what would be distributed under the alternative consideration provisions of the Purchase Agreement discussed in Section IV(C)(7). Debtor estimates, however, that total distributions would be $3,250,000 if the alternative considerations was received.
2. Cash as of February 24, 1989 includes $1.0 million of WOW International cash, amounts in Debtor's bank accounts and amounts being held by FNBC for Debtor against which Debtor can borrow.
3. Accounts receivable collections are assumed to be lower in a liquidation because of the increased difficulty of collecting disputed amounts.
4. The Effective Date of the Plan is assumed to be May 20, 1989.
5. Royalties, if any, on the transfer of assets to New WOW under the Plan will be paid by New WOW, and, therefore, do not reduce the Total Estimated Distributions to Creditors.
6. Projected Chapter 11 administrative costs have been reduced for amounts paid prior to Confirmation, current liabilities to be assumed by New WOW at Closing and costs and expenses expected to be paid out of the trust funds established by the Debtor for payment of certain expenses. No amounts have been included in relation to objecting to disputed Claims.
7. Assets are shown at assumed realization values. The values represent the Debtor's best estimate based on the February 28, 1989 balance sheet, projected forward through May 20, 1989, taking into account expected cash disbursements, sales revenues and collections of receivables. Assuming a value of $21 million for the Selected Net Assets at Closing, the amount of the Selected Net Assets Adjustment Note would be $2 million.
8. Valuation is based on the Redemption Price of Series A, B, and C Preferred Stock to be distributed under the Plan, reduced to present value based on a 10% interest factor, and assuming a "best case" scenario that all dividends to which shareholders are entitled are paid. The valuations of the Preferred Stock set forth in Exhibits E and H are based on projections by New WOW and attempt to forecast the valuation of the stock to reflect more accurately the performance of New WOW. Under a "worst case" scenario that no dividends are paid on the Preferred Stock prior to redemption, the present value of the distributions to Creditors would be reduced by approximately $4.2 million, but would still be significantly greater than the liquidation alternative. For purposes of Debtor's analysis of distributions under the Plan, however, Debtor has assumed best case and worst case scenarios to indicate the range of potential distributions. Interest on the Notes is assumed to be paid in full.

Although Debtor's and New WOW's estimates of distributions to creditors are comparable, reported asset balances shown in Exhibit G (Debtor's Estimates) vary somewhat from the beginning balances in New WOW's financial projections incorporated in Exhibit H. This results from: (1) reporting on

Exhibit G only the realizable value of those assets included in the calculation of the Selected Net Assets Adjustment Note, (2) asset valuation and accounting methods to be used after Closing vary from those used for preparation of Exhibit G, (3) New WOW's assumption that arrangements will be made to sell significant quantities of Inactive Inventory prior to the Closing Date, thus reducing the amount of Inactive Inventory being purchased at Closing and (4) New WOW's projections assume a Closing Date of May 31 rather than May 20, 1989.

9. Together with proceeds previously paid to ABN through February 24, 1989, ABN will receive a total distribution of approximately $32.5 million under the Plan. This will result in $7 million being reimbursed by ABN to the Debtor under the terms of the ABN Settlement. Five-sevenths of this amount will be distributed to Unsecured Creditors under the Plan. (In a liquidation, however, this amount would be subject to the fees and expenses of a trustee.) ABN's portion of the Total Estimated Distributions to Creditors will be reduced by the ABN Payment, but since it will be paid to Debtor for distribution to the Unsecured Creditors, it is included in the Total Estimated Distributions to Creditors.

**Exhibit H-1** Worlds of Wonder, Inc.
Projected Pro Forma Balance Sheet
As of June 1, 1989 (Dollars in Thousands)

| | Projected Pre-Transaction Balances | Elimination of Assets not Purchased | Estimated Book Balances of Acquired Assets | Pro Forma Reorganization Adjustments | Projected Post-Transaction |
|---|---|---|---|---|---|
| ASSETS: | | | | | |
| Cash | $ — | $ — | $ — | $ 1,000 | $ 1,000 |
| Accounts receivable, net | 12,715 | (12,715) | — | — | — |
| Inventories | 22,746 | (1,466) | 21,280 | — | 21,280 |
| Other Assets | 8,038 | (296) | 7,742 | (107) | 7,635 |
| Total current assets | 43,499 | (14,477) | 29,022 | 893 | 29,915 |
| Property & equipment, net | 2,001 | — | 2,001 | (2,001) | — |
| Other assets | 3,805 | (78) | 3,727 | (3,727) | — |
| Total assets | $ 49,305 | $(14,555) | $ 34,750 | $ (4,835) | $29,915 |
| LIABILITIES AND SHAREHOLDERS EQUITY: | | | | | |
| Short-term debt | $ 70,950 | $ — | $ 70,950 | $ (61,450) | $ 9,500 |
| Accounts payable | 500 | — | 500 | — | 500 |
| Accrued expenses | 2,185 | (240) | 1,945 | — | 1,945 |
| Total current liabilities | 73,635 | (240) | 73,395 | (61,450) | 11,945 |

**Exhibit H-1**  (*continued*)

| | Projected Pre-Transaction Balances | Elimination of Assets not Purchased | Estimated Book Balances of Acquired Assets | Pro Forma Reorganization Adjustments | Projected Post-Transaction |
|---|---|---|---|---|---|
| Liabilities subject to reorganization proceedings | 83,489 | — | 83,489 | (83,489) | — |
| Long-term debt | 105,576 | — | 105,576 | (101,576) | 4,000 |
| Shareholders' equity: | | | | | |
| Series A, 8% redeemable preferred stock; $33.33 stated and liquidation value; 60,000 shares authorized, issued and outstanding | — | — | — | 1,931 | 1,931 |
| Series B, 8% redeemable preferred stock; $76.66 stated and liquidation value; 150,000 shares authorized, issued and outstanding | — | — | — | 10,628 | 10,628 |

| | | | | | |
|---|---:|---:|---:|---:|---:|
| Series C, 8% redeemable preferred stock; $33.33 stated and liquidation value; 45,000 shares authorized, issued and outstanding | — | — | — | 1,386 | 1,386 |
| Common stock; $.10 par value; 245,000 shares authorized, issued and outstanding on June 1, 1989 | 72,315 | — | 72,315 | (72,290) | 25 |
| Retained earnings | (285,710) | (14,315) | (300,025) | 300,025 | — |
| Total shareholders' equity | (213,395) | (14,315) | (227,710) | 241,680 | 13,970 |
| Total liabilities and shareholders' equity | $ 49,305 | $(14,555) | $ 34,750 | $ (4,835) | $29,915 |

(See summary of significant accounting policies and assumptions in Section IX(D)(5)(b))

130

**Exhibit H-2**  Worlds of Wonder, Inc.
Projected Pro Forma Balance Sheets (Dollars in Thousands)

| | | | March 31 | | |
|---|---|---|---|---|---|
| | 1990 | 1991 | 1992 | 1993 | 1994 |
| **ASSETS:** | | | | | |
| Cash and cash equivalents | $ 3,851 | $ 1,631 | $ 3,522 | $ 7,129 | $14,938 |
| Accounts receivable, net | 9,203 | 12,355 | 13,592 | 14,950 | 16,446 |
| Inventories | 7,504 | 7,557 | 8,160 | 8,976 | 9,874 |
| Other assets | 1,670 | 1,779 | 1,779 | 1,848 | 1,924 |
| Total current assets | 22,228 | 23,322 | 27,053 | 32,903 | 43,182 |
| Property & equipment, net | 706 | 654 | 630 | 676 | 661 |
| Total assets | $22,934 | $23,976 | $27,683 | $33,579 | $43,843 |
| **LIABILITIES AND SHAREHOLDERS' EQUITY:** | | | | | |
| Short-term debt and current portion of long-term debt | $ 2,000 | $  — | $ 2,000 | $  — | $  — |
| Accounts payable | 189 | 244 | 278 | 322 | 374 |
| Accrued expenses | 2,392 | 1,955 | 2,126 | 2,338 | 2,572 |
| Total current liabilities | 4,581 | 2,199 | 4,404 | 2,660 | 2,946 |
| Long-term debt | 2,000 | 2,000 | — | — | — |
| Shareholders' equity: Series A, 8% redeemable preferred stock; | | | | | |

| | | | | |
|---|---|---|---|---|
| $33.33 stated and liquidation value; 60,000 shares authorized, issued and outstanding | 1,965 | 2,000 | — | — | — |
| Series B, 8% redeemable preferred stock; $76.66 stated and liquidation value; 150,000 shares authorized, issued and outstanding | 10,753 | 10,933 | 11,124 | 11,311 | 11,500 |
| Series C, 8% redeemable preferred stock; $33.33 stated and liquidation value; 45,000 shares authorized, issued and outstanding | 1,402 | 1,424 | 1,449 | 1,474 | 1,500 |
| Common stock; $.10 par value; 245,000 shares authorized, issued and outstanding | 25 | 25 | 25 | 25 | 25 |
| Retained earnings | 2,208 | 5,395 | 10,681 | 18,109 | 27,872 |
| Total shareholders' equity | 16,353 | 19,777 | 23,279 | 30,919 | 40,897 |
| Total liabilities and shareholders' equity | $22,934 | $23,976 | $27,683 | $33,579 | $43,843 |

(See summary of significant accounting policies and assumptions in Section IX(D)(5)(b))

**Exhibit H-3**  Worlds of Wonder, Inc.
Projected Statement of Income (Dollars in Thousands)

| | Ten Months Ended March 31, 1990 | Year Ended March 31, | | | |
|---|---|---|---|---|---|
| | | 1991 | 1992 | 1993 | 1994 |
| Revenues | $72,807 | $79,339 | $87,407 | $96,308 | $106,132 |
| Costs and expenses: | | | | | |
| Cost of goods sold | 43,350 | 42,510 | 45,902 | 50,492 | 55,541 |
| Selling, general and administrative | 24,981 | 30,153 | 32,476 | 35,012 | 37,768 |
| | 68,331 | 72,663 | 78,378 | 85,504 | 93,309 |
| Operating income | 4,476 | 6,676 | 9,029 | 10,804 | 12,823 |
| Non-operating income (expense): | | | | | |
| Interest, net | (1,828) | (1,539) | (1,583) | (1,161) | (582) |
| Income before income taxes | 2,648 | 5,137 | 7,446 | 9,643 | 12,241 |
| Income taxes | 265 | 513 | 744 | 963 | 1,223 |
| Net income | $ 2,383 | $ 4,624 | $ 6,702 | $ 8,680 | $ 11,018 |

(See summary of significant accounting policies and assumptions in Section IX(D)(5)(b)

**Exhibit H-4**  Worlds of Wonder, Inc.
Projected Statement of Changes in Shareholders' Equity
(Dollars in Thousands)

| | Redeemable Preferred Stock | | | Comon Stock | Retained Earnings | Total |
|---|---|---|---|---|---|---|
| | Series A | Series B | Series C | | | |
| Balances at June 1, 1989 | $1,931 | $10,628 | $1,386 | $25 | $ — | $13,970 |
| Net income | — | — | — | — | 2,383 | 2,383 |
| Accretion of preferred stock | 34 | 125 | 16 | — | (175) | — |
| Balances at March 31, 1990 | 1,965 | 10,753 | 1,402 | 25 | 2,208 | 16,353 |
| Net income | — | — | — | — | 4,624 | 4,624 |
| Cash dividends | — | — | — | — | (1,200) | (1,200) |
| Accretion of preferred stock | 35 | 180 | 22 | — | (237) | — |
| Balances at March 31, 1991 | 2,000 | 10,933 | 1,424 | 25 | 5,395 | 19,777 |
| Net income | — | — | — | — | 6,702 | 6,702 |
| Cash dividends | — | — | — | — | (1,200) | (1,200) |
| Accretion of preferred stock | — | 191 | 25 | — | (216) | — |
| Redemption of preferred stock | (2,000) | — | — | — | — | (2,000) |
| Balances at March 31, 1992 | — | 11,124 | 1,449 | 25 | 10,681 | 23,279 |
| Net income | — | — | — | — | 8,680 | 8,680 |
| Cash dividends | — | — | — | — | (1,040) | (1,040) |
| Accretion of preferred stock | — | 187 | 25 | — | (212) | — |
| Balances at March 31, 1993 | — | 11,311 | 1,474 | 25 | 18,109 | 30,919 |
| Net income | — | — | — | — | 11,018 | 11,018 |
| Cash dividends | — | — | — | — | (1,040) | (1,040) |
| Accretion of preferred stock | — | 189 | 26 | — | (215) | — |
| Balances at March 31, 1994 | $ — | $11,500 | $1,500 | $25 | $27,872 | $40,897 |

(See summary of significant accounting policies and assumptions in Section IX(D)(5)(b))

**Exhibit H-5**  Worlds of Wonder, Inc.
Projected Statement of Cash Flows (Dollars in Thousands)

| | Ten Months Ended March 31, 1990 | For the Years Ended March 31, | | | |
|---|---|---|---|---|---|
| | | 1991 | 1992 | 1993 | 1994 |
| Cash flows from operating activities: | | | | | |
| Net income | $ 2,383 | $4,624 | $6,702 | $8,680 | $11,018 |
| Adjustments to reconcile net income to net cash provided by operating activities: | | | | | |
| Depreciation and amortization | 79 | 172 | 204 | 255 | 315 |
| Net effect of changes in: | | | | | |
| Accounts receivable | (9,203) | (3,152) | (1,236) | (1,359) | (1,495) |
| Inventories | 13,776 | (54) | (603) | (816) | (898) |
| Other current assets | 5,965 | (109) | — | (69) | (76) |
| Accounts payable | (311) | 56 | 33 | 44 | 51 |
| Accrued liabilities | 447 | (437) | 171 | 212 | 234 |
| Total adjustments | 10,753 | (3,524) | (1,431) | (1,733) | (1,869) |
| Net cash provided by operating activities | 13,136 | 1,100 | 5,271 | 6,947 | 9,149 |

| | | | | | |
|---|---|---|---|---|---|
| Cash flows from investing activities: | | | | | |
| Capital expenditures | (785) | (120) | (180) | (300) | (300) |
| Net cash used in investing activities | (785) | (120) | (180) | (300) | (300) |
| Cash flows from financing activities: | | | | | |
| Repayments under debt agreements | (9,500) | (2,000) | — | (2,000) | — |
| Dividends paid | — | (1,200) | (1,200) | (1,040) | (1,040) |
| Redemption of preferred stock | — | — | (2,000) | — | — |
| Net cash used in financing activities | (9,500) | (3,200) | (3,200) | (3,040) | (1,040) |
| Net increase (decrease) in cash and cash equivalents | 2,851 | (2,220) | 1,891 | 3,607 | 7,809 |
| Cash and cash equivalents at beginning of period | 1,000 | 3,851 | 1,631 | 3,522 | 7,129 |
| Cash and cash equivalents at end of year | $ 3,851 | $1,631 | $3,522 | $7,129 | $14,938 |
| Supplemental disclosure of cash flow information: | | | | | |
| Cash paid during the period for interest | 1,666 | 1,799 | 1,637 | 1,276 | 945 |

(See summary of significant accounting policies and assumptions in Section IX(D)(5)(b))

**EXHIBIT 5-4  SAMPLE DISCLOSURE STATEMENT BY
UNSECURED CREDITORS' COMMITTEE
(SELECTED ITEMS)**

This exhibit consists of selected provisions for a disclosure statement prepared by the unsecured creditors' committee. In order to illustrate all of the items that were included in the disclosure statement the table of contents of the disclosure statement precedes the following excerpts:

**Table of Contents**

COMMITTEE'S DISCLOSURE STATEMENT

**Exhibit 5-4   Sample Disclosure Statement by Creditors**                    **137**

      **C.** Operations

          **1.** Health Care Operations

          **2.** Health Care Reimbursement Programs

          **3.** Regulations

          **4.** Competition

          **5.** Employees

**III.** RECENT HISTORY OF THE LONG-TERM CARE INDUSTRY

**IV.** COMPANY HISTORY—1985 THROUGH JUNE 1987

**V.** ACTIONS REPORTEDLY TAKEN BY CARE TO ADDRESS ITS OPERATING PROBLEMS

      **A.** Facility Management Changes

      **B.** Current Revenue Enhancement Efforts

      **C.** Quality Assurance Department

      **D.** Nursing Cost Reduction

      **E.** Regulatory Compliance

**VI.** COMPANY HISTORY—BANKRUPTCY FILING THROUGH PRESENT

**VII.** RECENT FINANCIAL RESULTS

      **A.** Comparison of Fiscal 1987 to Fiscal 1986

      **B.** 1988 Results (Unaudited)

**VIII.** LIQUIDATION ANALYSIS

      **A.** Assumptions

          **1.** Liquidation Scenarios

          **2.** Liquidation Values

              **a.** Cash

              **b.** Accounts Receivable

              **c.** Inventory

              **d.** Prepaid Assets

              **e.** Notes Receivable

              **f.** Refundable Taxes

              **g.** Property and Equipment/Net

              **h.** Mortgage Notes Receivable

              **i.** Other Assets

              **j.** Restricted Funds

              **k.** Excess of Costs Over Net Assets Acquired

**Exhibit 5-4  Sample Disclosure Statement by Creditors**                    **139**

C. Treatment of Interests

D. Estimation of Claims

E. Description of New Common Stock

F. Description of Shareholder Warrants

G. Securities Law Considerations

H. Executory Contracts and Unexpired Leases

I. Disputed C/I Reserve

J. Unclaimed Property

K. Surrender of Old Notes and Old Debentures

L. Distribution of Fractions

M. Creditor's Committee

N. Conditions to Confirmation

XI. CERTAIN FEDERAL INCOME TAX CONSEQUENCES OF THE PLAN

A. General Tax Considerations

B. Tax Consequences to the Company

1. Net Operating Losses

2. Discharge of Indebtedness

3. Alternative Minimum Tax

4. Consolidated Federal Income Tax Return Issues

5. Tax Reorganization

XII. LITIGATION

A. Ramona Manor Convalescent Hospital v. Care Enterprises, et al.

B. Weinberger v. Care Enterprises, Inc.

C. Litigation Between the Debtor and its Affiliates and the former Shareholders of First Ohio Investment Group and their Affiliates

1. The Managed Facilities Litigation

a. Americare Corp., v. Alliance Health Care Corp., et al.

b. Americare Corp., Americare Southwest, Inc. and Americare Southwest of Arizona, Inc. v. Alliance Health Care Company, et al.

c. Roswell Health Care Company v. Lee R. Bangerter, et al.

d. Americare Corp. v. Las Cruces Health Care Company, Ralph E. Hazelbaker and John M. Haemmerle

Exhibit 5-4    Sample Disclosure Statement by Creditors                    **141**

# VIII.
# LIQUIDATION ANALYSIS

When evaluating the terms of the Plan, each creditor and shareholder should compare their treatment under the Plan with how they would be treated if the Debtor were liquidated under chapter 7 of the Bankruptcy Code. A liquidation analysis was prepared by the Debtor based on available 1987 year end balance sheet information. Although a number of months have elapsed since year end, the Debtor expects that the net result of the liquidation analysis would not differ significantly from an analysis based on more current information. The Debtor's Liquidation Analysis is attached as Exhibit "2".

## A. Assumptions

### 1. Liquidation Scenarios

The liquidation analysis sets forth two scenarios: (1) a "forced" liquidation over twelve months; and (2) a "orderly" liquidation over thirty-six months. All assets were assumed to be converted to cash within the time frame or each scenario.

### 2. Liquidation Values

#### a. Cash
Assumed to be liquidated at 100% under both scenarios.

#### b. Accounts Receivable
All long-term care ("LTC") facility receivables were assumed to be collected at an average rate of 80% under an orderly liquidation to reflect the difficulty of collecting receivables for discontinued facilities and 60% under a forced liquidation to reflect further discounts that might to be taken to convert to cash within the shorter time frame. The value of government program receivables net of deposits, retentions, and adjustments/allowances was assumed to be collected at 75% under an orderly liquidation and 50% under a forced liquidation, again to reflect the difficulties that would be encountered in converting to cash within

the shorter time frame. Health Care Network ("HCN") receivables were assumed to be included in the HCN sales price.

### c. Inventory

The value of inventory at the LTC facilities was included in the liquidated facility values. The balance of the inventory consists primarily of pharmaceuticals at HCN and was assumed to be included in the HCN liquidated value.

### d. Prepaid Assets

Prepaid items such as insurance, rent, licenses and fees were assumed to have a liquidated value of 100% either through cash refunds or direct reductions in the administrative costs of a chapter 7. Items such as deferred expenses and fees were assumed to have no liquidation value.

### e. Notes Receivable

It was assumed that notes receivable which represent the current portion of mortgage notes receivable would be collected at 100% under either liquidation scenario.

### f. Refundable Taxes

It was assumed that refundable taxes would be converted to cash at 100% under either liquidation scenario.

### g. Property and Equipment/Net

The liquidation value of the LTC facilities was derived by the Debtor from independent appraisals of each facility previously prepared by Valuation Counselors. It was assumed that the LTC facilities would be sold on a one-off basis or in small blocks. Discounts from appraised values were assumed to be 20% for owned facilities and 30% for leaseholds in an orderly liquidation. Discounts from appraised values were assumed to be 40% for owned facilities and 50% for leaseholds in a forced liquidation. Appraised values were assumed to be further reduced by reductions such as landlord consent fees in leaseholds, employee benefits payable, typical physical plant problems, and brokers' commission.

It was assumed that the net cash value of HCN would be $9,600,000 in an orderly liquidation and 15% less or $8,100,000 in a forced liquidation. The sales price would include all HCN assets. While HCN has generated profits in the past, it is believed that it would sell at a significant discount since approximately 70% of its business is with Care and the balance is on thirty day contracts. Valuation Counselors appraised HCN at $11,600,000.

It was also assumed for both LTC facilities and HCN that the value of capitalized lease assets would equal the value of capitalized lease liabilities. LTC facility and HCN equipment was assumed to be included in the facility/HCN sales prices. The remaining equipment, primarily located at Corporate, was assumed to be worth 10% under either liquidation scenario.

### h. Mortgage Notes Receivable

It was assumed that mortgage notes receivable could be liquidated at a rate that would provide a 15% return to potential buyers. Individual notes were

Exhibit 5-4   Sample Disclosure Statement by Creditors                    143

analyzed and the principal balance discounted where necessary to provide a 15% return. The net result was a 26% average reduction in the principal amount which was assumed to be valid under both liquidation scenarios.

### i. Other Assets

Items such as lease deposits were assumed to have a liquidated value of 100% either through cash refunds, additions to sales prices or direct reductions in the administrative costs of a chapter 7. Items such as deferred expenses and fees were assumed to have a liquidated value of 0%.

### j. Restricted Funds

Restricted funds held in escrow for the payment of industrial revenue bonds were assumed to have a liquidated value of 100% either through conversion to cash or through the direct reduction of debt.

### k. Excess of Costs Over Net Assets Acquired

It was assumed that goodwill would not have any value under either liquidation scenario.

### l. Administrative Expenses

Administrative expenses for chapter 7 legal and accounting/transaction costs/general administration are rough estimates, which may be unrealistically high. Estimates for chapter 7 trustee's fees were based on the statutory payment of 3% of the gross proceeds of the estate to be distributed. Chapter 11 administrative expenses consisted of estimates of expenditures to date and rough estimates of future expenditures.

### m. Priority Claims

Priority claims were based on rough extrapolations of known priority claims for the Debtor and its Affiliates.

## B.  Adjustment for Facilities Sold Since Analysis

Since the Liquidation Analysis was prepared, Care sold or disposed of five facilities. The sales resulted in a reduction of the liquidation value for all facilities from $530,000 to $717,000 depending on whether the liquidation was "forced" or "orderly." Of that amount, the sale of the Hillcrest facility reduced the liquidation value for all facilities from $150,000 to $210,000. The Hillcrest sale was a unique situation, with the facility being sold to a nearby Catholic hospital for a price exceeding the facility's appraised value.

## C.  Liquidation Analysis Conclusions

The Debtor estimates the gross liquidation value of Care's December 31, 1987 assets to be approximately $118,000,000 in a "forced" liquidation and $154,000,000 in an "orderly" liquidation given the nature of the assets and today's market conditions. The Debtor estimated administrative costs of liquidating the assets to be $22,000,000 in a "forced" liquidation and $33,000,000 in an "orderly" liquidation, which may be unrealistically high. It is estimated that there would be approximately $3,000,000 in priority claims under either liquidation scenario. The estimated net liquidation proceeds available for both secured and unsecured claims are approximately $93,000,000 in a "forced" liquidation and $117,000,000 in an "orderly" liquidation. In liquidation, secured creditors would receive 100¢ on the dollar and unsecured creditors would receive from 3¢ to 18¢ on the dollar, depending upon whether the liquidation was "forced" or "orderly." Under the Committee's Plan of Reorganization, secured creditors receive 100¢ on the dollar and all unsecured creditors will receive cash or securities worth significantly more than the estimated chapter 7 dividend.

## IX.
## THE REORGANIZED DEBTOR

The Committee's Plan of Reorganization is based upon its Business Plan, which projects the cash the Company expects to generate during the period 1989–1995. Described below are: (1) the methodology used to develop the Committees Business Plan; and (2) a summary of the Business Plan and the elements of the Committee's Plan of Reorganization affecting the forecasted financial performance of the Company.

### A. Development of the Committee's Business Plan

The Committee's accountants, Ernst & Whinney, assisted the Committee in preparing its Business Plan. Attached to this Disclosure Statement as Exhibit "3" is the most recent Accountants' Report prepared for the Committee. A detailed description of the services provided by Ernst & Whinney to the Committee is set forth below. Specifically, the Committee's accountants:

1. Obtained and read the Debtor's Business Plan (including consolidated projected financial statements and projected financial statement data for Care's facilities, Health Care Network and corporate and regional expenses), the Debtor's Disclosure Statement and "Care Enterprises—Analysis of Catastrophic Health Legislation."

2. Interviewed key management personnel, industry experts and analysts as to the underlying assumptions used in the preparation of the consolidated projected financial statements.

3. Utilizing long-term care specialists, analyzed the facility/regional data supporting Care's assumptions used in preparing the consolidated projected financial statements.

4. Analyzed June through December utilization, to supplement the 1988 five month (January through May) "running rate" calculations prepared by Care.

5. Revised the assumptions used by Care in formulating the projected consolidated financial statements. Made additional assumptions as necessary to account for items not included in the original projected consolidated financial

Exhibit 5-4    Sample Disclosure Statement by Creditors                    145

statements prepared by Care, and to account for differences between the Debtor's Plan of Reorganization and the Committee's Plan.

6. Obtained the micro-computer model used by Care to prepare the projected consolidated financial statements and modified the model to reflect the revised assumptions and additional assumptions referred to above. Assembled projected consolidated financial statements and the pro-forma 1988 year end balance sheet for the Committee's Business Plan.

## B.  Summary of Business Plan

The Committee's 1989–1995 Business Plan projects the generation of additional cash to service the New Notes to be issued to the Banks and other indebtedness of the Company, principally from the following sources:

1. The sale of approximately thirty percent (30%) of the Company's nursing home facilities and the subsequent reduction of regional and corporate costs by approximately twenty percent (20%) as a result.

2. The implementation of profit improvement programs, which were scheduled to begin in August 1988 and be implemented by mid-1989. These are in addition to profit improvement programs instituted by the Company in 1987 and early 1988.

3. Medi-Cal reimbursement rates are assumed to increase by five percent (5%) in 1989 from their 1988 levels. In 1990 and years thereafter, Medi-Cal reimbursement levels are projected to increase by amounts equal to the rate of inflation.

4. The positive financial impact of the Medicare Catastrophic Coverage Act of 1988. A copy of the Company's December 1988 "Analysis of Catastrophic Health Legislation" is attached for informational purposes as Exhibit "4" [not included].

5. The conversion of virtually all unsecured debt to New Common Stock in the reorganized Debtor.

The Committee's projected consolidated financial statements for 1989–1995 are presented in Exhibit "3".

The following is a more detailed discussion of the items summarized above as well as the Committee's major planning assumptions.

### a.  Sale of Facilities

The Business Plan calls for the sale of twenty-three facilities between January 1989 and June 1990, including all of the facilities in the Utah region. This is in addition to nine other facilities which have been or will be sold, closed, or otherwise disposed of by Care during the second half of 1988. The Committee assumes that the facilities will be sold for one hundred percent (100%) of appraised value in all cash sales. After 1990, the Company will own only sixty-nine (69) facilities.

Shown in Exhibit "5" [not included] are the facilities which are being sold, closed or otherwise disposed of together with the actual expected cash proceeds from each. The facilities to be eliminated were determined based on the Company's analysis of financial, operational, logistical and legal considerations. Shown in Exhibit "6" [not included] are the facilities which will continue to be operated by the Company.

### b. Profit Improvement Actions

The profit improvement programs called for by the Business Plan are described below (figures shown are for the Company at its current size):

*(1) Facilities Profit Improvements, $5.3 million*

Reduction of nursing, housekeeping, laundry, dietary, food, patient activities, social services, education, and administrative expenses at the facilities through the implementation of improvement programs and other means. The changes are assumed to have no negative impact on patient care. Timing of the profit improvements: sixty percent (60%) by December 31, 1988, eighty-five percent (85%) by March 31, 1989; 100% by June 30, 1989. The Committee is currently unable to verify the impact, if any, of the profit improvement programs implemented by the Company to date.

*(2) Facilities Ancillary Charge Recovery, $0.4 million*

Improved recovery of ancillary charges through improved record keeping.

*(3) Facilities Private Pay Price Increases, $3.2 million*

Increases in private pay rates, cost reductions and other industry factors are assumed to result in payor mix shift of five percent (5%) of private pay patients to Medicaid. This projected shift will erode the dollar impact of the projected private pay rate increases. The decrease in private pay census comes as a result of: (i) rates being raised at some facilities to levels higher than the highest rates of local competitors; (ii) rates being raised at some facilities disproportionate to the quality level of the facility; (iii) loss of some historical rate "advantages"; (iv) a general trend toward obtaining Medi-Cal eligibility for a greater number of patients who were previously self-pays; and (v) the impact of cost-savings on the real or perceived quality of care at various facilities. While the private pay rate increases are expected to have a positive dollar impact of $3.2 million per year, after taking into account decreases in private pay census the financial impact is expected to be reduced by approximately one-third in each year of the projection period.

*(4) HCN Cost Reductions, $0.5 million.*

Reduced cost of goods sold as a result of taking prompt pay discounts and more aggressive product contracting. Projected reduction based on comparisons of prices paid by similar companies.

*(5) Corporate Expense Reductions, $4.4 million.*

Reduction of personnel and non-personnel costs through elimination of non-vital, low-value-added and redundant activities, procedural improvements, upgrading the quality of people in certain positions, and replacement of the existing general ledger system.

Exhibit 5-4    Sample Disclosure Statement by Creditors                    **147**

*(6)  Employee Benefit Program, $1.2 million.*

Modification of Care's employee benefit program to eliminate the Company's 401K Plan, change employee/Care share of contributions to insurance plans. Impact on people employed at the facilities is assumed to be relatively minor.

### c.  Increased Medi-Cal Reimbursement

Historically, Medi-Cal reimbursement has lagged behind nursing home cost inflation in California. The assumption of a five percent (5%) increase in 1989 and the general assumption that Medi-Cal reimbursement increases will equal the rate of inflation are based primarily upon interviews with the Rates Development Branch of Medi-Cal and the California Association of Health Facilities, as well as recent experience in annual rate increases for the Medical Program. Eventually, the response to industry pressure for rate increases is likely to be a total redesign of the reimbursement system rather than the one-time inflation "catch-up" predicted by Care. Because the timetable for and details of any system redesign are currently unknown, assumptions based on historical precedent have been used.

### d.  Financial Impact of Medicare Catastrophic Coverage Act of 1988.

A portion of Care's patients requiring a high level of care and whose Medicare coverage has lapsed will, as of January 1, 1989, be re-eligible for Medicare coverage under the new 150-day annual eligibility provision of the Medicare Catastrophic Coverage Act of 1988 (the "Act"). In addition to "tube feeders," other classes of patients are assumed to be re-eligible for Medicare coverage, including patients requiring intravenous therapy and total parenteral nutrition, tracheotomy patients, respirator patients, insulin-dependent diabetic patients, and patients with stage III and IV pressure sores.

Additionally, it is assumed that a portion of patients requiring a high level of care will be eligible for an additional 50 days of Medicare coverage per annum due to the expansion of Medicare coverage under the new legislation. The categories of patients eligible for the additional coverage is assumed to include insulin-dependent diabetic patients as well as tube feeders. Finally, it is assumed that a percentage of patients in Care's facilities who become acutely ill during the course of the year and remain in the facilities during the acute phase of their illness will qualify for Medicare coverage during their post-acute stays in Care's facilities.

The Committee has incorporated into its projected consolidated financial statements Care's December 1988 estimate of the financial impact of the Act. Because the Committee has not yet been able to review Care's actual operating results with respect to the impact of the Act since its implementation on January 1, 1989, there are likely to be further revisions to the financial impact estimates. (In fact, Care has already revised its December 1988 estimates based upon certain as yet unsubstantiated assumptions.) Additionally, the Committee believes that Care has failed to present or consider the negative impact on reimbursable costs of additional patient volume; the probable loss in revenue associated with conversion of private pay days to Medicare; the likely overstatement of days of eligibility in view of the historical distribution of patient stays; and the possible narrowing of the scope of Medicare benefits as Regulations and Instructions to intermediaries are promulgated. When these items are taken into account, the assumptions about the positive financial impact of the Act may decrease significantly. Finally, as noted elsewhere in the Disclosure Statement, numerous bills have been introduced in Congress which would have the effect of delaying or repealing these Medicare benefits.

### e. Major Assumptions.

Historical data, adjusted where appropriate, was used as the basis for projecting revenues and expenses in addition to capital spending and balance sheet items. Economic projections specific to the nursing home industry provided by Data Resources Inc. (DRI) were utilized, where available, to forecast rates of inflation going forward.

### f. Operating Revenues and Expenses

REVENUE/EXPENSE
ELEMENT

*MAJOR ASSUMPTIONS*

*Revenue Related*

| | |
|---|---|
| Occupancy | Changed at certain facilities. Care's analysis modified by twelve month (January to December 1988) year-to-date utilization statistics, re-examination of preliminary market information, and interviews with Care's Management. See Exhibit "7" [not included]. |
| Mix | No significant change except for a mix shift from Medicaid and private to Medicare as a result of recent changes in federal government reimbursement programs. |
| Medicare Rates | Adjusted downward to reflect impact of cost reductions in 1988 and 1989 (rates are cost-based); Assumed to increase in relation to cost inflation thereafter. |
| Medicaid (in cost-based states) | Same as treatment of Medicare rates, except for an upward adjustment made to reflect increased nursing salaries. |
| Medi-Cal | Described in prior section; assumed to keep pace with inflation. |
| Private Pay Rates | Adjusted to market levels in January 1989; increase 1% more than inflation |

**Exhibit 5-4    Sample Disclosure Statement by Creditors**                                    **149**

in 1989 and 1990; increase with inflation thereafter.

HMO

Increase at 50% of the rate of inflation going forward reflecting increasing competition for HMO business

All Other

Increase with inflation.

*EXPENSES* (After Cost Reductions)

Nursing in California

10 to 15% (planned at 12.5%) for the first three years of the plan; increase with DRI's overall projected rate of inflation for nursing costs thereafter.

Nursing Costs Outside California

Nursing costs projected to increase in accordance with DRI projections.

Secondary Effect of Increase in Minimum Wage

Implementation of the new wage will result in a 5% raise in salaries for 15% of Care's California workforce in 1989.

Leases, Mortgage Payments, Other Fixed Expenses

In accordance with lease, mortgage and other contractual terms.

Depreciation

Based on history and future capital spending.

Income Taxes

A federal tax rate of 34% is assumed. A state tax rate of 9.3% is assumed. The special insolvency limitation for the utilization of net operating loss ("NOL") carryovers which is available under § 382 of the Internal Revenue Code is used. A NOL carryover of $55 million for federal tax purposes and $27 million for state tax purposes is assumed. No assumptions relating to alternative minimum tax and investment tax credit carryover provisions have been included in the calculations of taxes other than the limitation of NOL utilization under alternative minimum tax rules.

Interest

In accordance with the Committees Plan of Reorganization, and mortgages, leases and other contracts.

It has been assumed that regulatory changes will not significantly impact Care's operating costs going forward. A $1,000,000 contingency (in 1988 dollars) has been included in the projections to reflect the cost of responding to the estimated three decertification actions per year.

### g. Capital Spending Requirements

Capital spending requirements in 1988 dollars have been projected at $350 per bed in 1989, $400 per bed in 1990, $450 per bed in 1991, and $500 per bed in 1992, and thereafter at the facilities, $200,000 per year for corporate and regional expenditures, and approximately $200,000 per year for the Health Care Network. The Company contends that these spending levels are needed to maintain physical plant and equipment in working order and provide for necessary refurbishment of facilities when required.

The future capital spending requirement projections are less than actual capital spending requirements in 1986 ($1,200 per bed) and 1987 ($727 per bed) when the Company completely remodeled a number of facilities. The future projections contemplate making required capital improvements to all facilities on an ongoing basis.

### h. Balance Sheet Items

With some exceptions, working capital items are projected to increase with revenue and expenses going forward, based on their historical relationships. Before the elimination of any facilities, Care believes that it will reduce receivables by $1,000,000 between the beginning and the middle of 1989 as a result of better management of receivables.

Certain current liabilities, particularly reserves for bankruptcy and litigation, are left unchanged or reduced going forward as actual payments are made. Fixed assets increase or decrease in the future based on capital spending and depreciation. Prepetition debt is projected in accordance with the Plan.

### i. Bankruptcy Related Expenses

Bankruptcy related professional expenses are estimated by the Debtor to be $8,180,000 in total as detailed in Exhibit "8" [not included]. Of this amount, $1,160,000 was paid in 1988. The remaining portion of $7,020,000 is assumed paid in 1989. Professional fees are difficult to project with precision and the Debtor believes that, depending upon the length of time the chapter 11 case continues, actual professional costs may be higher or lower than those projected.

### j. Hazelbaker Litigation

The Hazelbaker litigation is discussed, along with other litigation, at Article XII of this Disclosure Statement. For planning purposes, it was assumed that $500,000 in cash/expense would be expended net of any recoveries in 1989 and that the various litigation actions would be self-funding thereafter. The Business Plan projects no net cash to be received as a result of the litigation even though the Company is optimistic that a substantial recovery will be obtained in 1990 or 1991.

Exhibit 5-4    Sample Disclosure Statement by Creditors                    **151**

## C. Funding of the Plan

### 1. Sources of Funding for Plan

The Plan will be funded through operating and sales activities. Below is a summary of the funds estimated to be generated by each activity in excess of amounts expended for operations and debt service to lenders other than the Banks.

| Activities | Estimated Amount of Funds to be Generated ($ millions) |
|---|---|
| 1. Business Operations | $75 |
| 2. Sale or disposition of facilities | 5 |
| Total | $80 |

This Committee is currently negotiating with Paradigm Corp. for the sale of additional facilities and the settlement of the litigation pending between the Company and the former controlling shareholders of Americare and first Ohio and their affiliates. Additionally, the Committee may also obtain, prior to the Confirmation Date, commitments for financing from one or more financial institutions or investors to satisfy the cash requirements of the Plan. The terms of any such financing may include the issuance of debt and/or equity securities to the prospective lender or investor. Under the Plan, Reorganized Care is also free to sell, refinance or otherwise dispose of one or more facilities between the Confirmation Date and the Effective Date to fund the Plan.

### 2. Estimated Funds Necessary to Satisfy New Notes

The total estimated funds necessary to satisfy the New Notes to be paid over the 1989–1995 period is approximately $40,000,000. This amount may decrease by the payment of Excess Cash, if any, to the Banks which would decrease the interest paid over the 3-1/2 year period. The cost of replacing the letters of credit issued by the Banks, which are to be cancelled three months after repayment of the New Notes, has not been included in the $45,000,000 estimates.

## D. Reorganization Value of the Company

The Committee's investment bankers, Houlihan, Lokey, Howard & Zukin Capital ("HLHZ"), have conducted a preliminary investigation and analysis of the Company. The purpose of the investigation and analysis is to determine the fair market value of the Company as a going concern on a debt-free basis. HLHZ's preliminary opinion, attached hereto as Exhibit "9", is that the fair market value of the Company on a debt-free basis is in the range of $140–160 million. While this opinion is preliminary in nature and subject to further investigation, HLHZ believes that its final conclusion will fall near the bottom end of the range. By comparison, the liabilities of the Company far exceed $180.0 million.

## E. Transfer of Property Interests to the Reorganized Debtor

As of the Effective Date of the Plan, the Reorganized Care shall retain and be revested with all property of the Estate.

## F. Officers and Directors of the Reorganized Debtor

The Plan contemplates a change in the Debtors' Board of Directors and senior management. The Committee is presently identifying candidates to serve on the Board and has selected candidates to replace the Chief Executive Officer, _____ and the Chief Financial Officer, _____.

The Committee plans to have selected new Board members by the time the Court approves the form of this Disclosure Statement, and to the extent feasible, this Disclosure Statement shall be amended to identify the persons who have been selected. In any event, such persons shall be designated at least 15 days prior to the Confirmation Date in order to comply with section 1129(a)(5) of the Bankruptcy Code.

### 1. Officers

Reorganized Care will replace _____ and _____, but will otherwise continue with current management. Richard E. Matthews will assume the position of Care's Chief Executive Officer and John Rasmussen will act as Care's Chief Financial Officer. The officers of Reorganized Care and their post reorganization salaries are as follows:

| NAME | POSITION | SALARY |
|---|---|---|
| Richard E. Matthews | Chief Executive Officer, President | $_____ |
| John Rasmussen | Chief Financial Officer | $_____ |
| Richard Matros | Executive Vice President | $120,000 |
| Lance Samuelson | Secretary and Vice President of Administration | $ 79,764 |
| Barbara Garner | Vice President Quality Assurance | $ 75,000 |
| John Goates | Vice President Marketing | $ 66,000 |
| Mike Anderson | Chief Information Officer, Vice President Financial Information Services | $116,000 |

Exhibit 5-4 Sample Disclosure Statement by Creditors 153

Roger Randall      Asst. Vice                       $62,000
President Risk
Management

## 2. Background of New Officers

Richard E. Matthews, selected by the Committee to serve as Care's Chief Executive Officer, has more than 16 years experience as a consultant/chief executive for companies in corporate restructuring, workout and reorganization proceedings. Mr. Matthews' prior health care related experience includes his service as the court appointed trustee in the successful reorganization of Pacific Homes and service as a consultant to Watts Health Foundation/United Health Plan in its successful reorganization proceeding. Mr. Matthews has also served as a special consultant to the United States Department of Health, Education and Welfare and the State Department. In 1972, Mr. Matthews served as the President and Chief Executive Officer of Olympic Plastics Company, which commenced proceedings under Chapter XI of the former Bankruptcy Act. Mr. Matthews continued to manage and operate the business during the reorganization proceeding, located a purchaser for the stock of the company and negotiated the terms of a successful plan.

John W. Rasmussen, selected by the Committee to serve as Care's Chief Financial Officer, has for the past six years served as a consultant/chief financial officer for a variety of companies involved in reorganization proceedings and workouts. Mr. Rasmussen is a Certified Public Account with ten years auditing experience with Peat, Marwick, Mitchell & Co. Mr. Rasmussen's industry experience is extremely broad, and includes health maintenance organization; savings and loan; real estate; construction; and business software development and distribution.

## 3. Directors

Reorganized Care will have a new five-member Board of Directors. Richard E. Matthews, Care's new Chief Executive Officer will serve on the Board. The four additional Directors will be identified by the Committee at least 15 days before the Confirmation Date.

## G. Affiliates Remaining in Chapter 11 Proceedings

The Committee's Plan concerns only the Chapter 11 case of Care Enterprises, Inc., the parent company. Immediately after the Confirmation Date, _____ and _____ will be removed from the management and boards of directors of all debtor and non-debtor subsidiaries. The Committee anticipates that new management will promptly formulate and pursue confirmation of a chapter 11 plan or plans for the subsidiaries remaining under the Bankruptcy Court's jurisdiction.

## X.
## SUMMARY OF PLAN OF REORGANIZATION

This Disclosure Statement summarizes the Committee's Plan of Reorganization, but is qualified in its entirety by the full text of the Plan itself. The Plan is proposed only for Care Enterprises, Inc. All terms defined in the Plan have the same meaning in this Disclosure Statement. The Plan, if confirmed, will bind the Debtor, any entity acquiring property under the Plan or otherwise transferring property pursuant to the Plan, and all creditors and shareholders of the Debtor. All creditors, shareholders, and other interested parties are urged to read the Plan carefully.

### A. Classification of Claims

The Plan designates fifteen (15) classes of Allowed Claims and Interests. Administrative Claims, reclamation claims, claims for set-off and priority tax claims specified in Bankruptcy Code sections 507 (a)(1), 546, 553 and 507(a)(7), respectively, have not been classified and are excluded from the designation of classes. A claim or Interest is in a particular class only to the extent that the claim is an Allowed Claim, Allowed Secured Claim or Allowed Interest in that class.

1. *Class 1:* Class 1 consists of all Allowed Claims entitled to priority under sections 507(a)(3), (4), (5) and (6) of the Bankruptcy Code.

2. *Class 2:* Class 2 consists of the Allowed Secured Claim of Santa Barbara Savings secured by a Lien on Colonial Convalescent Hospital and Hilltop Convalescent Hospital.

3. *Class 3:* Class 3 consists of the Allowed Secured Claim of Home Federal Savings & Loan secured by a Lien on Hilltop Convalescent Hospital and Georgian Court Convalescent Hospital.

4. *Class 4:* Class 4 consists of the Allowed Secured Claim of Union Bank which is secured by a lien on Washington Manor and Cedarhaven Convalescent Hospital.

5. *Class 5:* Class 5 consists of the Allowed Secured Claim of FTC Servicing Corp., as agent, which is secured by a lien on an apartment building located in Phoenix, Arizona.

6. *Class 6:* Class 6 consists of the Allowed Secured Claim of California Federal Savings and Loan which is secured by a lien on a deposit account located in Los Angeles, California.

7. *Class 7:* Class 7 consists of the Allowed Secured Claims of Citibank, N.A. as agent for Wells Fargo Bank, N.A. and Citibank, N.A.

8. *Class 8:* Class 8 consists of all Allowed Claims against the Debtor in an amount equal to or less than $500.00, or which have been reduced by an election in writing by the holder of such claim to the sum of $500.00, in full and complete satisfaction of such claim. To be included in Class 8, holders of Al-

**Exhibit 5-4  Sample Disclosure Statement by Creditors**                    **155**

lowed Claims that exceed $500.00 must file a written election to reduce their claim to $500.00 within the time allowed for filing ballots accepting or rejecting the Plan.

9. *Class 9:* Class 9 consists of all Allowed Claims arising out of guarantees executed by the Debtor before the Petition Date, pursuant to which the Debtor guaranteed the obligation of any Affiliate.

10. *Class 10:* Class 10 consists of Allowed Claims held by Affiliates of the Debtor.

11. *Class 11:* Class 11 consists of all Allowed Claims for goods purchased by the Debtor or services rendered to the Debtor, other than legal, accounting or investment banking services, prior to the date the Debtor commenced its chapter 11 case.

12. *Class 12:* Class 12 consists of all Allowed Claims for personal injury which are covered by insurance and Allowed Claims for Worker's Compensation.

13. *Class 13:* Class 13 consists of all Allowed Claims other than personal injury claims covered by insurance, which (i) were the subject of litigation pending against the Debtor in a court of competent jurisdiction or before an administrative tribunal as of the date the Debtor commenced its chapter 11 case or (ii) were scheduled as disputed in the list of creditors filed by the Debtor with the Bankruptcy Court.

14. *Class 14:* Class 14 consists of all unsecured Allowed Claims, other than claims in Classes 8, 9, 10, 11, 12 and 13. Class 14 includes, without limitation, the Allowed Claims of the holders of Public Debt, the deficiency claims of secured creditors, and claims arising from the rejection of executory contracts and leases.

15. *Class 15:* Class 15 consists of all Allowed Interests of the Debtor.

## B.  Treatment of Claims

THE HOLDER OF A CLAIM WILL RECEIVE A DISTRIBUTION UNDER THE PLAN ONLY IF IT IS AN "ALLOWED CLAIM." An Allowed Claim means a claim against the Debtor to the extent that the claim was listed on the schedules filed by the Debtor and not listed as disputed, contingent, or unliquidated or as to which proof of such claim was timely filed and which, if it is a Disputed Claim, is allowed by the Court. Distributions to the holders of Allowed Claims under the Plan are in full satisfaction of those Allowed Claims (including any interest accrued thereon). Except as otherwise provided in the Plan, all claims against and Interests in the Debtor arising prior to the Confirmation Date will be discharged by the Plan on the Effective Date. (See Article XIII below).

*Class 1* (Priority Claims): The Priority portion of Allowed Claims for wages, contributions to employee benefit plans, and those arising from consumer deposits, if any, will be paid in cash in full on the Effective Date, or as soon thereafter as is practicable, unless otherwise ordered by the Court. Accrued and unpaid vacation and sick leave will be reinstated and used by current employees pursuant to company policy.

*Class 2, 3, 4, 5 and 6* (Secured Claims other than the Banks): The Allowed Secured Claims in Classes 2, 3, 4, 5 and 6 will retain unaltered the legal, equitable and contractual rights to which such claims entitle the holder thereof. If the Debtor is in default to the holder of any such claims, the Debtor shall, on the Effective Date, as soon as is practical thereafter (i) cure all existing defaults, other than defaults relating to the insolvency or financial condition of the Debtor, defaults arising from the commencement of the Debtor's case or defaults based upon the appointment of or taking possession by a trustee or custodian; (ii) reinstate the original maturity of the Allowed Secured Claim as though no such default had occurred and pay the allowed secured claim according to that original maturity; (iii) compensate the holder of the Allowed Secured Claim under which there was a default for any damages incurred based upon that claimant's reasonable reliance on the contractual provision under which there was a default or applicable loss; and (iv) comply with all other terms of the obligations without alteration.

*Class 7* (Secured Claims of the Banks): The Banks will receive on the Effective Date (i) a cash payment of $500,000 or less on account of agent fees, letter of credit fees and related expenses; (ii) the Initial Cash Payment; (iii) the Net Available Cash, if any, remaining on the Effective Date; and (iv) the New Notes to be issued to the Banks. The New Notes mature approximately three and one-half years after the Effective Date, with interest accruing at a rate equal to prime plus 2%. Interest will be paid monthly on the New Notes. Commencing on the last day of the third full calendar quarter after the Confirmation Date, the New Notes call for quarterly payments of $1.5 million escalating thereafter to $3.5 million (less the interest payments) with a final payment at the maturity of the New Notes equal to all unpaid principal and accrued interest. The New Notes may be further reduced by the payment of Excess Cash as provided for in the Plan. This payment of Excess Cash would enable the Banks to receive an accelerated payment of the New Notes if the performance of Reorganized Care is better than that projected by the Committee. With respect to contingent claims arising from the Bank's issuance of pre-petition letters of credit, the Plan provides for the payment, annually in advance, of a letter of credit fee equal to 2% of the face amount of letters of credit outstanding. The letters of credit will be cancelled no later than three months after payment in full of the New Notes. Under the Plan, the Banks will retain their pre-petition liens and, to the extent legally and contractually permissible, receive a lien on all other property of the Debtor and its subsidiaries, except for the Unencumbered Property, to secure the New Notes and the Debtor's repayment obligation in the event of a drawing under any letter of credit.

*Class 8* (Small Claims): The Bankruptcy Code permits the separate classification of claims consisting of unsecured claims that are less than or reduced to

**Exhibit 5-4    Sample Disclosure Statement by Creditors**                    **157**

an amount approved by the Bankruptcy Court for purposes of administrative convenience. Class 8 consists of all unsecured Allowed Claims against the Debtor which were $500.00 or less, or more than $500.00, but have been reduced to $500.00 at the election of the holder thereof. Where a creditor has filed multiple proofs of claim for different indebtedness owed to such creditor by the Debtor, the claims will be aggregated so that, for example, if five claims, each for $400.00 arising from separate transactions were filed, the creditor would have one claim for $2,000, not five claims of $400.00 each. Holders of Class 8 Allowed Claims will receive cash in the full amount of such Allowed Claims (up to a maximum of $500.00) on or shortly after the Effective Date. An election by any holder to be included in Class 8 must be indicated on such holder's ballot and received by the Committee on or before the deadline for receipt of ballots accepting or rejecting the Plan.

*Class 9 and 10* (Pre-Petition Guaranties and Affiliates Claims): From time to time, the Debtor has guaranteed or entered into agreements to cause support and performance of the obligations of its Affiliates to third parties. These guaranties will remain in place following confirmation of the Plan. The Debtor has also incurred obligations to its Affiliates in the ordinary course of its business. Likewise, from time to time, the Affiliates have incurred obligations to the Debtor. The Debtor's schedules reflect that, as of the Petition Date, the amounts owed by the Affiliates to the Debtor exceeded the amounts owed by the Debtor to its Affiliates. The Allowed Claims, if any, held by the Affiliates net of amounts owing to the Debtor are unaffected by the Plan.

*Class 11* (Trade Claims): Class 11, consisting of Allowed Claims for goods purchased by the Debtor and certain services rendered to the Debtor, will receive, on the Effective Date, or as soon as practicable thereafter, a cash distribution equal to 50% of their Allowed Claims. The holder of any Class 11 Allowed Claim may elect, in lieu of a cash distribution, to receive one share of New Common Stock for each $10.00 of such holder's Allowed Claim. Unless waived by a vote of the Committee, confirmation of the Plan is conditioned upon the allowed claims in Class 11 totalling to no more than $1,500,000.

*Class 12* (Personal Injury and Worker's Compensation Claims): Allowed Claims for personal injuries which are covered by insurance and allowed claims for Worker's Compensation will retain unaltered the legal, equitable and contractual rights to which such claim entitles the holder thereof.

*Class 13 and 14* (Claims for damages and all other unsecured claims): Class 13 and 14 consist of all unsecured Allowed Claims against the Debtor other than those classified in Classes 8, 9, 10, 11 and 12. The holders of Class 13 and Class 14 Allowed Claims will receive one share of New Common Stock for each $10.00 of Allowed Claim. In making the distribution to the holders of Class 13 and 14 claims, subordination agreements will be enforced to the same extent that such agreements are enforceable under applicable non-bankruptcy law.

## C.  Treatment of Interests

THE HOLDER OF AN EQUITY SECURITY INTEREST MAY RECEIVE A DISTRIBUTION UNDER THE PLAN ONLY IF IT IS AN "ALLOWED INTEREST". An Allowed Interest means an equity security interest of the Debtor to the extent listed in the List of Equity Security Holders filed with the Court or otherwise of record, or as to which proof of such interest was filed and which, if it is a Disputed Interest, is allowed by the Court. Distributions under the Plan will be made to the holders of Allowed Interests of record as of the time of the commencement of distribution.

*Class 15* (Equity Security Holders): The Debtor has issued an outstanding two classes of Common Stock, Class A and Class B. Additionally, the Debtor has authorized, but not issued, Preferred Stock. The holders of Allowed Interests in Class 15 will receive, subject to certain conditions, a Pro Rata Distribution of Shareholder Warrants to purchase up to twenty-percent (20%), in the aggregate, of the outstanding New Common Stock of Reorganized Care on a fully diluted basis. The Distribution of Shareholder Warrants is conditioned upon (i) acceptance of the Plan by the holders of Allowed Interests, excluding negative votes cast by insiders and (ii) the Committee's ability to confirm the Plan under § 1129(b) of the Code if any class of Allowed Claims fails to accept the Plan. In any event, all Common Stock and Preferred Stock of the Debtor will be cancelled, annulled and extinguished.

## D.  Estimation of Claims

The claims against the Debtor's Estate are estimated as follows:

| *Class of Claim* | *Estimated Amounts* |
|---|---|
| 1.  Priority Claims (Class 1) | $     50,000 |
| 2.  Secured Claims other than the Secured Claims of Wells Fargo Bank, N.A. and Citibank, N.A. (Class 2, 3, 4, 5 and 6) | 5,500,000 |
| 3.  Secured Claims of Citibank, N.A. and Wells Fargo Bank N.A. (Class 7) | 39,000,000 |
| 4.  Allowed Claims of less than $500.00 (Class 8) | unknown |
| 5.  Allowed Claims arising from guarantees of Affiliate Obligations (Class 9) | contingent, unknown |
| 6.  Unsecured Claims of Affiliates (Class 10) | -0- |
| 7.  All unsecured Allowed Claims for goods and services, excluding legal, accounting and investment banking services (Class 11) | 750,000 |

**Exhibit 5-4  Sample Disclosure Statement by Creditors**          **159**

8.  Allowed Claims for personal injury, Workers' Com-          contingent
    pensation (Class 12)                                       unknown

9.  Allowed Claims for damages, excluding personal            contingent
    injury, or which are the subject of litigation (Class     unknown
    13)

10. Allowed Claims of holders of 9% Convertible Sen-          72,000,000
    ior Subordinated Debentures and 16% Senior Sub-
    ordinated Notes (Class 14)

11. All unsecured Allowed Claims, other than Public           2,400,000
    Debt and Class 8, 9, 10, 11, 12 and 13 claims
    (Class 14)

Administrative Claims                                         5,000,000

## E.  Description of New Common Stock.

The Plan contemplates the issuance of New Common Stock, having a par value of $.01 per share, to the holders of Public Debt and other unsecured creditors in Classes 13 and 14. The New Common Stock will be issued at the rate of one share per $10.00 of each holder's Allowed Claim. Additional shares of New Common Stock may be authorized to fulfill any management stock programs. Common stockholders will be entitled to cast one vote for each share held of record, to receive, subject to limitations in the New Notes, such dividends as may be declared by the Board of Directors out of legally available funds and to share pro rata in any distribution of the Debtor's assets after payment of all debts and other liabilities. Stockholders will not have pre-emptive rights or other rights to subscribe, except those, if any, specified in the Plan, for additional shared and the New Common Stock is not subject to conversion or redemption. The New Common Stock will be, when issued, fully paid and non-assessable. Finally, no other classes of stock are currently contemplated for issuance by Reorganized Care, nor can any such class be authorized or issued except with the concurrence of a majority of the shares of New Common Stock voting at a meeting called for such purpose and an appropriate amendment to the Certificate of Incorporation.

## F.  Description of Shareholder Warrants

Shareholder Warrants to purchase a number of shares of New Common Stock equal to twenty-five percent (25%) of the number of shares Distributed to the holders of Allowed Claims will be issued to the holders of Allowed Interests in Class 15. Warrant certificates will be issued (each entitling the holder to purchase one share of New Common Stock) and will expire on the fifth anniversary of the date of their issue. The exercise price will be $10.00 per share for the first twelve (12) months, escalating thereafter by $1.00 per year on each anniversary of the date of issuance. In the event of a merger, sale of all or substantially all of Reorganized Care's assets or other similar transaction respecting Reorganized Care, which shall be defined to exclude transactions with Affiliates, the Shareholder Warrants shall be callable after appropriate notice for $.25 per warrant share, but will not otherwise be subject to call.

The Shareholder Warrants will be issued pursuant to a warrant agreement containing customary antidilution adjustment provisions. The Shareholder Warrants will be transferable, and may be exercised by delivery of the Warrants, together with the notice of exercise properly completed, and payment of the exercise price, either by certified or cashier's check payable to Reorganized Care.

As noted elsewhere in the Disclosure Statement, HLHZ's preliminary opinion is that the fair market value of the Company on a debt-free basis is in the range of $140–160 million. Assuming a value of $150 million, secured indebtedness of $100 million (leaving $50 million of net reorganization value), and a Distribution of New Common Stock to the holders of Allowed Claims totalling to $80 million, the New Common Stock should have a value of $6.25 per share. If the market price of the New Common Stock were $6.25 immediately after the Confirmation Date, the Shareholder Warrants would have substantial time or speculative value. In any event, if, as the Committee believes, the Company is insolvent, the value of the Shareholder Warrants will be much greater than the current value of all Allowed Interests, which is zero.

## G. Securities Law Considerations.

Pursuant to the exemption from registration afforded by Section 1145 of the Bankruptcy Code, the New Common Stock and Shareholder Warrants issuable pursuant to the Plan, and any New Common Stock issued upon exercise of the Shareholder Warrants will not be registered under the Securities Act of 1933, as amended (the "1933 Act") or under any state securities laws. In general, such securities may be freely traded by a creditor receiving them under the Plan without registration under the 1933 Act or other laws, unless such creditor is an "underwriter" with respect to such securities, as that term is defined in the Bankruptcy Code.

Under Section 1145(b) of the Bankruptcy Code, an underwriter is a person or entity who (i) purchases a claim against or interest in the Debtor with a view to the distribution of the securities received on account of such claim or interest, (ii) offers to sell such securities on behalf of the holders thereof (except offers to sell fractional interests); (iii) offers to buy such securities with a view to the distribution thereof pursuant to an agreement made in connection with the Plan, or (iv) is an "issuer" with respect to the Debtor, as the term "issuer" is defined in Section 2(11) of the 1933 Act.

In this context, an "issuer" under Section 2(11) includes any person directly or indirectly controlling, controlled by or under direct or indirect common con-

Exhibit 5-4  Sample Disclosure Statement by Creditors    **161**

trol with the Debtor. Whether a person is an "issuer," and therefore an "underwriter" for purposes of Section 1145(b) depends upon a number of factors, including: the relative size of the person's voting securities in the Debtor; the distribution and concentration of other voting securities in the Debtor; whether the person, either alone or acting in concert with others, has a contractual or other relationship giving that person power over management policies and decisions; and whether the person actually has such power notwithstanding the absence of formal indicia of control. An officer or director of the Debtor may be deemed to be a controlling person, particularly if his position is coupled with ownership of a significant percentage of voting stock. In addition, the legislative history of Section 1145 suggests that a creditor receiving at least 10% of the securities of a reorganized debtor would be deemed to be a controlling person.

Based on the published views of the Securities and Exchange Commission, the Committee believes that a person who receives less than 1% of a class of securities generally would not be deemed to be an underwriter and that creditors receiving more than 1% (but less than 10%) are not necessarily deemed to be underwriters. Persons who are not issuers, but are otherwise underwriters under section 1145(b) of the Bankruptcy Code, may resell the securities received under the Plan in ordinary trading transactions. Because of the complex and subjective issues involved in determining underwriter status and what constitutes an ordinary trading transaction engaged in by an entity which is not an issuer, creditors are urged to consult with their counsel concerning whether they will be able to trade freely the securities received.

The Committee believes that most recipients should be in a position to resell such securities in reliance upon an exemption from the 1933 Act registration requirements. If the Committee has reason to believe that a recipient of the securities issued pursuant to the Plan may be an underwriter, it may require assurances from such recipient that he is aware of Section 1145 of the Bankruptcy Code and the requirements of the 1933 Act regarding resale of such securities, and that any of the securities held by him would be sold in compliance with the Code and the 1933 Act.

The Securities Act of 1934 (the "1934 Act") provides for the registration of classes of securities (i) listed on a national securities exchange; or (ii) traded in the over-the-counter market where the Company's assets exceed $5.0 million and shareholders total to more than 500 in number. The Committee will use its best efforts to cause the Debtor to apply for a listing for the New Common Stock and the Shareholder Warrants on a nationally recognized securities exchange. In the event such a listing cannot be obtained, the Committee believes that it is likely that such securities will be traded in the over-the-counter market. Registration under section 12 of the 1934 Act will obligate the Reorganized Debtor to file periodic reports with the Securities and Exchange Commission pursuant to section 13 of the 1934 Act. Additionally, Reorganized Care will become subject to the proxy and tender offer rules and its officers, directors and principal shareholders will become subject to the insider reporting and short swing profit recovery provisions of the 1934 Act. The Committee will use its best effort to cause the Debtor to register the New Common Stock and the Shareholder Warrants before confirmation of its Plan to avoid any lapse in such reporting.

## H. Executory Contracts and Unexpired Leases

1. Under the Plan, all executory contracts and unexpired leases which have not been assumed pursuant to a prior order of the Bankruptcy Court or which are subject to a motion already filed with the Bankruptcy Court are rejected, except the following, which are assumed under the plan:

a. Software Licensing Agreement with Collier-Jackson, Inc.

b. Master Lease Agreement with Comdisco, Inc. for telephone equipment.

c. Software Licensing and Development Agreement with Automated Programming Technologies, Inc.

d. Equipment lease with Maryland National Leasing Corporation.

e. Purchase Agreement with Development Corp. of America and Ralph E. Hazelbaker.

f. Automobile lease agreements (three) with Galles Rental.

g. Duplicator lease agreement with Eastman Kodak Company.

h. Telephone equipment lease agreement and amendments with AT&T Information Systems.

i. Software Licensing Agreements (two) with Infocentre.

j. Software Agreement and Customer Support Services Agreement with Hewlett-Packard.

k. Agreement for equipment sale with Amcare Microsoftware Systems.

l. Agreement for AMS License Programs with Amcare Microsoftware Systems.

Claims arising from such rejection must be filed no later than thirty (30) days following the Confirmation Date.

## I. Disputed C/I Reserve.

On the Effective Date, the Distributions reserved for the holders of Disputed Claims and Disputed Interests will be held in trust by Reorganized Care in a segregated account. The cash and New Common Stock to be deposited into the Disputed C/I Reserve will be equal to that which would be distributed on account of all Disputed Claims if such Disputed Claims were allowed in full, or such lesser amount of cash and New Common Stock as may be found by the Court constitute a sufficient reserve for all Disputed Claims.

Any interest or dividends which are paid in cash or in kind on account of cash and New Common Stock attributable to the Disputed Claims prior to the disbursements will be added to the Disputed C/I Reserve. The cash contained in the Disputed C/I Reserve will be invested as permitted by order of the Bankruptcy Court. All New Common Stock held in the Disputed C/I Reserve will deemed to be issued and outstanding and with respect to any matter requiring a

**Exhibit 5-4    Sample Disclosure Statement by Creditors**                    **163**

vote of shareholders, will be deemed to vote on such matter in the same proportions as the votes actually cast by all holders of New Common Stock.

When any Disputed Claim or Disputed Interest becomes an Allowed Claim or Allowed Interest subsequent to the Effective Date, the distributions on account of such Allowed Claim or Allowed Interest will be deposited with the Disbursing Agent, Indenture Trustees and/or stock transfer agent for delivery to the holder as soon as practicable thereafter.

### J.  Unclaimed Property.

Any Distributions from the Indenture Trustees, Disbursing Agent and/or stock transfer agent under the Plan which are unclaimed after 180 days following the Effective Date will be returned to Reorganized Care. Reorganized Care will then deposit this unclaimed property in the Unclaimed Property Reserve. Any principal, interest, or dividends payable in cash or in kind which may have been paid on account of Unclaimed Property will be held for the benefit of holders of Allowed Claims which have failed to claim Unclaimed Property. For a period of five years following the Effective Date, any Unclaimed Property and any interest, principal or dividend payment attributable to such unclaimed property will be delivered to the holders thereof upon presentation of evidence satisfactory to Reorganized Care that such holder is entitled to such Unclaimed Property. All rights to claim Unclaimed Property will terminate five years following the Effective Date, and Unclaimed Property will then be returned to Reorganized Care as its property free and clear of any claims or obligations or Reorganized Care under the Plan.

### K.  Surrender of Old Notes and Old Debentures.

As a condition to receiving any Distribution under the Plan, the holders of Public Debt must surrender their Old Notes and Old Debentures. Following confirmation, the holders of Public Debt will receive specific instructions regarding the time and manner in which the Old Notes and Old Debentures are to be surrendered. Old Notes and Old Debentures may be surrendered to receive the Distributions to which the holders of Public Debt are entitled for a period of five years after the Effective Date. If no surrender occurs during this period, no Distribution may be made to such holders of Public Debt.

### L.  Distributions of Fractions.

The Plan provides that one share of New Common Stock will be issued for each $10.00 of Allowed Claim. All fractions of New Common Stock and Shareholder Warrants which would otherwise have been distributed will be aggregated in separate pools ("the Fractional Pools") on the date of such Distribution. Holders of Allowed Claims and Allowed Interests who would otherwise be entitled to receive fractions will be ranked according to the size of the fractions to which such holder would otherwise be entitled. If two or more holders are entitled to the same fraction (as rounded to the second decimal place), the ranking of such holders will be determined by lot. Based on such ranking, the whole shares of New Common Stock and Shareholder Warrants will be distributed to the holders entitled to the largest fractions of each until all of the whole units of New Common Stock and Shareholder Warrants in the Fractional Pools have been distributed.

## M. Creditors' Committee.

Following confirmation of the Plan, the Creditors Committee will continue in its current form until the Effective Date, after which it will continue on a reduced basis. The Committee will have the right to participate in hearings which take place after the Effective Date, such as hearings to modify or amend the Plan, hearings on applications for professionals' compensation, and on objections to claims. Members of the Committee will continue to serve without compensation, but shall be reimbursed for their reasonable and necessary expenses. Attorneys, accountants and other professionals employed by the Committee, who continue to be employed after the effective date, will be compensated by Reorganized Care. If Reorganized Care objects to the compensation requested by such professionals, it may apply to the Bankruptcy Court for a determination of the compensation due.

## N. Conditions to Confirmation

Unless waived by a vote of the Committee, confirmation of the plan is expressly conditioned upon: (i) the Committee obtaining, prior to the Confirmation Date, the Banks' agreement to restructure the indebtedness of certain Affiliates to the Banks; and (ii) Class 11 Allowed Claims totaling in amount to no more than $1,500,000.

## XI.
## CERTAIN FEDERAL INCOME TAX CONSEQUENCES OF THE PLAN

### A. General Tax Considerations

Certain significant federal income tax consequences of the Plan under the Internal Revenue Code of 1986, as amended (the "Tax Code"), are described below. The Plan will limit Care's ability to use its net operating loss carryovers ("NOLS") and its general business tax credit carryovers ("BTCs") to reduce its federal income tax liabilities on future earnings. The tax consequences of the Plan are subject to many uncertainties due to the complexity of the Plan, the unsettled nature of several of the tax issues presented by the Plan and the lack

Exhibit 5-4    Sample Disclosure Statement by Creditors                    165

of interpretative authority regarding certain changes in the tax law, including changes made to the applicable sections of the Tax Code by the Bankruptcy Tax Act of 1980, the Tax Reform Act of 1984 and the Tax Reform Act of 1986. The Committee has not received an opinion of counsel as to the tax consequences of the Plan. Uncertainties with regard to federal income tax consequences of the Plan also arise due to the fact that certain information, including the Company's federal and state income tax returns have not been reviewed or audited by the Committee.

Events subsequent to the date of this Disclosure Statement, such as the enactment of additional tax legislation, could also change the federal income tax consequences of the Plan and the transactions contemplated thereunder. CREDITORS ARE ADVISED TO CONSULT THEIR OWN TAX ADVISORS, TO REVIEW THIS MATERIAL AND TO CONSIDER THE TAX CONSEQUENCES OF THE PLAN TO THEM, INCLUDING THE EFFECT OF FOREIGN, STATE AND LOCAL TAXES. THIS DISCLOSURE STATEMENT IS NOT INTENDED TO BE AND SHOULD NOT BE CONSTRUED AS LEGAL OR TAX ADVICE TO ANY CREDITOR.

## B.  Tax Consequences to the Company

### 1.  Net Operating Losses

During recent years, the Company has incurred substantial net operating losses. The Company estimates that, as of the taxable year ending December 31, 1988, its NOL carryovers and other tax shields total to approximately $78 million. Operating losses incurred in a taxable year may be carried forward for 15 years and used to offset income earned in those years. The NOLs expire at various dates through the year 2002. In addition, the Company estimates that it has consolidated BTCs of approximately $4,021,000 (adjusted pursuant to the Tax Reform Act of 1986) which can be used as a credit against future federal income tax liabilities. The BTCs will expire in the year 2002. Certain provisions of the Tax Code, including the limitations imposed by Sections 382 and 383 of the Tax Code, the regulations governing the filing of consolidated federal income tax returns and the rules governing debt cancellation income, may affect the amount of NOL and BTC carryovers which will be available to the Company if certain events occur, including changes in the nature of its business and changes in the ownership of its stock. Each of these provisions is discussed below.

Section 382 of the Tax Code imposes limitations on a corporation's use of its NOLs against future taxable income if the ownership of the stock of the corporation changes by certain prescribed percentages. Section 383 of the Tax Code provides limitations on the use of tax credit carryovers under rules essentially identical to those contained in Section 382 of the Tax Code.

Section 382(a) of the Tax Code provides that the amount of income which may be offset by a debtor's NOLs is limited to an annual amount (hereinafter described) after any "ownership change." An ownership change occurs, in general, if the percentage of stock held by any one or more 5% shareholders has increased by more than 50 percentage points over the lowest percentage of stock held by those shareholders during the applicable testing period. Generally, the testing period is the 3-year period ending on the date any 5% shareholder's ownership interest changes. The term "5% shareholders" is broadly defined and certain groups of less than 5% shareholders are aggregated together and treated as one 5% shareholder. It is anticipated that under the present Committee Plan that an ownership change will occur.

If an ownership change occurs, the taxpayer's use of its NOLs thereafter is limited to an annual amount (the "annual limitation amount") equal to the product of (i) the federal long-term tax-exempt rate in effect at the time of the ownership change (currently approximately 7.5%) times (ii) the fair market value of the stock immediately prior to the ownership change. However, if the ownership change occurs as a result of an exchange of stock for debt in a bankruptcy proceeding, the annual limitation amount is increased to reflect any increase in the value of the stock which is attributable to any surrender or cancellation of creditor's claims in exchange for stock, pursuant to Section 382(1)(6) of the Tax Code (the "special insolvency limitation"). The special insolvency limitation thus reflects any increase in value of the stock attributable to debt cancellation in the bankruptcy reorganization. For example, if the value of a corporation's stock before its reorganization is $200 and the value of its stock increases to $1,000 after its reorganization as a result of the surrender of its creditors' claims for stock in the reorganization, the use of NOLs will be limited to $75 ($1,000 × 7.5%) using the annual limitation amount. It is estimated that there is no value in the Company's stock before reorganization under the Committee's Plan, and that the value of the stock immediately subsequent to the reorganization may be $50,000,000, which is the midpoint of the range identified in HLHZ's preliminary opinion of value. No assurance can be given that the value of the stock for Section 382 purposes will be determined to be $50 million, and a higher or lower value may ultimately apply. In the event the value is less than $50 million, the utilization of the NOL would be reduced in accordance with the foregoing formula.

Section 382(1)(5) of the Tax Code provides an alternative to the special insolvency limitation for a corporation in a bankruptcy proceeding if two requirements are met (the "bankruptcy alternative"). First, any ownership change must occur as part of a plan of reorganization approved by the court during that bankruptcy proceeding. Second, persons who were shareholders or creditors of the corporation immediately before the ownership change must own, immediately after the ownership change as a result of the ownership of their prior interests, stock which has at least 50% of the total voting power and 50% of the total value of all of the stock. For purposes of this 50% ownership test, stock transferred to a creditor in satisfaction of indebtedness is only taken into account if such indebtedness was either held by the creditor for at least 18 months prior to the filing of the bankruptcy proceeding or arose in the ordinary course of the trade or business. Such indebtedness will be referred to as "qualifying indebt-

**Exhibit 5-4    Sample Disclosure Statement by Creditors**              **167**

edness." Since a substantial portion of the new common stock will be distributed under the Committee's Plan to those who hold publicly traded debt, there is a significant doubt that that Committee can demonstrate that it can satisfy the requirements of Section 382(b)(5).

If a corporation meets the foregoing requirements, neither the annual limitation amount nor the special insolvency limitation will apply to limit the amount of annual income which can be offset by NOLs. Instead, the corporation's NOLs will be reduced by (a) the interest paid or accrued by the corporation during the current taxable year prior to the ownership change and in the three preceding taxable years on that portion of the indebtedness with respect to which stock is issued under the plan (the "interest reduction") and (b) one-half of the excess of the amount of debt discharged in the bankruptcy reorganization over the fair market value of the stock exchanged therefor. Furthermore, if a second ownership change occurs within two years after the use of the bankruptcy alternative, all of the NOLs will be eliminated for periods subsequent to the second ownership change.

## 2. Discharge of Indebtedness

As a result of the Plan, the Allowed Claims of Class 8 and Class 11 debtholders will be settled in exchange for cash, but Class 11 holders have the option to receive one share of new common stock for each $10 of such holder's Allowed Claim. It is probable that the IRS will treat the Company as if it settled the claim for cash at an amount less than the full amount of the claim and in turn purchased the shares for cash. As a general rule when debt is discharged in a bankruptcy proceeding in exchange for cash or other property having a value less than the face amount of the debt discharged, the debtor's NOLs are reduced by the amount of such difference (the "debt discharge rule"). However, in the case of Class 13 and 14 debtholders who receive only new common stock for each $10 of the Allowed Claim in exchange for the debt discharged, the debt discharge rule does not apply, even though the stock has a fair market value less than the face amount of the debt discharged. In such a case the debtor does not sustain a reduction in its NOLs. This concept is commonly referred to as the "stock-for-debt exception" to the debt discharge rule. In order to qualify for the stock-for-debt exception, the stock transferred to creditors must not be considered "de minimis" within the meaning of Section 108(e)(8) of the Tax Code. This section generally defines a "de minimis" case as one where nominal or token shares are issued.

The Committee believes that the New Common Stock to be issued under the Plan should not be considered as nominal or token. Therefore, the Company should sustain no reduction of its NOLs with respect to the Allowed Claims of the Class 13 and 14 creditors exchanged for New Common Stock. The Company will sustain a reduction of its tax attributes where debts are satisfied only for cash (or considered to be satisfied only for cash) at less than face value without any stock being issued as in the case of Class 8 and 11 claims. However, Section 108(e)(2) of the Tax Code provides that there will be no reduction of

NOLs if the payment of the liability discharged would have given rise to a deduction for federal income tax purposes such as a purchase of office supplies with less than one year's useful life. Under the Committee's Plan the number and amount of claims in Class 8 and 11 claims have not yet been estimated but it does not appear to represent a significant amount in relation to the overall amount of debt being restructured or the amount of NOL being preserved.

### 3. Alternative Minimum Tax

The Tax Reform Act of 1986 added an alternative minimum tax applicable to corporations which replaces the "add on" corporate minimum tax. The tax equals 20% of the corporation's alternative minimum taxable income ("AMTI") in excess of a $40,000 exemption (which is phased out at higher income levels) and is payable only to the extent it exceeds the corporation's regular federal income tax liability. Because certain deductions in determining a corporation's taxable income are added back and other adjustments are made in calculating AMTI, it is quite possible for a corporation to have no taxable income or even a loss and still owe an alternative minimum tax. AMTI is computed by modifying the corporation's taxable income for certain adjustments and preferences. One adjustment which will increase the Company's liability for the alternative minimum tax is the limitation on the use of NOLs in computing AMTI.

A corporation may use its NOLs in calculating its regular taxable income and its AMTI. However, the NOLs that are allowable against AMTI may not exceed 90% of AMTI, so that a corporation's AMTI can never be reduced solely through use of its NOLs. As a result, the Company would be liable for an alternative minimum tax even if its taxable income in a year is less than the available NOLs, so that it has no regular taxable income. For example, if the Company earns taxable income in 1990 of $10 million and has an allowable net operating loss carryover equal to at least $10 million, its taxable income would be zero. However, assuming no other adjustments, its AMTI would be $1 million and its alternative minimum tax liability would be $200,000 because only 90% of AMTI can be offset by NOLs.

### 4. Consolidated Federal Income Tax Return Issues

The ability of the Company to use its NOLs in future years may be affected by the Treasury Department Regulations governing the filing of consolidated federal income tax returns. The major limitations are the separate return limitations year rules (the "SRLY Rules") and the consolidated return change of ownership rules (the "CRCO Rules"). Neither of these rules will completely eliminate the NOLs. If the SRLY rules apply, a net operating loss can be used only to offset the income of the entity which incurred the loss and cannot offset the income of other companies in the affiliated group. If the CRCO Rules apply, the losses of the members of an affiliated group cannot be used to offset income of any corporation which becomes a member of the group after the year in which the loss was incurred.

The CRCO Rules should apply to the Company because there likely will be

**Exhibit 5-4    Sample Disclosure Statement by Creditors**                    **169**

a change in the ownership of the Debtor's stock (as defined in the consolidated return Treasury Regulations). Thus, if the Company's consolidated group acquires a profitable new member of the group, the income of such member could not be offset by the current affiliated group's NOLs. Moreover, the SRLY Rules should apply to the Debtor's bankruptcy reorganization. Accordingly, each of the Debtor's subsidiaries that remains in existence following the reorganization will only be able to use its NOLs to offset its own income and not to offset the income of other subsidiaries of the Company's consolidated group. Since the losses are almost entirely at the parent level, as a practical matter the SRLY Rules should not have negative tax consequences unless the company acquires or is acquired by an outside corporation or changes its line of business. Although the Committee's business plan does not contemplate the reorganized Debtor acquiring or being acquired by another corporation or changing its line of business during the 1989–95 period, the Committee has not ruled out this possibility.

### 5. *Tax Reorganization*

Under the Plan, the holders of unsecured debt (excluding ordinary trade debt) and Public Debt will exchange their Allowed Claims for shares of New Common. Trade creditors of the Company will exchange their Allowed Claims for cash or be considered to do so. If any Allowed Claims constitute "securities" for federal income tax purposes ("tax securities"), exchange of such tax securities should qualify as a recapitalization of Care Enterprises, Inc. under Section 368(a)(1)(E) of the Tax Code. Under Section 1032 of the Tax Code, the Company should recognize no gain or loss on the issuance of its New Common in the bankruptcy reorganization.

**Exhibit "2"**    Care Enterprises
Liquidation Analysis
Gross Proceeds ($ 000's)

| Current Assets | Forced Liquidation Value | Orderly Liquidation Value |
|---|---|---|
| Cash | $ 2,500 | $ 2,500 |
| Accounts Receivable/Net | | |
|   Facility Receivables | 11,000 | 11,000 |
|   HCN Receivables | N/A | N/A |
|   Government Program | | |
|     Receivables | 4,200 | 6,200 |
| Inventory | | |
|   Facility Inventory | N/A | N/A |
|   HCN Inventory | N/A | N/A |
| Prepaid Assets | 3,600 | 3,600 |
| Notes Receivable | 1,000 | 1,000 |
| Refundable Taxes | 600 | 600 |
| TOTAL CURRENT ASSETS | $ 22,900 | $ 24,900 |
| | | |
| *Other Assets* | | |
| Property and Equipment/Net | | |
|   LTC Facilities | $ 72,300 | $101,200 |
|   HCN | 8,100 | 9,600 |
|   Misc. Equipment | 500 | 500 |
| Mortgage Notes Receivable | 8,600 | 8,600 |
| Other Assets | 1,900 | 1,900 |
| Restricted Funds | 3,700 | 3,700 |
| Excess of Costs Over Net | | |
|   Assets Acquired | 0 | 0 |
| TOTAL OTHER ASSETS | $ 95,100 | $125,500 |
| TOTAL ESTIMATED | | |
|   GROSS PROCEEDS | $118,000 | $150,400 |

**Exhibit 5-4   Sample Disclosure Statement by Creditors**     **171**

**Exhibit "2"**   Care Enterprises
Liquidation Analysis
Net Proceeds ($ 000's)

| Current Assets | Forced Liquidation Value | Orderly Liquidation Value |
|---|---|---|
| Total Estimated Gross Proceeds | $118,000 | $150,400 |
| Chapter 7 Administrative Expenses | | |
| Legal and Accounting | (3,000) | (6,000) |
| Transaction Costs | (3,000) | (3,000) |
| Trustee's Fees | (3,500) | (3,000) |
| General Administration | (7,500) | (4,600) |
| | | (15,000) |
| Chapter 7 Administrative Expenses | (5,000) | (5,000) |
| Estimated Proceeds Available for Claims | $ 96,000 | $116,800 |
| Estimated Priority Claims | | |
| Wages/Benefits | (1,500) | (1,500) |
| Taxes | (1,500) | (1,500) |
| Estimated Proceeds Available for Secured and Unsecured Claims | $ 93,000 | $113,800 |
| Secured Liabilities at 12/31/87 | 88,000 | 88,000 |
| Unsecured Liabilities at 12/31/87 | 161,000 | 161,000 |

**Exhibit "3"**

---

The Official Creditors' Committee of
Care Enterprises, Inc.

At your request, we have performed the agreed-upon procedures enumerated below, to the projected consolidated financial statements of Care Enterprises, Inc., Debtor in Possession ("Care") as prepared by Care in connection with and included in Care's Amended Joint Disclosure Statement dated March 17, 1989 ("Care's Amended Disclosure Statement") filed with the United States Bankruptcy Court. The projected financial statements include projected consolidated balance sheets as at December 31, 1988, 1989, 1990, 1991, 1992, 1993, 1994 and 1995 and projected consolidated income statements and projected consolidated cash flows for the years ended December 31, 1989, 1990, 1991, 1992, 1993, 1994 and 1995. It is understood that this report and the projected consolidated financial statements accompanying this report are solely for your information to assist you in effectuating a Plan of Reorganization ("Creditors' Plan") to be filed with the United States Bankruptcy Court and not for any other purpose.

Our procedures were as follows:

1. We obtained and read the projected consolidated financial statements included in Care's Amended Disclosure Statement as discussed above.
2. We applied adjustments to Care's projected consolidated financial statements resulting from differences between (i) assumptions used in the projected consolidated financial statements included in Care's Amended Disclosure Statement and (ii) assumptions used in the accompanying projected consolidated financial statements.
3. We applied the pro forma adjustments reflecting the Creditors' Plan to the December 31, 1988 year end projected balance sheet.
4. We assembled (i) the accompanying projected consolidated financial statements utilizing the financial model used by Care and provided to us and (ii) the pro forma 1988 year end balance sheet.

Because the procedures described above do not constitute an examination of the projected consolidated financial statements in accordance with standards established by the American Institute of Certified Public Accountants ("AICPA"), pursuant to the standards set forth in Statement on Standards for Accountants' Services on Prospective Financial Information issued by the AICPA, we do not express an opinion on whether the projected consolidated financial statements are presented in conformity with AICPA presentation guidelines or on whether the underlying assumptions provide a reasonable basis for the presentation.

Had we performed additional procedures or had we made an examination of the projected consolidated financial statements in accordance with standards estab-

**Exhibit 5-4    Sample Disclosure Statement by Creditors**                173

lished by the AICPA, matters might have come to our attention that would have been reported to you. Furthermore, there will usually be differences between forecasted and actual results, because events and circumstances frequently do not occur as expected, and those differences may be material. We have no responsibility to update this report for events and circumstances occurring after the date of this report.

ERNST & WHINNEY

Century City
Los Angeles, California
April 14, 1989


CARE ENTERPRISES, INC.

DIFFERENCES BETWEEN (i) ASSUMPTIONS USED IN THE ACCOMPANYING PROJECTED CONSOLIDATED FINANCIAL STATEMENTS AND (ii) ASSUMPTIONS USED IN PROJECTED CONSOLIDATED FINANCIAL STATEMENTS FOUND IN CARE'S AMENDED DISCLOSURE STATEMENT

APPENDIX A

| Assumptions Used in Care's Amended Disclosure Statements | Assumptions Used in the Accompanying Projected Consolidated Financial Statements |
| --- | --- |
| *Occupancy Levels*<br>With certain specified exceptions, future facility occupancy levels are projected to be the same as May 31, 1988 year-to-day levels. | Projected occupancy levels for some facilities are changed from those used in Care's Amended Disclosure Statement to reflect changes in occupancy levels experienced subsequent to May 31, 1988. |
| *Medi-Cal Catch-Up*<br>In 1989 and 1990, Medi-Cal reimbursement increases are assumed to be 1% greater than inflation, i.e., are assumed to increase from 1988 levels by 7.7% in 1989 and 8.2% in 1990. In 1991, Medi-Cal reimbursement is assumed to 4% greater than inflation. In years thereafter, Medi-Cal reimbursement increases are assumed to equal the rate of inflation. | In 1989, Medi-Cal reimbursement rates are assumed to increase 5% from their 1988 levels. In 1990 and years thereafter, Medi-Cal reimbursement rates are projected to increase by amounts equal to the general rate of inflation. |

*Private Pay Census Shift*
The rate increases and cost cuts assumed in Care's Amended Disclosure Statement will have no effect on the facilities' private pay census.

For each year of the 1989–1995 projection period, Care facilities will experience a shift in payor mix from private pay to Medicaid of 5% of private pay levels assumed in Care's Amended Disclosure Statement.

*Ripple Effect*
The implementation of the new California minimum wage is not assumed to have a "ripple" effect (i.e., it will not result in salary increases for any class of workers other than those directly affected).

Implementation of the minimum wage is estimated to have the effect of raising the salaries of 15% of Care's California workforce by 5% in 1989.

*Impact of Catastrophic Health Legislation*
Medicare patient days are projected to increase as of 1989 based on Care's review of the impact of the passage of the Medicare Catastrophic Coverage Act of 1988 (the "Act") included in Care's January 1989 document "Care Enterprises - Analysis of Catastrophic Health Legislation" included as Exhibit "1" in the Care's Amended Disclosure Statement.

All assumptions are as detailed in Care's December 1988 document, "Care Enterprises - Analysis of Catastrophic Health Legislation" included elsewhere in this disclosure statement. The projected consolidated financial statements of Care included in Care's Amended Disclosure Statement reflect subsequent revisions to such assumptions which revisions resulted in increases in projected revenues. Such revisions have not been incorporated in the accompanying projected consolidated financial statements.

*Nursing Costs*
Care will achieve its targeted nursing cost reductions by June 30, 1989 and will maintain these levels in subsequent years.

Nursing costs will exceed targeted levels by 3.4%, the same percentage by which actual December 1988 nursing costs exceed levels targeted by Care.

*Decertification Contingency*
The cost of curing threatened decertification actions ranging from $800,000 to $1,100,000 is assumed.

The cost of curing decertification actions are assumed to be greater than Care's assumptions by $200,000 each year.

**Exhibit 5-4    Sample Disclosure Statement by Creditors**                    **175**

*Interest on Cash Balances*
Interest is calculated on outstanding cash balances at interest rates of 7% to 16%.

Interest on outstanding cash balances is calculated at 7%.

*Terms of Reorganization Plan*
*Bank Debt*
All bank debt is assumed to be paid over over the course of the three year period from 1989 to 1991.

A new note of $37,200,000 will be issued. Such amount is subject to change based upon the actual amount of accrued interest and certain fees through the effective date. The terms of the note are as follows:

(i)   A $10 million principal payment within 120 days of the confirmation date.

(ii)  Interest payable monthly at prime plus 2%. Prime rate assumed to be 11.5%.

(iii) Quarterly principal payments (less interest component) beginning March 31, 1990 as follows:

March 31, 1990—$1.5 million

June 30 and September 30, 1990—$2.5 million per quarter

December 31, 1990—$3.5 million

March 31, 1991 through September 1992—$3.5 million per quarter

December 31, 1992—remaining unpaid balance

(iv)  Beginning March 31, 1990, quarterly payments equal to excess net operating cash, as defined, payable 60 to 120 days after the end of each quarter.

(v)   Estimated bank fees of $300,000 paid annually in advance for Agents' and letter of credit fees.

In addition, an estimated payment of $350,000 to cover outstanding letter of credit fees, outstanding Agent fees and other miscellaneous fees are paid within 120 days of the confirmation date.

*Bank Letter of Credit*

A non-cash collateralized letter of credit will be issued to cover workers' compensation claims at a fee of $82,000 in 1989 and $110,000 in the years 1990–1995.

A non-cash collateralized letter of credit will be issued to cover workers' compensation claims. Letter of credit expires March 31, 1993. Fee included in (v) above.

*Trade Debt*

All trade debt will be paid over the course of the three-year period from 1989 to 1991.

A maximum of $3 million in "true trade debt" (as defined in the Creditors' Plan) will be paid at a rate of $.50 per $1.00 of value. A $1.5 million fund will be available to pay these trade claims. Remaining trade debt will be converted to equity.

*Bondholder Debt*

All bondholder debt will be paid over the course of the seven-year period from 1989 to 1995.

All bondholder debt will be converted to equity.

*Additional Financing*

Additional mortgage debt incurred. The cash flow and interest expense on such new mortgage debt is reflected in all financial statements for the years 1990 to 1995.

Debt financing in the amount of $10 million is obtained within 120 days of the confirmation date. Certain assets of the Company are pledged as security for such debt. To the extent that cash proceeds are received from sales of assets in excess of those amounts assumed in Care's Amended Disclosure Statement, the need for such additional financing would be reduced.

*Income Taxes*

Net operating losses (NOL) carried forward for tax computation purposes are not assumed to be subject to limitation.

The special insolvency limitation for the utilization of net operating loss ("NOL") carryovers which is available under § 382(1)(6) of the Internal Revenue Code is used.

Consolidated Balance Sheet
($ in Thousands)

| Assets | 1988 Year-End Projected (1) | 1989 | 1990 | 1991 | 1992 | 1993 | 1994 | 1995 |
|---|---|---|---|---|---|---|---|---|
| Current | | | | | | | | |
| Cash | $ (500) | $ 4,591 | $ 5,286 | $ 1,624 | $ 1,584 | $ 12,544 | $ 25,187 | $ 38,443 |
| Accounts Receivable, Open Facilities | 22,915 | 24,037 | 25,358 | 26,993 | 28,670 | 30,156 | 31,757 | 33,443 |
| Accounts Receivable, Eliminated Facilities | 8,706 | 3,902 | 59 | 0 | 0 | 0 | 0 | 0 |
| Inventory, Open Facilities | 3,181 | 3,340 | 3,527 | 3,714 | 3,911 | 4,118 | 4,336 | 4,566 |
| Inventory, Eliminated Facilities | 587 | 141 | 0 | 0 | 0 | 0 | 0 | 0 |
| Prepaids | | | | | | | | |
| Normal Course of Business, Open Facilities | 2,065 | 2,168 | 2,290 | 2,411 | 2,539 | 2,673 | 2,815 | 2,964 |
| Normal Course of Business, Eliminated Facil. | 79 | 12 | 0 | 0 | 0 | 0 | 0 | 0 |
| Bankruptcy Related & Refundable | 1,800 | 1,600 | 1,600 | 0 | 0 | 0 | 0 | 0 |
| Subtotal Prepaids | 3,944 | 3,780 | 3,890 | 2,411 | 2,539 | 2,673 | 2,815 | 2,964 |
| Notes Receivable | 245 | 269 | 294 | 315 | 346 | 380 | 417 | 457 |
| Receivables from Prior Owner of Americare | 100 | 100 | 100 | 100 | 100 | 100 | 100 | 100 |
| Total Current Assets | 39,177 | 40,160 | 38,512 | 35,157 | 37,149 | 49,971 | 64,611 | 79,972 |
| Property, Plant & Equipment, Net—Open | 101,215 | 96,163 | 92,039 | 88,681 | 86,135 | 83,876 | 81,884 | 80,881 |
| Property, Plant & Equipment, Net—Eliminated | 19,008 | 2,625 | 20 | 20 | 20 | 20 | 20 | 20 |
| Mortgage Notes Receivable | 11,998 | 11,729 | 11,436 | 11,120 | 10,774 | 10,395 | 9,978 | 9,521 |
| Other Assets—Open Facilities | 7,853 | 7,853 | 7,853 | 7,853 | 7,853 | 7,853 | 7,853 | 7,853 |
| Other Assets—Eliminated Facilities | 518 | 227 | 0 | 0 | 0 | 0 | 0 | 0 |
| Restricted Funds—Open Facilities | 4,086 | 4,351 | 4,616 | 4,881 | 5,146 | 5,411 | 5,676 | 5,941 |
| Excess of Cost Over Net Assets Acquired—Open | 3,738 | 3,645 | 3,551 | 3,458 | 3,364 | 3,271 | 3,177 | 3,084 |
| Excess of Cost Over Net Assets Acquired—Elim. | 3,380 | 1,591 | 0 | 0 | 0 | 0 | 0 | 0 |
| Total Assets | $190,972 | $168,343 | $158,026 | $151,169 | $150,441 | $160,796 | $173,199 | $187,272 |

(1)Assumed confirmation date of January 1, 1989. Actual confirmation date would most likely be in the third quarter of fiscal year 1989.

Care Enterprises
Consolidated Balance Sheet
($ in Thousands)

| Liabilities | 1988 Year-End Projected (1) | 1989 | 1990 | 1991 | 1992 | 1993 | 1994 | 1995 |
|---|---|---|---|---|---|---|---|---|
| Current Liabilities Excluding Reorganized Debt & New Mortgages | | | | | | | | |
| Accounts Payable, Open Facilities | $ 7,336 | $ 7,703 | $ 8,134 | $ 8,565 | $ 9,019 | $ 9,497 | $ 10,001 | $ 10,531 |
| Accounts Payable, Eliminated Facilities | 1,587 | 246 | 0 | 0 | 0 | 0 | 0 | 0 |
| Accrued Liabilities | | | | | | | | |
| Normal Course of Business—Open Facilities | 16,265 | 16,265 | 16,265 | 16,265 | 16,265 | 16,265 | 16,265 | 16,265 |
| Normal Course of Business—Eliminated Facil. | 519 | 114 | 0 | 0 | 0 | 0 | 0 | 0 |
| Workmens Comp. | 4,800 | 4,701 | 4,508 | 4,307 | 4,106 | 3,905 | 3,803 | 3,795 |
| Reserve for Discontinued Operations | 1,700 | 1,047 | 494 | 46 | 0 | 0 | 0 | 0 |
| Contingency Reserve | 1,200 | 580 | 580 | 580 | 580 | 580 | 580 | 580 |
| Accrued Consulting Fees | 280 | 280 | 280 | 280 | 280 | 280 | 280 | 280 |
| Subtotal Accrued Liabilities | 24,764 | 22,987 | 22,127 | 21,478 | 21,231 | 21,030 | 20,928 | 20,920 |
| Current Portion of Long Term Debt—Open | 1,727 | 1,686 | 1,730 | 2,334 | 2,012 | 2,192 | 2,379 | 2,475 |
| Current Portion of Long Term Debt—Eliminated | 100 | 100 | 125 | 125 | 125 | 111 | 105 | 100 |

| | | | | | | | | |
|---|---|---|---|---|---|---|---|---|
| Total Current Liabilities Excl. Reorg. Debt | 35,514 | 32,722 | 32,116 | 32,502 | 32,387 | 32,830 | 33,412 | 34,025 |
| Long Term Debt (Facilities)—Open | 54,493 | 52,807 | 51,077 | 48,743 | 46,731 | 44,539 | 42,160 | 39,685 |
| Long Term Debt (Facilities)—Eliminated | 6,694 | 1,191 | 1,042 | 917 | 792 | 681 | 576 | 476 |
| Deferred Income Taxes | 2,500 | 2,500 | 2,500 | 2,500 | 2,500 | 2,500 | 2,500 | 2,500 |
| Other Liabilities | | | | | | | | |
| L.T. Workmens Comp | 4,600 | 4,501 | 4,308 | 4,107 | 3,906 | 3,705 | 3,603 | 3,595 |
| Bankruptcy Reserves | 6,394 | 0 | 0 | 0 | 0 | 0 | 0 | 0 |
| Litigation Reserves | 8,116 | 7,616 | 7,616 | 7,616 | 7,616 | 7,616 | 7,616 | 7,616 |
| Other Adjustments | 200 | 200 | 200 | 200 | 200 | 200 | 200 | 200 |
| Subtotal Other Liabilities | 19,310 | 12,317 | 12,124 | 11,923 | 11,722 | 11,521 | 11,419 | 11,411 |
| Reorganization Debt | | | | | | | | |
| Bondholder Debt | 0 | 0 | 0 | 0 | 0 | 0 | 0 | 0 |
| Subordinated Unsecured Promissory Notes | 0 | 0 | 0 | 0 | 0 | 0 | 0 | 0 |
| Preferred Stock | 0 | 0 | 0 | 0 | 0 | 0 | 0 | 0 |
| Notes Payable, Citicorp & Wells | 27,200 | 27,200 | 20,872 | 9,690 | 0 | 0 | 0 | 0 |
| Convenience Claims | 0 | 0 | 0 | 0 | 0 | 0 | 0 | 0 |
| Trade Payables | 0 | 0 | 0 | 0 | 0 | 0 | 0 | 0 |
| Accrued Interest Not Paid—Bank Debt | 0 | 0 | 0 | 0 | 0 | 0 | 0 | 0 |
| Accrued Interest Not Paid—Bonds | 0 | 0 | 0 | 0 | 0 | 0 | 0 | 0 |
| Additional Financing | 10,000 | 10,000 | 7,500 | 5,000 | 2,500 | 0 | 0 | 0 |
| Equity | 35,261 | 29,607 | 30,796 | 39,895 | 53,810 | 68,726 | 83,132 | 99,175 |
| Total Liabilities and Equity | $190,972 | $168,343 | $158,026 | $151,169 | $150,441 | $160,796 | $173,199 | $187,272 |

(1) Assumed confirmation date of January 1, 1989. Actual confirmation date would most likely be in the third quarter of fiscal year 1989.

179

Care Enterprises
Consolidated Income Statement
($ in thousands)

| | 1989 | 1990 | 1991 | 1992 | 1993 | 1994 | 1995 |
|---|---|---|---|---|---|---|---|
| Medicare Revenues | $ 11,683 | $ 10,883 | $ 11,503 | $ 12,119 | $ 12,768 | $ 13,452 | $ 14,174 |
| Medicaid Revenues | 109,336 | 97,900 | 102,215 | 110,177 | 116,126 | 122,396 | 129,006 |
| Private Revenues | 49,462 | 49,476 | 53,202 | 56,074 | 59,102 | 62,293 | 65,656 |
| Veteran Revenues | 1,558 | 1,470 | 1,546 | 1,630 | 1,718 | 1,810 | 1,908 |
| HMO Revenues | 3,887 | 3,940 | 4,076 | 4,186 | 4,299 | 4,415 | 4,534 |
| Ancillary Revenues | 48,482 | 48,967 | 51,729 | 54,424 | 57,259 | 60,242 | 63,379 |
| Other Revenues | 8,291 | 8,259 | 8,430 | 8,543 | 8,699 | 9,158 | 9,641 |
| Revenues | 232,699 | 220,895 | 232,701 | 247,152 | 259,970 | 273,766 | 288,299 |
| Nursing | 62,061 | 58,179 | 63,180 | 66,566 | 70,133 | 73,892 | 77,851 |
| Building Expenses | 3,911 | 3,460 | 3,568 | 3,757 | 3,957 | 4,166 | 4,387 |
| Utilities | 5,010 | 4,611 | 4,776 | 5,020 | 5,275 | 5,545 | 5,827 |
| Housekeeping | 5,493 | 4,887 | 5,052 | 5,335 | 5,633 | 5,948 | 6,282 |
| Laundry Expenses | 3,359 | 2,992 | 3,096 | 3,269 | 3,452 | 3,645 | 3,850 |
| Dietary Expenses | 8,999 | 8,078 | 8,389 | 8,858 | 9,353 | 9,876 | 10,428 |
| Food Expenses | 7,216 | 6,440 | 6,581 | 6,831 | 7,091 | 7,360 | 7,640 |
| Patient Activity Expenses | 2,070 | 1,795 | 1,830 | 1,933 | 2,041 | 2,155 | 2,276 |
| Social Service Expenses | 1,098 | 996 | 1,041 | 1,099 | 1,161 | 1,225 | 1,295 |
| Education Expenses | 2,111 | 1,843 | 1,910 | 2,016 | 2,130 | 2,248 | 2,375 |
| Ancillary Expenses | 33,747 | 33,157 | 34,664 | 36,459 | 38,346 | 40,332 | 42,420 |
| Employee Benefits | 24,340 | 22,703 | 23,462 | 24,657 | 25,914 | 27,234 | 28,620 |
| Administrative Expenses | 23,254 | 21,767 | 22,684 | 23,928 | 25,242 | 26,628 | 28,089 |
| Direct Expenses | 182,669 | 170,908 | 180,234 | 189,729 | 199,727 | 210,255 | 221,340 |
| Cost Reductions to be Realized | 712 | N.A. | N.A. | N.A. | N.A. | N.A. | N.A. |
| Gross Profit | 49,318 | 49,988 | 52,467 | 57,423 | 60,243 | 63,511 | 66,959 |

| | | | | | | | |
|---|--:|--:|--:|--:|--:|--:|--:|
| Rent Expense | 7,512 | 6,486 | 6,541 | 6,707 | 6,874 | 7,052 | 7,253 |
| Other Indirect Expense | 4,615 | 4,181 | 4,429 | 4,663 | 4,910 | 5,169 | 5,442 |
| Corporate Expenses | 12,733 | 12,668 | 13,011 | 13,714 | 14,455 | 15,236 | 16,058 |
| SG&A Expense | 24,860 | 23,335 | 23,981 | 25,084 | 26,238 | 27,457 | 28,754 |
| Depreciation Expense | 8,587 | 7,607 | 7,354 | 7,261 | 7,209 | 7,188 | 6,460 |
| Operating Profit | 15,870 | 19,046 | 21,132 | 25,078 | 26,795 | 28,867 | 31,745 |
| Interest Expense (Facilities) | 5,620 | 5,215 | 5,096 | 4,970 | 4,831 | 4,675 | 4,474 |
| Interest Expense—Bank Debt | 3,672 | 3,672 | 2,818 | 1,308 | 0 | 0 | 0 |
| Interest Expense—Trade Credit | 0 | 0 | 0 | 0 | 0 | 0 | 0 |
| Loan Fees | 850 | 300 | 300 | 300 | 75 | 0 | 0 |
| Interest Expense—Add. Financing | 1,550 | 1,550 | 1,163 | 775 | 388 | 0 | 0 |
| Interest Income (Notes Recvbl.) | 1,199 | 1,175 | 1,149 | 1,120 | 1,090 | 1,056 | 1,019 |
| Interest Income—Cash Reserves | (35) | 321 | 370 | 114 | 111 | 878 | 1,763 |
| HCN, Facility Duplicate Profit | 2,600 | 2,800 | 2,900 | 3,100 | 3,200 | 3,400 | 3,600 |
| Decertification Contingency | 1,000 | 1,000 | 1,100 | 1,100 | 1,200 | 1,200 | 1,300 |
| Gain/(Loss) on Sale of Facilities | (6,845) | (4,333) | 0 | 0 | 0 | 0 | 0 |
| Cont. Losses at Closed Fclts. | 0 | 0 | 0 | 0 | 0 | 0 | 0 |
| A/R Writeoffs at Closed Facilities | 368 | 271 | 451 | 451 | 438 | 433 | 430 |
| Recapture of Unused Reserves | 0 | 0 | 0 | 0 | 0 | 0 | 0 |
| Amortization of Goodwill | 94 | 94 | 94 | 94 | 94 | 94 | 94 |
| Earnings Before Taxes | (5,564) | 1,308 | 9,181 | 14,214 | 17,771 | 20,999 | 24,630 |
| Income Taxes | 90 | 119 | 82 | 299 | 2,855 | 6,593 | 8,587 |
| Net After Tax Income | $ (5,654) | $ 1,189 | $ 9,099 | $ 13,915 | $ 14,916 | $ 14,406 | $ 16,043 |

Care Enterprises
Consolidated Cash Flow
($ in Thousands)

| | 1989 | 1990 | 1991 | 1992 | 1993 | 1994 | 1995 |
|---|---|---|---|---|---|---|---|
| Revenues | $232,699 | $220,895 | $232,701 | $247,152 | $259,970 | $273,766 | $288,299 |
| Operating and G&A Expenses | (208,241) | (194,242) | (204,215) | (214,813) | (225,966) | (237,712) | (250,094) |
| HCN-Facilities Duplicate Profit | (2,600) | (2,800) | (2,900) | (3,100) | (3,200) | (3,400) | (3,600) |
| Facility Interest Expense | (5,620) | (5,215) | (5,096) | (4,970) | (4,831) | (4,675) | (4,474) |
| Change in Restricted Funds | (265) | (265) | (265) | (265) | (265) | (265) | (265) |
| Decertification Contingency | (1,000) | (1,000) | (1,100) | (1,100) | (1,200) | (1,200) | (1,300) |
| Cash Operating Income | 14,972 | 17,373 | 19,125 | 22,904 | 24,509 | 26,515 | 28,566 |
| | | | | | | | |
| Change in Accounts Receivable | (1,123) | (1,320) | (1,636) | (1,676) | (1,487) | (1,600) | (1,686) |
| Change in Inventory | (159) | (187) | (187) | (197) | (207) | (218) | (230) |
| Change in Accounts Payable | 367 | 431 | 431 | 454 | 478 | 503 | 530 |
| Change in Prepaid Expenses | (103) | (121) | (121) | (128) | (135) | (142) | (149) |
| Change in Accrued Liabilities | 0 | 0 | 0 | 0 | 0 | 0 | 0 |
| Subtotal Change in Working Capital | (1,018) | (1,197) | (1,513) | (1,547) | (1,351) | (1,457) | (1,535) |
| Cash after Operations | 13,954 | 16,176 | 17,612 | 21,357 | 23,158 | 25,058 | 27,031 |
| | | | | | | | |
| Change in Prepaid Expenses (Non-Operating) | 200 | 0 | 1,600 | 0 | 0 | 0 | 0 |
| Change in Accrued Liabilities (Non-Operating) | (719) | (193) | (201) | (201) | (201) | (102) | (8) |

| | | | | | | | |
|---|---|---|---|---|---|---|---|
| Change in Other Liabilities | (6,993) | (193) | (201) | (201) | (201) | (102) | (8) |
| Change in Reserve for Discontinued Operations | (653) | (553) | (448) | (46) | 0 | 0 | 0 |
| Cont. Losses at Closed Facil. after Reserves | 0 | 0 | 0 | (451) | (438) | (433) | (430) |
| Gain/(Loss) on Sale of Facilities | (6,845) | (4,333) | 0 | 0 | 0 | 0 | 0 |
| Receivables Writeoff at Eliminated Facilities | (368) | (271) | 0 | 0 | 0 | 0 | 0 |
| Change in Working Capital—Eliminated Facilities | 3,571 | 3,636 | 59 | 0 | 0 | 0 | 0 |
| Change in Long Term Debt (Facilities)—Eliminated | (5,503) | (124) | (125) | (125) | (125) | (111) | (105) |
| Recapture of Unused Reserves | 0 | 0 | 0 | 0 | 0 | 0 | 0 |
| Interest Income | 1,164 | 1,496 | 1,519 | 1,234 | 1,201 | 1,934 | 2,782 |
| Net Book Value of Prop. & Equip. Retired or Sold | 18,172 | 4,196 | 0 | 0 | 0 | 0 | 0 |
| Book Value of Other Assets Retired or Sold | 291 | 227 | 0 | 0 | 0 | 0 | 0 |
| Capital Spending | (3,535) | (3,483) | (3,996) | (4,715) | (4,950) | (5,196) | (5,457) |
| Cash after Capital Spending/Asset Disposition/Extraordinary Items | 12,735 | 16,581 | 15,819 | 16,851 | 18,443 | 21,048 | 23,805 |
| Tax Expense | (90) | (119) | (82) | (299) | (2,855) | (6,593) | (8,587) |
| Change in Deferred Income Taxes | 0 | 0 | 0 | 0 | 0 | 0 | 0 |
| Cash after Taxes | 12,645 | 16,462 | 15,737 | 16,552 | 15,588 | 14,455 | 15,218 |
| Change in Notes Receivable | (24) | (25) | (22) | (31) | (34) | (37) | (40) |
| Change in Rcvbl. from Prior Americare Owner | 0 | 0 | 0 | 0 | 0 | 0 | 0 |
| Change in Mortgage Notes Receivable | 269 | 294 | 315 | 346 | 380 | 417 | 457 |

## Consolidated Cash Flow (*continued*)

| | 1989 | 1990 | 1991 | 1992 | 1993 | 1994 | 1995 |
|---|---|---|---|---|---|---|---|
| Cash Available for Interest Payments and Principal Reductions | 12,890 | 16,731 | 16,030 | 16,868 | 15,934 | 14,835 | 15,635 |
| Change in Long Term Debt (Facilities)—Open | (1,727) | (1,686) | (1,730) | (2,334) | (2,012) | (2,192) | (2,379) |
| Additional Financing | 0 | (2,500) | (2,500) | (2,500) | (2,500) | 0 | 0 |
| Interest Expense—Additional Financing | (1,550) | (1,550) | (1,163) | (775) | (388) | 0 | 0 |
| Cash Available for Pre-Petition Debt | 9,613 | 10,995 | 10,638 | 11,259 | 11,035 | 12,643 | 13,256 |
| Change in Bank Debt | 0 | (6,328) | (11,182) | (9,690) | 0 | 0 | 0 |
| Interest on Bank Debt | (3,672) | (3,672) | (2,818) | (1,308) | 0 | 0 | 0 |
| Change in Bondholder Debt | 0 | 0 | 0 | 0 | 0 | 0 | 0 |
| Change in Promissory Notes | 0 | 0 | 0 | 0 | 0 | 0 | 0 |
| Loan Fees | (850) | (300) | (300) | (300) | (75) | 0 | 0 |
| Change in Preferred Stock | 0 | 0 | 0 | 0 | 0 | 0 | 0 |
| Cash Dividends | 0 | 0 | 0 | 0 | 0 | 0 | 0 |
| Payments in Kind | 0 | 0 | 0 | 0 | 0 | 0 | 0 |
| Change in Convenience Claims | 0 | 0 | 0 | 0 | 0 | 0 | 0 |
| Change in Trade Debt | 0 | 0 | 0 | 0 | 0 | 0 | 0 |
| Interest on Trade Debt | 0 | 0 | 0 | 0 | 0 | 0 | 0 |
| Change in Cash | $5,091 | $695 | ($3,662) | ($39) | $10,960 | $12,643 | $13,256 |

**Exhibit 5-4    Sample Disclosure Statement**                                      **185**

Care Enterprises, Inc.
Adjusted Projected Balance Sheet
December 31, 1988
($ in thousands)

| | 1988 Year-End as Projected | Pro-Forma Adjustments Amount | Ref # | 1989 Year-End Projected Pro-Forma |
|---|---|---|---|---|
| **Assets** | | | | |
| **Current** | | | | |
| Cash | 1,000 | | | 1,000 |
| Accounts Receivable—Open Facilities | 22,915 | | | 22,915 |
| Accounts Receivable—Eliminated Facilities | 8,706 | | | 8,706 |
| Inventory—Open Facilities | 3,181 | | | 3,181 |
| Inventory—Eliminated Facilities | 587 | | | 587 |
| Prepaids | | | | 0 |
|   Normal Course of Business—Open Facilities | 2,065 | | | 2,065 |
|   Normal Course of Business—Eliminated Facil. | 79 | | | 79 |
|   Bankruptcy Related & Refundable | 1,800 | | | 1,800 |
|    SUBTOTAL PREPAIDS | 3,944 | | | 3,944 |
| Notes Receivable | 245 | | | 245 |
| Receivables from Prior Owner of Americare | 100 | | | 100 |
|    TOTAL CURRENT ASSETS | 40,677 | | | 40,677 |
| Property, Plant & Equipment, Net—Open | 101,215 | | | 101,215 |
| Property, Plant & Equipment, Net—Eliminated | 19,008 | | | 19,008 |
| Mortgage Notes Receivable | 11,998 | | | 11,998 |
| Other Assets—Open Facilities | 7,853 | | | 7,853 |
| Other Assets—Eliminated Facilities | 518 | | | 518 |
| Restricted Funds—Open Facilities | 4,086 | | | 4,086 |
| Excess of Cost over Net Assets Acquired—Open | 3,738 | | | 3,738 |
| Excess of Cost over Net Assets Acquired—Elim. | 3,380 | | | 3,380 |
|    TOTAL ASSETS | 192,472 | | | 192,472 |

Adjusted Projected Balance Sheet ($ in thousands) *(continued)*

| | 1988 Year-End as Projected | Pro-Forma Adjustments Amount | Ref # | 1988 Year-End Projected Pro-Forma |
|---|---|---|---|---|
| **Liabilities** | | | | |
| Current Liabilities Excluding Reorganized Debt & New Mortgages | | | | |
| Accounts Payable—Open Facilities | 7,336 | | | 7,336 |
| Accounts Payable—Eliminated Facilities | 1,587 | | | 1,587 |
| Accrued Liabilities | 16,265 | | | 16,265 |
| Normal Course of Business—Open Facilities (1) | 519 | | | 519 |
| Normal Course of Business—Eliminated Facil. | 4,800 | | | 4,800 |
| Workmens Comp. | 1,700 | | | 1,700 |
| Reserve for Discontinued Operations | 1,200 | | | 1,200 |
| Contingency Reserve | 280 | | | 280 |
| Accrued Consulting Fees | | | | |
| SUBTOTAL ACCRUED LIABILITIES | 24,764 | | | 24,764 |
| Current Portion of Long Term Debt—Open | 1,727 | | | 1,727 |
| Current Portion of Long Term Debt—Eliminated | 100 | | | 100 |
| TOTAL CURRENT LIABILITIES EXCL. REORG. DEBT | 35,514 | | | 35,514 |

186

| Account | Amount | Adjustment | Note | Net |
|---|---|---|---|---|
| Long Term Debt (Facilities)—Open | 54,493 | | | 54,493 |
| Long Term Debt (Facilities)—Eliminated | 6,694 | | | 6,694 |
| Deferred Income Taxes | 2,500 | | | 2,500 |
| Other Liabilities | 4,600 | | | 4,600 |
| L.T. Workmens Comp | | | | |
| Bankruptcy Reserves | 6,394 | | | 6,394 |
| Litigation Reserves | 8,116 | | | 8,116 |
| Other Adjustments | 200 | | | 200 |
| SUBTOTAL OTHER LIABILITIES | 19,310 | | | 19,310 |
| Reorganization Debt | 67,712 | (67,712) | (1) | 0 |
| Bondholder Debt | 0 | | | 0 |
| Subordinated Unsecured Promissory Notes | 0 | | | 0 |
| Preferred Stock | 0 | | (2) | |
| Notes Payable—Citicorp & Wells | 34,800 | 2,400 | (6) | 27,200 |
| | | (10,000) | | |
| Convenience Claims | 300 | ( 300) | (3) | |
| Trade Payables | 5,400 | ( 3,900) | (3) | |
| | | ( 1,500) | (7) | |
| Accrued Interest—Bank Debt | 2,400 | ( 2,400) | (2) | |
| Accrued Interest Not Paid—Bonds | 5,524 | ( 5,524) | (4) | |
| Additional Mortgage Debt | 0 | 10,000 | (5) | 10,000 |

Adjusted Projected Balance Sheet ($ in Thousands) (*continued*)

| | 1988 Year-End as Projected | Pro-Forma Adjustments | | 1988 Year-End Projected Pro-Forma |
|---|---|---|---|---|
| | | Amount | Ref # | |
| EQUITY | (42,175) | 67,712 | (1) | 35,261 |
| | | 3,900 | (3) | |
| | | 5,524 | (4) | |
| | | 300 | (3) | |
| TOTAL LIABILITIES AND EQUITY | 192,472 | | | 192,472 |

ADJUSTMENTS:
(1) Conversion of Bondholder Debt into Equity
(2) Accrued Interest on Bank Debt
(3) Convert Non-"True Trade Payables" into Equity
(4) Conversion of Bondholder Accrued Interest into Equity
(5) Additional Mortgage-Based Borrowings
(6) Initial Bank Pay Down
(7) Pay-off of "True Trade Payables"

**Exhibit 5-4    Sample Disclosure Statement by Creditors**          **189**

## EXHIBIT "9"

---

January 9, 1989

The Official Committee of
    Unsecured Creditors of
    Care Enterprises, Inc.
c/o Perry L. Landsberg, Esq.
Sidley & Austin
1049 Century Park East
Suite 3500
Los Angeles, CA 90067

Gentlemen:

At your request, on behalf of the Official Committee of Unsecured Creditors of Care Enterprises, Inc. (the "Committee") we have conducted a preliminary analysis of Care Enterprises, Inc. (hereinafter sometimes referred to as "Care" or the "Company") and herewith submit this letter on our preliminary findings. Our conclusions are preliminary in nature and subject to further investigation and analysis.

The purpose of this preliminary analysis was to express an opinion regarding the fair market value, as of approximately the date of letter, of the Company as a going concern on a debt-free basis.

Care Enterprises, Inc., headquartered in Tustin, California, operates skilled and intermediate nursing facilities. On March 28, 1988, Care filed a voluntary petition with the United States Bankruptcy Court for relief under Chapter 11 of Title 11 of the United States Code. The Company is currently operating as a debtor in possession.

The term "fair market value", as used herein, is defined as the amount at which the Company, on a debt-free basis, would change hands between a willing buyer and a willing seller, each having reasonable knowledge of all relevant facts, neither being under any compulsion to act, with equity to both.

In the course of our preliminary investigation, we have, among other things:

1. visited Company headquarters and toured several of the Company's facilities:
2. discussed with certain members of the management of the Company the history, nature and future prospects of the business;
3. reviewed a 1987 SEC 10-K filing for the Company which contained, among

other things, audited financial statements for the three fiscal years ended December 31, 1987;

4. reviewed unaudited financial statements for the 10 months ended October 31, 1988;
5. reviewed the Care Enterprises Business Plan dated October, 1988;
6. reviewed the Debtor's Joint Disclosure Statement;
7. reviewed publicly-available information on companies we deemed similar to Care;
8. reviewed various schedules prepared by Ernst & Whinney, accounting experts retained by the Committee; and
9. conducted such other reviews and studies as we deemed appropriate.

These data have been accepted, without further verification, as correctly reflecting the results of the operations and financial condition of the Company, in accordance with generally accepted accounting principles applied on a consistent basis. With respect to the financial forecasts, we have assumed that they have been reasonably prepared and reflect management's estimates of the future financial results and condition of the Company, and that there has been no material adverse change in the assets, financial condition, business or prospects of the Company since the date of the most recent financial statements and projections made available to us. All such assumptions have been made only for the purpose of this letter, and are subject to future adjustment as the circumstances may warrant.

In our preliminary analysis of Care, we have taken into account the income- and cash-generating capability of the Company. Typically, an investor contemplating an investment in a company on a going-concern basis with income- and cash-generating capability similar to that of Care will evaluate the potential returns of his investment weighted with the potential investment risks. Accordingly, we have utilized market comparative approaches and discounted future cash flow approaches in our preliminary analysis of the Company.

In market comparison approaches, appropriate measures of the Company's earnings and cash flow potential are developed. These levels of earnings and cash flow are meant to be representative of the potential levels the Company can generate in the near-term future. In our preliminary analysis of Care, the Company's historical financial results, the Company's business plan, and financial schedules prepared by Ernst and Whinney were utilized to develop various representative levels of cash flow. Since the Company's recent historical results have been very poor, we gave significant weighting to the Company's projections as modified by Ernst & Whinney.

The second component of market comparative approaches entails the development of capitalization rates. Price to earnings and other ratios derived from the public marketplace reflect investors' sentiments toward particular industries in

**Exhibit 5-4    Sample Disclosure Statement by Creditors**                    **191**

general and certain companies specifically. Our preliminary analysis compared the investment attributes of Care to those of a group of comparable, publicly-traded companies. This analysis served as a basis for the selection of appropriate risk-adjusted capitalization rates for Care.

The third component of a market comparison approach is the selection and application of control premiums. Price to earnings and other ratios derived from the public marketplace represent transactions in minority blocks of stock. To reflect the value of a company on a control or enterprise basis, a control premium must be applied. Our preliminary analysis included a premium for Care we felt appropriate based on an analysis of premiums paid for control in the public marketplace.

The discounted future cash flow approach takes various measures of projected cash flow and discounts them back at an appropriate risk adjusted discount rate to present value. In our preliminary analysis of Care, we utilized projections prepared by management modified by certain adjustments determined by Ernst and Whinney. Discount rates were developed considering the Company's capital structure, rates of return required in the public marketplace, and the risk of realizing the Company's projected cash flow.

Based on the investigation, premises, provisos and analyses outlined above and described more fully in the forthcoming report, it is our preliminary opinion that the fair market value of Care Enterprises Inc. on a debt-free basis is reasonably stated in range of ONE HUNDRED FORTY MILLION DOLLARS ($140,000,000) to ONE HUNDRED SIXTY MILLION DOLLARS ($160,000,000). Furthermore, while this opinion is preliminary in nature and subject to further investigation, we currently believe that our final conclusion will fall near the bottom end of this range.

In accordance with recognized professional ethics, our professional fees for this service are not contingent upon the opinion expressed herein, and neither Houlihan, Lokey, Howard & Zukin Capital, nor any of its employees have a present or intended financial interest in the Company.

HOULIHAN, LOKEY, HOWARD & ZUKIN CAPITAL,
    A California Limited Partnership

**EXHIBIT 5-5    SAMPLE DISCLOSURE STATEMENT FOR
PREPETITION SOLICITATIONS**

From July 10, 1986 through September 26, 1986, Crystal Oil Company obtained the approval of all impaired classes of claims and interests. A bankruptcy
petition was filed on October 1, 1986 and on December 31, 1986, the plan was
confirmed. The following excerpts from the Disclosure Statements are included
in this Exhibit:

Solicitation of Ballots
Disclosure Statement Summary
Anticipated Operations During the Chapter 11 Case
Feasibility of the Plan (Including Projections)
Alternative to the Plan (Including Liquidation Analysis)
Bankruptcy Considerations

**Exhibit 5-5   Disclosure Statement for Prepetition Solicitations**          **193**

DISCLOSURE STATEMENT

# CRYSTAL OIL COMPANY

Solicitation of Ballots
to
Plan of Reorganization
to be filed under
Chapter 11 of the United States Bankruptcy Code

This Disclosure Statement (this "Disclosure Statement") and the accompanying forms of ballot are being furnished by Crystal Oil Company, a Louisiana corporation (the "Company"), to its known impaired creditors pursuant to Sections 1125(a) and 1126(b) of the United States Bankruptcy Code (the "Bankruptcy Code") in connection with a solicitation by the Board of Directors of the Company of ballots for the acceptance of a Plan of Reorganization (the "Plan") of the Company prior to the commencement of a case under Chapter 11 of the Bankruptcy Code. **The Company is not currently a debtor in a case under Chapter 11 of the Bankruptcy Code. However, if the Company receives ballots accepting the Plan from the holders of at least two-thirds in amount and more than half in number of each class of its impaired creditors voting on the Plan, the Company, subject to certain conditions described herein, intends to file a voluntary petition for reorganization under Chapter 11 of the Bankruptcy Code and to seek as promptly as practicable confirmation of the Plan using the acceptances received pursuant to this solicitation to satisfy the requirements of Section 1129 of the Bankruptcy Code relating to class approval of the Plan by such creditors.** Further, even if the Company does not receive the requisite approval of the Plan from each class of its impaired creditors, or if an involuntary petition under Chapter 11 of the Bankruptcy Code is filed against the Company prior to the Company's receipt of such approval, the Company may nevertheless use any of the acceptances received pursuant to this solicitation to seek confirmation of the Plan or of any modification of the Plan that does not adversely change the treatment of the claim of any impaired creditor who has accepted the Plan. See "VOTING PROCEDURES AND REQUIREMENTS—Possible Reclassification of Creditors and Interest Holders".

Pursuant to Rule 3018 of the Bankruptcy Rules under the Bankruptcy Code, the Board of Directors of the Company has fixed the close of business on June 16, 1986, as the record date for the determination of creditors from whom acceptances or rejections of the Plan will be accepted. The solicitation period for ballots with respect to the Plan will expire at 5:00 p.m., New York City time, on Friday, August 8, 1986, unless and until the Company, in its sole discretion, shall have extended the period of time for which ballots will be accepted. Except to the extent allowed by the Bankruptcy Court, ballots that are received after the expiration of the solicitation period may not be accepted or used by the Company in connection with the Company's request for confirmation of the Plan or any modification thereof. See "VOTING PROCEDURES AND REQUIREMENTS—Ballots and Voting Deadline".

*While the successful implementation of the Plan contemplates and requires a reorganization of the Company under Chapter 11 of the Bankruptcy Code, the Company believes that the Plan provides for the maximum and earliest recovery for all creditors of the Company and that if the Company can obtain the necessary acceptances of the Plan from its impaired creditors prior to the commencement of a case under Chapter 11, the cost and time related to such a reorganization could be substantially reduced. Accordingly, the Board of Directors believes that approval of the Plan is in the best interests of the Company and its creditors, and recommends that all its impaired creditors vote to accept the Plan.*

THIS TRANSACTION HAS NOT BEEN APPROVED OR DISAPPROVED BY THE SECURITIES AND EXCHANGE COMMISSION NOR HAS THE COMMISSION PASSED UPON THE FAIRNESS OR MERITS OF SUCH TRANSACTION NOR UPON THE ACCURACY OR ADEQUACY OF THE INFORMATION CONTAINED IN THIS DOCUMENT. ANY REPRESENTATION TO THE CONTRARY IS UNLAWFUL.

The Date of this Disclosure Statement is July 9, 1986.

This Disclosure Statement may not be relied upon for any purpose other than to determine how to vote on the Plan, and nothing contained herein shall constitute an admission of any fact or liability by the Company, or be admissible in any proceeding involving the Company or any other party, or be deemed advice on the tax or other legal effects of the Plan on holders of claims or interests. Certain of the information contained in this Disclosure Statement, by its nature, is forward looking, contains estimates and assumptions which may prove not to have been the case, and contains financial projections which may be materially different from actual future experiences.

The securities to be issued pursuant to the Plan have not been registered with the Securities and Exchange Commission (the "Commission") under the Securities Act of 1933 (the "Securities Act") or under any state securities act or similar state law in reliance upon an exemption from registration provided by Section 1145 of the Bankruptcy Code. Further, such securities have not been approved by the Commission or any state securities commission or similar authority. Neither the Commission nor any state commission has passed upon the accuracy or adequacy of the information contained in this Disclosure Statement or upon the merits of the Plan. Any representation to the contrary is unlawful.

Pursuant to Section 1126 of the Bankruptcy Code, each holder of an impaired claim or interest under the Plan will be entitled to accept or reject the Plan. Although the holders of the Company's Common Stock, $.01 par value (the "Common Stock"), may be considered impaired under the Plan, the Company does not currently intend to solicit the acceptance of the Plan by such holders until such time as it has obtained the acceptance of the Plan by all classes of its impaired creditors and has filed a petition for reorganization under Chapter 11 of the Bankruptcy Code. Further, the Company may submit to the Bankruptcy Court for determination the issue whether, in light of all circumstances, the holders of the Common Stock are impaired under the Plan and may seek confirmation of the Plan without soliciting the holders of the Common Stock pursuant to the "cram-down" provisions of Section 1129(b) of the Bankruptcy Code on the basis that the Plan does not discriminate unfairly and is fair and equitable to the holders of the Common Stock. In addition, if the Company does solicit the holders of the Common Stock and is unable to obtain the acceptance of the Plan by such holders, the Company will likely seek confirmation of the Plan pursuant to such provisions. The ability of the Company to obtain confirmation of the Plan pursuant to the cram-down provisions of the Bankruptcy Code, however, is subject to the Bankruptcy Court making certain factual and legal determinations with respect to the Plan. Therefore, there can be no assurance that the Company would be able to have the Plan confirmed if the Company does not solicit the holders of the Common Stock or if the Company does solicit the holders of the Common Stock and such holders do not vote to accept the Plan. See "VOTING PROCEDURES AND REQUIREMENTS—Classes Entitled to Vote" and "CONFIRMATION OF THE PLAN".

Amendments to the Plan's classification and treatment of one or more classes under the Plan that do not materially and adversely change the treatment of the other classes may be made to the Plan either before or after a petition under Chapter 11 of the Bankruptcy Code is filed. Such amendments may be approved by the Bankruptcy Court at the confirmation hearing without resolicitation of creditors who are not further impaired. See "THE PLAN—Modification of the Plan".

The Plan contemplates the issuance of a substantial number of new shares, and rights to receive new shares, of the Company's common stock and voting preferred stock. Accordingly, if the Plan is confirmed, the percentage of ownership of the Company's common stock held by the current holders of the Company's common stock, and percentage of the total voting power with respect thereto, will be reduced to approximately 36% and 17%, respectively, which interest could be further reduced to as low as approximately 11% and 8%, respectively, if certain new warrants to purchase the Company's common stock are exercised. See "RISK FACTORS—Risks with Respect to the New Securities—Dilution and Possible Change in Control", "PURPOSE AND EFFECTS OF THE PLAN—CERTAIN CONSID-ERATIONS—Effects on Ownership of Common Stock" and "PURPOSE AND EFFECTS OF THE PLAN—CERTAIN CONSIDERATIONS—Effects on Voting Power".

If the Plan is accepted and confirmed, the Company will have authorized 2,300,000,000 shares of common stock, of which approximately 142,448,000 will be issued and outstanding as of the effective date of the Plan and 2,015,822,000 will be reserved for future issuance upon conversion of certain convertible securities and the exercise of certain warrants. Although the Company believes that such capitalization is

**Exhibit 5-5    Disclosure Statement for Prepetition Solicitations**                    **195**

desirable in order to gain approval of and to implement the Plan, the potential issuance of over 2,000,000,000 shares of common stock will likely result in an extremely low market price for the Company's common stock for the foreseeable future and may restrict the marketability of such stock. Accordingly, there can be no assurance as to the price or marketability of the Company's common stock if the Plan is confirmed.

The Company is required under Section 1122 of the Bankruptcy Code to classify the claims or interests of its creditors and interest holders into classes that contain claims and interests that are substantially similar to the other claims or interests in such class. While the Company believes that it has classified all claims or interests in compliance with the provisions of Section 1122, it is possible that once a case has been commenced in bankruptcy, a creditor or interest holder may challenge the Company's classification of such holder's claim or interest and the Bankruptcy Court may find that a different classification is required for the Plan to be confirmed. In such event, it is the present intent of the Company to modify the Plan to provide for whatever reasonable classification might be required by the Bankruptcy Court for confirmation and to use the acceptances received by the Company from any creditor pursuant to this solicitation for the purpose of obtaining the approval of the class or classes of which such creditor is ultimately deemed to be a member. Any such reclassification of creditors could adversely affect the class in which such creditor was initially a member, or any other class under the Plan, by changing the composition of such class and the required vote thereof for approval of the Plan. Further, a reclassification of the claims of creditors after approval of the Plan and its classification of such creditors could necessitate the resolicitation of a completely new plan of reorganization. See "THE PLAN—Classification and Treatment of Claims and Interests".

Although this solicitation relates to a plan of reorganization of the Company to be filed under Chapter 11 of the Bankruptcy Code, no such filing has been made or is contemplated to be made by the Company until such time as the Plan has been accepted by the requisite number of the Company's impaired creditors or the Company shall have determined that such a filing is necessary to protect the Company's property and interests. The Company, however, is currently in default under several covenants with respect to its secured bank debt and is or soon will be in default with respect to all of its other long-term debt because of its decisions in April and May 1986 to suspend all payments of principal and interest on such debt. As a result of such defaults, it is possible that an involuntary Chapter 11 case could be commenced against the Company pursuant to Section 303 of the Bankruptcy Code prior to the completion of this solicitation. If such an involuntary case were to be commenced, the Plan could become inoperative. In such event, the Company may elect to prepare and send to its creditors an alternative plan of reorganization which may contain various alternative terms and conditions, including, for example, payments and treatment of allowed claims and allowed interests different than those set forth in the Plan. In addition, if the Company is required to modify the Plan, the Company could be required to resolicit from its creditors acceptances and rejections concerning the Plan as modified.

The statements contained in this Disclosure Statement are made as of the date hereof unless another time is specified herein, and neither the delivery of this Disclosure Statement nor any exchange of rights made in connection with the Plan shall, under any circumstances, create any implication that the information contained herein is correct as of any time subsequent to the date hereof.

For the definitions of certain capitalized terms used herein, see "GLOSSARY OF TERMS".

# DISCLOSURE STATEMENT SUMMARY

The following is a brief summary of certain information contained elsewhere in this Disclosure Statement. The summary is necessarily incomplete and selective and is qualified in its entirety by reference to the more detailed information, the consolidated financial statements, including the notes thereto, the financial projections, including the notes thereto, the capitalization table, including the notes thereto, and the Annexes and Exhibits appearing elsewhere in this Disclosure Statement. See "GLOSSARY OF TERMS" for the meaning of certain capitalized terms used herein.

## THE COMPANY

The Company was incorporated in 1926 under the laws of the State of Maryland and became principally engaged in crude oil and natural gas exploration and production when it merged with Roberts Petroleum Company during 1963. In 1984, the Company moved its state of incorporation to the State of Louisiana. In recent years, the Company emphasized the development of its crude oil and natural gas exploration and production activities. This emphasis, together with present economic conditions, resulted in a decision by the Company in 1985 to discontinue its refinery operations and to sell or hold for sale its refinery assets. Since 1980, the Company has devoted a significant portion of its drilling activity to its properties in the Vernon, Arkana and North Missionary Lake Fields located primarily in northern Louisiana. Numerous properties located outside of these principal operational areas were sold during 1984 and 1985, with the proceeds used primarily to reduce indebtedness of the Company. High interest costs on borrowings made to finance the Company's previously active drilling program have combined with falling crude oil and natural gas prices to render the Company unable to service any of its indebtedness other than its secured bank debt and, possibly, part of its secured indebtedness to Halliburton, and to threaten the Company's ability to continue as a going concern. In response to the Company's financial problems, the Company's drilling activities have been substantially curtailed since the third quarter of 1984, and the Company has been forced to postpone indefinitely certain development drilling which might improve its cash flow by bringing certain proved developed non-producing and proved undeveloped reserves into production. However, under most current crude oil and natural gas prices, it is doubtful that additional drilling and completions on the Company's development properties would contribute significantly to cash flow even if the Company had funds for such drilling.

The Company's executive offices are located at 400 Crystal Building, Shreveport, Louisiana 71101, and its telephone number is (318) 222-7791.

## CLASSIFICATION OF CREDITORS

Section 1123 of the Bankruptcy Code provides that a plan of reorganization shall classify the claims and interests of a debtor's creditors and interest holders into classes that contain claims and interests that are substantially similar. The Plan divides the Company's creditors and interest holders into the following classes:

Class 1 —Administrative Expenses
Class 2 —Wage Related Claims
Class 3 —Employee Benefit Plan Claims
Class 4 —Tax Claims
Class 5 —Additional Priority Claims
Class 6 —The Bank's Secured Claims
Class 7 —Halliburton Claim
Class 8A —15% Senior Note Secured Claims
Class 8B —15% Senior Note Unsecured Claims
Class 9 —Mechanics and Materialmen Lien Claims

Exhibit 5-5   Disclosure Statement for Prepetition Solicitations                     197

Class 10 —Secured Trustee Claim
Class 11 —Unsecured Claims
Class 12 —14⅞% Debenture Claims
Class 13 —Subordinated Debenture Claims
Class 14 —Intercompany Claims
Class 15 —Shareholder Claims of Interest

## VOTING PROCEDURE

Pursuant to Rule 3018 of the Bankruptcy Rules under the Bankruptcy Code, the Board of Directors of the Company has fixed the close of business on June 16, 1986, as the record date for the determination of creditors from whom acceptances or rejections of the Plan will be accepted. The solicitation period for ballots with respect to the Plan will expire at 5:00 p.m., New York City time, on Friday, August 8, 1986, unless and until the Company, in its sole discretion, shall have extended the period of time for which ballots will be accepted. Except to the extent allowed by the Bankruptcy Court, ballots that are received after the expiration of the solicitation period may not be accepted or used by the Company in connection with the Company's request for confirmation of the Plan or any modification thereof. See "VOTING PROCEDURES AND REQUIREMENTS—Ballots and Voting Deadline".

Only classes that are impaired under the Plan are entitled to vote to accept or reject the Plan. Generally, Section 1124 of the Bankruptcy Code provides that a class of claims or interests is considered to be impaired under a plan of reorganization unless the plan does not alter the legal, equitable and contractual rights of the holders of such claims or interests. In addition, such classes will be considered impaired unless all outstanding defaults, other than defaults relating to the insolvency or financial condition of the debtor or the commencement of a bankruptcy case, are to be cured and the holders of claims or interests in such classes are to be compensated for any damages incurred as a result of any reasonable reliance by such holders on any contractual provisions or applicable law to demand accelerated payment. For the reasons discussed in "THE PLAN—Classification and Treatment of Claims and Interests", the Company has determined that only the following classes of its creditors and interest holders may or will be impaired under the Plan:

Class 6   —The Bank
Class 7   —Halliburton
Class 8A —15% Senior Note Holders (Secured Claims)
Class 8B —15% Senior Note Holders (Unsecured Claims)
Class 12 —14⅞% Debenture Holders
Class 13 —Subordinated Debenture Holders
Class 14 —Intercompany Claim—CEPCO
Class 15 —Common Stock Holders*

---

* The determination of whether this class is impaired under the Plan may be submitted to the Bankruptcy Court.

All other classes will not be impaired under the Plan, and therefore, will not be entitled to vote with respect to the acceptance or rejection of the Plan. Further, although the holders of the Common Stock, whose interests are classified in Class 15, may be considered impaired under the Plan and may be entitled to vote to accept or reject the Plan, the Company is not soliciting the acceptance of the Plan by such holders pursuant to this solicitation and does not currently intend to solicit such acceptance until such time as it has obtained the acceptance of the Plan by all classes of its impaired creditors and has filed a petition for the reorganization of the Company under Chapter 11 of the Bankruptcy Code. In addition, the

Company may submit to the Bankruptcy Court for determination the issue whether, in light of all circumstances, the holders of the Common Stock are impaired under the Plan and may seek Confirmation of the Plan pursuant to the cram-down provisions of Section 1129(b) of the Bankruptcy Code in lieu of or notwithstanding a vote by the holders of the Common Stock. See "CONFIRMATION OF THE PLAN". **Accordingly, no acceptances or rejections of the Plan by any holder of the Common Stock with respect to such holder's interest in the Common Stock is being requested nor will they be accepted by the Company in connection with this solicitation.**

## VOTE REQUIRED

Once a petition for reorganization of the Company has been filed, the Bankruptcy Court will determine whether the impaired classes described above have accepted the Plan by determining whether sufficient acceptances have been received from the holders of Allowed Claims and Allowed Interests in such classes. An impaired class of claims will be determined to have accepted the Plan if the holders of Allowed Claims in that class casting votes in favor of the Plan (i) hold at least two-thirds of the dollar amount of all the Allowed Claims of the holders in such class *voting* on the Plan and (ii) comprise more than half in number of the holders of the Allowed Claims in such class *voting* on the Plan. An impaired class of interests, if one exists, will be determined to have accepted the Plan if the holders of the Allowed Interests casting votes in favor of the Plan hold at least two-thirds in amount of the Allowed Interests as to which votes are cast. As discussed above, the Company may submit to the Bankruptcy Court for determination the issue of whether, in light of all circumstances, the holders of the Common Stock are impaired under the Plan and may seek confirmation of the Plan without soliciting the holders of the Common Stock pursuant to the cram-down provisions of Section 1129(b) of the Bankruptcy Code on the basis that the Plan does not discriminate unfairly and is fair and·equitable to the holders of the Common Stock. *Ballots of holders of impaired claims received pursuant to this solicitation that are signed and returned, but not expressly voted either for acceptance or rejection of the Plan, will be counted as ballots for acceptance of the Plan. Except as may be allowed by the Bankruptcy Court, a ballot accepting the Plan may not be revoked.*

## PURPOSE AND EFFECTS OF THE PLAN

### General

Beginning in 1984, the effects of the worldwide decline in demand and excess supply of crude oil and natural gas and the corresponding decline in crude oil and natural gas prices began to seriously affect the operations of the Company. This decline in prices, coupled with the high interest costs associated with the funds borrowed by the Company to finance a portion of its exploration and development activities, began to threaten the Company's financial condition in 1984. While the Company had experienced losses from operations in the two years prior to 1984, the Company was able in such years to obtain outside financing for its activities. As the severity and extended duration of the recession in the oil and gas industry became more apparent, management of the Company in late 1984 and in 1985 began implementing steps to reduce and restructure the Company's outstanding indebtedness to a level that management believed the Company could service while carrying on the development drilling activities necessary to improve its cash flow by bringing proved non-producing and other reserves into production. Principal among the Company's efforts to reduce and restructure its indebtedness in 1985, were (i) its agreement with Halliburton in April 1985 to extend (with a monthly amortization schedule) the term of a sizeable trade payable to Halliburton through April 1987 and (ii) its Exchange Offers for its Debentures that were closed on October 3, 1985. Pursuant to the Exchange Offers, the Company exchanged approximately

**Exhibit 5-5   Disclosure Statement for Prepetition Solicitations**                    **199**

$125,155,000 face amount of the 15% Senior Notes and 7,418,000 shares of Common Stock for approximately $234,216,000 face amount of the Debentures, having a net book value of approximately $217,846,000. As a result of the Exchange Offers, the Company reduced the face amount of its outstanding indebtedness by approximately $109,000,000 and its annual cash interest costs by approximately $12,719,000. On December 5, 1985, the Company obtained from its shareholders approval of an amendment to its Articles of Incorporation increasing the number of its authorized shares of Common Stock from 35,000,000 to 90,000,000 and decreasing the par value thereof from $1.00 to $.01 so as to provide the Company with the ability to exercise an option with respect to the 15% Senior Notes to pay accrued interest thereon and to make certain redemptions of the 15% Senior Notes with shares of Common Stock. On December 15, 1985, the Company exercised its option to pay the first semi-annual interest payment due on the 15% Senior Notes with shares of Common Stock by issuing to the holders of the 15% Senior Notes approximately 23,150,000 shares of Common Stock valued at approximately $.54 per share. The Company's exercise of this option saved the Company approximately $9,400,000 in cash.

While past restructuring efforts (see "PURPOSE AND EFFECTS OF THE PLAN—CERTAIN CONSIDERATIONS—Purpose of the Plan and Background") together with the Company's efforts to decrease, where possible or advisable, its fixed general and administrative costs, provided the Company with some temporary relief from its heavy debt burden, it has become apparent to management of the Company, particularly in light of the recent substantial decline in prices for crude oil and natural gas, that the anticipated results of the Exchange Offers have not been fully achieved and that more dramatic debt restructuring efforts are necessary if the Company is to continue as a going concern. In that regard, management has concluded that for any restructuring of the Company to be successful, a substantial portion of the Company's outstanding indebtedness must be converted into equity. Accordingly, the Plan provides for a reduction in the outstanding face amount of the Company's indebtedness (excluding intercompany indebtedness and $33,100,000 in Letters of Credit) from $277,399,000 to $129,022,000 ($75,093,000 of which will be non-interest bearing), with the holders of the eliminated debt to receive a combination of Preferred Stock, New Common Stock and Warrants.

The Plan was conceived by management as an alternative to the more drastic measures available to the Company for restructuring its debt, such as a liquidation of its properties in the current depressed market or an immediate filing for protection under Chapter 11 of the Bankruptcy Code. The terms of the Plan were arrived at after consultation with the Company's financial advisors as to what type of plan might be feasible and after lengthy negotiations with certain of the Company's senior secured creditors and certain other parties in interest. The Company believes that the Plan provides the Company's creditors and shareholders with distributions of property in the form of new securities having a value not less than the amount that such holders would receive if the Company were to be liquidated under Chapter 7 of the Bankruptcy Code and should provide for the maximum possible recovery for all classes of the Company's creditors and shareholders. While the successful implementation of the Plan contemplates and requires a reorganization of the Company under Chapter 11 of the Bankruptcy Code, the Company believes that if it can obtain the necessary acceptances of the Plan from its creditors prior to the commencement of a case under Chapter 11 of the Bankruptcy Code, the costs and time related to such a reorganization could be substantially reduced. *While there can be no assurance that the Plan, if approved, will be successful or confirmed or that no further restructuring of the Company's indebtedness will be required, the Company believes that reorganization under the Plan is feasible and that the Plan does provide for the greatest and earliest possible recoveries for its creditors and shareholders.*

**Negotiations with Certain Creditors**

During the past few months, the Company has conducted negotiations with the Bank and Halliburton, the Company's two most senior creditors, with respect to a possible reorganization of the Company. While the terms of the Plan reflect the Company's understanding of an approach that might be acceptable to the Bank, the terms of the Plan have not been definitely agreed to by the Bank. The Company has also discussed the terms of the Plan with Halliburton, but does not have any understanding that such terms will be acceptable to Halliburton. To date, the most important unresolved points with Halliburton relate to the terms of a proposed intercreditor agreement between Halliburton and the Bank and, specifically, the sharing ratio between the Bank and Halliburton as to the Company's cash flow available for debt service and whether and to what extent Halliburton will have an obligation to repay to the Bank any amounts paid to Halliburton by the Company if in the future the Company is unable to satisfy its obligations to the Bank. The resolution of such issues is not expected to materially affect the rights of other impaired creditors under the Plan because the Plan contemplates that the Company will, in effect, dedicate all available cash flow to the payment of indebtedness to the Bank and to Halliburton in recognition of their senior security positions prior to applying any cash flow to the payment of obligations under any of the other New Securities. The Company is also negotiating with Halliburton as to the amount of interest that will accrue on the New Halliburton Note and as to whether some additional principal and interest payments will be made on the Halliburton Note prior to the Company's commencement of the Chapter 11 case contemplated by this Disclosure Statement. However, the Company in preparing the Plan has provided that the New Halliburton Note will accrue interest at a reasonable annual rate of interest, $\frac{3}{4}\%$ above prime, and has taken into consideration the possibility of making certain additional payments to Halliburton prior to the Company's filing for reorganization. Accordingly, the Company believes that if the Plan is ultimately modified to provide for a different rate of interest on the New Halliburton Note or if the Company does decide to make any further payments of principal or interest to Halliburton prior to filing for reorganization, such events would not materially adversely affect the feasibility of the Plan or further impair the claims of the holders of any of the other impaired claims under the Plan. See "FEASIBILITY OF THE PLAN". The Company will continue to attempt to persuade Halliburton as to the merits of the Plan after this Disclosure Statement is distributed and while ballots are being solicited. However, there can be no assurance that Halliburton, the Bank or any other impaired creditor under the Plan will accept the Plan and there is the possibility that a revised plan of reorganization will be negotiated with creditors for future presentation thereto.

The Company has also conducted negotiations with the representatives of holders believed by the Company to control in excess of $85,000,000 (68%) of the 15% Senior Notes. While such negotiations were preliminary and limited to ascertaining the basic terms that such holders might be willing to agree upon in any comprehensive restructuring of the Company's outstanding indebtedness, the Company believes that such holders might be willing to accept the Plan as currently proposed. However, the Company emphasizes that all such negotiations were preliminary in form and that the specific terms of the Plan have not been definitely agreed upon with such holders. Accordingly, there can be no assurance that any of such holders will accept the Plan.

**Effects of the Plan**

The following table sets forth the aggregate face amount, the book value and the estimated aggregate Allowed Amounts of Allowed Claims of the Old Securities (other than the Common Stock) and the Letters of Credit at June 16, 1986, the record date for this solicitation, and the aggregate face amount or number of shares or Warrants of the New Securities to be issued under the Plan to the holders of the Bank Note, the Halliburton Note, the 15% Senior Notes, the 14⅞% Debentures and the Subordinated Debentures and to the issuer of the Letters of Credit. See "CAPITALIZATION".

| | Old Securities | | |
|---|---|---|---|
| | Face Amount | Book Value | Estimated Aggregate Amount of Allowed Claims(1) |
| | (In Thousands) | | |
| Bank Note(2) | $ 43,651 | $ 43,651 | $ 43,864 |
| Letters of Credit(3) | 33,100 | 747 | 33,100 |
| Halliburton Note(4) | 10,278 | 10,278 | 10,515 |
| 15 % Senior Notes | 125,155 | 200,581 | 134,542 |
| 14⅞% Debentures | 16,691 | 16,445 | 17,706 |
| 12⅝% Debentures due 1990 | 7,715 | 7,715 | 8,202 |
| 9 % Debentures | 14,259 | 14,259 | 15,061 |
| 11⅜% Debentures | 20,412 | 18,507 | 20,111 |
| 13¾% Debentures | 12,919 | 12,728 | 13,477 |
| 12⅝% Debentures due 2001 | 26,319 | 20,371 | 22,923 |
| Total | $310,499 | $345,282 | $319,501 |

(1) The Allowed Amounts of the Allowed Claims of the holders of the 14⅞% Debentures, the 11⅜% Debentures, the 13¾% Debentures and the 12⅝% Debentures due 2001 have been adjusted for the original issue discount with respect to such Debentures, assuming a petition for the reorganization of the Company had been filed on June 16, 1986. Such adjustments are required under the Bankruptcy Code because Section 502(b)(2) of the Bankruptcy Code provides that the Allowed Amount of a claim of a holder of a debt security may not reflect any unmatured interest. Accordingly, because the face amounts of the 14⅞% Debentures, the 11⅜% Debentures, the 13¾% Debentures and the 12⅝% Debentures due 2001 reflect some amounts of unmatured interest, the Allowed Amounts of the Allowed Claims with respect to such Debentures have been adjusted using the straight-line method of allocating interest so that only that portion of the original issue discount that represents matured interest on such Debentures is included in the estimated Allowed Amounts of the Allowed Claims. In all instances, estimated Allowed Amounts of Allowed Claims include accrued but unpaid interest to June 16, 1986, which, for purposes of the information contained in this table, is treated as the Petition Date. In addition, the estimated Allowed Amount of the Bank's claim with respect to the Bank Note includes $45,000 in expenses of the Bank required to be paid by the Company pursuant to the Loan Agreement.

| | | | | New Securities | | | | |
| --- | --- | --- | --- | --- | --- | --- | --- | --- |
| New Notes | | | Preferred Stock | | | Warrants | | |
| Bank Note | Halliburton Note | Convertible Secured Notes | Senior Preferred | Series A Preferred | New Common Stock | $0.075 Warrants | $0.10 Warrants | $0.125 Warrants |
| | | | (In Thousands) | | | | | |
| $43,651 | $ — | $ — | — | — | — | 20,000 | — | — |
| — | — | — | — | — | — | — | . — | — |
| — | 10,278 | — | — | — | 12,000 | 20,000 | — | — |
| — | — | 75,093 | 50,062 | — | 40,050 | 87,609 | 75,093 | — |
| — | — | — | — | 13,186 | 5,591 | — | 15,022 | 11,684 |
| — | — | — | — | 5,519 | 2,375 | — | 6,129 | 6,129 |
| — | — | — | — | 10,135 | 4,361 | — | 11,254 | 11,254 |
| — | — | — | — | 13,533 | 5,824 | — | 15,027 | 15,027 |
| — | — | — | — | 9,069 | 3,903 | — | 10,070 | 10,070 |
| — | — | — | — | 15,425 | 6,638 | — | 17,128 | 17,128 |
| $43,651 | $10,278 | $75,093 | 50,062 | 66,867 | 80,742 | 127,609 | 149,723 | 71,292 |

(2) The Company intends to continue, at least until the commencement of the Chapter 11 case contemplated by this Disclosure Statement, to make monthly installments of principal (currently approximately $1,147,000) and interest on the Bank Note, and may, with Bankruptcy Court approval, continue to make such payments at the same or at some reduced level after the commencement of such a proceeding and until Confirmation of the Plan.

(3) The Company will continue to be contingently obligated for possible reimbursement to the Bank for the full amount of the Letters of Credit under the Plan.

(4) The Company is currently negotiating with Halliburton as to whether some additional principal and interest payments will be made on the Halliburton Note prior to the Company's commencement of the Chapter 11 case contemplated by this Disclosure Statement, and may, with Bankruptcy Court approval, make some payments on the Halliburton Note after the commencement of such a proceeding and until Confirmation of the Plan.

Exhibit 5-5    Disclosure Statement for Prepetition Solicitations    203

stributions Under the Plan to the Holders of the
% Senior Notes and the Debentures per $1,000 Face Amount

The following table sets forth for each $1,000 face amount of the 15% Senior Notes and each issue of the
:bentures (i) the estimated Allowed Amounts of Allowed Claims with respect to the 15% Senior Notes and each issue
the Debentures, assuming a petition for the reorganization of the Company had been filed as of June 16, 1986, and
) the face amount of the New Convertible Secured Notes and the number of shares of the Preferred Stock and New
>mmon Stock and the number of Warrants to be issued to the holders of the 15% Senior Notes and each issue of the
:bentures assuming the Plan is confirmed. **Holders of the 15% Senior Notes and the Debentures should note that the
tual Allowed Amounts of their Allowed Claims with respect to their securities as of the Petition Date and the
tributions to be provided to such holders under the Plan with respect to each $1,000 face amount of such securities
,y be different than as set forth below as a result of the accrual of interest, including amortization of original issue
count, on such securities from June 16, 1986, to the Petition Date.**

| | Estimated Allowed Amount of Principal Per $1,000 Face Amount (1) | Estimated Allowed Amount of Interest Per $1,000 Face Amount | Face Amount or Number of New Securities to be issued for each $1,000 Face Amount of the 15% Senior Notes and the Debentures | | | | | | |
| --- | --- | --- | --- | --- | --- | --- | --- | --- | --- |
| | | | New Convertible Secured Notes | Senior Preferred Stock | Series A Preferred Stock | New Common Stock | $.075 Warrants | $0.10 Warrants | $.125 Warrants |
| % Senior Notes........ | $1,000 | $75 | $600 | 400 | — | 320 | 700 | 600 | — |
| ₄% Debentures.......... | 986 | 74 | — | — | 790 | 335 | — | 900 | 700 |
| ₄% Debentures due 990 ............................ | 1,000 | 63 | — | — | 715 | 308 | — | 794 | 794 |
| % Debentures.......... | 1,000 | 56 | — | — | 711 | 306 | — | 789 | 789 |
| ₄% Debentures.......... | 909 | 76 | — | — | 663 | 285 | — | 736 | 736 |
| ₄% Debentures.......... | 986 | 57 | — | — | 702 | 302 | — | 779 | 779 |
| ₄% Debentures due 001 ........................... | 806 | 63 | — | — | 586 | 252 | — | 651 | 651 |

) The Allowed Amounts of the Allowed Claims of the holders of the 14⅞% Debentures, the 11⅜% Debentures, the
13¾% Debentures and the 12⅝% Debentures due 2001 have been adjusted for the original issue discount with
respect to such Debentures. Such adjustment is required under the Bankruptcy Code because Section 502(b)(2) of
the Bankruptcy Code provides that the Allowed Amount of a claim of a holder of a debt security may not reflect any
unmatured interest. Accordingly, because the face amounts of the 14⅞% Debentures, the 11⅜% Debentures, the
13¾% Debentures and the 12⅝% Debentures due 2001 reflect some amounts of unmatured interest, the Allowed
Amounts of the Allowed Claims with respect to such Debentures have been adjusted using the straight-line method
of allocating interest so that only that portion of the original issue discount that represents matured interest on such
Debentures is included in the estimated Allowed Amounts of the Allowed Claims.

## THE PLAN

The concept of the Plan is to allow those creditors of the Company (secured, unsecured, senior and subordinated) to receive a claim against or interest in the Company, or combination thereof, that represents the true nature and character of their current interest in the Company and to provide to the shareholders of the Company the right to participate in the future of the Company when, and if, the Company has been successfully revitalized and the holders of all superior claims have been compensated for such claims in accordance with the Plan. In addition, the Plan seeks to provide to all parties in interest, from the most senior secured creditors, whose cooperation and assistance is essential for the successful reorganization of the Company, to management, whose skills and day-to-day efforts will be necessary for the continued operation of the Company during the Chapter 11 reorganization and for the success of the Company after reorganization, the opportunity to share in any future profits of the Company.

The Plan attempts to achieve the above goals in the following manner. First, the Plan provides for the elimination through the exchange of securities of approximately $164,244,000 of the Company's prepetition debt, including interest, and the restructuring of an additional $129,427,000 of such debt. Second, the Plan allows the holders of the Company's secured debt to retain their present secured positions in certain assets of the Company and provides to all the holders of debt, secured or unsecured, who, after giving effect to all existing subordination agreements, might receive a distribution in a liquidation of the Company (if the Company were to be liquidated in the near future) the right to continue to hold a claim as a creditor of the Company in an amount at least equal to the amount of such possible distribution. Third, the Plan provides that a significant portion of the Company's remaining prepetition debt (including all unsecured subordinated debt, which would likely receive nothing if the Company were to be liquidated today) shall be converted into equity, or rights to receive equity, in the Company. Fourth, the Plan provides that all trade debt and all debt incurred in the ordinary course of business ($9,960,000 at March 31, 1986) shall be paid in full because of the anticipated relative small amount of such debt and the necessity and importance of the services, goods and rights, including the right to develop many of the Company's crude oil and natural gas properties, provided by the holders thereof to the continuing operation of the Company. Further, a distinction exists between such trade debt and ordinary course of business debt from other unsecured debt represented by the Debentures (which is impaired under the Plan) in that the subordination provisions of the Debentures would, in effect, require in all likelihood the distribution of amounts otherwise distributable thereto but for the Plan to the holders of Senior Indebtedness.

With respect to the approach under the Plan as to trade debt and debt incurred in the ordinary course of business, a substantial portion of the amounts thereof $7,322,000 (74%) relates to the Company's obligations to royalty owners and to joint interest owners with respect to properties operated by the Company. Considering the amount of such indebtedness in relation to the Company's total indebtedness, and considering the nature of such indebtedness and the fact that it is not subordinated to Senior Indebtedness, the Company does not propose to impair the claims of its trade and ordinary course of business creditors and has provided in the Plan that such creditors will be paid in full. In that regard, the Company has attempted to keep such indebtedness current and the amount thereof to a minimum. The Company regards it as most important for its future and the preservation of its properties to keep royalty payments, working interest obligations and obligations as to which mechanics' and materialmens' liens could attach current and unimpaired. The Company believes that this approach is in the best interest of all interested parties.

The Plan calls for the issuance of four general forms of New Securities. The New Securities are (i) New Notes, (ii) Preferred Stock, (iii) New Common Stock and (iv) Warrants. The New Notes will be issued to the Bank, Halliburton and the holders of the 15% Senior Notes, with the principal amount of the New Notes to be issued to each of such holders to be equal to or greater than the amount which such

Exhibit 5-5    Disclosure Statement for Prepetition Solicitations                205

holders might receive if the Company were to be liquidated in a Chapter 7 case. The payment schedules for the New Notes to be issued to the Bank and Halliburton will be partially a function of the Company's cash flow and are intended to provide the Company with a flexible means of meeting its future debt obligations. The New Notes to be issued to the holders of the 15% Senior Notes will be non-interest bearing, will be convertible into approximately seven shares of New Common Stock per $1.00 face amount and will not be due until ten years after the Effective Date. The Preferred Stock will be issued in two series, with one series, the $.06 Senior Convertible Voting Preferred Stock (the "Senior Preferred Stock"), to be issued to the holders of the 15% Senior Notes and the other series, the Series A Convertible Voting Preferred Stock (the "Series A Preferred Stock"), to be issued to the holders of the 14⅞% Debentures and the Subordinated Debentures. Each series of the Preferred Stock will have a liquidation preference over the New Common Stock, will have full voting rights with the New Common Stock and will be convertible into shares of the New Common Stock. Each share of the Senior Preferred Stock will have a liquidation preference over the Series A Preferred Stock, will be entitled to a $.06 noncumulative annual dividend under certain limited circumstances and will be convertible into four and one-half shares of the New Common Stock. The Series A Preferred Stock will be entitled to no dividends and each share will be convertible into four shares of New Common Stock. The number of shares of the Series A Preferred Stock to be issued to the holders of the 14⅞% Debentures and the Subordinated Debentures will vary depending upon their current relative status as to right of payment. The New Common Stock will be the common stock of the Company to be issued to the holders of the Common Stock as of the Effective Date. In addition, a substantial additional number of shares of the New Common Stock will be issued to (i) Halliburton in partial consideration for its agreement to accept the modifications to the Halliburton Note, (ii) the holders of the 15% Senior Notes and the Debentures to reflect their true equity interest in the Company and (iii) members of current and future management in consideration for their agreement to remain or become employees of the Company during the Chapter 11 case and as additional incentive for them to continue as or become employees of the Company upon Confirmation of the Plan. Copeland and PWI, the Company's financial advisors, will also receive shares of the New Common Stock as partial compensation for their services to the Company with respect to the development and implementation of the Plan. Finally, Warrants to purchase shares of the New Common Stock will be issued to all of the above parties (other than PWI) in a manner intended to reflect each of the recipient's current and future interest in the Company. The Warrants will have exercise prices ranging between $.075 and $.25 per share, and the holders of the New Bank Note, the New Halliburton Note and the New Convertible Secured Notes will be entitled to pay all or any part of the exercise price of any of the Warrants held by them by surrendering all or any portion of the principal and accrued interest, if any, on such New Notes, with that portion of such New Notes so surrendered being valued at 110% of the amount thereof. Similarly, the holders of the Senior Preferred Stock will be entitled to pay all or any part of the exercise price of any of the Warrants held by them by surrendering any of such shares held by them to the Company, with the shares so surrendered being valued at 100% of their liquidation preference. For a more complete description of the New Securities and their relative rights and preferences, see "THE NEW SECURITIES".

In summary, the Plan attempts to balance the relative rights and interests of the Company's creditors and interest holders, and to resolve numerous potential priority, preference, subordination and similar issues affecting the relative claims of creditors and interest holders in the Company. The terms of the Plan were arrived at after lengthy discussions between the Company and certain of its senior secured creditors and other parties in interest and are based upon the Company's analysis of all claims, an evaluation of the relative merits of potential conflicting claims and a compromise between such claims consistent with the goal of reorganizing the Company into a viable operating entity, which management hopes will prosper for the benefit of all creditors and interest holders.

A brief description of the characteristics of the distribution to each class of creditors and interest holders under the Plan is set forth below:

| Class Description | Estimated Amount of Claims | Estimated Number of Claimants in Class | Brief Description of Distribution under the Plan |
|---|---|---|---|
| | (In Thousands) | | |
| **Class 1** | | | |
| Administrative Expenses(1) | $ 1,700 | 15 | Paid in full or provided for by escrow on the Effective Date. |
| **Class 2** | | | |
| Wage Related Claims(2) | $ 162 | 195 | Paid in full or provided for by escrow on the Effective Date. |
| **Class 3** | | | |
| Employee Benefit Plan Claims(2) | $ 0 | 0 | Paid in full or provided for by escrow on the Effective Date. |
| **Class 4** | | | |
| Tax Claims(2)(3) | $ 2,045 | 66 | Paid in full or provided for by escrow on the Effective Date; provided, however, payments may be deferred at the option of the Company and paid in full in six equal annual installments from the earlier of the date of assessment and the Effective Date. The Company intends to request the Bankruptcy Court to estimate, if possible, the amount of any unliquidated tax claims against the Company and order that an amount equal to such estimate be escrowed for the payment thereof. |
| **Class 5** | | | |
| Additional Priority Claims(2) | $ 0 | 0 | Paid in full or provided for by escrow on the Effective Date. |
| **Class 6** | | | |
| The Bank Secured Claims(4) | $76,964 | 1 | New Bank Note in the Allowed Amount of the Bank's Class 6 claim with respect to the Bank Note ($43,864,000 at June 16, 1986) less all amounts paid thereon during the Chapter 11 case, and $.075 Warrants to purchase 20,000,000 shares of New Common Stock. The Company will continue to be contingently obligated to the Bank for the full amount of the Letters of Credit ($33,100,000 at June 16, 1986) under the Plan. Further, the Bank will be paid in full on the Effective Date the Allowed Amount of its Class 6 claim with respect to its reimbursable expenses under the Loan Agreement. |
| **Class 7** | | | |
| Halliburton Claim(4) | $10,515 | 2 | New Halliburton Note in the Allowed Amount of Halliburton's Class 7 claim with respect to the Halliburton Note ($10,515,000 at June 16, 1986) less all amounts paid thereon during the Chap- |

*Table continued on next page.*

**Exhibit 5-5   Disclosure Statement for Prepetition Solicitations**                    **207**

| Class Description | Estimated Amount of Claims | Estimated Number of Claimants in Class | Brief Description of Distribution under the Plan |
|---|---|---|---|
| | (In Thousands) | | |
| | | | ter 11 case, $.075 Warrants to purchase 20,000,000 shares of New Common Stock and 12,000,000 shares of New Common Stock. |
| **Class 8** | | | |
| 15% Senior Note Claims(5)(6) ........ | $134,542 | 234 | |
| Class 8A | | | |
| 15% Senior Note Secured Claims(5) ........................... | | | Pro Rata distribution of $75,093,000 New Convertible Secured Notes. |
| Class 8B | | | |
| 15% Senior Note Unsecured Claims(5) ........................... | | | Pro Rata distribution of (i) 50,062,000 shares of Senior Preferred Stock, (ii) $.075 Warrants to purchase 87,609,000 shares of New Common Stock, (iii) $.10 Warrants to purchase 75,093,000 shares of New Common Stock and (iv) 40,050,000 shares of New Common Stock. |
| **Class 9** | | | |
| M&M Lien Claims(2) ....................... | $ 1,861 | 304 | Paid in cash not later than the first day of the first month beginning not later than 30 days after the Effective Date or provided for by escrow if not then determined. |
| **Class 10** | | | |
| Secured Trustee Claim(2) ................. | $    0 | 1 | Paid in cash not later than the first day of the first month beginning not later than 30 days after the Effective Date or provided for by escrow if not then determined. |
| **Class 11** | | | |
| Unsecured Claims(2) ........................ | $ 7,937 | 7,400 | Paid in cash not later than the first day of the first month beginning not later than 30 days after the Effective Date to the extent not paid during the course of the Chapter 11 case or provided for by escrow or other appropriate arrangement if the amount of the claim or name and location of the claimant is not then determined. |
| **Class 12** | | | |
| 14⅞% Debenture Claims(6)(7) ...... | $17,706 | 37 | Pro Rata distribution of (i) 13,186,000 shares of Series A Preferred Stock, (ii) $.10 Warrants to purchase 15,022,000 shares of New Common Stock, (iii) $.125 Warrants to purchase 11,684,000 shares of New Common Stock and (iv) 5,591,000 shares of New Common Stock. |

*Table continued on next page.*

| Class<br>Description | Estimated<br>Amount of<br>Claims | Estimated<br>Number of<br>Claimants<br>in Class | Brief Description of<br>Distribution under the Plan |
|---|---|---|---|
| | (In Thousands) | | |
| **Class 13**<br>Subordinated Debenture<br>  Claims(6)(7)............................ | $79,774 | 494 | Pro Rata distribution of (i) 53,681,000 shares of Series A Preferred Stock, (ii) $.10 Warrants to purchase 59,608,000 shares of New Common Stock, (iii) $.125 Warrants to purchase 59,608,000 shares of New Common Stock and (iv) 23,101,000 shares of New Common Stock. |
| **Class 14**<br>  Intercompany Claims(2)................... | $69,411 | 1 | Will receive no distributions. |
| **Class 15**<br>Shareholder Claims of<br>  Interest(8) ...................................... | 51,506<br>shares | 7,671 | Pro Rata distribution of (i) 51,705,723 shares of New Common Stock, (ii) $.125 Warrants to purchase 200,000,000 shares of New Common Stock, (iii) $.15 Warrants to purchase 200,000,000 shares of New Common Stock and (iv) $.25 Warrants to purchase 200,000,000 shares of New Common Stock. |
| **Copeland** ............................................... | * | 1 | $350,000 and not less than 2,700,000 shares of New Common Stock. In addition, Copeland will receive $.075 Warrants to purchase 7,000,000 shares of New Common Stock and $.10 Warrants to Purchase 7,000,000 shares of New Common Stock. |
| **PWI**........................................................ | * | 1 | $150,000 and not less than 1,500,000 shares of New Common Stock. |
| **Management**(8)(9)............................. | ** | ** | 5,000,000 shares of New Common Stock, $.075 Warrants to purchase 17,000,000 shares of New Common Stock and $.10 Warrants to purchase 17,000,000 shares of New Common Stock. |

\*    Copeland and PWI will receive the cash fee and New Securities to be issued to them under the Plan in consideration for the services rendered by them for the Company in developing and implementing the Plan. See "FEES AND EXPENSES OF SOLICITATION".

\*\*   Members of management will receive the New Securities to be issued to them under the Plan in consideration for their agreement to remain or become employees of the Company during the Chapter 11 case and as an additional incentive for them to continue or become employees of the Company upon Confirmation of the Plan. The estimated number of members of management that will receive such New Securities is not currently determinable.

(1) Excludes expenses incurred in the ordinary course of business and expenses associated with the Company's investment advisors and assumes (i) the Effective Date of the Plan is 122 days after the Petition Date and (ii) the Plan is accepted by all classes of impaired creditors pursuant to this solicitation and no material amendments to the Plan are made that would require a resolicitation of such creditors. See "THE PLAN—Classification and Treatment of Claims and Interests—Class 1—Administrative Expenses" and "FEES AND EXPENSES OF SOLICITATION".

*Notes continued on next page.*

**Exhibit 5-5  Disclosure Statement for Prepetition Solicitations**  **209**

(2) As of March 31, 1986.

(3) Calculated after all anticipated offsets, credits and refunds are considered.

(4) As of June 16, 1986, the record date for this solicitation. The Company intends to continue, at least until the filing of a petition for reorganization under Chapter 11, to make monthly installments of principal (currently approximately $1,147,000) and interest on the Bank Note and may, with Bankruptcy Court approval, continue to make such payments at the same or at some reduced level after such filing and until Confirmation of the Plan. The Company is also currently negotiating with Halliburton as to whether some additional principal and interest payments will be made on the Halliburton Note prior to the Company's filing of a petition for reorganization under Chapter 11 and may, with Bankruptcy Court approval, make some payments on the Halliburton Note after such filing and until Confirmation of the Plan.

(5) The Company has not attempted to estimate the specific amount of the claims in either Class 8A or Class 8B because of the integral relationship between such claims and the inherent uncertainties in valuing the collateral securing the payment of the 15% Senior Notes after giving effect to the Bank's and Halliburton's prior mortgages and security interests in such collateral. The Company, however, has calculated the aggregate amount of such claims ($134,542,000 at June 16, 1986) and has provided in the Plan for distributions to the holders thereof based on such aggregate amount. Under the Plan, each holder of a Class 8A or Class 8B claim will be entitled to receive with respect to his Allowed Claim in each such class a Pro Rata distribution (based on the aggregate Class 8A and Class 8B claims) of the consideration to be distributed to the holders in such class.

(6) The estimated Allowed Amounts of the Allowed Claims of the holders of the 15% Senior Notes and the Debentures are set forth as of June 16, 1986, the record date for this solicitation. The actual Allowed Amounts of Allowed Claims of the holders of the 15% Senior Notes and the Debentures as of the Petition Date will be different than is set forth above as a result of the accrual of interest, including amortization of original issue discount, on such securities from June 16, 1986, to the Petition Date.

(7) As of June 16, 1986. The estimated Allowed Amounts of the Allowed Claims of the holders of the 14⅞% Debentures, the 11⅜% Debentures, the 13¼% Debentures and the 12⅝% Debentures due 2001 have been adjusted for the original issue discount with respect to such Debentures, assuming a petition for the reorganization of the Company had been filed on June 16, 1986. Such adjustments are required under the Bankruptcy Code because Section 502(b)(2) of the Bankruptcy Code provides that the Allowed Amount of a claim of a holder of a security may not reflect any unmatured interest. Accordingly, because the face amounts of the 14⅞% Debentures, the 11⅜% Debentures, the 13¼% Debentures and the 12⅝% Debentures due 2001 reflect some amounts of unmatured interest, the estimated Allowed Amounts of the Allowed Claims with respect to such Debentures have been adjusted using the straight-line method of allocating interest so that only that portion of the original issue discount that represents matured interest on such Debentures is included in the estimated Allowed Amounts of the Allowed Claims.

(8) As of June 16, 1986. The estimated amount of claims excludes 200,000 shares of Common Stock issued to Mark A. Roberts pursuant to a severance and consulting agreement with the Company effective as of July 1, 1986. See "THE PLAN—Implementation of the Plan— Management of the Company".

(9) Excludes 800,000 shares of New Common Stock that may be issued to Robert F. Roberts and 800,000 $.25 Warrants that may be issued to Robert F. Roberts and Mark A. Roberts pursuant to the Plan. See "THE PLAN—Implementation of the Plan—Management of the Company".

## COMPARISON OF SECURITIES

The New Securities to be issued under the Plan to the holders of the 15% Senior Notes and the Debentures will have substantially different rights and characteristics than the 15% Senior Notes and the Debentures. A chart describing some of the principal differences between the 15% Senior Notes, the New Convertible Secured Notes and the Senior Preferred Stock is set forth in Exhibit H to this Disclosure Statement and is incorporated herein by reference. A chart describing some of the principal differences between the Series A Preferred Stock and each issue of the Debentures is set forth in Exhibit I to this Disclosure Statement and is incorporated herein by reference. In addition to reviewing the description of the New Securities set forth in this Disclosure Statement, holders of the 15% Senior Notes and the Debentures are urged to review the comparison charts set forth in Exhibits H and I to this Disclosure Statement.

## RISK FACTORS

Acceptance or rejection of the Plan is subject to a number of substantial risks relating to the Company, the Bankruptcy laws, the New Securities and the crude oil and natural gas industry in general. See "PURPOSE AND EFFECTS OF THE PLAN—CERTAIN CONSIDERATIONS" and "RISK FACTORS".

## CERTAIN INCOME TAX CONSEQUENCES

The Company believes that the Consummation of the Plan will constitute a "recapitalization" of the Company under the Internal Revenue Code of 1954, as amended (the "IRC"), and that the non-recognition provisions of Section 354(a) of the IRC will apply. Therefore, subject to certain exceptions, no' gain or loss will be recognized by the holders of the Old Securities (except with respect to the Halliburton Note) upon the exchange of such Old Securities for the New Securities (excluding the Warrants). Whether the holders of the Bank Note and the Halliburton Note will recognize any gain or loss in connection with the Plan will depend upon, among other things, whether the Bank Note, the Halliburton Note, the New Bank Note and the New Halliburton Note are securities. Gain, if any, will be recognized to the extent of the fair market value of the Warrants. Additional tax considerations will be applicable to Copeland, PWI, members of management, certain foreign persons and other entities subject to special tax rules. See "CERTAIN FEDERAL INCOME TAX CONSEQUENCES".

## VOTING AND BALLOT SOLICITOR

RepublicBank Dallas, National Association has agreed to act as Voting Agent, and D.F. King & Co., Inc. has agreed to act as Ballot Solicitor in connection with the Company's solicitation of ballots for the acceptance of the Plan. In addition, Copeland and PWI will provide certain solicitation services to the Company in connection with the Company's solicitation of ballots for the acceptance of the Plan.

## MARKET AND TRADING INFORMATION

As a result of the Company's financial condition, losses and inability to meet its public debt obligations, the American Stock Exchange, Inc. (the "AMEX") on May 19, 1986, suspended trading on the Common Stock, the 15% Senior Notes and the Debentures. Subsequently, on May 30, 1986, the Common Stock, the 15% Senior Notes and the Debentures were delisted from the AMEX. As a result of such actions, the Common Stock is currently listed only on the Pacific Stock Exchange, Incorporated (the "PSE") and the Intermountain Stock Exchange (the "ISE"), and the 15% Senior Notes and the

**Exhibit 5-5    Disclosure Statement for Prepetition Solicitations**                    **211**

Debentures are not listed on any national securities exchange and are traded only in the over-the-counter market. On July 7, 1986, the closing sale price of the Common Stock (symbol: COR) as reported by the PSE was $.25 per share. Since the AMEX's suspension and delisting of the 15% Senior Notes and the Debentures, reported trading with respect to such securities has been very limited and the Company has been unable to obtain any meaningful information with respect to the current market prices for such securities. Information on the historical market prices of the 15% Senior Notes, the Debentures and the Common Stock is set forth in "MARKET AND TRADING INFORMATION".

**TRADING OF THE NEW CONVERTIBLE SECURED NOTES,
THE PREFERRED STOCK, THE NEW COMMON STOCK AND THE WARRANTS**

The Company intends to explore the possibility of listing the New Common Stock, the Preferred Stock, the New Convertible Secured Notes and the Warrants on the PSE or on one or more other national securities exchanges upon the Effective Date. However, there can be no assurance that the Company will make an application to list any of such New Securities or if such an application is made that any of such New Securities would be approved for listing. The inability of the Company to secure the listing of any of such New Securities or the decision not to list such New Securities could affect the liquidity and marketability of such New Securities. In addition, the large number of shares of the New Common Stock that could potentially be outstanding upon Confirmation of the Plan, combined with the low conversion ratios and exercise prices of the New Convertible Secured Notes, the Preferred Stock and the Warrants, will likely depress the prices at which some or all of the New Securities will trade for the foreseeable future, limit the marketability of such New Securities and adversely affect the ability of the Company to list such New Securities on the PSE or on any other national securities exchange. Whether or not any such New Securities are approved for listing on the PSE or on any other national securities exchange, such New Securities may trade in the over-the-counter market. However, even if the New Common Stock, the Preferred Stock, the New Convertible Secured Notes and the Warrants are approved for listing on the PSE or on any other national securities exchange, there can be no assurance as to the prices at which any of such New Securities may be traded when issued or that an established market for any of such securities will develop.

**INFORMATION**

For assistance in voting and copies of the documents relating to the Plan, contact the Ballot Solicitor, telephone number (212) 269-5550 (collect), the Voting Agent, telephone number (214) 922-6147, or L. G. Caskey, Secretary of the Company, telephone number (318) 222-7791 (collect).

## ANTICIPATED OPERATIONS DURING THE CHAPTER 11 CASE

Upon the Company's commencement of a Chapter 11 case, the Company anticipates that it will operate its business as a debtor-in-possession pursuant to Sections 1107 and 1108 of the Bankruptcy Code. The Company intends to carry on its current crude oil and natural gas operations, which, as discussed earlier, would be primarily limited to attempting to maximize production from existing wells and possibly engaging in certain limited development drilling where the wells are considered acceptable risks and the costs associated therewith are expected to be recovered within a short period of time. During the Chapter 11 case, the Company may also seek authority to dispose of certain crude oil and natural gas properties, its remaining refinery assets or other assets. Such dispositions will be subject to the requirements set forth in Section 363 of the Bankruptcy Code.

Section 363 of the Bankruptcy Code prohibits the use of "cash collateral" by the Company without the consent of each entity that has an interest in such collateral, unless such use is permitted by the Bankruptcy Court after notice and hearing. Because substantially all the Company's crude oil and natural gas properties are currently mortgaged and the proceeds therefrom subject to a cash collateral agreement between the Company and the Bank, the Company believes that the vast majority of its cash receipts and other assets will be subject to security interests existing before the commencement of the Chapter 11 case. Accordingly, the Company's use of such cash receipts or other assets during the Chapter 11 case will be subject to the requirements of Section 363 of the Bankruptcy Code. In recognition of the senior position of the Bank Note, the Company, with the approval of the Bankruptcy Court, may continue to make principal payments thereon during the pendency of the Chapter 11 case not to exceed $1,147,000 per month and may continue to keep interest thereon current. Further, with the consent of the Bank and the approval of the Bankruptcy Court, the Company may make additional payments of interest, and perhaps principal, on the Halliburton Note.

Section 364 of the Bankruptcy Code authorizes the Company to obtain unsecured credit and incur unsecured debt in the ordinary course of its business. Any unsecured credit incurred by the Company after the Petition Date would be entitled to treatment as an Administrative Claim. In the event that the Company is required to obtain unsecured credit or to incur unsecured debt after the Petition Date outside the ordinary course of its business, the Company will be required to obtain Bankruptcy Court approval prior to incurring such unsecured credit.

If postpetition financing is necessary and the Company is unable to obtain unsecured credit, the Bankruptcy Court, after notice and a hearing, may authorize the Company to obtain secured credit. In such event, Section 364 of the Bankruptcy Code requires that the creditor extending such secured credit may be entitled to the following treatment: (i) priority treatment over any and all other Administrative Claims; (ii) security in the nature of a lien on property of the Company that is not otherwise subject to a lien; or (iii) security in the nature of a junior lien on property of the Company that is subject to a prior lien of a secured creditor. Furthermore, in the event that the Company is not able to obtain secured credit in the manner set forth above, Section 364(d) authorizes the Company, subject to a hearing on adequate protection to existing lien holders, to obtain secured credit secured by a prior or equal lien on property of the Company that is previously subject to the lien on the property of the Company. While the Company has no current intention to incur unsecured credit outside the ordinary course of its business or secured credit in order to operate its business, there can be no assurance that additional financing will not be necessary in order to continue operations prior to Confirmation of the Plan. Any such credit could ultimately, in effect, reduce the security that one or more classes of the Company's creditors currently has.

Finally, the Company or certain parties in interest may contest various matters or initiate certain adversary proceedings in the Bankruptcy Court during the pendency of the reorganization. These matters or proceedings may involve, *inter alia,* objections to claims, relief from the automatic stay, recovery of voidable preferences, or fraudulent conveyances. The Company will be a party to these matters and will, to the extent necessary, defend or assert the interest of its Estate versus other parties.

Exhibit 5-5   Disclosure Statement for Prepetition Solicitations                213

# FEASIBILITY OF THE PLAN

Assuming the Effective Date of the Plan is December 31, 1986, the Company is expected to have remaining approximately $120,565,000 ($75,093,000 of which will be non-interest bearing) in secured debt (excluding the $32,200,000 in Letters of Credit), and will have no other indebtedness outstanding other than normal and recurring trade indebtedness estimated at approximately $12,000,000, and, possibly, contingent obligations from claims against the Company not resolved or provided for in the Chapter 11 case.

The following tables set forth the Company's (i) Historical Consolidated Statement of Operations for the year ended December 31, 1985, and Statements of Projected Operations for each of the eleven years in the period ending December 31, 1996, and (ii) Historical Statement of Cash Flow for the year ended December 31, 1985, and Statements of Projected Cash Flow for each of the eleven years in the period ending December 31, 1996. In addition to the projected financial information discussed below, reference should be made to "THE COMPANY", "THE PLAN—Implementation of the Plan—Business of the Reorganized Company" and the discussion under the heading "Business" in the Company's Annual Report for a discussion of the business presently conducted and proposed to be conducted by the Company.

The financial projections present, to the best of the management's belief, the expected results of operations and cash flow for the projected periods, utilizing the hypothetical assumptions referred to below.  Accordingly, the projections reflect management's judgment, based on current facts and circumstances, of the expected conditions and management's anticipated course of action upon the Effective Date of the Plan.  WHILE MANAGEMENT BELIEVES THE ASSUMPTIONS SET FORTH BELOW ARE REASONABLE, THEIR VALIDITY MAY BE AFFECTED BY THE OCCURRENCE OF EVENTS AND THE EXISTENCE OF CONDITIONS NOT NOW CONTEMPLATED AND BY OTHER FACTORS, MANY OF WHICH ARE BEYOND THE CONTROL OF THE COMPANY.  THE PROJECTIONS ARE, THEREFORE, NOT INTENDED TO BE REPRESENTATIONS OF THE COMPANY'S FUTURE PERFORMANCE.  ACTUAL OPERATING RESULTS DURING THE PROJECTED PERIODS WILL VARY FROM THE PROJECTIONS AND SUCH VARIATIONS MAY BE MATERIAL.

THE FINANCIAL PROJECTIONS DO NOT ASSUME ANY FUTURE FINANCING BY THE COMPANY, THE CONVERSION OF ANY PRINCIPAL AMOUNT OF THE NEW CONVERTIBLE SECURED NOTES, THE CONVERSION OF ANY SHARES OF THE PREFERRED STOCK OR THE EXERCISE OF ANY OF THE WARRANTS BECAUSE OF THE UNCERTAINTY OF THE OCCURRENCE OF ANY OF SUCH EVENTS.  IF ANY SUCH EVENTS DO OCCUR, SUCH EVENTS WOULD LIKELY HAVE A BENEFICIAL EFFECT ON THE FUTURE CAPITALIZATION OF THE COMPANY AND COULD RESULT IN MATERIAL VARIATIONS IN THE PROJEC-TIONS. THE COMPANY, HOWEVER, EMPHASIZES THAT SUCH EVENTS ARE SPECULATIVE AND THAT THERE CAN BE NO ASSURANCE THAT ANY OF SUCH EVENTS WILL OCCUR.

Historical Statement of Operations for the Year Ended December 31, 1985,
and Statements of Projected Operations for Each of the Eleven Years
in the Period Ending December 31, 1996

(In Thousands)

| | Historical Year Ended December 31, 1985 | Projected Years Ending December 31, | | | |
|---|---|---|---|---|---|
| | | 1986 | 1987 | 1988 | 1989 |
| **REVENUES** | | | | | |
| Crude oil and natural gas ................... | $ 88,927 | $ 51,953 | $38,898 | $45,762 | $43,372 |
| Other income ....................................... | 5,439 | 916 | 623 | 743 | 693 |
| | 94,366 | 52,869 | 39,521 | 46,505 | 44,065 |
| **COSTS AND EXPENSES** | | | | | |
| Lease operating expense ..................... | 15,917 | 11,351 | 9,821 | 9,388 | 7,810 |
| Taxes other than windfall profit ......... | 7,197 | 3,619 | 2,625 | 2,765 | 2,752 |
| Windfall profit tax .............................. | 492 | 400 | — | — | — |
| General and administrative ................ | 13,574 | 13,400 | 7,300 | 7,100 | 7,100 |
| Contingencies ...................................... | — | 1,000 | 1,000 | 500 | 500 |
| Interest and debt expense ................... | 51,368 | 21,309 | 7,120 | 6,642 | 6,453 |
| Exploration costs ................................ | 4,306 | 2,710 | 1,000 | 1,000 | 1,000 |
| Write-down of inventory .................... | 2,500 | — | — | — | — |
| Depreciation and depletion ................ | 52,625 | 201,426 | 16,252 | 15,229 | 14,362 |
| | 147,979 | 255,215 | 45,118 | 42,624 | 39,977 |
| INCOME (LOSS) FROM CONTIN-UING OPERATIONS BEFORE IN-COME TAXES ...................................... | (53,613) | (202,346) | (5,597) | 3,881 | 4,088 |
| INCOME TAXES ...................................... | 60 | — | — | 957 | 1,320 |
| INCOME (LOSS) FROM CONTIN-UING OPERATIONS .......................... | (53,673) | (202,346) | (5,597) | 2,924 | 2,768 |
| LOSS FROM DISCONTINUED OPERATIONS ...................................... | (14,158) | (10,000) | — | — | — |
| NET INCOME (LOSS) ............................. | $(67,831) | $(212,346) | $(5,597) | $ 2,924 | $ 2,768 |

See Summary of Significant Financial Projection Assumptions.

**Exhibit 5-5    Disclosure Statement for Prepetition Solicitations**                          **215**

| | Projected Years Ending December 31. | | | | | | |
|---|---|---|---|---|---|---|---|
| 1990 | 1991 | 1992 | 1993 | 1994 | 1995 | 1996 |
| $44,267 | $39,460 | $35,169 | $32,168 | $28,702 | $23,705 | $18,261 |
| 768 | 1,167 | 2,027 | 2,670 | 3,783 | 4,084 | 1,529 |
| 45,035 | 40,627 | 37,196 | 34,838 | 32,485 | 27,789 | 19,790 |
| | | | | | | |
| 7,201 | 6,033 | 5,359 | 4,716 | 4,475 | 4,135 | 3,564 |
| 2,770 | 2,525 | 2,309 | 2,215 | 2,014 | 1,778 | 1,619 |
| — | — | — | — | — | — | — |
| 7,100 | 7,100 | 7,100 | 7,100 | 7,100 | 7,100 | 7,100 |
| 500 | 500 | 500 | 500 | 500 | 500 | 500 |
| 5,577 | 5,592 | 6,421 | 7,372 | 7,714 | 7,358 | 3,859 |
| 1,000 | 1,000 | 1,000 | 1,000 | 1,000 | 1,000 | 1,000 |
| — | — | — | — | — | — | — |
| 15,041 | 13,927 | 12,776 | 12,248 | 11,077 | 9,175 | 7,295 |
| 39,189 | 36,677 | 35,465 | 35,151 | 33,880 | 31,046 | 24,937 |
| | | | | | | |
| 5,846 | 3,950 | 1,731 | (313) | (1,395) | (3,257) | (5,147) |
| 2,057 | 1,155 | 25 | — | — | — | — |
| 3,789 | 2,795 | 1,706 | (313) | (1,395) | (3,257) | (5,147) |
| — | — | — | — | — | — | — |
| $ 3,789 | $ 2,795 | $ 1,706 | $  (313) | $(1,395) | $(3,257) | $(5,147) |

Historical Statement of Cash Flow for the Year Ended December 31, 1985, and
Statements of Projected Cash Flow for Each of the Eleven Years
in the Period Ending December 31, 1996

(In Thousands)

| | Historical Year Ended December 31, 1985 | Projected Years Ending December 31, | | | |
|---|---|---|---|---|---|
| | | 1986 | 1987 | 1988 | 1989 |
| Income (Loss) from continuing operations | $(53,673) | $(202,346) | $(5,597) | $ 2,924 | $2,768 |
| Add items not requiring cash and interest and debt expense: | | | | | |
| Depreciation and depletion | 52,625 | 201,426 | 16,252 | 15,229 | 14,362 |
| Exploration costs | 4,306 | 1,710 | — | — | — |
| Interest and debt expense | 51,368 | 21,309 | 7,120 | 6,642 | 6,453 |
| Income taxes | — | — | — | 957 | 1,320 |
| Other | 1,571 | 650 | — | — | — |
| Cash flow provided from continuing operations, before debt expense | 56,197 | 22,749 | 17,775 | 25,752 | 24,903 |
| Cash flow provided from discontinued operations | 5,675 | — | — | — | — |
| Other sources of cash flow, net | 15,531 | 1,934 | 921 | — | — |
| Cash flow provided before capital expenditures and debt service | 77,403 | 24,683 | 18,696 | 25,752 | 24,903 |
| Cash available for use (to be provided) at the beginning of year | 4,123 | 5,231 | (847) | — | (638) |
| Cash available | 81,526 | 29,914 | 17,849 | 25,752 | 24,265 |
| Capital expenditures for crude oil and natural gas properties | 9,032 | 6,957 | 1,736 | 13,733 | 6,287 |
| Cash available for debt service | 72,494 | 22,957 | 16,113 | 12,019 | 17,978 |
| Debt service, requiring use of cash: | | | | | |
| Old and New Bank and Halliburton Notes: | | | | | |
| Principal | 28,968 | 18,338 | 11,956 | 9,500 | 15,598 |
| Interest expense, including letters of credit | 8,374 | 5,392 | 4,157 | 3,157 | 2,380 |
| Other Debt (primarily the Debentures): | | | | | |
| Principal | 3,517 | — | — | — | — |
| Interest expense | 26,404 | 74 | — | — | — |
| New Convertible Secured Notes—Sinking Fund | — | — | — | — | — |
| Cash flow available | 5,231 | (847) | — | (638) | — |
| Senior Preferred Stock dividends | — | — | — | — | — |
| Cash available for use (to be provided) in subsequent year | $ 5,231 | $ (847) | $ — | $ (638) | $ — |
| Cash at end of year (See Note F) | $ 9,231 | $ 3,153 | $ 4,000 | $ 3,362 | $4,000 |

See Summary of Significant Financial Projection Assumptions.

Exhibit 5-5   Disclosure Statement for Prepetition Solicitations    217

| | | | Projected Years Ending December 31, | | | |
|---|---|---|---|---|---|---|
| 1990 | 1991 | 1992 | 1993 | 1994 | 1995 | 1996 |
| $ 3,789 | $ 2,795 | $ 1,706 | $ (313) | $(1,395) | $(3,257) | $(5,147) |
| 15,041 | 13,927 | 12,776 | 12,248 | 11,077 | 9,175 | 7,295 |
| — | — | — | — | — | — | — |
| 5,577 | 5,592 | 6,421 | 7,372 | 7,714 | 7,358 | 3,859 |
| 2,057 | 1,155 | 25 | — | — | — | — |
| — | — | — | — | — | — | — |
| 26,464 | 23,469 | 20,928 | 19,307 | 17,396 | 13,276 | 6,007 |
| — | — | — | — | — | — | — |
| — | — | — | — | — | — | — |
| 26,464 | 23,469 | 20,928 | 19,307 | 17,396 | 13,276 | 6,007 |
| — | 6,795 | 20,708 | 30,720 | 48,470 | 53,939 | 56,167 |
| 26,464 | 30,264 | 41,636 | 50,027 | 65,866 | 67,215 | 62,174 |
| 10,412 | 9,451 | 10,827 | 1,483 | 1,868 | 1,003 | 675 |
| 16,052 | 20,813 | 30,809 | 48,544 | 63,998 | 66,212 | 61,499 |
| 8,418 | — | — | — | — | — | — |
| 839 | 105 | 89 | 74 | 59 | 45 | 29 |
| — | — | — | — | — | — | — |
| — | — | — | — | — | — | — |
| — | — | — | — | 10,000 | 10,000 | 55,093 |
| 6,795 | 20,708 | 30,720 | 48,470 | 53,939 | 56,167 | 6,377 |
| — | — | — | — | — | — | — |
| $ 6,795 | $20,708 | $30,720 | $48,470 | $53,939 | $56,167 | $ 6,377 |
| $10,795 | $24,708 | $34,720 | $52,470 | $57,939 | $60,167 | $10,377 |

CRYSTAL OIL COMPANY AND SUBSIDIARIES
SUMMARY OF SIGNIFICANT FINANCIAL PROJECTION ASSUMPTIONS

The financial projections present, to the best of the Company's management's belief, the expected results of operation and cash flow for the projected periods utilizing the hypothetical assumptions referred to below. Accordingly, the projection reflect management's judgment, based on current facts and circumstances, of the expected conditions and its anticipate course of action upon the Effective Date of the Plan. However, while management believes these assumptions are reasonabl their validity may be affected by the occurrence of events and the existence of conditions not now contemplated and by othe factors, many of which are beyond the control of the Company. The projections are therefore not intended to b representations of the Company's future performance. Actual operating results during the projected periods will vary from th projections and such variations may be material. The historical information for the year ended December 31, 1985, extracted from the Company's consolidated financial statements for such year included in the Company's Annual Repor which should be read, including the related footnotes, for additional information. The Company's historical accountir policies have been consistently applied in the financial projections.

The principal hypothetical assumptions underlying the financial projections are as follows:

A.  The financial projections assume a Petition Date of September 1, 1986, and an Effective Date on December 31, 198 In addition, the financial projections assume that the New Convertible Secured Notes and the shares of Preferre Stock to be issued under the Plan are not converted into shares of New Common Stock and that the Warrants to b issued under the Plan are not exercised. The projections for the year ending December 31, 1986, consider unaudite financial results of the Company for the three months ended March 31, 1986, which, in the opinion of managemen include all normal and recurring adjustments and the $174,000,000 valuation adjustment described in the footnot to the Company's consolidated condensed financial statements included in the Company's Quarterly Report. Th remaining periods are based on the hypothetical assumptions discussed herein.

The Company's Board of Directors currently intends to approve a corporate readjustment of the recorded amounts its assets and liabilities to fair value, effected in a form similar to a quasi-reorganization simultaneous with th Effective Date of the Plan. Accordingly, such readjustment is considered in the financial projections.

The adjustments to the fair value of assets are based on the Company's estimates thereof. In addition, the princip amount of the New Convertible Secured Notes to be issued under the Plan is discounted to reflect an impute interest rate of 15% per annum. Therefore, the effects of the quasi-reorganization represent management's be estimates of the quasi-reorganization. The actual effects of the readjustment will be based on the fair values of th Company's assets and liabilities based·upon appraisals prepared by independent experts as of the Effective Dat which will likely be different than considered herein.

B.  Revenues, production costs (including lease operating expense and ad valorem, severance and windfall profit taxes and capital expenditures attributable to crude oil and natural gas production have been determined from the Gru Report, except for certain decreases in the assumptions for projected crude oil and natural gas prices made by th Company subsequent to the issuance of such report. However, it is not practical to have a full reserve repo prepared as often as market conditions are changing in the crude oil and natural gas industry, and the Company h therefore relied on the Gruy Report for purposes of the above information insofar as future volumes of productio and certain other matters are concerned. While pricing assumption adjustments to the Gruy Report data have bee made, such pricing adjustments are not expected to materially affect the production levels and cost informatio contained in the Gruy Report. The Gruy Report, attached hereto as Exhibit F, is referred to concerning th assumptions and procedures utilized in the preparation of such engineering evaluation. For certain information wi respect to reserve evaluations, see "RISK FACTORS—Reserve Values".

Exhibit 5-5   Disclosure Statement for Prepetition Solicitations                    219

The financial projections consider that proved developed non-producing and proved undeveloped reserves will be successfully developed and will have production as reflected in the engineering evaluation. The financial projections include cash available for debt service attributable to the successful development and production of proved nonproducing reserves as follows:

| | 1986 | 1987 | 1988 | 1989 | 1990 | 1991 | 1992 | 1993 | 1994 | 1995 | 1996 |
|---|---|---|---|---|---|---|---|---|---|---|---|
| | | | | | | (In Thousands) | | | | | |
| de oil and natural us revenues | $2,507 | $4,835 | $13,774 | $19,568 | $25,572 | $25,291 | $23,931 | $23,795 | $21,988 | $18,163 | $13,918 |
| duction costs | 303 | 695 | 1,212 | 1,649 | 2,185 | 2,232 | 2,334 | 2,596 | 2,664 | 2,465 | 2,358 |
| ease in cash flow ovided from con- nuing operations | 2,204 | 4,140 | 12,562 | 17,919 | 23,387 | 23,059 | 21,597 | 21,199 | 19,324 | 15,698 | 11,560 |
| ease in capital ex- enditures | 3,184 | 1,496 | 13,733 | 6,287 | 10,412 | 9,451 | 10,827 | 1,483 | 1,868 | 1,003 | 675 |
| ease (decrease) in ash available for ebt service | $ (980) | $2,644 | $(1,171) | $11,632 | $12,975 | $13,608 | $10,770 | $19,716 | $17,456 | $14,695 | $10,885 |

Year Ending December 31.

As reflected in the above table, the ability of the Company to fund the obligations contemplated by the Plan is dependent upon the success of the Company's future development drilling program.

The pricing assumptions utilized for determining future crude oil and natural gas reserves, as considered in the engineering evaluation, have been made by the Company based on advice of Copeland, the Company's principal financial advisor. Such pricing assumptions consider that the prices for the Company's crude oil for the last nine months of 1986, for the year ending December 31, 1987, and for each year thereafter in the projections will average approximately $13.00, $16.25, and $20.00 per barrel, respectively. The prices for the Company's natural gas for such periods are assumed to average approximately $2.60, $2.30 and $3.00 per Mcf, respectively. If future prices differ, the level of reserves the Company will be able to economically produce could be affected. As of June 16, 1986, the Company's average price for the Company's crude oil and natural gas was approximately $12.50 per barrel and $2.45 per Mcf. To illustrate meaningfully the effect on the projected cash available for debt service (i.e., Available Cash Flow), the following table considers hypothetical assumed increases and decreases in crude oil and natural gas prices and the related increases and decreases to cash available for debt service reflected in the financial projections, without considering any changes in production, drilling activities, interest income resulting from fluctuations in cash available for short-term investment or debt service payments. Accordingly, the adjustments to cash flow available for debt service considered below may not reflect the maximum changes attributable to the hypothetical fluctuations in the crude oil and natural gas prices:

### Hypothetically Assumed Increase (Decrease) in Average Prices of Crude Oil and Natural Gas

| Percentage Change to Average Prices Considered in Financial Projections | Crude Oil (bbls.) | | | Natural Gas (Mcf) | | |
|---|---|---|---|---|---|---|
| | 1986 | 1987 | Thereafter | 1986 | 1987 | Thereafter |
| 20% | $15.60 | $19.50 | $24.00 | $3.12 | $2.76 | $3.60 |
| 15 | 14.95 | 18.69 | 23.00 | 2.99 | 2.65 | 3.45 |
| 10 | 14.30 | 17.88 | 22.00 | 2.86 | 2.53 | 3.30 |
| 5 | 13.65 | 17.06 | 21.00 | 2.73 | 2.42 | 3.15 |
| (5) | 12.35 | 15.44 | 19.00 | 2.47 | 2.19 | 2.85 |
| (10) | 11.70 | 14.63 | 18.00 | 2.34 | 2.07 | 2.70 |
| (15) | 11.05 | 13.81 | 17.00 | 2.21 | 1.96 | 2.55 |
| (20) | 10.40 | 13.00 | 16.00 | 2.08 | 1.84 | 2.40 |

**Effects of Hypothetical Assumed Increases (Decreases)
in Average Prices of Crude Oil and Natural Gas and Corresponding
Increase (Decrease) to "Projected Cash Flow Available for Debt Service"
Reflected in the Financial Projections**

| Percentage Change to Average Prices Considered in Financial Projections | Projected Years Ending December 31, | | | | | | | | | | |
|---|---|---|---|---|---|---|---|---|---|---|---|
| | 1986 | 1987 | 1988 | 1989 | 1990 | 1991 | 1992 | 1993 | 1994 | 1995 | 1996 |
| | (In Thousands) | | | | | | | | | | |
| 20% | $6,966 | $7,526 | $8,843 | $8,335 | $8,432 | $7,608 | $6,825 | $6,432 | $5,729 | $4,691 | $3,665 |
| 15 | 5,225 | 5,645 | 6,633 | 6,251 | 6,324 | 5,706 | 5,119 | 4,824 | 4,297 | 3,518 | 2,748 |
| 10 | 3,483 | 3,763 | 4,422 | 4,167 | 4,216 | 3,804 | 3,412 | 3,216 | 2,865 | 2,346 | 1,832 |
| 5 | 1,742 | 1,882 | 2,211 | 2,084 | 2,108 | 1,902 | 1,706 | 1,608 | 1,432 | 1,173 | 916 |
| (5) | (1,742) | (1,882) | (2,211) | (2,084) | (2,108) | (1,902) | (1,706) | (1,608) | (1,432) | (1,173) | (916) |
| (10) | (3,483) | (3,763) | (4,422) | (4,167) | (4,216) | (3,804) | (3,412) | (3,216) | (2,865) | (2,346) | (1,832) |
| (15) | (5,225) | (5,645) | (6,633) | (6,251) | (6,324) | (5,706) | (5,119) | (4,824) | (4,297) | (3,518) | (2,748) |
| (20) | (6,966) | (7,526) | (8,843) | (8,335) | (8,432) | (7,608) | (6,825) | (6,432) | (5,729) | (4,691) | (3,665) |

The engineering evaluation considers that production costs and capital expenditures will remain constant at the same levels as that considered in the Company's December 31, 1985, reserve report. See the Company's Annual Report.

Capital expenditures for crude oil and natural gas properties do not consider that the Company's inventory of lease and well equipment will be utilized. To the extent that the Company currently has an inventory of lease and well equipment that can be utilized in the projected drilling activities, future cash expenditures could be reduced and cash available for debt service could be increased. In addition, the value of lease and well equipment salvaged from abandoned crude oil and natural gas properties is assumed to be less than abandonment and refurbishment costs by $1,200,000 in the financial projections.

C.  The financial projections consider that the Company will continue monthly payments on the Bank Note of $1,147,000 plus accrued interest through August 1986, and thereafter the monthly installments on the Bank Note and the New Bank Note, as the case may be, will be equal to the Minimum Payment described in "THE NEW SECURITIES—The New Bank Note and the Letters of Credit". The financial projections also consider that beginning in 1987 an additional principal payment will be made on the New Bank Note in an amount equal to a specified percentage of Available Cash Flow to the extent the amount calculated exceeds the principal and interest payments previously paid on such debt during the year. The percentage of Available Cash Flow to be applied to the New Bank Note is currently being negotiated between the Bank and Halliburton, but is expected to be between 70% and 91%. In addition, it is considered that an additional principal payment of $2,250,000 will be paid on the Halliburton Note during 1986. Such additional payment reflects the Company's latest offer to Halliburton with respect to the Company's resumption of payments on the Halliburton Note. Principal payments on the New Halliburton Note are considered to be determined in an amount equal to the Available Cash Flow less any amounts paid on the New Bank Note (including interest) and interest payments previously paid on the New Halliburton Note during the year.

The Bank Note and New Bank Note are considered to accrue interest at prime plus ¼%. The Halliburton Note and New Halliburton Note are considered to accrue interest at 12% through July 5, 1986, and thereafter at prime plus ¼%. The reduction in the annual rate of interest on the Halliburton Note from 12% to prime plus ¼% reflects the Company's latest offer to Halliburton with respect to the Company's resumption of payments of principal and interest on the Halliburton Note. The prime interest rate in the last nine months of 1986, 1987, and thereafter is assumed to average 8½%, 9%, and 9½%, respectively.

Exhibit 5-5   Disclosure Statement for Prepetition Solicitations                     221

Although the Bank and Halliburton have not agreed on an allocation of Available Cash Flow, the allocation of the amount attributable to the payment of principal on the New Bank Note and the New Halliburton Note is based on the percentages of each of the aggregate amount of both Notes at the beginning of the year. It is not presently determinable whether the amount of the Letters of Credit outstanding will be considered in determining the annual allocation of Available Cash Flow between the New Bank Note and New Halliburton Note. Therefore, the following tables reflect the effect on the debt service of such obligations considering whether the Letters of Credit are included or excluded:

### Allocation of Payments Including Letters of Credit

| | Projected Years Ending December 31, | | | | | | | | | | |
|---|---|---|---|---|---|---|---|---|---|---|---|
| | 1986 | 1987 | 1988 | 1989 | 1990 | 1991 | 1992 | 1993 | 1994 | 1995 | 1996 |
| **Bank Note and New Bank Note:** | | | | | | | | | | | |
| Minimum monthly principal payment | $13,088 | $10,500 | $ 9,500 | $ 5,000 | $3,177 | $ — | $— | $— | $— | $— | $— |
| Cash sweep principal payment | — | 628 | — | 8,639 | — | — | — | — | — | — | — |
| Interest expense, including letters of credit fee paid | 4,412 | 3,374 | 2,419 | 1,642 | 302 | 105 | 89 | 74 | 59 | 45 | 29 |
| Total debt service on Bank Note and New Bank Note | 17,500 | 14,502 | 11,919 | 15,281 | 3,479 | 105 | 89 | 74 | 59 | 45 | 29 |
| **Halliburton Note and New Halliburton Note:** | | | | | | | | | | | |
| Principal payments | 5,250 | — | — | — | — | — | — | — | — | — | — |
| Cash sweep principal payments | — | 828 | — | 1,959 | 5,241 | — | — | — | — | — | — |
| Interest expense | 980 | 783 | 738 | 738 | 537 | — | — | — | — | — | — |
| Total debt service on Halliburton Note and New Halliburton Note | 6,230 | 1,611 | 738 | 2,697 | 5,778 | — | — | — | — | — | — |
| **TOTAL** | $23,730 | $16,113 | $12,657 | $17,978 | $9,257 | $105 | $89 | $74 | $59 | $45 | $29 |

### Allocation of Payments Excluding Letters of Credit

| | Projected Years Ending December 31, | | | | | | | | | | |
|---|---|---|---|---|---|---|---|---|---|---|---|
| | 1986 | 1987 | 1988 | 1989 | 1990 | 1991 | 1992 | 1993 | 1994 | 1995 | 1996 |
| **Bank Note and New Bank Note:** | | | | | | | | | | | |
| Minimum monthly principal payment | $13,088 | $10,500 | $ 9,500 | $ 5,000 | $5,000 | $ — | $— | $— | $— | $— | $— |
| Cash sweep principal payment | — | — | — | 6,417 | 1,027 | — | — | — | — | — | — |
| Interest expense, including letters of credit fee paid | 4,412 | 3,374 | 2,483 | 1,707 | 501 | 105 | 89 | 74 | 59 | 45 | 29 |
| Total debt service on Bank Note and New Bank Note | 17,500 | 13,874 | 11,983 | 13,124 | 6,528 | 105 | 89 | 74 | 59 | 45 | 29 |
| **Halliburton Note and New Halliburton Note:** | | | | | | | | | | | |
| Principal payments | 5,250 | — | — | — | — | — | — | — | — | — | — |
| Cash sweep principal payments | — | 1,456 | — | 4,180 | 2,392 | — | — | — | — | — | — |
| Interest expense | 980 | 783 | 674 | 674 | 245 | — | — | — | — | — | — |
| Total debt service on Halliburton Note and New Halliburton Note | 6,230 | 2,239 | 674 | 4,854 | 2,637 | — | — | — | — | — | — |
| **TOTAL** | $23,730 | $16,113 | $12,657 | $17,978 | $9,165 | $105 | $89 | $74 | $59 | $45 | $29 |

The financial projections consider that the Letters of Credit are included in the allocation of principal payments between the New Bank Note and New Halliburton Note; however, the effect on the financial projections from excluding the Letters of Credit in the allocation of such payments would not be material.

D.  Other income primarily consists of interest earned on short-term cash investments and fees for the gathering and transportation of natural gas from certain field systems.  Short-term cash investments are assumed to earn interest at 6.5%, which approximates the rate currently being realized by the Company.  Other income for 1986 has been reduced by a loss of $325,000 which resulted from the sale of certain of the Company's transportation assets.  The net proceeds from such sale are approximately $775,000.  In addition, the Company's other primary transportation assets are considered to be sold in June 1987 for approximately $850,000.

E.  General and administrative costs and expenses for 1986 include $5,250,000 of costs and expenses associated with the Plan (which amount represents $1,950,000 anticipated to be incurred prior to filing for reorganization and $3,300,000 of administrative expenses after filing for reorganization, including fees to Copeland and PWI).  In addition, general and administrative costs and expenses assume that current levels of staffing and expenditures are maintained through the projection period, except to the extent that adjustments can be reasonably estimated.  Such adjustments primarily relate to decreases in costs incurred for outside consulting and professional services, salary and related costs due to reductions in the number of employees, and costs and expenses related to assets assumed to be sold.  The Company has historically incurred and it is assumed that it will continue to incur costs and expenses attributable to its Land and Geological Departments, which are charged for financial reporting purposes to exploration costs.  Such costs and expenses were $1,239,000 in 1985, and are projected to be approximately $1,000,000 for each of the eleven years in the period ending December 31, 1996.

F.  The financial projections consider that cash provided from accounts receivable and other current assets will fund the Company's current accounts payable and accrued expenses, other than interest relating to the Company's debt obligations.  In addition, the financial projections consider that the Company will retain $4,000,000 in cash to fund its day-to-day operations, except to the extent such funds are needed to make the minimum payments on the New Bank Note and the New Halliburton Note.

G.  The amount of contingency costs and expenses is an estimate to provide for items not specifically identified or currently contemplated.  Such costs and expenses could relate to such items as workovers, litigation settlements, indemnification payments for tax benefits sold, tax claims, and other unspecified contingencies.

H.  The Company is currently considering various alternatives for its Longview Refinery, including, but not limited to, selling the refinery assets to a third party, entering into an agreement whereby a third party would operate such assets with the Company retaining a net profits interest, or salvaging the refinery.  It is not currently determinable when economic conditions will enable the Company to exercise these or any other alternatives relative to this refinery.  Consequently, the financial projections do not consider any benefit or detriment relating to the sale or operation of such assets.  The Company's Adobe Refinery is considered to be salvaged and sold for its metal value in 1986 and that the Company will receive approximately $80,000 in cash.

I.  The financial projections consider that the rules and regulations of the Service, as they relate to federal income and windfall profit taxes, and of the state and local taxing authorities remain as in effect on December 31, 1985.  Since the Company intends to account for the effects of the Plan in a manner similar to a quasi-reorganization and is not anticipated to incur any cash obligations for federal income tax consequences, the tax benefits from the prospective use of net operating losses, investment tax credits, and statutory depletion carryforwards for financial reporting purposes arising prior to the Effective Date of the Plan will be treated as an increase to additional paid-in capital.  See "CERTAIN FEDERAL INCOME TAX CONSEQUENCES".

**Exhibit 5-5    Disclosure Statement for Prepetition Solicitations**                223

# ALTERNATIVES TO THE PLAN

The Company believes that the Plan affords creditors and interest holders the potential for the greatest realization out of the Company's assets and, therefore, is in the best interests of creditors and shareholders. Management of the Company has considered alternatives to the Plan such as a liquidation and a sale of its assets in the context of a Chapter 11 or Chapter 7 case. In the opinion of management, such alternatives would not afford creditors or shareholders as great a realization potential as does the Plan.

## LIQUIDATION ANALYSIS

If the Plan is not confirmed, the theoretical alternatives include (i) liquidation or (ii) an alternative plan of reorganization.

In evaluating its business operations, the Company has considered the alternative of immediately liquidating its assets. In considering this alternative, the Company, both in the context of an ongoing concern and in a liquidation, has taken into account the nature, status, and underlying values of its tangible and intangible assets, the ultimate realizable value of such assets, and the extent to which certain of its assets are subject to the liens and security interests of its secured creditors. In arriving at the estimated liquidation value of its assets, the Company has taken into account its internal assessment of such assets and the likely net realizable liquidation value of such assets. The Company also considered a recent reserve report, the 10-Q Gruy Report, prepared by the Company's independent petroleum engineers. The Company, however, emphasizes that the determination of the hypothetical proceeds from the sale of its assets in a liquidation is an uncertain process involving numerous underlying assumptions. Accordingly, there can be no assurance that the assumptions employed by the Company in determining the liquidation value of its assets results in an accurate estimation of such liquidation values.

### Assets

The Company's assets consist primarily of producing crude oil and natural gas properties, cash, accounts receivable, land and buildings and related assets. The Company has analyzed and evaluated each of such assets, based upon, among other factors described herein, its unaudited Consolidated Balance Sheet at March 31, 1986, and the 10-Q Gruy Report reflecting the Company's proved crude oil and natural gas properties. As reflected in the following tables, management of the Company has concluded that the liquidation value of its assets is approximately $122,000,000 (the "Liquidation Proceeds").

## CRYSTAL OIL COMPANY AND SUBSIDIARIES
### ESTIMATED LIQUIDATION ANALYSIS

### ASSETS

| | Historical Amounts as of March 31. 1986 | Liquidation Amount |
|---|---|---|
| | (In Thousands) | |
| **Current Assets** | | |
| Cash | $ 8,406 | $ 8,406 |
| Accounts receivable | 11,150 | 11,100 |
| Inventories | 3,035 | 3,035 |
| Prepaid expenses and other | 1,924 | 1,300 |
| Total Current Assets | 24,515 | 23,841 |
| **Property, Plant and Equipment, net** | | |
| Producing crude oil and natural gas properties | 110,807 | 90,944 |
| Land and buildings | 3,363 | 2,500 |
| Furniture, office equipment, and other | 767 | 650 |
| Transportation equipment | 1,943 | 1,525 |
| Total Property, Plant and Equipment | 116,880 | 95,619 |
| **Other Assets** | | |
| Net assets of discontinued refinery operations held for sale | 2,003 | 2,003 |
| Miscellaneous other assets | 401 | 200 |
| Total Other Assets | 2,404 | 2,203 |
| TOTAL ASSETS | $ 143,799 | $121,663 |

### LIABILITIES AND DEFICIENCY IN STOCKHOLDERS' EQUITY

| | | |
|---|---|---|
| **Secured debt** | | |
| Bank Note | $ 47,092 | $ 47,092 |
| Bank Note interest and expenses | 372 | 3,762 |
| Letters of Credit | 762 | 32,200 |
| Letters of Credit fee | 73 | 480 |
| Halliburton Note | 11,028 | 11,028 |
| Halliburton Note interest | 99 | 2,361 |
| 15% Senior Notes ($125,155,000 face) | 200,581 | 14,919 |
| 15% Senior Notes interest | 3,230 | — |
| **Other claims** | | |
| Accounts payable, accrued expenses, taxes, and other | 13,703 | 7,821 |
| Administrative expenses | — | 2,000 |
| **Unsecured debt** | | |
| 12⅝% Debentures due 1990 | 7,715 | .— |
| 12⅝% Debentures due 1990 interest | 284 | — |
| 9 % Debentures | 14,259 | — |
| 9 % Debentures interest | 535 | — |
| 14⅞% Debentures ($16,691,000 face) | 16,443 | — |
| 14⅞% Debentures interest | 724 | — |
| 11⅜% Debentures ($20,412,000 face) | 18,492 | — |
| 11⅜% Debentures interest | 1,064 | — |
| 13¾% Debentures ($12,919,000 face) | 12,727 | — |
| 13¾% Debentures interest | 370 | — |
| 12⅝% Debentures due 2001 ($26,319,000 face) | 20,346 | — |
| 12⅝% Debentures due 2001 interest | 969 | — |
| Deficiency in Stockholders' Equity | (227,069) | — |
| TOTAL LIABILITIES AND STOCKHOLDERS' DEFICIENCY | $ 143,799 | $121,663 |

See Summary of Significant Assumptions to Estimated Liquidation Analysis.

**Exhibit 5-5   Disclosure Statement for Prepetition Solicitations**                    **225**

### CRYSTAL OIL COMPANY AND SUBSIDIARIES

### SUMMARY OF SIGNIFICANT ASSUMPTIONS TO ESTIMATED LIQUIDATION ANALYSIS

The liquidation analysis assumes that the Plan is not confirmed and that all assets of the Company and its subsidiaries are liquidated by December 31, 1987, in the context of a Chapter 7 case.   The hypothetical assumptions utilized in the analysis consider the estimated liquidation value of the Company's assets and estimated amount of claims that would be Allowed, together with an estimate of certain administrative costs and other expenses that would likely result during the liquidation process.   While management believes that the assumptions utilized in the liquidation analysis are reasonable, the validity of such assumptions may be affected by the occurrence of events and the existence of conditions not now contemplated and by other factors, many of which will be beyond the control of the Bankruptcy Court and the Company.   The liquidation analysis is therefore not intended to be representative of the Company's current liquidation value.   The actual liquidation value of the Company will vary from that considered herein and variations may be material.

The principal hypothetical assumptions underlying the liquidation analysis are primarily the same as those utilized in the financial projections, except as follows:

A.   The liquidation analysis considers that producing crude oil and natural gas properties will be sold in three equal installments on December 31, 1986, June 30, 1987, and December 31, 1987.   The proceeds from such sales have been estimated by the Company based on the 10-Q Gruy Report ( see "THE COMPANY—Additional Reserve Information"), adjusted to consider the Company's estimate of the depressed market condition for the sale of crude oil and natural gas properties, a buyer's allowance for return on investment, and other normal risks incidental to the crude oil and natural gas industry.   Based on such assumptions, the Company has estimated that its and its subsidiaries' total proved reserves could be sold for approximately $66,527,000 or $3.00 per equivalent barrel ( natural gas converted to barrels on the basis of approximate energy content) and, accordingly, the liquidation value of the Company's crude oil and natural gas properties is based on the estimated proved reserves attributable thereto valued at $66,527,000, plus cash flow of $24,417,000, net of operating, general and administrative costs and expenses ( see note F), estimated to be provided from operation of such properties prior to the assumed dates of the aforementioned property sales.   However, there can be no assurance that a buyer would exist for the Company's crude oil and natural gas properties or at what price the proposed sales would be consummated.   In addition, the sales price of the Company's crude oil and natural gas properties could be adversely affected because of the poor bargaining position of the Company if a forced liquidation were to occur.

The Company's undeveloped lease and mineral rights are primarily located in geographical areas in which the Company has properties with proved crude oil and natural gas reserves.   As such, the value of such leases is considered to be reflected in the value of the proved reserve of the surrounding properties, and no incremental value has been considered in the liquidation analysis for the Company's undeveloped lease and mineral rights.

B.   Certain of the Company's assets which are not converted to cash in the normal course of operations ( e.g., accounts receivables) or consumed in its business activities ( e.g., prepaid costs and expenses) are assessed to be sold for amounts estimated by the Company to represent their liquidation value.   Such assets are primarily described as follows along with the major assumptions considered in the liquidation analysis:

| Description of the Asset | Assumptions Considered in Liquidation Analysis |
|---|---|
| Inventory of lease and well equipment .......... | Sold in three equal installments on December 31, 1986, June 30, 1987, and December 31, 1987. |
| Land and buildings ....................................... | Primarily relates to the sale of the Company's principal executive office on December 31, 1987. |
| Furniture, office equipment and other............ | Sold in three equal installments on December 31, 1986, June 30, 1987, and December 31, 1987. |

| Description<br>of the Asset | Assumptions Considered<br>in Liquidation Analysis |
|---|---|
| Refinery assets............................................... | Considers that the Longview Refinery is sold in 1987 for an amount equal to its net book value of approximately $2,000,000. |

C. The liquidation analysis considers that the Company will continue monthly payments on the Bank Note of $1,147,000 plus accrued interest at prime plus ¼%. The prime interest rate is assumed to average 8½% during the last nine months of 1986 and 9% in 1987. In addition, the proceeds from the sale of assets are considered to be utilized to repay principal on the Bank Note to the extent such assets represent collateral under the Loan Agreement. Otherwise, the proceeds are considered to be retained and distributed on December 31, 1987, to creditors in order of their preferential claims.

It is assumed that no principal or interest payments will be made on the Halliburton Note, the 15% Senior Notes, or the Debentures prior to December 31, 1987. In addition, it is assumed that the principal amount outstanding under the Halliburton Note and all accrued interest, calculated at 12% compounded monthly, will be paid in full on December 31, 1987. The 15% Senior Notes are assumed to receive approximately $14,919,000 ($.11 per dollar of Allowed Claim) which represents $7,252,000 ($.05 per dollar of Allowed Claim) from the sale of assets mortgaged under the 15% Senior Note Indenture and $7,667,000 ($.06 per dollar of Allowed Claim) from the allocation of the proceeds from the liquidation of unsecured assets and the enforcement of subordination rights.

D. The liquidation values allocated to the Letters of Credit represent the aggregate claim outstanding. The actual obligation of the Company with respect to the Letters of Credit, however, is primarily dependent upon cash payments made for the indemnification to various third parties for the loss of tax benefits received by such third parties under safe harbor leases entered into by the Company. See "THE OLD DEBT SECURITIES—The Bank Note and the Letters of Credit". Accordingly, to the extent that the actual cash obligations attributable to the Letters of Credit are less than the amount considered in the liquidation analysis, the excess would primarily be allocated to the payment of the 15% Senior Notes because the property securing the Company's obligations with respect to the payment of the 15% Senior Notes also secures the payment of the Company's obligations with respect to the Letters of Credit. Therefore, the allocation of liquidation proceeds to the payment of the 15% Senior Notes could range from approximately $14,919,000 to approximately $46,882,000 ($.11 to $.35 per dollar of Allowed Claim).

E. Liquidation distributions for accounts payable, accrued expenses, taxes and other in the liquidation analysis are considered to be comprised of the following as of March 31, 1986 (in thousands):

| | |
|---|---:|
| Wage related claims........................................................................................................................ | $ 162 |
| Tax claims ................................................................................................................................. | 2,045 |
| Unsecured claims relating to royalty owners ..................................................................................... | 2,520 |
| Net accounts payable paid prior to Chapter 7 filing date and contingencies ...................................... | 2,894 |
| Claims considered to be paid in full................................................................................................ | 7,621 |
| Amount of unsecured assets allocated to unsecured claims other than Class 8B claims...................... | 200 |
| | $7,821 |

The liquidation analysis considers that the holders of secured claims will consent to the payment of royalty owners in order to protect their lien on the Company's producing properties. Accordingly, unsecured claims (Class 11 under the Plan), other than such claims considered to be paid in full, will receive liquidation proceeds in an amount ranging from approximately $.03 to $.04 per dollar of their claim depending on the final distribution of the Letters of Credit (see Note D above).

Exhibit 5-5   Disclosure Statement for Prepetition Solicitations                    227

F.  Administrative expenses are considered to exclude expenses incurred in the ordinary course of business and assume that the liquidation of assets and payment of liabilities will be completed by December 31, 1987.  The administrative expenses are considered to include $1,300,000 for legal expenses for the Company and all Creditor Committees, $100,000 for accountants and $600,000 for printing and other costs.

Administrative expenses incurred in the ordinary course of business are assumed to aggregate approximately $7,580,000.  Such estimate is based on historical levels of general and administrative costs and expenses and assumes, except to the extent that adjustments can be reasonably estimated, that such adjusted costs and expenses will be reduced by 25% and 40% on December 31, 1986, and June 30, 1987, respectively.  Costs and expenses associated with the Company's Land and Geological Departments are assumed to be eliminated by August 1, 1986.

### COMPARISON OF ESTIMATED DISTRIBUTIONS UNDER THE PLAN WITH ESTIMATED RECOVERIES IN LIQUIDATION
#### (Giving Effect to Subordination Rights)

The following sets forth a comparison of the estimated distributions under the Plan with the estimated recoveries in a liquidation of the Company after giving effect to all contractual subordination rights.  Such information should be read in conjunction with the information set forth under "FEASIBILITY OF THE PLAN—Summary of Significant Financial Projection Assumptions" and "ALTERNATIVES TO THE PLAN—Liquidation Analysis—Summary of Significant Assumptions to Estimated Liquidation Analysis".

| | | Estimated Distribution Under the Plan | | |
| | | | | |
| Class | Description | Cash Distribution for each $100 of Allowed Claim | New Securities | Estimated Cash Recovery in a Liquidation for each $100 of Allowed Claim |
|---|---|---|---|---|
| Class 1 | Administrative Expenses | $100 | | $100 |
| Class 2 | Wage Related Claims | 100 | | 100 |
| Class 3 | Employee Benefit Plan Claims | 100 | | 100 |
| Class 4 | Tax Claims | 100 | | 100 |
| Class 5 | Additional Priority Claims | 100 | | 100 |
| Class 6 | The Bank's Secured Claims | — | New Bank Note in the Allowed Amount of the Bank's Class 6 claim with respect to the Bank Note ($43,864,000 at June 16, 1986) less all amounts paid thereon during the Chapter 11 proceeding, and $.075 Warrants to purchase 20,000,000 shares of New Common Stock. | 100 |
| Class 7 | Halliburton Claim | — | New Halliburton Note in the Allowed Amount of Halliburton's Class 7 claim with respect to the Halliburton Note ($10,515,000 at June 16, 1986) less all amounts paid thereon during the Chapter 11 proceeding, $.075 Warrants to purchase 20,000,000 shares of New Common Stock and 12,000,000 shares of New Common Stock. | 100 |
| Class 8A | 15% Senior Note Secured Claims | — | Pro Rata distribution of $75,093,000 New Convertible Secured Notes. | 5 |

*Table continued on next page.*

| Class | Description | Cash Distribution for each $100 of Allowed Claim | New Securities | Estimated Cash Recovery in a Liquidation for each $100 of Allowed Claim |
|---|---|---|---|---|
| | | | Estimated Distribution Under the Plan | |
| Class 8B | 15% Senior Note Unsecured Claims | $ — | Pro Rata distribution of (i) 50,062,000 shares of Senior Preferred Stock, (ii) $.075 Warrants to purchase 87,609,000 shares of New Common Stock, (iii) $.10 Warrants to purchase 75,093,000 shares of New Common Stock and (iv) 40,050,000 shares of New Common Stock. | $ 6 |
| Class 9 | Mechanics and Materialmens Lien Claims | 100 | | 3 |
| Class 10 | Secured Trustee Claim | 100 | | 100 |
| Class 11 | Unsecured Claims | 100 | | 3 |
| Class 12 | 14⅞% Debenture Claims | — | Pro Rata distribution of (i) 13,186,000 shares of Series A Preferred Stock, (ii) $.10 Warrants to purchase 15,022,000 shares of New Common Stock, (iii) $.125 Warrants to purchase 11,684,000 shares of New Common Stock and (iv) 5,591,000 shares of New Common Stock. | 0 |
| Class 13 | Subordinated Debenture Claims | — | Pro Rata distribution of (i) 53,681,000 shares of Series A Preferred Stock, (ii) $.10 Warrants to purchase 59,608,000 shares of New Common Stock, (iii) $.125 Warrants to purchase 59,608,000 shares of New Common Stock and (iv) 23,101,000 shares of New Common Stock. | 0 |
| Class 14 | Intercompany Claims | — | — | 0 |
| Class 15 | Shareholder Claims of Interest | — | Pro Rata distribution of (i) 51,706,000 shares of New Common Stock, (ii) $.125 Warrants to purchase 200,000,000 shares of New Common Stock, (iii) $.15 Warrants to purchase 200,000,000 shares of New Common Stock and (iv) $.25 Warrants to purchase 200,000,000 shares of New Common Stock. | 0 |

## Analysis

As indicated above, the Company has concluded that the net realizable value of its assets in a liquidation is approximately $122,000,000. Based on such conclusion, unsecured creditors, secured creditors having an unsecured deficiency claim after liquidation of the collateral securing the Company's obligation to them, and general unsecured creditors of the Company would receive substantially less (probably only nominal amounts) in a liquidation than under the Plan and the holders of the Debentures, whose claims are subordinated to those of the holders of the Bank Note, the Halliburton Note and the 15% Senior Notes, and the shareholders of the Company would receive nothing in a liquidation.

Exhibit 5-5   Disclosure Statement for Prepetition Solicitations          229

The foregoing determination is derived from an analysis of certain claims that are required to be paid from the Liquidation Proceeds before any distribution to unsecured creditors and an analysis of a probable extent of the Allowed Claims of unsecured creditors eligible to share in the balance, if any, of the Liquidation Proceeds. In a liquidation, creditors and interest holders of the Company are paid from available assets in the following general order, with no lower class receiving any payments until amounts due to prior classes have been paid fully or payment provided for:

1. Secured creditors (to the extent of the value of their collateral);

2. Priority creditors;

3. Unsecured creditors; and

4. Shareholders.

It should be noted that in the class of unsecured creditors the subordination agreements, where applicable, will in effect create priorities within that class.

#### Deficiency Claims

The Company has determined that the proceeds from the sale of the Company's secured assets would be insufficient to satisfy the claims of all secured creditors, in particular the holders of the 15% Senior Notes. Moreover, each secured creditor which would be unsatisfied from the proceeds from such a sale would be entitled to an unsecured claim in the amount of any deficiency after the sale of such creditors collateral. Accordingly, secured creditors would be allowed to participate with unsecured creditors in the distribution of proceeds from the sale of the Company's unsecured assets to the extent of their deficiency claim. Based upon the liquidation analysis, the Company believes that unsecured creditors (other than the holders of the Debentures who, because of their subordinated status, would likely receive no distributions in a liquidation) and any secured creditors having deficiency claims (including the holders of the 15% Senior Notes who would likely have a deficiency claim of between approximately $90,007,000 and $121,970,000 depending upon the final distribution with respect to the Letters of Credit) will only receive nominal amounts in a liquidation of the unencumbered assets of the Company. In contrast, under the Plan, the Company believes that secured and unsecured creditors (including the holders of the 15% Senior Notes and the Debentures) will receive a meaningful distribution in respect of their claims.

### ALTERNATIVES

If the Plan is not confirmed, the Company or any other party in interest could attempt to formulate a different plan. Such a plan might involve either a reorganization and continuation of the Company's business or an orderly liquidation of its assets. In respect of an alternative plan the Company has explored various other proposals in connection with the extensive negotiation process involved with the formulation and development of the Plan. The Company believes that the Plan, as described herein, enables creditors and interest holders to realize the most under the circumstances.

THE COMPANY BELIEVES THAT CONFIRMATION AND IMPLEMENTATION OF THE PLAN IS PREFERABLE TO ANY OF THE BANKRUPTCY ALTERNATIVES DESCRIBED HERE-IN BECAUSE IT WILL PROVIDE GREATER RECOVERIES THAN THOSE AVAILABLE IN LIQUIDATION TO ALL CLASSES OF CREDITORS AND INTEREST HOLDERS, INCLUDING THE HOLDERS OF THE DEBENTURES AND THE COMMON STOCK WHO WOULD RECEIVE NOTHING IN A LIQUIDATION. IN ADDITION, OTHER ALTERNATIVES WOULD INVOLVE SIGNIFICANT DELAY, UNCERTAINTY AND SUBSTANTIAL ADDITIONAL ADMINIS-TRATIVE COSTS.

## BANKRUPTCY CONSIDERATIONS

In general, in order to have the Plan confirmed, each class of impaired claims and interests is or will be given the opportunity to vote to accept or reject the Plan. With regard to such classes, the Plan will be deemed accepted by a class if the members who hold at least two-thirds in amount and more than half in number of the total Allowed Claims of the class vote for acceptance. The Plan will be deemed accepted by a class of interests if it is accepted by the members who hold at least two-thirds in amount of the total Allowed Interests. Only those members who vote to accept or reject the Plan will be counted as class members for voting purposes. In the event any class of claims or interests that is impaired under the Plan fails to accept the Plan by the minimum percentage of votes, the Company may request Confirmation pursuant to the cram-down provisions of Section 1129(b) of the Bankruptcy Code, which would allow Confirmation of the Plan regardless of the fact that a particular class of claims or interests has not accepted the Plan. Further, the Company may request the Bankruptcy Court to confirm the Plan pursuant to the cram-down provisions of the Bankruptcy Code in lieu of a vote of the holders of the Common Stock. There, however, can be no assurance that any class of creditors or interest holders under the Plan will accept the Plan or that the Company would be able to use the cram-down provisions of the Bankruptcy Code for Confirmation of the Plan.

Additionally, the following specific risks exist with respect to a Confirmation of the Plan in a Chapter 11 case:

(i) The Bankruptcy Code provides that acceptances or rejections obtained prior to the Petition Date will be effective for Chapter 11 purposes only if the prepetition solicitation of the acceptances or rejections complies with applicable non-bankruptcy law governing the adequacy of disclosure or, if no such law exists, the information distributed prior to or with the solicitation meets the "adequate information" requirements of Chapter 11 set forth in section 1126(b) of the Bankruptcy Code. The Company intends to continue the effectiveness of the ballots received prior to Petition Date for purposes of voting on the Plan once it has filed a petition under Chapter 11. There can be no assurance that (a) a party in interest will not successfully object to the continued effectiveness of the ballots or (b) that the Bankruptcy Court will deem the ballots effective for purposes of Confirmation of the Plan.

(ii) Any objection to the Plan filed in the Chapter 11 case by a member of a class of claims or interests could either prevent Confirmation of the Plan or delay such Confirmation for a significant period of time.

(iii) In the event that certain creditors contest the amount of their Allowed Claim and successfully contend that such amount should be higher than the amount reflected on the Schedule of Liabilities, the Bankruptcy Court may deem the Plan not feasible, and may deny Confirmation of the Plan.

(iv) In the event that any class of impaired claims or interests fails to provide acceptance levels to meet the minimum class vote requirements as described above, the Company may request a cram-down. In order to effectuate a cram-down, the Bankruptcy Court must determine that the Plan is fair and equitable with respect to the dissenting class. The Bankruptcy Code contains guidelines for the application of the fair and equitable standard to secured creditors and interest holders. As indicated earlier, the Company may submit to the Bankruptcy Court for determination the issue whether, in light of all circumstances, the holders of the Common Stock are impaired under the Plan and may seek Confirmation of the Plan without soliciting the holders of the Common Stock pursuant to the cram-down provisions under Section 1129(b) of the Bankruptcy Code on the basis that the Plan does not discriminate unfairly and is fair and equitable to the holders of the Common Stock. See "CONFIRMATION OF THE PLAN—Requirements for Confirmation of the Plan".

**Exhibit 5-5    Disclosure Statement for Prepetition Solicitations**                    **231**

### Treatment of Claims or Interests Under the Plan

Section 1123(a)(4) of the Bankruptcy Code provides that a debtor must provide the same treatmen for each claim or interest on a particular class, unless the holder of a particular claim or interest agrees to  less favorable treatment of such particular claim or interest. The Company believes that it has complie with Section 1123(a)(4) by its classification and treatment of various creditors under the Plan. In th event that the Bankruptcy Court finds that the Plan violates Section 1123(a)(4), and the creditors affecte do not consent to the treatment afforded them under the Plan, the Bankruptcy Court may den Confirmation of the Plan. See "THE PLAN—Classification and Treatment of Claims and Interests".

### Risk of Chapter 11 Filing Prior to Expiration of Solicitation Period

In the event that an unforeseen circumstance occurs, including the filing of an involuntary Chapter or Chapter 11 case against the Company pursuant to Section 303 of the Bankruptcy Code, the Plan ma become inoperative. In such event, the Company may elect to prepare and send to its creditors an interest holders alternative plans of reorganization which may contain various alternative terms an conditions, including, for example, payments and treatment of its Allowed Claims and Allowed Intere different from that set forth in the Plan. In addition, if the Company is required to modify the Plan, t Company may need to resolicit from its creditors acceptances and rejections concerning the Plan.

### General Litigation Disclaimer

Upon the Company's filing of a petition under Chapter 11 of the Bankruptcy Code, the Company v be subject to the jurisdiction of the Bankruptcy Court and the Company's business will be operat pursuant to the requirements of the Bankruptcy Code. The Bankruptcy Code contains numer provisions which set forth various causes of action which are unique to the Bankruptcy Code and r otherwise assertable outside of a bankruptcy case. These causes of action include, but are not limited: matters relating to preferences, fraudulent conveyances, adequate protection, enforceability of, and rel from, the automatic stay, turnover of property of the Company's estate, avoidance of liens, abandonm of property of the Company's estate and certain other matters relating specifically to reorganization un Chapter 11 of the Bankruptcy Code, such as classification of claims and interests, treatment of claims : interests, impairment of claims and interests and disclosure and solicitation in connection with a plan reorganization.

The Plan, at Article IX grants the Company the exclusive right to maintain causes of action to reco preferences and fraudulent conveyances. While the Company is not currently aware of any spec circumstances that would clearly entitle a party in interest to assert any cause of action against Company in a bankruptcy proceeding, there can be no assurance that such circumstances do not exist : that one or more parties in interest will not assert such causes of action against the Company. In the ev that any cause of action is asserted against the Company which materially affects the operation of Company's business or its ability to have the Plan confirmed, it is unlikely that the Company will be : to achieve Confirmation of the Plan within the time hoped for to avail the Company of the benefits of prepetition solicitation contemplated by this Disclosure Statement. If such is the case, the Company r be forced to seek other alternatives to the Plan.

## EXHIBIT 5-6   STANDING CHAPTER 12 TRUSTEE'S INSTRUCTIONS TO DEBTOR'S COUNSEL

_____, Esq.
926 South Hill Street
Denver, CO.

RE:  Chapter 12 Bankruptcy Case No. _____Debtors: _____


Dear _____.

You have filed a petition for relief for a family farmer under Chapter 12 of the Bankruptcy Code on behalf of the above debtor. I am hereby notifying the debtor and you, as attorney for the debtor, of the following:

1. Section 521 of the Bankruptcy Code and Bankruptcy Rule X-1007, require the debtor to cooperate with the United States Trustee and the Standing Chapter 12 Trustee appointed in this case. The debtor is also required to furnish information required by the United States Trustee and the Standing Chapter 12 Trustee in supervising the administration of this case, including regular reports of operations of the debtor's farming enterprise. Also as required by Bankruptcy Rule X-1008, you and the debtor are required to give the Standing Chapter 12 Trustee and the United States Trustee notice of all motions and other pleadings filed in this case.

2. The debtor must provide the Standing Chapter 12 Trustee with the following financial and informational reports:

a. Summary of Operations for Chapter 12 case. The enclosed report is an informational report showing the debtor's acreage, results from last year's operation and estimates or projections for the current or next crop year. This form should be completed and received in the Standing Chapter 12 Trustee office at least five days prior to the first meeting of creditors.

b. Monthly Cash Receipts and Disbursements Statement. The enclosed form should be self-explanatory. The debtor must report no later than the 10th day following the end of the month all of his receipts or income, in cash or by check, received during the month. The receipts should be itemized by kind, quantity and dollar amount, for example: "Sold 2,000 bushels of corn—$2,000", "Sold 10 beef cattle—$4,000", "Sold 5 tons of hay—$275". Likewise, all expenses paid in cash or by check should be itemized. As indicated, household or family living expenses need not be itemized but a lump-sum of cash used or spent for household or family living expenses should be shown. Operating expenses should be itemized under appropriate headings such as fuel, feed, veterinary expense, repairs, etc. Be sure the debtor knows how to complete that part of the form which calls for a monthly reconciliation of cash.

c. Tax Deposit Statement. If the debtor is a family farm corporation or if the debtor has employees for which he must withhold income taxes or pay social security taxes, he must complete the tax deposit statement enclosed with this letter, and provide evidence of payment.

d. Insurance Statement. *Within ten days after the date of this letter, the debtor must provide the Standing Chapter 12 Trustee with a verified statement or written evidence from his insurance carrier or broker that he has fire and extended coverage* on his buildings and equipment and also motor vehicle insurance on all vehicles operated on public highways. If no such insurance is currently in effect, the debtor must explain why it is not in force. The debtor shall immediately notify the Standing Chapter 12 Trustee of any lapse, cancellation or proposed cancellation of any insurance coverage.

3. Under Section 1231 of Chapter 12 of the Bankruptcy Code, a separate taxable entity is created for state and local tax purposes commencing on the day the Chapter 12 petition was filed. Therefore, the debtor is required to commence keeping books and records for the new separate taxable entity. This means that the debtor should do the following:

a. The books and records of the debtor are to be closed as of the date of filing the bankruptcy petition, and a new set of books and records must be kept thereafter for the debtor-in-possession under Chapter 12.

b. All of the debtor's bank accounts must be closed immediately upon the filing of the Chapter 12 petition, and new bank accounts opened. All amounts from the old accounts and all receipts are to be deposited in the new bank accounts, and all disbursements should be made by check. The new bank accounts must be in the name of the debtor as "Chapter 12 Debtor-in-possession", and this description should also appear on the new bank pre-numbered blank checks for his checking account.

c. The debtor must keep a file (or envelope) for copies of all bills, invoices and sales slips for purchases or payments he makes after the petition is filed.

d. The debtor, if an individual, must file a state and local (if required) tax return for that part of the taxable year which ended on the date the Chapter 12 petition was filed as provided by Section 1231 of the Bankruptcy Code.

4. You will receive a separate notice of the date, time and place for the first meeting of creditors under Section 341 of the Bankruptcy Code. Both the debtor and his attorney must attend that meeting, at which the debtor will be examined, under oath, by the Standing Chapter 12 Trustee and by any creditors who may attend. The debtor must bring with him to that meeting a copy of his last year's federal, state, and local (if required) income tax returns, Form 1040, and all Schedules filed with the return, including Schedule F. The copy of the income tax returns must be filed with the Standing Chapter 12 Trustee at the First Meeting as an Exhibit.

5. In addition to the Monthly Cash Receipts and Disbursements Statement referred to in paragraph 2.b. above, within 60 days after the end of a calendar year (or fiscal year), the debtor must complete and file with the Standing Chapter 12 Trustee a Schedule F and Form 4835 of IRS Form 1040 for any part of the first calendar or taxable period ending after the date on which the Chapter 12 petition was filed. The Schedule F and Form 4835 must report all income

234 of Chapter 12 requires

and all expenses to the end of the calendar (fiscal) year. Since Section 1231(b) of Chapter 12 requires the Standing Chapter 12 Trustee to make a state or local tax return for an individual debtor-in-possession, the Standing Chapter 12 Trustee will consult further with you and the debtor-in-possession in order to live up to the joint responsibilities to prepare the tax returns. The debtor is responsible for filing and paying all federal taxes as usual.

6. Since Congress specified that Chapters 1, 3 (except for Section 361) and 5 of the Bankruptcy Code also apply to cases under Chapter 12 of the Bankruptcy Code, you should emphasize to your client that he may not:

a. Retain or employ attorneys, accountants, appraisers, auctioneers or other professional persons without court approval. This includes employing the attorney who filed the petition to provide services after the filing. See 11 U.S.C. Section 327.

b. Compensate any attorney, accountant, appraiser, auctioneer or other professional except as allowed by the Court. See 11 U.S.C. Section 330.

c. Use cash collateral (or cash equivalents) without the consent of the secured creditors or court authorization. See 11 U.S.C. Section 363(c)(2). Cash collateral includes proceeds, products, offspring, rents, or profits of property subject to a security interest when reduced to cash.

d. Obtain credit or incur unsecured debt other than in the ordinary course of business without court authorization. See 11 U.S.C. Section 364(b).

e. Incur secured debt without court authorization. See 11 U.S.C. Section 364(c).

f. Pay any creditor for goods or services provided before the filing of the petition except as provided in a confirmed plan. See 11 U.S.C. Section 549.

7. *A Chapter 12 plan must be filed within 90 days of the date of filing of the petition* (11 U.S.C. Section 1221). Failure to comply is cause for dismissal under 11 U.S.C. Section 1208. The statement of current income and current expenditures required to be filed under 11 U.S.C. Section 521(1) should be accurate and should be reviewed and modified, if necessary, prior to the Section 341 meeting. Failure to provide an accurate statement may result in denial of confirmation, dismissal, or conversion to a Chapter 7 liquidation. Also, be advised that the Trustee will oppose all plans that call for payments outside the plan, including payments to secured creditors during the 3 to 5 year time period the plan is administered by the Trustee.

8. Liquidation Analysis. Under Section 1225(a)(4) of Chapter 12, you must be able to provide at the hearing on confirmation of the plan that the amount that will be distributed under the plan for each allowed unsecured claim is not less than the amount that would be paid on the claim if the debtor were liquidated under Chapter 7. A claim filed by an unsecured creditor is allowed unless the debtor or the Chapter 12 Trustee files an objection to it in Court and the Court sustains the objection. I would suggest that you give consideration to the early preparation of an accurate analysis of the liquidation value of all of the property of the debtor's estate which you must be prepared to offer as an Exhibit at the confirmation hearing, or the Court may not be able to confirm your plan.

9. *Failure to Comply.* Failure of the debtor to comply with the instructions contained in this letter may be grounds for dismissal of this Chapter 12 case under Section 1208 of the Bankruptcy Code.

I am providing your client with a copy of this letter. If you or the debtor have any question about this letter or the enclosed instructions, please call or write to me at 303 East Seventeenth Avenue, Suite 1000, Denver, Colorado 80203, (303) 839-1204.

The trustee's percentage fee to be collected on all payments under plans has been set by the Attorney General at 10 percent on the first $450,000 paid under the plan, and three percent on the overage.

Sincerely,

_____

Standing Chapter 12 Trustee

## EXHIBIT 5-7   REPORTS BY EXAMINER

This Exhibit consists of the following:
Belle Apparel—Examiners' Report, page 236
ABC Systems—Ex-Parte Request for Expedited Hearing on Immediate Appointment of a Trustee, page 245.
ABC Systems—Examiners' Request for Immediate Appointment of a Trustee, page 246

### UNITED STATES BANKRUPTCY COURT
### CENTRAL DISTRICT OF TENNESSEE

**In re:**          ⎫   Case No. 99-99999-XX
Belle             ⎬   EXAMINER'S REPORT
Debtors.          ⎭

In accordance with an order entered by this court on December 15, 1988 and the subsequent appointment by the United States Trustee of _____, CPA as the Examiner of this bankruptcy estate, the Examiner submits this report of initial investigation.

### Outline

### SECTION I - *DESCRIPTION OF DEBTOR*

#### A) Business

The Debtor operates a sole proprietorship doing business as Belle Apparel. In the past, the Debtor owned or controlled related entities which were formed to operate in conjunction with Belle Apparel. These businesses were known as Superior Apparel and Blue Textile. Both entities are defunct according to the Debtor.

Exhibit 5-7   Reports by Examiner                                    237

Historically, the Debtor operated his business as an apparel jobber. This involved the wholesaling of primarily men's apparel goods to Southeastern area retailers. During 19X5, the Debtor expanded his business to include contract sewing services. At present, in the post-petition period, the Debtor is operating exclusively as a contract sewing business.

### B) Location

The Debtor's opperating facility is located at:
  2010 First Avenue
  Nashville, Tennessee
The facility is owned by the Debtor's parents. The building, formerly owned by the Debtor, was sold to the Debtors's parents in July, 19X7, at a gain of approximately $10,000 (according to the Debtor's 19X7 tax return). The building is occupied on a rent-free basis. The Debtor's statement of affairs indicates that a lease agreement exists requiring monthly rent payments of $1,300 which have been "deferred."

### C) Management

The Debtor's business is managed entirely by James Smith. Mr. Smith negotiates all of the business' sewing contracts, oversees production, is responsible for customer and creditor relationships and makes daily deliveries of completed goods. During the period when the Debtor also operated as an apparel jobber, Mr. Smith handled all of the purchasing and resale functions such operations entailed.

## SECTION II - *LEGAL AND ACCOUNTING PROFESSIONALS*

The Debtor informed the Examiner that his attorney since the date of filing has been Tom North. During 19X8, the Debtor has also engaged other attorneys to handle various legal matters.

The Debtor's tax returns are prepared by Lynn Tims an enrolled agent. Prior to 19X8, Ms. Tims also summarized certain of the Debtor's accounting records on a periodic basis and used such data to prepare the Debtor's tax returns. Since 19X8, the Debtor has engaged Ms. Faye Fields to summarize certain of its accounting records on a periodic basis. In prior years, the Debtor also engaged a CPA to compile periodic financial statements.

## SECTION III - *ACCOUNTING RECORDS AND OPERATING REPORTS*

The Examiner spoke with both Ms. Tims and Ms. Fields regarding the Debtor's accounting records and the specific procedures they used to summarize such records. Based on these interviews, the Examiner determined that:

a) The accounting records of the Debtor are maintained using a single-entry bookkeeping system.

b) Bank reconciliations are not performed. Neither of the Debtor's bookkeepers obtained or reviewed the Debtor's bank statements, cancelled checks or bank memoranda

c) No formal cash disbursements or cash receipts journals existed prior to the bankruptcy.

d) The bookkeepers recorded expenses on the basis of vendor invoices marked paid and recorded sales from sales invoices, all based upon only those specific records provided by the Debtor; accounts receivable at any point in time were determined by the Debtor.

A single-entry accounting system cannot be relied upon to yield accurate accounting data. Such a system lacks controls designed to provide a reasonable degree of assurance that all transactions have been recorded. For example, when expenses are recorded from paid invoices and sales are recorded from sales invoices, to the extent such data is misplaced or not turned over to a person responsible for recording such activity, the accounting records of the business will be inaccurate. Further, there are no compensating procedures which would make it known that any data had been omitted.

Based upon the foregoing, the Examiner has determined that the available accounting records of the Debtor are not reliable. The Debtor does not have an accounting system (in the classical sense with *double-entry* journals and ledgers). As such, the Debtor's lack of accounting system procedures and controls leaves a high degree of uncertainty as to the completeness of its financial records and reports.

The Examiner reviewed the October, 19X8 operating report filed by the Debtor as well as a draft copy of the November, 19X8 operating report. The Examiner also discussed how these reports were being prepared with the Debtor's bookkeeper. The Debtor's bookkeeper informed the Examiner that she does not understand the reports and has completed them to her best ability. The Examiner noted that the October, 1988 operating report reflects the collection of pre-petition accounts receivable although the pre-petition accounts receivable balance remain unchanged. The Examiner also determined that the reported inventory balance ($56,000) of the Debtor is overstated. The balance reflected in the operating report includes certain operating equipment which the Debtor has valued at approximately $35,000. Further, the Examiner is not satisfied that the true inventory is actually worth the remaining $21,000 value assigned to it. These factors, together with the problems cited above regarding the Debtor's accounting system, cast significant doubt as to the accuracy or reliability of the operating reports being filed by the Debtor.

Exhibit 5-7    Reports by Examiner                                          239

## SECTION IV - *INVESTIGATION BY EXAMINER*

The proposed Order directing the appointment of an Examiner (lodged by counsel to the Debtor) delineates specific issues which the Examiner was commissioned to investigate. These issues primarily involve transactions between the Debtor and CIB, Inc. (a creditor). Based upon its investigation, the Examiner was ordered to determine ". . . whether the Debtor committed fraud as to CIB which would justify the appointment of a trustee in this case." While the Examiner is not an attorney and, therefore, is unable to render a legal opinion as to whether or not the Debtor committed a fraud upon CIB, the Examiner has learned important facts relating to the transactions entered into between the Debtor, CIB, Inc. and others. The following summarizes information obtained from interviews of James Smith, who cooperated fully with the Examiner, various current and former bank officials, representatives of certain creditors and a selective review of the Debtor's accounting and financial records.

In July, 19X8, the Debtor began purchasing Levi jeans from CIB. According to a declaration filed by CIB, the Debtor purchased approximately $434,000 of jeans from CIB during the period July to September, 19X8. Acting as an apparel jobber, the Debtor, in turn sold these jeans to Atlanta area retailers. During this time, the Debtor also operated his contract sewing operation.

Beginning in late August and continuing through early September until purchases were halted, certain checks written by the Debtor in payment of CIB invoices were returned unpaid by the bank on which the checks were drawn. Although it appears that some of the checks were returned by the bank because the date of the check was altered, the checks were primarily returned unpaid because there were insufficient funds in the Debtor's account. The Examiner has not been able to obtain the Debtor's bank records for the month of September, 1988 and therefore is unable to determine the total amount of checks returned unpaid in the subject time period.

Nevertheless, a review of the Debtor's available bank and accounting records indicates that the Debtor was able to operate its business despite an ongoing chronic shortage of cash. The bank statements of the Debtor reveal numerous check handling and NSF charges for an extended period of time. According to the Debtor's tax returns, such charges totaled approximately $6,500 in 19X5 and 1986 and approximately $20,000 in 19X7. Other data provided by the Debtor's bookkeeper indicated that the Debtor has incurred in excess of $14,000 of bank charges in the nine month period ended September 30, 19X8. Upon substantiation of these facts, the Examiner interviewed available bank officials (including former bank officials) employed by the banks at which the Debtor held accounts. The Examiner also reviewed transactions between checking accounts maintained by the Debtor at different banks. On the basis of these procedures, the Examiner determined that:

a) The Debtor was in daily contact with its primary bank—People Bank.

b) The Debtor informed the Examiner that he would contact the bank daily to determine what deposit amount was necessary to cover checks drawn on its account which had been presented to the bank for payment.

c) The Debtor would then attempt to collect available receipts from customers, borrow funds from various parties or draw checks on his other accounts in sufficient amounts to cover the checks presented to the bank for payment.

d) According to former bank officials, the bank observed checks regularly drawn on the Debtor's parents' checking account and, later, drawn on other accounts of the Debtor. These checks were used by the Debtor to make deposits to cover checks drawn on its account at First International Bank.

e) The Examiner was advised by these same former bank officials that representatives of the bank confronted James Smith and informed him that the bank suspected he was kiting checks, and requested that he stop doing so.

f) In 19X7, the Debtor began cashing checks at XYZ Money Exchange (XYZ) on a recurring basis in order to obtain sufficient cash to cover checks drawn on his accounts. According to the Debtor, XYZ would deduct 2% from the face amount of the check and would give the Debtor cash for the remainder of the check amount.

g) In connection with his practice of cashing checks at XYZ, the Debtor drew multiple checks, payable to XYZ, from multiple accounts on any given day. In reviewing records provided by the Debtor's attorney, the examiner picked one day at random and noted a total of 11 checks, totaling approximately $42,000, drawn on accounts at four different banks.

h) According to the Debtor, XYZ agreed to hold checks for up to two days before depositing them in their account.

i) According to the Debtor and one of the former bank officials interviewed by the Examiner, the bank contacted XYZ and spoke with a representative regarding the Debtor's practice of cashing checks (at XYZ) to cover checks that would otherwise be returned NSF by the bank. According to the former bank official, the XYZ representative advised the bank that XYZ knew what it was doing in dealing with Mr. Smith.

j) The practice of cashing checks at XYZ continued from around February, 19X7 through the middle of August, 19X7. During this approximately six-month time period, the Debtor wrote checks to XYZ exceeding $1.7 million in total. The practice was apparently stopped when approximately $72,000 in checks made payable to XYZ were returned unpaid by the Debtor's banks.

k) A review of the bank account transactions occurring during the period of time that the Debtor was purchasing jeans from CIB indicate that the Debtor was drawing checks on accounts at other banks (even though these bank accounts did not have sufficient funds on deposit to cover these checks) to cover checks drawn on his First International Bank checking account. The Examiner discussed this practice with the Debtor and was informed by the Debtor, that although funds did not exist to cover the check when such

**Exhibit 5-7   Reports by Examiner**                                              **241**

checks were drawn, the Debtor fully intended to be able to cover such checks before they were presented for payment. The Debtor represented that he intended to cover such checks with receipts from his business operations. Due to the Debtor's unadequate accounting records, the Examiner was unable to verify if the Debtor was in fact able to cover such checks with business receipts.

l) The Debtor also informed the Examiner that he believes officials of Peoples Bank were aware of his practices during this time. In fact, the Debtor informed the Examiner that on days when business receipts were not sufficient to cover the shortfall in his account, the Debtor would draw a check from one of his other accounts to cover checks drawn on his Peoples Bank Account (that would otherwise have been NSF). The Debtor represents that he explained to Peoples Bank officers that the check he was depositing was not covered by sufficient funds at the moment it was written and would further explain how he intended to cover the check before it was presented to the other bank for payment. The Debtor claims that, because of the bank's awareness of the manner by which he was covering his NSF checks, he believed that such a method was an acceptable practice.

m) The Examiner attempted to verify the representations made by the Debtor, especially in regards to his banking arrangements, with current officials of Peoples Bank. However, such bank officials declined to speak with the Examiner other than to say that the bank always either honored or rejected the Debtor's checks within the time frame required by law and that at no time did the bank allow the Debtor's account to be overdrawn.

A review of the Debtor's tax returns reveals that historically, the Debtor's business has been only marginally profitable. Exhibit I summarizes the profit or loss reported on the Debtor's federal tax returns during the five-year period from 19X3 through 19X7.

As depicted in the exhibit, the Debtor's most profitable year was 19X4. In that year, the Debtor reported profits of $24,723. Further review of the Debtor's tax returns reveal no other material sources of income apart from the Debtor's business operation. The Debtor informed the Examiner that his living expenses during the five year period averaged approximately $40,000 a year. As depicted in Exhibit II, the Debtor has been unable to meet his living expenses solely from the profits of his business for an extended period of time. The Debtor informed the Examiner that he borrowed money on a short-term basis in order to pay his combined business and living expenses. This process of short-term borrowing gradually grew to a point where ultimately the Debtor was churning debt at an annual rate close to 3 to 4 times the annual gross receipts of its business operations. As previously described, in 19X7, the Debtor engaged in a check cashing scheme that exceeded $1.7 million in a six-month period alone via Gala.

It appears that the Debtor was only able to sustain his cash flow through a convoluted series of short-term borrowings, check kiting, and receipts from his business operations until the middle of 19X8 when a series of events combined to restrict the Debtor's ability to cover checks he had written. The Debtor informed the Examiner that these events were generally the following:

**a)** In mid-19X8, the Debtor lost a supply source of Levi jeans which he was jobbing at the rate of $25,000 to $30,000 per week. After a period of time, this source of jeans was replaced by CIB. In the interim, the Debtor was deprived of a major cash flow source.

**b)** In this same time period, the Debtor lost his two primary sewing contracts.

**c)** Rather than layoff staff, the Debtor chose to retain his employees while he attempted to obtain new sewing contacts and regain one of the lost contracts.

**d)** Creditors, including the IRS and a company with which the Debtor had factored receivables, began to pressure the Debtor for payment of past due balances. According to the Debtor, the IRS eventually levied his bank accounts in order to collect unpaid payroll taxes.

**e)** The Debtor fell behind in his mortgage payments, and incurred unexpected medical and automobile expenses during this period.

Eventually, with decreased cash inflow from his business operations and unabated cash outflow to satisfy creditors and pay living expenses, the Debtor was unable to honor checks he had written to his creditors, including CIB.

## SECTION V - *PROPOSED OWNER'S SALARY*

The Examiner was asked to determine whether a salary of $3,000 per month was reasonable and necessary to support James Smith and his family and necessary for the successful reorganization of the Estate. A salary set at this level, though perhaps necessary to support the Debtor's family, exceeds the recent five year profit history of the Debtor's business on an annual basis. Further, the Debtor's operating statements for the months of October and November, 19X8 reflect an average profit from operations of only approximately $1,800. Under the circumstances, it does not appear that the Debtor can support a monthly salary of $3,000 from its business operations without further detriment to its pre-and post-petition creditors. Serious doubt exists as to whether or not the Debtor's business can be profitable enough to maintain the Debtor's living expenses alone.

## SECTION VI - *RECOMMENDATIONS*

It is the undertanding of the Examiner that the Debtor has prepared a proposed plan of reorganization. The Examiner recommends the following steps be taken in determining the future course or this bankruptcy estate:

**Exhibit 5-7   Reports by Examiner**                                      **243**

1) The Debtor should be required to provide a supportable cash flow forecast showing business profits sufficient to cover his current operating expenses, payments to creditors in accordance with the proposed plan of reorganization and sufficient remaining cash flow to pay the Debtor's personal living expenses.

2) The Debtor must provide accurate operating reports on a timely basis. The Examiner understands that the Debtor has hired a new accountant for this purpose.

3) Subject to the viability of the cash flow forecast described at Item 1 above, three alternatives exist for control of the bankruptcy estate:

   a) Appointment of a trustee to take over the affairs of the estate.
   b) A sale of the business or its assets.
   c) Allow the Debtor to continue to operate his business subject to his ability to attain profitability, adhere to his reorganization plan and file accurate timely operating reports.

In evaluating these alternatives, the Examiner believes that if a trustee were appointed, the trustee would require the services of Mr. Smith in order to operate the business. Any sale of the business or its assets would most likely not generate significant benefits to the creditors. In reviewing the bankruptcy schedules filed by the Debtor, the Examiner noted that the assets of the Debtor, excluding the Debtor's personal residence, are of nominal value and subject to multiple, secured interests. Such assets include the Debtor's business accounts receivable, inventory and sewing machines. Finally, in evaluating the last alternative, the Court should consider that in order to adhere to his plan of reorganization and meet his present living expenses, the Debtor would have to attain levels of profitability far in excess of his historical profit levels.

DATED: January 20, 19X9

                              Respectfully submitted,


                              _____, CPA
                              Examiner

## BELLE APPAREL
## EXHIBIT I - SUMMARY OF SCHEDULE C INFORMATION

|                      | 19X3     | 19X4     | 19X5     | 19X6      | 19X7     |
|----------------------|----------|----------|----------|-----------|----------|
| Gross Receipts       | 562,888  | 769,979  | 543,172  | 408,602   | 597,590  |
| Gross Profit         | 51,105   | 91,604   | 97,726   | 86,038    | 196,552  |
| Operating Expenses   | 36,776   | 66,881   | 76,463   | 102,003   | 183,577  |
| Profit <Loss>        | 14,329   | 24,723   | 21,263   | <15,965>  | 12,975   |

SOURCE: Debtor's United States Individual Tax Returns, Schedule C - Profit or [Loss] from Business or Profession

NOTE 1: As described elsewhere in this report, the accounting records of the Debtor are not reliable because they do not include all of the transactions entered into by the Debtor. For example, the Debtor incurred approximately $34,000 in check cashing fees in 1987 which the Examiner believes are not reflected above. If this expense were included, the Debtor would have reported a *loss* from business operations in 1987 of approximately $21,000.

NOTE 2: According to the Debtor, the observed fluctuation in volume and relationship between gross profit, operating expenses and gross receipts is due to the relative transformation of the business from an apparel jobber to a contract sewing operation. The Debtor's jobbing activity increased again in 1988 (not shown above).

## BELLE APPAREL
## EXHIBIT II - ESTIMATED INCOME SHORTFALL

|                                          | 19X3       | 19X4       | 19X5       | 19X6       | 19X7       |
|------------------------------------------|------------|------------|------------|------------|------------|
| Business Profit <Loss> per Exhibit I     | $14,329    | $24,723    | $21,263    | $<15,965>  | $12,975    |
| Less: Estimated living expenses (per Debtor) | <40,000>   | <40,000>   | <40,000>   | <40,000>   | <40,000>   |
| Estimated Shortfall                      | $<25,671>  | $<15,277>  | $<18,737>  | $<55,965>  | $<27,025>  |

**Exhibit 5-7    Reports by Examiner**                                      **245**

_____, CPA

_____, CPA

2000 First Avenue
Nashville, Tennessee
(615) 555-1212
Examiners

## UNITED STATES BANKRUPTCY COURT
## CENTRAL DISTRICT OF TENNESSEE

| | |
|---|---|
| **In re**<br>ABC Systems<br>a Tennessee corporation<br>Debtor and Debtor-In-Possession | Case No. 99-99999-XX<br>(Chapter 11)<br>EX-PARTE REQUEST FOR EX-<br>PEDITED HEARING ON IMME-<br>DIATE APPOINTMENT OF A<br>TRUSTEE<br>Date:<br>Time:<br>Dept:   3 |

1. The Examiners' report has been served on the parties and is incorporated herein by reference.
2. Because of the conditions described in the Examiners' report, there is a continuing erosion of cash collateral and an unwillingness on the part of the Debtor to act responsibly as a Debtor-In-Possession.
3. The Examiners request an expedited hearing regarding the Examiners' request for the immediate appointment of a Trust.
4. The continuing actions of the Debtor constitute an emergency situation in the opinion of the Examiners.
5. The Examiners request telephonic notice of the date and time of the hearing.

October 14, 19X7                    Respectfully Submitted,
Nashville, Tennessee

_____, CPAs
Examiners

_____, CPA

_____, CPA

2000 First Avenue
Nashville, Tennessee
Examiners

## UNITED STATES BANKRUPTCY COURT CENTRAL DISTRICT OF TENNESSEE

| | |
|---|---|
| **In re** | Case No. 99-9999 |
| ABC SYSTEMS | (Chapter 11) |
| Debtor and Debtor-In-Possession | EXAMINERS' REQUEST FOR |
| | IMMEDIATE APPOINTMENT OF |
| | A TRUSTEE |
| | Date: |
| | Time: |
| | Dept:   3 |

**I.** *Description of ABC Systems*

    **A.** ABC holds an '8(a)' Certification as a Disadvantaged Minority-owned Business. Under certain circumstances, an 8(a) company is afforded a preference in government contract awards. ABC's 8(a) Certification expires in October of 19X8 and cannot be renewed under current law.

    **B.** ABC's contracts are with two governmental departments—DE and FG.

    **C.** The contracts with DE are both time and material for services ("logistics") and fixed unit price for manufactured products. The FG contracts are fixed unit prices for manufactured products.

    **D.** The Company is owned by the Jones family. James Jones, Sr. is the Chairman and James Jones, Jr. is the President.

**II.** *Bankruptcy Background*

    **A.** ABC's banking relationship has been with First Bank. Currently ABC owes First Bank approximately $2,200,000 in secured debt.

    **B.** ABC has used the maximum of its borrowing ability since early 19X6. For the year ended December 31, 19X5, ABC's auditors qualified their opinion on the financial statements to be subject to the availability of additional financing to allow ABC to continue operations.

    **C.** During 19X6, the FG suspended progress payments. ABC substantially suspended manufacturing in the fourth quarter of 19X6.

**Exhibit 5-7  Reports by Examiner**                                                **247**

**D.** In the first quarter of 19X7 ABC renegotiated the FG. contracts, eliminating the progress payment clauses.

**E.** ABC's financial condition continued to deteriorate, and it filed for Chapter 11 on May 1, 1987.

**F.** The court appointed the Examiners (_____, CPAs) to aid in a June, 1987 hearing regarding assumptions of contracts.

**G.** In August of 1987 the parties entered into a stipulation regarding the use of First Bank's cash collateral, the assumption of the DE and FG contracts and regarding progress payments by the FG.

**H.** The stipulation provides for default provisions if operating results vary by more than 10% from a forecast filed as an exhibit to the stipulation.

**I.** The duties of the Examiners were expanded by the cash collateral stipulation to include, among other things, approval of disbursements.

**J.** By mutual agreement of the parties, the role of the Examiners was expanded to that of general monitoring of operations and cash collateral issues.

**III.** *Financial Performance Since August, 1987*

**A.** The financial forecast filed as an exhibit to the cash collateral stipulation (the original forecast) was prepared in June of 1987. In August of 1987, the effective date of the stipulation, it became apparent, upon detailed review, that the original forecast was not reasonably attainable.

**B.** Upon the urging of the Examiners, a 1st revised forecast was prepared by ABC and presented by ABC as a worst case scenario. This forecast projected a cash shortfall of $200,000 in early December, 1987.

**C.** During August and September, 1987, ABC failed to meet the 1st revised forecast, and upon the urging of the Examiners, a 2nd revised forecast was prepared, showing a $300,000+ cash shortfall in early December, 1987.

**D.** Since ABC management was not able to provide a source for $300,000, the Examiners instructed management to extensively review cash needs and any possible revisions of production schedules to help cash flow.

**E.** A 3rd revised cash flow was prepared showing a cash shortfall of $100,000 in December, 1987. Management has not identified specific solutions to this shortfall.

**F.** As a result of past "broken promises" to suppliers, ABC is on a "Cash-In-Advance" or "Cash-On-Delivery" basis with nearly all suppliers.

**G.** ABC has lost over $300,000 in August and September, 1987 according to the operating reports prepared by ABC.

**IV.** *Financial Controls and Reporting*

**A.** ABC has provided to the Examiners financial statements and operating reports that do not agree with each other. Upon questioning by the Examiners, both the financial statements and the operating reports were found to be in error.

**B.** ABC has both a Controller and a Chief Financial Officer. Neither officer reviewed the August operating report before it was filed with the Court.

**C.** ABC has had substantial difficulty in maintaining adequate control over both pre- and post-petition accounts receivable. This is viewed by the Examiners as an intolerable situation, considering the relatively few number of transactions.

**D.** ABC keeps its books on a very sophisticated computer system. The Examiners believe that substantial savings in both time and payroll could be gained by simplifying the accounting and reporting systems. These recommendations have been ignored by ABC without providing contrary evidence.

**E.** Because of the problems noted and the inability of the Controller and the Chief Financial Officer to answer certain questions regarding the financial information and controls, the Examiners have lost confidence in ABC's ability to control and generate accurate, meaningful financial data.

**F.** The Examiners have noted a general lack of initiative on the part of ABC's financial management to take needed actions (the revisions to the financial forecasts were initiated by the Examiners as was an analysis of accounts receivable, cost reduction studies, etc.)

**V.** *Anticipated Operating Levels*

**A.** Critical to the success of this reorganization, protection of cash collateral and completion of DE and FG existing contracts, is a reasonably accurate prediction of the future operating level of ABC.

**B.** ABC is currently carrying an administrative and facilities overhead burden sufficient to support a $1,500,000+ per month sales level. The sales for September, 1987, were $180,000.

**C.** Obviously ABC needs to increase sales or decrease overhead to become profitable.

**D.** According to interviews of ABC and government personnel, the DE has substantially lost confidence in ABC's ability to deliver product timely, ABC's financial capabilities, and ABC's workforce capabilities and management expertise.

**Exhibit 5-7  Reports by Examiner**                                    **249**

**E.**  ABC is on the DE's Contractor Improvement Program (CIP) and as such, a contract officer at the DE must supplement any contract award to ABC with a memo stating the specific reasons as to ABC's ability to perform on such contract. The contract officers are reluctant to assume this additional personal career risk.

**F.**  ABC has signed *no* new manufacturing contracts since the Chapter 11 filing.

**G.**  In spite of the above lack of new contracts, J. Jones, Sr. & J. Jones, Jr. expect ABC to sign $3,000,000 in manufacturing contracts prior to January 1, 1988, and sufficient subsequent contracts such that ABC's revenues will be in the range of $12,000,000 to $20,000,000 per year.

**H.**  Carmen Munoz, Marketing Analyst for ABC, expects only $1,500,000 in new manufacturing contracts in the next 3 to 6 months. Randy Bromfield, V.P., Marketing, expects $1,500,000–$3,000,000 in new manufacturing contracts in the next 3 to 6 months.

**I.**  Nick Young of the Small Business Administration ("SBA") informed the Examiners that $46,000 in manufacturing contracts are possible in the next few months. He has indicated that, based upon the financial problems and the history of delinquent deliveries over the past one and one half years, it is very difficult to obtain new contracts for ABC. ABC has to prove its ability much as a new company would. (Mr. Young's position at the SBA is to aid ABC in obtaining contracts.) Mr. Young indicated that the larger the contract, the more difficult the "selling job" becomes with the DE.

**J.**  It is evident that the Joneses are substantially more optimistic about future manufacturing contracts than are others. The Joneses have not provided any evidence to support their optimism.

**K.**  Discussions with the SBA and DE and company personnel indicate that the company can regain creditability and thus contract awards; however, this process may take several years of proving itself.

**L.**  In September of 1987, DE conducted a "Pre-Award Survey" of ABC. This survey noted an unsatisfactory rating in technical ability, production capability and quality assurance capability and further noted ". . . the management deficiencies and weaknesses that lead to the termination of production precludes any realistic expectation of satisfactory performance." The end result was a "no award" recommendation.

**M.**  If ABC overestimates future sales and continues to maintain its high administrative and facilities overhead, it may be wasting cash collateral and unnecessarily jeopardizing completion of the DE and FG contracts.

**N.** The indicators lead the Examiners to believe that future contract awards will be less than expected by the Joneses. The Joneses have indicated a strong unwillingness to accept this possibility and are unwilling to accordingly reduce overhead.

**O.** It should be noted that a significant portion of ABC's revenues ($2–$4 million per year) were and are generated by "logistics" contracts which require relatively little overhead. Logistics contracts are time and materials for services that the company can bill semi-monthly. This reduces the cash flow needs and the business risk to both ABC and the DE, making contract awards easier to obtain. These contracts are attractive to ABC because they provide a basis for expansion of a service which should be profitable, while at the same time allow a reduction of the overhead now incurred by DE.

**VI.** *Actions of the Debtor-In-Possession*

**A.** ABC has made post-petition preference payments of approximately $20,000 to the Jones family or related entities. The Jones have ignored demands for repayment.

**B.** ABC executives continue to use leased autos even though CSA has agreed to reject the leases due to lack of equity in the leases, aside from the fact that this is a significant overhead expense not needed by a business in a bankruptcy proceeding.

**C.** ABC management has difficulty separating the concerns of the Jones family from their fiduciary responsibility to the Chapter 11 Estate.

**D.** ABC management has taken the position that significant salary awards should be provided to the Jones family and other management personnel in spite of a clear need to reduce management overhead (i.e., have only one Chief Executive Operating Officer and only one Financial Officer).

**E.** The financial management of ABC has proven ineffective and has lost credibility with the Examiners, First Bank and the DE by not being able to provide accurate, timely financial data and reduce overhead.

**F.** ABC is currently not in substantial compliance with the financial forecast filed as an exhibit to the cash collateral stipulation. Consequently, ABC is in default and, among other remedies, First Bank and/or the DE could call for the immediate appointment of a Trustee.

**G.** Management has a lack of understanding of the responsibilities of a "Debtor-In-Possession" coupled with an unwillingness to comply with such responsibilities as explained by the Examiners.

**H.** Without requesting prior court approval, the debtor approached the SBA for permission to assume approximately $175,000 in SBA guaranteed debts of another 8(a) company in bankruptcy. The re-

**Exhibit 5-7   Reports by Examiner**                                   **251**

quest was denied by the SBA with a further loss of ABC's credibility with the SBA.

I.   The continuing lack of financial controls and timely preparation of information make it impossible for the Examiners to monitor cash collateral. ABC's operating reports do not track contracts in progress. The amount for contracts in progress as shown on the operating report did not change from August to September even though production was occurring.

VII. *Other Comments*

A.   The Examiners would like noted the excellent cooperation received from the Counsel for the Debtor, Counsel for the Bank and the Counsel for the Creditor's Committee, and representatives of the SBA and the DE.

B.   The Examiners also note the very favorable performance of Wendell James, V.P. of Manufacturing, who has prepared an apparently coherent manufacturing plan and schedule.

C.   The Examiners do not believe that with certain existing management, its financial position and past performance, its lack of strong financial controls and management, its current lack of new contracts, and its lack of credibility, that it will be feasible to achieve a rapid reorganization as it now plans.

D.   ABC currently operates from three locations in the Nashville area. Not all space is utilized to justify this significant overhead expense (some of which involves economic ramifications with the Jones family).

VIII. *Recommendations of the Examiners*

A.   The Examiners recommend the *IMMEDIATE APPOINTMENT OF A TRUSTEE* with manufacturing management experience. The Examiners do not believe that the Debtor has the management ability nor the willingness to do what is necessary to reorganize ABC and operate under the responsibilities assigned to a Debtor-In-Possession.

B.   ABC should aggressively pursue all avenues to reduce overhead in line with the current level of operations. Only when new profitable contracts are awarded that raise sales levels should the company (very cautiously) increase overhead.

C.   The Examiners recommend the preparation of a coherent marketing plan that concentrates on time and material contracts ("logistics"), contracts with a reasonable possibility of award, and that care be taken not to "underbid" contracts. Also, the marketing plan should address the viability of the company after expiration of its 8(a) certification in October, 1988.

October 14, 1987                              Respectfully Submitted,
Nashville, Tennessee

_____, CPAs

Examiners

## PART THREE

# Accounting Services

# CHAPTER SIX

# Retention of the Accountant and Fees

## EXHIBIT 6-1   AFFIDAVIT OF ACCOUNTANT FOR DEBTOR

### UNITED STATES BANKRUPTCY COURT SOUTHERN DISTRICT OF NEW YORK

**In re:**
IONOSPHERE CLUBS, INC. and
EASTERN AIR LINES, INC.,
Debtors.

Chapter 11 Case Nos.
89 B 10448 and
89 B 10449 (BRL)

### AFFIDAVIT OF BARRY M. MONHEIT
*PURSUANT TO 11 U.S.C. SEC. 327 AND BANKRUPTCY RULE 2014*

STATE OF NEW YORK
COUNTY OF NEW YORK          } ss:

Barry M. Monheit, being duly sworn, deposes and says as follows:

1. I am a partner in the independent public accounting firm of Arthur Andersen & Co. ("Andersen"), whose New York offices are located at 1345 Avenue of the Americas, New York, New York, and am authorized to execute this affidavit on behalf of Andersen. I am a duly licensed certified public accountant in the states of New York and Texas.

2. Andersen is a firm of independent public accountants operating throughout the United States since 1913. Andersen has been retained as accountants to render professional services to debtors, creditors, creditors' committees, investors and others in numerous bankruptcy cases.

3. Andersen has provided professional services to Eastern Air Lines, Inc. ("Eastern") since February 1986 and Ionosphere Clubs, Inc. ("Ionosphere") since its inception (collectively the "Debtors"). To the best of my knowledge, neither Andersen, nor any of its professional personnel have any relationship with the Debtors that would impair Andersen's ability to continue to provide such professional services, including attest services as to which professional and regulatory requirements of independence exist.

4. To the best of my knowledge, Andersen has not had any prior business association with the Debtors, any creditors of the Debtors or any other parties in interest in this Chapter 11 case, or their respective attorneys and accountants, identified at the present time, except as follows:

a)  As independent auditors, Andersen has audited the consolidated financial statements of Eastern and its subsidiaries since December 1987 and was in the process of the examination of the annual financial statements for the year ended December 31, 1988 when the petition for relief under Chapter 11 Title 11 of the United States Code was filed on March 9, 1989. Andersen has also, since the date of appointment as auditors, performed various accounting, tax and management information systems consultation projects.

b)  Andersen is currently an unsecured creditor for work performed for the Debtors prior to the commencement of these cases, both billed and not yet billed, in an amount of approximately $245,000.

c)  Andersen has performed professional services for certain of the creditors whose names appear on the initial list of the Debtors' twenty largest creditors, including, General Electric Company, the Boeing Company, American National Bank & Trust Co. of Chicago, IBM Corporation, Telex Computer Products, AT&T Communications and Marriott Corporation. Andersen has provided to these companies and/or their affiliates various professional accounting, tax and management information systems services, including serving in certain cases as auditors.

d)  Andersen is currently the auditor for Jet Capital Corporation, an equity security holder in Texas Air Corporation, the sole shareholder of Eastern. Andersen is also the auditor for Texas Air Corporation and its other subsidiaries, including Continental Airlines, Inc., and its other affiliated entities.

e)  Andersen has provided personal tax consulting and compliance services to various individuals employed by the organizations enumerated above, along with certain of the Debtors' management.

f)  The Debtors have numerous additional creditors, equity security holders and other parties with whom it maintains significant business relationships beyond those identified in paragraph (c). Andersen may have audit, tax, consulting or other professional relationships with such entities or persons or Andersen may, from time to time, perform professional services for such entities or persons unrelated to the Debtors or its business affairs.

**Exhibit 6-1   Affidavit of Accountant for Debtor**                                         **257**

5. To the best of my knowledge, Andersen has not been retained to assist any entity or person other than the Debtors on matters relating to, or in connection with, these Chapter 11 cases. If Andersen's proposed retention by the Debtors is approved by this Court, Andersen will not accept any engagement or perform any service for any entity or person other than the Debtors in these Chapter 11 cases. Andersen will, however, continue to provide professional services to entities or persons that may be creditors or equity security holders of the Debtors or parties-in-interest in these Chapter 11 cases, provided that such services do not relate to, or have any direct connection with, these Chapter 11 cases or the Debtors.

6. To the best of my knowledge, information and belief, Andersen does not have or represent any interest materially adverse to the interest of the Debtors, or of any class of creditors or equity security holders of the Debtors, by reason of any direct or indirect relationship to, connection with, or interest in the Debtors or any investment banker for any securities of the Debtors, or for any other reason except as noted in paragraph 4 above.

7. By virtue of its prior engagement on behalf of the Debtors, Andersen is familiar with the books, records and financial information and other data maintained by the Debtors and is well-qualified by background information and experience to continue to provide professional services to the Debtors.

8. Andersen has been advised that the Debtors desire to retain it to provide professional services including the following:

    a)   Audit services, including:

      (1) completing the audit of the annual financial statements for the year ended December 31, 1988 and to review or audit subsequent financial statements;

      (2) assist in the preparation of various forms and reports required to be filed with the Securities and Exchange Commission ("SEC") and other regulatory entities;

      (3) review of the Debtors' quarterly consolidated financial reports;

      (4) review of the tax returns prepared by the Debtors, and

    b)   Consulting services, including:

      (1) rendering accounting assistance in connection with reports required by the Court;

      (2) reviewing cash or other projections and submissions to the Court of reports and statements of receipts, disbursements and indebtedness;

      (3) assisting the Debtors with the preparation of business plans;

      (4) assisting with the preparation for and negotiations with lending institutions and creditors;

      (5) providing appraisal services as requested by the Debtors and the Debtors' counsel;

      (6) reviewing existing accounting systems and procedures for purposes of rendering reports to management and other parties-in-interest;

(7) assisting with the analysis and revision of the Debtors' plan or plans or reorganization;

(8) consulting with the Debtors' management and counsel in connection with operating, financial and other business matters relating to the ongoing activities of the Debtors;

(9) reviewing the Debtors' liquidation analysis;

(10) assisting with the analysis of alternative restructuring scenarios and related tax effects;

(11) assisting with the feasibility analyses;

(12) providing expert testimony as required;

(13) interfacing with accountants and other financial consultants for committees and other creditor groups;

(14) assisting the Debtors with the preparation of the Schedules of Assets and Liabilities and the Statements of Financial Affairs;

(15) assisting with analysis of sale of various assets of Debtors;

(16) providing assistance to an examiner if one is appointed, in connection with the examination of related party transactions;

(17) assisting with such other matters as management or counsel to the Debtors may request from time to time;

9. Andersen's requested compensation for professional services rendered to the Debtors shall be based upon the time expended to render such services and at billing rates commensurate with the experience of the person performing such services and will be computed at the hourly billing rates customarily charged by Andersen for such services.

The customary hourly rates of Andersen are as follows:

| | |
|---|---|
| Partners/Principals | ____-____ |
| Managers | ____-____ |
| Seniors | ____-____ |
| Staff/Paraprofessionals | ____-____ |

In the normal course of business, Andersen revises its hourly rates on April 1 and October 1 of each year and Andersen requests that effective April 1 and October 1 of each year (beginning October 1, 1989), the aforementioned rates be revised to the regular hourly rates which will be in effect at that time. Expenses will be charged at actual costs incurred (and will include charges for typing, copying, telephone, computer rental, etc.).

10. Andersen requests that it be permitted to submit monthly invoices covering actual services rendered and out-of-pocket disbursements incurred, such invoices to contain reasonable detail. Further, Andersen requests that the Debtors make payment against such invoices when billed in the following amounts:

a)   With respect to invoices submitted for the services rendered as set forth in paragraph 8(a) hereof, at an amount equal to such invoice;

b)   With respect to invoices submitted for the services rendered as set forth in paragraph 8(b) hereof, at an amount equal to seventy-five (75%) percent of services rendered; and

**Exhibit 6-1  Affidavit of Accountant for Debtor**                                    **259**

c)  One hundred (100%) percent of all out-of-pocket expenses reasonably incurred in the performance of the aforementioned services.

11. With respect to the services to be rendered as set forth in paragraph 8(b) hereof, based on information presently available, we expect that our work will result in time charges not to exceed $1,000,000, plus out-of-pocket disbursements. If Andersen determines that it will be necessary to render services to the Debtors, the charges for which will exceed $1,000,000, Andersen will apply to this Court for an order increasing the compensation ceiling.

12. Andersen understands that, in accordance with the Bankruptcy Code, final payment and all interim payments, are subject to approval by this Court. All sums received pursuant to paragraph 10(a) through (c) above shall be credited against the amount ultimately allowed Andersen upon the filing by Andersen of an appropriate application for allowance of compensation and reimbursement of expenses.

13. No payments have been made to Andersen for services rendered, or to be rendered, in connection with these Chapter 11 cases. Subject to the approval of this Court, the source of all compensation for professional services to be rendered on behalf of the Debtor shall be funds of the Debtors' estates.

14. No agreement exists between Andersen or any other person (other than partners of Andersen) for the sharing of compensation to be received by Andersen in connection with services rendered in these cases.

WHEREFORE, affiant respectfully requests that an order be entered authorizing the retention of Arthur Andersen & Co. to perform the services described above.

Barry M. Monheit

Sworn to
before me on this 14th
day of March, 1989

Notary Public

**EXHIBIT 6-2    APPLICATION FOR RETENTION OF ACCOUNTANT
FOR DEBTOR**

---

## UNITED STATES BANKRUPTCY COURT SOUTHERN DISTRICT OF NEW YORK

In re:
IONOSPHERE CLUBS, INC. and
EASTERN AIR LINES, INC.,
Debtors.

Chapter 11 Case Nos.
89 B 10448 and
89 B 10449 (BRL)

## APPLICATION FOR RETENTION OF ARTHUR ANDERSEN & CO., INDEPENDENT PUBLIC ACCOUNTANTS, *AS CONSULTANTS AND AUDITORS FOR THE DEBTORS*

TO THE HONORABLE BURTON R. LIFLAND, UNITED STATES
BANKRUPTCY JUDGE:

The above-captioned Debtors make this application pursuant to Section
327(a) of the Bankruptcy Code, 11 United States Code, Sections 101 *et seq.*

1. On March 9, 1989, Ionosphere Clubs, Inc. ("Ionosphere") and Eastern
Air Lines, Inc. ("Eastern") collectively referred to as the "Debtors", filed with
the Bankruptcy Court for the Southern District of New York their respective
petitions for relief under Chapter 11 of Title 11 of the United States Code.
Pursuant to an order dated March 9, 1989, the Ionosphere and Eastern chapter
11 cases were consolidated for procedural purposes only. The Debtors are continuing to operate their business and manage their property as debtors-in-
possession.

2. Ionosphere, a New York corporation, is a wholly-owned subsidiary of
Eastern, a certificated air carrier engaged primarily in scheduled air passenger
transportation. Ionosphere's principal business is the ownership and operation
of a network of 27 hospitality club rooms, known as "Ionosphere Clubs", located at 25 airports serviced by Eastern.

3. Eastern is a certified air carrier that was incorporated in Delaware in 1938.
Eastern is one of the nation's original four trunk carriers and was, in 1988, the
9th largest airline in the United States (in terms of revenue passenger miles). As
of December 31, 1988, Eastern provided scheduled air transportation between
approximately 63 metropolitan areas in the United States and Canada, 17 cities
in the Caribbean and 18 cities in Central and South America.

4. Substantial and continuing accounting services are required in the ongoing
businesses and operations of the Debtors. In particular, accountants will be required to undertake accounting, auditing, appraisal tax and other consulting
services that include (i) attest audit services, including completion of the audit
of the annual financial statements for the year ended December 31, 1988, (ii)
assisting in the preparation of various forms and reports required to be filed with

**Exhibit 6-2   Application for Retention of Accountant for Debtor**          **261**

the Securities and Exchange Commission ("SEC") and other regulatory entities; (iii) reviewing the Debtors' quarterly consolidated financial reports, (iv) rendering tax return preparation and other tax consulting services; (v) rendering accounting assistance in connection with reports required by the Court, (vi) reviewing cash or other projections and submissions to the Court of reports and statements of receipts, disbursements and indebtedness, (vii) assisting the Debtors with the preparation of business plans, (viii) assisting with the preparation for and negotiations with lending institutions and creditors, (ix) providing appraisal services as requested by Debtors and Debtors' counsel, (x) reviewing existing accounting systems and procedures for purposes of rendering reports to management and other parties-in-interest, (xi) assisting with the analysis and revision of Debtors' plan or plans of reorganization, and (xii) consulting with the Debtors' management and counsel in connection with operating, financial and other business matters relating to the ongoing activities of the Debtors.

5. By this application, the Debtors seek to retain Arthur Andersen & Co., independent public accountants ("Andersen"), to perform those services fully described in the affidavit (the "Monheit Affidavit") of Barry M. Monheit ("Monheit") annexed hereto and made part hereof as Exhibit "A". As set forth therein, it is proposed that Andersen be retained (i) as special accounting consultants, to assist the Debtors, *inter alia* in the development, negotiation and confirmation of a plan or plans of reorganization and to provide such other financial consulting services as may be required by the Debtors (collectively the "Consulting Services"); and (ii) as auditors, to complete the examination of the Debtors' consolidated financial statements as of December 31, 1988 and for the year then ended and to review or audit subsequent financial statements and to issue such reports in connection therewith as may be required by applicable law or requested by the Debtors (collectively the "Audit Services").

6. For both internal and external reasons, the retention of a firm such as Andersen is essential to a successful reorganization of the Debtors. Andersen, and particularly Monheit, the partner in charge of this engagement for Andersen, have had extensive experience in reorganization proceedings, and enjoy an excellent reputation for services which they have rendered in large and complex Chapter 11 proceedings throughout the United States on behalf of both creditors and debtors. For this reason, the Debtors believe that the Consulting Services to be rendered by Andersen will add an additional dimension of accounting and financial expertise to these cases.

7. The Audit Services which Andersen proposes to render to the Debtors are akin to those which have been performed by Andersen on the Debtors' behalf for several years. The Debtors clearly require the services of an independent public accounting firm to conduct an audit of their financial statements. In light of Andersen's acquired familiarity with the Debtors' financial affairs and the quality of services previously rendered, the Debtors believe that retaining Andersen to render Audit Services is preferable to retaining a new and different firm to service this distinct accounting need.

8. The services which Andersen will render to the Debtors will be confined to those outlined in the Monheit Affidavit.

9. To the best of the Debtors' knowledge, Andersen has no connection with, and holds no interest adverse to, the Debtors, the creditors of their estates or any other party in interest herein or their respective attorneys, except for (a) Andersen's general unsecured claim against the Debtor for services rendered prior to the Chapter 11 filings and (b) matters set forth in the Monheit Affidavit. Consequently, the Debtors believe that Andersen is a "disinterested person" herein (as defined in S101(13) of the Bankruptcy Code), as required by Section 327(a) of the Bankruptcy Code.

10. The Debtors propose to compensate Andersen at:

(i)   seventy-five (75%) percent of its monthly billings for fees generated in connection with the Audit Services rendered;*

(ii)  seventy-five (75%) percent of its monthly billings for fees generated in connection with the Consulting Services rendered; and

(iii) one-hundred (100%) percent of its reasonable and necessary out-of-pocket expenses;

all subject to final approval by this Court after the filing by Andersen of an application for interim or final allowance of compensation in accordance with Sections 330 and 331 of the Bankruptcy Code and the then applicable Bankruptcy Rules. In addition as the annexed order provides, it is proposed that Andersen's aggregate billings for Consulting Services (exclusive of disbursements) shall not exceed $1,000,000 without further order of this Court.

11. The Debtors believe that Andersen is eminently qualified to represent them herein and that the retention of Andersen is in the best interests of the Debtors and their estates.

12. Notice of this application has been given to the United States Trustee. No creditors' committee has been appointed in this case. Applicants submit that no further notice need be given.

---

* Initial proposal was for 100 percent.

**Exhibit 6-2  Application for Retention of Accountant for Debtor**          **263**

WHEREFORE, the Debtors pray for entry of the annexed order and for such other and further relief as is just and proper.
Dated:  New York, New York
        March 14, 1989

EASTERN AIR LINES, INC.
Debtor and Debtor in Possession

By: _____
        Rolf S. Andresen
        Vice President: Finance
        and Chief Financial Officer

WEIL, GOTSHAL & MANGES
Attorneys for Debtors-In-Possession
767 Fifth Avenue
New York, New York 10153
(212) 310–8000

By: _____
        A Member of the Firm

IONOSPHERE CLUBS, INC.

By: _____
        Charline Dawkins
        Vice President and
        General Manager

**EXHIBIT 6-3   ORDER AUTHORIZING RETENTION OF ACCOUNTANT FOR DEBTOR**

## UNITED STATES BANKRUPTCY COURT
## SOUTHERN DISTRICT OF NEW YORK

| | |
|---|---|
| In re:<br>IONOSPHERE CLUBS, INC. and<br>EASTERN AIR LINES, INC.,<br>Debtors. | Chapter 11 Case Nos.<br>89 B 10448 and<br>89 B 10449 (BRL) |

## ORDER AUTHORIZING RETENTION OF ARTHUR ANDERSEN & CO., INDEPENDENT PUBLIC ACCOUNTANTS, AS CONSULTANTS AND AUDITORS FOR THE DEBTORS

Upon the annexed application (the "Application") of Ionosphere Clubs, Inc. ("Ionosphere") and Eastern Air Lines Inc. ("Eastern"), as Debtors-in-Possession (collectively the "Debtors"), dated March 14, 1989, seeking authority for the Debtors to retain and employ the firm of Arthur Andersen & Co. ("Andersen"), independent public accountants, for the purpose set forth in the Application and upon the annexed affidavit of Barry M. Monheit, a partner in the firm of Andersen, sworn to on March 14, 1989 (the "Monheit Affidavit"); and the Court being satisfied that Andersen represents no interest adverse to the Debtors, their creditors, or the estates with respect to the matters upon which it is to be engaged, that Andersen and its professional personnel are disinterested persons with the meaning of Bankruptcy Code Section 101(13), as modified in Section 1107(b), that its employment is necessary and in the best interests of the Debtors, their creditors and their estates, and sufficient cause appearing therefore; and no notice being required; it is

ORDERED, that the Debtors, be, and they are hereby authorized and empowered to retain the firm of Andersen, *nunc pro tunc,* to March 9, 1989, to perform the accounting, auditing, appraisal, tax and consulting services as set forth in the Application and the Monheit Affidavit; and it is further

ORDERED, that the Debtors, be, and they hereby are authorized and empowered to pay Andersen, upon its periodic submission of bills;

(i)    seventy-five (75%) percent of Andersen's fees for the rendition of those services described in paragraph 8(a) of the Monheit Affidavit ("Audit Services");

(ii)    seventy-five (75%) percent of Andersen's fees for the rendition of those services described in paragraph 8(b) of the Monheit Affidavit ("Consulting Services"); and

(iii)   seventy-five (75%) percent of all reasonable and necessary out-of-

**Exhibit 6-3   Order Authorizing Retention of Accountant for Debtor**        **265**

pocket expenses incurred by Andersen in performance of the services authorized hereunder;

and it is further
ORDERED, that:

(i)     Each bill submitted by Andersen shall set forth in reasonable detail the services rendered, the time spent and by whom;
(ii)    Andersen shall not submit bills to the Debtors for payment more frequently than every (30) days;
(iii)   Simultaneously with the submission of a bill by Andersen to the Debtors, Andersen shall submit a copy of such bill to each committee appointed in the Debtors' Chapter 11 cases or in the alternative to such committee's counsel and the U.S. Trustee's office;
(iv)    Notwithstanding anything contained hereinabove to the contrary, the Debtors shall not pay any bill submitted to them by Andersen for fees or reimbursement of expenses prior to the tenth (10th) business day following receipt by the Debtors of such bill; and
(v)     The aggregate billings made by Andersen to the Debtors for Audit and Consulting Services rendered to the Debtors by Andersen (exclusive of reimbursement of Andersen's expenses) shall not exceed $2,000,000, except as may otherwise be authorized by subsequent order of this Court;

and it is further
ORDERED, that all payments made by the Debtors to Andersen pursuant to this Order shall be credited against such amounts as may be ultimately allowed to Andersen by the Court upon the filing by Andersen of an application for an allowance of interim or final compensation in accordance with Sections 330 or 331 of the Bankruptcy Code and such Bankruptcy Rules as may then be applicable.

Dated:  New York, New York
        March 21, 1989

UNITED STATES
BANKRUPTCY JUDGE

NO OBJECTION:

United States Trustee
for the Southern District
of New York

**EXHIBIT 6-4   AFFIDAVIT OF ACCOUNTANT FOR UNSECURED CREDITORS' COMMITTEE**

## UNITED STATES BANKRUPTCY COURT
## SOUTHERN DISTRICT OF NEW YORK

| | |
|---|---|
| **In re**<br>IONOSPHERE CLUBS, INC. and<br>EASTERN AIR LINES, INC.,<br>Debtors, | Chapter 11<br>Case Nos. 89 B 10448 (BRL)<br>and 89 B 10449 (BRL) |
| STATE OF NEW YORK<br>COUNTY OF NEW YORK | ss.: |

ARTHUR B. NEWMAN, being duly sworn, deposes and says:

1. I am a member of the firm of Ernst & Whinney, Independent Certified Public Accountants, whose New York offices are located at 787 Seventh Avenue, New York, New York 10019. I make this affidavit in support of the application of the Official Committee of Unsecured Creditors (the "Creditors' Committee") of Eastern Air Lines, Inc. ("Eastern") and Ionosphere Clubs, Inc. ("Ionosphere"; Eastern and Ionosphere are collectively referred to herein as the "Debtors") for the entry of an order authorizing the retention of Ernst & Whinney as accountants.

2. To the best of my knowledge, neither my firm nor any member thereof has any connection with the Debtors, any company affiliated with the Debtors, their respective officers, or attorneys except that during 1988, Ernst & Whinney performed certain limited accounting services for Eastern in connection with its decision to close its Kansas City operations. The Debtors have many creditors and accordingly, my firm may have rendered accounting services to certain of these creditors. Additionally, our many partners (approximately 1,200) may have business associations with certain creditors. We have apprised the Debtors of our proposed engagement by the Creditors' Committee and we have been advised that the Debtors have no objection thereto.

3. The nature and extent of the services that my firm proposes to render herein include, but are not limited to, the following:

(a) To review all financial information prepared by the Debtors or their accountants as requested by the Creditors' Committee including, but not limited to, a review of the Debtors' financial statements as of the date of the filing of the petitions, showing in detail all assets and liabilities and preferred, priority and secured creditors;

(b) To attend meetings of the Creditors' Committee and of the Debtors, creditors, their attorneys and with federal, state and local tax, regulatory and other governmental authorities, if requested;

(c) To render such assistance as may be necessary in these cases and in other actions and proceedings related thereto including, but not limited to,

**Exhibit 6-4    Affidavit of Accountant**                                    **267**

(i) review and advise in connection with any plan of reorganization suggested or proposed with respect to the Debtors; and

(ii) the determination of whether the financial condition of the Debtors is such that a plan of reorganization is likely or feasible.

(d) To review the Debtors' monthly operating and cash flow statements;

(e) Where appropriate, to review the books and records of the Debtors for related party transactions, including those with their parent company and other affiliates;

(f) Where appropriate, to review the books and records of the Debtors for potential voidable transactions and unenforceable claims;

(g) To prepare a liquidation analysis of the value of the assets of the estates;

(h) To review the current operations of the Debtors;

(i) To render such assistance as may be necessary in any investigation which may be undertaken with respect to the pre-petition accounts, conduct, property, liabilities and financial condition of the Debtors, including the operation and financing of their businesses and the desirability of the continuance thereof;

(j) To review any business plans, operating projections and other reports prepared by the Debtors;

(k) To review and analyze proposed transactions for which the Debtors seek Court approval, including any transactions involving the sale of assets or stock of the Debtors; and

(l) To render such other assistance as the Creditors' Committee and its counsel may deem necessary.

4. My firm will use its regular hourly rates in performing the aforementioned services. These rates by classification, at present, are partners (_____–_____), senior managers (_____–_____), managers (_____–_____) and staff accountants (_____–_____). In the normal course of business, my firm revises its regular hourly rates as on October 1 of each year and my firm requests that effective October 1 of each year, the aforementioned rates be revised to the regular hourly rates which will be in effect at that time.

5. My firm requests that it be permitted to submit monthly invoices to the Debtor for actual services rendered and out-of-pocket disbursements incurred, such invoices to contain reasonable detail. Further, my firm requests that the Debtors make payments against such invoices when billed at 75% of the fees for professional services rendered and 100% of the out-of-pocket disbursements reasonably incurred in the performance of the aforementioned services, within ten (10) days of receiving such invoices.

6. With respect to the services to be rendered as set forth in paragraph 3 hereof, based on information presently available, we expect that our work will result in time charges not to exceed $500,000, plus out-of-pocket disbursements. If my firm determines that it will be necessary to render services to the Creditors' Committee, the charges for which will exceed $500,000, my firm will apply to this Court for an order increasing the compensation ceiling.

7. All sums so received pursuant to paragraph 5 shall be credited against the amount ultimately allowed Ernst & Whinney upon the filing by Ernst & Whinney of an appropriate application for allowance of compensation and reimbursement of expenses.

8. Deponent represents that Ernst & Whinney does not, and will not, represent any entity other than the Creditors' Committee in connection with these cases.

9. I have read the application of the Creditors' Committee for an order approving the retention of Ernst & Whinney as accountants accompanying this affidavit and, to the best of my knowledge, information and belief, the contents of said application are true and correct.

WHEREFORE, deponent respectfully requests that an Order be entered authorizing the retention of Ernst & Whinney to perform the accounting and general financial consulting as described above.

 

 

 
                                                  _____

                                                Arthur B. Newman

Sworn to before me this
_____day of April, 1989.

 

_____
Notary Public

Exhibit 6-5    Application for Retention of Accountant                    **269**

# EXHIBIT 6-5  APPLICATION FOR RETENTION OF ACCOUNTANT FOR UNSECURED CREDITORS' COMMITTEE

## UNITED STATES BANKRUPTCY COURT
## SOUTHERN DISTRICT OF NEW YORK

| | |
|---|---|
| **In re**<br>IONOSPHERE CLUBS, INC. and<br>EASTERN AIR LINES, INC.,<br>Debtors. | Chapter 11<br>Case Nos. 89 B 10448 (BRL) and<br>89 B 10449 (BRL) |

## APPLICATION FOR AN ORDER AUTHORIZING RETENTION OF ERNST & WHINNEY AS ACCOUNTANTS FOR THE OFFICIAL COMMITTEE OF UNSECURED CREDITORS

TO THE HONORABLE BURTON R. LIFLAND,
CHIEF UNITED STATES BANKRUPTCY JUDGE:

The Official Committee of Unsecured Creditors (the "Creditors' Committee") of Eastern Airlines, Inc. ("Eastern") and Ionosphere Clubs, Inc. ("Ionosphere") (Eastern and Ionosphere are collectively referred to herein as the "Debtors"), by its attorneys Kramer, Levin, Nessen, Kamin & Frankel, respectfully represents:

1. On March 9, 1989, Eastern, and its affiliate Ionosphere, filed voluntary petitions for reorganization relief under the provisions of chapter 11, title 11, United States Code (the "Bankruptcy Code") with the United States Bankruptcy Court for the Southern District of New York (the "Bankruptcy Court"). By order of the Bankruptcy Court dated March 9, 1989, the Chapter 11 cases of Eastern and Ionosphere were consolidated for procedural purposes only.

2. The Debtors are continuing to operate their businesses and manage their properties as debtors in possession in accordance with Sections 1107 and 1108 of the Bankruptcy Code.

3. At the meeting of creditors of the Debtors held on March 22, 1989, the United States Trustee for the Southern District of New York, pursuant to Section 1102 of the Bankruptcy Code, appointed the Creditors' Committee, currently consisting of 14 members, to represent the interests of the creditors of both Eastern and Ionosphere in these cases, with claims exceeding $1.2 billion.

4. Upon information and belief, Eastern, a subsidiary of the Texas Air Corporation and an affiliate of Continental Airlines, Inc., is a certificated air carrier engaged primarily in the transportation of persons and property both within the United States and internationally, providing scheduled air transportation to approximately 63 cities in North America, 18 cities in the Caribbean and 17 cities in Central and South America. Eastern also transports mail and freight over portions of its routes in scheduled and charter services.

5. During the past 30 days, Eastern's operations have been severely curtailed due to a strike by its machinists and pilots unions and its operations and financial condition are in a state of extreme uncertainty.

6. In view of the magnitude and complexity of Eastern's operations and the uncertainty surrounding its business and financial condition, the Creditors' Committee believes that it is imperative that it retain accountants to investigate and advise it on the myriad of issues that have already arisen and will continue to arise in these cases. The Creditors' Committee therefore wishes to retain the firm of Ernst & Whinney to perform necessary accounting services for the Creditors' Committee as set forth herein.

7. The Creditors' Committee represents more than $1 billion of claims against the Debtors' estates, and makes this request in order to properly discharge its duties to the creditors it represents. The Creditors' Committee has chosen Ernst & Whinney based, in large measure, upon that firm's broad based experience and expertise as accountants in large and complex bankruptcy and reorganization proceedings.

8. As accountants to the Creditors' Committee, Ernst & Whinney, at the Creditors' Committee's request, will, among other things:

(a) Review all financial information prepared by the Debtors or their accountants as requested by the Creditors' Committee, including, but not limited to, a review of the Debtors' financial statements as of the date of the filing of the petitions, showing in detail all assets and liabilities and preferred, priority and secured creditors;

(b) Attend meetings of the Creditors' Committee and of the Debtors, creditors, their attorneys and with federal, state and local tax, regulatory and other governmental authorities, if requested;

(c) Render such assistance as may be necessary in these cases and in other actions and proceedings related thereto including, but not limited to:

(i) review and advise in connection with any plan of reorganization suggested or proposed with respect to the Debtors; and

(ii) the determination of whether the financial condition of the Debtors is such that a plan of reorganization is likely or feasible;

(d) Review the Debtors' operating and cash flow statements;

(e) Where appropriate, review the books and records of the Debtors for related party transactions, including those with their parent company and other affiliates;

(f) Where appropriate, review the books and records of the Debtors for potential voidable transactions and unenforceable claims;

(g) Prepare a liquidation analysis of the value of the assets of the estates;

(h) Review current operations of the Debtors;

(i) Render such assistance as may be necessary in any investigation which may be undertaken with respect to the pre-petition accounts, conduct,

**Exhibit 6-5   Application for Retention of Accountant**                              **271**

property, liabilities and financial condition of the Debtors, including the operation and financing of their businesses and the desirability of the continuance thereof;

(j) Review any business plans operating projections and other reports prepared by the Debtors;

(k) Review and analyze proposed transactions for which the Debtors seek Court approval, including any transactions involving the sale of assets or stock of the Debtors; and

(l) Render such other assistance as the Creditors' Committee and its counsel may deem necessary.

9. To the best of the Creditors' Committee's knowledge, Ernst & Whinney has no connection (as that term is used in Bankruptcy Rule 2014(a)) with the Debtors, their creditors, or any other party in interest, or with the respective attorneys or accountants of any of the foregoing, except as may be set forth in the affidavit of Arthur B. Newman, annexed hereto as Exhibit A and made a part hereof.

10. It is respectfully requested that Ernst & Whinney be permitted to render monthly statements to the Debtors computed in accordance with regular hourly rates, as set forth in the annexed affidavit. It is further requested that the Debtors be authorized and directed to pay 75% of time charged and 100% of out-of-pocket disbursements set forth and properly documented in such monthly statements, *provided, however,* that payments for time charged shall not exceed $500,000, subject and without prejudice to further application to and order of this Court. All monthly payments of compensation and reimbursement of disbursements to Ernst & Whinney shall be subject to approval of the Bankruptcy Court upon the filing of applications by Ernst & Whinney in accordance with Section 330 and 331 of the Bankruptcy Code.

WHEREFORE, the Creditors' Committee respectfully requests that this Court enter an order, substantially in the form annexed hereto as Exhibit B (i) approving the selection and retention by the Creditors' Committee of Ernst & Whinney as accountants to provide the professional services set forth in this application *nunc pro tunc* to March 30, 1989; (ii) permitting Ernst & Whinney to render to the Debtors monthly statements for compensation and reimbursement of expenses; (iii) authorizing and directing the Debtors to pay 75% of time charged and 100% of out-of-pocket disbursements as set forth and reasonably documented in such statements; (iv) declaring that all payments received by Ernst & Whinney from the Debtors shall be subject to approval of the Court upon the filing of an application by Ernst & Whinney in accordance with Sections 330 and 331 of the Bankruptcy Code; and (v) directing that the aggregate compensation to be paid to Ernst & Whinney by the Debtors shall not exceed $500,000 plus out-of-pocket disbursements, subject and without prejudice to further application to and order of this Court; and granting such other and further relief as may be just and proper.

Dated:  New York, New York
       April 5, 1989

KRAMER, LEVIN, NESSEN,
KAMIN & FRANKEL
Attorneys for the Official Committee
of Unsecured Creditors of Eastern
Air Lines, Inc. and Ionosphere
Clubs, Inc.

By: _____
A Member of the Firm
919 Third Avenue
New York, New York 10022
(212) 715-9100

**EXHIBIT 6-6**    **ORDER AUTHORIZING RETENTION OF ACCOUNTANT FOR UNSECURED CREDITORS' COMMITTEE**

---

## UNITED STATES BANKRUPTCY COURT
## SOUTHERN DISTRICT OF NEW YORK

| | |
|---|---|
| **In re**<br>IONOSPHERE CLUBS, INC. and<br>EASTERN AIR LINES, INC.,<br>Debtors. | Chapter 11<br>Case Nos. 89 B 10448 (BRL) and 89<br>B 10449 (BRL) |

## ORDER AUTHORIZING RETENTION OF ERNST & WHINNEY AS ACCOUNTANTS FOR THE OFFICIAL COMMITTEE OF UNSECURED CREDITORS

Upon the application (the "Application") of the Official Committee of Unsecured Creditors (the "Creditors' Committee") of Eastern Air Lines, Inc. and Ionosphere Clubs, Inc. (collectively, the "Debtors"), dated April 5, 1989, for an order pursuant to Section 1103(a) of Title 11, United States Code (the "Bankruptcy Code"), approving the Creditors' Committee's retention and employment of the accounting firm of Ernst & Whinney, Independent Certified Public Accountants ("Ernst & Whinney") as of March 30, 1989, as its accountants; and upon the affidavit of Arthur B. Newman, a member of the firm of Ernst & Whinney, sworn to on April 4, 1989; and the Court being satisfied that said firm represents no interest adverse to the estates and the Debtors, that Ernst & Whinney and its professional personnel are disinterested persons within the meaning of Bankruptcy Code Section 101(13), that its employment is necessary and in the best interests of the estates; and no adverse interest being represented and sufficient cause appearing therefor, it is

ORDERED, that the Creditors' Committee hereby is authorized to employ and retain Ernst & Whinney as its accountants as of March 30, 1989 to perform the accounting services described in the Application; and it is further

ORDERED, that all payments of compensation and reimbursement of disapplication therefor in accordance with Sections 330 and 331 of the Bankruptcy Code; and it is further

Dated:  New York, New York
      April _____, 1989

—————————————
UNITED STATES
BANKRUPTCY JUDGE

NO OBJECTION:
  WEIL, GOTSHAL & MANGES
  Attorneys for Eastern Air Lines,
    Inc. and Ionosphere Clubs, Inc.

By: _____            April 13, 1989
  A Member of the Firm
  767 Fifth Avenue
  New York, New York 10153
  (212) 310–8000

NO OBJECTION:

—————————————————     April 17, 1989
Office of the United States Trustee

**Exhibit 6-7    Accountant for Debtor**                                                           **275**

## EXHIBIT 6-7    ACCOUNTANT FOR DEBTOR

Exhibit 6-7 consists of the following:

## IN THE UNITED STATES BANKRUPTCY COURT FOR THE EASTERN DISTRICT OF MICHIGAN SOUTHERN DIVISION

**In the Matter of:**
HERCULES FENCE & SUPPLY CO., a Michigan corporation, Debtor.

Bankruptcy No. 87-05031-G
Chapter 11

### APPLICATION FOR AUTHORITY TO RETAIN RON OSSIPOVE AS ACCOUNTANT

NOW COMES Debtor Hercules Fence & Supply Co., a Michigan corporation, by and through his attorney, ARNOLD SCHAFER of SCHAFER AND WEINER, P.C., and for its Application for Authority to Retain Ron Ossipove as Accountant for Debtor, states as follows:

1. That on August 19, 1987, the above-named Debtor filed its Chapter 11 petition with this Honorable Court.

2. That the Debtor is in need of accounting services to assist it in the performance of the following duties:

(a) To properly review the books and records of the Debtor;

(b) Compile the annual and interim balance sheets and related statements of income and retained earnings, and change in financial position, for the year ended March 31, 1987 and December 31, 1987;

(c) Advise on how to report monthly cash statements of income and expenses;

(d) General ledger work;

(e) Preparation of annual income tax returns, Federal and State;

(f) Preparation of all payroll tax returns and annual wage and tax statements; and

(g) To perform various other functions in order for the proper maintenance of the company records.

3. That the Debtor has consulted with an accountant by the name of Ron Ossipove and he has indicated a willingness to serve as the accountant for the Debtor.

4. That the Debtor believes that it is essential that an accountant be appointed in this matter. Further, the Debtor is informed, and based upon such information, that Ron Ossipove is competent and qualified to perform the necessary accounting services outlined in this Application.

5. That attached hereto and made a part hereof as Exhibit "1" is an Affidavit of Ron Ossipove stating that (a) he, to the best of his knowledge, has no connection with the Debtor, its creditors or any other party in interest in this case; and (b) he, to the best of his knowledge, does not represent any interest adverse to that of the estate of the Debtor, its creditors or any other party in interest in this case in matters upon which Ron Ossipove is to be employed. Also, that he was the accountant for this Debtor in pre-Chapter 11 and as a result $1,500.00 is due and owing to him.

6. That attached hereto and made a part hereof as Exhibit "2" is a proposed engagement letter from Ron Ossipove outlining the services which he will perform on behalf of the Debtor and the accounting fees requested for said services.

WHEREFORE, Debtor prays that this Honorable Court enter an Order authorizing Debtor to retain the accountant Ron Ossipove to perform various accounting services for the Debtor, as outlined in this Application and attached engagement letter.

SCHAFER and WEINER, P.C.

By:_____
Arnold Schafer (P24694)
Attorneys for Debtor
255 East Brown Street
Suite 315
Birmingham, MI 48011
(313) 540-3340

DATED:

**Exhibit 6-7   Accountant for Debtor**                                                    **277**

# IN THE UNITED STATES BANKRUPTCY COURT FOR THE EASTERN DISTRICT OF MICHIGAN SOUTHERN DIVISION

**In the Matter of:**
HERCULES FENCE & SUPPLY CO.,
a Michigan corporation,
Debtor.

Bankruptcy No. 87-05031-G
Chapter 11

## AFFIDAVIT IN SUPPORT OF APPLICATION FOR APPOINTMENT OF ACCOUNTANT FOR DEBTOR

STATE OF MICHIGAN
COUNTY OF OAKLAND } ss

RON OSSIPOVE, being first duly sworn, deposes and says as follows:

1. I am an accountant and have been authorized under applicable law to practice public accounting in the State of Michigan.

2. I practice my accounting services at 29226 Orchard Lake Road, Suite 150, Farmington Hills, Michigan.

3. I am familiar with Sections 101(13), 327 and 330 of the Bankruptcy Code and Rules 2014 and 5002 of the Bankruptcy Rules concerning the appointment of professional persons to perform services in a bankruptcy estate.

4. I, to the best of my knowledge, have no connection with the Debtor, its creditors or any other party in interest in this case.

5. I, to the best of my knowledge, do not represent any interest adverse to that of the estate of the Debtor, its creditors or any other party in interest in this case in matters upon which this accounting firm is to be employed. I have been the accountant for this Debtor in pre-Chapter 11 and as a result there is due and owing to me the sum of $1,500.00.

6. Based upon the foregoing, I believe that I am eligible for the appointment as the accountant, and my appointment is in the best interest of this estate and is consistent with Sections 101(13), 327 and 330 of the Bankruptcy Code. Further, deponent sayeth not.

_____
RON OSSIPOVE

Subscribed and sworn to before
me, a Notary Public on this _____
day of _____, 1987.

_____

## ENGAGEMENT LETTER

September 1, 1987

Mr. Bernard Conn
President
Hercules Fence & Supply Company
319 W. Eight Mile Road
Detroit, Michigan 48203

Dear Mr. Conn:

This letter is to confirm our understanding of the terms and objectives of our engagement and the limitations of the services I will provide.

I will provide the following services:

1. I will compile, from information you provide, the annual and interim balance sheets and related statements of income and retained earnings, and change in financial position of Hercules Fence & Supply Company, for the year ended March 31, 1987 and December 31, 1987. We will not audit or review such financial statements. My report on the annual and interim financial statements of Hercules Fence & Supply Company is presently expected to read as follows:

   The accompanying balance sheet of Hercules Fence & Supply Company, as of March 31, 1987 and December 31, 1987 and the related statements of income, retained earnings, and changes in financial positions for the year then ended have been compiled by me.

   A compilation is limited to presenting in the form of financial statements, information that is representation of management. I have not audited or reviewed the accompanying financial statements, and accordingly, do not express an opinion or any other form of assurance on them.
2. Advise your staff on how to report monthly cash statements of income and expenses.
3. Make the necessary adjustments and posts to your General Ledger.
4. Prepare annual income tax returns, Federal and State.
5. Prepare all payroll tax returns and annual wage and tax statements.
6. I will assist you in assembly of any information for preparation of required reports for filing in proceedings for reorganization under Chapter 11 of the Bankruptcy Code, as mutually agreed upon.

My fees for these services will be based on our normal hourly rate of _____ Dollars ($_____) per hour.

**Exhibit 6-7  Accountant for Debtor**                                             **279**

I will continue my services for future periods under the above terms of this engagement until such time as the terms are not suitable and upon notification of change or cancellation of such terms by you.

If the foregoing is in accordance with your understanding, please sign the copy of this letter in the space provided and return it to me.

Yours truly,

_____

Ron Ossipove
Accountant

Acknowledged:

_____

President

_____

Date

## IN THE UNITED STATES BANKRUPTCY COURT
## FOR THE EASTERN DISTRICT OF MICHIGAN
## SOUTHERN DIVISION

**In the Matter of:**
HERCULES FENCE & SUPPLY CO.,          Bankruptcy No. 87-05031-G
a Michigan corporation,                Chapter 11
Debtor.

## ORDER AUTHORIZING DEBTOR TO RETAIN RON OSSIPOVE
## AS ITS ACCOUNTANT

At a session of said Court held in the United States Courthouse, City of Detroit, Wayne County, Michigan, on _____.
PRESENT: HON. _____
BANKRUPTCY JUDGE

This matter having come to be heard on the Application of the Debtor, by and through its attorneys, Schafer and Weiner, P.C., seeking authority to retain the accountant Ron Ossipove to perform various accounting services outlined herein, and the Court being fully advised in the premises;
IT IS HEREBY ORDERED that the Debtor is hereby authorized to retain

Ron Ossipove as its accountant to (a) properly review the books and records of the Debtor; (b) compile the annual and interim balance sheets and related statements of income and retained earnings, and change in financial position, for the year ended March 31, 1987 and December 31, 1987; (c) advise on how to report monthly cash statements of income and expenses; (d) general ledger work; (e) preparation of annual income tax returns, Federal and State; (f) preparation of all payroll tax returns and annual wage and tax statements; and (g) to perform various other functions in order for the proper maintenance of the company records.

_____

BANKRUPTCY JUDGE

Exhibit 6-8    Application Retaining Financial Advisor                    **281**

**EXHIBIT 6-8    APPLICATION RETAINING FINANCIAL ADVISOR FOR UNSECURED CREDITORS' COMMITTEE**

## UNITED STATES BANKRUPTCY COURT
## DISTRICT OF NEW HAMPSHIRE

In re
PUBLIC SERVICE COMPANY
  OF NEW HAMPSHIRE,
Debtor.

## APPLICATION OF THE OFFICIAL COMMITTEE OF UNSECURED CREDITORS FOR AN ORDER AUTHORIZING RETENTION OF *SALOMON BROTHERS INC AS FINANCIAL ADVISOR*

The application of the Official Committee of Unsecured Creditors (the "Committee") of Public Service Company of New Hampshire ("PSNH" or the "Debtor"), for an order pursuant to 11 U.S.C. §§ 1103(a) and 328(a) authorizing the retention of a financial advisor, respectfully represents:

### A. Background

1. On January 28, 1988, the Debtor filed a voluntary petition for relief under the provisions of Chapter 11, Title 11, United States Code (the "Bankruptcy Code") with the United States Bankruptcy Court for the District of New Hampshire (the "Bankruptcy Court"). The Debtor is continuing to operate its business and manage its property as debtor-in-possession.

2. At a meeting of creditors of the Debtor held on February 10, 1988, the United States Trustee, pursuant to Section 1102(a)(1) of the Bankruptcy Code, appointed the Committee, presently comprised of seven members and one *ex officio* member representing the interests of the general unsecured institutional and trade creditors of the Debtor in this case, with claims exceeding $916,000,000.00.

3. The Debtor is the largest electric utility in New Hampshire, operating a single integrated system which supplies electricity to approximately three-quarters of the state's population.

4. The Debtor is the fourth-largest company in the United States to file a Chapter 11 petition and the first investor owned utility to file a reorganization case since the Depression. Its capital structure includes 24 secured debt issues of three different levels of priority, with interest rates ranging from 4⅝% to 18% and 10 unsecured debt issues with interest rates ranging from 12¼% to 17½%. The Company produces electrical power at more than 17 different facilities and is subject to state and federal regulation.

## B. The Necessity for Prompt Retention of a Financial Advisor

5. The Committee respectfully submits that the services of a financial advisor are essential now to enable it to evaluate the complex financial and economic issues raised by the unique nature of the Debtor's reorganization proceedings and to fulfill its statutory and fiduciary duties to the creditors it represents. As part of this process, it will be necessary for the Committee, with the assistance of a financial advisor, to evaluate and take positions on a broad range of complex financial and economic issues, including (i) the terms of any proposed sale or other disposition of the Debtor's operating assets such as is presently under discussion by the Debtor with both New England Electric System and Northeast Utilities; (ii) the financial factors which would support an increase in existing rates, whether or not Seabrook operates; (iii) the Debtor's business plan and forecasts leading to a plan of reorganization; (iv) the financial impact of alternative uses of the Seabrook facility; and (v) the structure, terms, conditions and elements of a plan of reorganization in this case.

6. Notwithstanding that the Debtor has indicated its general willingness to share the work product of its financial advisor, The First Boston Corporation, with the Committee, it is critical that the Committee retain its own investment advisor. Although the interests of the Debtor and the unsecured creditors represented by the Committee will at times be aligned, the Committee often can be expected to represent interests and advocate positions which may be in conflict with the Debtor and other constituencies and may be unique to the general unsecured creditors of this estate. Just as, based on the inherently adversarial nature of the relationship between the Committee and the Debtor, each requires its own attorneys, the Committee requires its own financial advisor independent of the Debtor's interests, to test and review positions taken by the Debtor in light of the special and independent vantage point of unsecured creditors.

7. The Committee is strongly of the belief that just as it is necessary to retain counsel at the start of the case, it is critical to have the services of an investment banker from the inception. That is particularly true in this case where complex issues relating to the restructuring of the Debtor must be evaluated and addressed based on such early developments as the proposed purchase of the Debtor's non-Seabrook assets. It is the Committee's intention to address the available alternative means to maximize the value of the Debtor's assets very promptly, and for this purpose the investment banker's services at this juncture are absolutely necessary. Furthermore, this Court has made clear its intention to police exclusivity carefully. Thus, early attention to plan of reorganization issues by the Committee, with financial advisors, will be essential.

8. The Committee submits that, for good reason, it is common in every Chapter 11 reorganization of a large, publicly-held company for a committee of unsecured creditors to retain the services of an investment banker/financial advisor. The Committee clearly requires such services in this case.

9. In the process of selecting a financial advisor, the Committee has inter-

**Exhibit 6-8** **Application Retaining Financial Advisor** 283

viewed five leading investment banking firms which were available to represent the Committee. Included among the candidates was Salomon Brothers Inc ("Salomon Brothers"), which is recognized as one of the nation's leading investment banks. Salomon Brothers has broad based expertise in all major areas of investment banking. In particular, Salomon Brothers has a Corporate Liability and Asset Restructuring Group, which has extensive experience in advising and representing clients involved in troubled situations both in and out of Chapter 11. The expertise of Salomon Brothers' Corporate Liability and Asset Restructuring Group is supplemented by the other departments of the firm, including Equity and Fixed Income Research, Capital Markets, High Yield Finance, Project Finance, Mergers and Acquisitions and Merchant Banking, as necessary to properly deal with the wide variety of matters which arise in reorganization cases and corporate debt restructurings.

10. In addition to Salomon Brothers' broad based experience and expertise in investment banking and corporate reorganization, Salomon Brothers, through its Electric and Gas Utility Finance Group, provides the Committee with a high degree of knowledge and expertise in the utility industry and a unique understanding of the financial condition of the Debtor and the financial issues surrounding this Chapter 11 case. The Electric and Gas Utility Finance Group of Salomon Brothers provides a full range of investment banking, analytical and financial advisory services to companies in the utility industry numbering approximately 50 of the 75 largest utilities in the United States, and can provide important expertise to the Committee. Salomon Brothers' qualifications are described more fully in the accompanying affidavit of Ronald J. Calise annexed hereto as Exhibit A (the "Calise Affidavit").

11. As a result of Salomon Brothers' knowledge and experience in investment banking generally, including its familiarity and experience in financial restructuring, coupled with its knowledge of the utility industry and the financial issues relating to this case, the Committee concluded that Salomon Brothers was well positioned to serve the interests of the general creditors of this Debtor. At a meeting of the Committee held on March 17, 1988 the Committee determined to retain Salomon Brothers as its financial advisor, subject to the Bankruptcy Court's approval.

## C. Terms of Salomon Brothers' Retention

12. The engagement letter dated March 18, 1988 from Ronald J. Calise, Managing Director of Salomon Brothers, to James Neidhart of Equitable Capital Management Corp., Chairman of the Committee (the "Retention Agreement") sets forth the services which Salomon Brothers has agreed to perform for the Committee and the compensation it will receive therefor. A copy of the Retention Agreement is annexed hereto as Exhibit B.

13. In summary, the Retention Agreement provides that Salomon Brothers will provide the following services as financial advisor to the Committee:

(a) Assisting in an analysis of the Company's business, operations, properties, financial condition and ability to operate under its current rate structure;

(b) Assisting in the review of financial forecasts showing projected revenues and cash flows for the Company under a range of business and financial assumptions;

(c) Assisting in a valuation analysis of PSNH and its components as a going concern and in liquidation;

(d) Assisting in the review of a business plan based on the above analysis, which may include recommendations as to appropriate corporate organizational structure, mergers, divestitures, joint ventures or other similar combinations, and the sale or disposition of assets;

(e) Assisting in the review and development of an appropriate capital structure for PSNH on a reorganized basis;

(f) Assisting in the negotiation and implementation of a plan of reorganization and analyzing and developing alternatives with respect to any proposed plans of reorganization including advising as to the reasonableness and feasibility of any such plans and the value to the creditors of any plan distributions, including any publicly tradeable securities included therein;

(g) Participating in hearings in connection with the foregoing including confirmation of the reorganization plan and, if requested, providing expert testimony in connection with any hearings before the United States Bankruptcy Court or before any relevant regulatory body;

(h) Assisting in the review and analysis of the impact of various rate levels upon reorganization values and distributions;

(i) Assisting in the review of the impact of proposed sales or other dispositions of assets upon unsecured creditors, and advising the Committee with respect to any proposed sales;

(j) Reviewing and analyzing reports by and work product of the Company's financial advisors; and

(k) Rendering such other financial advisory services as may, from time to time, be requested by the Committee in the performance of its duties.

14. The services to be performed by Salomon Brothers pursuant to the Retention Agreement shall not include other investment banking services, such as the sale or disposition of assets, the raising of capital, or any other specific transaction requested by the Committee. Terms of additional compensation for such other investment banking services, if any, will be in line with industry practice, subject to mutual agreement and Bankruptcy Court approval.

15. As consideration for the financial advisory services which Salomon Brothers proposes to perform on behalf of the Committee, subject to Bankruptcy Court approval, the Committee has agreed that Salomon Brothers will receive an advisory fee in the amount $150,000 per month effective March 18, 1988, payable in arrears by the Debtor at the end of each month, upon the submission of monthly invoices to the Debtor and the Committee setting forth in reasonable detail the nature and scope of the services rendered and the names

**Exhibit 6-8  Application Retaining Financial Advisor**          **285**

and titles of the persons rendering the services during such month, subject to final application to the Bankruptcy Court for approval of all fees. To the extent that the services performed by Salomon Brothers in any month are *de minimis,* then the monthly fee shall be reduced accordingly. In addition, Salomon Brothers will be reimbursed by the Debtor for all necessary and reasonable out-of-pocket expenses incurred in connection with the retention. Furthermore, Salomon Brothers is reserving its right to apply to this Court, upon confirmation of a plan of reorganization or other successful completion of this Chapter 11 case, for an additional fee reflective of Salomon Brothers' contribution to this case. The Debtor and the Committee reserve the right to take a position on such an application based upon the facts and circumstances, and this Court, of course, will rule upon such application based upon the relevant facts and circumstances and applicable law.

16. The Retention Agreement further provides that Salomon Brothers (including any affiliates and their respective officers, directors, employees, agents or controlling persons) shall be indemnified and held harmless by the Debtor against losses, claims, damages or liabilities to which Salomon Brothers may become subject. Salomon Brothers shall be reimbursed by the Debtor for any legal or other expenses reasonably incurred in connection with investigating or defending any such loss, claim, damage or liability (or action in respect thereof). However, Salomon Brothers will not be protected or held harmless from any losses, claims, damages, liabilities or expenses to the extent it is finally determined that they resulted primarily from actions taken or omitted to be taken by Salomon Brothers in bad faith or from its negligence.

17. As stated in paragraph 2 of the Calise Affidavit, the terms and conditions of employment and compensation provided for in the Retention Agreement are consistent with employment and compensation arrangements typically entered into by other major investment banks in large and complex corporate reorganization cases.

18. The Committee submits that obtaining immediate access to the services of a financial advisor is necessary to a successful and prompt resolution of this case. Without the immediate services of an investment banker, the Committee will be ill-prepared to effectively address the numerous financial and economic issues which will arise in the near future in connection with the disposition of assets or other restructuring proposals.

19. The Committee submits that Salomon Brothers has the experience and expertise necessary to effectively represent the Committee's substantial interests in this case. Salomon Brothers' experience will be of particular value in assisting in the formulation of a suitable plan of reorganization benefiting the unsecured creditors in this case.

20. Based upon Salomon Brothers' affidavit, the Committee believes that Salomon Brothers has no interest adverse to the interests of the estate or the unsecured creditors with respect to the matters on which Salomon Brothers will be employed; nor does it have any actual bias or conflict that might justify denying its retention and compensation.

21. Notice of this Application has been given to the Debtor, the office of the United States Trustee, and those parties listed on the Special Notice List and 2002(i) List. It is respectfully submitted that no other notice need or should be given.

22. No previous application for the relief requested herein has been made to this or any other court.

WHEREFORE, the Committee requests that the annexed proposed order be entered authorizing (i) the retention of Salomon Brothers as financial advisor to the Committee under the terms of the Retention Agreement and (ii) the payment of fees and expenses in accordance with the terms of the Retention Agreement, and that this Court grant such other and further relief as is just and proper.

Dated: New York, New York
      April 1, 1988

KRAMER, LEVIN, NESSEN,
KAMIN & FRANKEL
Counsel for the Official Creditors
Committee

By: _____
    A Member of the Firm
919 Third Avenue
New York, New York 10022
(212) 715–9100

**Exhibit 6-9   Employment of Accountant as Expert Witness**                    **287**

## EXHIBIT 6-9   EMPLOYMENT OF ACCOUNTANT AS EXPERT WITNESS

Exhibit 6-9 consists of the following:

_____.

2049 Century Park East
Suite 3500
Los Angeles, California 90067
(213) 553–8100

Attorneys for Official Committee of Creditors Holding Unsecured Claims

## UNITED STATES BANKRUPTCY COURT
## CENTRAL DISTRICT OF CALIFORNIA

**In re**

Debtor.

Case No. LA 89 99999 XX
Chapter 11

APPLICATION BY OFFICIAL CREDITORS'
COMMITTEE TO EMPLOY _____ AS EX-
PERT WITNESS; DECLARATION OF _____,
COMMENTS OF THE UNITED STATES
TRUSTEE; AND ORDER THEREON

Date: No hearing set
Time: No hearing set
Place: Courtroom C, 8th Floor
312 North Spring Street
Los Angeles, CA 90012

TO THE HONORABLE _____, UNITED STATES BANKRUPTCY
JUDGE:

The Official Committee of Creditors Holding Unsecured Claims (the "Committee") respectfully represents and alleges as follows:

1. _____ ("_____" or the "Debtor") filed its voluntary petition under chapter 11 of the Bankruptcy Code on March 28, 1989.

2. The Committee was appointed pursuant to 11 U.S.C. § 1102 on April 11, 1988. On or about May 3, 1988, the Bankruptcy Court made and entered its Order authorizing the Committee to employ _____ as the accountants for the Committee.

3. A hearing to determine whether the Court's May 3, 1988 authorization to employ _____ as accountants for the Committee included authorization to permit _____ to provide the Committee with management consultant services rendered by members of _____ health care group (the "Fee Hearing") is currently scheduled for _____. Pursuant to Order of the Bankruptcy Court entered on or about _____,

Exhibit 6-9   **Employment of Accountant as Expert Witness**          **289**

the Committee is authorized to employ such accounting experts as may be appropriate to appear and testify at the Fee Hearing.

4. The Committee seeks an Order authorizing the retention of _____ ("_____"), to appear and testify as an expert witness at the Fee Hearing. Among other qualifications, Mr. _____ is _____. A copy of Mr. _____ resume is attached hereto as Exhibit "A" [omitted].

5. As a _____, the Committee believes that _____ is well qualified to testify as an accounting expert at the Fee Hearing. _____ has agreed to be employed as an expert witness on the following terms and conditions:

a. _____ will be paid at the rate of _____ per hour plus receive reimbursement for all actual and necessary out-of-pocket expenses.

b. _____ will submit an itemized fee statement to _____ following the Fee Hearing covering the services rendered and expenses incurred in connection with providing expert testimony at such hearing. The statement shall be due and payable by _____ ten (10) days after receipt.

c. Because _____ is to be engaged as an expert witness only, he shall not be required to file a fee application in this chapter 11 case. If the Debtor disputes any portion of the fee statement issued by _____, the undisputed portion of the statement shall be paid immediately and the Debtor shall be obliged to file within ten (10) days an objection to payment of the disputed portion and request a hearing thereon.

d. To the best of the Committee's knowledge, information and belief, _____ has no connection with the Debtor, its attorneys or agents or _____ creditors with respect to the matters upon which _____ is to be engaged, except as set forth in the declaration of _____ attached hereto and made a part hereof.

WHEREFORE, the Committee respectfully requests that the Court make and enter its Order authorizing the Committee's retention of _____ effective _____, the date of the Court's Order authorizing the Committee to employ expert witnesses, on the terms and conditions set forth hereinabove.

DATED: May 19, 19X9

BY:_____
Attorneys for Official
Creditors Committee

## DECLARATION OF _____

I, _____, declare as follows:

1. I _____. I have personal knowledge of the facts stated herein, and if called as a witness I could and would competently thereto.

2. I have been selected by the Official Unsecured Creditors Committee of _____(the "Committee") to serve as an expert witness on the terms and conditions described in the attached Application. A copy of my resume is attached to the Application as Exhibit "A".

3. To the best of my knowledge, information and belief, I have no connection with _____, its creditors, or any other party in interest in the chapter 11 case pertaining to _____or its attorneys, accountants or other professionals except as follows:

    a. I have agreed to serve as an expert witness for the Committee at the expense of the estate if so authorized by the Court; and

    b. With more than twenty (20) years experience in the accounting profession I may, from time to time, have rendered services to various entities which may be creditors or parties in interest herein. Any such engagement has been with respect to matters not connected with this case and not involving _____ or its estate.

4. To the best of my knowledge, information and belief, I do not hold or represent any interest adverse to the Committee or the _____estate and am a disinterested person within the meaning of section 101(13) of the Bankruptcy Code.

I declare under penalty of perjury that the foregoing is true and correct.

Executed this __day of _____at _____, California.

_____

**Exhibit 6-9   Employment of Accountant as Expert Witness**                    **291**

## COMMENTS OF OFFICE OF UNITED STATES TRUSTEE

( ) THE U.S. TRUSTEE TAKES NO POSITION.
( ) THE U.S. TRUSTEE HAS NO OBJECTION.
( ) THE U.S. TRUSTEE OBJECTS AND REQUESTS A HEARING.
( ) AN OBJECTION IS RAISED AS SET FORTH BELOW.

COMMENTS:

DATED: May ___, 19X9

OFFICE OF THE U.S. TRUSTEE

BY: _____
NAME: _____

Case Name:
Case Number: LA89 99999 XX
Type of Document: APPLICATION TO EMPLOY EXPERT WITNESS

## ORDER

Upon the Application of the Official Committee of Creditors Holding Unsecured Claims (the "Committee") for authority to employ _____ ("_____") as an expert witness, and upon the Declaration of _____ attached thereto, and the Court being satisfied that _____ represents no interest adverse to the Committee or the estate with respect to the matters upon which he is to be engaged; that _____ is a disinterested person as that term is defined in section 101(13) of the Bankruptcy Code; that _____'s employment is necessary and would be in the best interest of the Committee and the estate; and notice of the Application having been given to the United States Trustee and to _____ (the "Debtor"); and good cause appearing therefor, it is hereby

ORDERED that the Committee is authorized to employ _____ as an expert witness on the terms and conditions set forth in the Application; and it is

ORDERED that the Debtor is authorized and directed to compensate _____ and reimburse _____ reasonable and necessary out-of-pocket expenses within ten (10) days after receipt of an invoice, all in accordance with the terms of the Application.

DATED: _____


                                        _____
                                        UNITED STATES
                                        BANKRUPTCY JUDGE

Exhibit 6-10    Order Establishing Interim Fees                         **293**

## EXHIBIT 6-10    ORDER ESTABLISHING INTERIM FEES AND EXPENSE REIMBURSEMENT PROCEDURE

BERNARD SHAPIRO and MICHAEL A. MORRIS, members of
GENDEL, RASKOFF, SHAPIRO & QUITTNER
1801 Central Park East, Suite 600
Los Angeles, California 90067
Telephone: (213) 277–5400; and

BRUCE H. SPECTOR and STEPHEN P. FELDMAN, members of
STUTMAN, TREISTER & GLATT
PROFESSIONAL CORPORATION
3701 Wilshire Boulevard, Penthouse Suite
Los Angeles, California 90010
Telephone: (213) 380–1360

Attorneys for Debtors and Debtors in Possession

### UNITED STATES BANKRUPTCY COURT
### CENTRAL DISTRICT OF CALIFORNIA

| | |
|---|---|
| **In re**<br>WICKES COMPANIES, INC.,<br>a Delaware corporation;<br>THE WICKES CORPORATION,<br>a Delaware corporation;<br>GAMBLE-SKOGMO, INC.,<br>a Delaware corporation;<br>and affiliates,<br>    Debtors. | Case Nos. LA-82-06657WL<br>through LA-82-06665WL;<br>LA-82-06755WL;<br>LA-82-06756WL;<br>LA-82-06933WL;<br>through LA-82-06935WL;<br>LA-82-07139WL through<br>LA-82-07144WL<br><br>ORDER ESTABLISHING<br>INTERIM FEE AND EXPENSE<br>REIMBURSEMENT PROCEDURE |

The application of all the Debtors-in-Possession for an order establishing a procedure for the payment of interim compensation and for the reimbursement of expenses incurred by professionals employed herein as authorized by this court, the examiner and members of committees of creditors appointed by the United States Trustee came on for hearing before the undersigned Bankruptcy Judge on June 24, 1982 at 9:00 A.M. The court has duly considered the application, the files and records in these cases and the statements of counsel present. The court finds that notice of the said hearing was duly given to the creditors of these estates and to all other parties entitled thereto, and that the adoption of an interim fee procedure is necessary in connection with the administration of the estates. Now, therefore, it is,

ORDERED that, unless and until otherwise ordered by this Court, the procedure for reimbursement of expenses to committee members and for awarding interim compensation and reimbursement of expenses to the examiner, all attorneys, accountants and other professionals employed pursuant to order of this Court shall be as follows:

A. *On or before the twentieth day of each month* the committee members, the examiner and the attorneys, *accountants* and other professionals whose employment by a debtor in possession, a committee appointed under 11 U.S.C. § 151102 or the examiner shall have been authorized by this court *may submit statements to Wickes Companies, Inc. (1) for reimbursement of expenses paid or incurred on or before the last day of the preceding month in the instance of committee members or (2) for compensation and reimbursement of expenses paid or incurred on or before the last day of the preceding month in the instance of the examiner, attorneys, accountants and other professionals.* Any expenses or compensation not billed for in one month may be billed for in a subsequent month.

B. All statements submitted to one or more of the debtors in possession in accordance with this order shall be delivered to the attention of Arthur E. Kirchheimer (in the case of all law firm billings), *J. M. Van Tatenhove (in the case of all accountants' billings),* or Jeffrey Chanin (in the case of all other professionals and committee members) at *WICKES COMPANIES, INC., 3340 Ocean Park Boulevard, Suite 2000, Santa Monica, California 90405,* and shall contain the following information in either schedule or narrative form:

1. *With respect to all expenses incurred by committee members and those expenses of professional persons incurred away from their respective offices,* the amount, the date incurred and the nature thereof. The debtors in possession and the committees of creditors appointed herein shall develop for use in these cases (subject to this court's approval) a uniform set of guidelines as to reimburseable expenses and a uniform procedure (which may include appropriate forms) by which such requests for reimbursement shall be submitted.

2. *With respect to compensation to be paid there shall be provided a daily accounting of the services rendered which shall include* the date of the service rendered, an identification of the person or persons who performed the service, the time devoted in rendering the service on the day in question, a description of the services so rendered, and, to the extent practicable, the identity of the debtor estate (by case number) in which or for which the services were rendered.

3. *With respect to office expenses, costs and other special charges,* a monthly description of all such charges (*e.g.,* "long distance phone charges," "duplicating expense," *etc.*), and a description of the method by which such charges are calculated.

**Exhibit 6-10    Order Establishing Interim Fees**                                    **295**

C. Statements submitted by attorneys, accountants and other professionals shall be based upon their respective normal and customary hourly rates for a case of this type as they exist from time to time. At least 10 days before the first interim payment is sought, a schedule of such rates, together with a brief biographical sketch of each professional who is expected to devote a substantial portion of his/her time in rendering services in connection with these cases, shall be filed by each with the Court and served upon Wickes Companies, Inc., 3340 Ocean Park Boulevard, Santa Monica, Ca. 90405, Attention: Sanford C. Sigiloff, President, and c/o Cathy Cooke, Gibson, Dunn & Crutcher, 2029 Century Park East, Los Angeles, California 90067, upon the United States Trustee, upon the Securities and Exchange Commission, and upon the chairperson(s) and counsel of each of the creditors' committee appointed in any of these cases. Not less than 10 days notice of any proposed change in such hourly rates shall be given in the same manner. Any party in interest may request a hearing before this Court as to the reasonableness of any such rates, and no payments based on those rates questioned shall be made until this Court shall have ruled thereon.

D. All these statements and schedules submitted in accordance with paragraph B above shall be reviewed by Wickes Companies, Inc. and, if acceptable and if no hearing under paragraph C above is pending, *such statements will be paid within twenty days of receipt as follows:*

(1) Each statement or portion thereof which has been reasonably identified by the sender as relating to a particular case shall be attributed by Wickes Companies, Inc. to that case and the debtor in that case shall pay the statement or portion thereof in accordance with subparagraph E below.

(2) Wickes Companies, Inc. shall attribute the statements of counsel, accountants or other professionals employed in a particular case to that case and cause the debtor in that case to pay the statement in accordance with subparagraph E below.

(3) Wickes Companies, Inc. shall allocate the unallocated portions of the statements of committee members, counsel, the examiner, accountants or other professionals serving or employed in more than one case in accordance with this Court's Order of April 24, 1982 granting "Application of Debtors In Possession To Continue Historic Allocation of Overhead" and cause the debtor in each case to pay the statements in accordance with subparagraph E below. (This allocation and payment shall be without prejudice to adjustment by the Court upon motion of a party in interest.)

E. Payments shall be made as follows:

(1) To committee members, 100% of actual and reasonable expenses incurred;

(2) *To accountants* and other professionals (other than counsel and the examiner), *100%* of expenses and of compensation for services rendered;

(3) To the examiner and counsel, 100% of expenses and 75% of compensation for services rendered.

F. *Within 15 days following the end of each three-month period, commencing with the period ending July 31, 1982, each party who has sought reimbursement of expenses or interim compensation shall file with the Court and serve upon counsel to the debtors in possession, counsel to and the chairpersons of each committee of creditors appointed herein, the United States Trustee and the Securities and Exchange Commission an application for approval of the payments actually billed for during the preceding three-month period.* Provided, however, that the time reports and time records of the examiner which would normally accompany its application for approval of compensation may be separately filed with the Court to be held under seal and copies thereof need only be served upon the United States Trustee and the Securities and Exchange Commission. A hearing on these applications shall be held before the Court at 10 o'clock a.m. on the first Friday of the month following the month in which the applications are filed. (The first of these hearings shall be on *September 3, 1982, at 9 o'clock a.m.*) If any party who has received one or more payments during a three month period in accordance with paragraph E above shall fail to file an application for approval of those payments so received as required by this paragraph F, then Wickes Companies, Inc. shall not pay such party any further monthly payments (whether for reimbursement of expenses or for compensation) unless and until an application for approval of previously made payments shall have been filed and ruled upon by the Court, or unless otherwise ordered by the Court.

G. That portion of the interim compensation paid to accountants and other professionals in accordance with paragraph E. (2) which is ultimately approved and allowed by this Court shall be in full satisfaction of the claims of all such persons to receive reasonable compensation under 11 U.S.C. § 330.

H. At any time on or after August 15, 1983, the examiner or any counsel who has theretofore received interim compensation at 75% of customary hourly rates, may file an application with the Court to receive (as interim compensation) amounts equal to the previously unpaid 25% ("Special Interim Compensation"). No examiner or counsel shall apply for Special Interim Compensation more often than annually. All applications for Special Interim Compensation shall be filed and heard at the same time and in the same manner as the applications described in paragraph F above. Nothing contained herein shall be construed as giving any party any right to be awarded any such Special Interim Compensation nor to prejudice the right of any entity to object to the court's awarding all or any portion of the Special Interim Compensation sought.

I. The debtors in possession shall give notice of the filing of all applications filed pursuant to this order to all entities entitled to notice under this Court's order of April 24, 1982 granting the "Application For Order Establishing Notice Procedure."

J. In connection with the administration of these estates, the parties may from time to time seek to employ counsel, accountants, appraisers and other profes-

Exhibit 6-10    Order Establishing Interim Fees                                                297

sionals for a limited period of time or for a very limited purpose. In those instances the parties may, with the court's approval, employ such persons on terms and conditions different from those set forth herein, including on a retainer, on an hourly basis or on a contingent fee basis. It is further,

ORDERED, that nothing contained herein or done pursuant hereto shall be deemed to prejudice the right of any counsel or of the examiner to seek an award of such additional compensation at the conclusion of one of these cases as may be appropriate under the provisions of Section 330 of the Bankruptcy Code, 11 U.S.C. § 330.

AND IT IS FURTHER ORDERED, that any entity whose employment has not been previously approved by this Court, but who desires the allowance and payment of an administrative expense under Bankruptcy Code § 503, 11 U.S.C. § 503, shall file an application for such allowance with this Court and shall serve a copy thereof upon counsel for the debtors in possession, the United States Trustee, the Securities and Exchange Commission and counsel for each committee appointed under Bankruptcy Code § 151102, 11 U.S.C. § 151102. The form of each such application and the information contained therein shall conform to the fullest extent appropriate to the other provisions of this Order. All such applications filed and served on or before the fifteenth day of the month preceding the month in which a regularly scheduled fee hearing is to be held, shall be heard at the same time as the regularly filed requests for interim compensation. Any such applications not timely filed shall be heard at the next scheduled quarterly hearing. The debtors in possession shall give notice of the filing of all such applications to all entities entitled thereto under this Court's order of April 24, 1982 granting the "Application for Order Establishing Notice Procedure." Nothing contained in this paragraph shall be construed as giving any person any right to have any administrative expense allowed or paid when sought, nor to prejudice the right of any party to object to the allowance or payment of all or any portion of the administrative expense alleged in any such application.

Dated: June 30, 1982.

William J. Lasarow
United States Bankruptcy Judge

**EXHIBIT 6-11   PETITION FOR ALLOWANCE OF INTERIM
COMPENSATION AND REIMBURSEMENT OF
EXPENSES**

---

### UNITED STATES BANKRUPTCY COURT
### SOUTHERN DISTRICT OF NEW YORK

| | |
|---|---|
| **In re:** | In proceedings for a Reorganization |
| CHATEAUGAY CORPORATION | under Chapter 11 |
| REOMAR INC., | |
| THE LTV CORPORATION, *et. al.* | Case Nos. 86B 11270 (BRL) |
| Debtors | through 86B 11334 (BRL) inclusive |
| | 86B 11402 (BRL) and 86B 11464 |
| | (BRL) |

**APPLICATION FOR ALLOWANCE OF INTERIM COMPENSATION
AND REIMBURSEMENT OF EXPENSES *BY ERNST & WHINNEY,
ACCOUNTANTS FOR THE DEBTORS***

### Index

APPLICATION FOR COMPENSATION
EXHIBIT A—  July 17, 1986 Application to retain Ernst & Whinney
EXHIBIT B—  July 17, 1986 Affidavit—Arthur B. Newman
EXHIBIT C—  July 17, 1986 Order authorizing retention of Ernst & Whinney
EXHIBIT D—  April 2, 1987 Application for an order supplementing an order
dated July 17, 1986 authorizing the retention of Ernst & Whin-
ney as consultants and accountants for the debtors
EXHIBIT E—  April 2, 1987 Affidavit—Arthur B. Newman
EXHIBIT F—  April 16, 1987 Order supplementing an order dated July 17,
1986 authorizing the retention of Ernst & Whinney as consul-
tants and accountants for the debtors
EXHIBIT G—  Cumulative charges for consulting services covering period of
February 1, 1987–May 31, 1987
EXHIBIT H—  Detail of consulting charges by month February 1, 1987–May
31, 1987

[Exhibits Omitted]

Exhibit 6-11    Petition for Allowance of Interim Compensation                    **299**

## UNITED STATES BANKRUPTCY COURT
## SOUTHERN DISTRICT OF NEW YORK

| | |
|---|---|
| **In re:**<br>CHATEAUGAY CORPORATION<br>REOMAR, INC.,<br>THE LTV CORPORATION, *et. al.,*<br>Debtors | In proceedings for a Reorganization<br>under Chapter 11<br><br>Case Nos. 86B 11270 (BRL)<br>through 86B 11334 (BRL) Inclusive,<br>86B 11402 (BRL) and 86B 11464<br>(BRL) |

## APPLICATION FOR ALLOWANCE OF INTERIM COMPENSATION AND REIMBURSEMENT OF EXPENSES *BY ERNST & WHINNEY, ACCOUNTANTS FOR THE DEBTORS*

The application of Ernst & Whinney respectfully represents:

1. Ernst & Whinney is a firm of independent public accountants employed by the above captioned debtors and debtors in possession (collectively, the "Debtors"), and makes this application for an allowance for compensation for professional services rendered and for reimbursement of actual out-of-pocket expenses incurred for services to the Debtors.

2. Ernst & Whinney was engaged to represent the Debtors by Order entered by this court on July 17, 1986 (the "Retention Order"), a copy of which is annexed here as Exhibit C, and to perform required accounting services for and on behalf of the Debtors, as enumerated in the accompanying Accountants' Affidavit of Arthur B. Newman dated July 17, 1986 (the "Newman Affidavit"), a copy of which is attached hereto as Exhibit B. The Retention Order, insofar as is germane here, provides as follows: "ORDERED, that the Debtors be, and they hereby are, authorized and empowered to retain E&W to perform those services set forth in the Application and Newman Affidavit; and it is further

"ORDERED, that the Debtors be, and they hereby are, authorized and empowered to pay E&W, upon its periodic submission of bills,

(i) one-hundred (100%) percent of E&W's fees for the rendition of those services described in paragraph 3(a) of the Newman Affidavit;

(ii) seventy-five (75%) percent of E&W's fees for the rendition of those services described in paragraph 3(b) of the Newman Affidavit ("Consulting Services"); and

(iii) one-hundred (100% percent of all reasonable and necessary out-of-pocket expenses incurred by E&W in the performance of those services hereunder;

and it is further
ORDERED, that;

★★★

(v)   the aggregate billings made by E&W to the Debtors for Consulting
      Services rendered to the Debtors by E&W (exclusive of reimbursement
      of E&W's expenses) shall not exceed $1,000,000, except as may other-
      wise be authorized by subsequent order of this Court.

3. The Newman Affidavit, insofar as is germane here, provides as follows:

The nature and extent of the services that my firm proposes to render herein are
as follows:

(a) to perform an examination of the Debtors' consolidated financial statements
as of December 31, 1986, and for the year then ended, and issue our reports
thereon, including reports on the financial statements of subsidiaries that may be
required by the Debtors (the "Auditing Services"), and

(b) to act as accounting consultants to the Debtors with respect to the development, negotiation and confirmation of a plan or plans of reorganization (the "Consulting Services").

4. A subsequent Order entered by this Court on April 16, 1987 (the "Supplemental Retention Order"), a copy of which is annexed here as Exhibit F, increased the Compensation Ceiling from $1 million to $1.75 million for
Consulting Services and authorized the Debtors to retain E&W to conduct an
examination of the Debtors' consolidated financial statements as of December
31, 1987 and for the year then ended and to issue such reports in connection
therewith as may be required by law or requested by the Debtors (the "1987
Auditing Services") The Supplemental Retention Order was accompanied by an
Accountants' Affidavit of Arthur B. Newman dated April 2, 1987 (the "Second
Newman Affidavit"), a copy of which is attached hereto as exhibit E, which
further enumerates the services performed by Ernst & Whinney on behalf of the
Debtors.

5. Ernst & Whinney is submitting this application for allowance of interim
compensation for Consulting Services only covering the period from February
1, 1987 through May 31, 1987. An application for fees and expenses related to
Auditing Services for the period from February 1, 1987 through May 31, 1987
will be included with the next application for fees and expenses related to Consulting Services.

6. During such period, Ernst & Whinney provided the following Consulting
Services to the Debtors:

(a)   Provided assistance and direction to the Debtors in preparing finan-
      cial data for reporting under Chapter 11.
(b)   Reviewed historical and projected financial data and reports pre-
      pared by the Debtors.
(c)   Interviewed personnel at subsidiaries and reviewed underlying sup-
      port and assumptions to understand historical and projected financial
      data.

**Exhibit 6-11    Petition for Allowance of Interim Compensation**    **301**

(d)   Attended numerous meetings with the Debtors' management, counsel and other advisors as requested.

(e)   Attended numerous meetings of the Debtors with the Bank Committee, the Committee of Unsecured Creditors and the Equity Committee and various subcommittees of each of those committees as requested.

(f)   Attended numerous meetings with financial advisors and counsel for the Bank Committee, Committee of Unsecured Creditors and Equity Committee as requested.

(g)   Provided review and analysis of various cash and operating projections prepared by the Debtors.

(h)   Reviewed corporate and overhead expenses of the Debtors' parent and subsidiary entities.

(i)   Reviewed Statement of Financial Affairs by entity in preparation for filing by Debtors with the Court.

(j)   Reviewed historical and proposed capital expenditures with Debtors

(k)   Analyzed debt agreements, covenants, security and other matters related to liabilities and assets pledged against those liabilities.

(l)   Participated extensively in negotiations for debtor-in-possession financing with the creditor banks and other parties in interest.

(m)   Provided financial analysis, input and assistance with respect to various applications submitted for approval by this Court.

(n)   Provided input on miscellaneous matters of concern to Debtors' management and related to the Chapter 11 environment as those matters arose in the course of business.

7. Exhibit H, attached hereto, sets forth the detailed analysis of the Consulting Services rendered during the period, including the identity of the consultants rendering such services, the hours expended by them and their hourly rates. The charges associated with such services, based upon standard hourly rates, have the value of $481,156.

8. In addition, Ernst & Whinney incurred necessary out-of-pocket expenses of $46,837.07 during such period related to Consulting Services.

9. Immediately prior to the Chapter 11 filing E&W received a retainer of $75,000 relating to the bankruptcy accounting and consulting services. Such retainer has not yet been applied to the monthly billings which have been at 75% of our time charges.

10. The first decretal paragraph of the Supplemental Retention Order provides that the "aggregate compensation to be paid to Ernst & Whinney for and on account of Consulting Services rendered to the Debtors by Ernst & Whinney (exclusive of reimbursement of Ernst & Whinney's expenses) be and hereby is increased from $1 million to $1.75 million, subject to further order of this Court." From July 17, 1986 through May 31, 1987, for the period during which the Debtors have been in Chapter 11 including the periods covered by this application and the previous fee application of March 31, 1987, E&W has rendered Consulting Services which, at standard hourly rates, are valued at

$1,507,439. It is anticipated that the addition of E&W's fees for consulting services rendered during the months of June and July will cause total E&W consulting fees to surpass the ceiling of $1.75 million. E&W will submit a request for an order from the Court separate from this fee application seeking an increase in the aggregate compensation for Consulting Services.

11. WHEREFORE, Ernst & Whinney respectfully requests this Court to approve its application for fees for Consulting Services rendered during the period February 1, 1987 through May 31, 1987 in the amount of $481,156 and necessary out-of-pocket expenses in the amount of $46,837.07.

Sworn to before me this
11 day of August, 1987

                                   Ernst & Whinney

                                   _____

                                   Partner
                                   787 Seventh Avenue
                                   New York, New York 10019
                                   (212) 830–6000

_____

Notary Public

Exhibit 6-12   Petition for Fee Allowance                                    303

## EXHIBIT 6-12   PETITION FOR FEE ALLOWANCE AND REIMBURSEMENT OF EXPENSES

---

### UNITED STATES BANKRUPTCY COURT
### SOUTHERN DISTRICT OF NEW YORK

**IN RE:**

> CASE NO. _____

### APPLICATION FOR FINAL COMPENSATION AND REIMBURSEMENT OF EXPENSES

To the Honorable _____, United States Bankruptcy Judge:

Pursuant to 11 U.S.C. Section 331, _____, accountants for the Unsecured Creditors' Committee (the "Committee") hereby applies for final compensation and reimbursement for out-of-pocket expenses for the period November 1, 19X5 through April 14, 19X6:

1. _____ filed their voluntary petitions under Chapter 11 of the Bankruptcy Code on December 6, 19X4.

2. On January 23, 19X5, effective January 2, 19X5, this Court authorized the retention of _____ as accountants for the Committee.

3. By order dated January 23, 1985, effective January 2, 1985, the Court established an initial maximum aggregate compensation for _____ of _____. The aggregate amount of _____ by orders to _____ efforts as accountants for the Committee.

4. _____ has submitted to the Debtors monthly invoices for fees and expenses incurred during the period January 2, 19X5 through October 31, 19X5 in the total amount of _____. This total amount was comprised of fees of _____ and expenses of _____. Of the fees and expenses which had been incurred, _____ had been billed by _____ and the remainder of _____ represented the 15% fee holdback ordered by this Court on January 23, 19X5. A copy of each invoice is attached hereto as Exhibits A–J. By order dated December 18, 19X5, the Court authorized payment of our Interim Fee Application which reflected _____ fees and expenses of _____, incurred from January 2, 19X5 through October 31, 19X5.

5. _____ has submitted to the Debtors and Trustee monthly invoices for fees and expenses incurred during the period November 1, 19X5 through April 14, 19X6 in the total amount of _____. This total amount is comprised of fees of _____ and expenses of _____. We have submitted invoices in the amount of _____. The remainder of _____ represents the 15% fee holdback ordered by the Court on January 23, 19X5. A copy of each invoice is attached hereto as exhibits K-P.

6. _____ has also submitted to the Debtors an invoice for fees incurred in the preparation of the Interim Fee Application and the monthly billings for January 19X5 through February 19X6. This invoice totals _____. A copy is attached as Exhibit Q. In addition, _____ requests that further invoices may be submitted, prior to the date of the hearing, to a total of _____ to allow for expenses incurred but not yet recorded in the firm's accounting systems, possible late submission of time records and our fees for preparing this Application and the monthly billings for March and April 19X6.

7. _____ respectfully submits that the fees requested in this Application constitute a reasonable and fair value of such services in view of time spent, complexity of matters and results achieved.

8. The number of hours charged, the hourly charges incurred and out-of-pocket expenses incurred were as follows:

Professional Fees:

(Detail omitted)

9. _____ maintains records of the time expended in the rendition of all professional services required in the administration of the Debtors' estate. The firm's time records were made concurrently with the rendition of professional services, and all such records are available for inspection, subject to any applicable privilege. Copies of these records will be sent to the U.S. Trustee prior to the date of the hearing of this Fee Application.

10. During the course of this reorganization case, as of April 14, 19X6, partners, managers, seniors and staff of _____ have devoted an aggregate of _____ hours on this engagement. The average hourly rate charged by _____ to date is _____. Exhibit R annexed hereto contains a detailed breakdown of the hours expended by each _____ professional.

11. _____ was engaged to assist the Committee in monitoring and investigating the affairs of the Debtors. During the period November 1, 19X5 through April 14, 19X6 our efforts have been focused in the following areas:

A. *Monitoring of cash receipts and disbursements.*

As stated in our interim fee application, in order for the Committee to be informed about the activities of the Debtors and certain of their subsidiaries, we were instructed to regularly review the operations and cash movements of these entities. This effort continued to require weekly visits to both the New York and Connecticut locations. Our frequent reports to the Committee focused on information regarding the operations of these entities and whether or not funds were being properly handled and applied.

B. *Services in connection with the sale of assets, the development of a plan of reorganization and the establishment of the _____ Trust.*

As stated previously, a significant amount of effort has been expended by the Committee, its Executive Committee, and its professional advisors in connection with the above. We have participated in many discussions and negotiating sessions and have provided a number of analyses and charts to assist the Committee in evaluating alternative proposals and scenarios. These dis-

**Exhibit 6-12** **Petition for Fee Allowance** **305**

cussions have continued through April 19X6 and include the negotiations in respect of the sale of the residual assets to the _____. We specifically assisted the Committee in the preparation of the closing statement for this sale. We have also advised on the tax issues arising from the establishment of the Trust including the Trustee's obligations in respect of withholding tax for both the Trust and its beneficiaries.

C. *Services in connection with the settlement of the claims of* _____. These claims against the Debtors were settled in February 19X6 after lengthy negotiations between the _____ Official Receiver as liquidator of _____, the Debtors and the Committee.

Our assistance in the negotiations included:

Gathering factual information from the Debtors' books and records and from discussions with the Debtors' management,

Facilitating the exchange of factual information between the parties,

Analyzing the _____ claims and reconciling these claims with the Debtors' records,

Preparing support for counterclaims to be made by the Debtors,

Meeting with the Official Receiver and counsel to each of the parties to discuss the factual basis for the various claims,

Meeting with counsel to the Creditors' Committee and the Executive Creditors' Committee to discuss the issues and structure a settlement.

The above services were of particular benefit to these estates in helping to reach a fair settlement with _____ and thus avoiding lengthy and expensive litigation.

D. *Recording of Creditors' Claims and Debtor Schedules filed with the Court for the initial purposes of distribution, calculation, reconciliation to Debtor Records, and Plan Ballot summary.*
Since the Bar Date for receipt of claims we have developed a complete detail listing of all Proofs of Claim filed with the Court prior to the Bar Date, provisionally identified multiple claims and performed certain reconciliation work, and established a Creditors' database incorporating both the Proofs of Claim and the Debtor Records. The database was utilized to evaluate and summarize votes case in the Plan Ballot, which totalled in excess of 1,400.

E. *Overall assistance to the Creditors' Committee.*
We have continued to provide assistance to the Committee in obtaining and evaluating financial information and, in general, acting as liaison between the Committee and the Debtors. We have attended numerous meetings of the Committee and its Executive Committee, held many discussions with management and accountants of the Debtors and non-debtors, prepared pertinent financial analyses and assisted with overall fact finding and document gathering activities.

12. All professional services for which allowance of compensation is requested were performed by _____ for and on behalf of the Committee and not on behalf of any other party.

13. _____ hereby represents that there is no agreement or understanding between _____ and any other person for sharing of compensation to be received for services rendered in this application, except that various members and professionals associated with _____ may share in such compensation.

WHEREFORE, _____ prays for the entry of an order approving total compensation of _____. In addition to the total compensation of _____, _____ requests that further invoices may be submitted, prior to the date of the hearing, to a total of _____ to allow for expenses incurred but not yet recorded in the firm's accounting systems, possible late submission of time records and our fees for preparing this Application and the monthly billings for March and April 19X6.

Respectfully submitted this 7th day of May, 19X6.

By_____

New York, N.Y.

Exhibit 6-13   Application for Allowance of Compensation                    **307**

**EXHIBIT 6-13   APPLICATION FOR ALLOWANCE OF COMPENSATION FOR ACCOUNTANT FOR DEBTOR**

---

## UNITED STATES BANKRUPTCY COURT
## EASTERN DISTRICT OF MICHIGAN

Re: CONTINENTAL  TRANSMISSION,
INC.,

      Debtor.

Case No. 87-00549-G

Chapter 11

## APPLICATION FOR ALLOWANCE OF COMPENSATION FOR ACCOUNTANT FOR DEBTOR

NOW COMES GARY L. FIGURSKI, P.C., by and through the LAW OF-FICES OF GREGORY L. GILBERT, attorneys for the Debtor, and for their Application for Allowance of Compensation for Accountant for Debtor states:

1. That Applicant has acted as accountant for Debtor since February 12, 1987, and would have been the accountant listed in the Order Appointing Debtor in Possession of February 4, 1987.

2. That during the period covered by this Application of February 12, 1987 through August 10, 1987, GARY L. FIGURSKI, P.C. has performed numerous services as accountant for Debtor, which are briefly summarized as follows:

    (a) Prepared opening balance sheet based on filings with Bankruptcy Court of assets and liabilities;

    (b) Compiled monthly financial statements on a cash basis for the months of February, March, April, May and June, 1987;

    (c) Prepared payroll and sales tax reports for the months of January through June, 1987; and

    (d) Attended various meetings.

3. That all services for which compensation is requested by Applicant were performed for and on behalf of the Debtor, and not on behalf of any other committee, creditor or other person. Moreover, no payments have heretofore been made to Applicant in this case.

4. That during the period covered by this Application, the services performed by Applicant involved 133.25 hours, at an average hourly rate of $50.29 per hour, which summary of services is attached hereto as Figure A.

5. That no agreement or understanding exists between Applicant and any other person for the sharing of compensation to be received for services rendered, or in connection with this case.

WHEREFORE, Applicant, GARY L. FIGURSKI, P.C., respectfully prays it be allowed compensation, as accountant for Debtor, for the time period of February 12, 1987 to August 10, 1987 of $6,710.25.

GARY L. FIGURSKI, P.C.

_____

GARY L. FIGURSKI, President
Accountant for Debtor
27850 Plymouth Road
Livonia, Michigan 48150
522–9110

DATED: August 14, 1987.

**Figure A**   Continental Transmission, Inc.
Summary of Hours and Fees by Staff
February 12, 1987 through August 10, 1987

| Staff | Total Hours | Rate | Amount |
|-------|-------------|------|--------|
| G. Figurski | 27.50* | $75.00 | $2,062.50 |
| J. Theeck | 99.75 | $45.00 | 4,488.75 |
| P. DeMay | 6.00 | $25.00 | 150.00 |
|  | *133.25 |  | $6,701.25 |

Average Rate per Hour   $50.29
[Editor's Note: As a general rule it is advisable to keep time in terms of ⅙ hours. Many courts will not accept ½ or ¼ hours.]

**Exhibit 6-13**   **Application for Allowance of Compensation**   **309**

**Figure B**   Continental Transmission, Inc.
Detail Analysis of Fees
February 12, 1987 through August 10, 1987

| Date | Description | Staff | Time | Dollars |
|---|---|---|---|---|
| 02/12/87 | Meeting with Joe Viviano | GLF | 2.00 | $  150.00 |
| 02/16/87 | Organize payroll files, prepare payroll reports | JT | 4.50 | 202.50 |
| 02/21/87 | Photocopy W-2's and payroll reports | PD | 1.00 | 25.00 |
| 02/24/87 | Creditors Meeting—Court | GLF | 2.75 | 206.25 |
| 02/25/87 | Phone calls—Joe Viviano, Aaron Conley, John Cidor | GLF | 1.25 | 93.75 |
| 03/03/87 | Meet Joe Viviano—review bankruptcy accounting filing requirements | GLF | 2.50 | 187.50 |
| 03/04/87 | Phone calls—Aaron Conley re: payroll depository | GLF | .50 | 37.50 |
| 03/12/87 | Phone call—John Cidor (IRS) | GLF | .50 | 37.50 |
| 03/12/87 | February Compiled Financial Statement Preparation | JT | 6.50 | 292.50 |
| 03/14/87 | Preliminary review of February Financial Statement | GLF | .50 | 37.50 |
| 03/14/87 | Preparation of sales tax and withholding reports—Feb '87 | JT | 4.50 | 202.50 |
| 03/16/87 | February Compiled Financial Statement Preparation | JT | 1.50 | 67.50 |
| 03/17/87 | February Compiled Financial Statement Preparation | JT | 4.75 | 213.75 |
| | subtotal | | 32.75 | 1,753.75 |

**Figure B**    Continental Transmission, Inc.
            Detail Analysis of Fees (*continued*)
            February 12, 1987 through August 10, 1987

| Date | Description | Staff | Time | Dollars |
|------|-------------|-------|------|---------|
|  | Balance Forward |  | 32.75 | 1,753.76 |
| 03/18/87 | February Compiled Financial Statement Preparation | JT | 1.50 | 67.50 |
| 03/21/87 | February Compiled Financial Statement Preparation | JT | 4.50 | 202.50 |
| 03/21/87 | Review February Compiled Financial Statement | GLF | 1.00 | 75.00 |
| 04/14/87 | Letter—Re: filing requirements and deadlines | JT | .75 | 33.75 |
| 04/14/87 | Review letter, phone calls to Vernon Conley and Jason Range | GLF | .50 | 37.50 |
| 04/20/87 | Meeting with Jason Range | GLF | 1.00 | 75.00 |
| 04/20/87 | March Compiled Financial Statement Preparation | JT | 8.00 | 360.00 |
| 04/21/87 | March Compiled Financial Statement Preparation | JT | 9.50 | 427.50 |
| 04/24/87 | Review March Compiled Financial Statement | GLF | 1.00 | 75.00 |
| 04/25/87 | First Quarter payroll update | PD | 5.00 | 125.00 |
| 04/28/87 | Complete March Compiled Financial Statement and 1st quarter payroll reports | JT | 5.00 | 225.00 |
| 05/12/87 | April Compiled Financial Statement Preparation | JT | 3.50 | 157.50 |
| 05/13/87 | April Compiled Financial Statement Preparation | JT | 5.00 | 225.00 |
|  | subtotal |  | 79.00 | 3,840.00 |

**Exhibit 6-13**  **Application for Allowance of Compensation**  **311**

**Figure B**  Continental Transmission, Inc.
Detail Analysis of Fees (*continued*)
February 12, 1987 through August 10, 1987

| Date | Description | Staff | Time | Dollars |
|------|-------------|-------|------|---------|
| | Balance Forward | | 79.00 | 3,840.00 |
| 05/14/87 | Complete April Compiled Financial Statement | JT | 8.00 | 360.00 |
| 05/14/87 | Review completed April Compiled Financial Statement | GLF | 1.00 | 75.00 |
| 05/21/87 | Appear at DIP hearing | JT | 2.50 | 112.50 |
| 06/09/87 | May Compiled Financial Statement Preparation | JT | 4.50 | 202.50 |
| 06/10/87 | May Compiled Financial Statement Preparation | JT | 7.00 | 315.00 |
| 06/13/87 | Complete May Compiled Financial Statement | JT | .75 | 33.75 |
| 06/13/87 | Review May Compiled Financial Statement | GLF | 1.00 | 75.00 |
| 06/30/87 | Letter—Re: status of payroll liability | JT | 1.50 | 67.50 |
| 07/14/87 | Phone calls re: June financial information: Ken Gadd, Jason Range, Vernon Conley, Sam Barr, Gregory Gilbert | GLF | 1.00 | 75.00 |
| 07/16/87 | June Compiled Financial Statement Preparation | JT | 8.00 | 360.00 |
| 07/17/87 | Complete June Compiled Financial Statement | JT | 8.00 | 360.00 |
| 07/17/87 | Review June Compiled Financial Statement | GLF | 1.00 | 75.00 |
| | subtotal | | 123.25 | 5,951.25 |

**Figure B**   Continental Transmission, Inc.
Detail Analysis of Fees (*continued*)
February 12, 1987 through August 10, 1987

| Date | Description | Staff | Time | Dollars |
|------|-------------|-------|------|---------|
| | Balance Forward | | 123.25 | 5,951.25 |
| 07/31/87 | Phone calls re: status of bankruptcy for meeting of August 3, 1987: Ken Gadd, Jason Range, Sam Barr, Gregory Gilbert, Vernon Conley | GLF | 1.00 | 75.00 |
| 08/03/87 | Attend meeting on bankruptcy status | GLF | 3.00 | 225.00 |
| 08/08/87 | Phone Call: Ken Gadd—set up appointment to review accounting procedures with Juanita | GLF | 1.00 | 75.00 |
| 08/09/87 | Letter to Vernon Conley on current status | GLF | 5.00 | 375.00 |
| | Total All Pages | | 133.25 | $6,701.25 |

# CHAPTER SEVEN

# Accounting Services for the Debtor in Possession or Trustee: Part 1

## EXHIBIT 7-1   SUMMARY FINANCIAL INFORMATION INCLUDED WITH PETITION

*[If petitioner is a corporation, this Exhibit shall be completed and attached to the petition pursuant to paragraph 7 thereof.]*

*[Caption, other than designation, as in Form No. 1.]*

FOR COURT USE ONLY

_____

Date Petition Filed

_____

Case Number

_____

Bankruptcy Judge

1. Petitioner's employer's identification number is _____.

2. If any of petitioner's securities are registered under section 12 of the Securities and Exchange Act of 1934, SEC file number is _____.

3. The following financial data is the latest available information and refers to petitioner's condition on _____.

    a. Total assets: $_____

    b. Liabilities:

|  | | Approximate number of holders |
|---|---|---|
| Secured debt, excluding that listed below | $_____ | _____ |
| Debt securities held by more than 100 holders: | $_____ | _____ |
|   Secured | $_____ | _____ |
|   Unsecured | $_____ | _____ |
| Other liabilities, excluding contingent or unliquidated claims | $_____ | _____ |
| Number of shares of common stock | $_____ | _____ |

Comments, if any: _____

_____

_____

4. Brief description of petitioner's business:_____

_____

5. The name of any person who directly or indirectly owns, controls, or holds, with power to vote, 20 percent or more of the voting securities of petitioner is _____

6. The names of all corporations 20 percent or more of the outstanding voting securities of which are directly or indirectly owned, controlled, or held, with power to vote, by petitioner are_____

_____

_____

_____

Exhibit 7-2    Schedules of Assets and Liabilities                    315

## EXHIBIT 7-2    SCHEDULES OF ASSETS AND LIABILITIES

### UNITED STATES BANKRUPTCY COURT FOR THE
### CENTRAL DISTRICT OF CALIFORNIA

In re:                              Case No. LA-XO-04065-JD
DEBTOR CORP.                        _____
Debtor*                                    SCHEDULES

### SCHEDULE A—STATEMENT OF ALL LIABILITIES OF DEBTOR

Schedules A-1, A-2, and A-3 must include all the claims against the petitioner or his property as of the date of the filing of the petition by or against him.

### SCHEDULE A-1—Creditors having priority (Cont'd.)

| 1 Nature of claim | 2 Name of creditor and complete mailing address including zip code | 3 Specify when claim was incurred and the consideration therefore; when claim is subject to setoff, evidenced by a judgment, negotiable instrument, or other writing, or incurred as partner or joint contractor, so indicate, specify name of any partner or joint contractor on any debt | 4 Indicate if claim is contingent, unliquidated or disputed | 5 Amount of Claim |
|---|---|---|---|---|

a Wages, salaries and commissions, including vacation, severance and sick leave pay owing to workmen, servants, clerks, or traveling or city salesmen on salary or commission basis, whole or part time, whether or not selling exclusively for the debtor, not exceeding $2000 to each earned within 90 days before filing of petition or cessation of business, if earlier (specify date)

                                (SEE RIDER A-1-a)                      $ 3,020.00

b Contributions to employee benefit plans for services rendered within 180 days before filing of petition or cessation of business, if earlier (specify date)       –0–

c Claims of farmers, not exceeding $2,000 for each individual, pursuant to 11 USC §507(a)(5)(A).

d Claims of United States fishermen, not exceeding $2,000 for each individual, pursuant to 11 USC Section 507(a)(5)(B).

## SCHEDULE A-1—Creditors having priority (Cont'd.)

| 1 Nature of claim | 2 Name of creditor and complete mailing address including zip code | 3 Specify when claim was incurred and the consideration therefore; when claim is subject to setoff, evidenced by a judgment, negotiable instrument, or other writing, or incurred as partner or joint contractor, so indicate, specify name of any partner or joint contractor on any debt | 4 Indicate if claim is contingent, unliquidated or disputed | 5 Amount of Claim |
|---|---|---|---|---|
| e Deposits by individuals, not exceeding $900 for each purchase, lease or rental of property or services for personal, family, or household use that were not delivered or provided | | | | –0– |
| f Taxes owing (itemize by type of tax and taxing authority) | | | | |
| (1) To the United States | | (See Schedule A-1 Supplement) | | 21,736.58 |
| (2) To any state | | (See Schedule A-1 Supplement) | | 39,589.70 |
| (3) To any other taxing authority | | | | –0– |

*Include here all names used by debtor within last 6 years.     Total $64,346.28

## RIDER A-1-a

| | | |
|---|---|---|
| Tom Jones<br>6420 Lexington Ave.<br>Cerritos, California 90701 | Sales Commission | $   500.00<br>(contingent and unliquidated) |
| Bill Thompson<br>1247 Main Street<br>Hacienda Heights,<br>California 91745 | Sales Commission | 500.00<br>(contingent and unliquidated) |
| William Robertson<br>4201 South Street<br>Woodland Hills, California<br>91634 | Sales Commission | 200.00<br>(contingent and unliquidated) |
| Denise Blank<br>5891 Smith Street<br>Huntington Beach, Calif.<br>92647 | Salary | 1,820.00<br>$3,020.00 |

**Exhibit 7-2  Schedules of Assets and Liabilities**                              **317**

## SCHEDULE A-1 SUPPLEMENT

d

(1)  Taxes owing to United States Internal Revenue Service

| | |
|---|---:|
| Federal withholding tax | $14,243.06 |
| FICA | 7,194.43 |
| Federal Unemployment tax | 299.09 |
| | $21,736.58 |

(2)  Taxes owing to State of California
(a) State Board of Equalization

| | |
|---|---:|
| Sales and use tax 1st quarter | 16,965.20 |
| April | 16,901.06 |
| May 1–7 | 3,215.95 |
| | $37,082.21 |

(b) Employment Development Department

| | |
|---|---:|
| State withholding tax | $ 1,512.45 |
| State Disability Insurance | 183.21 |
| State Unemployment tax | 811.83 |
| | $ 2,507.49 |

(3)  To any other taxing agency                                          –0–

Addresses:

Internal Revenue Service, 300 N. Los Angeles St.,
Los Angeles, Ca. 90012, Attn: Chief Special Procedures

State Board of Equalization, 1020 "N" Street, P.O.B. 1799
Sacramento, Ca. 95808

Employment Development Department, 800 Capitol Mall
Sacramento, Ca. 95814

Los Angeles County Tax Collector, 225 N. Hill St.,
Los Angeles, Ca. 90012

## SCHEDULE A-2—Creditors Holding Security

| 1. Name of creditor and complete mailing address including zip code | 2. Description of security and date when obtained by creditor | 3. Specify when claim was incurred and the consideration therefor; when claim is subject to setoff, evidenced by a judgment, negotiable instrument, or other writing, or incurred as partner or joint contractor, so indicate; specify name of any partner or joint contractor on any debt | 4. Indicate if claim is contingent, unliquidated or disputed | 5. Market value | 6. Amount of claim without deduction of value of security |
|---|---|---|---|---|---|
| 1) Bank of America<br>102 E. Las Tunas<br>San Gabriel, CA 91776<br>   Trade accounts receivable of the<br>   Debtor Corp. |      Accounts receivable financing<br>     loan opened July, 1977, with<br>     daily activity since that date | | | $590,781.76 | $419,540.91 |
| 2) Bank of America<br>102 E. Las Tunas<br>San Gabriel, CA 91776<br>   Equipment loan |      Loan date May 1, 1978 for purchase<br>     of film processing equipment<br>     which in turn is leased to<br>     customer, London Press<br>               Book Value | | | 22,500.00 | 25,710.00 |
| 3) Bank of America<br>102 E. Las Tunas<br>San Gabriel, CA 91776<br>   Auto Loan |      Loan date October 3, 1979<br>     1979 C-30 Chev. Van<br>               Book Value | | | 4,750.00 | 5,213.80 |
| | | | Total | $618,031.76 | $450,464.71 |

**Exhibit 7-2    Schedules of Assets and Liabilities**                                    **319**

# SCHEDULE A-3—Creditors Having Unsecured Claims Without Priority

| Name of creditor (including last known holder of any negotiable instrument) complete mailing address including zip code | Specify when claim was incurred and the consideration therefor; when claim is contingent, unliquidated, disputed, subject to setoff, evidenced by a judgment, negotiable instrument, or other writing, or incurred as partner or joint contractor, so indicate; specify name of any partner or joint contractor on any debt | Indicate if claim is contingent, unliquidated, or disputed | Amount of Claim |
|---|---|---|---|
| 1. Trade accounts payable (See Schedule A-3 Supplement [Schedule not included in Figure] for detail) | | | $586,437.20 |
| 2. Note payable  Nancy Southern  P. O. Box 6005  Booker, Texas 79005  Note dated May 1, 1978 for purchase of stock of J. P. Harwood Company at book value.  Evidenced by judgment for $95,625.04  Disputed and case appealed  Attorney: Jerome L. Daniels, Esq.  900 North Flower Street  Los Angeles, California 90017 | | | 86,673.04 (disputed) |
| 3. Lease/purchase contract  Daniel R. Mai, dba Jefferson Ltd.  P. O. Box 73056  Los Angeles, California 90018 | | | 16,000.00 (disputed and unliquidated) |
| 4. Consulting contract date October 26, 1979  Corporate Associates  1100 Fox Street  Los Angeles, California 92660 | | | Unknown |
| 5. Gustav Thompson  22505 West 8th  Los Angeles, California 90032 | Landlord | | –0– |
| 6. Gary Dodsman Insurance Agency  9567 Westwood Boulevard  Los Angeles, California 90047 | Note | | 1,418.50 |
| 7. American Corporation  Route 6  Somerville, New Jersey 08892 | Note | | 61,078.21 |
| | | Total | $751,606.95 |

## STATEMENT OF ALL PROPERTY OF DEBTOR

Schedules B-1, B-2, and B-4 must include all property of the debtor as of the date of the filing of the petition by or against him.

### SCHEDULE B-1—Real Property

| Description and location of all real property in which debtor has an interest (including equitable and future interests, interests in estates by the entirety, community property, life estates, lease-holds, and rights and powers exercisable for his own benefit) | Nature of interest (specify all deeds and written instruments relating thereto) | Market value of debtor's interest without deduction for secured claims listed in Schedule A-2 or exemptions claimed in Schedule B-4 |
|---|---|---|
| 2404 5th Avenue<br>South El Monte, California 91733 | | $    –0– |
| Leasehold interest in commercial building of approximately 8,000 sq. feet | Lease expires November 30, 1980 | |
| | Total | $    –0– |

### SCHEDULE B-2 SUPPLEMENT

### f. Automobiles, trucks, trailers, and other vehicles

| Make | Type | Year | Purchased | License | Cost |
|---|---|---|---|---|---|
| Dodge | B300 Van | 1977 | 5-2-77 | 1T95568 | |
| Dodge | Van | 1977 | 3-2-78 | 1T51194 | |
| Chevrolet | 16′ Flatbed | 1974 | 1-28-77 | 53679T | |
| Chevrolet | C-30 Van | 1979 | 9-27-79 | 1T62560 | |
| Ford | Pinto S/W | 1976 | 5-25-76 | 328T | |

|  |  |
|---|---|
| | $31,943.41 |
| Less Depreciation | 27,526.26 |
| Book Value | $   4,417.15 |

**Exhibit 7-2   Schedules of Assets and Liabilities**                                    **321**

## SCHEDULE B-2—Personal Property

| Type of Property | Description and Location | | Market value of debtor's interest without deduction for secured claims listed in Schedule A-2 or exemptions claimed in Schedule B-4 |
|---|---|---|---|
| a. Cash on hand | | | $    980.49 |
| b. Deposits of money with banking institutions, savings and loan associations, credit unions, public utility companies, landlords, and others | Bank of America 102 E. Las Tunas San Gabriel, CA | General Account #953216 | 18.87 |
| | Gustav Thompson 22505 West 8th Los Angeles, CA 90032 | Rent deposit | 1,700.00 |
| c. Household goods, supplies and furnishings | | | –0– |
| d. Books, pictures, and other art objects; stamp, coin, and other collections | | | –0– |
| e. Wearing apparel, jewelry, firearms, sports equipment, and other personal possessions | | | –0– |
| f. Automobiles, trucks, trailers, and other vehicles | See Schedule B-2 supplement | Book value | 4,417.15 |
| g. Boats, motors, and their accessories | | | –0– |
| h. Livestock, poultry, and other animals | | | –0– |
| i. Farming supplies and implements | | | –0– |
| j. Office equipment, furnishings, and supplies | Cost Less depreciation | $9,748.59 7,700.08 | 2,048.51 |
| k. Machinery, fixtures, equipment, and supplies (other than those listed in items i and j) used in business | Fork lift Shelving Computer | | 500.00 1,000.00 4,000.00 |

|  |  |
|---|---|
| Schedule B-2 Sub-Total | $14,665.02 |

## SCHEDULE B-2—Personal Property (Cont'd.)

| Type of property | Description and Location | Market value of debtor's interest without deduction for secured claims listed in Schedule A-2 or exemptions claimed in Schedule B-4 |
|---|---|---|
| | Schedule B-2 Sub-Total Forward | $ 14,665.02 |
| l. Inventory | | 250,000.00 |
| m. Tangible personal property of any other description | | –0– |
| n. Patents, copyrights, franchises, and other general intangibles (specify all documents and writings relating thereto) | | –0– |
| o. Government and corporate bonds and other negotiable and nonnegotiable instruments | | –0– |
| p. Other liquidated debts owing debtor | SEE RIDER [Not included in figure] Notes payable from employees | 590,781.76 7,667.64 |
| q. Contingent and unliquidated claims of every nature, including counterclaims of the debtor (give estimated value of each) | Causes of action against Nancy Southern to recover monies heretofore paid | Unknown |
| r. Interests in insurance policies (itemize surrender or refund values of each) | | –0– |
| s. Annuities | | –0– |
| t. Stock and interests in incorporated and unincorporated companies (itemize separately) | | –0– |
| u. Interests in partnerships | | –0– |
| v. Equitable and future interests, life estates, and rights or powers exercisable for the benefit of the debtor (other than those listed in Schedule B-1) (specify all written instruments relating thereto) | | –0– |
| | Total | $863,114.42 |

Exhibit 7-2    Schedules of Assets and Liabilities                                    323

## SCHEDULE B-3—Property Not Otherwise Scheduled

| Type of Property | Description and Location | Market value of debtor's interest without deduction for secured claims listed in Schedule A-2 or exemptions claimed in Schedule B-4 |
|---|---|---|
| a. Property transferred under assignment for benefit of creditors, within 120 days prior to filing of petition (specify date of assignment, name and address of assignee, amount realized therefrom by the assignee, and disposition of proceeds so far as known to debtor) | | $  –0– |
| b. Property of any kind not otherwise scheduled | | |
| | Notes receivable (equipment sale)<br>Graphic Reproductions<br>2424 So. San Gabriel Blvd.<br>Los Angeles, CA 90001<br>               Unpaid balance | 9,231.22 |
| | A & W Investments<br>5635 Palms Blvd.<br>Los Angeles, CA 90029<br>               Unpaid balance | 7,900.31 |
| | Lease-Sale Contract (equipment lease/ sale)<br>Surrey Press, Inc.<br>7311 Woodley Ave.<br>North Hollywood, CA 91605<br>               Unpaid balance | 43,204.30 |
| | Total | $60,335.83 |

## SCHEDULE B-4—Property claimed as exempt

Debtor selects the following property as exempt pursuant to 11 USC & 522(d) or the laws of the State of _____.

| Type of Property | Location, description and, if relevant, the present use of the property. | Statute and section creating the exemption. | VALUE CLAIMED EXEMPT | |
|---|---|---|---|---|
| | | | Dollars | Cents |
| None | | | | –0– |
| | | | Total | $  –0– |

## SUMMARY OF DEBTS AND PROPERTY

(From the Statements of the Debtor in Schedules A and B)

| Schedule | DEBTS | Dollars | Cents |
|---|---|---|---|
| A-1/a, b | Wages, contributions | $ | 3,020.00 |
| A-1/c | Deposits of money | | –0– |
| A-1/f (1) | Taxes owing United States | | 21,736.58 |
| A-1/f (2) | Taxes owing States | | 39,589.70 |
| A-1/f (3) | Taxes owing other taxing authorities | | –0– |
| A-2 | Secured claims | | 450,464.71 |
| A-3 | Unsecured claims without priority | | 751,606.95 |
| | SCHEDULE A TOTAL | | $1,266,417.94 |

PROPERTY

| | | | |
|---|---|---|---|
| B-1 | Real property (total value) | $ | –0– |
| B-2/a | Cash on hand | | 980.49 |
| B-2/b | Deposits | | 1,718.87 |
| B-2/c | Household goods | | –0– |
| B-2/d | Books, pictures, and collections | | –0– |
| B-2/e | Wearing apparel and personal possessions | | –0– |
| B-2/f | Automobiles and other vehicles | | 4,417.15 |
| B-2/g | Boats, motors, and accessories | | –0– |
| B-2/h | Livestock and other animals | | –0– |
| B-2/i | Farming supplies and implements | | –0– |
| B-2/j | Office equipment and supplies | | 2,048.51 |
| B-2/k | Machinery, equipment, and supplies used in business | | 5,500.00 |
| B-2/l | Inventory | | 250,000.00 |
| B-2/m | Other tangible personal property | | –0– |
| B-2/n | Patents and other general intangibles | | –0– |
| B-2/o | Bonds and other instruments | | –0– |
| B-2/p | Other liquidated debts | | 598,449.40 |
| B-2/q | Contingent and unliquidated claims | | –0– |
| B-2/r | Interests in insurance policies | | –0– |
| B-2/s | Annuities | | –0– |
| B-2/t | Interests in corporations and unincorporated companies | | –0– |
| B-2/u | Interests in partnerships | | –0– |
| B-2/v | Equitable and future interests, rights, and powers in personality | | –0– |
| B-3/a | Property assigned for benefit of creditors | | –0– |
| B-3/b | Property not otherwise scheduled | | 60,335.83 |
| B-4 | Amount of Property claimed as exempt $    –0– | | |
| | Total of Schedule B-1 thru B-3 | $ | 923,450.25 |

Exhibit 7-3   Statement of Executory Contracts                    325

## EXHIBIT 7-3   STATEMENT OF EXECUTORY CONTRACTS

---

### UNITED STATES BANKRUPTCY COURT
### SOUTHERN DISTRICT OF NEW YORK

| | |
|---|---|
| **In re**<br>ROE HOSIERY COMPANY INC.,<br>Debtor. | In Proceedings for a Reorganization<br>Case No. XI-B-10999 |

## STATEMENT OF EXECUTORY CONTRACTS OF DEBTOR

The following are all of the executory contracts of debtor on the date of the filing of the petition herein:

1. Conditional bill of sale dated *March 11, 19__,* from *Jones Auto Company, Inc.* to the debtor, covering *one* (1) 1940 *two ton International Truck*, Engine No. 3329145, Serial No. 2KH4–15282. Contract price is *two thousand one hundred and fifty* ($2,150) Dollars, of which *five hundred* ($500) Dollars was paid at time of contract, and balance of which was payable in monthly installments of *fifty* ($50) Dollars each over a period of *two* (2) years and *nine* (9) months, evidenced by promissory notes. The total amount of all unpaid notes is *eight hundred* ($800) Dollars.

2. Agreement made in *January, 19__,* between debtor and *Henry Jones*, for the employment of the latter from week to week at a weekly salary of *seventy-five* ($75) Dollars; the agreement may be terminated by either party upon *one* (1) week's notice to the other.

3. Lease dated *March 6, 19__,* between *Brown Holding Corporation*, as landlord, and debtor, as tenant, for space on the *fifth* floor of premises, *845 Bleeker* Street, *New York, New York*, for a term of *seven* (7) years and *two* (2) months, beginning *April 1, 19__,* and terminating *May 31, 19__,* at a rental of *four thousand eight hundred* ($4,800) Dollars per year, payable in equal monthly installments in advance.

[Set forth a similar statement of any other executory contract of the debtor.]

|  |  |
|---|---|
| (Signed) | *Arthur Smith*<br>Attorney for the Debtor. |
| (Address) | *22 Broadway*<br>*New York, New York 10005* |

**Source:** Adapted from *Collier Forms Manual*, Form 3012.

## EXHIBIT 7–4  PROJECTED PRO FORMA FINANCIAL STATEMENTS

This exhibit presents a pro forma balance sheet. Other examples of pro forma financial statements are shown in the excerpts of the disclosure statement in Chapter 5 of this volume.

**X COMPANY**
PROJECTED PRO FORMA CONSOLIDATED BALANCE SHEET
December 31,19X9

(Giving Pro Forma Effect to Consummation of the Trustees'
Joint Plan of Reorganization As of That Date)
(Unaudited—$000 Omitted)

| | Projected Historical December 31, 19X9 (prior to reorganization adjustments) | Reorganization adjustments | Projected Pro Forma December 31, 19X9 (after reorganization adjustments) |
|---|---|---|---|
| *Assets* | | | |
| Current assets | | | |
| Cash and cash equivalents | $15,977 | $ (5,000)(A) | $10,977 |
| Receivables | 5,374 | | 5,374 |
| Inventories | 1,590 | | 1,590 |
| Prepaid expenses | 1,029 | | 1,029 |
| Total current assets | 23,970 | (5,000) | 18,970 |
| Property and Equipment, net of accumulated amortization: | | | |
| Owned | 18,896 | | 18,896 |
| Capital leases | 10,441 | | 10,441 |
| Total property and equipment | 29,337 | | 29,337 |
| Deposits on aircraft purchase and lease agreements | 3,522 | | 3,522 |
| Other assets | | | |
| Excess paid for stock of consolidated subsidiary over equity in net assets acquired | 3,559 | | 3,559 |
| Other | 483 | | 483 |
| Total other assets | 4,042 | | 4,042 |
| Investment in and advances to discontinued operations (Seafood operations) | 14,171 | | 14,171 |
| | $75,042 | $ (5,000) | $70,042 |

**Exhibit 7-4   Projected Pro Forma Financial Statements**                327

## CONSOLIDATED BALANCE SHEET (*continued*)

| | Projected Historical December 31, 19X9 (prior to reorganization adjustments) | Reorganization adjustments | Projected Pro Forma December 31, 19X9 (after reorganization adjustments) |
|---|---|---|---|
| Liabilities, Preferred Stocks and Common Stockholders' Equity | | | |
| Current Liabilities | | | |
| Accounts payable and accrued liabilities | $ 9,023 | | $ 9,023 |
| Other current liabilities | 1,186 | | 1,186 |
| Current portion of long-term debt | 1,050 | | 1,050 |
| Current portion of capitalized lease obligations | 2,256 | | 2,256 |
| Total current liabilities | 13,515 | | 13,515 |
| Total current liabilities | $13,515 | | $13,515 |
| Other liabilities | 4 | | 4 |
| Deferred gain on sale and leaseback | 1,232 | | 1,232 |
| Long-term debt and capitalized lease obligations | | | |
| Long-term debt | 11,056 | | 11,056 |
| Capitalized lease obligations | 9,289 | | 9,289 |
| Long-term debt and capitalized lease obligations | 20,345 | | 20,345 |
| Prebankruptcy liabilities of Chapter X companies (Unsecured liabilities in Classes 5, 6 and 7) | 39,299 | $(39,299)(B) | |
| Stockholders' equity prior to reorganization | 647 | (647)(C) | |
| Series A preferred stock (Redeemable from available income, as defined, commencing in the fifth year following reorganization) at par, which equals liquidation preference | | 14,952 (D) | 14,952 |
| Series B convertible, preferred stock, at par, which equals liquidation preference | | 4,568 (D) | 4,568 |

## CONSOLIDATED BALANCE SHEET (*continued*)

| | Projected Historical December 31, 19X9 (prior to reorganization adjustments) | Reorganization adjustments | Projected Pro Forma December 31, 19X9 (after reorganization adjustments) |
|---|---|---|---|
| Common stockholders' equity: | | | |
| Common stock and additional paid-in-capital | | 15,426 (D) | 15,426 |
| Retained earnings (after reorganization adjustments) | | — | — |
| Total common stockholders' equity | | 15,126 | 15,426 |
| Total common stockholders' equity and preferred stocks | | 34,946 | 34.946 |
| | $75,042 | $ (5,000) | $70,042 |

(A) Payment of estimated costs of the case.
(B) Close out of prebankruptcy liabilities of Chapter X companies.
(C) Close out of stockholders' equity prior to reorganization.
(D) Creation of new preferred and common stocks.

Exhibit 7-5    Projected Operating Results                    **329**

## EXHIBIT 7-5   PROJECTED OPERATING RESULTS

*Note: For examples of projections that are included in the disclosure statements, see the excerpts from disclosure statement in Chapter 5.*

This exhibit contains an example of the breakdown of one year's projects into twelve periods based on the assumption that the plan is approved and that the debtor has a quasi-reorganization. If the proposed Statement of Position contained in Appendix C of the Practice and Procedure volume becomes effective all assets and liabilities would have to be restated at their going concern values.

**NO NAME INCORPORATED**

**PROJECTED OPERATING RESULTS**

**November 1, 19X1, Through October 31, 19X2**

———

**NO NAME INCORPORATED**

COMMENTS ON MANAGEMENT ASSUMPTIONS
INCLUDED IN ACCOMPANYING PROJECTIONS

1. The Balance Sheet as of October 31, 19X2, as shown in Exhibit I, has been adjusted to reflect the conditions set forth in the plan of reorganization. The adjustment is as follows:

| | | |
|---|---|---|
| Notes Payable-Unsecured | $89,592 | |
| Accounts Payable | 183,055 | |
| Retained Earnings | | $152,547 |
| Goodwill | | 62,600 |
| Leasehold Improvements | | 52,400 |
| Additional Paid-In Capital | | 5,100 |

All unsecured debt as of October 30, 19X1, the date the petition was filed under chapter 11, has been reduced by 60 percent for a total of $272,647. The deficit in Retained Earnings of $152,547 has been eliminated as a result of the anticipated debt forgiveness. The Goodwill account was completely written off and the Leasehold Improvements account was reduced by $52,400. The balance of the anticipated benefit from debt forgiveness of $5,100 has been credited to the Additional Paid-In Capital account.

2. Exhibit I reflects the Company's actual Balance Sheet after adjustments as of October 31, 19X1, and the projected balance sheet as of October 31, 19X2,

after giving consideration to the projected operating results and changes in cash flow reflected in the remaining Exhibits.

3. Exhibits II and III reflect projected operating results for the year ending October 31, 19X2, and are based on the following major assumptions:
   a. Sales are projected at $1,250,000 annual volume, and are based upon present backlog data as well as historical seasonal patterns.
   b. Cost of sales is projected at 73 percent of sales.
   c. Purchase costs are assumed to be 46 percent of sales, and purchase requirements are assumed to be three months prior to shipment.
   d. Payroll taxes are projected at 5.2 percent of payroll costs.
   e. Building rent is anticipated to increase from $2,000 per month to approximately $3,000 per month in April, 19X5, upon moving the Company's operations to new facilities. As of September 30, 19X2, the lease agreement would have required payments of $5,000 per month. The lessor has agreed to reduce the payments to $2,000 per month until the expiration of the lease, March 30, 19X2. At this time the debtor will be required to vacate the facilities.
   f. The officers of the Company have agreed to a 15 percent reduction in salary. This reduction is reflected in the Exhibits.

4. Exhibit IV reflects the projected cash flow for the year ending October 31, 19X2, and is based on the following major assumptions:
   a. Collections of Accounts Receivable are assumed to be as follows:

   | | |
   |---|---|
   | 10% | of current month's sales |
   | 80 | of previous month's sales |
   | 10 | of second previous month's sales |
   | 100% | |

   b. Additional long-term financing of $100,000 is anticipated. $38,000 will be used to acquire new equipment, which is essential if the company is to continue operating.
   c. All purchases are assumed to be paid for within 30 days of receipt of goods. Substantially all other creditors are paid within the same month of receipt of goods and services, except the ABC Advertising Company which has agreed to delay for one year the billings for advertising services rendered.

5. The forecast is based on the assumption that the plan of reorganization will be accepted.

# NO NAME INCORPORATED

## BALANCE SHEETS

### For the Year Ending October 31, 19X2

(Based Upon Management Assumptions as Set Forth in Accompanying Comments)

### Assets

| | October 31 | |
| --- | --- | --- |
| | 19X2 (Projected) | 19X1 (Actual) |
| **Current Assets** | | |
| Cash (Exhibit IV) | $ 14,690 | $ 33,545 |
| Accounts Receivable | 114,000 | 48,799 |
| Inventory | 258,049 | 254,875 |
| Prepaid Expenses | 3,388 | 3,388 |
| Total Current Assets | 390,127 | 340,607 |
| **Fixed Assets:** | | |
| Machinery and Equipment | 119,874 | 81,874 |
| Leasehold Improvements | 28,974 | 29,974 |
| Furniture and Fixtures | 13,058 | 13,058 |
| | 161,906 | 123,906 |
| Less: Accumulated Depreciation | 65,118 | 47,118 |
| | 96,788 | 76,788 |
| **Other Assets** | | |
| Deposits | 2,636 | 2,636 |
| Cash Surrender Value of Life Insurance | 2,594 | 2,594 |
| | 5,230 | 5,230 |
| Total Assets | $492,145 | $422,625 |

### Liabilities

| | October 31 | |
| --- | --- | --- |
| | 19X2 (Projected) | 19X1 (Actual) |
| **Current Liabilities:** | | |
| Current Notes Payable—Unsecured | $ 59,727 | $ 59,727 |
| Current Notes Payable—Secured | -0- | 33,748 |
| Accounts Payable | 52,844 | 122,038 |
| Accrued Expenses | 88,496 | 10,740 |
| Estimated Income Taxes Payable | 16,033 | -0- |
| Total Current Liabilities | 217,100 | 226,253 |
| Long-Term Debt | 95,823 | 48,061 |
| | 95,823 | 48,061 |
| **Owner's Equity** | | |
| Common Stock—$10 Par Value— 8,000 Shares | 80,000 | 80,000 |
| Additional Paid-In Capital | 68,311 | 68,311 |
| Retained Earnings | 30,911 | -0- |
| | 179,222 | 148,311 |
| Total Liabilities and Owners' Equity | $492,145 | $422,625 |

## NO NAME INCORPORATED

PROJECTED STATEMENT OF OPERATIONS

For the Year Ending October 31, 19X2

(Based Upon Management Assumptions As Set Forth in
Accompanying Comments)

| | Actual | Total | Period 1 | Period 2 | Period 3 | Period 4 |
|---|---|---|---|---|---|---|
| Net Sales, All Products | $ 0 | $1,250,000 | $ 85,000 | $120,000 | $ 90,000 | $190,000 |
| Cost of Sales: | | | | | | |
| Beginning Inventory | 0 | 254,875 | 254,875 | 304,719 | 280,703 | 258,754 |
| Purchases | 0 | 598,000 | 87,400 | 41,400 | 18,400 | 41,400 |
| Direct Labor | 0 | 141,920 | 11,700 | 9,360 | 12,350 | 9,880 |
| Manufacturing Burden | 0 | 175,754 | 12,794 | 12,824 | 13,001 | 14,281 |
| | 0 | 1,170,549 | 366,769 | 368,303 | 324,454 | 324,315 |
| Less: Ending Inventory | 0 | 258,049 | 304,719 | 280,703 | 258,754 | 185,615 |
| Cost of Sales | 0 | 912,500 | 62,050 | 87,600 | 65,700 | 138,700 |
| Gross Profit | 0 | 337,500 | 22,950 | 32,400 | 24,300 | 51,300 |
| Selling, General and Adm. | 0 | 282,333 | 23,885 | 22,595 | 23,764 | 22,664 |
| Operating Income | 0 | 55,167 | (935) | 9,805 | 536 | 28,636 |
| Interest Expense | 0 | 8,823 | 547 | 660 | 660 | 797 |
| Other Income | 0 | 600 | 50 | 50 | 50 | 50 |
| Income Before Tax | 0 | 46,944 | $ (1,432) | $ 9,195 | $ (74) | $ 27,889 |
| Provision for Tax | 0 | 16,033 | | | | |
| Net Income | 0 | 30,911 | | | | |
| Retained Earnings (Beg.) | 0 | 0 | | | | |
| Retained Earnings (End) | $ 0 | $ 30,911 | | | | |

**Exhibit 7-5   Projected Operating Results**                    333

| Period 5 | Period 6 | Period 7 | Period 8 | Period 9 | Period 10 | Period 11 | Period 12 |
|---|---|---|---|---|---|---|---|
| $ 90,000 | $ 40,000 | $ 90,000 | $110,000 | $115,000 | $100,000 | $105,000 | $115,000 |
| 185,615 | 195,706 | 245,455 | 254,584 | 249,163 | 247,622 | 254,711 | 258,200 |
| 50,600 | 52,900 | 46,000 | 48,300 | 52,900 | 52,900 | 52,900 | 52,900 |
| 9,880 | 9,880 | 13,650 | 11,400 | 14,300 | 11,960 | 11,960 | 15,600 |
| 15,311 | 16,169 | 15,179 | 15,179 | 15,209 | 15,229 | 15,279 | 15,299 |
| 261,406 | 274,655 | 320,284 | 329,463 | 331,572 | 327,711 | 334,850 | 341,999 |
| 195,706 | 245,455 | 254,584 | 249,163 | 247,622 | 254,711 | 258,200 | 258,049 |
| 65,700 | 29,200 | 65,700 | 80,300 | 83,950 | 73,000 | 76,650 | 83,950 |
| 24,300 | 10,800 | 24,300 | 29,700 | 31,050 | 27,000 | 28,350 | 31,050 |
| 23,074 | 23,656 | 24,236 | 23,106 | 24,236 | 23,300 | 23,310 | 24,507 |
| 1,226 | (12,856) | 64 | 6,594 | 6,814 | 3,700 | 5,040 | 6,543 |
| 797 | 798 | 798 | 798 | 742 | 742 | 742 | 742 |
| 50 | 50 | 50 | 50 | 50 | 50 | 50 | 50 |
| $    479 | $(13,604) | $   (684) | $  5,846 | $  6,122 | $  3,008 | $  4,348 | $  5,851 |

## NO NAME INCORPORATED
### PROJECTED STATEMENT OF OPERATING EXPENSES
For the Year Ending October 31, 19X2
(Based Upon Management Assumptions As Set Forth in Accompanying
Comments)

| | Actual | Total | Period 1 | Period 2 | Period 3 | Period 4 |
|---|---|---|---|---|---|---|
| **Manufacturing Burden** | | | | | | |
| Salaries and Wages: | | | | | | |
|   Engineering | $ 0 | $ 66,450 | $ 4,600 | $ 4,600 | $ 4,600 | $ 5,850 |
|   Indirect Labor | 0 | 14,000 | 1,000 | 1,000 | 1,000 | 1,000 |
| | 0 | 80,450 | 5,600 | 5,600 | 5,600 | 6,850 |
| Payroll Taxes | 0 | 11,556 | 963 | 963 | 963 | 963 |
| Building Rent | 0 | 26,802 | 1,613 | 1,613 | 1,750 | 1,750 |
| Heat, Light, and Power | 0 | 10,140 | 660 | 670 | 680 | 690 |
| Small Tools and Shop | 0 | 1,500 | 100 | 100 | 110 | 110 |
| Depreciation | 0 | 14,000 | 1,050 | 1,050 | 1,050 | 1,050 |
| Insurance | 0 | 2,200 | 160 | 160 | 160 | 160 |
| Property Taxes | 0 | 2,000 | 400 | 400 | 400 | 400 |
| Maintenance and Repairs | 0 | 3,400 | 400 | 400 | 400 | 400 |
| Engineering Supplies | 0 | 2,400 | 200 | 200 | 200 | 200 |
| Employee Benefits | 0 | 7,200 | 490 | 510 | 530 | 550 |
| Equipment Rental | 0 | 5,550 | 445 | 445 | 445 | 445 |
| Accrued Vacations | 0 | 8,556 | 713 | 713 | 713 | 713 |
|   Total (Exhibit II) | $ 0 | $175,754 | $ 12,794 | $ 12,824 | $ 13,001 | $ 14,281 |
| **Selling, General and Adm.** | | | | | | |
| Salaries and Wages: | | | | | | |
|   Officers | $ 0 | $ 87,000 | $ 7,250 | $ 7,250 | $ 7,250 | $ 7,250 |
|   Office | 0 | 57,015 | 5,325 | 4,260 | 5,325 | 4,260 |
| | 0 | 144,015 | 12,575 | 11,510 | 12,575 | 11,510 |
| Payroll Taxes | 0 | 7,492 | 654 | 599 | 654 | 599 |
| Employee Benefits | 0 | 3,640 | 270 | 280 | 290 | 300 |
| Accrued Vacations | 0 | 7,200 | 600 | 600 | 600 | 600 |
| Building Rent | 0 | 4,096 | 231 | 231 | 250 | 250 |
| Utilities | 0 | 2,220 | 150 | 160 | 170 | 170 |
| Depreciation | 0 | 4,000 | 200 | 200 | 200 | 200 |
| Telephone and Telegraph | 0 | 9,410 | 700 | 710 | 720 | 730 |
| Professional Fees | 0 | 8,000 | 667 | 667 | 667 | 667 |
| Freight-Out | 0 | 600 | 50 | 50 | 50 | 50 |
| Office Supplies | 0 | 3,900 | 325 | 325 | 325 | 325 |
| Travel and Entertainment | 0 | 7,560 | 630 | 630 | 630 | 630 |
| Insurance | 0 | 2,800 | 233 | 233 | 233 | 233 |
| Overtime Premium | 0 | 600 | 200 | 0 | 0 | 0 |
| Advertising | 0 | 72,000 | 6,000 | 6,000 | 6,000 | 6,000 |
| Equipment Rental | 0 | 1,200 | 100 | 100 | 100 | 100 |
| Miscellaneous | 0 | 3,600 | 300 | 300 | 300 | 300 |
|   Total (Exhibit II) | $ 0 | $282,333 | $ 23,885 | $ 22,595 | $ 23,764 | $ 22,664 |

**Exhibit 7-5   Projected Operating Results**                                           335

| Period 5 | Period 6 | Period 7 | Period 8 | Period 9 | Period 10 | Period 11 | Period 12 |
|---|---|---|---|---|---|---|---|
| $ 5,850 | $ 5,850 | $ 5,850 | $ 5,850 | $ 5,850 | $ 5,850 | $ 5,850 | $ 5,850 |
| 2,000 | 2,000 | 1,000 | 1,000 | 1,000 | 1,000 | 1,000 | 1,000 |
| 7,850 | 7,850 | 6,850 | 6,850 | 6,850 | 6,850 | 6,850 | 6,850 |
| 963 | 963 | 963 | 963 | 963 | 963 | 963 | 963 |
| 1,750 | 2,618 | 2,618 | 2,618 | 2,618 | 2,618 | 2,618 | 2,618 |
| 690 | 990 | 970 | 950 | 950 | 950 | 970 | 970 |
| 120 | 120 | 130 | 130 | 140 | 140 | 150 | 150 |
| 1,050 | 1,250 | 1,250 | 1,250 | 1,250 | 1,250 | 1,250 | 1,250 |
| 160 | 200 | 200 | 200 | 200 | 200 | 200 | 200 |
| 400 | 0 | 0 | 0 | 0 | 0 | 0 | 0 |
| 400 | 200 | 200 | 200 | 200 | 200 | 200 | 200 |
| 200 | 200 | 200 | 200 | 200 | 200 | 200 | 200 |
| 570 | 590 | 610 | 630 | 650 | 670 | 690 | 710 |
| 445 | 475 | 475 | 475 | 475 | 475 | 475 | 475 |
| 713 | 713 | 713 | 713 | 713 | 713 | 713 | 713 |
| $ 15,311 | $ 16,169 | $ 15,179 | $ 15,179 | $ 15,209 | $ 15,229 | $ 15,279 | $ 15,299 |
| | | | | | | | |
| $ 7,250 | $ 7,250 | $ 7,250 | $ 7,250 | $ 7,250 | $ 7,250 | $ 7,250 | $ 7,250 |
| 4,260 | 4,260 | 5,325 | 4,260 | 5,325 | 4,435 | 4,435 | 5,545 |
| 11,510 | 11,510 | 12,575 | 11,510 | 12,575 | 11,685 | 11,685 | 12,795 |
| 599 | 599 | 654 | 599 | 654 | 608 | 608 | 665 |
| 300 | 300 | 310 | 310 | 320 | 320 | 320 | 320 |
| 600 | 600 | 600 | 600 | 600 | 600 | 600 | 600 |
| 250 | 412 | 412 | 412 | 412 | 412 | 412 | 412 |
| 170 | 230 | 220 | 200 | 190 | 180 | 180 | 200 |
| 400 | 400 | 400 | 400 | 400 | 400 | 400 | 400 |
| 740 | 1,100 | 760 | 770 | 780 | 790 | 800 | 810 |
| 667 | 667 | 667 | 667 | 667 | 667 | 667 | 667 |
| 50 | 50 | 50 | 50 | 50 | 50 | 50 | 50 |
| 325 | 325 | 325 | 325 | 325 | 325 | 325 | 325 |
| 630 | 630 | 630 | 630 | 630 | 630 | 630 | 630 |
| 233 | 233 | 233 | 233 | 233 | 233 | 233 | 233 |
| 200 | 200 | 0 | 0 | 0 | 0 | 0 | 0 |
| 6,000 | 6,000 | 6,000 | 6,000 | 6,000 | 6,000 | 6,000 | 6,000 |
| 100 | 100 | 100 | 100 | 100 | 100 | 100 | 100 |
| 300 | 300 | 300 | 300 | 300 | 300 | 300 | 300 |
| $ 23,074 | $ 23,656 | $ 24,236 | $ 23,106 | $ 24,236 | $ 23,300 | $ 23,310 | $ 24,507 |

## NO NAME INCORPORATED
PROJECTED STATEMENT OF CASH FLOW
For the Year Ending October 31, 19X2
(Based Upon Management Assumptions As Set Forth
in Accompanying Comments)

| | Actual | Total | Period 1 | Period 2 | . . . | Period 12 |
|---|---|---|---|---|---|---|
| Beginning Balance (Exh. 1) | $    0 | $    33,545 | $ 33,545 | $   5,636 | | $ 24,740 |
| Add: | | | | | | |
| Accounts Receivable | 0 | 1,184,799 | 57,299 | 88,500 | | 95,500 |
| Other Income | 0 | 600 | 100 | 100 | | 100 |
| Financing Proceeds | 0 | 100,000 | 0 | 50,000 | | 0 |
| | 0 | 1,285,399 | 57,399 | 138,600 | | 95,600 |
| Deduct: | | | | | | |
| Accounts Payable | 0 | 122,038 | 45,122 | 19,200 | | 0 |
| Purchases | 0 | 545,100 | 0 | 87,400 | | 52,900 |
| Salaries and Wages | 0 | 366,385 | 29,875 | 26,470 | | 35,245 |
| Payroll Taxes | 0 | 19,048 | 1,617 | 1,562 | | 1,628 |
| Building Rent (Mfg.) | 0 | 26,802 | 1,613 | 1,613 | | 2,618 |
| Heat, Light, and Power | 0 | 10,140 | 660 | 670 | | 970 |
| Small Tools and Shop | 0 | 1,500 | 100 | 100 | | 150 |
| Property Taxes | 0 | 2,000 | 400 | 400 | | 0 |
| Maintenance and Repairs | 0 | 3,400 | 400 | 400 | | 200 |
| Engineering Supplies | 0 | 2,400 | 200 | 200 | | 200 |
| Employee Benefits (Mfg.) | 0 | 7,200 | 490 | 510 | | 710 |
| Equipment Rental (Mfg.) | 0 | 5,550 | 445 | 445 | | 475 |
| Employee Benefits (Non-Mfg.) | 0 | 3,640 | 270 | 280 | | 320 |
| Building Rent (Non-Mfg.) | 0 | 4,096 | 231 | 231 | | 412 |
| Utilities | 0 | 2,220 | 150 | 160 | | 200 |
| Telephone and Telegraph | 0 | 9,410 | 700 | 710 | | 810 |
| Freight-Out | 0 | 600 | 50 | 50 | | 50 |
| Office Supplies | 0 | 3,900 | 325 | 325 | | 325 |
| Travel and Entertainment | 0 | 7,560 | 630 | 630 | | 630 |
| Overtime Premium | 0 | 600 | 200 | 0 | | 0 |
| Advertising | 0 | 10,000 | 0 | 0 | | 1,000 |
| Equipment Rental (Non-Mfg.) | 0 | 1,200 | 100 | 100 | | 100 |
| Miscellaneous | 0 | 3,600 | 300 | 300 | | 300 |
| | 0 | 1,158,389 | 83,878 | 141,756 | | 99,243 |
| Insurance | 0 | 5,000 | 0 | 0 | | 2,500 |
| Professional Fees | 0 | 8,000 | 0 | 0 | | 1,000 |
| Capital Additions | 0 | 38,000 | 0 | 0 | | 0 |
| Interest Expense | 0 | 8,879 | 547 | 660 | | 742 |
| Notes Payable | 0 | 52,238 | 883 | 882 | | 2,165 |
| Income Taxes | 0 | 33,748 | 0 | 0 | | 0 |
| | 0 | 1,304,254 | 85,308 | 143,298 | | 105,650 |
| Ending Balance (Exhibit 1) | $    0 | $    14,690 | $   5,636 | $     938 | | $ 14,690 |

Exhibit 7-6    Sample Application                                                    337

**EXHIBIT 7-6    SAMPLE APPLICATION ALLOWING PAYMENTS TO
RETAIL CUSTOMERS (WARRANTY CLAIMS)**

## UNITED STATES BANKRUPTCY COURT
## CENTRAL DISTRICT OF CALIFORNIA

| | |
|---|---|
| **In re** | APPLICATION FOR ORDER PERMITTING PAY-MENTS TO RETAIL CUSTOMERS; AND ORDER |
| Debtors. | THEREON |

The application of the debtors and debtors in possession listed on Exhibit A hereto respectfully represents:

1. Applicants have filed voluntary petitions under Chapter 11 of the Bankruptcy Code and are debtors and debtors in possession in the above-captioned cases.

2. The debtor and its affiliates own and operate various retail stores, including department stores, furniture stores, supermarkets, drug stores, women's clothing stores and other retail outlets.

3. At the time that Applicants filed their respective Chapter 11 cases, various retail customers had credit balances on their charge accounts owing to overpayment, or had placed deposits on goods which they no longer want delivered. In addition, some of Applicants' customers desire to return unsatisfactory goods which were purchased pre-petition for either cash or credit.

4. Together with Applicants' affiliates who are not debtors in possession before this Court, Applicants comprise an enterprise doing business at more than 2,000 locations, located throughout the United States, Europe and the Middle East. A significant percentage of Applicants' business is in the retail sector, and consequently, maintaining the satisfaction of the consumer population is imperative to the success of any reorganization by Applicants.

5. The Court has previously entered orders recognizing the need for unusual relief in these Chapter 11 cases. For example, the Court has granted Applicants the authority to honor certain demands pursuant to 11 U.S.C. § 546(c). In addition, the Court has recognized the importance of keeping employee morale high and has authorized Applicants to pay pre-petition wage and related benefits and to honor accrued vacation days, sick leave days and employment and other personnel policies.

6. Applicants' customers are essential to its vitality. It is crucially important to Applicants' business that customer goodwill be maintained and that Applicants be permitted to:

(a) refund customer overpayments on charge accounts;

(b) accept for return unsatisfactory merchandise purchased pre-petition and issue cash or credit therefor; and

(c) refund pre-petition deposits made by customers on goods no longer wanted.

7. The requested relief is in the best interests of these estates as it will have a trivial economic impact on Applicants' creditors, while preserving for the creditors the invaluable assets of customer goodwill.

WHEREFORE, Applicants pray that this Court enter its order permitting Applicants, without further order of this Court, to:

(a) refund customer overpayments on charge accounts;

(b) accept for return unsatisfactory goods purchased pre-petition and issue cash or credit therefor; and

(c) refund to customers pre-petition deposits on goods no longer wanted.

DATED: May 11, 19X2.

_____,

a Member of
STUTMAN, TREISTER & GLATT
PROFESSIONAL CORPORATION
Attorneys for Debtors and
Debtors in Possession

THE OFFICE OF THE UNITED STATES
TRUSTEE HAS NO OBJECTION
TO THE RELIEF REQUESTED IN
THE FOREGOING APPLICATION.
By. _____

**Exhibit 7-7   Sample Application**                    **339**

**EXHIBIT 7-7   SAMPLE APPLICATION FOR ORDER TO PAY
                  PREPETITION WAGES**

## UNITED STATES BANKRUPTCY COURT
## CENTRAL DISTRICT OF CALIFORNIA

| | |
|---|---|
| **In re** | Cases Nos. LA-XX-  through LA-XX |
| | APPLICATION FOR ORDER |
| Debtors. | AUTHORIZING DEBTORS-IN- |
| | POSSESSION *TO PAY PREPETITION WAGES* |
| | AND RELATED BENEFITS AND TO |
| | HONOR OUTSTANDING PAYROLL |
| | CHECKS; AND ORDER THEREON |

The application of all the debtors-in-possession respectfully represents and shows:

1. The Debtors have heretofore filed petitions for relief under chapter 11 of the Bankruptcy Code. Applicants are the respective Debtors in Possession in those chapter 11 cases.

2. Within 90 days prior to the filing of the chapter 11 cases, the Debtors issued to their respective employees certain payroll checks from their general payroll accounts some of which checks may not have been cashed prior to the filing of the respective chapter 11 case. In addition, wages and related benefits for the pay period ending on or about April 23, 19X2 will be due on or about April 30, 19X2.

3. Applicants believe that in order to avoid the risk of massive resignations and of discontent or loss of morale among their essential employees, and in view of the priority awarded to wage claims, it is necessary and appropriate that Applicants be permitted to take the necessary steps to insure that the uncashed payroll checks of its employees be honored and the payroll be made for the pay period ending on or about April 23, 19X2. Applicants propose to accomplish this either by retaining the existing payroll accounts and permitting checks drawn on these accounts prior to or after the Chapter 11 filings to be paid or by other means.

WHEREFORE, Applicants pray that this Court enter its order authorizing Applicants to retain their present payroll accounts, to permit uncashed payroll checks drawn on said accounts to be honored, and to pay pre-petition wages by whatever procedures Applicants devise.

DATED: April 24, 19X2.

_____, a Member of
STUTMAN, TREISTER & GLATT
PROFESSIONAL CORPORATION
Attorneys for Debtors and
Debtors in Possession

## Order

IN LOS ANGELES, CALIFORNIA, IN SAID DISTRICT, ON THIS 24 DAY OF APRIL, 19X2.

Upon consideration of the foregoing Application and good cause appearing, it is hereby

ORDERED, that the Application is granted and that all the Debtors-in-Possession are authorized to pay pre-petition wages by whatever procedures they adopt including but not limited to the retention of their payroll accounts and the honoring of uncashed checks drawn thereon prior to the Chapter 11 filings.

_____
UNITED STATES
BANKRUPTCY JUDGE

THE OFFICE OF UNITED STATES
TRUSTEE HAS NO OBJECTION TO
THE RELIEF REQUESTED IN
THE FOREGOING APPLICATION

By_____

Exhibit 7-8    Sample Application                                    **341**

EXHIBIT 7-8    **SAMPLE APPLICATION FOR ORDER TO HONOR ACCRUED VACATION DAYS, SICK-LEAVE AND OTHER PERSONNEL POLICIES**

## UNITED STATES BANKRUPTCY COURT
## CENTRAL DISTRICT OF CALIFORNIA

| | |
|---|---|
| **In re** | APPLICATION FOR AUTHORIZATION TO HONOR ACCRUED VACATION DAYS, SICK-LEAVE DAYS AND EMPLOYMENT AND OTHER PERSONNEL POLICIES; AND ORDER THEREON |
| Debtors. | |

The application of all the debtors in possession respectfully represents and shows:

1. Applicants have commenced these cases by filing voluntary petitions under chapter 11 of the Bankruptcy Code. Applicants are the respective Debtors in Possession in these cases.

2. At the time the Debtors filed these chapter 11 cases, the Debtors had adopted corporate employment and personnel policies including policies allowing a certain number of vacation and sick-leave days per year to each employee.

3. At present, Applicants wish to continue the Debtors employment and personnel policies. Applicants believe that it is in the best interests of the estates to continue these policies to the extent practicable on a day-to-day basis, and to permit employees to utilize accrued benefits such as sick day and vacation leave even if they accrued prior to the chapter 11 filings. Continuing these policies will enable Applicants to retain employees and keep employee morale high, which is vital to the success of these chapter 11 cases.

WHEREFORE, Applicants pray that this Court enter its Order authorizing Applicants to honor for as long as they deem it advisable the existing employee and personnel policies including accrued vacation day and sick-leave day commitments to their employees.

DATED: April 24, 19X2.

                            _____, a Member of
STUTMAN, TREISTER & GLATT
PROFESSIONAL CORPORATION
Attorneys for Debtors and
Debtors-in-Possession

## Order

AT LOS ANGELES, IN SAID DISTRICT, ON THIS 24 DAY OF APRIL, 19X2.

The Court having considered the foregoing Application of all the Debtors-in-Possession; and good cause appearing, now, therefore, it is hereby

ORDERED, that the foregoing application of the Debtors-in-Possession is granted; and it is further

ORDERED, that the Debtors-in-Possession are authorized to honor, in their discretion, existing employee and personnel policies including but not limited to vacation day and sick-leave day commitments to their employees; and it is further

ORDERED, that the Debtors-in-Possession may, in their discretion, choose not to honor such policies or to change them as the circumstances may require, and it is further

ORDERED, that by honoring existing employee and personnel policies or any modifications thereof, the Debtors-in-Possession shall not be deemed to have assumed any executory contracts.

Any such assumption of executory contracts shall be provided for by an Order of this Court or through a confirmed plan or plans of reorganization.

_____

UNITED STATES
BANKRUPTCY JUDGE

THE OFFICE OF UNITED STATES
TRUSTEE HAS NO OBJECTION TO
THE RELIEF REQUESTED IN
THE FOREGOING APPLICATION

By_____

Exhibit 7-9   Determination of Prepetition Claims                                  343

## EXHIBIT 7-9   DETERMINATION OF PREPETITION CLAIMS

### Determination of Prepetition Claims

In many engagements, the accountant for the debtor is not authorized to render services until some time after the case is filed. It is necessary for the debtor to determine the liabilities immediately prior to the filing of the petition. However, in most cases the balance at the end of the day prior to the filing of the petition is used. Listed on page 344 is a suggested format for a worksheet that may be used to help work back from the claim as determined once engaged to the balance that existed before the petition was filed.

DETERMINATION OF PREPETITION LIABILITIES

| | Balance subsequent to petition date | Less Additions | Plus Payments | Plus Other Deductions | Prepetition Balance |
|---|---|---|---|---|---|
| Trade payables | $ | $ | $ | $ | $ |
| Credit memos | | | | | |
| Taxes (Identify) | | | | | |
| —Withholding | | | | | |
| —FICA | | | | | |
| —Sales & Use | | | | | |
| —Property | | | | | |
| —Other | | | | | |
| Severance compensation or wages payable | | | | | |
| Customer deposits | | | | | |
| Notes payable | | | | | |
| Accrued interest | | | | | |
| Commissions due third parties | | | | | |
| Other (Identify) | | | | | |
| Total | $ | $ | $ | $ | $ |

**Exhibit 7-10   Special Instruction**                                    **345**

# EXHIBIT 7-10   SPECIAL INSTRUCTION FOR THE DETERMINATION OF PREPETITION CLAIMS

Listed below is a summary of some of the procedures that were used by one debtor to determine that all prepetition liabilities were recorded:

1. Record and accrue all liabilities
   a. If not billed, make an estimate and record
   b. Record all taxes including
      • Payroll (record the actual liability existing immediately before the petition is filed)
      • Sales taxes (record all taxes up to the filing of the petition)
      • Use Taxes
      • Property taxes
   c. Record all actual advertising incurred and other related accruals.
   d. Accrue all sales commissions and unpaid wages
   e. Accrue all possible liabilities
2. Subsequently discovered liabilities existing at petition date
   a. Do not pay
   b. Adjust prepetition liability account to reflect these items.
3. Bank Accounts
   a. Payment was stopped on all checks outstanding as of petition date.
   b. As checks are returned, record the amount as a prepetition claim.
   c. Reconcile bank accounts as soon as possible after filing and record any previously unrecorded liabilities as prepetition when appropriate.
4. Subsequent payment of liabilities
   a. Do not pay any prepetition liabilities without approval from _____.
   b. Carefully review all invoices that were received after the petition was filed to be sure they are not a prepetition claim.

# Accounting Services for the Debtor in Possession or Trustee: Part 2

## EXHIBIT 8-1  OPERATING GUIDELINES FOR CENTRAL DISTRICT OF CALIFORNIA

**U.S. Department** of Justice

*United States Trustee*
*Central District of California*

| | |
|---|---|
| *3101 Federal Building* | *213/894-6811  CH* |
| *300 N. Los Angeles Street* | *FTS 798-6811* |
| *Los Angeles, California 90012* | *213/894-6387  CH* |
| | *FTS 798-6387* |

Dear Attorney:

The United States Trustee for the Central District of California has determined that it is in the best interest of the public to establish **Guidelines** for practice before the United States Bankruptcy Court in this District when related to matters within his responsibility or supervision under 28 U.S.C. § 586.

The attached are the first in a series of practical **Guidelines** which will be released from time to time. For counsel's convenience in setting up a permanent storage system for the **Guidelines,** they have been printed so that they can be punched and placed in a three-ring notebook.

Each **Guideline** is subject to revision as is deemed necessary by the United States Trustee. In order to ensure the continued timeliness of your set of **Guidelines,** a separate *Table of Contents* of current **Guidelines** and their Revision Dates will also be released on an as-needed basis.

The United States Trustee reserves the right to vary any and all requirements set forth in these **Guidelines** as is considered appropriate on a case by case basis.

Sincerely,


UNITED STATES TRUSTEE
CENTRAL DISTRICT OF CALIFORNIA

OFFICE OF THE UNITED STATES TRUSTEE

# GUIDELINES*

## FOR FULFILLING THE REQUIREMENTS

## OF THE UNITED STATES TRUSTEE

---

* Editor's Note: The format for Operating Statements recommended by the U.S. Trustee for this region is shown in Chapter 8 of the *Practice and Procedure* volume.

OFFICE OF THE UNITED STATES TRUSTEE

# GUIDELINE NO. 1
*(June, 1987)*

## INITIAL REQUIREMENTS OF U.S. TRUSTEE UPON FILING OF CHAPTER 11 CASES AND USE OF COVER SHEET

Debtors in Possession and Chapter 11 Trustees shall submit each of the following documents to the United States Trustee within seven (7) days after the filing of the Chapter 11 Petition. Such documents (and copies of them) are *not* to be filed with the Bankruptcy Court. Such documents shall have attached to them the INITIAL FILING REQUIREMENTS COVER SHEET (Form UST-2), a copy of which is attached to this **Guideline**. Debtors are to check off the boxes on the form indicating which documents are attached, which documents have been previously submitted, and which explanations are attached instead of the required documents.

If any document is not attached or has not been previously submitted, an explanation for such non-inclusion must be given. The sufficiency of the explanation will be subject to review by the United States Trustee. Insufficient explanations may result in the filing of a motion to dismiss or convert the case.

If any document is not filed initially, any subsequent filings require use of an additional INITIAL FILING REQUIREMENTS COVER SHEET (Form UST-2) indicating the particular document being filed at that time.

### REQUIRED DOCUMENTS:

1. **REAL PROPERTY QUESTIONNAIRE** (Form UST-5) for each parcel of real property leased or owned, or in the process of being purchased, by the Debtor.
2. Proof of Insurance Coverage (Submit Declaration Pages for Each Policy):
   A. General Comprehensive Public Liability Insurance
   B. Fire and Theft Insurance
   C. Worker's Compensation Insurance
   D. Vehicle Insurance
   E. Product Liability Insurance
   F. Any other Insurance coverage customary in the Debtor's Business
3. Most recently filed State and Federal Payroll Tax Returns with all schedules and attachments
4. Most recently filed State Sales Tax Return with all schedules and attachments
5. Most recently prepared audited and unaudited Financial Statements
6. Proof of Establishment of Debtor in Possession Bank Accounts:
   A. General Account
   B. Payroll Account
   C. Tax Account
   D. Declaration under Penalty of Perjury from the Debtor verifying that all Pre-Petition Bank Accounts have been closed
7. Projected Operating Statement for first Thirty (30) days of Operation
8. Applications for Compensation to Principals, Partners, Officers or Directors of the Debtor
9. Copy of any trust agreements or conveyances (other than leases) to which Debtor is a party or under which Debtor holds, has possession of, or operates any property or business as a trustee or otherwise.

Debtors in Possession and Chapter 11 Trustees are directed to review the NOTICE OF REQUIREMENTS OF THE UNITED STATES TRUSTEE FOR DEBTORS IN POSSESSION IN CHAPTER 11 CASES (Form UST-1) which sets forth further details as to the above documents and sets forth additional requirements and time limits for compliance with the requirements of the United States Trustee.

Attorney Name, Address and Telephone

File with U.S. Trustee within Seven (7) Days after Filing
of Chapter 11 Petition.  Do Not File in Bankruptcy Court.

## Office of the United States Trustee

In re:

Chapter 11 Proceeding

Case Number:  _____ – _____

Debtor.

## INITIAL FILING REQUIREMENTS COVER SHEET

| Mark One Box for Each Required Document | | | You must attach each of the following documents or a satisfactory explanation for your failure to attach a document.  Failure to meet these requirements may result in the filing of a motion to dismiss or convert the case. |
|---|---|---|---|
| Document Attached | Previously Submitted | Explanation Attached | **REQUIRED DOCUMENTS:** |
| ☐ | ☐ | ☐ | 1.   Real Property Questionnaire (UST-5) for each Parcel of Real Property |
| | | | 2.   Proof of Insurance Coverage:  (Submit Declaration Pages) |
| ☐ | ☐ | ☐ | A.   General Comprehensive Public Liability Insurance |
| ☐ | ☐ | ☐ | B.   Fire and Theft Insurance |
| ☐ | ☐ | ☐ | C.   Worker's Compensation Insurance |
| ☐ | ☐ | ☐ | D.   Vehicle Insurance |
| ☐ | ☐ | ☐ | E.   Product Liability Insurance |
| ☐ | ☐ | ☐ | F.   Other Customary Insurance Coverage |
| ☐ | ☐ | ☐ | 3.   Most recently filed State and Federal Payroll Tax Return with all Schedules |
| ☐ | ☐ | ☐ | 4.   Most recently filed State Sales Tax Return with all Schedules and Attachments |
| ☐ | ☐ | ☐ | 5.   Most recently prepared Audited and Unaudited Financial Statements |
| | | | 6.   Proof of Establishment of Debtor-in-Possession Bank Accounts: |
| ☐ | ☐ | ☐ | A.   General Account |
| ☐ | ☐ | ☐ | B.   Payroll Account |
| ☐ | ☐ | ☐ | C.   Tax Account |
| ☐ | ☐ | ☐ | D.   Debtor Declaration verifying Closing of all Pre-Petition Bank Accounts |
| ☐ | ☐ | ☐ | 7.   Projected Operating Statement for first Thirty (30) days of Operation |
| ☐ | ☐ | ☐ | 8.   Applications for Compensation by Partners, Officers or Directors of the Debtor |
| ☐ | ☐ | ☐ | 9.   Copies of Trust Agreements to which Debtor is a party or under which holds Property |

Dated: _____, 19 _____

_____

Attorney for Debtor in Possession or Trustee

6/87                INITIAL  FILING  REQUIREMENTS  COVER  SHEET               **UST-2**

OFFICE OF THE UNITED STATES TRUSTEE

# GUIDELINE NO. 2
*(June, 1987)*

## REAL PROPERTY QUESTIONNAIRE IN CHAPTER 11 CASES WITH ANY REAL PROPERTY

In all Chapter 11 cases in which the Debtor leases or owns, or is in the process of purchasing, any parcels of real property, the Debtor shall file with the United States Trustee a REAL PROPERTY QUESTIONNAIRE (Form UST-5) within seven (7) days after the filing of the Chapter 11 petition.

A separate QUESTIONNAIRE shall be filed for each parcel of real property leased or owned, or in the process of being purchased, by the Debtor.

Failure to timely file the QUESTIONNAIRE may result in the filing of a motion to convert or dismiss the Chapter 11 case.

OFFICE OF THE UNITED STATES TRUSTEE

# GUIDELINE NO. 3
*(June, 1987)*

## MATTERS REQUIRING SUBMISSION TO UNITED STATES TRUSTEE PRIOR TO FILING WITH THE BANKRUPTCY COURT

Matters dealing with the following topics shall first be submitted to the attorney for the United States Trustee assigned to the case for review and comment.  In order to facilitate that process, a separate page should be provided in each written document required to be submitted for review and execution by the United States Trustee in the form set forth in **Guideline No. 4.**  Non-inclusion of matters in this **Guideline** does not constitute an opinion by the Office of the United States Trustee that it does not have a right to review or comment on such matters:

1. Applications to extend the time to file Schedules and/or Statement of Affairs.

2. Applications for approval of the employment of professional persons.  (These Applications are to be submitted prior to the time employment is to commence.  If it is impossible to do so prior to the commencement of services, a request for an appropriate *nunc pro tunc* order is required together with a Declaration showing good cause for such late application.  *Nunc pro tunc* employment applications are not favored in the Central District.  It is understood that there will be some delay between the filing of the petition and filing of the initial application to employ Debtor's general bankruptcy counsel, but that delay should not exceed fourteen (14) days.)

3. Stipulations for appointment of a Chapter 11 Trustee or Examiner or any other person or entity to be given possession, control or operation of any of the property of the Debtor outside the ordinary course of business of the Debtor.

4. Motions by Debtors to dismiss their Chapter 11 cases.  (Such motions must demonstrate, by way of declaration, that all United States Trustee Quarterly Fees have been paid in full.  Counsel should review **Guideline No. 10** for further information regarding the calculation and payment of Quarterly Fees.)

5. Such other documents as may from time to time be designated by the United States Trustee or the Court for submission to the United States Trustee for review or comment.

OFFICE OF THE UNITED STATES TRUSTEE

# GUIDELINE NO. 4
*(June, 1987)*

## FORM FOR COMMENTS AND EXECUTION BY OFFICE OF UNITED STATES TRUSTEE

Each document required to be submitted for review and comment by the Office of the United States Trustee pursuant to **Guideline No. 3** shall contain an entirely separate page in the form set forth below:

```
 1        COMMENTS OF OFFICE OF UNITED STATES TRUSTEE
 2
 3     ( )THE U.S. TRUSTEE TAKES NO POSITION.
 4     ( )THE U.S. TRUSTEE HAS NO OBJECTION.
 5     ( )THE U.S. TRUSTEE OBJECTS AND REQUESTS A HEARING.
 6     ( )AN OBJECTION IS RAISED AS SET FORTH BELOW.
 7
 8     COMMENTS:
 9
10
11
12
13
14
15
16
17
18     Dated: _____, 19 __
19                         OFFICE OF THE U.S. TRUSTEE
20
21                         By: _____
22
23                         Name: _____
24                               Attorney for the
                                 United States Trustee
25
26     Case Name: John Doe Enterprises
27     Case Number: LA-87-12345-XX
28     Type of Document: Application to Employ Attorney
```

OFFICE OF THE UNITED STATES TRUSTEE

# GUIDELINE NO. 5
*(June, 1987)*

## INTERIM STATEMENTS AND OPERATING REPORTS

Biweekly INTERIM STATEMENTS are to be filed within seven (7) days and MONTHLY OPERATING REPORTS are to be filed within twenty (20) days after the close of the applicable period.   Failure to file timely REPORTS and STATEMENTS may result in the filing of a motion to convert or dismiss the Chapter 11 case.   All blanks in the STATEMENTS and REPORTS must be filled out completely. If any item is not applicable, so state.   Filing of incomplete STATEMENTS or REPORTS will be treated as if no STATEMENT or REPORT had been filed.

If an unusual event occurs which will delay filing of any REPORT or STATEMENT, it is expected that the Debtor in Possession or Chapter 11 Trustee will deliver a letter to the United States Trustee explaining such extraordinary delay.   Insufficient explanations may result in the filing of a motion to convert or dismiss.

Unless prior **written** permission has been obtained from the United States Trustee, INTERIM STATEMENTS and OPERATING REPORTS may not be filed on a more or less frequent basis than that established under this **Guideline**. The United States Trustee reserves the right to vary these reporting requirements as is considered appropriate on a case by case basis.

United States Trustee **Forms UST-3 (INTERIM STATEMENTS)** and **UST-4 (OPERATING REPORTS)**, copies of which are attached to the NOTICE OF REQUIREMENTS OF THE UNITED STATES TRUSTEE (Form UST-1), set forth the actual form upon which REPORTS and STATEMENTS must be submitted.   Written permission must be obtained prior to use of any other form for such REPORTS and STATEMENTS.

INTERIM STATEMENTS are to be prepared *only* on a cash basis and the Profit and Loss Statement contained in the OPERATING REPORTS is to be prepared *only* on an accrual basis.   For financial analysis purposes, it is crucial for Debtors in Possession and Chapter 11 Trustees to comply with these cash and accrual bases requirements.

OFFICE OF THE UNITED STATES TRUSTEE

# GUIDELINE NO. 6
*(June, 1987)*

## APPLICATIONS TO EMPLOY PROFESSIONAL PERSONS

An Application to employ a professional person must, at a minimum, comply with BANKRUPTCY RULE 2014 (a), LOCAL RULE 2006 and the following requirements:

1.  It must be signed by a person authorized to make the Application such as the Debtor in Possession, the Chapter 11 Trustee, or an officer, general partner or other principal of the Debtor in Possession.

2.  It must state facts showing the necessity for such employment.

3.  It must state the name of the person or firm to be employed.

4.  It must state the reason for the selection of the particular professional to be employed. (Attachment of a statement of the past experience of the professional should be included.)

5.  It must state the specific services to be rendered in connection with the employment.

6.  It must set forth by way of verified declaration that, to the best of the professional's knowledge, the professional has no connection to any party in interest to the case and has no interest adverse to the estate of the Debtor. The declaration should not merely state legal conclusions, but should state the professional's connections, if any, to the Debtor, creditors or any other party in interest, including their respective attorneys and accountants. [See BANKRUPTCY RULE 2014]

7.  It must state the amount of the retainer previously received and the terms and conditions of employment, including the then current hourly rate(s) charged by each professional expected to render services, including partners, associates, and paraprofessional persons employed by the professional and whose services will be utilized for the benefit of and whose time will be charged to the Estate. The terms of employment may not violate applicable provisions of the BANKRUPTCY CODE. Payment by the Debtor in Possession or Chapter 11 Trustee of professional fees and/or expenses and payment by the Debtor in Possession or Chapter 11 Trustee of a retainer to a professional in monthly post-petition installments cannot be approved without prior application to the Court under § 331 of the BANKRUPTCY CODE.

8.  It must include a statement that no compensation will be paid by the Debtor in Possession or Chapter 11 Trustee except upon application to and approval by the Bankruptcy Court after notice and a hearing.

9.  It must provide a separate "Comments" page as provided for in **Guideline No. 4.**

10. It must include a copy of the proposed Order.

11. If an Application to employ a professional by the Debtor in Possession or Chapter 11 Trustee is made more than thirty (30) days after the date of commencement of post-petition services by that professional, an explanation of the delay in the form of a declaration under penalty of perjury must accompany the Application. Unsatisfactory explanations will result in an objection to the Application by the United States Trustee.

12. If an Application to employ a professional by the Debtor in Possession or Chapter 11 Trustee is made more than sixty (60) days after the date of commencement of post-petition services by that professional, the United States Trustee will object unless the Application is made on notice and an opportunity to be heard given to all creditors and interested parties. An explanation of the delay in the form of a declaration under penalty of perjury must accompany the Application. Any *nunc*

---

*pro tunc* Application must state the amount of fees and expenses which have accrued during the period between the date of the commencement of post petition services and the date of the Application to Employ.

13. Applications providing for payment by the Debtor in Possession or Chapter 11 Trustee of a post petition retainer are not acceptable and will be objected to unless a showing of unusual circumstances has been made to the satisfaction of the United States Trustee. In any event, such Applications must be made upon notice with an opportunity to request a hearing.

14. If more than one counsel is being retained to represent the Debtor in Possession, the Chapter 11 Trustee or the Creditors' Committee, there should be some statement in the Application as to the need for dual counsel, the services to be performed by each, and an affirmative statement in each Application that there will be no duplication of services. A separate Application is required for each professional.

## SPECIAL NOTES:

1. Refer to **Guideline No. 7 (Applications for Payment of Professional Fees)** for further details as to items in Fee/Expense Applications which are considered appropriate and inappropriate by the United States Trustee.

2. Applications to Employ will be processed by the United States Trustee in the regular course of business unless there is a demonstrated emergency. In an emergency case, counsel is to telephone the Attorney for the United States Trustee assigned to the case and set up an appointment to hand-deliver the Application for review and comment. The Staff Attorney so assigned will determine if expedited processing is appropriate.

3. No fees or reimbursement of costs can be paid by the Debtor in Possession or Chapter 11 Trustee to a professional person until the request for such fees and costs has been reviewed and allowed by the Bankruptcy Court after notice. Any Application must conform to the requirements of BANKRUPTCY RULE 2016(a).

4. Professionals who have received a pre-petition retainer and professionals who have entered into a contingency fee arrangement with the Debtor are required to file statements pursuant to § 329(a) of the BANKRUPTCY CODE, and such payments and agreements are subject to review by the Bankruptcy Court pursuant to § 329(b) of the BANKRUPTCY CODE. (Note: Rules of professional ethics and bankruptcy court decisions limit the use of contingency fee arrangements in certain circumstances.)

5. Normally, professional persons may apply to the Bankruptcy Court for payment of fees and expenses not more often than once every 120 days after the filing of the Petition, except when the Court permits Applications to be filed more frequently. The United States Trustee will oppose a request to permit Applications to be filed more often than once every 120 days in all but unusual cases. Any request for more frequent compensation must be justified and must be made by way of motion with notice and an opportunity to request a hearing.

6. If the Court permits professional persons to file Fee Applications more often than once every 120 days, then such short-term Applications must contain the detailed information specified in **Guideline No. 7 (Applications for Payment of Professional Fees)**.

GUIDELINE NO. 6                                                                                    PAGE 3
*(June, 1987)*

### APPLICATIONS TO EMPLOY PROFESSIONAL PERSONS

---

7.  The Bankruptcy Court can limit notice on Fee Applications. The United States Trustee will oppose requests to limit notice to less than ten (10) days or notice which does not include at least the United States Trustee, any committees, any secured creditors claiming cash as collateral, and any parties who have requested special notice.

8.  Within a reasonable time after confirmation of a plan of reorganization, professionals who have received a pre-petition retainer from the Debtor and professionals who have entered into a contingency fee arrangement with the Debtor are required to file Fee Applications.

9.  When the Debtor in Possession or Chapter 11 Trustee have made an application to employ a professional person, any successor professional must obtain similar court authorization for such employment pursuant to § 327 of the BANKRUPTCY CODE and BANKRUPTCY RULE 2014. The Application to Employ must be submitted and approved prior to the successor professional commencing services on behalf of the Debtor in Possession or Chapter 11 Trustee. When there is a change in attorney, the filing of a Substitution of Attorney form is also required.

OFFICE OF THE UNITED STATES TRUSTEE

# GUIDELINE NO. 7
### *(June, 1987)*

## APPLICATIONS FOR PAYMENT OF
## PROFESSIONAL FEES AND EXPENSES

Applications for payment of professional fees and expenses shall conform with the following substantive requirements. Failure to fulfill such requirements may result in an objection by the Office of the United States Trustee to such fee and/or expense payment application.

1.  The Application shall recite the date of entry of the Order of the Bankruptcy Court approving the employment of the individual or firm for whom payment of fees and/or expenses is sought and the date of the last Fee Application for that professional.

2.  The Application shall include a listing of the amount of fees and expenses previously requested, approved by the Court and received.

3.  The Application shall include a detailed listing of all time spent by the professional on matters for which compensation is sought, including the following:

    A.   Date service was rendered

    B.   Description of service -- (It is not sufficient to merely state "Research", "Telephone Call", "Court Appearance", etc. Reference must be made to the particular persons, motions, discrete tasks performed and other matters related to such service. Summaries that list a number of services under only one time period will not be satisfactory.)

    C.   Amount of time spent -- (Summaries are not adequate. Time spent is to be broken down in detail by the specific task performed. Lumping services together is not satisfactory)

    D.   Designation of the particular person who rendered the service -- (If more than one person's services are included in the Application, specify which person performed each item of service)

4.  An Application that seeks reimbursement of expenses shall include a summary listing of all expenses by category (i.e., long distance telephone, copy costs, messenger and computer research). As to unusual or costly expense items, as to each such item, the Application must state:

    A.   Date the expense was incurred

    B.   Description of the expense

    C.   Amount of the expense

    D.   Explanation of the expense

5.  The Application shall contain a listing of the hourly rates charged by each person whose services form a basis for the fees requested in the Application. The Application must contain a Summary in substantially the following form:

*Attorney Name*      *Hourly Rate*      *Total Hours this Application*      *Total Fee Due*

---

6.  The burden of proof in all Fee Applications is on the Applicant. The Application must contain sufficient evidence to justify the charges made by specifically detailing the services rendered and the tasks performed.

7.  The following items are considered inappropriate for Fee and/or Expense Applications. Any Application containing such items will be objected to automatically by the United States Trustee:

    A.  **Minimum** hourly billing increments of greater than **0.10** hours (effective 7/1/87).

    B.  Compensation sought for services rendered prior to the effective date of the Order approving employment of the professional. (This does not apply to pre-petition services rendered by Bankruptcy counsel in preparing the case for filing or services rendered during the maximum fourteen (14) day delay between the filing of the petition and the filing of the application to employ Debtor's general bankruptcy counsel.)

    C.  Compensation sought from the estate for services rendered prior to the date of the filing of the Petition except for bankruptcy-related services.

    D.  Requests for a bonus unless supported by a declaration setting forth facts sufficient to warrant a bonus.

    E.  Requests for compensation for services performed by an attorney employed by a trustee if for matters properly within the responsibility of the trustee.

    F.  An attorney/trustee failing to segregate properly those services performed as an "attorney" versus those performed in the capacity of "trustee."

    G.  Requests for compensation for services rendered which were unnecessary, unreasonable, or in error.

    H.  Requests for reimbursement of overhead expenses such as secretarial and word processing costs. (Reimbursement of reasonable Westlaw and Lexis costs is acceptable.)

    I.  Requests for reimbursement of expenses not yet incurred.

    J.  Photocopy charges in excess of the actual cost or twenty-five (25) cents per page, whichever is less.

    K.  Failure to give adequate written notice of the Fee and/or Expense Application.

    L.  Filing of a Fee and/or Expense Application more frequently than once every 120 days without a prior Bankruptcy Court Order allowing more frequent applications.

    M.  Requests for compensation at the full rate of the professional for performing non-professional services such as document delivery or filing of pleadings.

    N.  Charging current hourly rates for services performed at a time when the professional charged a lesser rate, if the professional reasonably should have applied for, and would likely have been paid, interim compensation under § 331 of the BANKRUPTCY CODE.

OFFICE OF THE UNITED STATES TRUSTEE

GUIDELINE NO. 7
*(June, 1987)*                                                                                          PAGE 3

APPLICATIONS FOR PAYMENT OF PROFESSIONAL FEES AND EXPENSES

---

O.  Submitting Fee Applications at a time when the Debtor in Possession or Chapter 11 Trustee have failed to pay Quarterly Fees or have failed to file timely Operating Reports or Interim Statements.

P.  Interim Fee requests seeking 100% of requested compensation.  The United States Trustee generally requests a hold back of an appropriate percentage on the award of interim compensation.

8.  **Special Note regarding Required Final Fee Applications:**  Where a reorganization plan has been confirmed, Final Fee Applications under § 330 of the BANKRUPTCY CODE are required as to all professionals who have been employed to perform services on behalf of the Debtor in Possession, Chapter 11 Trustee or at the expense of the estate.  The Final Fee Application is to cover all of the services performed in the case and must seek approval of all prior interim fee awards.  The Application may not merely cover the last period for which fees are sought.

9.  See *In re Yermakov*, 718 F.2d 1465 (9th Cir. 1983) regarding Applications for payment of professional fees and expenses.

OFFICE OF THE UNITED STATES TRUSTEE

# GUIDELINE NO. 8
*(June, 1987)*

## APPLICATIONS TO USE, SELL OR LEASE PROPERTY OF THE ESTATE OUTSIDE THE ORDINARY COURSE OF BUSINESS

At a minimum, the Application must meet the following requirements:

1. It may only be filed by the Debtor in Possession or, if a Chapter 11 trustee has been appointed, only by that trustee. It is not acceptable for the Debtor to file the Application when a Chapter 11 trustee has been appointed in the case.

2. It must sufficiently identify the property of the estate which is the subject of the Application.

3. It must identify the proposed disposition of the property. This requires full disclosure of all consideration to be received as part of the transaction by the estate or any other party to the transaction. Disclosure must include any contingent or concurrent transactions tied to the property transaction. Disclosure must include the name of the prospective buyer and amount proposed to be paid to any person and/or entity from the proceeds of the sale.

4. It must provide parties in interest with at least twenty (20) days after service of the notice of the Application in which to request a hearing. If less time is provided, an appropriate order shortening time for notice must accompany the Application stating good cause for the shortening of time.

5. BANKRUPTCY RULE 6004(e)(1) must be complied with as to the each sale of property by the Debtor.

6. If a proposed sale will utilize an escrow, the following requirements must also be met:
   A. The Application must state the anticipated closing date; and
   B. A copy of the Escrow Closing Statement must be submitted to the United States Trustee within ten (10) days after the close of escrow. (The Closing Statement must include the name, address and telephone number of the escrow agent.)

7. The originals of these Applications are not to be submitted to the United States Trustee for review or comment prior to filing with the Bankruptcy Court. Counsel is merely required to serve a copy of the Application upon the United States Trustee.

OFFICE OF THE UNITED STATES TRUSTEE

# GUIDELINE NO. 9
*(June, 1987)*

## EX PARTE APPLICATIONS

It is not unusual for circumstances to arise in bankruptcy cases which require immediate action without providing for full notice and an opportunity to be heard.  Since Ex Parte Applications do not provide for a regular notice procedure, their use should be restricted to situations in which a true emergency exists.

At a minimum, every Ex Parte Application must meet the requirements set forth in the BANKRUPTCY CODE, the BANKRUPTCY RULES and the LOCAL BANKRUPTCY RULES.

The originals of these Applications are not to be submitted to the United States Trustee for review or comment prior to filing with the Bankruptcy Court.  Counsel is merely required to serve a copy of the Application upon the United States Trustee and give timely notice of such Application in accordance with LOCAL BANKRUPTCY RULES.

If the Ex Parte Application is one related to the incurring of debt or obtaining of financing, including use of cash collateral, the Application must:

A.   Set forth sufficient facts to indicate that no other source of funds is available to finance the Debtor's in Possession or Chapter 11 Trustee's operation until full notice and an opportunity for a hearing can be given; and

B.   Provide only for the necessary financing to fund the Debtor's in Possession or Chapter 11 Trustee's  operation until notice and an opportunity for a hearing for further financing are provided.  Applications for long-term financing are not to be made on an ex parte basis.

OFFICE OF THE UNITED STATES TRUSTEE

# GUIDELINE NO. 10
### *(June, 1987)*

## CHAPTER 11 QUARTERLY FEE PAYMENTS

On October 27, 1986, the President signed into law the BANKRUPTCY JUDGES, UNITED STATES TRUSTEES, AND FAMILY FARMER BANKRUPTCY ACT OF 1986, PUB. L. NO. 99-554, which became effective November 26, 1986, in the United States Bankruptcy Court for the Central District of California.

Section 117 of the ACT imposes a new responsibility upon Debtors in Possession and Chapter 11 Trustees under Chapter 11 of the BANKRUPTCY CODE. That section requires that a quarterly fee be paid in all Chapter 11 cases. The fee applies to all Chapter 11 cases on November 26, 1986, unless a plan was confirmed or the case was dismissed or converted before that date. The fee must be paid to the United States Trustee every calendar quarter from the time the Petition is filed until the date of entry of an order confirming a plan or an order dismissing or converting the case.

The Chapter 11 Debtor in Possession and Chapter 11 Trustee are responsible for paying this fee. The amount of the fee varies depending on the disbursements made during the calendar quarter; however, a minimum fee of $150 is due each quarter even if no disbursements are made during the quarter.

Fee payments are due no later than one (1) month following the quarterly reporting period. In order for a plan to be confirmed in the case, the plan must provide that payment of quarterly fees will be made on or before the effective date of the plan.

### FEE SCHEDULE

| TOTAL QUARTERLY DISBURSEMENTS | | | QUARTERLY FEE |
|---|---|---|---|
| $ 0 | to | $ 14,999.99 | $ 150 |
| 15,000 | to | 149,999.99 | 300 |
| 150,000 | to | 299,999.99 | 750 |
| 300,000 | to | 2,999,999.99 | 2,250 |
| 3,000,000 | | and above | 3,000 |

Failure to pay the quarterly fee is cause for conversion or dismissal of the Chapter 11 case. [§ 1112(b)(10) of the BANKRUPTCY CODE] All unpaid fees must have been paid in full as of the effective date of the Plan of Reorganization. [§ 1129(a)(12) of the BANKRUPTCY CODE]

Requests for voluntary dismissals or conversions will be objected to unless all fees have been paid in full. If a Debtor in Possession or Chapter 11 Trustee have failed to provide reports that substantiate disbursements during the applicable quarter, the United States Trustee will require payment of the maximum fee for each unpaid quarter.

Quarterly fees are to be made payable to **THE UNITED STATES TRUSTEES** and are to be mailed to the address in Georgia set forth below. Fees are **not** to be mailed or delivered to the local Office of the United States Trustee. If any check is returned "unpaid" for any reason, all subsequent payments must be made by way of cashier's check, certified check or money order.

To ensure proper credit, it is imperative that Debtors in Possession and Chapter 11 Trustees write the case Account Number on each check and return it with the Payment Coupon provided with the quarterly billings. A separate check and coupon are required for each quarterly payment even if more than one quarterly fee is paid at the same time.

Send all payments to:

**UNITED STATES TRUSTEES
P.O. Box 198246
Atlanta, GA 30384**

OFFICE OF THE UNITED STATES TRUSTEE

# GUIDELINE NO. 11
*(June, 1987)*

## RESTRICTION AGAINST NAMING OF U.S. TRUSTEE
## OR MEMBERS OF HIS OFFICE AS PARTIES TO LITIGATION

The United States Trustee has the duty to supervise the administration of cases and trustees in cases under Chapters 7, 11, 12, and 13 of the BANKRUPTCY CODE. [See 28 U.S.C. § 586.]

The United States Trustee may raise and may appear and be heard on any issue in any case or proceeding under Title 11, United States Code. [See 11 U.S.C. § 307.] Copies of all papers filed with the Bankruptcy Court in this District are to be served upon the United States Trustee.

Due to a misunderstanding of the role of the United States Trustee, it is not uncommon for the United States Trustee or members of his office to be named as parties Defendant in various pleadings.

Neither the United States Trustee nor any member of his office is to be named as a "party" in any pleading filed in any court where the United States Trustee is not an actual party to the proceeding. The United States Trustee is to be added as an additional person with whom a copy of the pleading is to be filed and must be included in the Proof of Service form attached to all filed pleadings.

Naming the United States Trustee or any member of his office as a party Defendant may result in the filing of a motion to dismiss such improperly named person if counsel fails to correct such error upon request by the United States Trustee. Repeated refusal to follow this **Guideline** will result in the seeking of a court order to halt such abuse and for imposition of sanctions.

OFFICE OF THE UNITED STATES TRUSTEE

# GUIDELINE NO. 12
*(June, 1987)*

## SUBSTITUTION OF DEBTOR'S ATTORNEY IN CHAPTER 11 CASES

Whenever there is a substitution of Debtor's in Possession or Chapter 11 Trustee's counsel in a Chapter 11 case, withdrawing counsel shall file a final Fee and Expense Application within sixty (60) days after the date provided in the order allowing withdrawal of representation.

Failure to file a timely Fee and Expense Application will result in the filing of a motion by the United States Trustee which will seek an accounting and return of any pre-petition retainer or post-petition fees paid to withdrawing counsel.

New counsel must obtain court authorization for employment pursuant to § 327 of the BANKRUPTCY CODE and BANKRUPTCY RULE 2014. The Application to Employ must be submitted and approved prior to the successor counsel commencing services on behalf of the Debtor in Possession or Chapter 11 Trustee. (See **Guideline No. 6.**)

OFFICE OF THE UNITED STATES TRUSTEE

# GUIDELINE NO. 13
### *(June, 1987)*

## DEBTOR IN POSSESSION BANK ACCOUNTS

Debtors in Possession and Chapter 11 Trustees are required to open and maintain a minimum of three (3) Debtor in Possession or Chapter 11 Trustee bank accounts in a depository designated by the Bankruptcy Court.   The three (3) required accounts are the General Account, Payroll Account and Tax Account.  Instructions and a list of Court approved banking institutions are contained in the **NOTICE OF REQUIREMENTS OF THE UNITED STATES TRUSTEE FOR DEBTORS IN POSSESSION IN CHAPTER 11 CASES** (Form UST-1).

Debtors in Possession and Chapter 11 Trustees are not permitted to vary from this established procedure unless prior written permission has been obtained from the United States Trustee.  If a change is sought due to different circumstances in a particular case, the Debtor in Possession or Chapter 11 Trustee must submit a written request for a modification which must contain a showing of sufficient facts warranting the modification.

Checks are to be pre-numbered by the bank and should include the Case Name, Case Number, the words "Debtor in Possession" and the type of account (General, Payroll or Tax), in substantially the following form:

```
Ace Machine Shop                                    No. 4546
Debtor-in-Possession, LA-86-28432-NP
GENERAL ACCOUNT                             _____, 19 ___
1234 Market Street
Los Angeles, California 90071


Pay to the
Order of      _____      $ _____


_____      Dollars


                                     _____
```

OFFICE OF THE UNITED STATES TRUSTEE

# GUIDELINE NO. 14
*(June, 1987)*

## REQUESTS FOR FIXING OF BAR DATES FOR FILING OF CHAPTER 11 PROOFS OF CLAIM

The United States Trustee will object to any Application seeking the fixing of a bar date for the filing of proofs of pre-petition claims within the first 120 days after the filing of a Chapter 11 Petition.

The United States Trustee will also object to any Application seeking to give less than ninety (90) days' written notice of the bar date to all creditors and other interested persons.

Notwithstanding the foregoing, if unusual circumstances require the fixing of a bar date within the first 120 days or with less than ninety (90) days notice, a Declaration must accompany the Application specifying sufficient facts to warrant variance from the requirements set forth in this Guideline.

The originals of these Applications are not to be submitted to the United States Trustee for review or comment prior to filing with the Bankruptcy Court. Counsel is merely required to serve a copy of the Application upon the United States Trustee.

OFFICE OF THE UNITED STATES TRUSTEE

# GUIDELINE NO. 15
*(June, 1987)*

## SPECIAL AREAS OF INTEREST TO THE OFFICE OF THE U.S. TRUSTEE IN CHAPTER 11 CASES

Although the United States Trustee is concerned with all aspects of Chapter 11 cases, the public interest requires that it take a deeper interest in certain matters. These matters are set forth below. Failure to comply with United States Trustee requirements in these areas may result in an action to dismiss or convert the case or for appointment of a trustee or examiner.

1.  Payment in full of all administrative priority State and Federal Income, Employment, and other taxes that accrue after the date of the filing of the Petition.

2.  Payment in full of all administrative priority wages and other employee-related payments that accrue after the date of the filing of the Petition.

3.  Maintenance and proof of all necessary insurance, including sufficient general liability, property, theft, vehicle, product liability, worker's compensation insurance, and all other types of insurance customary in the Debtor's business.

4.  Compliance with the BANKRUPTCY CODE, LOCAL RULES OF COURT, and general requirements of the Office of the United States Trustee as set forth in the NOTICE OF REQUIREMENTS (Form UST-1) including, but not limited to, the following:

    A.  Timely filing of Schedules and Statement of Affairs;
    B.  Attendance at the U.S. Trustee's Creditors' Conference;
    C.  Attendance at 341(a) Meetings of Creditors;
    D.  Filing of periodic reports per LOCAL RULES and the Requirements of the United States Trustee; and
    E.  Payment of post-petition administrative obligations as they become due when properly perfected under § 503 of the BANKRUPTCY CODE.

5.  Operation of the business of the Debtor at a level sufficient to pay expenses of administration without an operating loss.

6.  Operation of the business of the Debtor without risk to the public.

7.  Operation of the business of the Debtor at a sufficient level of profitability to demonstrate that reorganization is feasible.

8.  Such other activities or conduct by the Debtor in Possession which, in the opinion of the United States Trustee, warrant close scrutiny.

OFFICE OF THE UNITED STATES TRUSTEE

# GUIDELINE NO. 16
*(June, 1987)*

## DISCLOSURE STATEMENTS

The following is a checklist of items that the United States Trustee believes should generally appear in Disclosure Statements. The list is neither exclusive nor exhaustive and, depending upon the size and nature of the Debtor and the Plan, may vary considerably. However, it may serve as a useful guide .

Whether or not a Disclosure Statement contains adequate information is not governed by any otherwise applicable non-bankruptcy statute, rule or regulation. [See 11 U.S.C. § 1125(d).] Since the enactment of the BANKRUPTCY CODE, Bankruptcy Judges in this District have generally looked to the comments of the United States Trustee and creditors as advisory input in determining whether or not a Disclosure Statement contains adequate information.

1. **Purpose of the Disclosure Statement:** The Disclosure Statement should indicate that its purpose is to provide "adequate information" of a kind, and in sufficient detail, as far as is reasonably practicable in light of the nature and history of the Debtor and the condition of the Debtor's books and records, that would enable a hypothetical reasonable investor typical of holders of claims (creditors) or interests (shareholders) of the relevant class to make an informed judgment concerning the Plan. [See 11 U.S.C. § 1125(a).] The Statement should not resort to "boilerplate" language found in *Colliers* that disclaims all of the assumptions and dollar amounts contained in the Disclosure Statement. Such a disclaimer is not only confusing, but makes the Statement somewhat meaningless.

2. **Vote Required for Approval:** The Disclosure Statement should briefly indicate the vote required for approval of the Plan and should clearly indicate that creditors or interest holders have a choice: They can either vote for *or* against the Plan. It should also state that creditors have accepted the Plan if voting creditors holding at least two-thirds in amount and more than one-half in number of the allowed claims voting, have voted for the Plan. [See 11 U.S.C. § 1126(c).] The Disclosure Statement should also state that a class of interests have accepted the Plan if voting members of that class holding at least two-thirds in amount of the allowed interests voting, have voted for the Plan. [See 11 U.S.C. § 1126(d).]

3. **Description of the Plan:** The Disclosure Statement should give a description of the major provisions of the Plan, including, where feasible, an estimated date by which creditors could expect to receive payment, an expected percentage return on their claims, and a summary of the treatment of various classes under the Plan. Generally, the description does not have to be detailed and may merely refer to the Plan which contains such detailed information. Further, the summary should contain a description of each class of creditors and the approximate dollar amount of the claims in each class.

4. **Means of Effectuating the Plan:** The Disclosure Statement should indicate how the Debtor intends to accomplish the goals of the Plan, i.e., whether by infusion of cash by an investor, sale of real or personal property, continued business operations, issuance of stock or otherwise. If an investor is to provide funds, financial information regarding the investor's ability to provide such funds should be included.

5. **Cash Requirements:** The Disclosure Statement should indicate the amount of cash to be paid upon confirmation of the Plan and the expected source of such cash. If the Debtor expects a cash infusion from an outside source or from principals which is to be repaid in the future, then the identity of the source as well as the repayment terms should be disclosed. Similarly, the effect of such infusions (i.e., principal and interest payments) should be reflected in the projections.

# Exhibit 8-1    Operating Guidelines for Central District of California    371

---

Futhermore, since the BANKRUPTCY CODE contemplates payment of administrative claims in cash upon confirmation, any waiver by administrative claim holders of this requirement should be disclosed.

6. **Administrative Expenses:**  The Disclosure Statement should indicate whether any administrative expenses have accrued which must be paid at the time of confirmation, unless the party to whom the expenses are owed has consented to an alternative treatment. [See 11 U.S.C. § 1129(a)(9)(A).]  Such disclosure should include the expected amounts owed, the identity of the claimants, and the source of the funds from which they will be paid upon confirmation.

7. **Legal Proceedings:**  The Disclosure Statement should briefly describe all material legal proceedings to which the Debtor is a party, proceedings which the Debtor contemplates instituting, and legal proceedings which are known to be threatened against the Debtor.  The information should include the court in which the litigation is pending, its present status, the relief sought, the Debtor's prognosis for the outcome, if appropriate, and the effect, if any, on the Plan.

8. **Description of the Business:**  The Statement should describe the Debtor's business, including those factors which may be unusual or peculiar to the business, such as seasonal cycles and unique product lines.

9. **Reasons for Financial Difficulties and Corrections of those Factors:**  The Disclosure Statement should contain a brief narrative description of the reasons for the Debtor's financial difficulties and the steps taken to alleviate the situation since the inception of the case.

10. **Valuation of Assets:**  In conjunction with any projections or any liquidation analysis, the Disclosure Statement should contain a current Balance Sheet and Profit and Loss Statement.  The Balance Sheet should indicate whether or not such Statement was audited and the basis for the valuation of indicated items.  Further, the Disclosure Statement should indicate, possibly in a separate schedule, the Debtor's estimate of current values of assets and the source of such estimated values (i.e., cost or appraisals).

11. **Historical and Current Financial Information:**  The Disclosure Statement should include historical financial data such as Cash Flow Statements, Profit and Loss Statements, and Balance Sheets to give creditors some perspective on both the Debtor's current financial situation and its prospects under the Plan.  Of equal importance is post-petition financial data including a pro forma Balance Sheet as of the date that the plan will be confirmed indicating the financial condition of the reorganized Debtor.  Use of spreadsheets is encouraged.  In order to allow full analysis, financial information must be provided on both a *cash* and *accrual* basis.

12. **Liquidation Analysis:**  A creditor cannot make an informed judgment regarding a Plan without information as to available alternatives.  Consequently, there should be some analysis as to what creditors would receive in a Chapter 7 liquidation.  The Disclosure Statement should clearly indicate the difference between treatment accorded in the Plan and that which creditors would receive under a Chapter 7 liquidation.  Such a comparison might indicate the percentage return to creditors under each alternative and might include assumptions regarding liquidation values, administrative costs, etc.  A disclosure of any assumptions utilized by management in formulating a liquidation alternative should be disclosed. [See 11 U.S.C. § 1129(a)(7)(A)(ii).]  It is generally insufficient to merely indicate that the Plan will provide a better return than liquidation without any supporting information.  A simple tabular presentation setting forth estimated administrative expenses, priority expenses, secured and unsecured claims, together with the Debtor's estimated asset values (including sources of such values) is appropriate.  The liquidation analysis should also provide a present value calculation of the payments to creditors under the proposed Plan versus its respective class liquidation amount.

---

13. **Projections:** Projections are critical to a creditor's ability to assess the viability of the Plan, especially where the Plan calls for deferred payments to creditors and is based upon future earnings. The Statement should include projections as far into the future as is practicable, including assumptions used by the Debtor in formulating the projections, such as expected sales levels, gross and net profit levels, and inventory acquisition. At a minimum, the period covered by the projections should be commensurate with the period of payment deferral under the Plan. Use of spreadsheets is encouraged. Financial projections must be provided on both a *cash* and *accrual* basis.

14. **Marketing Efforts:** The Statement should indicate what efforts the Debtor has made since the filing to market its properties that are currently for sale. Such a description should include the identity of the listing agent, the listing price, any offers received or anticipated, pending litigation which might affect the sale of the property, the equity in the property (including the source of the valuation), and any alternatives for marketing the property in the future.

15. **Post-Petition Events:** The Disclosure Statement should indicate whether any major post-petition events have occurred which might affect the case, such as the appointment of a Creditors' Committee, a trustee, an examiner or the existence of litigation with significant consequences to the ability of the Debtor to meet the Plan requirements.

16. **Management Compensation:** The Statement should disclose the identities of top management, a description of their qualifications, and their salary levels. [See 11 U.S.C. § 1129(a)(5).] Further, any disclosure should include the identity and affiliations of any individual proposed to serve, after confirmation of the Plan, as a director, officer or voting trustee of the Debtor, an affiliate of the Debtor participating in a joint Plan with the Debtor, or a successor to the Debtor under the Plan, and the identity of any insider who will be employed or retained by the reorganized Debtor and the nature of any compensation for such insider.

17. **Insider and Affiliate Claims:** The Statement should disclose the claims asserted by insiders as defined by 11 U.S.C. § 101(30). This disclosure should include the identity of the claimant, the affiliation of the insider with the Debtor, the circumstances giving rise to the claim and the amount of the claim, the amount of any claims the insider is asserting as a creditor and/or whether any or all of his claims have been subordinated.

18. **Stock Issued for Debt.** If the Debtor plans to issue stock for all or part of its debt, the Statement should indicate if such stock is exempt from securities laws under 11 U.S.C. § 1145 and should describe the nature of the stock or securities, such as voting rights, interest rate, cummulation of dividends, liquidation preference, potential markets and market values after confirmation, and the existence of other classes of stock. The Debtor should state whether stock is registered under § 5 of the S.E.C. Act or, if not, what exemption from registration is claimed and the basis for such claim.

Further, if the exemption of 11 U.S.C. § 1145 is relied upon, then the Disclosure Statement should indicate, as required by LOCAL RULE 914, that the following legend, with appropriate changes, will be included on any issued securities:

> *"The securities represented by this certificate have not been registered under the Securities Act of 1933 and were issued pursuant to an exemption provided by 11 U.S.C. § 1145, under an order confirming Plan in a case entitled _____ , Debtor, Case No._____ , in the United States Bankruptcy Court for the Central District of California. The holder of this certificate is referred to 11 U.S.C. § 1145(b) and (c) for guidance as to the sale of these securities."*

OFFICE OF THE UNITED STATES TRUSTEE

# GUIDELINE NO. 17

*(June, 1987)*

## CHAPTER 11 TIMETABLE AND CHECKLIST

At each designated point in time, the following documents are to be provided or the following tasks are to be performed. Counsel should review the current United States Trustee **Notice of Requirements** (Form UST-1) and these **Guidelines** for more detailed procedural and substantive information.

1. **Simultaneously with Filing of Petition**
    A.  Documents to be filed with Clerk of Bankruptcy Court   (Check current requirements)
    B.  Tasks to be performed:
        (1)  Take physical inventory as of date of filing
        (2)  Close all pre-petition bank accounts and books and records
        (3)  Change loss payee/beneficiary of all insurance policies to "_____ , Debtor in Possession"
        (4)  Prepare applications to employ professional persons, including Debtor's in Possession or Chapter 11 Trustee's general bankruptcy counsel. (Must be filed no more than fourteen (14) days after the commencement of post petition services.)

2. **Immediately after Filing**
    A.  Tasks to be performed:
        (1)  Record copy of bankruptcy petition at offices of appropriate county recorder for each parcel of real property owned by the Debtor
        (2)  Open a minimum of three (3) new Debtor in Possession bank accounts (General, Payroll and Tax Accounts)

3. **Within Seven (7) days after Filing**
    A.  Documents to be filed with the United States Trustee (use *Initial Filing Cover Sheet*):
        (1)  *Real Property Questionnaire* (Form UST-5) for each parcel of real property leased or owned, or in the process of being purchased, by the Debtor
        (2)  Proof of appropriate insurance coverage
        (3)  Copies of most recently filed state and federal payroll and state sales tax returns
        (4)  Copies of most recently prepared audited and unaudited financial statements
        (5)  Proof of establishment of minimum of three (3) new Debtor in Possession bank accounts
        (6)  Declaration verifying the closing of all pre-petition bank accounts and transferring of all funds to new "Debtor in Possession" bank accounts
        (7)  Projected Operating Statement for first thirty (30) days of operation by the Debtor in Possession or Chapter 11 Trustee
        (8)  Local Rule 920 Applications to compensate principals, partners, officers or directors
        (9)  Copies of trust agreements or conveyances to which Debtor is a party or under which Debtor holds, has possession of, or operates any property or business as a trustee or otherwise

4. **Within Fourteen (14) days after Filing**
    A.  Documents to be filed with the United States Trustee:
        (1)  Applications by the Debtor in Possession or Chapter 11 Trustee to employ counsel and other professionals

5. **Within Twenty-One (21) days after Filing**
    A.  Tasks to be performed:
        (1)  Prepare and submit to the United States Trustee *Interim Statement Number 1* covering the first two (2) weeks of post-petition operations. (These recaps are due seven (7) days after the close of every two (2) week period throughout the pendency of the Chapter 11 proceeding.)

OFFICE OF THE UNITED STATES TRUSTEE

GUIDELINE NO. 17
*(June, 1987)*

CHAPTER 11 TIMETABLE AND CHECKLIST

---

6. **At the Creditors' Conference or within Thirty (30) days after Filing (Whichever occurs first)**
   A. Documents to be filed with the United States Trustee:
      (1) Copies of final statements of closed pre-petition bank accounts
      (2) Conformed copies of Chapter 11 petition evidencing recording of same on each parcel of real property owned by the Debtor
      (3) Copies of declaration pages from insurance policies showing loss payee/beneficiary to be "_____ , Debtor in Possession"
      (4) Copies of signature cards evidencing opening of "Debtor in Possession" bank accounts
      (5) Physical inventory as of date of filing of the petition

7. **Within Fifty (50) days after Filing**
   A. Documents to be filed with the United States Trustee:
      (1) *Operating Report Number 1* covering the first thirty (30) days of post-petition operations. (These statements are due twenty (20) days after every thirty (30) day period of operation throughout the pendency of the Chapter 11 proceeding.)

8. **On a continuing basis:**
   A. Documents to be filed with the United States Trustee:
      (1) Local Rule 920 Applications regarding salaries for any new officers, directors, partners, or principals, or for any change in the nature of compensation to such persons
      (2) Copies of quarterly state and federal payroll tax and state sales tax returns when filed
      (3) Copies of any and all documents filed with the Bankruptcy Court
   B. Tasks to be performed:
      (1) Prepare and submit to the United States Trustee *Interim Statements* for each two (2) week period and *Operating Reports* for each thirty (30) day period of operation throughout the pendency of the Chapter 11 proceeding. These documents are due seven (7) days and twenty (20) days, respectively, after the close of the applicable reporting period.
      (2) Submit proof of current insuance coverage as to all types of insurance appropriate to the activities of the Debtor in the form of declaration pages. (As each policy of insurance expires, a new declaration page must be submitted indicating that insurance has been obtained to replace the expired policy.)

☆ U S. GOVERNMENT PRINTING OFFICE: 1987-181-493/65035

OFFICE OF THE UNITED STATES TRUSTEE

# GUIDELINE NO. 18
*(Revised May 1988)*

## PRE-PETITION PAYMENTS TO PROFESSIONALS AND FILING OF MONTHLY POST-PETITION PROFESSIONAL FEE STATEMENTS

Where a professional has received pre-petition payments, the professional shall file a **Professional Fee Statement** (Form UST-6) on a monthly basis as set forth herein. The **Professional Fee Statement** shall be filed with the Office of the United States Trustee and a copy shall be served upon the Creditors' Committee and upon all parties who have requested special notice. If no committee has been appointed, the twenty (20) largest unsecured creditors shall be served with a copy of the **Professional Fee Statement**. For service purposes, the list of twenty (20) largest unsecured creditors filed by the Debtor with the Petition (together with any amendments or corrections thereto) may be relied upon as accurately listing such creditors and their addresses. *Neither the original nor any copy of the Professional Fee Statement is to be filed with the Bankruptcy Court.*

The **Professional Fee Statement** shall disclose the total amount of pre-petition payments received during the year prior to the date of the filing of the Petition, the total amount of the pre-petition services rendered and expenses incurred during such year, and the balance of the funds remaining for post-petition services as of the date of the filing of the Petition. In addition, each **Statement** shall disclose the total amount of post-petition services rendered during the applicable reporting period and the balance of the pre-petition funds remaining for services to be rendered during the next reporting period.

The original of the **Professional Fee Statement** filed with the United States Trustee shall have attached to it sufficient supporting time and expense documentation to justify the fees earned and expenses incurred during the post-petition reporting period. (See Paragraphs 3, 4, 5 and 7 of **Guideline No. 7** for the specific detail required in such post-petition listings, for the format to be utilized and for a list of items deemed inappropriate.)

Supporting documentation is not required to be attached to the **Professional Fee Statement** as to the portion of the pre-petition payments against which services were rendered or expenses were incurred prior to the filing of the Petition. The United States Trustee, however, reserves the right to require the production of supporting documentation as to pre-petition services and/or expenses as he deems appropriate on a case-by-case basis.

The copies of the **Statement** served upon the Creditors' Committee, those who have requested special notice and the twenty (20) largest unsecured creditors need not contain a copy of the supporting documentation. Only the original filed with the United States Trustee must contain the required supporting documentation.

OFFICE OF THE UNITED STATES TRUSTEE

GUIDELINE NO. 18                                             PAGE 2
*(Revised May 1988)*

PRE-PETITION PAYMENTS TO PROFESSIONALS AND FILING OF MONTHLY
POST-PETITION PROFESSIONAL FEE STATEMENTS

---

**Professional Fee Statements** shall be filed as follows:

1. *Statement No. 1:* The first **Professional Fee Statement** shall be filed no later than the twentieth (20th) day of the month following the month during which the Petition was filed. This **Statement** shall provide detail regarding the services rendered from the date of the filing of the Petition until the last day of the month in which the Petition was filed. Since most Petitions will not have been filed on the first day of the month, it is anticipated that *Statement No. 1* will cover a period of less than thirty (30) days.

2. *Statements No. 2 and following:* These **Statements** shall be filed on a monthly basis and are due within twenty (20) days after the end of the prior calendar month. Each such **Statement** shall disclose the fees earned and expenses incurred during the prior calendar month and the remainder of the pre-petition funds available for services to be rendered in the future.

If the professional fails to timely file a **Professional Fee Statement**, the United States Trustee may file a motion to disgorge the unused funds as disclosed in the last filed **Statement**.

The requirements set forth in Paragraphs 3, 4, 5 and 7 of **Guideline No. 7** (**Applications for Payment of Professional Fees and Expenses**) apply to the **Professional Fee Statements** required under this **Guideline**.

The United States Trustee reserves the right to raise an objection to any fee or expense application filed in any case whether or not an objection has been raised as to any **Professional Fee Statement** filed in the case.

*This Guideline only applies to pre-petition payments to professionals. Requests for post-petition retainers and all post-petition fee applications must fully comply with the requirements set forth in Guideline No. 6 and Guideline No. 7.*

This **Guideline** is applicable to all Chapter 11 cases filed on or after December 1, 1987.

| ...ey or Professional Name, Address and Telephone Number | FILE WITH U.S. TRUSTEE ONLY – DO NOT FILE IN BANKRUPTCY COURT |
|---|---|

...plicable)  *Attorney for*

**OFFICE OF THE UNITED STATES TRUSTEE
CENTRAL DISTRICT OF CALIFORNIA**

...:                                                                CHAPTER 11 CASE NUMBER

**PROFESSIONAL FEE STATEMENT**

**NUMBER:** _____

**MONTH OF** _____, 19____

                                                            Debtor.

Name of Professional:
Date of entry of Order approving employment of the Professional:

Total amount of Pre-Petition payments received by the Professional:   $
*Less*: Total amount of all Pre-Petition services rendered and expenses:   < _____ >
Balance of funds remaining on date of filing of Petition:   $
*Less*: Total amount of all services rendered per prior Fee Statements:   <               >
*(Line 6 is not used when filing Statement No. 1)*
*Less*: Total amount of services and expenses this reporting period:   < _____ >
Balance of funds remaining for next reporting period:   $ _____

> YOU MUST ATTACH DETAILED DOCUMENTATION SUPPORTING THE PROFESSIONAL FEES EARNED AND THE
> EXPENSES INCURRED DURING THIS REPORTING PERIOD. (THE AMOUNT SPECIFIED ON LINE 7 ABOVE.) THE
> REQUIREMENTS SET FORTH IN PARAGRAPHS 3, 4, AND 5 OF U.S. TRUSTEE **GUIDELINE NO. 7** APPLY TO THE
> DETAIL REQUIRED IN THIS **STATEMENT.** *(Attach only to U.S. Trustee's Original of this Statement.)*

Total number of pages of supporting documentation attached hereto: _____
The above is a true and correct statement of fees earned and expenses incurred during the indicated reporting period.

...d:

_____                    _____
... Name of Professional                                        Signature of Professional



_____                    _____
... Name of Attorney for Professional                          Signature of Attorney for Professional
...plicable)                                                    *(If applicable)*

Professional Fee Statement (Form UST-6) - Page Two (2)

| In re | (SHORT TITLE) | CHAPTER 11 CASE NUMBER: |
|---|---|---|
| | Debtor. | |

## PROOF OF SERVICE BY MAIL

STATE OF CALIFORNIA
COUNTY OF _____

I am employed in the County of _____, State of California, in the office of a member of the b
this Court at whose direction the service was made; I am over the age of 18 and not a party to the within action; and my busi
address is as follows:

On _____, I served the foregoing **PROFESSIONAL FEE STATEMENT** on the intere
parties at their last known addresses in this action by placing a true and correct copy thereof in a sealed envelope with postage the
fully prepaid in the United States Mail at _____, California, addressed as follows:

I declare under penalty of perjury that the foregoing is true and correct.

Dated:

_____          _____
*Print Name*                                                      *Signature*

Exhibit 8-2   Operating Guidelines for Southern District of New York          379

## EXHIBIT 8-2   OPERATING GUIDELINES FOR SOUTHERN DISTRICT OF NEW YORK

---

As Revised January 14, 1987

TO:       Debtors-in-Possession and Trustees

FROM:   Harold Jones
         United States Trustee

RE:       Operating Guidelines and Financial Reporting Requirements
          Required in all cases under Chapter 11, and cases with operating
          businesses under Chapters 7 & 13 of the Bankruptcy Code.

In furtherance of the duties imposed on the United States Trustee by 28 U.S.C 586(a)(3), as added by Section 224(a) of Title 11 of the Bankruptcy Code, trustees and debtors-in-possession (11 U.S.C § 721 or § 1108) are required, as of the date of the filing of a petition commencing a case under Chapter 7, 11, or 13, to comply with the following guidelines relating to the opening and maintenance of bank accounts and the filing of operating reports with the United States Trustee. (*See,* Bankruptcy Rule X-1007).

## BANK ACCOUNT

A debtor-in-possession shall open new bank accounts to; (a) process all post-petition receipts and disbursements from operations of the business, and (b) a separate tax account into which all funds (including but not limited to funds held in trust for employee's withholding taxes, sales taxes, employer contributions, and any other taxes) as may be collected and or payable during the pendency of the case. A trustee who operates a business is also required to open and maintain such accounts. A bank in which those accounts are maintained must be in compliance with the provisions of 11 U.S.C. § 345(a).

In a case in which the trustee supersedes a debtor-in-possession, the trustee, upon ascertaining that such account previously had been opened and maintained, may continue such account with appropriate changes in the title of the account and signatory powers.

Each trustee or debtor-in-possession responsible for maintaining such account shall provide to the United States Trustee a copy of the check form ("Specimen" check) for each of the accounts, and a listing of the authorized signatories (not the signature cards). These specimen checks and the list shall be provided to the United States Trustee not later than the first meeting of creditors, or in the case of a trustee, the first scheduled meeting of creditors following the appointment of the trustee.

Deposits to the separate tax account of withholding and sales taxes, together with any necessary federal depository receipts, shall be made as follows:

I.  Within two business days from the date on which salaries are paid to employees
    A.  that portion of such salaries as are required to be withheld for federal, state and local taxes and for social security, and
    B.  the employer's portion of social security and disability and unemployment insurance; and
II.  In those cases in which a debtor (or debtor's business) is required to collect sales taxes, such taxes must be deposited in the tax account not later than the Monday following each business week for that week's tax liability; and
III.  Any other taxes which the debtor is required to collect, or for which it incurs liability in the ordinary course of the operation of its business (such as federal excise taxes, property taxes, rental taxes, etc.) must be deposited in this tax account no later than Wednesday of the week following the week in which such taxes were collected or in which the liability was incurred.

The debtor-in-possession or operating trustee shall within one calendar week after making any remittances to a depository on account of federal taxes, furnish the District Director of Internal Revenue Service (ATTN: Special Procedures Unit) with evidence, on forms provided by the District Director (IRS Form 6123, or equivalent) that such deposits have been made on behalf of the debtor, (the Form 6123 is not a substitute for a deposit slip or card, but should be submitted for verification to the Special Procedures Unit with the appropriate IRS Form [940, 941, etc.], to verify that deposits have been made to the Government (not the tax account) to meet the tax obligations for the period); and monthly serve copies of such forms with the operating report on the United States Trustee.

## INSURANCE

Within one week subsequent to the entry of the order for relief, the debtor-in-possession or trustee shall supply to the United States Trustee adequate proof that the debtor has all appropriate insurance coverage. This proof may be in the form of a copy of a binder or current policy. The insurance coverage should include such items as loss due to fire, theft, business interruption, workmen's compensation, liability, etc.

## MONTHLY FINANCIAL STATEMENTS

All debtors-in-possession, Chapter 11 trustees and Chapter 7 trustees who are authorized to operate business are required to file *verified*, periodic financial

**Exhibit 8-2   Operating Guidelines for Southern District of New York**     **381**

statements/operating reports (described below) in duplicate with the United States Trustee, with a copy to the creditors committee (if one has been appointed).[1] The original provided to the United States Trustee will be forwarded to the Clerk of the Bankruptcy Court for filing.

Reports shall be filed not later than the 15th calendar day following the end of each calendar month, covering all transactions, on an accrual basis, by the debtor-in-possession (or the trustee) for the calendar month immediately preceding the due date. The first report shall include all transactions for the first full calendar month *and* whatever portion of a month was involved for the prior month from the date of the filing of the petition.

Monthly reports shall include:

A.  A cover sheet showing the name of the debtor, case number, identifying the preparer, the debtor, and/or the debtor's attorney. If the operating report is prepared by a party other than the debtor, or its principals or employees, there should also be included an opinion letter or report specifying audit or review standards employed, and any deviations from the consistent application of generally accepted accounting principles.

B.  An Accrual Basis Profit & Loss Statement and Balance Sheet prepared in accordance with generally accepted accounting principles (GAAP) with all disclosure appropriate for interim reporting.

C.  A Schedule of Cash Receipts & Disbursements, either listing each transaction classed by ledger account, or if over 50 transactions per month, then grouped and categorized by ledger account. A Chart of Accounts should be provided with the first report.

D.  A Schedule of Accounts Payable.[2] This schedule should list each account (or group if more than 25) showing by columnar classification amounts which are:

1.  Pre-Petition
2.  Current/not yet due
3.  1–30 days past due
4.  31–60 days
5.  61–90 days
6.  91–180 days
7.  180 & over

---

[1] These reports must be filed *whether or not* the business is operating.

[2] Payable transactions, other than third party trade payables, i.e., with related parties, intercompany, and notes payable should be segregated. Any items which are disputed, or which have financially significant terms, conditions or covenants should be explained by appropriate disclosure. Pre-petition liabilities should also be segregated for presentation and disclosure purpose during the pendency of the proceeding. Any transaction effecting the balance of the pre-petition receivables should be fully explained by appropriate disclosure.

E.    A Schedule of Accounts Receivable. This should list accounts as described in "D" above. Disclosure is required wherever accounts are subject to factoring, discounting or other financing practice.

F.    A Schedule of Federal State and Local Taxes Collected, Received, Due or Withheld. For each month, this schedule should provide the following information:

     1.    All wages and salaries paid (gross) or incurred.

     2.    The amount of payroll taxes withheld.

     3.    The amount of employer payroll tax contributions incurred.

     4.    The gross taxable sales.

     5.    Sales taxes collected.

     6.    The date and amount paid over to each taxing agency for taxes identified in items 2, 3 and 5 above.

G.    A Schedule of Cost of Goods Sold classifying inventory by manufacturing process (raw materials, component, goods-in-process and finished goods) or by product line for a distributor-type business showing beginning inventory, purchases and ending inventory. The Schedule should show by ledger account all other items incurred or "expensed" as a cost of product, i.e., labor, overhead, etc.

## WAIVER OR MODIFICATION OF REPORTING REQUIREMENTS

The reporting requirements of the United States Trustee may be waived or modified only after a request in writing demonstrating both sufficient cause for the requested action, and specifying what alternative is to be provided in the form and detail of reporting for the estate. No waiver or modification shall be effective unless in writing and signed by the United States Trustee or an authorized delegate.

Debtors should be advised that a request to modify the Profit & Loss Statements to "cash basis", if approved, only modifies the recognition of revenue, and *will not release* the debtor-in-possession or trustee of the duty to report all costs or liabilities incurred in operating the business of the debtor.

## DISCLOSURE REQUIREMENTS

Interim financial reports (monthly and annual operating reports) shall comply with at least the minimum disclosure requirements established in AICPA Accounting Principles Board Opinion #28 for interim reporting. A mere compilation report and even a "review", without adequate disclosure, does not comply with these operating report requirements.

**Exhibit 8-2    Operating Guidelines for Southern District of New York**    **383**

## ANNUAL FINANCIAL STATEMENTS

All debtors-in-possession, and any trustee who operates a business is required to file in duplicate with the United States Trustee, with a copy to the creditors committee, if any, no later than 90 days after the close of the debtor's fiscal year, or each taxable year (if a short tax year election is made pursuant to Internal Revenue Code § 1398(d)(2)) the following annual financial statements prepared, to the extent possible, in accordance with generally accepted accounting principles (including GAAP disclosure requirements):

**A.**   A balance sheet with comparative figures for the prior fiscal year.

**B.**   A profit and loss statement with comparative figures for the prior fiscal year.

**C.**   A copy of the 10K for the period, for a publicly-held corporation.

We recognize that each debtor-in-possession is different and that the ability of a debtor-in-possession to comply with the monthly financial reporting also may vary. Thus, counsel should feel free to advise the United States Trustee as to the circumstances making it burdensome or otherwise difficult to provide the requested information and to indicate, for example, the type of financial statements the debtor-in-possession can provide, the form of such reports, and the timing. While the United States Trustee is willing to consider, on the basis of the facts of each case, any reasonable alternative that the debtor-in-possession may wish to propose, we wish to receive at least as much information as the debtor-in-possession provides to a creditors committee.

A copy of any communication sent to this Office concerning compliance with the financial reporting requirements should be served on the creditors committee, if any. Questions regarding these guidelines should be addressed to the staff attorney handling the case.

**EXHIBIT 8-3    OPERATING REPORTS FOR NORTHERN DISTRICT
OF TEXAS (SELECTED REPORTS)**

Included with the sample operating reports required by the Northern District California was a cash flows statement. This report was issued prior to the effective date of FASB Statement No. 95 and has been omitted here. It would appear that the issuance of a report, with month to month comparisons, that meets the requirements of FASB Statement No. 95 would be acceptable.

Form OPR-1

Case Name _____

Case Number _____

Comparative Balance Sheets

| | Filing Date | Month | Month | Month | Month | Month | Month | Month |
|---|---|---|---|---|---|---|---|---|
| **Assets** | | | | | | | | |
| **Current Assets** | | | | | | | | |
| Cash | | | | | | | | |
| Accounts Receivable, Net (OPR-3) | | | | | | | | |
| Inventory, at lower of cost or market | | | | | | | | |
| Prepaid expenses & deposits | | | | | | | | |
| Other _____ | | | | | | | | |
| Total Current Assets | | | | | | | | |
| Property, Plant & Equipment, at Cost | | | | | | | | |
| Less accumulated depreciation | | | | | | | | |
| Net Property | | | | | | | | |
| Other Assets | | | | | | | | |
| Total Other Assets | | | | | | | | |
| Total Assets | | | | | | | | |

I certify under penalty of perjury that the following operating reports, consisting of _____ pages are true and correct.

Date submitted _____ Signed _____

(Print name of signatory)

385

Case Name _____

Case Number _____

Comparative Balance Sheets

Form OPR-2

| | Filing Date | Month | Month | Month | Month | Month | Month | Month |
|---|---|---|---|---|---|---|---|---|
| **Liabilities** | | | | | | | | |
| Post Petition Liabilities (per form OPR-4) | | | | | | | | |
| Pre Petition Liabilities | | | | | | | | |
| Notes Payable—Secured | | | | | | | | |
| Priority Debt | | | | | | | | |
| Unsecured Debt | | | | | | | | |
| Other | | | | | | | | |
| Total Pre Petition Liabilities | | | | | | | | |
| Total Liabilities | | | | | | | | |
| **Shareholders' Equity (Deficit)** | | | | | | | | |
| Preferred Stock | | | | | | | | |
| Common Stock | | | | | | | | |
| Paid-In Capital | | | | | | | | |
| Retained Earnings | | | | | | | | |
| Through filing date | | | | | | | | |
| Post filing date | | | | | | | | |
| Total Shareholders' Equity (Net Worth) | | | | | | | | |
| Total Liabilities and Shareholders' Equity | | | | | | | | |

Form OPR-3

Case Name —————————

Case Number —————————

## Summary of Accounts Receivable

| | Total Accts. Receivable | 0–30 days | 31–60 days | 61–90 days | Over 90 days |
|---|---|---|---|---|---|
| Date of Filing: | | | | | |
| % to Total | | | | | |
| Month: | | | | | |
| % to Total | | | | | |
| Month: | | | | | |
| % to Total | | | | | |
| Month: | | | | | |
| % to Total | | | | | |
| Month: | | | | | |
| % to Total | | | | | |
| Month: | | | | | |
| % to Total | | | | | |
| Month: | | | | | |
| % to Total | | | | | |

387

Schedule of Post Petition Liabilities

Case Name _____

Case Number _____

| | Month | Month | Month | Month | Month | Month | Month | Month |
|---|---|---|---|---|---|---|---|---|
| Trade Account Payable | | | | | | | | |
| Taxes Payable | | | | | | | | |
| Federal Payroll Taxes | | | | | | | | |
| State Payroll & Sales | | | | | | | | |
| Ad Valorem Taxes | | | | | | | | |
| Other | | | | | | | | |
| Total Taxes Payable | | | | | | | | |
| Secured Debt—Post Petition | | | | | | | | |
| Accrued Interest Payable | | | | | | | | |
| Other Accrued Liabilities | | | | | | | | |
| 1. _____ | | | | | | | | |
| 2. _____ | | | | | | | | |
| 3. _____ | | | | | | | | |
| 4. _____ | | | | | | | | |
| 5. _____ | | | | | | | | |
| Total Post Petition Liabilities | | | | | | | | |

Post-Petition Taxes & Accounts Payable

| Account Name | Date Incurred | Date Due | 0–30 | 31–60 | 61–90 | Over 90 |
|---|---|---|---|---|---|---|
| FICA/WH | | | | | | |
| Sales Tax | | | | | | |
| TEC | | | | | | |
| | | | | | | |
| | | | | | | |
| | | | | | | |
| | | | | | | |
| | | | | | | |
| | | | | | | |
| | | | | | | |
| | | | | | | |
| | | | | | | |
| | | | | | | |
| | | | | | | |
| | | | | | | |
| | | | | | | |
| | | | | | | |
| | | | | | | |
| | | | | | | |
| | | | | | | |
| | | | | | | |
| | | | | | | |
| Totals: | | | | | | |

I hereby swear (or affirm) that all post petition debts or obligations (especially taxes to taxing authorities) are being paid on a timely basis. (If not, please explain below.)

_____

Signature

_____

PRINT name of signatory

Case Name _____

Case Number _____

Statement of Income (Loss)

| | Month | Month | Month | Month | Month | Month | Month | Year to Date |
|---|---|---|---|---|---|---|---|---|
| Net Revenue (Income) | | | | | | | | |
| Cost of Goods Sold | | | | | | | | |
| Material | | | | | | | | |
| Labor—Direct | | | | | | | | |
| Mfg. Overhead | | | | | | | | |
| Total Cost of Goods | | | | | | | | |
| Gross Profit | | | | | | | | |
| Operating Expenses | | | | | | | | |
| Selling & Marketing | | | | | | | | |
| General & Admin. | | | | | | | | |
| Other | | | | | | | | |
| Total Operating Expenses | | | | | | | | |
| Income Before Interest, Depreciation, or Taxes | | | | | | | | |
| Interest Expense | | | | | | | | |
| Depreciation | | | | | | | | |
| Extraordinary Expenses* | | | | | | | | |
| Income Tax Expense (Benefit) | | | | | | | | |
| Net Income (Loss) | | | | | | | | |

*Requires Footnote

Exhibit 8-4    Monthly Operating Report                                          391

## EXHIBIT 8-4    MONTHLY OPERATING REPORT OF CASH
## RECEIPTS AND DISBURSEMENTS

(The following format for the cash receipts and disbursements was suggested by the Association of Insolvency Accountants in a report filed with the U.S. Trustee's Office in Washington, D.C.)

|  | Current Period | Cumulative Date Of Filing Through— |
|---|---|---|
| Receipts |  |  |
| (Detail as needed) |  |  |
| Total Receipts | _____ | _____ |
|  |  |  |
| Less: |  |  |
| Disbursements |  |  |
| (By category) |  |  |
| Total Disbursements | _____ | _____ |
|  |  |  |
| Net Cash | _____ | _____ |
|  |  |  |
| Bank Balance Per Books, Beginning | _____ | _____ |
|  |  |  |
| Bank Balance Per Books, Ending | _____ | _____ |

# Accounting Services for the Creditors' Committee

## EXHIBIT 9-1    SAMPLE REPORT TO CREDITORS' COMMITTEE

*This draft is furnished solely for the purpose of indicating the form of the letter that we would expect to furnish to the Unsecured Creditors' Committee of Big Container Corporation in response to their request and the matters expected to be covered in the letter. Based on our discussions with representatives of the Committee, it is our understanding that the procedures outlined in this draft letter are those that they wished us to follow.*

Mr. Bill Brown
Chairman of the Committee of
Unsecured Creditors of Big Container Corporation
c/o Kentucky Corporation
1 Thomas Way
Lexington, KY

We have performed the procedures enumerated below with respect to (1) the operating statement of Big Container Corporation ("Big Container") as filed June 30, 19X7 which covers the period April 24, 19X7 to May 31, 19X7 and (2) extrapolating operating results for the months of June and July, 19X7. These procedures were performed solely to assist you in evaluating the reasonableness of Big Container's interim operating statements for the period of April 24, 19X7 to May 31, 19X7 and our report is not to be used for any other purpose. We make no representation as to the sufficiency of these procedures for your purposes.

Schedule I presents the financial report of Big Container for the period of April 24, 19X7 through May 31, 19X7 which was provided to the Committee by Big Container. Schedule II presents unaudited amounts provided by Big Container adjusted as follows:

Case I—Reflects adjustments made as the result of the procedures performed which are enumerated below.

Case II—Adjusts Case I to reflect a gross profit margin to a percentage determined by Stifford Corporation ("Stifford").

All the information presented herewith has been compiled from documentation supplied to us by Big Container as well as from interviews, discussions with employees of Big Container, CH & Company (Stifford's Accountants), G&F (Big Container's Accountants), and our reading of the interim operating statement for the period of April 24, 19X7 to May 31, 19X7 filed with the Bankruptcy Court.

For purposes of our agreed-upon procedures of necessity we accepted as accurate the financial records of Big Container. Except as noted below, we did not examine corroborating evidential matter such as checks, invoices, minutes, confirmations, written confirmations, or other support documents nor did we agree information back to the supporting subsidiary ledgers.

The procedures we performed related to the period April 24, 19X7 to May 31, 19X7 as reflected in Schedule I were as follows:

1.  *CASH*—We obtained Big Container's bank statements as of May 31, 19X7 and the bank statement reconciliation prepared by Big Container personnel. We compared cash balance per bank statement to cash balance per the interim operating statement. The reconciling items consisted of outstanding checks and petty cash of $2,500. No tests were performed on petty cash. We verified that the outstanding checks as of May 31, 19X7, cleared the bank in June 19X7 or were still shown as outstanding on the June 30, 19X7 reconciliation. Outstanding checks from May 19X7 not cleared in June 19X7 totaled $2,287. The reconciled amount of Cash on hand at May 31, 19X7 was $428,263 as presented on Schedule I.

2.  *NET SALES*—We obtained Big Container's gross sales journal, randomly selected two sales invoices from each bill date during the period April 24, 19X7 to May 31, 19X7 on which invoices were rendered, and agreed 4% of sales journal entries to sales invoices. The invoices selected agreed to amounts recorded without exception.

3.  *COST OF GOODS SOLD*—We attempted to analyze Big Container's calculation for cost of goods sold but we were unable to verify purchases and beginning and ending inventory. We performed alternative testing to determine an approximate gross margin percentage. From the sales invoices that we selected in the previous procedure, we selected and costed out one item from each invoice. Inventory cost was obtained from Big Container's inventory listing of product costs. This procedure resulted in 1.4% of sales being tested and showed a 11.3% gross profit margin which has been used as the adjusted gross margin percentage in Case I.

**Exhibit 9-1   Sample Report to Creditors' Committee**                                    **395**

4.  *MANAGEMENT SALARY AND PAYROLL EXPENSE*—We reviewed supporting documents for the period April 23, 19X7 to May 31 19X7 to determine if the expense was properly stated on Schedule II.

5.  *RENT EXPENSE*—We reviewed prior year's expense and supporting schedules for the period April 24, 19X7 to May 31 19X7 and compared to the expense on Schedule II. An adjustment is reflected in "Schedule II" (Cases I and II) to reflect the fact that the "as provided" column did not include amounts for the period April 24, 19X7 to April 30, 19X7.

6.  *UTILITIES EXPENSE*—We reviewed utility bills for the period April 24 19X7 to May 31, 19X7 to determine if the expense was properly stated on Schedule II. An adjustment is reflected in "Schedule II" (Cases I and II) to reflect the fact that the "as provided" column did not include amounts for the period April 24 19X7 to April 30, 19X7.

7.  *PROPERTY TAXES*—We reviewed source documents for the period April 24, 19X7 to May 31, 19X7 to determine if the expense was properly stated on Schedule II. An adjustment is reflected in "Schedule II" (Cases I and II) to reflect the fact that the "as provided" column did not include amounts for the period April 24, 19X7 to April 30, 19X7.

8.  *INTEREST EXPENSE*—We recalculated Stifford's interest billing for the period April 24, 1987 to May 31 19X7 to determine if the expense was properly stated on the interim operating statement. An adjustment is reflected in "Schedule II" (Cases I and II) to reflect the fact that the "as provided" column did not include amounts for the period April 24, 19X7 to April 30, 19X7.

9.  *INSURANCE EXPENSE*—We reviewed insurance bills for the period April 24, 19X7 to May 31 19X7 to determine if the expense was properly stated on the interim operating statement. This expense appears to be properly accrued.

10. *DEPRECIATION EXPENSE*—Big Container obtained an appraisal from M. A. Company, Inc. dated May 14, 19X7 which states assets at an appraised value of $1,354,172. Using the M. A. value and assuming a five year asset life we have estimated a depreciation amount of $27,454 to provide for this expense for the period of April 24, 19X7 to May 31, 19X7 (or an annualized amount of $270,834).

11. Because of the unavailability of financial information on outside services and contractors, supplies, repairs and maintenance, advertising, auto expense, delivery, travel and entertainment, and interest income on repo agreements we used Big Container's amounts without adjustment as listed in the "as provided" column of Schedule II.

Schedule III presents unaudited amounts for June and July, 19X7 provided by Big Container adjusted as described below.

The procedures we performed related to the period of June and July, 1987 were as follows:

*TOTAL REVENUE*—We used the revenue amount as provided by Big Container for the month of June, 19X7. We used the revenue amount for the first twenty-four days in July, 19X7 as provided by Big Container and extrapolated that amount to derive a revenue figure for the month of July, 19X7.

*COST OF SALES*—Revenue multiplied by the gross margin as derived in procedure 3 above has been used in determining amounts of cost of sales for the months of June and July, 19X7.

*OPERATING EXPENSES—EXCLUDING DEPRECIATION*—We used the operating expenses excluding depreciation as provided by Big Container for the month of June, 1987. Big Container did not provide operating expenses for the month of July, 1987. We used the operating expense for June, 19X7 in July, 19X7.

*DEPRECIATION EXPENSE*—We used a depreciation amount as derived in procedure 10 above for the month of June and July, 19X7.

Related party transactions were examined by reviewing accounts payable ledger sheet for Slippery Company to determine the amount of purchases made from and payments made to Slippery Company for the period of November 1, 19X6 to June 30, 19X7. These amounts are summarized on Schedule IV.

Schedules I, II, III and IV omit all the disclosures (and the balance sheet and the statement of changes of financial position) required by the generally accepted accounting principles. If the omitted disclosures were included the accompanying schedule, they might influence users' conclusions about the financial condition of Big Container. Accordingly the accompanying schedules are not designed for those who are not informed about such matters.

Because the above described procedures do not constitute an examination made in accordance with generally accepted auditing standards, we do not express an opinion on the Schedules I, II, III and IV. Had we performed additional procedures or had we made an examination of the financial statements of Big Container in accordance with generally accepted auditing standards, other matters might have come to our attention that would have been reported to you. This report relates only to the Schedules I, II, III and IV specified above and does not extend to any financial statements of Big Container, taken as a whole.

July, 19X7

**Exhibit 9-1  Sample Report to Creditors' Committee**                    397

## SCHEDULE I
## BIG CONTAINER CORPORATION
### CASH RECEIPTS AND DISBURSEMENTS

| | |
|---|---|
| Cash on Hand Start of Period | $ 132,197 |
| Receipts | 4,229,055 |
| Disbursements | (3,932,989) |
| Surplus/(Deficit) | $ 428,263 |
| Cash on Hand End of Period (1) | $ 428,263 |

## SCHEDULE II
## BIG CONTAINER CORPORATION

| | As Provided | | Case 1 Adjusted | | Case 2 Adjusted | |
|---|---:|---:|---:|---:|---:|---:|
| Total Revenue (Sales) (2) | 3,123,692 | 100% | 3,123,692 | 100% | 3,123,692 | 100% |
| Cost of Sales (3) | 980,989 | 31% | 2,765,432 | 89% | 2,718,577 | 87% |
| Gross Profit | 2,142,703 | 69% | 358,260 | 11% | 405,115 | 13% |
| Operating Expenses: | | | | | | |
| Management Salary (4)(A) | 23,456 | 1% | 23,456 | 1% | 23,456 | 1% |
| Payroll Expense (4)(A) | 228,729 | 7% | 228,729 | 7% | 228,729 | 7% |
| Outside Services & Contractors (12)(E) | 42,316 | 1% | 42,316 | 1% | 42,316 | 1% |
| Supplies (Office & Operating) | 12,650 | 0% | 12,650 | 0% | 12,650 | 0% |
| Repairs & Maintenance | 10,519 | 0% | 10,519 | 0% | 10,519 | 0% |
| Advertising | 319 | 0% | 319 | 0% | 319 | 0% |
| Auto Expense | 123 | 0% | 123 | 0% | 123 | 0% |
| Delivery | 45,863 | 1% | 45,863 | 1% | 45,863 | 1% |
| Accounting & Legal (B) | | 0% | | 0% | | 0% |
| Rent (5) | 58,638 | 2% | 72,320 | 2% | 72,320 | 2% |
| Telephone (6) | 11,320 | 0% | 13,961 | 0% | 13,961 | 0% |
| Travel & Entertainment | 16,654 | 1% | 16,654 | 1% | 16,654 | 1% |
| Utilities (6) | 8,277 | 0% | 10,208 | 0% | 10,208 | 0% |
| Insurance (6)(C) | 45,411 | 1% | 45,411 | 1% | 45,411 | 1% |
| Taxes (Real Estate, Property, etc.) (7)(D) | 8,200 | 0% | 10,113 | 0% | 10,113 | 0% |
| Interest (8) | 68,874 | 2% | 84,944 | 3% | 84,944 | 3% |
| Depreciation (10) | | 0% | 27,454 | 1% | 27,454 | 1% |
| Total Operating Expenses | 581,349 | 19% | 645,040 | 21% | 645,040 | 21% |
| Net Profit/(Loss) from Operations | 1,561,354 | 50% | (286,780) | -9% | (239,925) | -8% |
| Interest Income on Repo Agreements | 473 | 0% | 473 | 0% | 473 | 0% |
| Total Nonoperating Income/Expenses | 473 | 0% | 473 | 0% | 473 | 0% |
| Net Profit/(Loss) | 1,561,827 | 50% | (286,307) | -9% | (239,452) | -8% |

See accompanying notes

398

Exhibit 9-1   Sample Report to Creditors' Committee                    399

## NOTES TO SCHEDULE II

(A) Includes wages earned during the period April 24, 19X7 through May 31, 19X7 and related employer FICA expenses of $18,594 and unemployment tax of $9,075.

(B) Big Container has indicated that the charges for accounting and legal services related to the bankruptcy and related matters will be borne by the parent, Slippery Company. We have been told these items will not be charged or allocated to Big Container by the parent. We have also been told that the parent bears all charges for computer processing done for Big Container.

(C) Insurance expense is based on actual expense for the period less amount of health insurance reimbursed by employees to Big Container for the period of April 24, 19X7 through April 30, 19X7. As of May 1, 19X7, Big Container no longer provides health insurance benefits.

(D) Property taxes are based on historical 19X6 property tax bills without any anticipated tax increases.

(E) Big Container has represented that this item is sales commissions.

## SCHEDULE III
## BIG CONTAINER CORPORATION

|  | Extrapolated June | | Extrapolated July | |
|---|---|---|---|---|
| Total Revenue (Sales) | $1,250,000 | 100% | $1,033,333 | 100% |
| Cost of Sales | 1,108,750 | 89% | 916,567 | 89% |
| Gross Profit | 141,250 | 11% | 116,767 | 11% |
| Operating Expenses Excluding Depreciation | 450,000 | 36% | 450,000 | 44% |
| Depreciation Expenses | 22,569 | 2% | 22,569 | 2% |
| Total Operating Expenses | 472,569 | 38% | 472,569 | 46% |
| Net Profit/(Loss) from Operations | (331,319) | −27% | (355,802) | −34% |
| Net Profit/(Loss) | (331,319) | −27% | (355,802) | −34% |

Revenue of 800,000 for the period of July 1, through July 24, 19X7 was provided by Big Container.

$$800,000 \times (31/24) = 1,033,333$$

### SCHEDULE IV
### BIG CONTAINER CORPORATION
TRANSACTIONS WITH SLIPPERY COMPANY

| Month-Year | Purchases from Slippery | Payments Made to Slippery |
|---|---|---|
| Nov-X6 | $ 16,455 | $ 0 |
| Dec-X6 | 37,221 | 0 |
| Jan-X7 | 20,200 | 0 |
| Feb-X7 | 0 | 31,427 |
| Mar-X7 | 11,344 | 40,533 |
| Apr-X7 | 15,980 | 53,061 |
| May-X7 | 216,718 | 143,879 |
| Jun-X7 | 97,508 | 142,274 |
| Total | $415,426 | $411,174 |

Note that $145,295 of 19X7 purchases made from Slippery were for inventory purchases from suppliers that would not sell to Big Container directly.
Note that there was a zero balance due to Slippery at 4-23-X7.

# Valuation of a Business in Bankruptcy Proceedings

**EXHIBIT 10-1   EXAMPLE OF VALUE DETERMINED BY APPRAISAL**

## ARTHUR YOUNG & COMPANY

515 South Flower Street
Los Angeles, California 90071

Richard E. Matthews
Trustee—Pacific Homes

The accompanying schedule of assets at estimated values and liabilities of Richard E. Matthews, as Trustee of Pacific Homes (Debtor) under Chapter X at December 9, 1977 was not audited by us and accordingly we do not express an opinion on it.

The schedule mentioned above has been prepared on a basis which includes an estimate of the value of the assets that the Trustee may call upon to settle existing liabilities and future obligations as it goes forward in operating its home and hospital facilities. It is subject to the many uncertainties which are described in the notes to the schedule of assets at estimated values and liabilities. It neither purports to nor does it present the financial condition of the Trustee as of December 9, 1977 in accordance with generally accepted accounting principles on a historical cost/accrual basis of accounting.

Arthur Young & Company

February 14, 1978

## RICHARD E. MATTHEWS AS TRUSTEE OF PACIFIC HOMES (DEBTOR) UNDER CHAPTER X

### NOTES TO SCHEDULE AND ASSETS AT ESTIMATED VALUES AND LIABILITIES

**December 9, 1977**

**(Unaudited)**

### 1. General

The accompanying schedule of assets at estimated values and liabilities of Richard E. Matthews as Trustee of Pacific Homes (Debtor) under Chapter X of the Bankruptcy Act has been prepared without audit utilizing the books and records of the predecessor entity, Pacific Homes, a California nonprofit corporation, as of December 9, 1977 and other available data including the appraisals discussed in Note 2. On December 9, 1977, the Bankruptcy Court converted the Chapter XI proceedings of the Federal Bankruptcy Act of Pacific Homes to Chapter X proceedings.

The accompanying schedule of assets at estimated values and liabilities has been prepared on a basis which includes an estimate of the value of the assets

## RICHARD E. MATTHEWS AS TRUSTEE OF
## PACIFIC HOMES (DEBTOR) UNDER CHAPTER X
### SCHEDULE OF ASSETS AT ESTIMATED VALUES AND LIABILITIES
December 9, 1977
(Unaudited)

| Assets | | Liabilities | |
|---|---:|---|---:|
| Cash | $ 875,039 | Chapter X liabilities | $ — |
| Accounts and notes receivable, less allowance for doubtful accounts of $100,000 | 203,387 | Chapter X liabilities | |
| | | Accounts payable | 202,025 |
| | | Accrued payroll and taxes | 290,198 |
| | | Accrued property taxes | 39,287 |
| | | Accrued expenses | 11,246 |
| Prepaid expenses and supplies | 74,969 | Unearned care fees to December 31, 1977 (Note 4) | 601,000 |
| Deposits with vendors | 126,496 | | |
| Trust deed receivable | 23,834 | Long-term secured debt (Note 5) | 1,143,756 |
| Home and hospital properties, at appraised market values (Note 2) | 53,555,000 | Accrued interest on long-term secured debt (Note 5) | 20,699,481 |
| | | | 1,688,000 |
| | | Resident drawing and deposit accounts | 31,956 |
| Other assets: | | Unexpended designated gifts | 63,104 |
| Funds held in trust pending final order of Court (Note 3) | 1,467,332 | Pre-Chapter XI liabilities (Note 6) | 1,716,526 |
| Funds held in trust for resident drawing and deposit accounts | 31,956 | Commitments and contingencies: | |
| Other | 210,104 | Future obligations for the accommodation and care of residents and other claims (Note 7) | |
| Total other assets | 1,709,392 | | |
| | $56,568,117 | | $25,342,822 |

See accompanying notes.

that the Trustee may call upon to settle existing liabilities and future obligations as it goes forward in operating its home and hospital facilities. It neither purports to nor does it present the financial condition of the Company as of December 9, 1977, and the related results of operations for the period then ended in accordance with generally accepted accounting principles on an historical cost/ accrual basis.

The Trustee is currently operating the homes and hospital facilities from funds provided by monthly billings to the residents at rates dependent upon type of accommodation and level of care provided. Until such time as a plan or reorganization can be developed the future operations are dependent upon receipt of funds from such billings. It is anticipated that a plan of reorganization can be developed and approved by the Court whereby the homes and hospital facilities can continue to operate as a nonprofit organization.

Although the Trustee believes the assumptions are reasonable in the circumstances, it can provide no assurance that a plan of reorganization will be developed that will permit the Company to operate as contemplated by the assumptions nor can management provide assurances that actual future events will not differ materially from those contemplated by the assumptions used herein.

## 2. Valuation of Home and Hospital Properties

The values of home and hospital properties as of December 9, 1977 represent appraised market values based on a going concern nonprofit operation. These appraisals are as of October 13, 1977 and have been prepared by two outside real estate consulting firms.

All of these properties are security for long-term indebtedness (See Note 5).

## 3. Funds Held in Trust

These funds represent the proceeds from the sale of certain land and office buildings owned by Pacific Homes. Litigation subsequent to the sale as to whether such properties were security for certain long-term indebtedness caused such funds to be held in trust (in an interest bearing savings account) until the Court could rule upon the disposition of such funds. On January 30, 1978 a preliminary judgment was reached to release the funds to the Trustee. Approximately $850,000 of the funds are to be used in refurbishing of facilities and the remainder for working capital. This judgment is subject to the final findings of the judge. An appeal of the final decision may be made within 10 days after the decision is reached.

## 4. Unearned Care Fees

Prior to December 9, 1977, Pacific Homes while operating under Chapter XI had billed fees for the accommodation and/or care of residents for the month of December, 1977. The amount reflected as a liability as of December 9, 1977 is the amount of these fees to be earned during the period December 10 to December 31, 1977. The residents, approximately 1,700, will continue to be billed

Exhibit 10-1　Example of Value Determined by Appraisal　405

monthly in advance for their accommodations and/or care of rates which are dependent upon the level of care provided.

## 5. *Long-Term Secured Debt*

Long-term secured debt obligations and accrued interest thereon are as follows at December 9, 1977:

|  | Total Debt | Accrued Interest |
|---|---|---|
| 6% notes with mortgages or trust deeds on specified home properties and furnishings as collateral | $ 3,398,318 | $ 187,000 |
| First mortgage bonds, date July 1, 1970, on specified home properties and furnishings: | | |
| (1) Series B, Principal due serially from April 1, 1975 to April 1, 1988; 9% interest payable semi-annually on April 1 and October 1 | 4,610,00 | 115,250 |
| (2) Series C, principal due serially from February 1, 1977 to August 1, 1996; 10% interest payable semi-annually on February 1 and August 1 | 6,000,000 | 799,800 |
| 10% first mortgage notes due $52,654 monthly | 5,991,971 | 549,500 |
| State of California Department of Health 5% loan to bring certain facilities up to required standards | 699,192 | 36,450 |
| | $20,699,481 | $1,688,000 |

## 6. Pre-Chapter XI Liabilities

Pre-Chapter XI liabilities represent the liabilities and claims of unsecured creditors as of February 18, 1977, the date Pacific Homes entered Chapter XI proceedings, and consists of the following:

| | |
|---|---|
| Trade creditors-moratorium | $ 399,524 |
| Trade creditors | 206,905 |
| Prospective resident deposits and resident prepayments (a) | 98,888 |
| Resident loans and advances (b) | 497,013 |
| Refunds due residents who left facilities under terms of contractual agreements (c) | 514,196 |
| | $1,716,526 |

**EXHIBIT 10-2    EXAMPLE OF REORGANIZATION VALUE
DETERMINED BY DISCOUNTED CASH FLOWS**

In chapter 10 of the *Practice and Procedure* volume, the discounted cash flow approach to determining the value of a company in bankruptcy is described. This Exhibit contains an illustration of this approach. The period for which the cash flows are discounted is eleven years. The residual value is calculated by using the operating net income for the eleventh year and dividing it by a cost of capital of fifteen percent. The assumption is made that the capital expenditure after year eleven will be $115,000 per year and that depreciation after year thirteen will be relatively small. It is also assumed that at some point beyond the eleventh year the debtor will be subject to income taxes. An average tax expense of $500,000 per year after the eleventh year is used.

The reorganization value is determined by discounting the net annual cash flow before debt service less capital expenditure and estimated cost of capital of 15 percent and by adding to this value a residual value based on discounted cash flows. The fifteen percent rate may be too high in this case since the problem indicates that the debtor will be able to borrow at a rate of 8 percent. Of course, a lower cost of capital would have increased the value of the business.

The reorganized value is presented on the next page. The cash flows that served as the basis of the calculation of the reorganization value and the notes to the projections are presented on the pages following the reorganization value.

Exhibit 10-2   Example of Reorganization Value                        **407**

## DIP Corporation
## Reorganization Value

| Year | Operating cash flow | Capital expenditure | Net cash flow | Present value factor* | Present value amount |
|---|---|---|---|---|---|
| 19W9 | $ 413 | $ 0 | $ 413 | .8696 | $ 359 |
| 19X0 | 1,364 | 70 | 1,294 | .7561 | 978 |
| 19X1 | 1,605 | 75 | 1,530 | .6575 | 1,006 |
| 19X2 | 1,637 | 85 | 1,552 | .5718 | 887 |
| 19X3 | 1,869 | 90 | 1,779 | .4972 | 885 |
| 19X4 | 1,964 | 95 | 1,869 | .4323 | 808 |
| 19X5 | 2,141 | 100 | 2,036 | .3759 | 767 |
| 19X6 | 2,237 | 100 | 2,137 | .3269 | 699 |
| 19X7 | 2,034 | 110 | 1,924 | .2843 | 547 |
| 19X8 | 2,140 | 110 | 2,030 | .2472 | 502 |
| 19X9 | 2,250 | 115 | 2,135 | .2149 | 459 |
| Total discounted value of cash flows for 11 years | | | | | $7,897 |

Residual Value:
   The residual value is based on the assumption
that depreciation after the eleventh year
will be approximately $100,000.

| | |
|---|---|
| Cash flow 11th and subsequent years | $ 2,150 |
| Taxes (After considering tax benefit of depreciation) | 500 |
| Net cash flow | 1,650 |
| Cost of capital | − .15 |
| Residual value at the end of the eleventh year | 11,000 |
| Present value of residual value | × .2149 |

Present value of residual value: 2,364

Total reorganization value**: $10,261

*Based on year end values.
**Included in the reorganization value would be the value of any assets that are not
needed by the reorganized company.

Debtor-in-Possession
Projected Statement of Annual Operating Results and Annual Cash Flows Assuming
a Three-Year Deferral of Property Tax Payments and aThree-Year Deferral of Debt
Principal Payments
For the Years Ending April 30, 1989 to April 30, 1999

|  | 1989 | 1990 | 1991 | 1992 |
|---|---|---|---|---|
| REVENUES: | | | | |
| Room | $3,523,085 | $4,430,897 | $ 4,912,972 | $ 5,576,749 |
| Food and beverage | 3,263,654 | 4,171,771 | 4,576,704 | 5,116,886 |
| Other | 979,514 | 1,114,042 | 1,219,447 | 1,355,843 |
| Total revenues | 7,766,253 | 9,716,710 | 10,709,123 | 12,049,478 |
| Cost of Revenues | 4,404,700 | 5,191,669 | 5,658,512 | 6,279,481 |
| Gross Margin | 3,361,553 | 4,525,041 | 5,050,611 | 5,769,997 |
| OPERATING EXPENSES: | | | | |
| Sales, marketing and advertising | 426,553 | 326,310 | 356,112 | 394,529 |
| Management fees | 220,000 | 107,157 | 121,882 | 130,478 |
| Franchise fees | | 145,858 | 161,547 | 182,372 |
| Property operation and maintenance | 527,455 | 874,594 | 964,748 | 1,072,628 |
| Utilities | 656,937 | 637,731 | 699,127 | 782,209 |
| Property taxes | 105,000 | 105,000 | 105,000 | 429,945 |
| General and administrative | 1,012,828 | 964,756 | 1,037,228 | 1,140,218 |
| Total operation expenses | 2,948,773 | 3,161,406 | 3,445,644 | 4,133,379 |
| Net annual cash flow before debt service and capital expenditures | 412,780 | 1,363,635 | 1,604,967 | 1,636,618 |
| OTHER EXPENSES: | | | | |
| Interest | 540,000 | 1,080,000 | 1,080,000 | 1,073,201 |
| Depreciation | 475,000 | 947,350 | 947,350 | 947,350 |
| Total other expenses | 1,015,000 | 2,027,350 | 2,027,350 | 2,020,551 |
| Total expenses | 3,963,773 | 5,188,756 | 5,472,994 | 6,153,930 |
| Income (loss) before income taxes | (602,220) | (663,715) | (422,383) | (383,933) |
| Provision for Income Taxes | | | | |
| Net Income (loss) | (602,220) | (663,715) | (422,383) | (383,933) |
| Add Depreciation Expense | 475,000 | 947,350 | 947,350 | 947,350 |
| Less cash contribution to reserve for replacement | | 70,000 | 75,000 | 85,000 |
| Less principal portion of bond payments | | | | 139,829 |
| Positive (negative) cash flow | $(127,220) | $  213,635 | $  449,967 | $  338,588 |

See summary of significant projection assumptions and accounting policies.

Exhibit 10-2    Example of Reorganization Value                409

| 1993 | 1994 | 1995 | 1996 | 1997 | 1998 | 1999 |
|---|---|---|---|---|---|---|
| $ 6,217,561 | $ 6,491,350 | $ 6,784,448 | $ 7,090,970 | $ 7,411,410 | $ 7,746,447 | $ 8,096,751 |
| 5,711,268 | 5,968,775 | 6,238,123 | 6,519,730 | 6,814,162 | 7,122,004 | 7,443,875 |
| 1,509,563 | 1,577,435 | 1,648,180 | 1,722,127 | 1,799,420 | 1,880,215 | 1,964,671 |
| 13,438,392 | 14,037,560 | 14,670,791 | 15,332,827 | 16,024,992 | 16,748,666 | 17,505,297 |
| 7,022,672 | 7,342,198 | 7,676,089 | 8,025,291 | 8,390,509 | 8,772,488 | 9,171,998 |
| 6,415,720 | 6,695,362 | 6,994,702 | 7,307,536 | 7,634,483 | 7,976,178 | 8,333,299 |
| 439,574 | 459,675 | 480,559 | 502,399 | 525,239 | 549,125 | 574,106 |
| 136,736 | 140,339 | 146,186 | 152,277 | 158,623 | 165,234 | 172,121 |
| 194,158 | 202,631 | 211,342 | 220,428 | 229,905 | 239,792 | 250,105 |
| 1,179,522 | 1,230,321 | 1,304,719 | 1,361,059 | 1,419,857 | 1,481,217 | 1,545,253 |
| 876,091 | 915,862 | 957,558 | 1,001,169 | 1,046,782 | 1,094,489 | 1,144,389 |
| 450,387 | 453,064 | 363,141 | 378,884 | 698,250 | 715,417 | 733,345 |
| 1,270,658 | 1,328,990 | 1,390,142 | 1,454,125 | 1,521,072 | 1,591,124 | 1,664,422 |
| 4,547,126 | 4,730,882 | 4,853,657 | 5,070,341 | 5,599,728 | 5,836,398 | 6,083,741 |
| 1,868,594 | 1,964,480 | 2,141,055 | 2,237,195 | 2,034,755 | 2,139,780 | 2,249,558 |
| 1,049,108 | 1,024,462 | 997,769 | 968,861 | 937,554 | 903,648 | 866,928 |
| 947,350 | 947,350 | 947,350 | 947,350 | 947,350 | 947,350 | 947,350 |
| 1,996,458 | 1,971,812 | 1,945,119 | 1,916,211 | 1,884,904 | 1,850,998 | 1,814,278 |
| 6,543,584 | 6,702,694 | 6,798,766 | 6,986,552 | 7,484,632 | 7,687,396 | 7,898,019 |
| (127,864) | (7,332) | 195,936 | 320,984 | 149,851 | 288,782 | 435,280 |
| (127,864) | (7,332) | 195,936 | 320,984 | 149,851 | 288,782 | 435,280 |
| 947,350 | 947,350 | 947,350 | 947,350 | 947,350 | 947,350 | 947,350 |
| 90,000 | 95,000 | 100,000 | 100,000 | 110,000 | 110,000 | 115,000 |
| 296,951 | 321,597 | 348,290 | 377,198 | 408,505 | 442,411 | 479,131 |
| 432,535 | $ 523,421 | $ 694,996 | $ 791,136 | $ 578,696 | $ 683,721 | $ 788,499 |

## NOTES

### 1. Introduction

Management has formulated a refinancing proposal which is described in Note 3. The projected statement of annual operating results and annual cash flows assuming no deferral of property taxes and no deferral of debt principal payments (the "No Deferral Projection") is prepared using the assumption that property taxes are paid in the year assessed and the retirement of debt begins in the year that such debt is obtained, both of which are more fully described in Note 3. The projected statement of annual operating results and annual cash flows assuming a three-year deferral of debt principal payments (the "Debt Deferral Projection"), which is more fully described in Note 3, assumes that no debt principal payments will be made in the first three years of such debt being outstanding. The projected statement of annual operating results and annual cash flows assuming a three-year deferral of property taxes and a three-year deferral of debt principal payments (the "Tax and Debt Deferral Projection") assumes the current year assessed property taxes for the first three years in the No Deferral Projection will be deferred to 19X7, 19X8 and 19X9 and the deferral of debt principal payments during the first three years the debt is outstanding. The accompanying financial projections do not reflect the interest expense, if any, related to any borrowings to fund annual negative cash flows and interest income, if any, related to investment of annual positive cash flows.

### 2. Summary of Significant Accounting Policies

The accounting and reporting policies of the Company conform to generally accepted accounting principles and to general practices within the hotel industry. Depreciation is computed using the straight-line method over the estimated useful lives of the related assets. Such useful lives are twenty-five years for buildings and six years for furniture, fixtures and equipment.

### 3. Summary of Significant Projection Assumptions

As described in Note 1, the projected net annual cash flows before debt service and capital expenditures for the years ending April 30, 19X0 to April 30, 19X9 are the average of the relevant information in the Pannell, McColgan and Schultz studies. The McColgan and Schultz studies were for ten years and the Pannell study was for five years. The projected annual operating results for fiscal years 19X5 through 19X9 were not prepared by _____ but are based on management's assumption that such years will experience increases of an average of 4.5% each year. Such assumption is based on operations being stabilized by 19X4 and the average Consumer Price Index increases being an average of 4.5% for the fiscal years 19X5 through 19X9.

The _____ reports were for the periods beginning in 19W9. Because of current operating results, management believes that its projection for 19W9 is more likely to occur than the first year results reflected in the three

**Exhibit 10-2    Example of Reorganization Value**                                        **411**

studies. Accordingly, the projection for 19W9 is based on the actual operating results for the four months ended August 31, 19W8 and management's assumptions for the operating results for the eight months ending April 30, 19W9. Management believes the more likely operating results for the fiscal years 19X0 to 19X9 will be the average of the information included in the Pannell, McColgan and Schultz studies for years 19W9 to 19W8 and, accordingly, have used such information for years 19X0 to 19X9. The Pannell, McColgan and Schultz studies information for fiscal years 19X0 to 19X9 from which the averages were computed is listed on pages 10, 11 and 12 of the summary of significant projection assumptions.

## Revenues:

*Room*—Room revenues for 19W9 are projected using an occupancy rate of 44.0% and an average daily room rate of $60.94. Room revenues for 19X0 through 19X9 are the average of the room revenue information in the three studies.

*Food and Beverage*—Food and beverage revenues for 19W9 are projected to be 42% of total revenues. Food and beverage revenues for fiscal years 19X0 to 19X9 are the average of the food and beverage revenues information in the three studies.

*Other*—Other revenues are comprised of telephone, retail, amusements, rental and other operating revenues. Other revenues for 19W9 are projected to be 12.6% of total revenue. Other revenues for fiscal years 19X0 to 19X9 are the average of the relevant information in the three studies.

*Cost of Revenues*—Cost of revenues is comprised of the cost of room, food and beverage, and other revenues. The cost of revenues for 19W9 is projected to be 56.7% of total revenues. Cost of revenues for fiscal years 19X0 to 19X9 are the average of the cost of revenue information in the three studies.

## Expenses:

*Sales, Marketing and Advertising*—Sales, marketing and advertising expenses for 19W9 are projected to be 5.5% of total revenues. Sales, marketing and advertising expenses for fiscal years 19X0 to 19X9 are the average of the sales, marketing and advertising information in the three studies.

*Management Fees and Franchise Fees*—Management fees for 19W9 are projected to be 2.8% of total revenues. There is assumed to be no franchise fees expense for fiscal year 19W9. Management fees and franchise fees for fiscal years 19X0 to 19X9 are the average of the management fees and franchise fees information from the Pannell and McColgan studies. The Schultz study did not separately identify management fees and franchise fees. Schultz grouped management fees in the administrative and insurance expense category and franchise fees in the rooms cost of sales category.

*Property Operation and Maintenance*—Property operation and maintenance expenses for 19W9 are projected to be 6.8% of total revenues. Property operation and maintenance expenses for fiscal years 19X0 to 19X9 are the average of the information from the three studies.

*Utilities*—Utilities expense for fiscal 19W9 is projected to be 8.5% of total revenues. Utilities expense for fiscal years 19X0 to 19X9 is the average of the information from the three studies.

*Property Taxes*—Property tax expenses for the first six years of all three projections include an additional $105,000 which represents the payout over six annual installments of the approximate $630,000 of outstanding property taxes as of November 6, 19W7. Property tax expense for 19W9 in the No Deferral Projection and the Debt Deferral Projection includes a projected amount that approximates the property taxes assessed to the Company for fiscal year 19W8. Such amount, which also includes Tennessee franchise taxes, is $298,356. Property taxes for fiscal years 19X0 to 19X9 in the No Deferral Projection and the Debt Deferral Projection are the average of the information in the three studies. Such average is increased for fiscal years 19X0 to 19X5 by the $105,000 annual amount described above. Property taxes for the Tax Deferral Projection for fiscal years 19X0 to 19X5 include the $105,000 described above with the projected average amount of property taxes for fiscal years 19X0, 19X1 and 19X2 derived from the three studies deferred to fiscal years 19X7, 19X8 and 19X9, respectively.

*General and Administrative*—General and administrative expenses for 19W9 are projected to be 13% of total revenues. General and administrative expenses for fiscal years 19X0 to 19X9 are the average of the information in the three studies.

### Proposed Refinancing of Debt:

The Company proposes to issue tax-exempt bonds with a twenty-year term to bear interest at 8% annually. Payments of interest will be made annually from the beginning of the issue. Payments of principal are assumed to be made beginning the fourth year that the bonds are outstanding in the Debt Deferral Projection and in the Tax and Debt Deferral Projection. Payments of principal are assumed to be made from the beginning of the issue in the No Deferral Projection. It is the interest and principal related to these bonds that are shown and discussed in these projections.

### Depreciation:

A restatement of property and equipment book values to fair value during fiscal 19W9 is assumed as a result of reorganization under Chapter 11 protection of the United States Bankruptcy Court. Such restated depreciable property and equipment values are based on the information received in two of the three studies and approximately $12,800,000. Depreciation expense for 19W9 is projected to be approximately $475,000 which is a composite depreciation expense of the historical book values and the restated fair values. Depreciation expense for fiscal years 19X0 to 19X9 is projected to be approximately $947,350 based on the restated fair values.

Exhibit 10-2   Example of Reorganization Value                                  413

## *Provision for Income Taxes:*

The Company has net operating loss carryforwards which are assumed to be available to offset future tax liabilities during the projection period. Actual utilization of these losses will depend upon the final structuring of equity interests and, under certain structures, the utilization of the net operating loss carryforwards might *not* be available.

## *Reserve for Replacement:*

The reserve for replacement represents approximately 67% of the reserve for replacement projected amount included in the McColgan study. The remaining projected amount for reserve for replacement is reflected as normal maintenance expenses in property operation and maintenance.

## PART FOUR

# Auditing Procedures and Reports

# CHAPTER ELEVEN

# Audit Procedures and Special Areas of Inquiry

**EXHIBIT 11-1   REPORT ON SPECIAL INVESTIGATION**

Mr. _____                    November 23, 19X1
Attorney for the Creditors
   Committee of

Atlanta, Georgia 30303

Dear Sir:

We have performed the procedures requested by you as described on the following pages with respect to the activities of the debtor-in-possession of _____ Inc. This report is solely for your information and that of the Court and the members of the unsecured creditors committee of _____ Inc. in considering the activities of the debtor-in-possession and is not to be used for any other purpose. Because the procedures described on the following pages were not specified by the Court or the claimants, such procedures may not be sufficient for their purposes.

Also, because these procedures were not sufficient to constitute an examination made in accordance with generally accepted auditing standards, we do not express an opinion on the amounts or items described on the following pages. In connection with performing such procedures, however, nothing came to our attention, other than that which is described in the following pages, which would cause us to believe that the amounts or items should be adjusted. Had we performed additional procedures that might have been requested by the Court or the claimants, or had we made an examination of the financial statements of _____ Inc. in accordance with generally accepted auditing standards, other matters might have come to our attention that would have been reported to you.

This report relates only to the matters described herein, and does not extend to the financial statements of _____ Inc. taken as a whole for any date or period.

Yours very truly,

CPA & Company

## Index and Summary of Areas Investigated to Date

1. Pro-Forma Liquidation Recovery Estimates
2. Post-Filing Methods of Handling Receipts and Disbursements
3. XYZ Loan Documents and Meeting with Concerning Monitoring of Collateral
4. ABC Loan Documents and Meeting with Concerning Fixed Asset Appraisal
5. Meeting with PCPA
6. Corporate Controls in the Area of Inventory
7. Related Party Transactions
8. Consolidated Tax Returns
9. Omitted
10. Post Filing Timeliness of Financial Data
11. Forward Commitments
12. Omitted

### 1. Pro-Forma Liquidation Recovery Estimates

We agreed amounts from the October 1, 19X1 financial statements to the divisional general ledgers.

We discussed the miscellaneous other asset accounts and the miscellaneous other liability accounts with Controller, as to their content.

Observations:

1. The balance sheet includes some deferred costs, approximately $204,000, which would probably not be recoverable upon liquidation of the Company.
2. Accounts payable accounts include a "pad" of approximately $100,000 to cover possible unrecorded liabilities and "accrued other" includes an amount relating to an employee benefit accrual relating to the purchase of the Plant amounting to approximately $139,000.

We adjusted, in the manner indicated below, the amounts reflected in the above-described balance sheet to derive a pro-forma estimate of an amount that might have been recoverable by the unsecured creditors upon liquidation at October 1, 19X1 based on the indicated assumptions. The assumptions are not intended to reflect the actual amounts recoverable but are used only for illustra-

**Exhibit 11-1    Report on Special Investigation**                                                                **419**

tive purposes. Actual results achieved during any liquidation would vary from the assumptions, and such variations could be significant.

The adjustments were based on the following assumptions:

1. The collection of 70% of existing receivables
2. The recovery of 75% of the book value of existing inventories
3. Realization of the preliminary estimate of net proceeds of $2,215,000 on liquidation of property, plant and equipment, based upon preliminary discussions with _____ Bank.
4. Payment of certain priority liabilities of approximately $440,000.
5. No recovery of deferred costs of approximately $204,000
6. No payment with respect to the "pad" in accounts payable of approximately $100,000 and the employee benefit accrual of approximately $139,000 relating to the purchase of the _____ Plant.

Given the above, the unsecured creditors could have expected to receive approximately 24 cents on the dollar upon liquidation at October 1, 19X1 prior to administrative fees and any amounts potentially due or receivable with respect to the _____ at the _____ location. If the assumption as to inventory recovery were changed to 40%, the potential payment to unsecured creditors before administrative fees would have been approximately 4 cents on the dollar.

## 2. Post Filing Methods of Handling Receipts and Disbursements

We discussed with _____, Vice-President and _____, Controller, the Company's post-filing methods of handling cash receipts and disbursements at the various locations and we were informed of the following:

(1) Cash Receipts
Customer remittances are mailed to a lock box at the C&S Bank in Atlanta. However, ABC is no longer handling the depositing and recording of the daily remittances. Each day a courier delivers the sealed receipts to the general offices. A clerk opens the sealed receipts, prepares a listing of checks, prepares the deposit to First Atlanta Bank, and then makes the deposit to _____ account. The check listings are then sent to the various divisions where accounts receivable are relieved. Although a single clerk handles cash receipts with no dual participation, she appears to have no other accounting duties which would conflict with her cash receipts duties.

(2) Cash Disbursements
Prior to filing of the Chapter 11, disbursements greater than $500 required dual signatures of officers at the Corporate offices in Atlanta. Subsequent to the filing, with the exception of _____ settlements, all disbursements are made at the divisional level. We observed the procedures being followed at the _____ location and at the _____ location and discussed the procedures being utilized at the other locations with com-

pany officials. Dual signatures are required with both checksigners looking at the supporting documentation which includes the related receiving reports. The supporting documentation is then either stamped "paid" or perforated and the checks are mailed independently of the check preparation and signing functions. Copies of all released checks are then sent to the Corporate headquarters.

Observation: It appears that post-filing controls over the handling of cash disbursements are less stringent than pre-filing controls but because of the COD status of many divisional purchases, it may not be possible to strengthen such controls immediately. However, we were informed that not all of the local banks being utilized by the division have been given signature cards and dual signature instructions. We feel that this should be done immediately.

### 3. XYZ Loan Documents and Meeting with XYZ Concerning Monitoring Collateral

* We read the XYZ loan documents
* We met with XYZ representative, _____, and discussed XYZ monitoring of collateral.
* Mr. _____ indicated that XYZ had continuously monitored collateral to the date of filing via periodic confirmation of accounts receivable balances and monitoring of monthly physical inventories. In addition, XYZ performed trend analysis on this data and on other financial information received from _____ Inc. XYZ would not allow examination of their working papers.
* Observation: No conclusions can be reached concerning the extent of reliance which could be placed on work performed by XYZ.

### 4. ABC Loan Documents and Meeting with ABC Concerning Fixed Asset Appraisal

* We read the ABC loan documents
* We met with an ABC representative, Mr. _____ and their attorney, Mr. _____. They indicated that ABC is in the process of obtaining an appraisal of the property, plant and equipment from TBC Appraisers, this appraisal should be available around the first week in December, and that they would make the appraisal available to us.

### 5. Meeting with Prior CPA (PCPA)

* We discussed with Mr. _____, partner and Mr. _____, manager, from PCPA the professional services performed for _____ over the last several years to determine whether there were any significant problems encountered by PCPA in the conduct of their audits and whether there had been any significant disagreements with management.
* Observation: Messrs. _____ and _____ indicated that the only significant problem area related to inventory controls. In addition, Messrs. _____ and _____ indicated that there had been no significant dis-

**Exhibit 11-1   Report on Special Investigation**                                    **421**

agreements with the management of _____ Inc. We did not review PCPA's workpapers. Review of the PCPA's workpapers and further inventory testing appears to be warranted.

## 6. Corporate Controls in the Area of Inventory

- We discussed _____ Inc.'s method of accounting for inventory with management personnel at the _____ and _____ locations.
- We visited the _____ Division Plant while a physical inventory "count" was in progress.
- We read the report issued by Arthur Andersen & Company dated April 21, 19X1 describing the limited procedures performed by them with respect to the January 31, 19X1 physical inventory.
- Observation: In performing the above procedures, we noted that the majority of the _____ and _____ raw materials inventories are estimated, these estimates are only as reliable as the estimating capability of the inventory teams accordingly, such estimates may or may not be reliable. We have recommended that a controlled physical inventory be taken at all locations as soon as practicable.

## 7. Related Party Transactions

- We discussed with _____, Controller, the changing corporate structure of _____ Inc., a related company operating as a _____ broker (ie: from a subsidiary of _____ Inc. to a division of _____ Inc. to a subsidiary of _____). Such changes are reflected in the consolidated corporate tax returns for the indicated periods. We also looked at supporting documentation for all direct transactions between _____ as reflected by _____ accounts payable vendor analysis computer run, for the period February 1, 19X1 through October 31, 19X1
- Observation: Based upon our limited procedures, it appears that transactions between _____ should be reviewed further as to possible recovery as preferential.
- We discussed with management the allocation of income tax benefits between _____ and _____ the parent. The information received was agreed to worksheets prepared by _____ and to the consolidated tax returns.
- Observation: There should be further investigation into the possible recovery of approximately $66,000 from _____ Industries relating to allocation of an income tax benefit in 19X0.
- We read the non-competition agreements between _____ and _____ relating to the purchase of the _____ division in 19W1 and discussed with management the payments made pursuant to these agreements since 19W1.
- Observation: There should be further investigation into the possible recovery of approximately $36,000 paid to _____ during 19X1 and 19X2 after the expiration of the original 10 year term of the original agreement.
- We agreed officer's compensation and "perks" for the twelve months ended October 30, 19X1 to the payroll records, and read the officer's compensation

as shown on the Company's consolidated income tax returns for the years ended January 31, 19W1, January 31, 19X0 and January 31, 19X1.
- Observation: Most family members were removed from the payroll in October, 19X1.
- Observation: There is a possibility that a portion of _____ salary (paid by _____) from October, 19X0 to October, 19X1, approximately $34,000, may be recoverable due to his employment by _____.
- Observation: Further investigation into the area of "reasonable compensation" may be desired.

### 8. Consolidated Tax Returns

- We read the _____ consolidated tax returns for the years ended January 31, 19W1, 19X0 and 19X1.
- Observation: It appears that the $5,000,000 upstream dividend to _____ in 19X0 was invested in various "blue-chip" stocks and bonds. The consolidated returns indicate that there are numerous transactions in this portfolio during each year and there has been a general preservation of equity. It appears _____ only activity is investment transactions relating to its liquid assets.

### 10. Post-Filing Timeliness of Financial Data

- We inquired as to the timeliness of monthly financial statements with _____ personnel. Currently divisional financial statements are available by approximately the 10th business day following month end; however consolidated statements are not ready until approximately the 20th business day.
- Observation: In order for creditors and the debtor-in-possession to make timely decisions, we believe this information should be and could be available much earlier in the month.

### 11. Forward Commitments

- We have discussed with _____, Vice-President, and _____ Controller, the possibility of the Company having significant forward commitments and we were told that the Company does have some forward contracts to provide materials. However, these contracts are based upon current _____ prices plus or minus a percentage. Company officials have indicated to us that they do not hedge their metal purchases.
- We have read the contract with _____ related to the _____ at the _____ Plant and discussed the contract with Company officials at the _____ location and at the corporate offices.
- Observation: The Company has a contract with _____ to mine and reprocess the _____. This contract includes the purchase of reprocessed materials from the _____ at current _____ prices. In order to determine the net present value to _____ of the _____ further analysis of the _____ would be necessary in order to estimate the size and recoverable _____ content.

# CHAPTER TWELVE

# Financial Statements

**EXHIBIT 12-1   BALANCE SHEET: LIQUIDATION ANALYSIS**

Listed on the following pages is a financial statement that reflects the action taken to convert the assets to cash. Note that the fixed assets with a book value of $6,738,000 were sold for $596,000.

# EXHIBIT 12-1 BALANCE SHEET

Liquidation Analysis
March, 19X5

| | February 28 19X5 | Liquidation Adjustments Debits | Liquidation Adjustments Credits | Liquidation Balance Sheet |
|---|---|---|---|---|
| ASSETS | | | | |
| Current Assets: | | | | |
| Cash | 4,000 | 1) 1,970,000 2) 2,291,000 3) 20,000 4) 596,000 7) 61,000 | | 4,942,000 |
| Accounts Receivable | 2,189,000 | | 1) 2,189,000 | 0 |
| Inventories | 2,864,000 | | 2) 2,864,000 | 0 |
| Notes Receivable | 30,000 | | 3) 30,000 | 0 |
| Refundable Income Tax | 61,000 | | 7) 61,000 | 0 |
| Deferred Expenses | 9,000 | | 8) 9,000 | 0 |
| Total Current Assets | 5,157,000 | | | 4,942,000 |
| Property, Plant & Equipment | 6,738,000 | | 4) 6,738,000 | 0 |
| Deferred Costs—Net of Amortization | 416,000 | | 6) 416,000 | 0 |
| Funds Held by Trustee | 138,000 | | 5) 138,000 | 0 |
| TOTAL ASSETS | 12,449,000 | | | 4,942,000 |

## LIABILITIES & STOCKHOLDERS' DEFICIT

| | | | | |
|---|---|---|---|---|
| Current Liabilities: | | | | |
| Current Maturities of Long-Term Debt | 23,000 | | | 23,000 |
| Notes Payable | 6,226,000 | | | 6,226,000 |
| Accounts Payable-Pre | 2,435,000 | | | 2,435,000 |
| Post | 372,000 | | | 372,000 |
| Accrued Federal & State Income Taxes | 1,000 | | | 1,000 |
| Other Accrued Liabilities | 904,000 | | | 904,000 |
| Total Current Liabilities | 9,961,000 | | | 9,961,000 |
| Long-Term Debt-Bonds/SBA | 4,492,000 | 5) | 138,000 | 4,354,000 |
| Stockholders' Deficit: | | | | |
| Capital Stock | 400,000 | | | 400,000 |
| Deficit | (2,404,000) | 1) | 219,000 | (9,773,000) |
| | | 2) | 573,000 | |
| | | 3) | 10,000 | |
| | | 4) | 6,142,000 | |
| | | 6) | 416,000 | |
| | | 8) | 9,000 | |
| Total Stockholders' Deficit | (2,004,000) | | | (9,373,000) |
| TOTAL LIABILITIES & STOCKHOLDERS' DEFICIT | 12,449,000 | | | 4,942,000 |

LIQUIDATION ASSUMPTIONS:
1) Accounts Receivable converted at 90%
2) Inventory liquidated at 80%
3) Notes Receivable of $10,000 written off
4) Fixed assets sold for $596,000
5) Funds Held by Trustee applied to SBA Bond
6) Deferred Costs are worthless
7) Refundable Income Tax of $61,000 received
8) Deferred Expenses of $9,000 worthless

## EXHIBIT 12-2   BALANCE SHEET: PROFORMA REORGANIZATION

Balance Sheet
Proforma Reorganization
(000's omitted)

| | January 31 19X5 Consolidated | Adjustments Debits | Adjustments Credits | Reorganization Balance Sheet |
|---|---|---|---|---|
| *ASSETS:* | | | | |
| Cash | $ 3,549 | 5) 1,500<br>9) 100 | 3) 600<br>4) 2,150<br>6) 150<br>7) 250<br>8) 150 | $ 1,849 |
| Accounts Receivable (Net) | 5,628 | | | 5,628 |
| Inventory | 4,164 | | | 4,164 |
| Net Fixed Assets | 3,506 | | | 3,506 |
| Other Assets | 408 | | 10) 100 | 308 |
| Total | $17,255 | | | $15,455 |
| *LIABILITIES:* | | | | |
| Notes Payable—GECC | $ 6,871 | 7) 250 | 2) 2,345 | $ 8,966 |

| | | | | | |
|---|---|---|---|---|---|
| Notes Payable—C & S | 4,842 | 4) 4,842 | | | 0 |
| Accounts Payable—Unsecured | 5,820 | 3) 5,220 | | | 600 |
| Accounts Payable—Post Petition | 1,219 | | | | 1,219 |
| Other Liabilities | 136 | | | | 136 |
| Total Liabilities | 18,888 | | | | 10,921 |
| Net Worth | (1,633) | 2) 2,345<br>6) 150<br>8) 150 | | 3) 4,620<br>4) 2,692<br>5) 1,500 | 4,531 |
| Total | $17,255 | $14,557 | | $14,557 | $15,455 |

### Reorganization Adjustments

1. Prices assumed stable
2. GECC interest is accrued for period October 1, 19X2 through December 31, 19X4
3. Unsecured:
   a. Paid $600,000
   b. $4,620,000 as part of capital stock
4. C & S: Paid $2,150,000
5. Investment in Company of $1,500,000
6. EPA: $150,000 payment at settlement
7. Pay $250,000 to GECC
8. Additional Administrative Expense at closing, $200,000.
9. Fixed Assets at book value
10. Prepaid inventory will be changed to COD

## EXHIBIT 12-3 BALANCE SHEET: COMPARISON OF GOING CONCERN VALUES WITH LIQUIDATION VALUES

TGC Company, Inc. and Subsidiaries
Balance Sheet
Book Value-Historical Financials
April 30, 19X1

ASSETS:

CURRENT:

| | | |
|---|---:|---:|
| Cash | | $142,450 |
| Accounts Receivable (Net of | | |
| Allowance of $280,500) | $425,785 | |
| Inventories | $1,158,449 | |
| | $307,589 | |
| Prepaid Expenses | $23,244 | |
| TOTAL CURRENT ASSETS | | $2,057,517 |

LIABILITIES:

| | |
|---|---:|
| Current Maturities—Long-Term Debt | $17,725 |
| Current Maturities—Capital Leases | $29,154 |
| Notes Payable | $342,047 |
| Trade Accounts Payable | $983,882 |
| Floor Plan Payable | $307,589 |
| Salaries and Wages | $46,961 |
| Reserve For Warranty Claims | $175,800 |
| Interest | $29,333 |
| Taxes | $103,378 |

| | | |
|---|---|---|
| PROPERTY, PLANT & EQUIPMENT: | | |
| Land, Buildings & Leasehold Improvements | $1,267,457 | |
| Machinery & Equipment | $975,299 | |
| | $2,242,756 | |
| Accumulated Depreciation | ($1,116,538) | |
| | $1,126,218 | |
| OTHER | $1,568 | |
| TOTAL ASSETS | $3,185,303 | |

| | | |
|---|---|---|
| Long-Term Debt (Less Current Maturities) | | $55,263 |
| Long Term Capital Lease Obligations (Less Current Maturities) | | $78,317 |
| Deferred Tax Liability | | $550,321 |
| Note Payable-UAB Memphis Plus Interest | | $4,617,667 |
| Subordinated Capital Notes Plus Interest | | $1,477,776 |
| TOTAL LIABILITIES | | $8,815,213 |
| COMMON STOCK | | $1,450,000 |
| ACCUMULATED DEFICIT | | ($7,079,910) |
| TOTAL STOCKHOLDERS' DEFICIT | | ($5,629,910) |
| TOTAL LIABILITIES AND STOCKHOLDERS' DEFICIT | | $3,185,303 |

TGC Company, Inc. and Subsidiaries
Statement of Affairs
Book Value-Historical Financials
April 30, 19X1

| | Consolidated April 30, 19 | Encumbered Assets | Unencumbered Assets |
|---|---|---|---|
| ASSETS: | | | |
| Cash | $142,450 | $0 | $142,450 |
| Accounts Receivable (Net) | $425,785 | $425,785 | $0 |
| Inventory | $1,158,449 | $1,158,449 | $0 |
| | $307,589 | $307,589 | $0 |
| | $2,034,273 | | |
| PROPERTY PLANT & EQUIPMENT: | | | |
| Land Buildings & Leasehold | | | |
| Improvements | $1,267,457 | | |
| Machinery and Equipment | $975,299 | | |
| Accumulated Depreciation | ($1,116,538) | | |
| | $1,126,218 | $1,053,019 | $73,199 |
| OTHER | $24,812 | $0 | $24,812 |
| TOTAL | $3,185,303 | $2,944,842 | $240,461 |
| LESS: Secured Claims—Banks | | $4,840,008 | |
| —Floor Plan | | $307,589 | |

SECURED CLAIMS WHICH
BECOME UNSECURED                                    ($2,202,755)

LESS:
  Priority Claims                                                    $119,276
  Liquidation Expenses                                               $150,000

AVAILABLE FOR UNSECURED CLAIMS                                      ($28,815)

UNSECURED CLAIMS
Secured Which Has Become
  Unsecured                                                       $2,202,755
Other Bank Claims and
  Interest                                                          $329,333
Subordinated Capital Notes
  (Debentures) and Interest                                       $1,477,776
Trade Accounts Payable                                            $1,756,964

TOTAL UNSECURED CLAIMS                                            $5,766,828

TGC Company, Inc. and Subsidiaries
Statements of Going Concern Value and Estimated Liquidation Values
April 30, 19X1

| | Going Concern Value | ESTIMATED LIQUIDATION VALUES (ROUNDED) | | | |
|---|---|---|---|---|---|
| | | Liquidation Value | Encumbered Assets | Unencumbered Assets | Assumptions |
| ASSETS: | | | | | |
| Cash | $142,450 | $142,000 | $0 | $142,000 | 100% |
| Accounts Receivable (Net) | $425,785 | $213,000 | $213,000 | $0 | 50% |
| Inventories: | $1,158,449 | $579,000 | $579,000 | $0 | 50% |
| | $307,589 | $154,000 | $154,000 | $0 | 50% |
| Land, Buildings and Leasehold Improvements | $5,509,900 | $3,000,000 | $3,000,000 | $0 | 55% |
| Machinery and Equipment | $487,650 | $73,000 | $62,000 | $11,000 | 15% |
| Other | $24,812 | $10,000 | $0 | $10,000 | 40% |
| TOTAL | $8,056,635 | $4,171,000 | $4,008,000 | $163,000 | |
| LESS: Secured Claims—Banks | | | $4,840,008 | | |
|     —Floor Plan | | | $307,589 | | |

SECURED CLAIMS WHICH BECOME
UNSECURED                                                          ($1,139,597)

LESS:
Priority Claims                                                                      $119,276
Liquidation Expenses                                                                 $150,000

AVAILABLE FOR UNSECURED CLAIMS                                                       ($106,276)

UNSECURED CLAIMS:
Secured Which Has Become
Unsecured                                                                         $1,139,597
Other Bank Claims and Interest                                                      $329,333
Subordinated Capital Notes
(Debentures) and Interest                                                         $1,477,776
Accounts Payable                                                                  $1,756,964

TOTAL UNSECURED CLAIMS                                                             $4,703,670

PERCENTAGE PAID TO SECURED                                         78%

PERCENTAGE PAID TO UNSECURED                                                              0%

# EXHIBIT 12-4   BALANCE SHEET: GOING CONCERN VALUES

TTM COMPANY
Statement of Assets, Liabilities and Plan Equity (Deficiency)
February 28, 19X5

|  | Approximate Book Value | Estimated Market Value | Reference |
|---|---|---|---|
| **ASSETS** | | | |
| Cash, operating accounts | $     8,000 | $     8,000 | |
| Cash, disbursing agent account | 285,000 | 285,000 | Schedule A* |
| Anticipated cash proceeds from sale of Jones Street property | 511,000 | 511,000 | Schedule A* |
| Estimated earnings on cash through August 1, 1985 | 16,000 | 16,000 | |
| Trade accounts receivable | 352,000 | 352,000 | |
| Fixed assets, net of accumulated depreciation | 574,000 | 3,188,000 | Schedule B* |
| Total assets | 1,746,000 | 4,360,000 | |
| **LIABILITIES** | | | |
| Pre-petition claims, statutory interest and administrative expenses | 1,475,000 | 1,475,000 | Schedule C |
| Administrative trade creditors | 108,000 | 108,000 | |
| Secured claims | 457,000 | 457,000 | Schedule D* |
| Total liabilities | 2,040,000 | 2,040,000 | |
| PLAN EQUITY (DEFICIENCY) | ($   294,000) | $2,320,000 | |

*Schedules A, B and D are omitted

TTM COMPANY
Schedule of Pre-Petition Claims, Statutory Interest and Administrative Expenses
February 28, 19X5

| | Approximate Balance | Estimated Payment Effective Date of Proposed Plan | Unsecured Claims to be Paid Through Proposed Plan | Priority Claims to be Paid Through Proposed Plan | Claims to be Paid by the End of the Proposed Plan |
|---|---|---|---|---|---|
| Unsecured trade creditors | $ 336,000 | $161,000 | $175,000 (1) | $ — | $ — |
| Unsecured priority creditors | 32,000 | 1,000 | — | 31,000 (1) | — |
| Southern Railway claim—estimated | 58,000 | — | — | — | 58,000 |
| First Tennessee Bank—secured—note | 145,000 | — | — | — | 145,000 (3) |
| First Tennessee Bank—unsecured—note | 30,000 | 14,000 | 16,000 (2) | — | — |
| Internal Revenue Service—payroll taxes, penalties and interest—estimated | 349,000 | 349,000 | — | — | — |
| Internal Revenue Service—corporate taxes, penalties and interest—estimated | 61,000 | — | — | — | 61,000 (4) |
| State of Tennessee—secured priority—taxes, penalties and interest—estimated | 115,000 | — | — | 115,000 (1) | — |
| Statutory interest to be paid through proposed plan on allowed claims—estimated | 101,000 | — | 45,000 | 36,000 | 20,000 |
| Administrative expenses—estimated | 248,000 (5) | 248,000 | — | — | — |
| | $1,475,000 | $773,000 | $236,000 | $182,000 | $284,000 |

**Exhibit 12-4** Schedule of Pre-Petition Claims, Statutory Interest and Administrative Expenses (*continued*)

| | Approximate Balance | Estimated Payment Effective Date of Proposed Plan | Unsecured Claims to be Paid Through Proposed Plan | Priority Claims to be Paid Through Proposed Plan | Claims to be Paid by the End of the Proposed Plan |
|---|---|---|---|---|---|
| Summary of cash to be disbursed on effective date of plan: | | | | | |
| Cash, disbursing agent account | | $285,000 | | | |
| Anticipated cash proceeds from sale of Jones Street property | | 511,000 | | | |
| Estimated earnings on cash through August 1, 19X5 | | 16,000 | | | |
| Estimated total cash available | | 812,000 | | | |
| Less payments required to cure defaults under executory contracts or unsecured leases | | ( 39,000) | | | |
| Other amounts to be disbursed, as above | | $773,000 | | | |

NOTES

(1) Interest to be paid through the proposed plan at the estimated rate of 9.25% per annum.
(2) Interest is to be paid by the debtor from operating income at the rate of 12.5% per annum.
(3) Interest is to be paid by the debtor from operating income at the rate of 14.0% per annum.
(4) Interest is to be accrued through the proposed plan at the estimated rate of 11.0% per annum.
(5) Estimated administrative expenses include all fees and expenses for attorneys and accountants for the period May 21, 1984 through July 1, 1985.

# CHAPTER THIRTEEN

# Reporting on an Insolvent Company

---

**EXHIBIT 13-1  EXAMINATION REPORT FOR PROJECTED FINANCIAL STATEMENTS**

---

The Board of Directors
XYZ Technologies, Inc.

We have examined the accompanying projected income statement, balance sheet and statement of cash flow for XYZ Technologies, Inc. (the "Company") for the year ending December 31, 19X9, which projection hypothetically assumes that the Company will have sales of approximately 10,000 units of the ABC products at selling prices of $295 for Issue 3 ($275 selling price to distributors); and sales of approximately $2.2 million to Delta Communications. The projection also hypothetically assumes that the Company will be able to obtain new short term borrowings to meet expected cash needs during the projection period. There is no assurance that the Company will be able to obtain such new borrowings. Our examination was made in accordance with standards for an examination of a projection established by the American Institute of Certified Public Accountants and, accordingly, included such procedures as we considered necessary to evaluate both the assumptions used by management and the preparation and presentation of the projection.

The accompanying projection and this report were prepared for presentation to the Company's current lenders and should not be used for any other purpose.

In our opinion, the accompanying projection is presented in conformity with guidelines for presentation of a projection established by the American Institute of Certified Public Accountants, and the underlying assumptions as described in the summary of significant accounting policies and key assumptions underlying the projection provide a reasonable basis for management's projection. However, even if the hypothetical assumptions as described above occur there will usually be differences between the actual and projected results, because events and circumstances frequently do not occur as expected and those differences may be material. We have no responsibility to update this report for events and circumstances occurring after the date of this report.

CPA & Company
Date

Exhibit 13-2   Compilation Report                                439

## EXHIBIT 13-2   COMPILATION REPORT FOR PROJECTED FINANCIAL STATEMENTS

Date

XYZ Partners (an Illinois limited partnership)
Debtor in Possession

We have compiled the accompanying projected financial statements of XYZ Partners ("Partnership"), which consist of the following presentations for the calendar years 1989 through 1995 and for the three months ending March 31, 1996:

Notes and Assumptions Underlying Projections;
Projected Statements of Taxable Income (Loss) Prepared on the Income Tax Basis of Accounting;
Projected Statements of Cash Flows; and
Projected Statement of Capital Contributions, Ordinary Income (Loss) From Real Estate Rental Activities, Cancellation of Indebtedness Income, and Gain on Termination of Partnership Interest for a Class A Limited Partner Who Invested Pre-Petition Capital of $36,000 in the Partnership and Who Elects Not to Contribute Additional Post-Petition Capital to the Partnership, With Historical Information Presented For Years Prior to 1989.

The Partnership became the subject of a voluntary proceeding for reorganization under Chapter 11 of the United States Bankruptcy Code ("Bankruptcy Code") on April ___, 1988. Accordingly, pre-petition obligations of the Partnership (including those arising under agreements entered into prior to the commencement of the Chapter 11 proceeding) are subject to adjustment and modification pursuant to the Bankruptcy Code.

The Partnership filed a Plan of Reorganization ("Plan") in the United States Bankruptcy Court for the Northern District of Illinois, Eastern Division ("Court") on March _____, 1989. The aforementioned projections are prepared on the assumption that the Plan will be confirmed by the Court as filed. The confirmation of the Plan is subject to a vote of creditors and is contingent upon the Plan's satisfaction of certain provisions of the Bankruptcy Code.

The accompanying projections, prepared on the income tax basis of accounting as described in Note 5, are not intended to present the overall projected financial position, results of operations, and cash flows in the projection period in conformity with guidelines for presentation of a projection established by the American Institute of Certified Public Accountants. The projections and this report are prepared solely for purposes of their use as exhibits to the disclosure statement of the Partnership with respect to its Plan, and any other use without the prior written consent of CPA & Company is prohibited.

A compilation is limited to presenting projected financial information that is the representation of management and does not include evaluation of the support for the assumptions underlying the projected information. We have not audited the projected information (or the historical information presented for years prior to 1989) and, accordingly, do not express an opinion or any other form of assurance on the accompanying projections, assumptions, or historical information. Furthermore, even if the Plan is confirmed by the Court and consummated in accordance with the described provisions, the reader can expect that there will be differences between the projected and actual results, because events and circumstances frequently do not occur as expected, and those differences may be material. We have no responsibility to update this report for events or circumstances occurring after the date of this report.

We have not audited, reviewed or compiled the historical information included for years prior to 1989; accordingly we do not express an opinion or any other form of assurance on said information.

Under section 10.33 of the Treasury regulations, prospective financial statements that are predicated upon assumptions regarding the federal tax aspects of an investment may be construed as a "tax shelter opinion". The regulations require that the practitioner issuing a tax shelter opinion provide, where possible, (1) an opinion on each material tax issue with respect to the investment, and (2) an overall evaluation of whether the material tax benefits in the aggregate more likely than not will be realized. If not possible, the practitioner is required to state the reasons preventing the rendering of such an opinion and evaluation. However, section 1125(e) of the Bankruptcy Code provides that a person, acting in good faith and in compliance with the applicable provisions of the Bankruptcy Code, who (1) solicits acceptance or rejection of a plan or (2) participates in the offer, issuance, sale, or purchase of a security offered or sold under the plan, is not liable for violation of any applicable law, rule, or regulation governing solicitation of acceptance or rejection of a plan for the offer, issuance, sale, or purchase of securities. Pursuant to its order dated February ___, 1989, the Court has held that this compilation report is not governed by section 10.33 of the Treasury Regulations nor is this compilation report to be construed as a "tax shelter opinion" pursuant to such regulations. Insofar as the discussion of federal tax matters included as Note 11 to the accompanying projections contains a discussion significantly less in scope than would be required under the standards of Treasury regulation section 10.33, each limited partner and prospective limited partner in the Partnership is urged to consult his or her personal tax advisor as to the tax considerations of the Partnership's Plan.

CPA & Company

Exhibit 13-3   Report Issued Where Client Uses Computer                    **441**

## EXHIBIT 13-3   REPORT ISSUED WHERE CLIENT USES COMPUTER TO PROCESS CLIENT'S DATA

(Note: The following report is an illustration of the type of report that might be issued when the CPA has been requested to process data supplied by client on CPA's microcomputer and utilize CPA's software for the purpose of producing prospective financial statements. So that the specified users agree on the procedures, as required by the Statement, the CPA would issue this report in draft requiring that the users let us know whether the procedures are adequate for their use.)

### DRAFT

Based on our discussions with management, it is our understanding that the procedures outlined in this draft letter are the ones that certain specified users wish us to follow. Unless the specified users inform us otherwise, we shall assume there are no other additional procedures that such users wish us to follow.

ABC Trustee
XYZ Company

At your request, we have performed the agreed-upon procedures enumerated below with respect to the accompanying forecasted balance sheet, statements of income, retained earnings, and cash flows of XYZ Company as of December 31, 1989, and for the year then ending. These procedures, which were specified by ABC Trustee and XYZ Company, were performed solely to assist you, and this report is solely for your information and should not be used by those who did not participate in determining the procedures. We make no representations as to the sufficiency of these procedures for your purposes.

The agreed-upon procedures that we performed were as follows:

- We assisted the management of XYZ Company in assembling the prospective financial statements by entering data provided by XYZ Company into our computer and using our model to generate a forecasted balance sheet and statements of income, retained earnings, and cash flows.

Because the procedures described above do not constitute an examination of prospective financial statements in accordance with standards established by the American Institute of Certified Public Accountants (AICPA), we do not express an opinion on whether the prospective financial statements are presented in conformity with AICPA presentation guidelines or on whether the underlying assumptions provide a reasonable basis for the presentation.

Had we performed additional procedures or had we made an examination of the forecast in accordance with standards established by the AICPA, matters might have come to our attention that would have been reported to you. Furthermore, there will usually be differences between the forecasted and actual results, because events and circumstances frequently do not occur as expected, and those differences may be material. We have no responsibility to update this report for events and circumstances occurring after the date of this report.

CPA & Company
Date

Exhibit 13-4    Disclaimer of Opinion                                                    443

## EXHIBIT 13-4    DISCLAIMER OF OPINION ON PROJECTED FINANCIAL STATEMENTS

To the Board of Directors of
   XYZ, Inc.

We have examined the projected balance sheet, statement of income, and cash flows of XYZ, Inc. as of and for each of the six fiscal years in the period ended May 31, 19X6 (the projected statements), included in the XYZ, Inc. Five Year Business Plan dated April 4, 19X1, which have been prepared based on the assumptions included therein. Except as explained in the fourth paragraph, our examination was made in accordance with standards for an examination of a financial projection established by the American Institute of Certified Public Accountants and, accordingly, included such procedures as we considered necessary to evaluate both the assumptions used by management and the preparation and presentation of the projection.

The accompanying projection and this report were prepared to communicate the Company's Five Year Business Plan to the unsecured Creditors' Committee XYZ, Inc. bankruptcy case in connection with the Company's efforts to develop a plan of reorganization. They should not be used for any other purpose.

The projected statements do not include information regarding provisions or credits for income taxes or net earnings and earnings per share, which are required for prospective financial statements in the guidelines established by the American Institute of Certified Public Accountants. If the omitted information were included in the projected statements, it might influence the users' conclusions about the XYZ, Inc. projected financial position, results of operations and cash flow for the plan periods. Accordingly, this presentation is not designed for those who are not informed about such matters.

As noted in the projected statements, management has assumed that XYZ, Inc. will implement a plan of reorganization and emerge from bankruptcy during the first quarter of fiscal 19X3. However, management believes that there is no reasonable basis, at this time, upon which to formulate assumptions regarding the form and effects of a plan of reorganization. Accordingly, management has not made any assumptions in the projected statements to reflect the effects of a plan of reorganization, except that certain expenses related to the bankruptcy process have been assumed to cease as of the first quarter of fiscal 19X3. The effects that a plan of reorganization and the related tax implications will have on the historical carrying values of assets and liabilities and the capital structure of a reorganized entity could be material. Further, should XYZ, Inc. not emerge, as assumed, from bankruptcy in the first quarter of fiscal 19X3, additional bankruptcy expenses would be incurred in fiscal 19X3 and until such time as XYZ would emerge from bankruptcy protection. Those expenses could significantly affect XYZ's projected results of operations and cash flows. We were, therefore, unable to obtain suitable support for assumptions related to these matters.

As described in the preceding paragraph, because of the significance of the assumptions related to the implementation of an approved plan of reorganization and its effects on the projected statements, we are unable to and do not express an opinion with respect to the basis for the underlying assumptions. We have no responsibility to update this report for events and circumstances occurring after the date of this report.

CPA & Company
Date

Exhibit 13-5   Internal Use Only Report                                          445

## EXHIBIT 13-5   INTERNAL USE ONLY REPORT ON PROJECTED FINANCIAL STATEMENTS

To Mr. John Jones, President
XYZ Company

We have assembled, from information provided by management, the accompanying projected balance sheet, statements of income, retained earnings, and cash flows and summaries of significant assumptions and accounting policies of XYZ Company as of December 31, 19XX, and for the year then ending. (This financial projection omits the summary of significant accounting policies.)[1] The accompanying projection and this report were prepared for presentation to the Board of Directors of XYZ Company for its considerations as to whether to reduce the retail outlets to forty stores and should not be used for any other purpose. We have not compiled or examined the financial projection and express no assurance of any kind on it. Further, even if the retail outlets are reduced to forty there will usually be differences between the projected and actual results because events and circumstances frequently do not occur as expected, and those differences may be material. In accordance with the terms of our engagement, this report and the accompanying projection are restricted to internal use and may not be shown to any third party for any purpose.

February 14, 19XX

---

[1] This sentence would be included, if applicable.

**EXHIBIT 13-6   REPORT FOR AGREED-UPON PROCEDURES RELATING TO LEVERAGED BUYOUT TRANSACTION**

The staff of the AICPA's Audit Standards' Division issued an Auditing Interpretation (AU Section 2012, May, 1988) that precludes the CPA from providing any form of assurance through examination, review or agreed-upon procedures engagements that an entity is not solvent or would not become insolvent as a result of the issuance of debt, does not have unreasonably small capital, or has the ability to pay its debts as they mature. The interpretation includes the following type of report which the CPA could issue.

**Illustrative Agreed-Upon Procedures Report (Leveraged Buyout Transaction)**

March 24, 19X2

XYZ Bank and ABC Corporation:

This report is furnished at the request of XYZ Bank and ABC Corporation pursuant to the Credit Agreement dated as of March 24, 19X2 (the "Credit Agreement"), between ABC Corporation (the borrower) and XYZ Bank (the lender) in connection with the financing transaction set forth therein.

The sufficiency of the agreed-upon procedures we have been requested to perform, as set forth in subsequent paragraphs of this report, is the sole responsibility of the borrower and lender. Consequently, we make no representation regarding the sufficiency of the procedures described below either for the purposes for which this report has been requested or for any other purpose. Further, we make no representations regarding questions of legal interpretation, nor do we provide any assurance as to any matters relating to the borrower's solvency, adequacy of capital or ability to pay its debts. The agreed-upon procedures described below should not be taken to supplant any additional inquiries and procedures that the lender should undertake in its consideration of the proposed financing transaction contemplated by the Credit Agreement.

We have previously audited the consolidated balance sheet of the borrower as of December 31, 19X1, and the related consolidated statements of income, stockholders' equity and cash flow for the year then ended, and have rendered our unqualified report thereon dated February 27, 19X2. We have not audited any financial statements of the borrower as of any date or for any period subsequent to December 31, 19X1.

As requested, we have performed the following agreed-upon procedures as of and for the periods set forth below (our procedures did not extend to the period from March 21, 19X2, to March 24, 19X2, inclusive):

1. We have read the minutes of the 19X2 meetings of the stockholders and board of directors of the borrower as set forth in the minute books at March 20, 19X2, officials of the borrower having advised us that the minutes of all such meetings through that date were set forth therein.

**Exhibit 13-6    Report for Agreed-Upon Procedures**                                    **447**

2. We have read the accompanying unaudited consolidated financial statements of the borrower as of February 28, 19X2, and for the two-month period then ended, officials of the borrower having advised us that no financial statements as of any date or for any period subsequent to February 28, 19X2, were available.

3. We have made inquiries of certain officials of the borrower who have responsibility for financial and accounting matters regarding whether

a. The unaudited consolidated financial statements referred to above are in conformity with generally accepted accounting principles applied on a basis substantially consistent with that of the December 31, 19X1, audited consolidated financial statements.

b. At March 20, 19X2, there was any decrease in consolidated net assets or consolidated net current assets as compared with the amounts shown in the February 28, 19X2, unaudited consolidated balance sheet.

Based on the results of the procedures described in steps 1 through 3, above, nothing came to our attention that caused us to believe that the February 28, 19X2, financial statements are not in conformity with generally accepted accounting principles applied on a basis substantially consistent with that of the December 31, 19X1, audited financial statements or that, at March 20, 19X2, there was any decrease in consolidated net assets or consolidated net current assets as compared with the amounts shown on the February 28, 19X2, unaudited consolidated balance sheet.

4. With respect to the accompanying unaudited pro forma consolidated balance sheet as of February 28, 19X2,[1] which has been prepared on the basis set forth in the notes and assumptions thereto, we have

a. Read the unaudited pro forma consolidated balance sheet and supporting notes and assumptions.

b. Made inquiries of certain officials of the borrower who have responsibility for financial and accounting matters as to whether all adjustments necessary to present the unaudited pro forma consolidated balance sheet in accordance with the basis set forth in the notes thereto have been made.

c. Discussed with certain officials of the borrower their assumptions regarding the effects of the transaction set forth in the notes to the unaudited pro forma consolidated balance sheet.

d. Compared the amounts shown in the unaudited consolidated balance sheet of the borrower at February 28, 19X2, and in the unaudited pro forma consolidated balance sheet to the corresponding amounts shown on worksheets prepared by the borrower and found them to be in agreement; tested the mathematical accuracy of such worksheets.

Based on the results of the procedures described in 4a-d, above, no matters came to our attention that caused us to believe that the unaudited pro forma consolidated balance sheet does not reflect the proper application of the pro forma adjustments to the historical unaudited consolidated balance sheet.

---

[1] For example, this presentation might reflect a *business combination* accounted for as a purchase under Accounting Principles Board Opinion No. 16, *Business Combinations*.

5. With respect to the accompanying forecasted statement of consolidated cash flows for the three years ending December 31, 19X4, (the forecast), prepared by the borrower, we have

a. Read the forecast for compliance in regard to format with the preparation guidelines established by the American Institute of Certified Public Accountants (AICPA) for presentation of a forecast.

b. Tested the mathematical accuracy of the forecast.

Based on the results of the procedures referred to in steps 5a-b, no matters came to our attention to cause us to believe that the format of the forecast should be modified or that the forecast is mathematically inaccurate.

Because the foregoing procedures in steps 1–4 do not constitute an audit made in accordance with generally accepted auditing standards or an examination made in accordance with attestation standards established by the AICPA, we do not express an opinion on the February 28, 19X2, unaudited historical consolidated financial statements or unaudited pro forma consolidated balance sheet. Because the procedures described in steps 1 and 5a-b above do not constitute an examination of prospective financial statements in accordance with standards established by the AICPA, we do not express an opinion on whether the forecase referred to above is presented in conformity with AICPA presentation guidelines or on whether the underlying assumptions provide a reasonable basis for the presentation. Furthermore, there will usually be differences between the forecasted and actual results, because events and circumstances frequently do not occur as expected, and those differences may be material.

Had we performed additional procedures or had we audited the borrower's February 28, 19X2, consolidated financial statements in accordance with generally accepted auditing standards or had we examined the borrower's unaudited pro forma consolidated balance sheet or the forecast in accordance with standards established by the AICPA, other matters might have come to our attention that would have been reported to you.

This report is intended solely for use by the borrower and the lender in connection with the loan contemplated under the Credit Agreement and is not to be otherwise used, circulated, quoted or referred to by the borrower or the lender and should not be used by any party who did not participate in determining the foregoing procedures.

We have no responsibility to update this report for events and circumstances occurring after March 20, 19X2.

## PART FIVE

# Taxes

# Tax Awareness

## EXHIBIT 14-1    IRS, FORM 1041

| | |
|---|---|
| Form **1041**<br>Department of the Treasury<br>Internal Revenue Service | **U.S. Fiduciary Income Tax Return**<br>For the calendar year 1988 or fiscal year<br>beginning _____ , 1988, and ending _____ , 19 ___ |

OMB No. 1545

198

**Check applicable boxes:**
- ☐ Decedent's estate
- ☐ Simple trust
- ☐ Complex trust
- ☐ Grantor type trust
- ☐ Bankruptcy estate
- ☐ Family estate trust
- ☐ Pooled income fund
- ☐ Initial return
- ☐ Amended return
- ☐ Final return

Name of estate or trust (grantor type trust, see instructions)

Name and title of fiduciary

Address of fiduciary (number and street or P.O. Box)

City, state, and ZIP code

Number of Schedules K-1 attached *(See instructions)* . . . ▶

**Employer identification number**

**Date entity created**

Nonexempt charitable and split- trusts, check applicable boxes (s instructions):
- ☐ Described in section 4947(a
- ☐ Not a private foundation
- ☐ Described in section 4947(a

### Income

| | | |
|---|---|---|
| 1 | Dividends . . . . . . . . . . . . . . . . . . | 1 |
| 2 | Interest income . . . . . . . . . . . . . . . | 2 |
| 3 | Income (or losses) from partnerships, other estates or other trusts (see instructions) . . . | 3 |
| 4 | Net rent and royalty income (or loss) (attach Schedule E (Form 1040)). | 4 |
| 5 | Net business and farm income (or loss) (attach Schedules C and F (Form 1040)) | 5 |
| 6 | Capital gain (or loss) (attach Schedule D (Form 1041)) . . . . . | 6 |
| 7 | Ordinary gain (or loss) (attach Form 4797) . . . . . . . . | 7 |
| 8 | Other income (state nature of income) _____ . . . ▶ | 8 |
| 9 | **Total** income (add lines 1 through 8) . . . . . . . . . | 9 |

### Deductions

| | | |
|---|---|---|
| 10 | Interest . . . . . . . . . . . . . . . | 10 |
| 11 | Taxes . . . . . . . . . . . . . . . . | 11 |
| 12 | Fiduciary fees . . . . . . . . . . . . . | 12 |
| 13 | Charitable deduction (from Schedule A, line 6) . . . | 13 |
| 14 | Attorney, accountant, and return preparer fees . . . | 14 |
| 15 | Other deductions (attach schedule) . . . . . . . | 15 |
| 16 | **Total** (add lines 10 through 15) . . . . . . . . . ▶ | 16 |
| 17 | Adjusted total income (or loss) (subtract line 16 from line 9) . . . . . . | 17 |
| 18 | Income distribution deduction (from Schedule B, line 17) (see instructions) (attach Schedule K-1 (Form 1041)) | 18 |
| 19 | Estate tax deduction (including generation-skipping transfer taxes) (attach computation) | 19 |
| 20 | Exemption . . . . . . . . . . . . . . . . | 20 |
| 21 | **Total** (add lines 18 through 20) . . . . . . . . . . ▶ | 21 |
| 22 | Taxable income of fiduciary (subtract line 21 from line 17) . . . . . . . ▶ | 22 |

### Tax and Payments

| | | |
|---|---|---|
| 23 | Total tax (enter amount from line 7, Schedule G) . . . . . . . . . | 23 |
| 24a | Payments: 1988 estimated tax payments and amount applied from 1987 return | 24a |
| b | Treated as paid by trust beneficiaries (attach Form 1041-T) | 24b |
| c | Subtract line 24b from line 24a . . . . . . . | 24c |
| d | Tax paid with extension of time to file ☐ Form 8736 ☐ Form 8800 ☐ Form 2758 . | 24d |
| e | Federal income tax withheld . . . . . . . . . . . . . | 24e |
| | Credits: | |
| f | Form 2439 _____ ; **g** Form 4136 _____ ; **h** Form 6249 _____ ; Total . | 24i |
| 25 | **Total** (add lines 24c through 24e, and 24i) . . . . . . . . . ▶ | 25 |
| 26 | If line 23 is larger than line 25, enter **TAX DUE** . . . . . . . | 26 |
| 27 | If line 25 is larger than line 23, enter **OVERPAYMENT** . . . . . . | 27 |
| 28 | Amount of line 27 to be: **a** Credited to 1989 estimated tax ▶ _____ ; **b** Refunded . ▶ | 28 |
| 29 | **Penalty** for underpayment of estimated tax. Check ☐ If Form 2210 (Form 2210F) is attached. . . | 29 |

**Please Sign Here**

Under penalties of perjury, I declare that I have examined this return, including accompanying schedules and statements, and to the best of my knowled belief, it is true, correct, and complete. Declaration of preparer (other than fiduciary) is based on all information of which preparer has any knowledge.

▶ _____

Signature of fiduciary or officer representing fiduciary    Date

▶ _____ Date

EIN of fiduciary *(see instructions)*

**Paid Preparer's Use Only**

| | | | |
|---|---|---|---|
| Preparer's signature ▶ | | Date | Check if self-employed ▶ ☐ |
| Firm's name (or yours if self-employed) and address ▶ | | E.I. No. ▶<br>ZIP code ▶ | Preparer's social securit |

Exhibit 14-2   IRS, Form 982

453

# EXHIBIT 14-2   IRS, FORM 982

| Form **982** (Rev. December 1986)<br>Department of the Treasury<br>Internal Revenue Service | **Reduction of Tax Attributes Due to Discharge of Indebtedness**<br>**(Also, Section 1082 Basis Adjustment)**<br>▶ Attach this form to your income tax return. | OMB No. 1545-0046<br>Expires 11-30-89<br><br>Attachment<br>Sequence No. **51** |
|---|---|---|

| Name | Identifying number (SSN or EIN) |
|---|---|

### Part I   General Information

**1** Amount excluded is due to (check applicable box(es)):

  **a** Discharge of indebtedness in a title 11 case . . . . . . . . . . . . . . . . . . . . . . . . . . ☐

  **b** Discharge of indebtedness to the extent insolvent (not in a title 11 case) . . . . . . . . . . . . . . ☐

  **c** Discharge of "qualified business indebtedness" occurring before January 1, 1987 (not in a title 11 case nor to the extent the taxpayer is insolvent) . . . . . . . . . . . . . . . . . . . . . . . . . . . . . . . . . . . ☐

  **d** Discharge of "qualified farm indebtedness" (See instructions for line 1d before completing Part II) . . . . . ☐

**2** Total amount of discharged indebtedness excluded from gross income . . . . . . . . . . **2**

**3** Do you elect to treat all real property described in section 1221(1), relating to property held for sale to customers in the ordinary course of a trade or business, as if it were depreciable property? . . . . . . . . . ☐ Yes ☐ No

### Part II   Reduction of Tax Attributes

Note: *You must attach a description of the transactions resulting in the reduction in basis under section 1017.*

**Enter amount excluded from gross income:**

**4** Under 1a and/or 1b which you elect to apply first to reduce the basis (under section 1017) of depreciable property . . . . . . . . . . . . . . . . . . . . . . . . . . . . . . **4**

**5** Applied to reduce any net operating loss which occurred in the tax year of the discharge or carried over to the tax year of the discharge . . . . . . . . . . . . . . . . . . . . . . **5**

**6** Applied to reduce certain credit carryovers comprising the general business credit to or from the tax year of the discharge . . . . . . . . . . . . . . . . . . . . . . . . . . **6**

**7** Applied to reduce any net capital loss for the taxable year of the discharge including any capital loss carryovers to the tax year of discharge . . . . . . . . . . . . . . . . . . . . **7**

**8** Applied to reduce the basis of nondepreciable assets and depreciable assets if not reduced on line 4 except in the case of discharge of qualified farm indebtedness . . . . . . . . . . . . . **8**

**9** Applied to reduce any carryover to or from the taxable year of the discharge for determining the foreign tax credit . . . . . . . . . . . . . . . . . . . . . . . . . . . . **9**

**10** Which you elect to treat as qualified business indebtedness and apply to reduce the basis of depreciable property . . . . . . . . . . . . . . . . . . . . . . . . . . . . . **10**

**11** For discharge of qualified farm indebtedness, applied to reduce the basis of property other than the basis of land used or held for use in the trade or business of farming . . . . . . . . . . . . **11**

**12** For discharge of qualified farm indebtedness, applied to reduce the basis of land used or held for use in the trade or business of farming . . . . . . . . . . . . . . . . . . . . . **12**

### Part III   Consent of Corporation to Adjustment of Basis of its Property Under Section 1082(a)(2) of the Internal Revenue Code

The corporation named above has excluded under section 1081(b) of the Internal Revenue Code $ _____

from its gross income for the tax year beginning _____, and ending _____

Under that section the corporation consents to have the basis of its property adjusted in accordance with the regulations prescribed under section 1082(a)(2) of the Internal Revenue Code in effect at the time of filing its income tax return for that year. The corporation is

organized under the laws of _____
(State of incorporation)

Note: *You must attach a description of the transactions resulting in the nonrecognition of gain under section 1081.*

### Signature

Under penalties of perjury, I declare that I have examined this form, including accompanying schedules and statements, and to the best of my knowledge and belief, it is true, correct, and complete.

_____      _____
(Signature—if individual taxpayer)      (Date)

_____   _____   _____
(Signature of officer—if corporate taxpayer)   (Title)   (Date)

# General Instructions

*(Section references are to the Internal Revenue Code unless otherwise noted.)*

**Paperwork Reduction Act Notice.—** We ask for this information to carry out the Internal Revenue laws of the United States. We need it to ensure that taxpayers are complying with these laws and to allow us to figure and collect the right amount of tax. You are required to give us this information.

**Changes You Should Note.—**

● Discharges of qualified business indebtedness that occur after December 31, 1986 (other than discharges that occur when a taxpayer is insolvent or in a title 11 case) will result in the current recognition of income in the amount of the discharge. In these situations, taxpayers cannot elect to exclude the amount of the discharge from gross income.

● Certain solvent farmers will be treated as insolvent for discharges of qualified farm indebtedness owed to an unrelated lender. This rule applies to discharges occurring after April 9, 1986, in tax years ending after that date. See the instructions for line 1d and section 108(g) for additional information.

**Purpose of Form.—** Generally, a discharge of indebtedness is included in your gross income. However, if the discharge occurred in one of the situations described below, you may be able to exclude the amount from your gross income. Use Form 982 for this purpose.

Use Parts I and II to report amounts you are excluding from income because they are due to:

● Discharge of indebtedness in a title 11 case;

● Discharge of indebtedness to the extent insolvent (not in a title 11 case);

● Discharge of "qualified business indebtedness" occurring before January 1, 1987 (not in a title 11 case nor to the extent insolvent); or

● Discharge of "qualified farm indebtedness" occurring after April 9, 1986, in tax years ending after that date.

Use Part III to exclude from gross income under section 1081(b) any amounts of income attributable to the transfer of property described in that section.

**When To File.—** File Form 982 with your original income tax return for the tax year in which the discharge of indebtedness was obtained or the transfer of property occurred. If you fail to file this form with your original return, you must file it with an amended return or claim for credit or refund if the discharge of indebtedness occurred in a title 11 case, involved qualified farm indebtedness, or occurred to the extent you were insolvent.

You must establish reasonable cause for not making the applicable elections on this form with your original return before you are entitled to make them with an amended return or claim for credit or refund. These elections include the section 1017(b)(3)(E)

election to treat certain inventory as depreciable property (line 3), the section 108(b)(5) election to reduce basis ahead of other tax attributes (not applicable to qualified farm indebtedness) (line 4), and the election to reduce the basis of depreciable property under section 108(d)(4) for a qualified business indebtedness (line 10).

# Specific Instructions

## Part I

**Lines 1a and 1b.—** If you checked line 1a and/or line 1b (but not line 1c), you may elect, by completing line 4, to apply all or a portion of the debt discharge amount to first reduce the basis in depreciable property (including property you elected on line 3 to treat as depreciable property). Any balance of the debt discharge amount will then be applied to reduce the tax attributes in the order listed on lines 5–9. Do not complete line 10. You must attach a statement describing the transactions which resulted in the reduction in basis and identifying the property of which the basis was reduced. If you do not make the election on line 4, go directly to lines 5–9 to reduce your attributes. See section 1017(b)(2) and (c) for limitations of reductions in basis on line 8.

**Line 1c.— Qualified business indebtedness** is the amount of indebtedness that was incurred or assumed either:

(1) By a corporation, or

(2) By an individual in connection with property used in the individual's trade or business. Also, you must make an election under section 108 with respect to the indebtedness. If the discharge amount exceeds the basis available for reduction with respect to qualified business indebtedness, the excess must be included in gross income.

If you checked only line 1c, you may elect, by completing line 10, to exclude the debt discharge amount and reduce your basis in depreciable property (including property you elected on line 3). Do not complete lines 4–9.

You must attach a statement describing the transactions which resulted in the reduction in basis and identifying the property of which the basis was reduced.

For more information, see **Publication 908**, Bankruptcy.

**Line 1d.— Qualified farm indebtedness** is the amount of indebtedness incurred directly in connection with the trade or business of farming. Among the other provisions is a requirement that 50% or more of the average annual gross receipts of the taxpayer for the 3 tax years preceding the tax year in which the discharge of indebtedness occurs be attributable to the trade or business of farming. Additional rules will be provided in a forthcoming revenue ruling.

If you checked line 1d, the debt discharge amount will be applied to reduce the tax attributes in the order listed on lines 5, 6, 7, and 9. Any remaining amount will be applied first to reduce the basis of property other than the basis of land used or held for use in the trade or business of farming (line 11), and then to reduce the basis of land used or held for use in the trade or business of farming (line 12).

**Line 2.—** Enter the total amount excluded from your gross income due to discharge of indebtedness under sections 108 and 1017. If you checked line 1a, 1b, and/or 1d, this amount will not necessarily equal the total reductions on lines 4–9 because the debt discharge amount may exceed the total tax attributes.

**Line 3.—** You may elect to treat all real property held as inventory in a trade or business as if it were depreciable property. You make the election by checking the "Yes" box on this line.

## Part II

**Line 6.—** If you use **Form 3800**, General Business Credit, you must refigure the amount of the carryover to be claimed without including the ESOP credit. If you do not use Form 3800, you may arrive at the total credit by combining the carryovers from the following forms:

● **Form 3468**, Computation of Investment Credit;

● **Form 5884**, Jobs Credit;

● **Form 6478**, Credit for Alcohol Used As Fuel;

● **Form 6765**, Credit for Increasing Research Activities (or for claiming the orphan drug credit); and

● **Form 8586**, Low-Income Housing Credit.

## Part III

**Adjustment to Basis.—** Unless it specifically states otherwise, the corporation, by filing this form, agrees to have the general rule for adjusting the basis of property (as described in regulations section 1.1082-3(b)) applied.

If the corporation desires to have the basis of its property adjusted in a manner different from the general rule, it must attach a request for variation from the general rule. The request must show the precise method used and the allocation of amounts.

Consent to the request for variation from the general rule will be effective only if incorporated in a closing agreement entered into by the corporation and the Commissioner of Internal Revenue under the provisions of section 7121. If no agreement is entered into, then the general rule will apply in the determination of the basis of the corporation's property.

**Signature.—** Form 982 must be signed by the taxpayer. If the taxpayer is a corporation, this form must be signed either by the president, vice president, treasurer, assistant treasurer, chief accounting officer, or by any other corporate officer (such as tax officer) who is authorized to sign. A receiver, trustee, or assignee must sign any form that is required to be filed on behalf of a corporation.

# OFFICIAL FORMS

# OFFICIAL FORM NO. 1

## Form 1. Voluntary Petition (Official Form No. 1)

## UNITED STATES BANKRUPTCY COURT FOR THE
## ———— DISTRICT OF ——————

### In re

————————————————,
Debtor [set forth here all names
including trade names used by
Debtor within last 6 years].
Social Security No.————————
and Debtor's Employer's Tax
Identification No.————————

Case No.————————

### Voluntary Petition

1. Petitioner's mailing address, including county, is ————————

2. Petitioner has resided [*or* has been domiciled *or* Petitioner's principal place of business has been *or* the principal assets of the petitioner have been] within this district for the preceding 180 days [*or* for a longer portion of the preceding 180 days than in any other district].

3. Petitioner is qualified to file this petition and is entitled to the benefits of title 11, United States Code as a voluntary debtor.

4. [*If appropriate*] A copy of petitioner's proposed plan, dated ————————, is attached [or Petitioner intends to file a plan pursuant to chapter 11 *or* chapter 13] of title 11, United States Code.

5. [*If petitioner is a corporation*] Exhibit "A" is attached to and made part of this petition.

6. [*If petitioner is an individual whose debts are primarily consumer debts.*] Petitioner is aware that [*he or she*] may proceed under chapter 7, 11, 12, or 13 of title 11, United States Code, understands the relief available under each such chapter, and chooses to proceed under chapter 7 of such title.

7. [*If petitioner is an individual whose debts are primarily consumer debts and such petitioner is represented by an attorney.*] A declaration or an affidavit in the form of Exhibit "B" is attached to and made a part of this petition.

WHEREFORE, petitioner prays for relief in accordance with chapter 7 [*or* chapter 11 *or* chapter 13] of title 11, United States Code.

Signed: _____,
*Attorney for Petitioner*

Address: _____,
_____

[*Petitioner signs if not represented by attorney.*]
_____,
*Petitioner.*

I, _____ , the petitioner named in the foregoing petition, declare under penalty of perjury that the foregoing is true and correct.
Executed on _____

Signature: _____
*Petitioner.*

**Exhibit "A"**

[*If petitioner is a corporation, this Exhibit "A" shall be completed and attached to the petition pursuant to paragraph 5 thereof.*]

[*Caption as in Form No. 1*]

FOR COURT USE ONLY
_____
Date Petition Filed
_____
Case Number
_____
Bankruptcy Judge

1. Petitioner's employer identification number is \_\_\_\_\_
2. If any of petitioner's securities are registered under section 12 of the Securities and Exchange Act of 1934, SEC file number is \_\_\_\_\_
3. The following financial data is the latest available information and refers to petitioner's condition on \_\_\_\_\_
   a. Total assets:         $_____
   b. Total liabilities:    $_____

|                                                  |            | Approximate number of holders |
|--------------------------------------------------|------------|-------------------------------|
| Secured debt, excluding that listed below        | $\_\_\_\_  | _____                   |
| Debt securities held by more than 100 holders    | $\_\_\_\_  | _____                   |
| Secured                                          | $\_\_\_\_  | _____                   |
| Unsecured                                        | $\_\_\_\_  | _____                   |
| Other liabilities, excluding contingent or unliquidated claims | $\_\_\_\_ | _____ |
| Number of shares of common stock                 | $\_\_\_\_  | _____                   |

Comments, if any: _____

4.  Brief description of petitioner's business: _____

5.  *[If presently available, supply the following information]* The name of any person who directly or indirectly owns, controls, or holds, with power to vote, 20% or more of the voting securities of petitioner is _____

6.  *[If presently available, supply the following information]* The names of all corporations 20% or more of the outstanding voting securities of which are directly or indirectly owned, controlled, or held, with power to vote, by petitioner are _____

### Exhibit "B"

[If petitioner is an individual whose debts are primarily consumer debts, this Exhibit "B" shall be completed and attached to the petition pursuant to paragraph (7) thereof].

*[Caption as in Form No. 1]*

FOR COURT USE ONLY.

_____

Date Petition Filed

_____

Case Number

_____

Bankruptcy Judge

I, _____, the attorney for the petitioner named in the foregoing petition, declare that I have informed the petitioner that [he or she] may proceed under chapter 7, 11, 12, or 13 of title 11, United States Code, and have explained the relief available under each such chapter.

Signature _____

*Attorney for Petitioner*

**Advisory Committee note.** This form may be used to commence a voluntary case under chapter 7, 11, or 13 of the Bankruptcy Code. A chapter 9 petition requires other allegations (see § 109(c) of the Code) but this form may be adapted for such use.

The title of the case, in the caption of the form, should include all names used by the debtor, such as trade names, names used in doing business, married names and maiden names. This will enable creditors to properly identify the debtor when they receive notices and orders.

A joint petition, available for an individual and spouse, may be filed under chapter 7, 11, or 13. See § 302 of the Code. This form may be adapted for such use.

The unsworn declaration at the end of the petition conforms with 28 U.S.C. § 1746 (1976) which permits the declaration to be made in the manner indicated with the same force and effect as a sworn statement. The form may be adapted for use outside of the United States by adding the words "under the laws of the United States" after the word "perjury.

"Exhibit "A" to be attached to the petition of a corporate debtor is for the purpose of supplying the Securities and Exchange Commission with the information it requires at the beginning stages of a chapter 11 case.

**Advisory Committee note to 1986 amendment.** Paragraphs 6 and 7 and Exhibit B were added by § 322 of the 1984 amendments. The references to chapters 11 and 12 of title 11 of the United States Code found in paragraph 6 and Exhibit B were added by § 283(aa) of the 1986 amendments.


## OFFICIAL FORM NO. 2

### Form 2. Application and Order to Pay Filing Fee in Installments (Official Form No. 2)


### UNITED STATES BANKRUPTCY COURT

_____ **District of** _____

**In re**

} Bankruptcy Case No.

**Debtor**


### APPLICATION TO PAY FILING FEES IN INSTALLMENTS

In accordance with Bankruptcy Rule 1006, application is made for permission to pay the filing fee on the following terms

$_____with the filing of the petition, and the balance of
$_____ in _____ installments, as follows:

$_____ on or before _____

$_____ on or before _____

$_____ on or before _____

$_____ on or before _____.

I certify that I have not paid any money or transferred any property to an attorney or any other person for services in connection with this case or in connection with any other pending bankruptcy case and that I will not make any payment or transfer any property for services in connection with the case until the filing fee is paid in full.

_____     _____
Date     Applicant

_____
Address of Applicant

## ORDER

IT IS ORDERED that the debtor pay the filing fee in installments on the terms set forth in the foregoing application.

IT IS FURTHER ORDERED that until the filing fee is paid in full the debtor shall not pay, and no person shall accept, any money for services in connection with this case, and the debtor shall not relinquish, and no person shall accept, any property as payment for services in connection with this case.

_____     _____
Date     Bankruptcy Judge

**Advisory Committee note.** The application for permission to pay filing fees in installments may be filed in accordance with 28 U.S.C. § 1930(a), and Rule 1006. Only an individual debtor in a voluntary case, or individual debtors filing a joint petition may pay the fee in installments.

If a joint petition is filed, this form may be adapted for use by both petitioners.

**Advisory Committee note to 1986 amendment.** Official Forms 2 and 3 have been combined.

## OFFICIAL FORM NO. 3

### Form 3. Order for Payment of Filing Fee in Installments (Official Form No. 3)

### [Abrogated]

## OFFICIAL FORM NO. 4

### Form 4. Unsworn Declaration under Penalty of Perjury on Behalf of a Corporation or Partnership (Official Form No. 4)

I, _____, [the president *or other officer or* an authorized agent of the corporation] [*or* a member *or* an authorized agent of the partnership] named as petitioner in the foregoing petition, declare under penalty of perjury that the foregoing is true and correct, and that the filing of this petition on behalf of the [corporation] [*or* partnership] has been authorized.

Executed on _____

                                        Signature: _____

> **Advisory Committee note.** Rule 1008 requires all petitions to be verified. This form is to be used on behalf of a corporation or partnership. It may be adapted for use in connection with other papers required by these rules to be verified. See the Note to Rule 9011. 28 U.S.C. § 1746 permits an unsworn declaration to be used in lieu of a verification. See Advisory Committee Note to Form No. 1.

# OFFICIAL FORM NO. 5

## Form 5. Certificate of Commencement of Case (Official Form No. 5)

### United States Bankruptcy Court

_____ District of _____

**In re**

**Debtor\***               }    Bankruptcy Case No.
Social Security No.:
Employer Tax I.D. No.:

## CERTIFICATE OF COMMENCEMENT OF CASE

I certify that on_____
(date)

☐ the above named debtor filed a petition requesting relief under chapter _____ of the Bankruptcy Code (title 11 of the United States Code), or

☐ a petition was filed against the above named debtor under chapter _____ of the Bankruptcy Code (title 11 of the United States Code), and

☐ that as of the date below the case has not been dismissed.

_____
Clerk of the Bankruptcy Court

By:_____

_____
Date                          Deputy Clerk

---

*\*Set forth all names, including trade names, used by the debtor within the last 6 years. (Bankruptcy Rule 1005). For joint debtors set forth both social security numbers.*

**Advisory Committee note.** This form is adapted from certificates that have been in use in several districts. The certificate may be used to alert persons dealing with the debtor or property of the debtor of the pendency of a case under the Code before the notice of the meeting of creditors is sent.

## OFFICIAL FORM NO. 6

### Form 6. Schedules of Assets and Liabilities (Official Form No. 6)

*[Caption as in Form No. 1]*

### Schedule A.—Statement of All Liabilities of Debtor.

Schedules A-1, A-2 and A-3 must include all the claims against the debtor or the debtor's property as of the date of the filing of the petition by or against the debtor.

### Schedule A-1.—Creditors having priority.

| (1) | (2) | (3) | (4) | (5) |
|---|---|---|---|---|
| *Nature of claim* | *Name of creditor and complete mailing address including zip code* | *Specify when claim was incurred and the consideration therefor; when claim is subject to setoff, evidenced by a judgment, negotiable instrument, or other writing, or incurred as partner or joint contractor, so indicate; specify name of any partner or joint contractor on any debt* | *Indicate if claim is contingent, unliquidated, or disputed* | *Amount of claim* |

a.  Wages, salary, and commissions, including vacation, severance and sick leave pay owing to employees not exceeding $2,000 to each, earned within 90 days before filing of petition or cessation of business (if earlier specify date).                                                   $_____

b.  Contributions to employee benefit plans for services rendered within 180 days before filing of petition or cessation of business (if earlier specify date).                                                                  $_____

c.  Claims of farmers, not exceeding $2,000 for each individual, pursuant to 11 U.S.C. § 507(a)(5)(A).                                       $_____

d.  Claims of United States fishermen, not exceeding $2,000 for each individual, pursuant to 11 U.S.C. § 507(a)(5)(B).                       $_____

e.  Deposits by individuals, not exceeding $900 for each for purchase, lease, or rental of property or services for personal, family, or household use that were not delivered or provided.                      $_____

**f.** Taxes owing [itemize by type of tax and taxing authority]
    (1) To the United States                                          $_____
    (2) To any state                                                $_____
    (3) To any other taxing authority                       $_____

          Total                                              $_____

## Schedule A-2.—Creditors holding security

| (1) | (2) | (3) | (4) | (5) | (6) |
|---|---|---|---|---|---|
| *Name of creditor and complete mailing address including zip code* | *Description of security and date when obtained by creditor* | *Specify when claim was incurred and the consideration therefor; when claim is subject to setoff, evidenced by a judgment, negotiable instrument, or other writing, or incurred as partner or joint contractor, so indicate; specify name of any partner or joint contractor on any debt* | *Indicate if claim is contingent, unliquidated, or disputed* | *Market Value* | *Amount of claim without deduction of value of security* |
| | | Total | | | _____ |
| | | | | | $_____ |

**466**

Appendix A

## Schedule A-3.—Creditors having unsecured claims without priority.

| (1) | (2) | (3) | (4) |
|---|---|---|---|
| Name of creditor [including last known holder of any negotiable instrument] and complete mailing address including zip code | Specify when claim was incurred and the consideration therefor; when claim is contingent, unliquidated, disputed, subject to setoff, evidenced by a judgment, negotiable instrument, or other writing, or incurred as partner or joint contractor, so indicate; specify name of any partner or joint contractor on any debt | Indicate if claim is contingent, unliquidated, or disputed | Amount of claim |
| | Total | | $_____ |

## Schedule B—Statement of All Property of Debtor

Schedules B-1, B-2, B-3, and B-4 must include all property of the debtor as of the date of the filing of the petition by or against the debtor.

### Schedule B-1.—Real Property

| Description and location of all real property in which debtor has an interest [including equitable and future interests, interests in estates by the entirety, community property, life estates, leaseholds, and rights and powers exercisable for the debtor's own benefit] | Nature of interest [specify all deeds and written instruments relating thereto] | Market value of debtor's interest without deduction for secured claims listed in Schedule A-2 or exemptions claimed in Schedule B-4 |
|---|---|---|
| | Total | $_____ |

## Schedule B-2.—Personal Property

| Type of Property | Description and Location | Market value of debtor's interest without deduction for secured claims listed on Schedule A-2 or exemptions claimed in Schedule B-4 |
|---|---|---|
| | | Total $_____ |
| **a.** Cash on hand | | $_____ |
| **b.** Deposits of money with banking institutions, savings and loan associations, brokerage houses, credit unions, public utility companies, landlords and others | | $_____ |
| **c.** Household goods, supplies and furnishings | | $_____ |
| **d.** Books, pictures, and other art objects; stamp, coin and other collections | | $_____ |
| **e.** Wearing apparel, jewelry, firearms, sports equipment and other personal possessions | | $_____ |
| **f.** Automobiles, trucks, trailers and other vehicles | | $_____ |
| **g.** Boats, motors and their accessories | | $_____ |
| **h.** Livestock, poultry and other animals | | $_____ |
| **i.** Farming equipment, supplies and implements | | $_____ |
| **j.** Office equipment, furnishings and supplies | | $_____ |
| **k.** Machinery, fixtures, equipment and supplies [other than those listed in Items j and l] used in business | | $_____ |
| **l.** Inventory | | $_____ |
| **m.** Tangible personal property of any other description | | $_____ |
| **n.** Patents, copyrights, licenses, franchises and other general intangibles [specify all documents and writings relating thereto] | | $_____ |
| **o.** Government and corporate bonds and other negotiable and nonnegotiable instruments | | $_____ |
| **p.** Other liquidated debts owing debtor | | $_____ |
| **q.** Contingent and unliquidated claims of every nature, including counterclaims of the debtor [give estimates value of each] | | $_____ |
| **r.** Interests in insurance policies [name insurance company of each policy and itemize surrender or refund value of each] | | $_____ |
| **s.** Annuities [itemize and name each issuer] | | $_____ |
| **t.** Stock and interests in incorporated and unincorporated companies [itemize separately] | | $_____ |
| **u.** Interests in partnerships | | $_____ |

v.   Equitable and future interests, life estates, and rights or powers exercisable for the benefit of the debtor (other than those listed in schedule B-1) [specify all written instruments relating thereto]     $_____

Total     $_____

## Schedule B-3.—Property not otherwise scheduled

| Type of Property | Description and Location | Market value of debtor's interest without deduction for secured claims listed in Schedule A-2 or exemption claimed in Schedule B-4 |
|---|---|---|
| a. Property transferred under assignment for benefit of creditors, within 120 days prior to filing of petition [specify date of assignment, name and address of assignee, amount realized therefrom by the assignee, and disposition of proceeds so far as known to debtor] | | $_____ |
| b. Property of any kind not otherwise scheduled | | $_____ |
| | Total | $_____ |

Debtor selects the following property as exempt pursuant to 11 U.S.C. § 522(d) [*or* the laws of the State of _____]

## Schedule B-4.—Property claimed as exempt

| Type of Property | Location, description, and, so far as relevant to the claim of exemption, present use of property | Specify statute creating the exemption | Value claimed exempt |
|---|---|---|---|
| | | | $_____ |
| | | Total | $_____ |

# Summary of debts and property.

*[From the statements of the debtor in Schedules A and B]*

| Schedule | | Total |
|---|---|---|
| | Debts | |
| A-1/a,b | Wages, etc. having priority | $_____ |
| A-1(c) | Deposits of money | _____ |
| A-1/d(1) | Taxes owing United States | _____ |
| A-1/d(2) | Taxes owing states | _____ |
| A-1/d(3) | Taxes owing other taxing authorities | _____ |
| A-2 | Secured claims | _____ |
| A-3 | Unsecured claims without priority | _____ |
| | Schedule A total | $_____ |
| | Property | |
| B-1 | Real property [total value] | $_____ |
| B-2/a | Cash on hand | _____ |
| B-2/b | Deposits | _____ |
| B-2/c | Household goods | _____ |
| B-2/d | Books, pictures, and collections | _____ |
| B-2/e | Wearing apparel and personal possessions | _____ |
| B-2/f | Automobiles and other vehicles | _____ |
| B-2/g | Boats, motors, and accessories | _____ |
| B-2/h | Livestock and other animals | _____ |
| B-2/i | Farming supplies and implements | _____ |
| B-2/j | Office equipment and supplies | _____ |
| B-2/k | Machinery, equipment, and supplies used in business | _____ |
| B-2/l | Inventory | _____ |
| B-2/m | Other tangible personal property | _____ |
| B-2/n | Patents and other general intangibles | _____ |
| B-2/o | Bonds and other instruments | _____ |
| B-2/p | Other liquidated debts | _____ |
| B-2/q | Contingent and unliquidated claims | _____ |
| B-2/r | Interests in insurance policies | _____ |
| B-2/s | Annuities | _____ |
| B-2/t | Interests in corporations and unincorporated companies | _____ |
| B-2/u | Interests in partnerships | _____ |
| B-2/v | Equitable and future interests, rights, and powers in personalty | _____ |

B-3/a          Property assigned for benefit of creditors              _____
B-3/b          Property not otherwise scheduled                        _____

                                        Schedule B total        $_____

---

### Unsworn Declaration under Penalty of Perjury
### of Individual to Schedules A and B

I, _____, declare under penalty of perjury that I have read the foregoing schedules, consisting of _____ sheets, and that they are true and correct to the best of my knowledge, information and belief.

Executed on _____

                                        Signature: _____

### Unsworn Declaration under Penalty of Perjury
### on Behalf of Corporation or Partnership
### to Schedules A and B

I, _____, [the president *or other officer* or an authorized agent of the corporation] [*or* a member *or* an authorized agent of the partnership] named as debtor in this case, declare under penalty of perjury that I have read the foregoing schedules, consisting of _____ sheets, and that they are true and correct to the best of my knowledge, information, and belief.

Executed on _____

                                        Signature: _____

**Advisory Committee note.** These schedules may be used pursuant to § 521(1) of the Code.

The unsworn declarations at the end of the form are in conformity with 28 U.S.C. § 1746. See Advisory Committee Note to Form No. 1

**Advisory Committee note to 1986 amendment.** Paragraphs c and d in Schedule A-1 have been added to reflect new priorities added to § 507 of the Code by the 1984 amendments.

# OFFICIAL FORM NO. 6A

## Form 6A. Schedule of Current Income and Current Expenditures for Individual Debtor (Official Form No. 6A)

*[Caption as in Form No. 2]*

### Schedule of Current Income and Current Expenditures for Individual Debtor

[Complete this form by answering each question. If your answer to a question is "none" or "not applicable" so state.]

A. *Family Status*
1. The debtor is: (check one of the following
   Married _____ Single _____ Separated _____ Divorced _____
2. The name of the debtor's spouse is _____
3. The debtor supports the following dependents (*other than the debtor's spouse*):

| *Name* | *Age* | *Relationship to Debtor* |
|--------|-------|--------------------------|
| _____ | \_\_\_\_ | _____ |
| _____ | \_\_\_\_ | _____ |
| _____ | \_\_\_\_ | _____ |
| _____ | \_\_\_\_ | _____ |

B. *Employment and Occupation*
1. The debtor is employed by _____, (*name of employer*) as _____ (*nature of position*)
2. The debtor is self-employed as _____(*nature of business or profession*) at the following principal place of business: _____(*address*)
3. The debtor's spouse is employed by _____, (*name of employer*) as _____ (*nature of position*)
4. The debtor's spouse is self-employed as _____, (*nature of business or profession*) at the following principal place of business: _____ (*address*)

C. *Current Income*
Give estimated average current monthly income of debtor and spouse, consisting of:

|   |   | *Debtor* | *Spouse* |
|---|---|----------|----------|
| 1. | Gross pay (*wages, salary, or commissions*) | $_____ | $_____ |
| 2. | Take home pay (*gross pay less all deductions*) | $_____ | $_____ |
| 3. | Regular income available from the operation of a business or profession | $_____ | $_____ |

**4.** Other income:
    Interest and dividends                        $_____   $_____
    From real estate or personal property     $_____   $_____
    Social security                               $_____   $_____
    Pension or other retirement income      $_____   $_____
    Other (*specify*)

    _____   $_____   $_____
    _____   $_____   $_____

**5.** Alimony, maintenance or support payments:
    Payable to the debtor for the debtor's use   $_____   $_____
    Payable to the debtor for the support of an-
    other (*Attach additional sheet listing the
    name, age, and relationship to the debtor of
    persons for whose benefit payments are
    made.*)                                   $_____   $_____

Total estimated current monthly income   $_____   $_____

If you anticipate receiving additional income on other than a monthly basis in the next six months (such as an income tax refund), attach additional sheet of paper and describe.

If you anticipate a substantial change in your income in the immediate future, attach additional sheet of paper and describe.

D. *Schedule of Current Expenditures*

Give estimated average current monthly expenditures of debtor and spouse, consisting of

**1.** Home expenses:

**a.** Rent or home loan payment
    (*including any assessment or maintenance fee*)   $_____

**b.** Real estate taxes   $_____

**c.** Utilities:
    Electricity   $_____
    Gas   $_____
    Water   $_____
    Telephone   $_____
    Other (*specify*)
    _____   $_____

  Total utilities   $_____

**d.** Home maintenance (repairs and upkeep)   $_____

Total, all home expenses   $_____

**2.** Other expenses:

**a.** Taxes (*not deducted from wages or included in home loan payment or included in real estate taxes*)     $____

**b.** Alimony, maintenance, or support payments (*attack additional sheet listing name, age, and relationship of beneficiaries*)     $____   (

**c.** Insurance (*not deducted from wages*)

    Life     $____

    Health     $____

    Auto     $____

    Homeowner's or Renter's     $____

    ____     $____

Total insurance expenses     $____

**d.** Installment payments:     $____

    Auto     $____

    Other (*specify*) ____     $____

    ____     $____

**e.** Transportation (*not including auto payments*)     $____

**f.** Education (*including tuition and school books*)     $____

**g.** Food     $____

**h.** Clothing     $____

**i.** Medical, dental, and medicines     $____

**j.** Laundry and cleaning     $____

**k.** Newspapers, periodicals, and books     $____

**l.** Recreation, clubs, and entertainment     $____

**m.** Charitable contributions     $____

**n.** Other expenses (*specify*)

    ____     $____

    ____     $____

    ____

*Total estimated current monthly expenses*     $____

If you anticipate a substantial change in your expenses in the immediate future attach additional sheet of paper and describe.

*Unsworn Declaration under Penalty of Perjury*

    I, _____, declare under penalty of perjury that I have read the foregoing schedule and any attachment, consisting of ____ sheets in all, and that they are true and correct to the best of my knowledge, information and belief.

Date _____                       _____

                                    *Signature of Debtor*

**Advisory Committe note.** Section 521(1), as amended by the 1984 amendments, requires debtors to file a schedule of current income and current expenditures. This form is designed for use by individual debtors and is modeled on Official Form No. 10, the Chapter 13 Statement. No official form is prescribed for partnerships and corporations.

Only the original schedule need be signed and verified, but copies must be conformed to the original. See Bankruptcy Rules 1008 and 9011(c).

### OFFICIAL FORM NO. 7

### Form 7. Statement of Financial Affairs for Debtor Not Engaged in Business (Official Form No. 7)

*[Caption as in Form No. 1]*

Statement of Financial Affairs for Debtor
Not Engaged in Business

[Each question shall be answered or the failure to answer explained. If the answer is "none" or "not applicable" so state. If additional space is needed for the answer to any question, a separate sheet, properly identified and made a part hereof, should be used and attached.

The term, "original petition," used in the following questions, shall mean the petition filed under Rule 1002 or 1004.]

1. *Name and residence.*
    a. What is your full name?
    b. Have you used, or been known by, any other names within the six years immediately preceding the filing of the original petition herein? (If so, give particulars.)
    c. Where do you now reside?
    d. Where else have you resided during the six years immediately preceding the filing of the original petition herein?
2. *Occupation and income.*
    a. What is your occupation?
    b. Where are you now employed? (Give the name and address of your employer, or the address at which you carry on your trade or profession, and the length of time you have been so employed or engaged.)

    c.    Have you been in a partnership with anyone, or engaged in any business during the six years immediately preceding the filing of the original petition herein? (If so, give particulars, including names, dates, and places.)

    d.    What amount of income have you received from your trade or profession during each of the two calender years immediately preceding the filing of the original petition herein?

    e.    What amount of income have you received from other sources during each of these two years? (Give particulars, including each source, and the amount received therefrom).

3.    *Tax returns and refunds.*

    a.    Where did you file your federal, state and municipal income tax returns for the two years immediately preceding the filing of the original petition herein?

    b.    What tax refunds (income and other) have you received during the year immediately preceding the filing of the original petition herein?

    c.    To what tax refunds (income or other), if any, are you, or may you be, entitled? (Give particulars, including information as to any refund payable jointly to you and your spouse or any other person.)

4.    *Financial accounts, certificates of deposit and safe deposit boxes.*

    a.    What accounts or certificates of deposit or shares in banks, savings and loan, thrift, building and loan and homestead associations, credit unions, brokerage houses, pension funds and the like have you maintained, alone or together with any other person, and in your own or any other name within the two years immediately preceding the filing of the original petition herein? (Give the name and address of each institution, the name and number under which the account or certificate is maintained, and the name and address of every other person authorized to make withdrawals from such account.)

    b.    What safe deposit box or boxes or other depository or depositories have you kept or used for your securities, cash, or other valuables within the two years immediately preceding the filing of the original petition herein? (Give the name and address of the bank or other depository, the name in which each box or other depository was kept, the name and address of every other person who had the right of access thereto, a brief description of the contents thereof, and, if the box has been surrendered, state when surrendered, or, if transferred, when transferred, and the name and address of the transferee.)

5.    *Books and records.*

    a.    Have you kept books of account or records relating to your affairs within the two years immediately preceding the filing of the original petition herein?

    **b.**   In whose possession are these books or records? (Give names and addresses.)

    **c.**   If any of these books or records are not available, explain.

    **d.**   Have any books of account or records relating to your affairs been destroyed, lost, or otherwise disposed of within the two years immediately preceding the filing of the original petition herein? (If so, give particulars, including date of destruction, loss, or disposition, and reason therefor.)

**6.**  *Property held for another person.*
What property do you hold for any other person? (Give name and address of each person, and describe the property, or value thereof, and all writings relating thereto.)

**7.**  *Property held by another.*
Is any other person holding anything of value in which you have an interest? (Give name and address, location and description of the property, and circumstances of the holding.)

**8.**  *Prior bankruptcy.*
What cases under the Bankruptcy Act or title 11, United States Code have previously been brought by or against you? (State the location of the bankruptcy court, the nature and number of each case, the date when it was filed, and whether a discharge was granted or denied, the case was dismissed, or a composition, arrangement, or plan was confirmed.)

**9.**  *Receiverships, general assignments, and other modes of liquidation.*

    **a.**   Was any of your property, at the time of the filing of the original petition herein, in the hands of a receiver, trustee, or other liquidating agent? (If so, give a brief description of the property, the name and address of the receiver, trustee, or other agent, and, if the agent was appointed in a court proceeding, the name and location of the court, the title and number of the case, and the nature thereof.)

    **b.**   Have you made any assignment of your property for the benefit of your creditors, or any general settlement with your creditors, within one year immediately preceding the filing of the original petition herein? (If so, give dates, the name and address of the assignee, and a brief statement of the terms of assignment or settlement.)

**10.**  *Suits, executions, and attachments.*

    **a.**   Were you a party to any suit pending at the time of the filing of the original petition herein? (If so, give the name and location of the court and the title and nature of the proceeding.)

    **b.**   Were you a party to any suit terminated within the year immediately preceding the filing of the original petition herein? (If so, give the name and location of the court, the title and nature of the proceeding, and the result.)

    c.   Has any of your property been attached, garnished, or seized under any legal or equitable process within the year immediately preceding the filing of the original petition herein? (If so, describe the property seized or person garnished, and at whose suit.)

**11.**   (a) *Payment of loans, installment purchases and other debts.*

What payments in whole or in part have you made during the year immediately preceding the filing of the original petition herein on any of the following: (1) loans; (2) installment purchases of goods and services; and (3) other debts? (Give the names and addresses of the persons receiving payment, the amounts of the loans or other debts and the purchase price of the goods and services, the dates of the original transactions, the amounts and dates of payments and, if any of the payees are your relatives or insiders, the relationship; if the debtor is a partnership and any of the payees is or was a partner or a relative of a partner, state the relationship; if the debtor is a corporation and any of the payees is or was an officer, director, or stockholder, or a relative of an officer, director, or stockholder, state the relationship.)

(b) *Setoffs.*

What debts have you owed to any creditor, including any bank, which were setoff by that creditor against a debt or deposit owing by the creditor to you during the year immediately preceding the filing of the original petition herein? (Give the names and addresses of the persons setting off such debts, the dates of the setoffs, the amounts of the debts owing by you and to you and, if any of the creditors are your relatives or insiders, the relationship.)

**12.**   *Transfers of property.*

    a.   Have you made any gifts, other than ordinary and usual presents to family members and charitable donations, during the year immediately preceding the filing of the original petition herein? (If so, give names and addresses of donees and dates, description, and value of gifts.)

    b.   Have you made any other transfer, absolute or for the purpose of security, or any other disposition, of real or personal property during the year immediately preceding the filing of the original petition herein? (Give a description of the property, the date of the transfer or disposition, to whom transferred or how disposed of, and, if the transferee is a relative or insider, the relationship, the consideration, if any, received therefor, and the disposition of such consideration.)

**13.**   *Repossessions and returns.*

Has any property been returned to, or repossessed by, the seller or by a secured party during the year immediately preceding the filing of the original petition herein? (If so, give particulars, including the name and address of the party getting the property and its description and value.)

**14.** *Losses.*

    **a.**  Have you suffered any losses from fire, theft, or gambling during the year immediately preceding or since the filing of the original petition herein? (If so, give particulars, including dates, names, and places, and the amounts of money or value and general description of property lost.)

    **b.**  Was the loss covered in whole or part by insurance? (If so, give particulars.)

**15.** *Payments or transfers to attorneys and other persons.*

    **a.**  Have you consulted an attorney during the year immediately preceding or since the filing of the original petition herein? (Give dates, name and address.)

    **b.**  Have you during the year immediately preceding or since the filing of the original petition herein paid any money or transferred any property to the attorney, to any other person on the attorney's behalf, or to any other person rendering services to you in connection with this case? (If so, give particulars, including amount paid or value of property transferred and date of payment or transfer.)

    **c.**  Have you, either during the year immediately preceding or since the filing of the original petition herein, agreed to pay any money or transfer any property to an attorney at law, to any other person on the attorney's behalf, or to any other person rendering services to you in connection with this case? (If so, give particulars, including amount and terms of obligation.)

I, _____, declare under penalty of perjury that I have read the answers contained in the foregoing statement of financial affairs and that they are true and correct to the best of my knowledge, information, and belief.

Executed on _____

_____
*Debtor*

    **Advisory Committee note.** See Advisory Committee Note to Form No. 1 for discussion of unsworn statement at the end of this form.

    **Advisory Committee note to 1986 amendment.** The introduction preceding paragraph 1 is amended to delete the reference to Rule 1003(a), which has been combined into Rule 1002.

    Paragraph 15 is amended to implement the amendments to Rule 1006(b), which prohibits payments not only to attorneys but to any other person who renders services to the debtor in connection with the case.

## OFFICIAL FORM NO. 8

## Form 8. Statement of Financial Affairs for Debtor Engaged in Business (Official Form No. 8)

*[Caption as in Form No. 1]*

Statement of Financial Affairs for Debtor Engaged in Business

[Each question shall be answered or the failure to answer explained. If the answer is "none" or "not applicable," so state. If additional space is needed for the answer to any question, a separate sheet properly identified and made a part hereof, should be used and attached.

If the debtor is a partnership or a corporation, the questions shall be deemed to be addressed to, and shall be answered on behalf of, the partnership or corporation; and the statement shall be certified by a member of the partnership or by a duly authorized officer of the corporation.

The term, "original petition," used in the following questions, shall mean the petition filed under Rule 1002 or 1004.]

1. *Nature, location, and name of business.*
   a. Under what name and where do you carry on your business?
   b. In what business are you engaged? (If business operations have been terminated, give the date of termination.)
   c. When did you commence the business?
   d. Where else, and under what other names, have you carried on business within the six years immediately preceding the filing of the original petition herein? (Give street addresses, the names of any partners, joint adventurers, or other associates, the nature of the business, and the periods for which it was carried on.)

2. *Books and records.*
   a. By whom, or under whose supervision, have your books of account and records been kept during the six years immediately preceding the filing of the original petition herein? (Give names, addresses, and periods of time.)
   b. By whom have your books of account and records been audited during the six years immediately preceding the filing of the original petition herein? (Give names, addresses, and dates of audits.)
   c. In whose possession are your books of account and records? (Give names and addresses.)
   d. If any of these books or records are not available, explain.
   e. Have any books of account or records relating to your affairs been destroyed, lost, or otherwise disposed of within the two years immediately preceding the filing of the original petition herein? (If so, give

particulars, including date of destruction, loss, or disposition, and reason therefor.)

3.  *Financial statements.*
    Have you issued any written financial statements within the two years immediately preceding the filing of the original petition herein? (Give dates, and the name and addresses of the persons to whom issued, including mercantile and trade agencies.)

4.  *Inventories.*
    a.  When was the last inventory of your property taken?
    b.  By whom, or under whose supervision, was this inventory taken?
    c.  What was the amount, in dollars, of the inventory? (State whether the inventory was taken at cost, market, or otherwise.)
    d.  When was the next prior inventory of your property taken?
    e.  By whom, or under whose supervision, was this inventory taken?
    f.  What was the amount, in dollars, of the inventory? (State whether the inventory was taken at cost, market, or otherwise).
    g.  In whose possession are the records of the two inventories above referred to? (Give names and addresses.)

5.  *Income other than from operation of business.*
    What amount of income, other than from operation of your business, have you received during each of the two years immediately preceding the filing of the original petition herein? (Give particulars, including each source, and the amount received therefrom.)

6.  *Tax returns and refunds.*
    a.  In whose possession are copies of your federal, state and municipal income tax returns for the three years immediately preceding the filing of the original petition herein?
    b.  What tax refunds (income or other) have you received during the two years immediately preceding the filing of the original petition herein?
    c.  To what tax refunds (income or other), if any, are you, or may you be, entitled? (Give particulars, including information as to any refund payable jointly to you and your spouse or any other person.)

7.  *Financial accounts, certificates of deposit and safe deposit boxes.*
    a.  What accounts or certificates of deposit or shares in banks, savings and loan, thrift, building and loan and homestead associations, credit unions, brokerage houses, pension funds and the like have you maintained, alone or together with any other person, and in your own or any other name, within the two years immediately preceding the filing of the original petition herein? (Give the name and address of each institution, the name and number under which the account or certificate is maintained, and the name and address of every person authorized to make withdrawals from such account.)

    **b.** What safe deposit box or boxes or other depository or depositories have you kept or used for your securities, cash, or other valuables within the two years immediately preceding the filing of the original petition herein? (Give the name and address of the bank or other depository, the name in which each box or other depository was kept, the name and address of every person who had the right of access thereto, a description of the contents thereof, and, if the box has been surrendered, state when surrendered or, if transferred, when transferred and the name and address of the transferee.)

**8.** *Property held for another person.*

What property do you hold for any other person? (Give name and address of each person, and describe the property, the amount or value thereof and all writings relating thereto.)

**9.** *Property held by another person.*

Is any other person holding anything of value in which you have an interest? (Give name and address, location and description of the property, and circumstances of the holding.)

**10.** *Prior bankruptcy proceedings.*

What cases under the Bankruptcy Act or title 11, United States Code have previously been brought by or against you? (State the location of the bankruptcy court, the nature and number of the case, and whether a discharge was granted or denied, the case was dismissed, or a composition, arrangement, or plan was confirmed.)

**11.** *Receiverships, general assignments, and other modes of liquidation.*

    **a.** Was any of your property, at the time of the filing of the original petition herein, in the hands of a receiver, trustee, or other liquidating agent? (If so, give a brief description of the property and the name and address of the receiver, trustee, or other agent, and, if the agent was appointed in a court proceeding, the name and location of the court, the title and number of the case, and the nature thereof.)

    **b.** Have you made any assignment of your property for the benefit of your creditors, or any general settlement with your creditors, within the two years immediately preceding the filing of the original petition herein? (If so, give dates, the name and address of the assignee, and a brief statement of the terms of assignment or settlement.)

**12.** *Suits, executions, and attachments.*

    **a.** Were you a party to any suit pending at the time of the filing of the original petition herein? (If so, give the name and location of the court and the title and nature of the proceeding.)

    **b.** Were you a party to any suit terminated within the year immediately preceding the filing of the original petition herein? (If so, give the name and location of the court, the title and nature of the proceeding, and the result.)

    **c.**   Has any of your property been attached, garnished, or seized under any legal or equitable process within the year immediately preceding the filing of the original petition herein? (If so, describe the property seized or person garnished, and at whose suit.)

**13.**  **a.**  *Payments of loans, installment purchases and other debts.*
    What payments in whole or in part have you made during the year immediately preceding the filing of the original petition herein on any of the following: (1) loans; (2) installment purchases of goods and services; and (3) other debts? (Give the names and addresses of the persons receiving payment, the amounts of the loans or other debts and of the purchase price of the goods and services, the dates of the original transactions, the amounts and dates of payments, and, if any of the payees are your relatives or insiders, the relationship; if the debtor is a partnership and any of the payees is or was a partner or a relative or a partner, state the relationship; if the debtor is a corporation and any of the payees is or was an officer, director, or stockholder, or a relative of an officer, director, or stockholder, state the relationship.)

    **b.**  *Setoffs.*
    What debts have you owed to any creditor, including any bank, which were setoff by that creditor against a debt or deposit owing by the creditor to you during the year immediately preceding the filing of the original petition herein? (Give the names and addresses of the persons setting off such debts, the dates of the setoffs, the amounts of the debts owing by you and to you and, if any of the creditors are your relatives or insiders, the relationship.)

**14.**  *Transfers of property.*
    **a.**  Have you made any gifts, other than ordinary and usual presents to family members and charitable donations during the year immediately preceding the filing of the original petition herein? (If so, give names and addresses of donees and dates, description, and value of gifts.)

    **b.**  Have you made any other transfer, absolute or for the purpose of security, or any other disposition which was not in the ordinary course of business during the year immediately preceding the filing of the original petition herein? (Give a description of the property, the date of the transfer or disposition, to whom transferred or how disposed of, and state whether the transferee is a relative, partner, shareholder, officer, director, or insider, the consideration, if any, received for the property, and the disposition of such consideration.)

**15.**  *Accounts and other receivables.*
Have you assigned, either absolutely or as security, any of your accounts or other receivables during the year immediately preceding the filing of

the original petition herein? (If so, give names and addresses of assignees.)

16. *Repossessions and returns.*

Has any property been returned to, or repossessed by, the seller, lessor, or a secured party during the year immediately preceding the filing of the original petition herein? (If so, give particulars, including the names and address of the party getting the property and its description and value.)

17. *Business leases.*

If you are a tenant of business property, what is the name and address of your landlord, the amount of your rental, the date to which rent had been paid at the time of the filing of the original petition herein, and the amount of security held by the landlord?

18. *Losses.*

a. Have you suffered any losses from fire, theft, or gambling during the year immediately preceding the filing of the original petition herein? (If so, give particulars, including dates, names, and places, and the amounts of money or value and general description of property lost.)

b. Was the loss covered in whole or part by insurance? (If so, give particulars.)

19. *Withdrawals.*

a. If you are an individual proprietor of your business, what personal withdrawals of any kind have you made from the business during the year immediately preceding the filing of the original petition herein?

b. If the debtor is a partnership or corporation, what withdrawals, in any form (including compensation, bonuses or loans), have been made or received by any member of the partnership, or by any officer, director, insider, managing executive, or shareholder of the corporation, during the year immediately preceding the filing of the original petition herein? (Give the name and designation or relationship to the debtor of each person, the dates and amounts of withdrawals, and the nature or purpose thereof.)

20. *Payments or transfers to attorneys and other persons.*

a. Have you consulted an attorney during the year immediately preceding or since the filing of the original petition herein? (Give date, name, and address.)

b. Have you during the year immediately preceding or since the filing of the original petition herein paid any money or transferred any property to the attorney, to any other person on the attorney's behalf, or to any other person rendering services to you in connection with this case? (If so, give particulars, including amount paid or value of property transferred and date of payment or transfer.)

c. Have you, either during the year immediately preceding or since the filing of the original petition herein, agreed to pay any money or transfer any property to an attorney at law, to any other person on the attorney's behalf, or to any other person rendering services to you in connection with this case? (If so, give particulars, including amount and terms of obligation.)

*(If the debtor is a partnership or corporation, the following additional questions should be answered.)*

21. *Members of partnership; officers, directors, managers, and principal stockholders of corporation.*

   a.  What is the name and address of each member of the partnership, or the name, title, and address of each officer, director, insider, and managing executive, and of each stockholder holding 20 percent or more of the issued and outstanding stock, of the corporation?

   b.  During the year immediately preceding the filing of the original petition herein, has any member withdrawn from the partnership, or any officer, director, insider, or managing executive of the corporation terminated his relationship, or any stockholder holding 20 percent or more of the issued stock disposed of more than 50 percent of the stockholder's holdings? (If so, give name and address and reason for withdrawal, termination, or disposition, if known.)

   c.  Has any person acquired or disposed of 20 percent or more of the stock of the corporation during the year immediately preceding the filing of the petition? (If so, give name and address and particulars.)

I, _____, declare under penalty of perjury that I have read the answers contained in the foregoing statement of affairs and that they are true and correct to the best of my knowledge, information, and belief.

Executed on _____

                                         *Signature:* _____

*[Person declaring for partnership or corporation should indicate position or relationship to debtor.]*

> **Advisory Committee note.** Many of the questions on this form are the same as on Form No. 7, Statement of Financial Affairs for Debtor Not Engaged in Business.
>
> The question regarding loans repaid (#13) includes installment credit sales of goods or services. The information is helpful with respect to possible preferences. Information regarding leases (#17) may be helpful with respect to lease termination or extension and whether the landlord may be holding a deposit.
>
> **Advisory Committee note to 1986 amendment.** Form 8 is amended in the same manner as Form 7.

## OFFICIAL FORM NO. 8A

### Form 8A. Chapter 7 Individual Debtor's Statement of Intention (Official Form No. 8A)

*[Caption as in Form No. 2]*

Chapter 7 Individual Debtor's Statement of Intention

1. I, _____, the debtor, have filed a schedule of assets and liabilities which includes consumer debts secured by property of the estate.

2. My intention with respect to the property of the estate which secures those consumer debts is as follows:

a. Property to Be Surrendered.

Description of property      Creditor's name

1. _____
2. _____
3. _____
4. _____
5. _____

b. Property to Be Retained. *[Check applicable statement of debtor's intention]*

| Description of property | Creditor's name | The debt will be reaffirmed pursuant to § 524(c) | The property is claimed as exempt and will be redeemed pursuant to § 722 | The creditor's lien will be avoided pursuant to § 522(f) and the property will be claimed as exempt |
|---|---|---|---|---|
| 1. | | | | |
| 2. | | | | |
| 3. | | | | |
| 4. | | | | |
| 5. | | | | |

3. I understand that § 521(2)(B) of the Bankruptcy Code requires that I perform the above stated intention within 45 days of the filing of this statement with the court, or within any extension of the 45 day period which the court may grant.

Date: _____

_____
*Debtor*

**Advisory Committee note.** Section 521(2), as added by the 1984 amendments, requires an individual debtor whose schedule of assets and liabilities includes consumer debts which are secured by property of the estate to file with the clerk a statement of the debtor's intention with regard to such property. This form is designed to implement this requirement.

## OFFICIAL FORM NO. 9

### Form 9. List of Creditors Holding 20 Largest Unsecured Claims (Official Form No. 9)

*[Caption as in Form No. 2]*

#### List of Creditors Holding 20 Largest Unsecured Claims

Following is the list of the Debtor's creditors holding the 20 largest unsecured claims which is prepared in accordance with Rule 1007(d) for filing in this chapter 11 [*or* chapter 9] case. The list does not include those (1) persons who come within the definition of insider set forth in 11 U.S.C. § 101(25), (2) secured creditors unless the value of the collateral is such that the unsecured deficiency places the creditor among the holders of the 20 largest unsecured claims, or (3) governmental units not within the definition of "person" in 11 U.S.C. § 101(35).

| (1) | (2) | (3) | (4) | (5) |
|---|---|---|---|---|
| *Name of creditor and complete mailing address including zip code* | *Name, telephone number and complete mailing address including zip code of employee, agent or department of creditor familiar with claim who may be contacted* | *Nature of claim (trade debt, bank loan, type of judgment, etc.)* | *Indicate if claim is contingent, unliquidated, disputed or subject to setoff* | *Amount of claim [if secured also state value of security]* |

*Date:* _____

_____

*Debtor.*

**Advisory Committee note.** This form is for use in chapter 11 reorganization and chapter 9 municipality debt adjustment cases to enable the appointment, pursuant to §§ 1102 and 901 of the Code, of a committee of unsecured creditors. The information contained on the form is to assist in expediting the formation of the committee and to assure adequate creditor representation.

In accordance with § 1102 of the Code, the form indicates that insiders should not be listed. "Insiders" is defined in § 101(25) of the Code to include, *inter alia,* persons who are related to the debtor, are partners, officers, directors, affiliates as further defined in § 101(2) of the Code, or are otherwise in control of the debtor. Reference should be made to § 101 for the complete listing of insiders.

The nature of the claim should be specified to indicate whether it is an institutional debt, a trade debt for merchandise or supplies, a debt based on a judgment and the underlying basis for the judgment, or the like.

In column (2), it is important to provide specific information with respect to the person to be contacted. In order to form the committee it may be necessary to write or telephone the creditors. If the creditor company is a large organization individual contact may otherwise be difficult or impossible.

A secured creditor should be listed among the 20 largest unsecured creditors only if that creditor is sufficiently undersecured so as to fall within that category.

**Advisory Committee note to 1986 amendment.** The form has been amended to reflect the definition of "person" in 11 U.S.C. § 101(35), as modified by the 1984 amendments and renumbered by the 1986 amendments.

## OFFICIAL FORM NO. 10

### Form 10. Chapter 13 Statement (Official Form No. 10)

*[Caption as in Form No. 1]*

### Chapter 13 Statement

[Each question shall be answered or the failure to answer explained. If the answer is "none" or "not applicable" so state. If additional space is needed for the answer to any question, a separate sheet, properly identified and made a part hereof, should be used and attached.

The term "original petition," used in the following questions, shall mean the original petition filed under § 301 of the Code or, if the chapter 13 case was converted from another chapter of the Code, shall mean the petition by or against you which originated the first case.

This form must be completed in full whether a single or a joint petition is filed. When information is requested for "each" or "either spouse filing a petition" it should be supplied for both when a joint petition is filed.]

1. *Name and residence.*
   a. Give full name.
      Husband [*or, if single, Debtor*] _____
      *Wife*_____
   b. Where does debtor, if single, or each spouse filing a petition now reside?
      (1) Mailing address of husband [*or* debtor]
      
      _____
      
      City or town, state and zip code
      
      _____

    **(2)**  Mailing address of wife

        City or town, state and zip code

    **(3)**  Telephone number including area code
        Husband [*or, if single, Debtor*]⎯⎯⎯⎯⎯⎯⎯⎯⎯⎯
        *Wife*⎯⎯⎯⎯⎯⎯⎯⎯⎯⎯⎯⎯⎯⎯⎯⎯⎯

  **c.**  What does debtor, if single, or each spouse filing a petition consider his or her residence, if different from that listed in b, above?
      Husband [*or* Debtor]⎯⎯⎯⎯⎯⎯⎯⎯⎯⎯⎯⎯
      Wife⎯⎯⎯⎯⎯⎯⎯⎯⎯⎯⎯⎯⎯⎯⎯

**2.**  *Occupation and income.*

  **a.**  Give present occupation of debtor, if single, or each spouse filing a petition. (If more than one, list all for debtor or each spouse filing a petition.)
      Husband [*or* Debtor]⎯⎯⎯⎯⎯⎯⎯⎯⎯⎯⎯⎯
      Wife⎯⎯⎯⎯⎯⎯⎯⎯⎯⎯⎯⎯⎯⎯⎯

  **b.**  What is the name, address, and telephone number of present employer (or employers) of debtor, if single, or each spouse filing a petition? (Include also any identifying badge or card number with employer.)
      Husband [*or* Debtor]⎯⎯⎯⎯⎯⎯⎯⎯⎯⎯⎯⎯
      Wife⎯⎯⎯⎯⎯⎯⎯⎯⎯⎯⎯⎯⎯⎯⎯

  **c.**  How long has debtor, if single, or each spouse filing a petition been employed by present employer?
      Husband [*or* Debtor]⎯⎯⎯⎯⎯⎯⎯⎯⎯⎯⎯⎯
      Wife⎯⎯⎯⎯⎯⎯⎯⎯⎯⎯⎯⎯⎯⎯⎯

  **d.**  If debtor or either spouse filing a petition has not been employed by present employer for a period of one year, state the name of prior employer(s) and nature of employment during that period.
      Husband [*or* Debtor]⎯⎯⎯⎯⎯⎯⎯⎯⎯⎯⎯⎯
      Wife⎯⎯⎯⎯⎯⎯⎯⎯⎯⎯⎯⎯⎯⎯⎯

  **e.**  Has debtor or either spouse filing a petition operated a business, in partnership or otherwise, during the past three years? (If so, give the particulars, including names, dates, and places.)
      Husband [*or* Debtor]⎯⎯⎯⎯⎯⎯⎯⎯⎯⎯⎯⎯
      Wife⎯⎯⎯⎯⎯⎯⎯⎯⎯⎯⎯⎯⎯⎯⎯

  **f.**  Answer the following questions for debtor, if single, or each spouse whether single or joint petition is filed unless spouses are separated and a single petition is filed:

    **(1)**  What are your gross wages, salary, or commissions per pay period?

|  | Husband [*or* Debtor] | Wife |
|---|---|---|
| (a) Weekly | | |
| (b) Semi-monthly | | |
| (c) Monthly | | |
| (d) Other (specify) | | |

**(2)** What are your payroll deductions per pay period for:

|  | Husband [*or* Debtor] | Wife |
|---|---|---|
| (a) Payroll taxes (including social security) | | |
| (b) Insurance | | |
| (c) Credit union | | |
| (d) Union dues | | |
| (e) Other (specify) | | |

**(3)** What is your take-home pay per pay period?

| Husband [*or* Debtor] | Wife |
|---|---|
| | |

**(4)** What was the amount of your gross income for the last calendar year?

| Husband [*or* Debtor] | Wife |
|---|---|
| | |

**(5)** Is your employment subject to seasonal or other change?

| Husband [*or* Debtor] | Wife |
|---|---|
| | |

**(6)** Has either of you made any wage assignments or allotments? (If so, indicate which spouse's wages assigned or allotted, the name and address of the person to whom assigned or allotted, and the amount owing, if any, to such person. If allotment or assignment is to a creditor, the claim should also be listed in Item 11a.)

3. *Dependents*. (To be answered by debtor if unmarried, otherwise for each spouse whether single or joint petition is filed unless spouses are separated and a single petition is filed.)

   **a.** Does either of you pay [*or* receive] alimony, maintenance, or support? _____ If so, how much per month? _____ For whose support? (Give name, age, and relationship to you.)
   Husband [*or* Debtor]_____
   Wife_____

**b.** List all other dependents, other than present spouse, not listed in a, above. (Give name, age and relationship to you.)
Husband [*or* Debtor]_____
Wife_____

**4.** *Budget.*

**a.** Give your estimated average future monthly income, if unmarried, otherwise for each spouse whether single or joint petition is filed, unless spouses are separated and a single petition is filed.

    **(1)** Husband's [or Debtor's] monthly take-home pay    _____

    **(2)** Wife's monthly take-home pay    _____

    **(3)** Other monthly income (specify)    _____

                                      Total    _____

**b.** Give estimated average future monthly expenses of family (not including debts to be paid under plan), consisting of:

    **(1)** Rent or home mortgage payment (include lot rental for trailer)    _____

    **(2)** Utilities (Electricity _____, Heat _____, Water _____, Telephone _____)    _____

    **(3)** Food    _____

    **(4)** Clothing    _____

    **(5)** Laundry and Cleaning    _____

    **(6)** Newspapers, periodicals, and books (including school books)    _____

    **(7)** Medical and drug expenses    _____

    **(8)** Insurance (not deducted from wages)
        (a) Auto    _____
        (b) Other    _____

    **(9)** Transportation (not including auto payments to be paid under plan)    _____

    **(10)** Recreation    _____

    **(11)** Dues, union, professional, social or otherwise (not deducted from wages)    _____

    **(12)** Taxes (not deducted from wages)    _____

    **(13)** Alimony, maintenance, or support payments    _____

    **(14)** Other payments for support of dependents not living at home    _____

    **(15)** Religious and other charitable contributions    _____

    **(16)** Other (specify)    _____
        _____    _____
        _____    _____

                                        Total    _____

    **c.**  Excess of estimated future monthly income (last line of Item 4a, above) over estimated future expenses (last line of Item 4b, above)          _____

    **d.**  Total amount to be paid each month under plan          _____

**5.** *Payment of attorney.*

    **a.**  How much have you agreed to pay or what property have you agreed to transfer to your attorney in connection with this case?          _____

    **b.**  How much have you paid or what have you transferred to the attorney?          _____

**6.** *Tax refunds.* (To be answered by debtor, if unmarried, otherwise for each spouse whether single or joint petition is filed, unless spouses are separated and a single petition is filed.)

To what tax refunds (income or other), if any, is either of you, or may either of you be, entitled? (Give particular, including information as to any refunds payable jointly to you or any other person. All such refunds should also be listed in Item 13b.)

---

**7.** *Financial accounts, certificates of deposit and safe deposit boxes.* (To be answered by debtor, if unmarried, otherwise for each spouse whether single or joint petition is filed unless spouses are separated and a single petition is filed.)

    **a.**  Does either of you currently have any accounts or certificates of deposit or shares in banks, savings and loan, thrift, building and loan and homestead associations, credit unions, brokerage houses, pension funds and the like? (If so, give name and address of each institution, number and nature of account, current balance, and name and address of every other person authorized to make withdrawals from the account. Such accounts should also be listed in Item 13b.)

---

    **b.**  Does either of you currently keep any safe deposit boxes of other depositories? (If so, give name and address of bank or other depository, name and address of every other person who has a right of access thereto, and a brief description of the contents thereof, which should also be listed in Item 13b.)

---

**8.** *Prior Bankruptcy.*

What cases under the Bankruptcy Act or Bankruptcy Code have previously been brought by or against you or either spouse filing a petition? (State the location of the bankruptcy court, the nature and number of each case, the date when it was filed, and whether a discharge was granted or denied, the case was dismissed, or a composition, arrangement, or plan was confirmed.)

---

**9.** *Foreclosures, executions, and attachments.* (To be answered by debtor, if unmarried, otherwise for each spouse whether single or joint petition is filed unless spouses are separated and a single petition is filed.)

    **a.** Is any of the property of either of you, including real estate, involved in a foreclosure proceeding, in or out of court? (If so, identify the property and the person foreclosing.)

    **b.** Has any property or income of either of you been attached, garnished, or seized under any legal or equitable process within the 90 days immediately preceding the filing of the original petition herein? (If so, describe the property seized, or person garnished, and at whose suit.)

**10.** *Repossessions and returns.* (To be answered by debtor, if unmarried, otherwise for each spouse whether single or joint petition is filed unless spouses are separated and a single petition is filed.)

Has any property of either of you been returned to, repossessed, or seized by the seller or by any other party, including a landlord, during the 90 days immediately preceding the filing of the original petition herein? (If so, give particulars, including the name and address of the party taking the property and its description and value.)

**11.** *Transfers of Property.* (To be answered by debtor, if unmarried, otherwise for each spouse whether single or joint petition is filed unless spouses are separated and a single petition is filed.)

    **a.** Has either of you made any gifts, other than ordinary and usual presents to family members and charitable donations, during the year immediately preceding the filing of the original petition herein? (If so, give names and addresses of donees and dates, description and value of gifts.)

    **b.** Has either of you made any other transfer, absolute or for the purpose of security, or any other disposition, of real or personal property during the year immediately preceding the filing of the original petition herein? (Give a description of the property, the date of the transfer or disposition, to whom transferred or how disposed of, and, if the transferee is a relative or insider, the relationship, the consideration, if any, received therefor, and the disposition of such consideration.)

**12.** *Debts.* (To be answered by debtor, if unmarried, otherwise for each spouse whether single or joint petition is filed.)

**a.** *Debts Having Priority.*

| (1) | (2) | (3) | (4) | (5) |
|---|---|---|---|---|
| *Nature of claim* | *Name of creditor and complete mailing address including zip code* | *Specify when claim was incurred and the consideration therefor; when claim is subject to setoff, evidenced by a judgment, negotiable instrument, or other writing* | *Indicate if claim is contingent, unliquidated, or disputed* | *Amount of claim* |

1. Wages, salary, and commissions, including vacation, severance and sick leave pay owing to employees not exceeding $2,000 to each, earned within 90 days before filing of petition or cessation of business (if earlier specify date).   $____

2. Contributions to employee benefit plans for services rendered within 180 days before filing of petition or cessation of business (if earlier specify date).   $____

3. Deposits by individuals, not exceeding $900 for each for purchase, lease, or rental of property or services for personal, family, or household use that were not delivered or provided.   $____

4. Taxes owing [itemize by type of tax and taxing authority]
   (A) To the United States   $____
   (B) To any state   ____
   (C) To any other taxing authority _____   ____
   
                                            Total   ____

**b.** *Secured Debts.* List all debts which are or may be secured by real or personal property. (Indicate in sixth column, if debt payable in installments, the amount of each installment, the installment period (monthly, weekly, or otherwise) and number of installments in arrears, if any. Indicate in last column whether husband or wife solely liable, or whether you are jointly liable.)

| Creditor's name, account number and complete mailing address including zip code | Consideration or basis for debt | Amount claimed by creditor | If disputed, amount admitted by debtor | Description of collateral [include year and make of automobile] | Installment amount, period, and number of installments in arrears | Husband or wife solely liable, or jointly liable |
|---|---|---|---|---|---|---|
| | | | | | | |
| | | | | | | |
| | | | | | | |
| | | | | | | |

                          Total secured debts _____

    **c.**  *Unsecured Debts*. List all other debts, liquidated and unliquidated, including taxes, attorneys' fees, and tort claims.

| Creditor's name, account number and complete mailing address including zip code | Consideration or basis for debt | Amount claimed by creditor | If disputed, amount admitted by debtor | Husband or wife solely liable, or jointly liable |
|---|---|---|---|---|
| | | | | |
| | | | | |
| | | | | |
| | | | | |
| | | | | |

Total unsecured debts _____

**13.**  *Codebtors*. (To be answered by debtor, if unmarried, otherwise for each spouse whether single or joint petition is filed.)

    **a.**  Are any other persons liable, as cosigners, guarantors, or in any other manner, on any of the debts of either of you or is either of you so liable on the debts of others? (If so, give particulars, indicating which spouse is liable and including names of creditors, nature of debt, names and addresses of codebtors, and their relationship, if any, to you.)

    **b.**  If so, have the codebtors made any payments on the debts? (Give name of each codebtor and amount paid by codebtor.)

    **c.**  Has either of you made any payments on the debts? (If so, specify total amount paid to each creditor, whether paid by husband or wife, and name of codebtor.)

**14.**  *Property and Exemptions*. (To be answered by debtor, if unmarried, otherwise for each spouse whether single or joint petition is filed.)

    **a.**  *Real Property*. List all real property owned by either of you at date of filing of original petition herein. (Indicate in last column whether owned solely by husband or wife, or jointly.)

| Description and location of property | Name of any co-owner other than spouse | Present market value (without deduction for mortgage or other security interest) | Amount of mortgage or other security interest on this property | Name of mortgagee or other secured creditor | Value claimed exempt (specify federal or state statute creating the exemption) | Owned solely by husband or wife or jointly |
|---|---|---|---|---|---|---|
| | | | | | | |
| | | | | | | |
| | | | | | | |
| | | | | | | |

**b.** *Personal Property.* List all other property, owned by either of you at date of filing of original petition herein.

| Description | Location of property if not at debtor's residence | Name of any co-owner other than spouse | Present market value (without deduction for mortgage or other security interest) | Amount of mortgage or other security interest on this property | Name of mortgagee or other secured creditor | Value claimed exempt, (specify federal or state statute creating the exemption) | Owned solely by husband or wife or jointly |
|---|---|---|---|---|---|---|---|
| Autos [give year and make] | | | | | | | |
| Household goods | | | | | | | |
| Personal effects | | | | | | | |
| Cash or financial account | | | | | | | |
| Other [specify] | | | | | | | |

[To be signed by both spouses when joint petition is filed.]

I, _____, [*if joint petition is filed* and I, _____,] declare under penalty of perjury that I have read the answers contained in the foregoing statement, consisting of _____ sheets, and that they are true and complete to the best of my knowledge, information, and belief.

_____
*Husband [or Debtor]*

_____
*Wife*

Executed on

**Advisory Committee note.** This form is adapted from former Chapter XIII Official Form No. 13-5. It may be used whether a single chapter 13 petition is filed or a joint petition is filed by husband and wife as authorized by § 302 of the Code.

Question 4 of the Statement, calling for a detailed family budget is particularly designed to insure that the debtor and the debtor's attorney will have compiled information relative to the feasibility of the plan prior to the creditors' meeting. Inquiry as to most transactions and developments affecting the financial condition of the debtor is limited to the year preceding the filing of the petition or to a shorter period. The scope of examination at the meeting or at any other time is not restricted by the scope of the inquiries in the Chapter 13 Statement. In Question 14a and b any claim of exempt property should be listed. This information assists the court in comparing the creditors' return under the plan and a possible chapter 7 case. Although Chapter 13 Statements are required by Rule 1007(f) to be filed in the same number as the petition they accompany, only the original need be signed and verified, but the copies must be conformed to the original. See Bankruptcy Rule 9011(c).

**Advisory Committee note to 1986 amendment.** In paragraph 8 the references to "proceedings" have been changed to "cases".

## OFFICIAL FORM NO. 11

### Form 11. Involuntary Case: Creditors' Petition (Official Form No. 11)

*[Caption as in Form No. 1]*

Involuntary Case: Creditors' Petition

1. Petitioners, _____, of * _____, and _____, of * _____, and _____, of * _____, are creditors of _____, of *_____ [*include county*], holding claims against the debtor, not contingent as to liability and not subject to bona fide dispute, amounting in the aggregate, in excess of the value of any lien held by them on the debtor's property securing such claims, to at least $5000. The nature and amount of petitioners' claims are as follows: _____

2. The debtor's principal place of business [*or* principal assets *or* domicile *or* residence] has been within this district for the 180 days preceding the filing of this petition [*or* for a longer portion of the 180 days preceding the filing of this petition than in any other district].

3. The debtor is a person against whom an order for relief may be entered under title 11, United States Code.

4. [The debtor is generally not paying its debts which are not subject to bona fide dispute as they become due as indicated by the following _____] *or* [Within 120 days preceding the filing of this petition, a custodian was appointed for *or* has taken possession of substantially all of the property of the debtor, as follows: _____]

* State mailing address.

WHEREFORE petitioners pray that an order of relief be entered against _____ under chapter 7 [*or* 11] of title 11, United States Code.

Signed: _____,
*Attorney for Petitioners.*

Address: _____
_____

[*Petitioners sign if not represented by attorney*]

_____,
_____,
_____,
*Petitioners.*

I, _____, one of the petitioners named in the foregoing petition, declare under penalty of perjury that the foregoing is true and correct according to the best of my knowledge, information, and belief.

Executed on _____

Signature: _____,
*Petitioner.*

**Advisory Committee note.** The requisites for an involuntary petition are specified in § 303 of the Code.

28 U.S.C. § 1746 permits the unsworn declaration in lieu of a verification. See Advisory Committee Note to Form No. 1.

**Advisory Committee note to 1986 amendment.** The inclusion in paragraphs 1 and 4 of the allegations that the debts are not subject to bona fide dispute reflects the requirements added to §§ 303(b)(i) and 303(h)(i) of the Code by the 1984 amendments.

## OFFICIAL FORM NO. 12

### Form 12. Involuntary Case Against Partnership: Partner's Petition (Official Form No. 12)

[*Caption as in Form No. 1*]

Involuntary Case Against Partnership: Partner's Petition

1. Petitioner, _____, of * _____ is one of the general partners of _____, a partnership, of * _____ [*include county*]
2. The other general partners of the debtor are _____, of * _____ and _____ of * _____

* State mailing address.

3.   The debtor has had its principal place of business [*or* its principal assets *or* its domicile *or* its residence] within this district for the 180 days preceding the filing of this petition [*or* for a longer portion of the 180 days preceding the filing of this petition than in any other district].

4.   The debtor is a person against whom an order for relief may be entered under title 11, United States Code.

5.   [The debtor is generally not paying its debts which are not subject to bona fide dispute as they become due as indicated by the following _____] *or* [Within 120 days preceding the filing of this petition, a custodian was appointed for *or* has taken possession of substantially all of the property of the debtor, as follows:

_____]

WHEREFORE, petitioner prays that an order of relief be entered against _____under chapter 7 [*or* 11] of title 11, United States Code.

                    Signed:   _____,
                              *Attorney for Petitioner.*
                    Address:  _____,
                              _____,
                              [*Petitioners sign if not
                              represented by attorney*]
                              _____,
                              *Petitioners.*

I, _____, the petitioner named in the foregoing petition, declare under penalty of perjury that the foregoing is true and correct according to the best of my knowledge, information and belief.

Executed on _____

                    Signature: _____,
                              *Petitioner.*

(As amended Order of the Judicial Conference of the United States, effective September 19, 1986).

**Advisory Committee note.** Pursuant to § 303(b)(3)(A) of the Code, a petition by fewer than all of the general partners seeking an order for relief with respect to the partnership is treated as an involuntary petition. It is adversarial in character because not all of the partners are joining in the petition.

Section 303(b)(3)(B) permits a petition against the partnership if relief has been ordered under the Code with respect to all of the general partners. In that event, the petition may be filed by a general partner, a trustee of a general partner's estate, or a creditor of the partnership. This form may be adapted for use in that type of case.

28 U.S.C. § 1472(1) specifies the proper venue alternatives for all persons, including partnerships as domicile, residence, principal place of business or location of principal assets. These options are set forth in paragraph (3)

of the form. The paragraph may be adapted for use when venue is based on a pending case commenced by an affiliate pursuant to 28 U.S.C. § 1472(2).

**Advisory Committee note to 1986 amendment.** The inclusion in paragraph 5 of the allegation that the debts are not subject to a bona fide dispute reflects the requirement added to § 303(h)(1) of the Code by the 1984 amendments.

## OFFICIAL FORM NO. 13

### Form 13. Summons to Debtor in Involuntary Case (Official Form No. 13)

### United States Bankruptcy Court

_____ **District of** _____

**In re**

**Debtor\***                                    Bankruptcy Case No.
Social Security No.:
Employer Tax I.D. No.:

## SUMMONS TO DEBTOR IN INVOLUNTARY CASE

**To the above named debtor:**

A petition under title 11, United States Code was filed against you on _____ in this bankruptcy court, requesting an order for relief under
(date)
chapter _____ of the Bankruptcy Code (title 11 of the United States Code).

YOU ARE SUMMONED and required to submit to the clerk of the bankruptcy court a motion or answer to the petition within 20 days after the service of this summons. A copy of the petition is attached.

Address of Clerk

At the same time you must also serve a copy of your motion or answer on petitioner's attorney.

```
┌─────────────────────────────────────────────────────────────────┐
│                                                                   │
│   Name and Address of Petitioner's Attorney                       │
│                                                                   │
│                                                                   │
│                                                                   │
│                                                                   │
└─────────────────────────────────────────────────────────────────┘
```

If you make a motion, your time to serve an answer is governed by Bankruptcy Rule 1011(c). If you fail to respond to this summons, the order for relief will be entered.

_____
Clerk of the Bankruptcy Court

_____          By:_____
Date                                                          Deputy Clerk

*Set forth all names, including trade names, used by the debtor within the last 6 years. (Bankruptcy Rule 1005). For joint debtors, set forth both social security numbers.*

## CERTIFICATE OF SERVICE

I, _____, certify that I am, and at all times during the
(name)

service of process was, not less than 18 years of age and not a party to the matter concerning which service of process was made. I further certify that the service of this summons and a copy of the complaint was made _____ by:
(date)

☐  Mail service; Regular, first class United States mail, postage fully prepaid, addressed to:

☐  Personal Service: By leaving the process with defendant or with an officer or agent of defendant at:

☐  Residence Service: By leaving the process with the following adult at:

☐  Publication: The defendant was served as follows: [Describe briefly]

☐  State Law: The defendant was served pursuant to the laws of the State of _____, as follows: [Describe briefly]
(name of state)

Under penalty of perjury, I declare that the foregoing is true and correct.

_____             _____
            Date                                                   Signature

| |
|---|
| Print Name |
| Business Address |
| City                       State           Zip |

**Advisory Committee note.** This form is to be used as provided in Rule 1010.

## OFFICIAL FORM NO. 14

### Form 14. Order for Relief Under Chapter 7 (Official Form No. 14)

**United States Bankruptcy Court**
**_____ District of _____**

In re

**Debtor***                        } Bankruptcy Case No.
Social Security No.:
Employer Tax I.D. No.:

## ORDER FOR RELIEF UNDER CHAPTER 7

On consideration of the petition filed on _____against

(date)

the above-named debtor, an order for relief under chapter 7 of the Bankruptcy
Code (title 11 of the United States Code) is granted.

_____                _____
Date                                           Bankruptcy Judge

*Set forth all names, including trade names, used by the debtor within the
last 6 years. (Bankruptcy Rule 1005). For joint debtors set forth both social
security numbers.

**Advisory Committee note.** This form is an adaptation of former Official Form No. 11. It is appropriate for use when relief is ordered on an involuntary petition filed under § 303 of the Code with respect to chapter 7 (liquidation) or chapter 11 (reorganization).

If a contested petition is tried by the court without a jury (or with an advisory jury), the findings of fact and conclusions of law thereon must be stated separately. See Rule 7052(a), which is made applicable to proceedings on a contested petition by Rule 1018.

## OFFICIAL FORM NO. 14A

## Form 14A. Order for Relief Under Chapter 11 (Official Form No. 14A)

### United States Bankruptcy Court

_____ District of _____

In re

Debtor*                              } Bankruptcy Case No.
Social Security No.:
Employer Tax I.D. No.:

## ORDER FOR RELIEF UNDER CHAPTER 11

On consideration of the petition filed on _____against

(date)

the above-named debtor, an order for relief under chapter 11 of the Bankruptcy
Code (title 11 of the United States Code) is granted.

_____              _____
Date                                              Bankruptcy Judge

*Set forth all names, including trade names, used by the debtor within the
last 6 years. (Bankruptcy Rule 1005). For joint debtors set forth both social
security numbers.

## OFFICIAL FORM NO. 15

### Form 15. Appointment of Committee of Unsecured Creditors in a Chapter 11 Reorganization Case (Official Form No. 15)

**United States Bankruptcy Court**
_____ District of _____

**In re**

**Debtor\***
Social Security No.:
Employer Tax I.D. No.:

Bankruptcy Case No.

## APPOINTMENT OF COMMITTEE OF UNSECURED CREDITORS IN A CHAPTER 11 REORGANIZATION CASE

☐ The following creditors of the above-named debtor holding the 7 largest unsecured claims and who are willing to serve are appointed to the committee of unsecured creditors:

☐ The following creditors of the above-named debtor who are members of a committee organized by creditors before commencement of this case under chapter 11 of the Bankruptcy Code (title 11 of the United States Code), which was fairly chosen and is representative of the different kinds of claims to be represented, and who are willing to serve, are appointed to the committee of unsecured creditors

| Name and Address | Name and Address | Name and Address |
|---|---|---|
| Name and Address | Name and Address | Name and Address |
| Name and Address | Name and Address | Name and Address |

*Set forth all names, including trade names, used by the debtor within the last 6 years. (Bankruptcy Rule 1005). For joint debtors set forth both social security numbers.*

Creditors that are partnerships or corporations should designate contact persons to whom correspondence should be directed. If a contact person is replaced, the court and other committee members must be advised in writing.

| | |
|---|---|
| _____ | _____ |
| Date | Bankruptcy Judge |

**Advisory Committee note.** This form is new. Pursuant to § 1102 of the Code the court is to appoint a committee of unsecured creditors which ordinarily is to consist of the creditors holding the 7 largest claims and who are willing to serve. If, however, a committee has been organized prior to the filing of the petition, is representative and was fairly chosen, that committee may be continued as the official or statutory committee.

This form can be adapted for use by the United States trustee who, pursuant to § 151102 of the Code, will appoint the committee. It may also be adapted for use if the court (or United States trustee on order of the court) appoints any other committee, e.g., of equity security holders.

Pursuant to § 901(a) of the Code, the provisions of § 1102, including subsection (a)(1) apply in a case under chapter 9, Adjustment of Debts of Municipality. In a chapter 9 case, only the court will appoint the committee. There is no provision in chapter 15 for a United States trustee to have any appointing function in that type of a case.

Subsection (a)(1) of § 1102 is not applicable in a railroad reorganization case and, therefore, the court will not appoint an unsecured creditors' committee.

**Advisory Committee note to 1986 amendment.** This form is amended to conform to the 1984 amendments to § 1102(b)(1) of the Code.

## OFFICIAL FORM NO. 16

### Form 16. Order for Meeting of Creditors and Related Orders, Combined with Notice Thereof and of Automatic Stay (Official Form No. 16)

*[Caption as in Form No. 1]*

Order for Meeting of Creditors and Fixing Times for Filing
Objections to Discharge and for Filing Complaints
to Determine Dischargeability of Certain Debts,
Combined with Notice Thereof and of Automatic Stay

To the debtor, creditors, and other parties in interest:
An order for relief under 11 U.S.C. chapter 7 [*or,* 11, *or* 13] having been entered on a petition filed by [*or* against] _____ of

\* _____,

on _____ it is ordered, and notice is hereby given, that:

\* State mailing address.

## [MEETING OF CREDITORS]

1.  A meeting of creditors pursuant to 11 U.S.C. § 341(a) has been scheduled for _____ at _____ o'clock __ m. at _____.

2.  The debtor shall appear in person [*or, if the debtor is a partnership,* by a general partner, *or, if the debtor is a corporation,* by its president *or other executive officer*] at that time and place for the purpose of being examined.

## [DEADLINE TO OBJECT TO DISCHARGE OR DETERMINE NONDISCHARGEABILITY OF CERTAIN DEBTS]

3.  [*If the debtor is an individual*] _____ is fixed as the last day for the filing of objections to the discharge of the debtor pursuant to 11 U.S.C. § 727.

4.  [*If the debtor is an individual*] _____ is fixed as the last day for the filing of a complaint to determine the dischargeability of any debt pursuant to 11 U.S.C. § 523(c).

## [ADDITIONAL INFORMATION CONCERNING THE MEETING, THE AUTOMATIC STAY AND THE DISCHARGE]

You are further notified that:

The meeting may be continued or adjourned from time to time by notice at the meeting, without further written notice to creditors.

Attendance by creditors at the meeting is welcomed, but not required. At the meeting the creditors may file their claims, [elect a trustee as permitted by law, designate a person to supervise the meeting, elect a committee of creditors,] examine the debtor, and transact such other business as may properly come before the meeting.

As a result of the filing of the petition, certain acts and proceedings against the debtor and property of the estate and of the debtor are stayed as provided in 11 U.S.C. § 362(a).

[*If the debtor is an individual*] If no objection to the discharge of the debtor is filed on or before the last day fixed therefor as stated in subparagraph 3 above, the debtor will be granted a discharge. If no complaint to determine the dischargeability of a debt under clause (2), (4), or (6) of 11 U.S.C. § 523(a) is filed within the time fixed therefor as stated in subparagraph 4 above, the debt may be discharged.

## [FILING OF CLAIMS]

[*For a chapter 7 or 13 case*] In order to have a claim allowed so that a creditor may share in any distribution from the estate, a creditor must file a claim, whether or not the creditor is included in the list of creditors filed by the debtor. Claims which are not filed within 90 days following the above date set for the meeting of creditors will not be allowed, except as otherwise provided by law. A claim may be filed in the office of the clerk of the bankruptcy court on an official form prescribed for a proof of claim.

[*If a no-asset or nominal asset case, the following paragraph may be used in lieu of the preceding paragraph.*] It appears from the schedules of the debtor that there are no assets from which any dividend can be paid to creditors. It is unnecessary for any creditor to file a claim at this time in order to share in any distribution from the estate. If it subsequently appears that there are assets from which a dividend may be paid, creditors will be so notified and given an opportunity to file their claims.

[*For a chapter 11 case*] The debtor [*or* trustee] has filed or will file a list of creditors and equity security holders pursuant to Rule 1007. Any creditor holding a listed claim which is not listed as disputed, contingent, or unliquidated as to amount, may, but need not, file a proof of claim in this case. Creditors whose claims are not listed or whose claims are listed as disputed, contingent, or unliquidated as to amount and who desire to participate in the case or share in any distribution must file their proofs of claim on or before _____, which date is hereby fixed as the last day for filing a proof of claim [*or, if appropriate,* on or before a date to be later fixed on which you will be notified]. Any creditor who desires to rely on the list has the responsibility for determining that the claim is accurately listed.

### [OBJECTION TO CLAIM OF EXEMPTIONS]

Unless the court extends the time, any objection to the debtor's claim of exempt property (Schedule B-4) must be filed within 30 days after the conclusion of the meeting of creditors.

### [TRUSTEE]

[*If appropriate*] _____ of * _____ has been appointed [*interim*] *trustee of the estate of the above-named debtor.*

\* State mailing address.

## United States Bankruptcy Court
## _____ District of _____

In re

}

Debtor*                                    Bankruptcy Case No.
Social Security No.:
Employer Tax I.D. No.:

## DISCHARGE OF ONE JOINT DEBTOR

It appears that _____** has joined in a petition
commencing a case under title 11, United States Code, which was filed on
_____, that an order for relief was entered under chapter
          (date)
7 and that no complaint objecting to the discharge of such debtor was filed
within the time fixed by the court [*or* that a complaint objecting to discharge of
the debtor was filed and, after due notice and hearing, was not sustained].

## IT IS ORDERED THAT:

1.  _____** is released from all dischargeable
    debts.

2.  Any judgment heretofore or hereafter obtained in any court other than this
    court is null and void as a determination of the personal liability of_____
    _____** with respect to any of the following:
    **(a)**  debts dischargeable under 11 U.S.C. § 523;
    **(b)**  unless heretofore or hereafter determined by order of this court to be
         nondischargeable, debts alleged to be excepted from the discharge
         under clauses (2), (4) and (6) of 11 U.S.C. § 523 (a);
    **(c)**  debts determined by this court to be discharged under 11 U.S.C.
         § 523.

3.  All creditors whose debts are discharged by this order and all creditors
    whose judgments are declared null and void by paragraph 2 above are en-
    joined from instituting or continuing any action or employing any process
    of engaging in any act to collect such debts as personal liabilities of _____
    _____**

_____                    _____
          Date                                     Bankruptcy Judge

*Set forth all names, including trade names, used by the debtor within the
last 6 years. (Bankruptcy Rule 1005). For joint debtors set forth both social
security numbers.*

*\*\*When only one of the debtors in a joint use is discharged, state here the name of the individual debtor being discharged.*

Dated _____

BY THE COURT

_____,

*Bankruptcy Judge.*

**Advisory Committee note:** This form can be used for cases filed under chapter 7, 11, or 13. It conforms with Rule 2003 which specifies that the court is to call the meeting of creditors even though, under the Code, it may not preside at such meeting.

This form revises former Official Form No. 12. The alternative paragraph is to be used when the court exercises the option under Rule 2002(e) to notify the creditors that no dividends are to be anticipated and no claims need be filed.

**OFFICIAL FORM NO. 17**

**Form 17. General Power of Attorney (Official Form No. 17)**

*[Caption as in Form No. 2]*

General Power of Attorney

To _____ of \* _____, and _____ of \* _____:
The undersigned claimant hereby authorizes you, or any one of you, as attorney in fact for the undersigned and with full power of substitution, to vote on any question that may be lawfully submitted to creditors of the debtor in the above-entitled case; [*if appropriate*] to vote for a trustee of the estate of the debtor and for a committee of creditors; to receive dividends; and in general to perform any act not constituting the practice of law for the undersigned in all matters arising in this case.

Dated: _____          Signed: _____

[*If appropriate*] By _____

as _____

Address: _____

[*If executed by an individual*] Acknowledged before me on _____

[*If executed on behalf of a partnership*] Acknowledged before me on _____,
by _____, who says that he [*or* she] is a member of the partnership named above and is authorized to execute this power of attorney in its behalf.

[*If executed on behalf of a corporation*] Acknowledged before me on _____,

\* State mailing address.

by _____, who says that he [or she] is _____ of the corporation named above and is authorized to execute this power of attorney in its behalf.

_____,

_____

[*Official character.*]

**Advisory Committee note.** Rule 9010(c) requires a general power of attorney to be prepared substantially in conformity with this form which is derived from former Official Form No. 13. While a power of attorney may of course be executed in favor of an attorney at law who is also retained as such to represent the creditor executing the form, the power of attorney does not purport to confer the right to act as an attorney at law. The corollary is that one not an attorney at law may act under a general power of attorney within the limitations prescribed in the form.

## OFFICIAL FORM NO. 18

### Form 18. Special Power of Attorney (Official Form No. 18)

[*Caption as in Form No. 2*]

Special Power of Attorney

To _____ of * _____, and _____ of * _____:
The undersigned claimant hereby authorizes you, or any one of you, as attorney in fact for the undersigned [*if desired:* and with full power of substitution,] to attend the meeting of creditors of the debtor or any adjournment thereof, and to vote in my behalf on any question that may be lawfully submitted to creditors at such meeting or adjourned meeting, and for a trustee or trustees of the estate of the debtor.

Dated: _____        Signed: _____
                      [*If appropriate*] By _____
                                 as _____
                          Address: _____

                                 _____

[*If executed by an individual*] Acknowledged before me on _____
[*If executed on behalf of a partnership*] Acknowledged before me on _____,
by _____, who says that he [*or* she] is a member of the partnership named above and is authorized to execute this power of attorney in its behalf.
[*If executed on behalf of a corporation*] Acknowledged before me on _____,
by _____, who says that he [or she] is _____ of the cor-

* State mailing address.

poration named above and is authorized to execute this power of attorney in its behalf.

_____,

_____

[*Official character.*]

**Advisory Committee note.** A special power of attorney shall conform substantially with this official form, as provided in Rule 9010(c), but it may grant either more or less authority in accordance with the language used. The form is derived from former Official Form No. 14.

## OFFICIAL FORM NO. 19

### Form 19. Proof of Claim (Official Form No. 19)

[*Caption as in Form No. 2*]

Proof of Claim

1. [*If claimant is an individual*] The undersigned, _____ who is the claimant herein, resides at* _____.
   [*If claimant is a partnership claiming through a member*] The undersigned, _____, who resides at * _____, is a member of _____, a partnership, composed of the undersigned and _____, of * _____, and doing business at * _____, and is authorized to make this proof of claim in behalf of the partnership.
   [*If claimant is a corporation claiming through an authorized officer*] The undersigned, _____, who resides at * _____, is the _____ of _____, a corporation organized under the laws of _____ and doing business at * _____, and is authorized to make this proof of claim on behalf of the corporation.
   [*If claim is made by agent*] The undersigned, _____, who resides at * _____, is the agent of _____, of * _____, and is authorized to make this proof of claim on behalf of the claimant.

2. The debtor was, at the time of the filing of the petition initiating this case, and still is indebted [*or* liable] to this claimant, in the sum of $_____.

3. The consideration for this debt [*or* ground of liability] is as follows: ____
   _____.

* State mailing address.

[*If filed in a chapter 7 or 13 case*] This claim consists of $_____ in principal amount and $_____ in additional charges [*or* no additional charges]. [*Itemize all charges in addition to principal amount of debt, state basis for inclusion and computation, and set forth any other consideration relevant to the legality of the charge.*]_____

_____

_____

_____.

4. [*If the claim is founded on writing*] The writing on which this claim is founded (or a duplicate thereof) is attached hereto [*or* cannot be attached for the reason set forth in the statement attached hereto].

5. [*If appropriate*] This claim is founded on an open account, which became [*or* will become] due on _____, as shown by the itemized statement attached hereto. Unless it is attached hereto or its absence is explained in an attached statement, no note or other negotiable instrument has been received for the account or any part of it.

6. No judgment has been rendered on the claim except _____

_____.

7. The amount of all payments on this claim has been credited and deducted for the purpose of making this proof of claim.

8. This claim is not subject to any setoff or counterclaim except _____

_____.

9. No security interest is held for this claim except _____
[*If security interest in property of the debtor is claimed*] The undersigned claims the security interest under the writing referred to in paragraph 4 hereof [*or* under a separate writing which (or a duplicate of which) is attached hereto, *or* under a separate writing which cannot be attached hereto for the reason set forth in the statement attached hereto]. Evidence of perfection of such security interest is also attached hereto.

10. This claim is a general unsecured claim, except to the extent that the security interest, if any, described in paragraph 9 is sufficient to satisfy the claim. [*If priority is claimed, state the amount and basis thereof*]._____

_____.

Dated_____

Signed:_____

*Penalty for Presenting Fraudulent Claim.* Fine of not more than $5,000 or imprisonment for not more than 5 years or both—Title 18, U.S.C., § 152.

**Advisory Committee note.** This form is derived from former Official Form No. 15. It may be used by any claimant, including a wage earner for whom alternative short forms have been specially prepared (Form Nos. 20 and No. 21), or by an agent or attorney for any claimant. Such a combined form is commonly used in practice.

If a security interest in the debtor's property is claimed, paragraph 9 requires that any security agreement (if not included in the writing on which the claim is founded and which is required by paragraph 4 to be attached) be attached to the proof of claim or that the reason why it cannot be attached be set forth. Paragraph 9 further requires evidence of perfection of the security interest to be attached to the proof of claim. See the Note to Rule 3001(d) as to what constitutes satisfactory evidence of perfection. The information so required will expedite determination of the validity of any claimed security interest as against the trustee.

Paragraph 10, requiring an explicit statement as to whether the claim is filed as a general, priority, or secured claim, will facilitate administration and minimize troublesome litigation over the question whether a proof of claim was intended as a waiver of security. See, e.g., *United States National Bank* v. *Chase National Bank,* 331 U.S. 28, 35–36 (1947); 3 Collier, *Bankruptcy* ¶ 57.07[3.1] (14th ed. 1961).

## OFFICIAL FORM NO. 20

### Form 20. Proof of Claim for Wages, Salary, or Commissions (Official Form No. 20)

*[Caption as in Form No. 2]*

Proof of Claim for Wages, Salary, or Commissions

1. The undersigned, _____, claimant herein resides at _____ and has social security number _____.

2. The debtor owes the claimant computed as follows:  $_____
   (a) wages, salary, or commissions for services performed from _____ to _____, at the following rate or rates of compensation _____  $_____
   *[if appropriate]*
   (b) allowances and benefits, such as vacation, severance and sick leave pay [specify]  $_____
   Total amount claimed  $_____

3. The claimant demands priority to the extent permitted by 11 U.S.C. § 507(a)(3).

4. The claimant has received no payment, no security, and no check or other evidence of this debt except as follows:_____.

Dated:_____

Signed:_____

*Claimant.*

*Penalty for Presenting Fraudulent Claim.* Fine of not more than $5,000 or imprisonment for not more than 5 years or both—Title 18, U.S.C., § 152.

> **Advisory Committee note.** This form is an adaptation of former Official Form No. 16 for the exclusive use of claimants for personal earnings in cases under the Code. Its limited purpose permits elimination of recitals that are appropriate for priority under § 507(a)(3) of the Code. If the claim as filed includes an amount not entitled to priority because, for example, not earned within the applicable 90 day period, reference to payroll records will ordinarily permit determination of the amount of the priority, if any, to which the claimant is entitled. If such records are unavailable, the claimant may be required to supply additional information as a condition to allowance of the claim with priority.

## OFFICIAL FORM NO. 21

### Form 21. Proof of Multiple Claims for Wages, Salary, or Commissions (Official Form No. 21)

*[Caption as in Form No. 2]*

Proof of Multiple Claims for Wages, Salary, or Commissions

1. The undersigned, whose address is* _____, is the agent of the claimants listed in the statement appended to this proof of claim and is authorized to make this proof of claims on their behalf.
2. The debtor owes the claimants $_____, computed as indicated in the appended statement. [Form BOF 21A may be used.]
3. The claimants demand priority to the extent permitted by 11 U.S.C. § 507(a)(3) and (4).
4. The claimants have received no payment, no security, and no check or other evidence of this debt except as follows:

Dated: _____            Signed: _____

*Penalty for Presenting Fraudulent Claim.* Fine of not more than $5,000 or imprisonment for not more than 5 years or both—Title 18, U.S.C., § 152.

* State mailing address.

Statement of Wage Claims

| Name, Address, & Social Security Numbers | Dates services rendered, rates of pay, and fringe benefits | Contributions to employee benefit plans | Amounts Claimed |
| --- | --- | --- | --- |

**Advisory Committee note.** This form is an alternative for Form No. 20 provided for use when there are numerous claimants for wages, salary, or commissions against a debtor's estate and they wish to have their proofs of claim executed and filed by a common agent. Use of the form should not only simplify the filing procedure for the claimants but facilitate the handling of the claims by the court.

## OFFICIAL FORM NO. 22

### Form 22. Order Appointing Interim Trustee and Fixing Amount of Bond (Official Form No. 22)

[Abrogated]

**Advisory Committee note:** This form may be promulgated by the Director of the Administrative Office pursuant to Rule 9009.

## OFFICIAL FORM NO. 23

### Form 23. Order Approving Election of Trustee and Fixing Amount of Bond (Official Form No. 23)

[Abrogated]

**Advisory Committee note:** This form may be promulgated by the Director of the Administrative Office pursuant to Rule 9009.

## OFFICIAL FORM NO. 24

**Form 24. Notice to Trustee of Selection and of Time Fixed for Filing a Complaint Objecting to Discharge of Debtor (Official Form No. 24)**

### United States Bankruptcy Court
_____ District of _____

**In re**

**Debtor\***                          } Bankruptcy Case No.
Social Security No.:
Employer Tax I.D. No.:

### NOTICE TO TRUSTEE OF SELECTION AND OF TIME FIXED FOR FILING A COMPLAINT OBJECTING TO DISCHARGE OF DEBTOR

To:

---
Name and Address of Trustee
---

You are notified of your election or appointment as trustee of the estate of the above-named debtor.

Your blanket bond is deemed sufficient. If you decide to reject this office, you are required to notify the clerk of the bankruptcy court in writing within 5 days after receipt of this notice. Such notice should be sent to:

---
Address of Clerk of the Bankruptcy Court
---

The amount of your bond has been fixed at $_____. The last date to file your bond is fixed at:

Date:

You are further notified that the last day for the filing by you or any other party in interest of a complaint objecting to the discharge of the debtor has been fixed at:

Date:

_____
Clerk of the Bankruptcy Court


_____          By:   _____
Date                                      Deputy Clerk

---

*Set forth all names, including trade names, used by the debtor within the last 6 years. (Bankruptcy Rule 1005). For joint debtors set forth both social security numbers.*

**Advisory Committee note.** This form is to be used in giving the notice required by Rule 2008. If a blanket bond has been authorized pursuant to Rule 2010(a), the second sentence of the form and the last sentence of the first paragraph may be deleted.

## OFFICIAL FORM NO. 25

### Form 25. Bond and Order Approving Bond of Trustee (Official Form No. 25)

### United States Bankruptcy Court
_____ District of _____

**In re**

**Debtor\*** } Bankruptcy Case No.
Social Security No.:
Employer Tax I.D. No.:

## BOND AND ORDER APPROVING BOND OF TRUSTEE

| |
|---|
| Trustee's Name and Address |

as principal, and

| |
|---|
| Surety's Name and Address |

as surety, bind ourselves to the United States in the sum of $_____ for the faithful performance by the undersigned principal of official duties as trustee of the estate of the above-named debtor.

_____          _____
        Date                                    Signature of Principal


                                      _____
                                        Signature of Surety

This bond filed by the trustee of the estate of above-named debtor is approved.

_____                    _____
              Date                                              Bankruptcy Judge

---

*Set forth all names, including trade names, used by the debtor within the last 6 years. (Bankruptcy Rule 1005). For joint debtors set forth both social security numbers.*

**Advisory Committee Note.** This form may be used in an individual case under § 322(a) of the Code, or, by modification of the caption, the reference in the bond to debtor, and where necessary, the reference to the principal, it may be adapted for use in a series of cases when a blanket bond is given pursuant to Rule 2010(a). Unless otherwise provided by local rule, the completed bond is to be filed with the court in accordance with § 322(a).

# OFFICIAL FORM NO. 26

## Form 26. Certificate of Retention of Debtor in Possession
### (Official Form No. 26)

### United States Bankruptcy Court
#### _____ District of _____

In re

**Debtor\***                              } Bankruptcy Case No.
Social Security No.:
Employer Tax I.D. No.:

### CERTIFICATE OF RETENTION
### OF DEBTOR IN POSSESSION

I certify that the above-named debtor continues in possession of its estate as debtor in possession, no trustee having been appointed.

_____
Clerk of Bankruptcy Court

By: _____

_____
Date                                         Deputy Clerk

*Set forth all names, including trade names, used by the debtor within the last 6 years. (Bankruptcy Rule 1005). For joint debtors set forth both social security numbers.*

**Advisory Committee note.** This form may be used in chapter 11 reorganization cases. Usually, a trustee will not be appointed in which event the debtor is automatically continued in possession pursuant to § 1101(a) of the Code.

When evidence of debtor in possession status is required, this certificate may be used in accordance with Rule 2011.

## OFFICIAL FORM NO. 27

### Form 27. Discharge of Debtor (Official Form No. 27)
### United States Bankruptcy Court
_____ District of _____

In re

Debtor*                                      } Bankruptcy Case No.
Social Security No.:
Employer Tax I.D. No.:

## DISCHARGE OF DEBTOR

It appears that the person named above filed a petition commencing a case under title 11, United States Code of _____, that an order for
(date)
relief was entered under chapter 7, and that no complaint objecting to the discharge of the debtor was filed within the time fixed by the court [*or* that a complaint objecting to discharge of the debtor was filed and, after due notice and hearing, was not sustained].

## IT IS ORDERED THAT:

1.  The above-named debtor is released from all dischargeable debts.
2.  Any judgment heretofore or hereafter obtained in any court other than this court is null and void as a determination of the personal liability of the debtor with respect to any of the following:
    **(a)**  debts dischargeable under 11 U.S.C. § 523;
    **(b)**  unless heretofore or hereafter determined by order of this court to be nondischargeable, debts alleged to be excepted from the discharge under clauses (2), (4) and (6) of 11 U.S.C. § 523 (a);
    **(c)**  debts determined by this court to be discharged.

3. All creditors whose debts are discharged by this order and all creditors whose judgments are declared null and void by paragraph 2 above are enjoined from instituting or continuing any action or employing any process or engaging in any act to collect such debts as personal liabilities of the above-named debtor.

_____                    _____
        Date                                Bankruptcy Judge

_____

*Set forth all names, including trade names, used by the debtor within the last 6 years. (Bankruptcy Rule 1005).*

**Advisory Committee note.** This form is a revision of former Official Form No. 24. It takes into account the features of § 523 of the Code which in turn, were derived from the 1970 amendments to the Bankruptcy Act.

## OFFICIAL FORM NO. 27J

**Form 27J. Discharge of Joint Debtors (Official Form No. 27J)**
**United States Bankruptcy Court**
**_____ District of _____**

**In re**                                    ⎫
                                             ⎪
**Debtor***                                  ⎬  Bankruptcy Case No.
Social Security No.:                          ⎪
Employer Tax I.D. No.:                        ⎭

## DISCHARGE OF JOINT DEBTORS

It appears that the persons named above have filed a petition commencing a joint case under title 11, United States Code on _____, that an
                                             (date)
order for relief was entered under chapter 7, and that no complaint objecting to the discharge of the debtors was filed within the time fixed by the court [*or* that a complaint objecting to discharge of one or both of the debtors was filed and, after due notice and hearing, was not sustained].

## IT IS ORDERED THAT:

1. The above-named debtors are released from all dischargeable debts.
2. Any judgment heretofore or hereafter obtained in any court other than this court is null and void as a determination of the personal liability of the debtors with respect to any of the following:
   **(a)** debts dischargeable under 11 U.S.C. § 523;

**(b)**   unless heretofore or hereafter determined by order of this court to be nondischargeable, debts alleged to be excepted from the discharge under clauses (2), (4) and (6) of 11 U.S.C. § 523 (a);

**(c)**   debts determined by this court to be discharged.

3.   All creditors whose debts are discharged by this order and all creditors whose judgments are declared null and void by paragraph 2 above are enjoined from instituting or continuing any action or employing any process or engaging in any act to collect such debts as personal liabilities of the above-named debtor.

_____                         _____
Date                                                              Bankruptcy Judge
                                                                   _____

*Set forth all names, including trade names, used by the debtor within the last 6 years. (Bankruptcy Rule 1005). For joint debtors set forth both social security numbers.*

## OFFICIAL FORM NO. 28

**Form 28. Order and Notice for Hearing on Disclosure Statement
(Official Form No. 28)
United States Bankruptcy Court
_____ District of _____**

**In re**

**Debtor***                                          Bankruptcy Case No.
Social Security No.:
Employer Tax I.D. No.:

## ORDER AND NOTICE FOR HEARING ON
## DISCLOSURE STATEMENT

**To all parties in interest:**
   A disclosure statement and plan under chapter 11 of the Bankruptcy Code was filed on _____ by:
                        (date)

Name and Address of Plan Proponent:

The disclosure statement and plan are on file with the bankruptcy clerk and may be viewed during regular business hours at the Court:

| |
|---|
| Address of the Court: |

Requests for copies of the disclosure statement and plan should be directed to:

| |
|---|
| Name and Address of Attorney for Plan Proponent |

## IT IS ORDERED AND NOTICE IS GIVEN THAT:

1. The hearing to consider approval of the disclosure statement will be held at the following place and time:

| Address | Room |
|---|---|
| | Date and Time |

2. Within ___ days after entry of this order, the proponent of the plan must:
   a. send each party in interest a copy of this order and notice;
   b. send a copy of the disclosure statement and plan to the debtor, trustee, each committee appointed pursuant to §1102 of the code, the Securities and Exchange Commission, the United States Trustee, and any party in interest who requests in writing a copy of the disclosure statement and plan.

3. An objection to the disclosure statement may be filed by any party in interest, pursuant to Bankruptcy Rule 3017(a). The last date to file an objection to the disclosure statement is:

```
┌─────────────────────────────────────────────────────────────────┐
│  Date:                                                            │
│                                                                   │
│                                                                   │
│                                                                   │
└─────────────────────────────────────────────────────────────────┘
```

_____                          _____
         Date                                         Bankruptcy Judge

---

*Set forth all names, including trade names, used by the debtor within the last 6 years. (Bankruptcy Rule 1005). For joint debtors, set forth both social security numbers.*

**Advisory Committee note.** This form is new and is related to Rule 3017(a). Section 1125 of the Code requires court approval of a disclosure statement before votes may be solicited for or against a plan in either chapter 11, reorganization or chapter 9, municipality cases. Before the court may approve a disclosure statement it must find that it contains adequate information to enable creditors whose votes will be solicited to be able to make an informed judgment about the plan.

Objections may be filed to the disclosure statement. Rule 3017(a) specifies that the court may fix a time for filing of objections or they can be filed at any time prior to approval of the statement.

Rule 3017(a) also specifies the persons who are to receive copies of the statement and plan prior to the hearing. These documents will not be sent to all parties in interest because at this stage of the case it could be unnecessarily expensive and confusing. However, any party in interest may request copies. The request should be made in writing (Rule 3017(a)), and sent to the person mailing the statement and plan which, as the form indicates, would usually be the proponent of the plan.

## OFFICIAL FORM NO. 29

### Form 29. Order Approving Disclosure Statement and Fixing Time for Filing Acceptances or Rejections of Plan, Combined with Notice Thereof (Official Form No. 29)

*[Caption as in Official Form No. 1]*

Order Approving Disclosure Statement and Fixing Time for Filing Acceptances or Rejections of Plan, Combined with Notice Thereof

A disclosure statement under chapter 11 of the Bankruptcy Code having been filed by _____, on _____ [*if appropriate,* and by _____, on _____], referring to a plan under chapter 11 of the Code filed by _____, on _____ [*if appropriate*, and by _____, on _____ respectively] [*if appropriate*, as modified by a modification filed on _____]; and

It having been determined after hearing on notice that the disclosure statement [*or* statements] contain[s] adequate information;

It is ordered, and notice is hereby given, that:

A. The disclosure statement filed by _____ dated _____ [*if appropriate*, and by _____, dated _____] is [are] approved.

B. _____ is fixed as the last day for filing written acceptances or rejections of the plan [*or* plans] referred to above.

C. Within _____ days after the entry of this order, the plan [*or* plans] [*or* a summary *or* summaries thereof approved by the court], [*if appropriate* a summary approved by the court of its opinion, if any, dated, approving the disclosure statement [*or* statements]], the disclosure statement [*or* statements] and a ballot conforming to Official Form No. 29 shall be transmitted by mail to creditors, equity security holders and other parties in interest as provided in Rule 3017(d).

D. If acceptances are filed for more than one plan, preferences among the plans so accepted may be indicated.

[*If appropriate*] E. _____ is fixed for the hearing on confirmation of the plan [*or* plans].

[*If appropriate*] F. _____ is fixed as the last day for filing and serving pursuant to Rule 3020(b)(1) written objections to confirmation of the plan.

Dated: _____             BY THE COURT

_____

*Bankruptcy Judge*

[*If the court directs that a copy of the opinion should be transmitted in lieu of or in addition to the summary thereof, the appropriate change should be made in paragraph C of this order.*]

**Advisory Committee note.** This form is new. As provided in § 1125 of the Code, a disclosure statement must be approved by the court prior to the solicitation of votes to a plan. This form may be used for such approval, to give notice of the time fixed for filing acceptances or rejections and the time fixed for the hearing on confirmation if such a time has been fixed.

## OFFICIAL FORM NO. 30

### Form 30. Ballot for Accepting or Rejecting Plan (Official Form No. 30)

*[Caption as in Form No. 1]*

Ballot for Accepting or Rejecting Plan

Filed by _____on _____

*The plan referred to in this ballot can be confirmed by the court and thereby made binding on you if it is accepted by the holders of two-thirds in amount and more than one-half in number of claims in each class and the holders of two-thirds in amount of equity security interests in each class voting on the plan. In the event the requisite acceptances are not obtained, the court may nevertheless confirm the plan if the court finds that the plan accords fair and equitable treatment to the class rejecting it. To have your vote count you must complete and return this ballot.*

*[If equity security holder]* The undersigned, the holder of *[state number]* _____ shares of *[describe type]* _____ stock of the above-named debtor, represented by Certificate(s) No. _____, registered in the name of _____

*[If bondholder, debenture holder, or other debt security holder]* The undersigned, the holder of *[state unpaid principal amount]* $_____ of *[describe security]* _____ of the above-named debtor, with a stated maturity date of _____ *[if applicable* registered in the name of _____]* *[if applicable* bearing serial number(s) _____]*

*[If holder of general claim]* The undersigned, a creditor of the above-named debtor in the unpaid principal amount of $_____,

[Check One Box]

☐     Accepts                    ☐     Rejects

the plan for the reorganization of the above-named debtor.

*[If more than one plan is accepted, the following may but need not be completed.]* The undersigned prefers the plans accepted in the following order: *[Identify plans]*

1. _____

2. _____

Dated:_____

Print or type name: _____

Signed: _____

*[If appropriate]* By: _____

as: _____

Address: _____

_____

Return this ballot on or before _____

to:<br>
Name:_____<br>
Address:_____

**Advisory Committee note.** This form may be modified as necessary to include identification of as many plans as may have been transmitted on which a vote will be taken.

The form can also be modified to take account of the types of parties who will vote as among equity security holders (see § 101(15) of the Code for definition of equity security), security holders (see § 101(35) for definition of security), secured creditors and unsecured creditors.

Before the form is transmitted, the blanks identifying the plan and the name and address of the person to whom it should be returned should be completed for the information of creditors and equity security holders.

## OFFICIAL FORM NO. 31

### Form 31. Order Confirming Plan (Official Form No. 31)

*[Caption as in Form No. 1]*

Order Confirming Plan

The plan under chapter 11 of the Bankruptcy Code filed by \_\_\_\_\_, on _____ [*if appropriate,* as modified by a modification filed on _____,] or a summary thereof having been transmitted to creditors and equity security holders; and

It having been determined after hearing on notice that:

1. The plan has been accepted in writing by the creditors and equity security holders whose acceptance is required by law; and
2. The provisions of chapter 11 of the Code have been complied with; that the plan has been proposed in good faith and not by any means forbidden by law; and
3. Each holder of a claim or interest has accepted the plan [*or* will receive or retain under the plan property of a value, as of the effective date of the plan, that is not less than the amount that such holder would receive or retain if the debtor were liquidated under chapter 7 of the Code on such date] [*or* The plan does not discriminate unfairly, and is fair and equitable, with respect to each class of claims or interests that is impaired under, and has not accepted the plan]; and
4. All payments made or promised by the debtor or by a person issuing securities or acquiring property under the plan or by any other person for ser-

vices or for costs and expenses in, or in connection with, the plan and incident to the case, have been fully disclosed to the court and are reasonable or, if to be fixed after confirmation of the plan, will be subject to the approval of the court; and

5. The identity, qualifications, and affiliations of the persons who are to be directors or officers, or voting trustees, if any, of the debtor [and an affiliate of the debtor participating in a joint plan with the debtor] [or a successor to the debtor under the plan], after confirmation of the plan, have been fully disclosed, and the appointment of such persons to such offices, or their continuance therein, is equitable, and consistent with the interests of the creditors and equity security holders and with public policy; and

6. The identity of any insider that will be employed or retained by the debtor and his compensation have been fully disclosed; and

7. [If applicable] Any regulatory commission with jurisdiction, after confirmation of the plan, over the rates of the debtor has approved any rate change provided for in the plan [or any rate change is expressly conditioned on approval of any regulatory agency having jurisdiction over the rates of the debtor; and

8. [If appropriate] Confirmation of the plan is not likely to be followed by the liquidation [or the need for further financial reorganization, of the debtor or any successor to the debtor under the plan]:

It is ordered that:

The plan filed by _____, on _____, a copy of which plan is attached hereto, is confirmed.

Dated: _____

BY THE COURT

_____

Bankruptcy Judge.

**Advisory Committee note.** The order of confirmation specifies those matters heard and determined by the court at the hearing on confirmation which are required by the Code in order for a plan to be confirmed.

In the case of an individual chapter 11 debtor, Form No. 27 may be adapted for use together with this form.

# OFFICIAL FORM NO. 32

## Form 32. Notice of Filing Final Account (Official Form No. 32)
## United States Bankruptcy Court
_____ District of _____

**In re**

**Debtor\***
Social Security No.:
Employer Tax I.D. No.:

Bankruptcy Case No.

## NOTICE OF FILING OF FINAL ACCOUNT[S] OF TRUSTEE, OF HEARING ON APPLICATIONS FOR COMPENSATION [AND OF HEARING ON ABANDONMENT OF PROPERTY BY THE TRUSTEE]

## TO THE CREDITORS:

1. NOTICE IS GIVEN that the final report and account of the trustee in this case has been filed and a hearing will be held by the court at the following place and time.

| Address | Room |
|---|---|
|  | Date and Time |

2. The hearing will be held for the purpose of examining and passing on the final report and account of the trustee, acting on applications for compensation, and transacting such other business as may properly come before the court. ATTENDANCE BY THE DEBTOR AND THE CREDITORS IS WELCOMED BUT IS NOT REQUIRED.

3. The following applications for compensation have been filed:

| Applicants | Commissions or Fees | Expenses |
|---|---|---|
| _____<br>Trustee | $_____ | $_____ |
| _____<br>Attorney for Trustee | $_____ | $_____ |
| _____ | $_____ | $_____ |
| _____ | $_____ | $_____ |
| _____ | $_____ | $_____ |
| _____ | $_____ | $_____ |

4.  The trustee's account shows total receipts of     $_____
                         and total disbursements of     $_____
                             for a balance on hand of     $_____

---

*\*Set forth all names, including trade names, used by the debtor within the last 6 years. (Bankruptcy Rule 1005). For joint debtors set forth both social security numbers.*

5.  In addition to the commissions and fees that may be allowed by the court, liens and priority claims which must be paid in advance of general creditors have been allowed in the total amount of          $_____
    General unsecured claims have been allowed in the amount of
                                                                   $_____

6.  ☐  The debtor has been discharged.
    ☐  The debtor has not been discharged.

7.  ☐  The trustee's application to abandon the following property will be heard and acted upon:

_____                              _____
Date                                                              Bankruptcy Judge

**Advisory Committee note.** This form is adapted from former Official Form No. 29 which is an adaptation of a form which has been made available to bankruptcy judges by the Administrative Office of the United States Courts and used for a number of years.

# OFFICIAL FORM NO. 33

## Form 33. Final Decree (Official Form No. 33)
### United States Bankruptcy Court
_____ District of _____

**In re**

**Debtor***
Social Security No.:
Employer Tax I.D. No.: } Bankruptcy Case No.

## FINAL DECREE

The estate of the above named debtor has been fully administered.

☐ The deposit required by the plan has been distributed.

IT IS ORDERED THAT:

☐ _____
    *(name of trustee)*
is discharged as trustee of the estate of the above-named debtor and the bond is cancelled:
☐ the chapter _____ case of the above named debtor is closed; and
☐ [other provisions as needed]

_____          _____
Date                      Bankruptcy Judge

---

*Set forth all names, including trade names, used by the debtor within the last 6 years (Bankruptcy Rule 1005). For joint debtors set forth both social security numbers.*

**Advisory Committee note.** This form is to be used in conjunction with Rule 3022. The final decree may discharge the trustee if one was appointed and if the trustee had not been discharged at an earlier time.

Section 350 of the Code requires the court to close the case after an estate has been fully administered and the trustee discharged. That section is applicable to chapter 7, 9, 11 and 13 cases and this form may be adapted to the circumstances of the particular case.

## OFFICIAL FORM NO. 34

### Form 34. Caption of Adversary Proceedings (Official Form No. 34)

**In re**                                            Bankruptcy Case No.

                  Debtor
                  Plaintiff

            v.                          Adversary Proceeding No.

                  Defendant

**Advisory Committee note.** Rule 7010 requires the caption of a pleading in an adversary proceeding to conform substantially to this form.

## OFFICIAL FORM NO. 35

### Form 35. Notice of Appeal to a District Court or Bankruptcy Appellate Panel from a Judgment of a Bankruptcy Court Entered in an Adversary Proceeding (Official Form No. 35)

UNITED STATES BANKRUPTCY COURT

_____ DISTRICT OF _____

_____ x

**In re**          Case No._____

_____

                Debtor,

_____

                Plaintiff,          ADV. PRO. NO._____

        v.

_____

                Defendant.

_____ x

NOTICE OF APPEAL

_____, the plaintiff [_or_ defendant _or_ other party] appeals to the district court [_or_ the bankruptcy appellate panel], from the final judgment [_or_ final order _or_ final decree (describe it)] of the bankruptcy court entered in this adversary proceeding on the _____ day of _____. The parties to the judgment [_or_ order *or* decree] appealed from and the names and addresses of their respective attorneys are as follows:

_____

Dated: _____

                                      Signed: _____
                                                  Attorney for Appellant.
                                   Address: _____

     **Advisory Committee note.** This form is an adaptation of the suggested form of notice of appeal which accompanies the Federal Rules of Appellate Procedure.

     If the appeal does not arise in an adversary proceeding the caption should conform to that in Official Form No. 2. This form may be modified for an appeal from an interlocutory order. See Rule 8001(b).

# Proposed Interim Chapter 12 Forms

## PROPOSED INTERIM FORM NO. 12-A

**Proposed Form No. 12-A. Chapter 12 Statement of Individual Debtor
(Proposed Interim Form No. 12-A)**

*[Caption as in Official Form No. 1]*

*Chapter 12 Statement of Individual Debtor*

[Each applicable question shall be answered or the failure to answer explained. If the answer is "none" or "not applicable," so state. If additional space is needed for the answer to any question, a separate sheet, properly identified and made a part hereof, should be used and attached.

The term "original petition," used in the following questions, shall mean the original petition filed under § 301 of the Code or, if the chapter 12 case was converted from another chapter of the Code, shall mean the petition by or against you which originated the first case.

Individual debtors must complete all questions. This form should be completed whether a married individual or a married individual and a spouse filed the petition. For convenience, the word "debtors" is used to refer to a married individual and spouse who have filed a chapter 12 petition. If such debtors' answers to any question are different, their respective answer shall be separately designated as the answer of the husband and the answer of the wife.]

1. *Filing status.* (Check appropriate status.)
   Unmarried individual      _____
   Married individual and spouse are debtors      _____
   Married individual is the sole debtor      _____

2. *Name and residence.*

    a. Full name
        Debtor or debtors _____

        _____

        Spouse who is not a debtor _____

        _____

    b. Residence of the debtor or debtors
        **(1)** Mailing address of debtor or debtors_____

              _____

              City or town, state and zip code.
        **(2)** Mailing address of spouse who is not a debtor _____

              _____

              City or town, state and zip code
        **(3)** Telephone number including area code
              Debtor or debtors _____

              _____

              Spouse who is not a debtor _____

              _____

3. *Summary of debt.*
    Give amounts as of the date of the filing of the
    petition.

    a. *Noncontingent, liquidated debt.*
        **(1)** Amount of noncontingent, liquidated
              debt from farming operations.         $_____
        **(2)** Amount of noncontingent, liquidated
              non-farm debt                   $_____
        **(3)** Total noncontingent, liquidated
              debt                         $_____

    b. Contingent or unliquidated debt.
        **(1)** Amount of contingent or unliquidated debt
              from farming operations        $_____
        **(2)** Amount of contingent or unliquidated
              non-farm debt                   $_____
        **(3)** Total contingent or unliquidated debt     $_____

    c. *Principal Residence.*
        Amount of non-farm debt that is secured by the
        principal residence of the debtor or debtors   $_____

4. *Summary of income from last tax year.*

    a. Debtor or debtors' last tax year before the
        current tax year was calender year 19_____.
    b. Debtor or debtors' gross income for the last
        tax year before the current year                 $_____

    **c.** Amount of debtor or debtors' gross income
    for last tax year before the current tax year
    from farming operations                   $_____

**5.** *Nature of farming operations.* (Place an "X" on the appropriate line to identify each type of farming operation in which the debtor or debtors are engaged and supply the other information requested below.)

    **a.** Crops          _____
        Kind(s) _____
        Acres owned _____ leased _____

    **b.** Dairy operations          _____
        Acres owned _____ leased _____

    **c.** Ranching          _____
        Kind(s) _____
        Acres owned _____ leased _____

    **d.** Poultry          _____
        Kind(s) _____
        Acres owned _____ leased _____

    **e.** Livestock          _____
        Kind(s) _____
        Acres owned _____ leased _____

    **f.** Production of poultry products          _____
        Kind(s) _____

    **g.** Production of livestock products          _____
        Kind(s) _____

**6.** *Non-farming activities.*

    **a.** If a debtor or debtors are self employed in other than farming operations, state the nature thereof

        _____

        _____

    **b.** If a debtor or debtors are employed by others in either farming operations or non-farming activity, state the nature thereof

        _____

        _____

    **c.** If a spouse who is not a debtor is either self employed in other than farming operations or employed by others in either farming operations or non-farming activity, state the nature thereof

        _____

    **d.** Give the name, address, and telephone number of each present employer of the debtor or debtors.

        _____

    **e.** Give the name, address, and telephone number of each present employer of a spouse who is not a debtor

        _____

**f.** State how long the debtor or debtors have been employed by each present employer.

_____

**g.** How long has the spouse who is not a debtor been employed by each present employer?

_____

7. *Budget.*
   **a.** *Current income.*
   **(1)** Estimated gross income from farming operations for the next twelve months. (Include all government program payments.)    $_____
   **(2)** Income from non-farming activities: Give estimated average monthly income of debtor and spouse, consisting of:

|  | Debtor | Spouse |
|---|---|---|
| **(A)** Gross pay from employer (wages, salary, or commissions) | $_____ | $_____ |
| **(B)** Take-home pay from employer (Gross pay less all deductions) | $_____ | $_____ |
| **(C)** Regular income available from self employment not included in item 7a(1) | $_____ | $_____ |
| **(D)** Other income: | | |
| Interest and dividends | $_____ | $_____ |
| From real estate or personal property | $_____ | $_____ |
| Social security | $_____ | $_____ |
| Pension or other retirement income | $_____ | $_____ |
| Other (*specify*) _____ | $_____ | $_____ |
| **(E)** Alimony, maintenance, or support payments: | | |
| Payable to the debtor for the debtor's use | $_____ | $_____ |
| Payable to the debtor for support of another (*Attach additional sheet listing the name, age, and relationship to the debtor of persons for whose benefit payments are made*) | $_____ | $_____ |
| **(F)** Total estimated average monthly income from non-farming activities | $_____ | $_____ |

If you anticipate receiving additional income on other than a monthly basis in the next year (such as an income tax refund) attach an additional sheet of paper and explain.

If you anticipate a substantial change in your income in the immediate future, attach an additional sheet of paper and explain.

(4) Total estimated income for next twelve months *(twelve times total estimated average monthly income from non-farming activities (item 7a(2)(F) with any adjustment for a substantial change in such income plus income from farming operations (item 7a(1)).* $_____

**b.** *Current expenses related to farming operations*

(1) Real Property expenses. *(Include expenses of the home of the debtor if the home is located on the debtor's property used in farming operations.)*

Give estimated current monthly expenditures consisting of

(A) Mortgage payment(s) $_____

(B) Rental or lease payment(s) $_____

(C) Real estate taxes $_____

(D) Repairs & upkeep $_____

Total real property expenses $_____

(2) Other expenses.

Give estimated current monthly expenditures for the debtor or debtors consisting of:

(A) Installment or lease payments on equipment

Specify _____ $_____

_____ $_____

_____ $_____

_____ $_____

Total Monthly installment or lease payments on equipment $_____

(B) Maintenance of equipment

Service contracts $_____

Other *(specify)*

_____ $_____

_____ $_____

Total maintenance of equipment $_____

(C) Utilities:

Electricity $_____

Fuel $_____

Water                                              $_____
 Telephone (business use)                          $_____
Total utilities                                                        $_____

**(D)** Production expenses
Labor (gross)                                      $_____
Seed                                               $_____
Fertilizer                                         $_____
Feed                                               $_____
Pesticides                                         $_____
Veterinary, etc.                                   $_____
Other *(specify)*

_____                   $_____
_____                   $_____
_____                   $_____

Total production expenses                                             $_____

**(E)** Miscellaneous expenses
Give any expenses of farming operation not reflected above.
(i)_____             $_____
(ii)_____             $_____
(iii)_____             $_____

Total miscellaneous expenses                                          $_____

**(3)** Total estimated monthly expenses                              $_____

**(4)** Total current yearly expenses related to
farming operations *(twelve times total esti-
mated monthly expenses (item 7c(3)))*                                 $_____

c.   *Current expenses not related to farming operations.*
Give estimated average current monthly expenditures for the individual debtor or debtors,
consisting of:

**(1)** Home expenses. *(Complete this item c(1)
only if the home is located on property not
used in farming operations)*
**(A)** Rent or home loan payment (including
any assessment or maintenance fee)                      $_____
**(B)** Real estate taxes                                    $_____
**(C)** Utilities:
Electricity                                 $_____
Gas                                         $_____
Water                                       $_____
Telephone (personal use)                    $_____
Other *(specify)*                           $_____
Total utilities                                              $_____

     **(D)** Home maintenance (repairs and up-
keep) $____

     **(E)** Total of all home expenses $____

  **(2)** Other expenses not related to farming activities.

     **(A)** Taxes *(not deducted from wages or included in home loan payment or included in real estate taxes)* $____

     **(B)** Alimony, maintenance, or support payments *(attach additional sheet listing name, age, and relationship of beneficiaries)* $____

     **(C)** Insurance *(not deducted from wages)*

| | |
|---|---|
| Life | $____ |
| Health | $____ |
| Auto | $____ |
| Homeowner's or Renter's | $____ |
| Other *(specify)* | |
| _____ | $____ |

       Total insurance expenses $____

     **(D)** Installment payments:

| | |
|---|---|
| Auto | $____ |
| Other *(specify)* | |
| _____ | $____ |
| _____ | $____ |

       Total installment payments $____

     **(E)** Transportation *(not including auto payments)* $____

     **(F)** Education *(including tuition and school books)* $____

     **(G)** Food $____

     **(H)** Clothing $____

     **(I)** Medical, dental, and medicines $____

     **(J)** Telephone $____

     **(K)** Laundry and cleaning $____

     **(L)** Newspapers, periodicals and books $____

     **(M)** Recreation, clubs and entertainment $____

     **(N)** Charitable contributions $____

     **(O)** Other expenses *(specify)*

       _____ $____

       _____ $____

     **(P)** Total of other expenses related to non-farming activities $____

If you anticipate a substantial change in your expenses in the immediate future, attach additional sheet of paper and explain.

    **(3)** Total expenses for next twelve months related to the debtor's non-farming activities *(twelve times the total estimated current monthly expenses (item 7c(1)(E) plus item 7c(2)(P) with an adjustment for any substantial change)*     $_____

  **d.** *Summary of budget information.*

    **(A)** Total income for next twelve months (item 7a(4))     $_____

    **(B)** Total estimated expenses for next twelve months (item 7b(4) plus 7c(3)).     $_____

    Available income ((A) minus (B))     $_____

**8.** *Dependents.*

The debtor supports the following dependents *(other than the debtor's spouse):*

| Name | Age | Relationship to Debtor |
|------|-----|------------------------|
| _____ | _____ | _____ |
| _____ | _____ | _____ |
| _____ | _____ | _____ |
| _____ | _____ | _____ |

**9.** *Payment of attorney*

  **a.** How much have you agreed to pay or what property have you agreed to transfer to your attorney in connection with the case?     $_____

  **b.** How much have you paid or what have you transferred to the attorney?     $_____

**10.** *Tax refunds and government program payments.* (To be answered by debtor or debtors and, unless spouses are separated, by a spouse who is not a debtor.)

To what tax refunds (income or other) and government program payments, if any, is either of you, or may either of you be, entitled? (Give particulars, including information as to any refunds payable jointly to you and any other person. All such refunds should also be listed in Item 18(b).)

_____

_____

**11.** *Financial accounts, certificates of deposit and safe deposit boxes.* (To be answered by debtor or debtors and, unless spouses are separated, by a spouse who is not a debtor.)

  **a.** Does either of you currently have any accounts or certificates of deposit or shares in banks, savings and loan, thrift, building and loan and homestead associations, credit unions, brokerage houses, pension funds and the like? (If so, give name and address of each institution, number and nature of account, current balance, and name and address of every other person authorized to make withdrawals from the account. Such accounts should also be listed in Item 18(b).)____

b. Does either of you currently keep any safe deposit boxes of other depositories? (If so, give name and address of bank or other depository, name and address of every other person who has a right of access thereto, and a brief description of the contents thereof, which should also be listed in Item 18(b).)____

12. *Prior bankruptcy.*
What cases under the Bankruptcy Act or Bankruptcy Code have previously been brought by or against you or either spouse filing a petition? (State the location of the bankruptcy court, the nature and number of each case, the date when it was filed, and whether a discharge was granted or denied, the case was dismissed, or a composition, arrangement, or plan was confirmed.)____

13. *Foreclosures, executions, and attachments.* (To be answered by debtor or debtors and, unless spouses are separated, by a spouse who is not a debtor.)
a. Is any of the property of either of you, including real estate, involved in a foreclosure proceeding, in or out of court? (If so, identify the property and the person foreclosing)____

b. Has any property or income of either of you been attached, garnished, or seized under any legal or equitable process within the 90 days immediately preceding the filing of the original petition herein? (If so, describe the property seized, or person garnished, and who filed the law suit.)____

14. *Repossessions and returns.* (To be answered by debtor or debtors and, unless spouses are separated, by a spouse who is not a debtor.)
Has any property of either of you been returned to, repossessed, or seized by the seller or by any other party, including a landlord, during the 90 days immediately preceding the filing of the original petition herein? (If so, give particulars, including the name and address of the party taking the property and its description and value.)

____

15. *Transfers of property.* (To be answered by debtor or debtors and, unless spouses are separated, by a spouse who is not a debtor.)
a. Has either of you made any gifts, other than ordinary and usual presents to family members and charitable donations, during the year im-

mediately preceding the filing of the original petition herein? (If so, give names and addresses of donees and dates, description and value of gifts.)_____

    **b.**   Has either of you made any other transfer, absolute or for the purpose of security, or any other disposition, of real or personal property during the year immediately preceding the filing of the original petition herein? (Give a description of the property, the date of the transfer or disposition, to whom transferred or how disposed of, and, if the transferee is a relative or insider, the relationship, the consideration, if any, received therefor, and the disposition of such consideration.)

**16.**   *Debts.* (To be answered by debtor or debtors and by a spouse who is not a debtor.)

    **a.**   *Debts Having Priority.*

| (1) Nature of claim | (2) Name of creditor and complete mailing address including zip code | (3) Specify when claim was incurred and the consideration therefor: whether claim is subject to setoff, evidenced by a judgment, negotiable instrument, or other writing | (4) Indicate if claim is contingent unliquidated, or disputed | (5) Amount of claim |
|---|---|---|---|---|

**1.**   Wages, salary, and commissions, including vacation, severance and sick leave pay owing to employees not exceeding $2,000 to each, earned within 90 days before filing of petition or cessation of business (if earlier specify date).

                                                                                   $_____

**2.**   Contributions to employee benefit plans for services rendered within 180 days before filing of petition or cessation of business (if earlier specify date).

                                                                                   $_____

**3.**   Deposits by individuals, not exceeding $900 for each purchase, lease, or rental of property or services for personal, family, or household use that were not delivered or provided.

                                                                                   $_____

**4.**   Taxes owing [itemize by type of tax and taxing authority]

                **(A)** To the United States                 $_____

                **(B)** To any state                         $_____

                **(C)** To any other taxing authority       $_____

                      Total                               $_____

    **b.**   *Secured Debts.* List all debts which are or may be secured by real or personal property. (Indicate in the next to last column, if debt payable in installments, the amount of each installment, the installment period (monthly, weekly, or otherwise) and number of installments in arrears, if any. Indicate in last column whether husband or wife solely liable, or whether you are jointly liable.)

| Creditor's name, account number and complete mailing address including zip code | Consideration or basis for debt | Amount claimed by creditor | If disputed, amount admitted by debtor | Description of collateral (include year and make of automobile) | Installment amount, period, and number of installments in arrears | Husband or wife solely liable, or jointly liable |
|---|---|---|---|---|---|---|
| | | | | | | |
| | | | | | | |
| | | | | | | |
| | | | | | | |

Total secured debts _____

   **c.** *Unsecured Debts.* List all other debts, liquidated and unliquidated, including taxes, attorney fees, and tort claims.

| Creditor's name, account number and complete mailing address including zip code | Consideration or basis for debt | Amount claimed by creditor | If disputed, amount admitted by debtor | Husband or wife solely liable, or jointly liable |
|---|---|---|---|---|
| | | | | |
| | | | | |
| | | | | |
| | | | | |
| | | | | |
| | | | | |

Total unsecured debts _____

**17.** *Codebtors.* (To be answered by debtor or debtors and by a spouse who is not a debtor.)

   **a.** Are any other persons liable, as cosigners, guarantors, or in any other manner, on any of the debts of either of you or is either of you so liable on the debts of others? (If so, give particulars, indicating which spouse is liable and including names of creditors, nature of debt, names and addresses of codebtors, and their relationship, if any, to you.)

_____

_____

   **b.** If so, have the codebtors made any payments on the debts? Give name of each codebtor and amount paid by codebtor.)

_____

_____

**c.** Has either of you made any payments on the debts? (If so, specify total amount paid to each creditor, whether paid by husband or wife, and name of codebtor.)

_____

_____

_____

**18.** *Property and exemptions.* (To be answered by debtor or debtors and a spouse who is not a debtor.)

    **a.** *Real Property.* List all real property owned at date of filing of original petition herein. (Indicate in the next to last column whether an exemption is claimed and in last column whether owned solely by husband or wife, or jointly.)

| Description and location of property | Name of any co-owner other than spouse | Present market value (without deduction for mortgage or other security interest) | Amount of mortgage or other security interest on this property | Name of mortgagee or other secured creditor | Value claimed exempt (specify federal or state statute creating the exemption) | Owned solely by husband or by wife, or jointly |
|---|---|---|---|---|---|---|
| | | | | | | |
| | | | | | | |
| | | | | | | |
| | | | | | | |

    **b.** *Personal Property.* List all other property owned by debtor or debtors and spouse who is not a debtor at date of filing of original petition herein. (Indicate in the next to last column whether an exemption is claimed and in last column whether owned solely by husband or wife, or jointly.)

| Description | Location of property if not at debtor's residence | Name of any co-owner other than spouse | Present market value (without deduction for mortgage or other security interest) | Amount of mortgage or other security interest on this property | Name of mortgagee or other secured creditor | Value claimed exempt (specify federal or state statute creating the exemption) | Owned solely by husband or wife, or jointly |
|---|---|---|---|---|---|---|---|
| Autos (give year and make) | | | | | | | |
| Farming equipment (give type & make) | | | | | | | |
| Household goods | | | | | | | |
| Personal effects | | | | | | | |
| Cash or financial account | | | | | | | |
| Other (specify) | | | | | | | |

Unsworn Declaration under Penalty of Perjury
of Individual to Chapter 12 Statement

[To be signed by debtor or debtors]

I, _____, [an unmarried individual] [*or* a married individual] [*if both husband and wife are debtors* and I, _____, the spouse], declare under penalty of perjury that I have read the answers contained in the foregoing statement, consisting of _____ sheets, and that they are true and complete to the best of my knowledge, information, and belief.

Executed on_____

_____
*Debtor*

_____
*Debtor*

## PROPOSED INTERIM FORM NO. 12-B

### Proposed Form No. 12-B. Chapter 12 Statement of Partnership or Corporate Debtor (Proposed Interim Form No. 12-B)

*[Caption as in Official Form No. 1]*

*Chapter 12 Statement of Partnership or Corporate Debtor*

[Each applicable question shall be answered or the failure to answer explained. If the answer is "none" or "not applicable," so state. If additional space is needed for the answer to any question, a separate sheet, properly identified and made a part hereof, should be used and attached.

The term "original petition," used in the following questions, shall mean the original petition filed under § 301 of the Code or, if the chapter 12 case was converted from another chapter of the Code, shall mean the petition by or against you which originated the first case.

The questions to be are addressed to, and shall be answered on behalf of, the corporation or partnership, and the statement shall be certified by a duly authorized officer of the corporation or by a member of the partnership.]

1. *Filing status.* (Place an "X" on the appropriate line.)
   Corporation                                                          _____
   Partnership                                                          _____
   Limited Partnership                                                  _____

2. *Name, and other information.*
   a. Full name _____
   b. Principal place of business of the debtor
      (1) Mailing address _____
          _____
          City or town, state and zip code.
      (2) Telephone number including area code
          _____
      (3) Date and the state of incorporation of the corporate debtor
          _____
      (4) Date and the state law under which the partnership debtor was formed
          _____
          _____
      (5) Name of the family or name of the family and relatives that conduct farming operations and own more than 50% of the stock or equity of the corporate or partnership debtor
          _____
          _____

3. *Summary of debt.*
   Give amounts as of the date of the filing of the petition.
   a. *Noncontingent, liquidated debt.*
      (1) Amount of noncontingent, liquidated debt from farming operations. $_____
      (2) Amount of noncontingent, liquidated non-farm debt $_____
      (3) Total noncontingent, liquidated debt $_____
   b. *Contingent or unliquidated debt.*
      (1) Amount of contingent or unliquidated debt from farming operations $_____
      (2) Amount of contingent or unliquidated non-farm debt $_____
      (3) Total contingent or unliquidated debt $_____
   c. *Principal Residence.*
      Amount of non-farm debt that is secured by a dwelling owned by the corporate or partnership debtor and used as a principal residence by a shareholder or partner of the debtor $_____

4. *Assets*
   a. Total value of assets $_____
   b. Value of assets related to farming operations $_____

5. *Summary of income from last tax year.*
   a. Debtor's last tax year before the current tax year was calendar year 19____ [*or* fiscal year _____, 19____ to _____, 19____]
   b. Debtor's gross income for the last tax year before the current tax year $_____
   c. Amount of debtor's gross income for last tax year before the current tax year from farming operations $_____

6. *Nature of farming operations.* (Place an "X" on the appropriate line to identify each type of farming operation in which the debtor is engaged and supply the other information requested below.)
   a. Crops _____
      Kind(s) _____
      Acres owned _____ leased _____
   b. Dairy operations _____
      Acres owned _____ leased _____
   c. Ranching _____
      Kind(s) _____
      Acres owned _____ leased _____
   d. Poultry _____
      Kind(s) _____
      Acres owned _____ leased _____

    **e.**  Livestock                                          ————
          Kind(s) _____
          Acres owned _____ leased _____

    **f.**  Production of poultry products           ————
          Kind(s)_____

    **g.**  Production of livestock products         ————
          Kind(s)_____

**7.** *Non-farming activities.*
If the debtor is engaged in business other than farming operations, state the nature thereof

_____

_____

**8.** *Budget.*

    **a.** *Current income.*

        **(1)** Estimated gross income from farming operations for the next twelve months. (Include all government program payments.)   $_____

        **(2)** Estimated gross income from non-farming activities for the next twelve months   $_____

        **(3)** Total income   $_____

    **b.** *Current expenses related to farming operations.*

        **(1)** Real Property expenses. *(Include expenses of a home of a shareholder or partner of the debtor if the home is located on the debtor's property used in farming operations.)*
Give estimated current monthly expenditures consisting of:

            **(A)** Mortgage payment(s)   $_____
            **(B)** Rental or lease payment(s)   $_____
            **(C)** Real estate taxes   $_____
            **(D)** Repairs & upkeep   $_____
               Total real property expenses   $_____

        **(2)** Other expenses.
Give estimated current average monthly expenditures consisting of:

            **(A)** Installment or lease payments on equipment
               Specify _____   $_____
               _____   $_____
               _____   $_____
               _____   $_____

               Total monthly installment or lease payments on equipment   $_____

**(B)** Maintenance of equipment
    Service contracts      $_____
    Other *(specify)*

    _____   $_____
    _____   $_____
    Total maintenance of equipment        $_____
**(C)** Utilities:
    Electricity      $_____
    Fuel      $_____
    Water      $_____
    Telephone (business use)      $_____
    Total utilities        $_____
**(D)** Production expenses:
    Labor (gross)      $_____
    Seed      $_____
    Fertilizer      $_____
    Feed      $_____
    Pesticides      $_____
    Veterinary, etc.      $_____
    Other *(specify)*

    _____   $_____
    _____   $_____
    _____   $_____
    Total production expenses        $_____
**(E)** Miscellaneous expenses
    Give any expenses of farming opera-
    tion not reflected above.
        (i) _____   $_____
        (ii) _____   $_____
        (iii) _____   $_____
    Total miscellaneous expenses        $_____
**(3)** Total estimated monthly expenses        $_____
**(4)** Total current expenses related to farming
    operations *(twelve times total estimated*
    *monthly expenses (item 8c(3))*        $_____
**c.** *Current expenses related to non-farming*
   *activities.*
   Estimated expenses of the debtor's non-farming
   activities for the next twelve months        $_____
**d.** *Summary of budget information.*
   **(A)** Debtor's total estimated income for next
       twelve months (item 8a(3)).      $_____
   **(B)** Debtor's total estimated expenses for next
       twelve months (item 8b(4) plus item 8c).        ($_____)
       Available income ((A) minus (B))        $_____

9. *Payment of attorney*
   a. How much has the debtor agreed to pay or what property has the debtor agreed to transfer to its attorney in connection with the case? $____
   b. How much has the debtor paid or what has the debtor transferred to its attorney? $____

10. *Tax refunds and government program payments.*
    To what tax refunds (income or other) and government program payments, if any, is the debtor entitled? (Give particulars, including information as to any refunds payable jointly to the debtor and any other person. All such refunds should also be listed in Item 18(b))

11. *Financial accounts, certificates of deposit and safe deposit boxes.*
    a. Does the debtor currently have any accounts or certificates of deposit or shares in banks, savings and loan, thrift, building and loan and homestead associations, credit unions, brokerage houses, pension funds and the like? (If so, give name and address of each institution, number and nature of account, current balance, and name and address of every person authorized to make withdrawals from the account. Such accounts should also be listed in Item 18(b).)____
    b. Does the debtor currently keep any safe deposit boxes or other depositories? (If so, give name and address of bank or other depository, name and address of every person who has a right of access thereto, and a brief description of the contents thereof, which should also be listed in Item 18(b))____

12. *Prior bankruptcy.*
    What cases under the Bankruptcy Act or Bankruptcy Code have previously been brought by or against the debtor? (State the location of the bankruptcy court, the nature and number of each case, the date when it was filed, and whether a discharge was granted or denied, whether the case was dismissed, or whether an arrangement or plan was confirmed.)

13. *Foreclosures, executions, and attachments.*
    a. Is any of the property of debtor, including real estate, involved in a foreclosure proceeding, in or out of court? (If so, identify the property and the person foreclosing.)____
    b. Has any property or income of debtor been attached, garnished, or seized under any legal or equitable process within the 90 days immediately preceding the filing of the original petition herein? (If so,

describe the property seized, or person garnished, and who filed the law suit.)_____

**14.** *Repossessions and returns.*
Has any property of debtor been returned to or been repossessed or seized by the seller or by any other party, including a landlord, during the 90 days immediately preceding the filing of the original petition herein? (If so, give particulars, including the name and address of the party obtaining the property and its description and value.)

_____

**15.** *Transfers of property.*
   **a.** Has the debtor made any gifts, during the year immediately preceding the filing of the original petition herein? (If so, give names and addresses of donees and dates, description and value of gifts.)_____

   **b.** Has the debtor made any other transfer, absolute or for the purpose of security, or any other disposition, of real or personal property during the year immediately preceding the filing of the original petition herein? (Give a description of the property, the date of the transfer or disposition, to whom transferred or how disposed of, and, if the transferee is an insider, the relationship, the consideration, if any, received therefor, and the disposition of such consideration.)_____

**16.** *Debts.*
   **a.** *Debts Having Priority.*

| (1) Nature of claim | (2) Name of creditor and complete mailing address including zip code | (3) Specify when claim was incurred and the consideration therefor: whether claim is subject to setoff, evidenced by a judgment, negotiable instrument, or other writing | (4) Indicate if claim is contingent unliquidated, or disputed | (5) Amount of claim |
|---|---|---|---|---|

**1.** Wages, salary, and commissions, including vacation, severance and sick leave pay owing to employees not exceeding $2,000 to each earned within 90 days before filing of petition or cessation of business (if earlier specify date).

$_____

**2.** Contributions to employee benefit plans for services rendered within 180 days before filing of petition or cessation of business (if earlier specify date).

$_____

3.  Deposits by individuals, not exceeding $900 for each purchase, lease, or rental of property or services for personal, family, or household use that were not delivered or provided.

    $_____

4.  Taxes owing [itemize by type of tax and taxing authority]
    (A) To the United States                          $_____
    (B) To any state                                  $_____
    (C) To any other taxing authority                 $_____
    Total                                             $_____

    **b.**  *Secured Debts.* List all debts which are or may be secured by real or personal property. (Indicate in the last column, if debt payable in installments, the amount of each installment, the installment period (monthly, weekly, or otherwise) and number of installments in arrears, if any.)

| Creditor's name, account number and complete mailing address including zip code | Consideration or basis for debt | Amount claimed by creditor | If disputed, amount admitted by debtor | Description of collateral (include year and make of vehicles) | Installment amount, period, and number of installments in arrears |
|---|---|---|---|---|---|
| | | | | | |
| | | | | | |
| | | | | | |
| | | | | | |
| | | Total secured debts _____ | | | |

    **c.**  *Unsecured Debts.* List all other debts, liquidated and unliquidated, including taxes, attorney fees, and tort claims.

| Creditor's name, account number and complete mailing address including zip code | Consideration or basis for debt | Amount claimed by creditor | If disputed, amount admitted by debtor |
|---|---|---|---|
| | | | |
| | | | |
| | | | |
| | | | |
| | | | |
| | Total unsecured debts _____ | | |

17.  *Codebtors.*
    **a.**  Are any other persons liable, as cosigners, guarantors, or in any other manner, on any of the debts of the debtor or is the debtor so liable on

the debts of others? (If so, give particulars including names of creditors, nature of debt, names and addresses of codebtors, and their relationship, if any, to the debtor.)

_____

_____

_____

**b.** If so, have the codebtors made any payments on the debts? (Give name of each codebtor and amount paid by codebtor.)

_____

_____

**c.** Has the debtor made any payments on the debts? (If so, specify total amount paid to each creditor and name of codebtor.)

_____

_____

_____

**18.** *Property.*

**a.** *Real Property.* List all real property owned at date of filing of original petition herein.

| Description and location of property | Name of any co-owner | Present market value (without deduction for mortgage or other security interest) | Amount of mortgage or other security interest on this property | Name of mortgagee or other secured creditor |
|---|---|---|---|---|
| | | | | |
| | | | | |
| | | | | |
| | | | | |

**b.** *Personal Property.* List all other property owned by debtor at date of filing of original petition herein.

| Description | Location of property if not at debtor's farm | Name of any co-owner | Present market value (without deduction for mortgage or other security interest) | Amount of mortgage or other security interest on this property | Name of mortgagee or other secured creditor |
|---|---|---|---|---|---|
| Autos (give year and make) | | | | | |
| Farming equipment (give type and make) | | | | | |
| Other Equipment and office furnishings | | | | | |
| Cash or financial account | | | | | |
| Other (specify) | | | | | |

## Unsworn Declaration under Penalty of Perjury
### on Behalf of Corporation or Partnership
### to Chapter 12 Statement

I, _____, [the president *or other officer* or an authorized agent of the corporation] [*or* a member *or* an authorized agent of the partnership] named as debtor in this case, declare under penalty of perjury that I have read the answers contained in the foregoing statement, consisting of _____ sheets, and that they are true and correct to the best of my knowledge, information, and belief. Executed on _____

Signature: _____

**Advisory Committee note.** A chapter 12 debtor must also prepare and file a statement of affairs as prescribed by Official Form No. 8. Rule 12.3.